Emma

5
FINAL

Kaoru
Mori

-Contents-

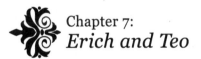

Chapter 7:
Erich and Teo

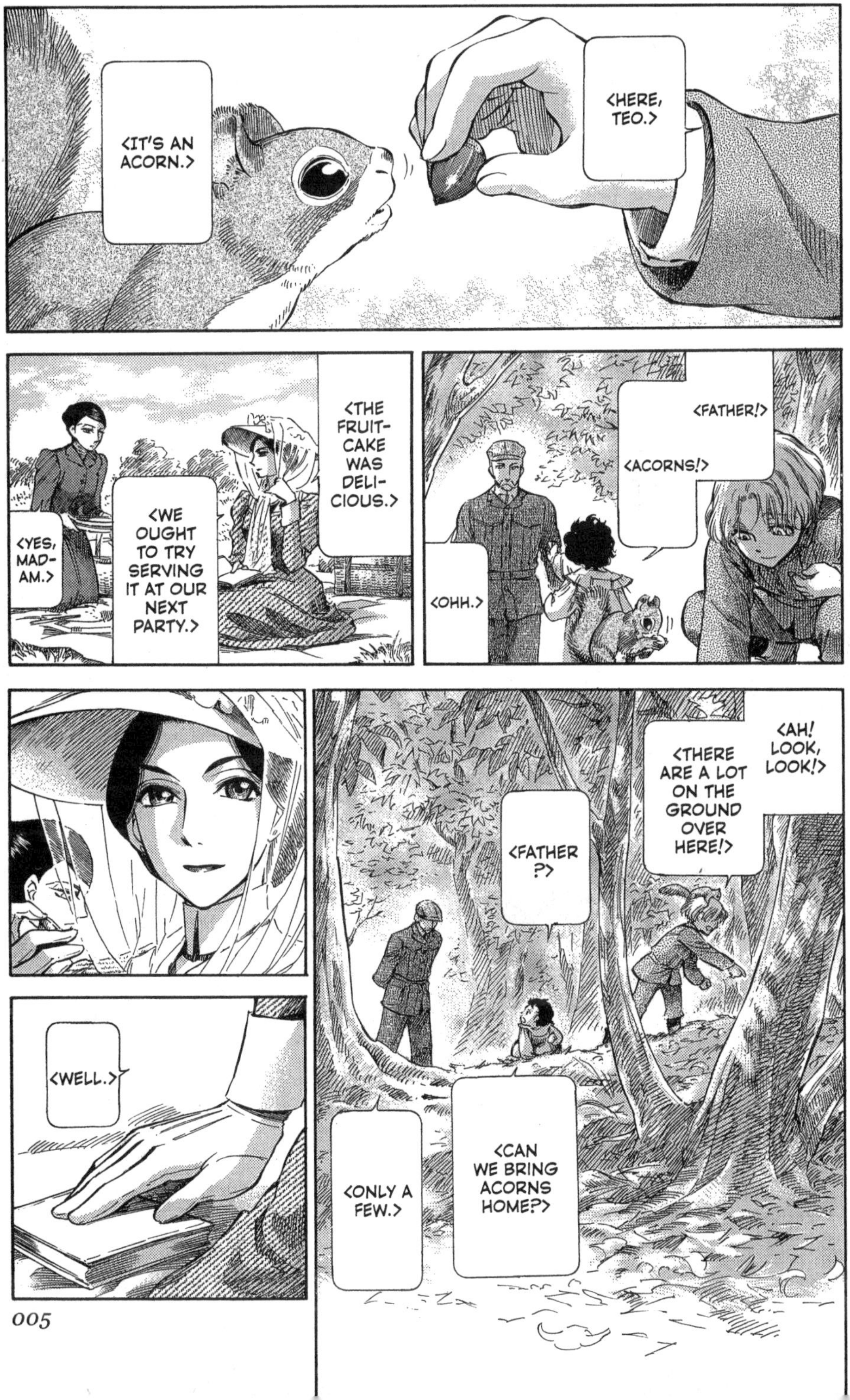
<HERE, TEO.>
<IT'S AN ACORN.>
<FATHER!>
<ACORNS!>
<OHH.>
<THE FRUIT-CAKE WAS DELI-CIOUS.>
<WE OUGHT TO TRY SERVING IT AT OUR NEXT PARTY.>
<YES, MAD-AM.>
<AH! LOOK, LOOK!>
<THERE ARE A LOT ON THE GROUND OVER HERE!>
<FATHER?>
<CAN WE BRING ACORNS HOME?>
<ONLY A FEW.>
<WELL.>

Chapter 7: *Erich and Teo*

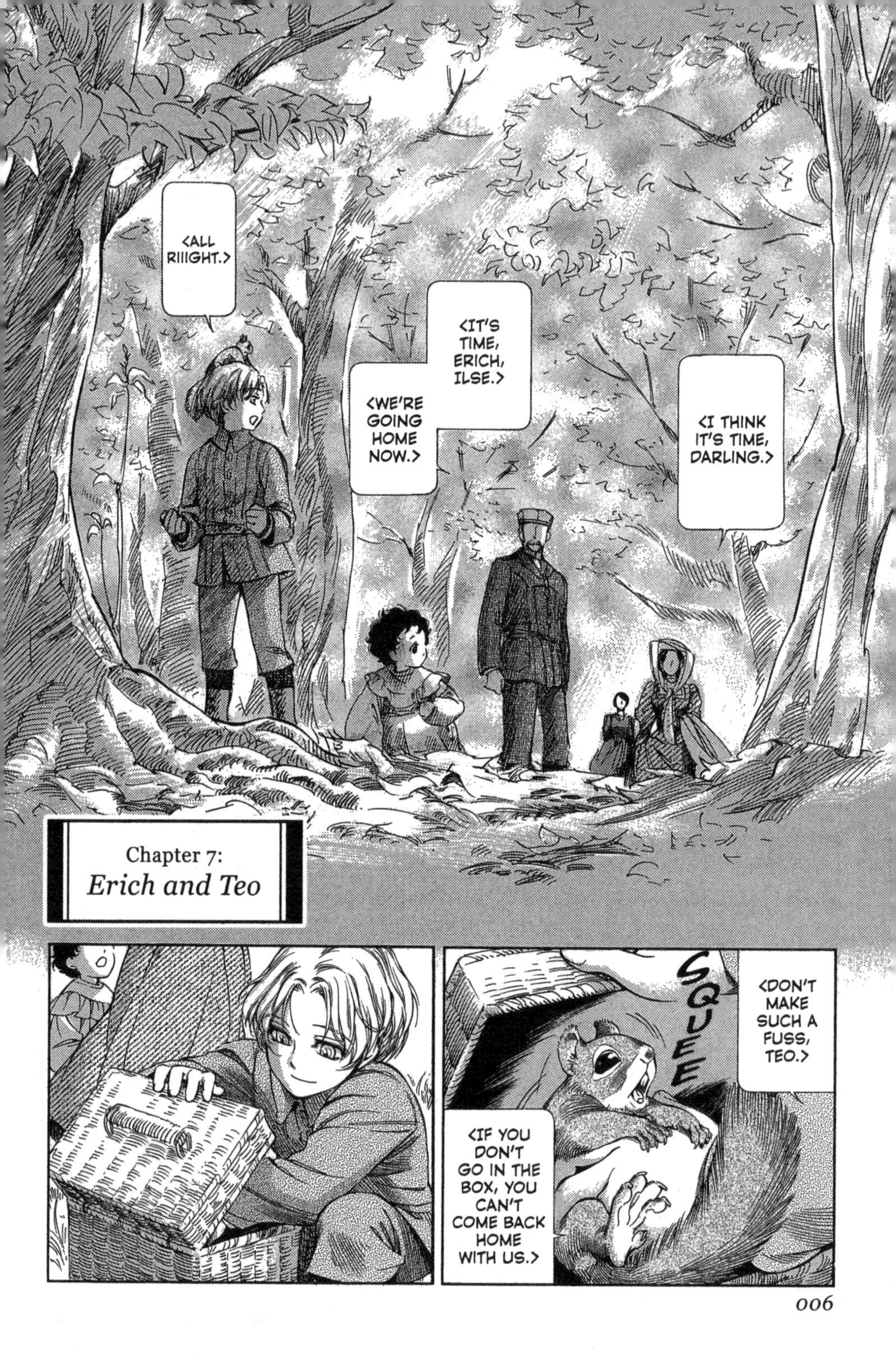
<I THINK IT'S TIME, DARLING.>
<IT'S TIME, ERICH, ILSE.>
<WE'RE GOING HOME NOW.>
<ALL RIIIGHT.>
<DON'T MAKE SUCH A FUSS, TEO.>
SQUEEE
<IF YOU DON'T GO IN THE BOX, YOU CAN'T COME BACK HOME WITH US.>

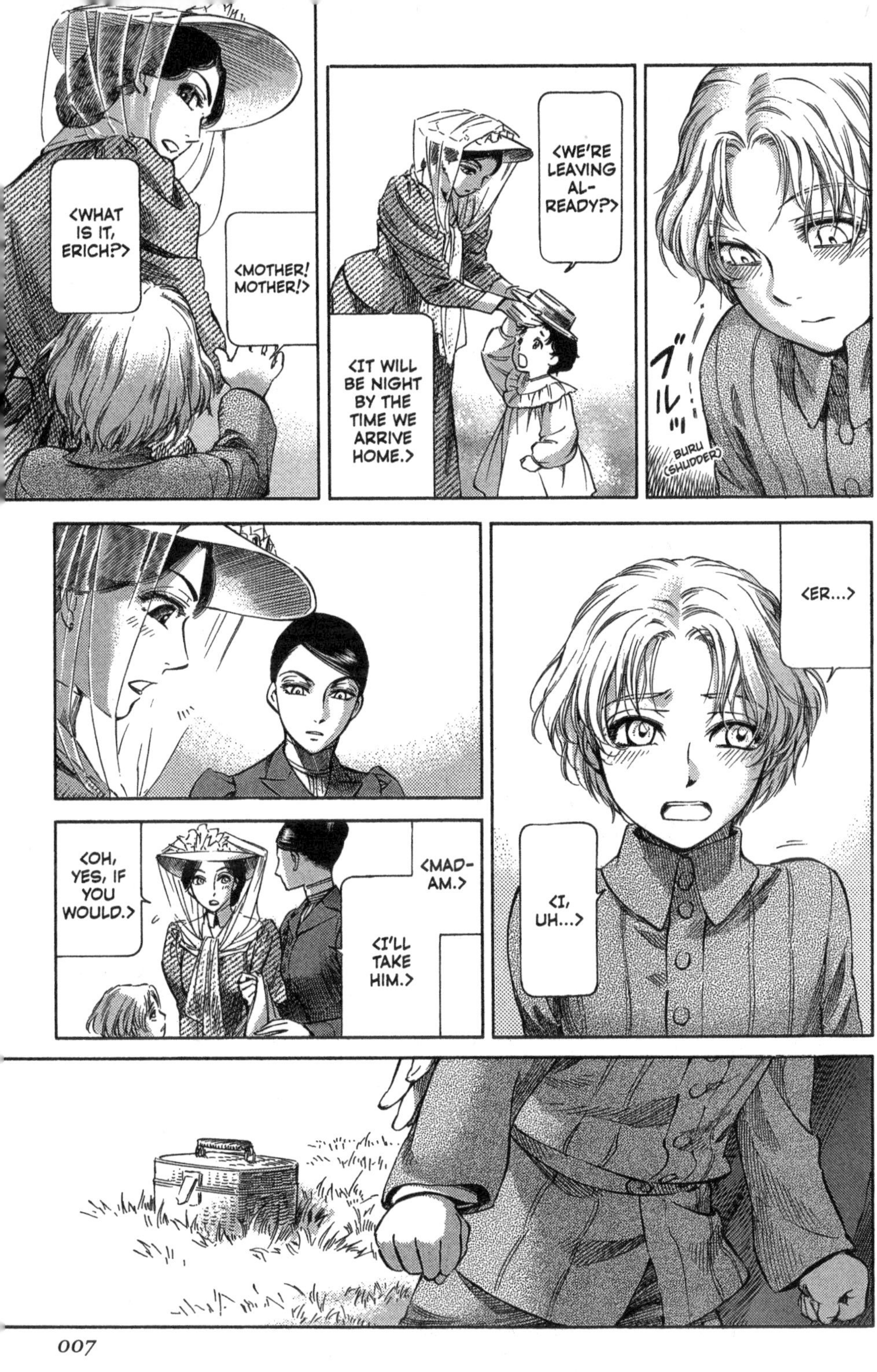
ブル
BURU (SHUDDER)
<WE'RE LEAVING AL-READY?>
<IT WILL BE NIGHT BY THE TIME WE ARRIVE HOME.>
<MOTHER! MOTHER!>
<WHAT IS IT, ERICH?>
<ER...>
<I, UH...>
<MAD-AM.>
<I'LL TAKE HIM.>
<OH, YES, IF YOU WOULD.>

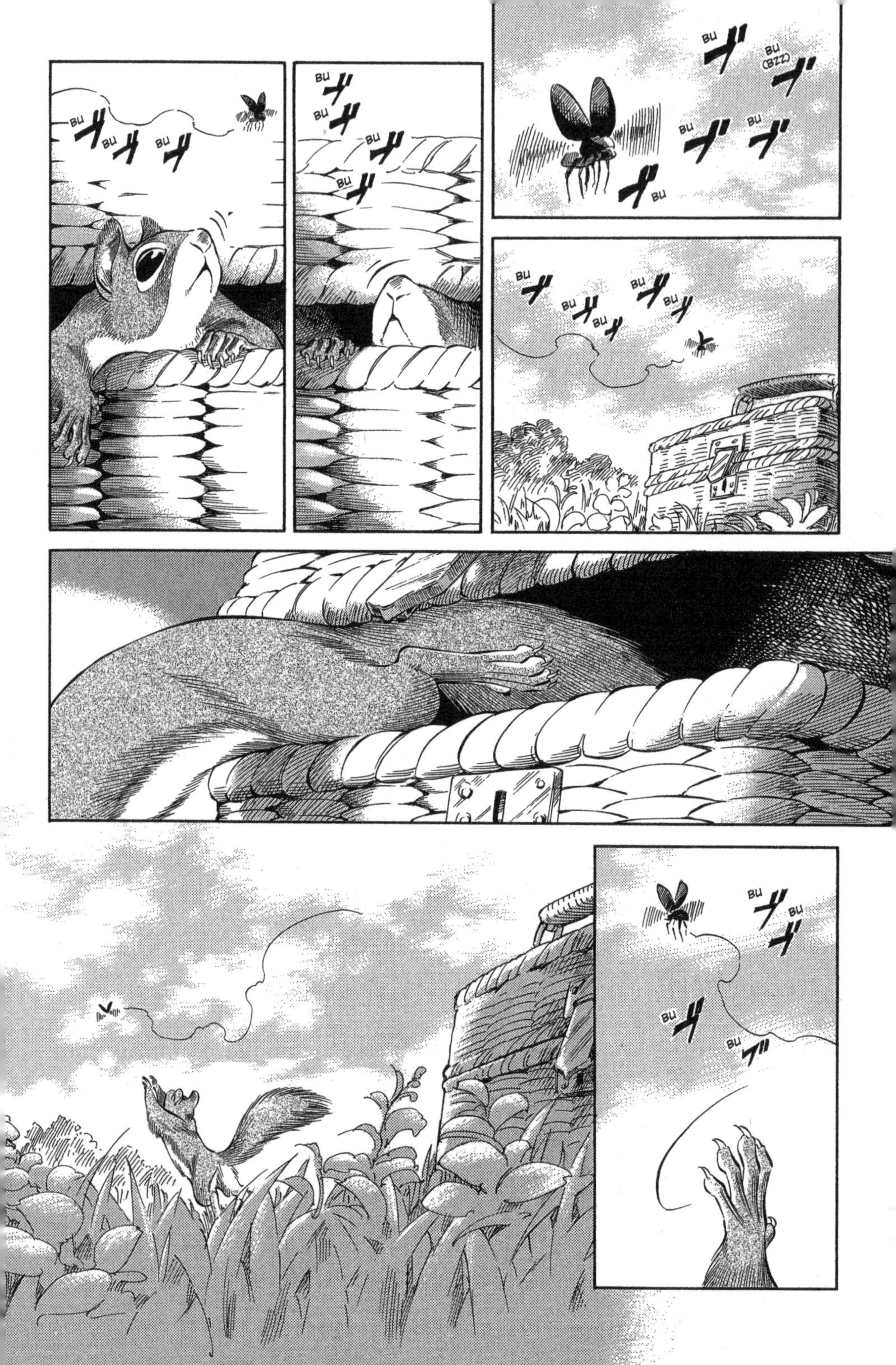

BU
BU (BZZ)
BU
BU
BU
BU
BU
BU
BU
BU
BU
BU
BU
BU
BU
BU
BU
BU
BU
BU
BU

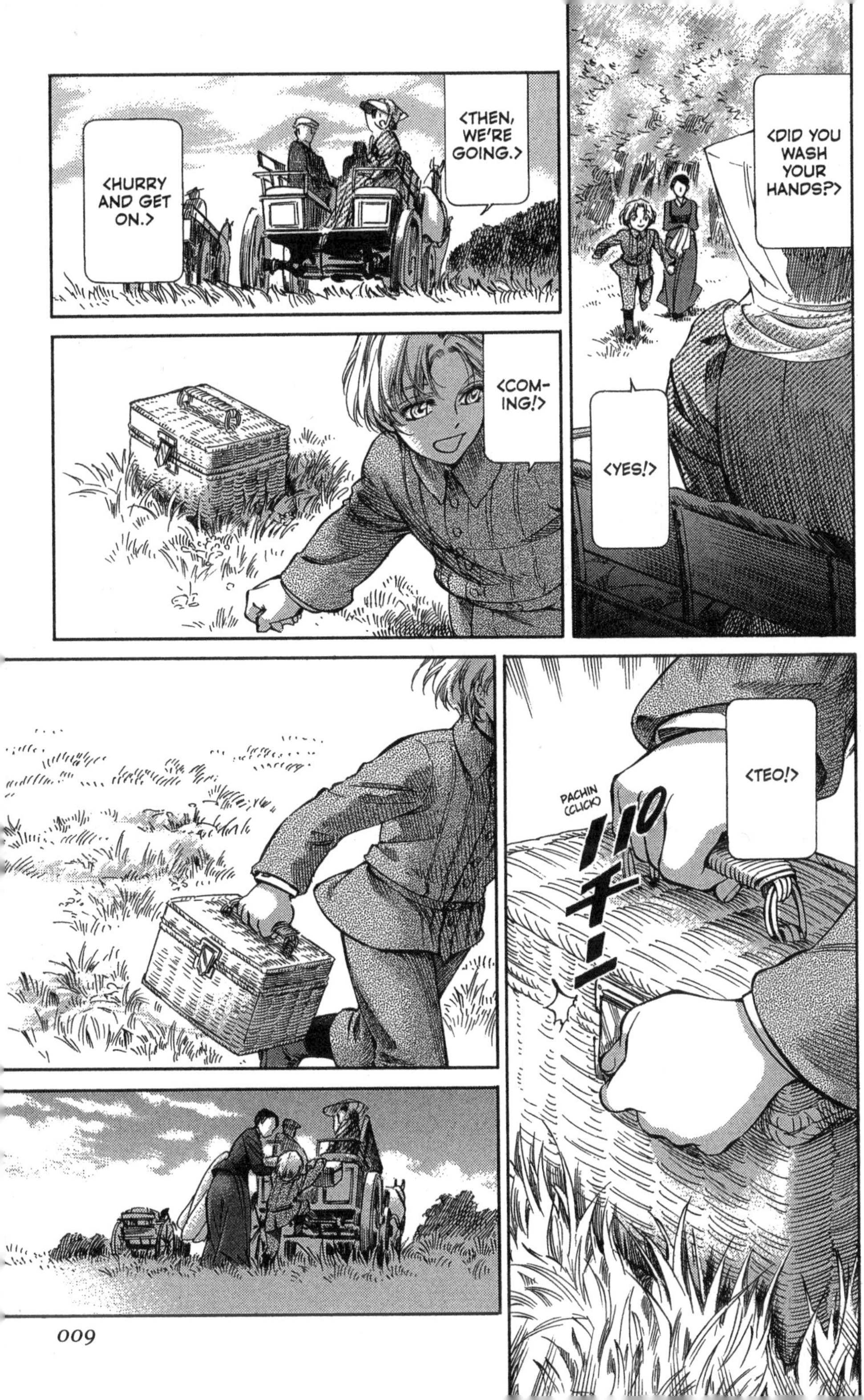
<DID YOU WASH YOUR HANDS?>
<YES!>
<THEN, WE'RE GOING.>
<HURRY AND GET ON.>
<COM-ING!>
<TEO!>
PACHIN (CLICK)

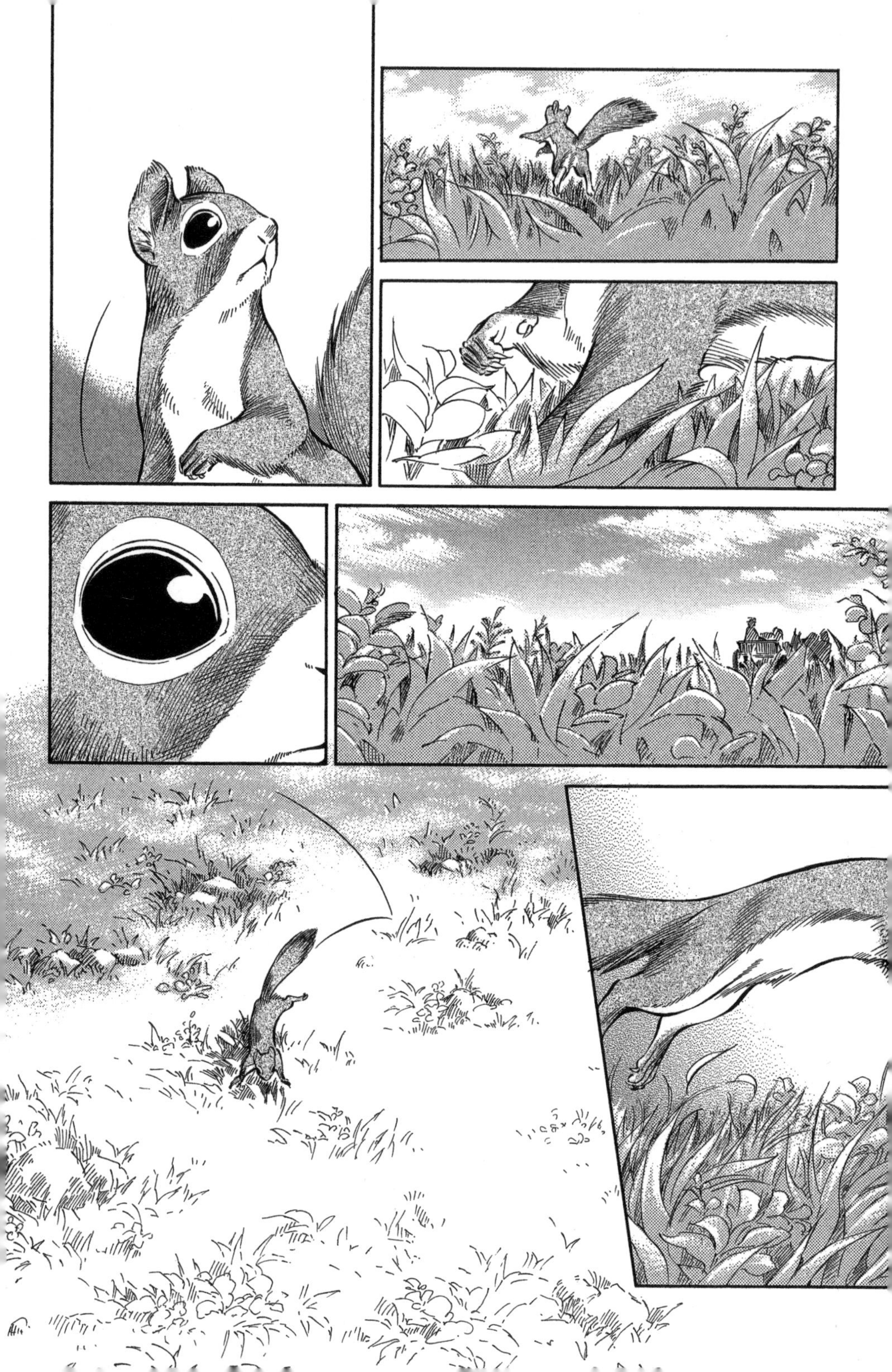

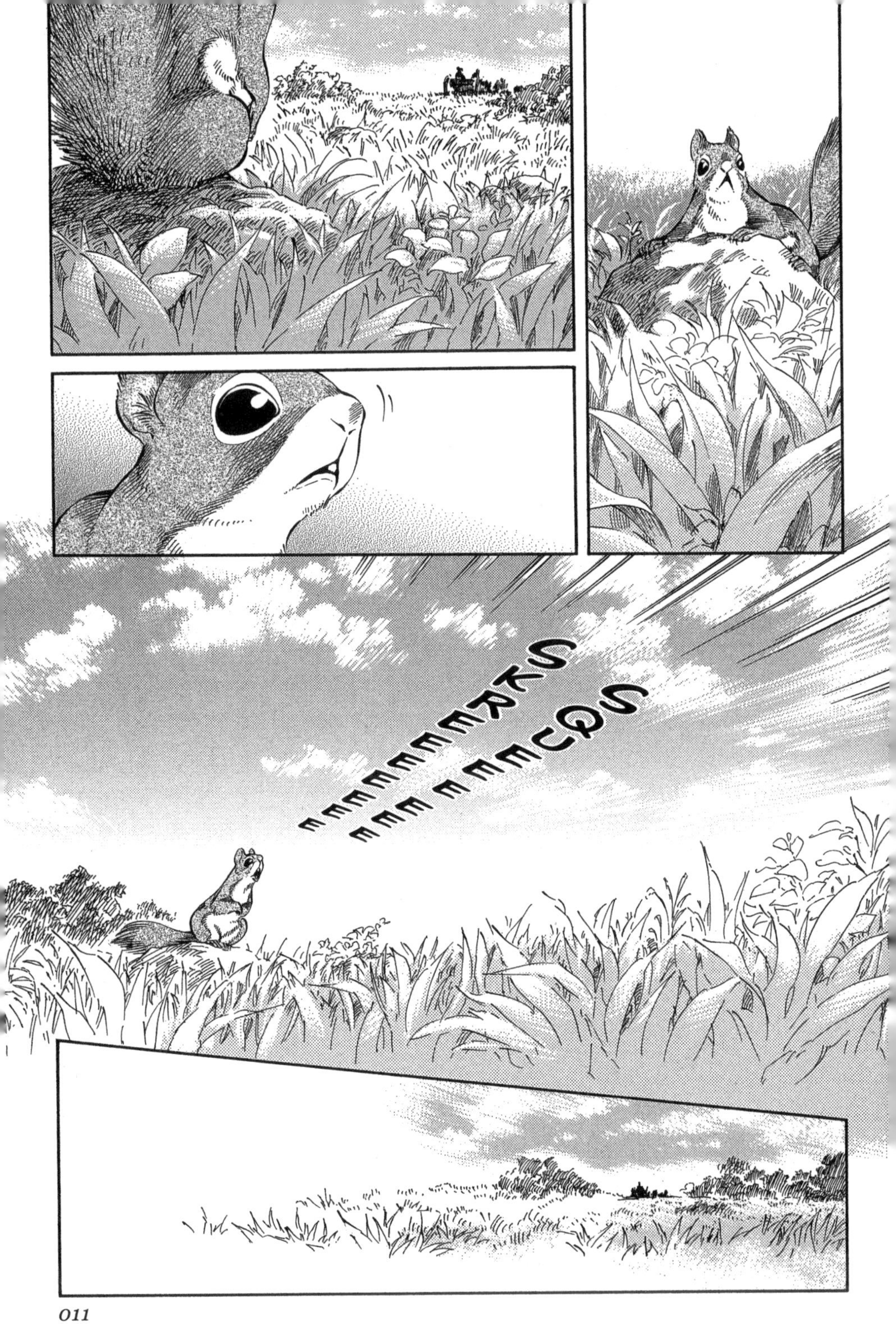
SQUEEEEEE
SKREEEEEEE

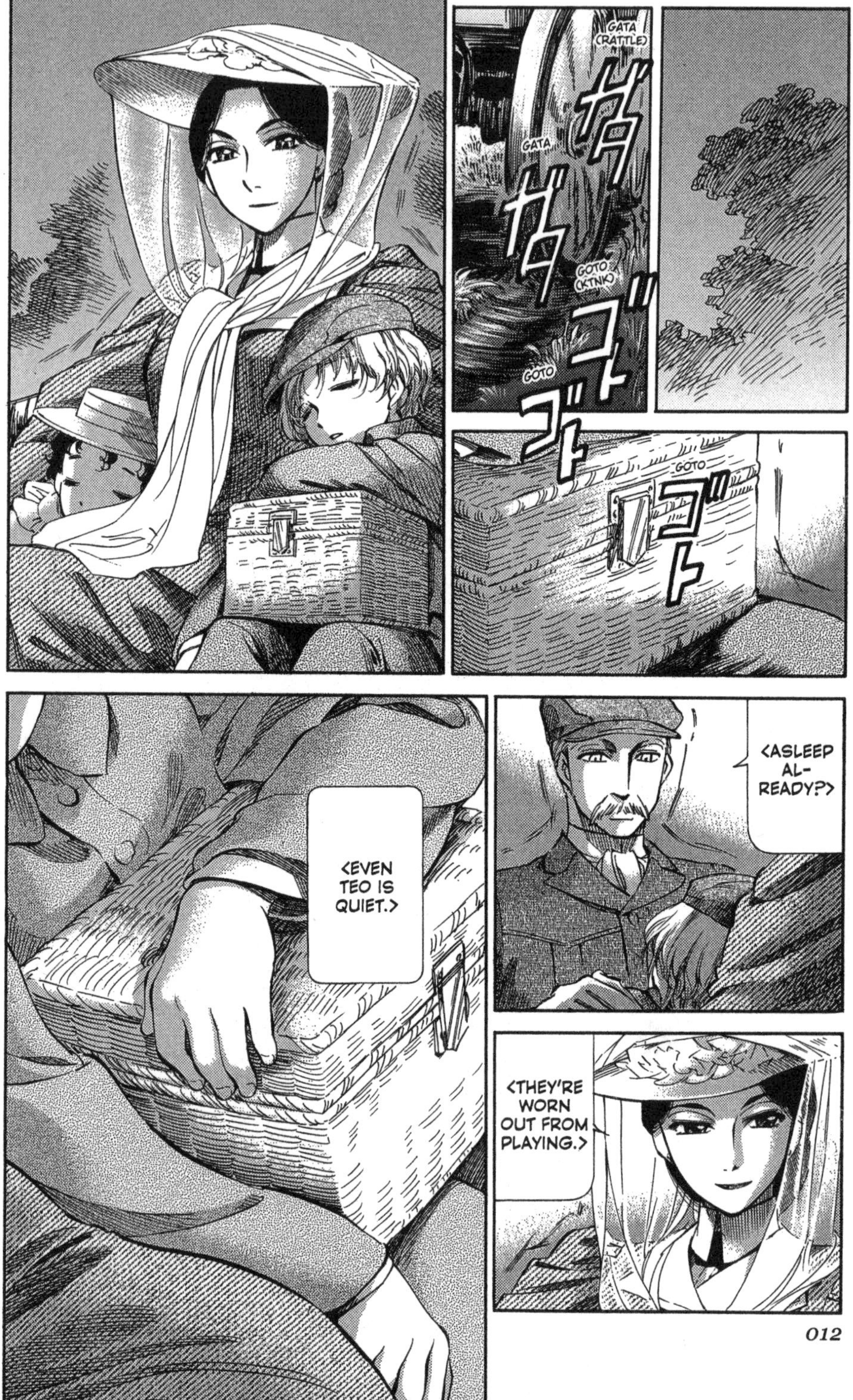
GATA (RATTLE)
ガタ
GATA
ガタ
GOTO (KTNK)
ゴト
GOTO
ゴト
GOTO
ゴト
<ASLEEP AL-READY?>
<THEY'RE WORN OUT FROM PLAYING.>
<EVEN TEO IS QUIET.>

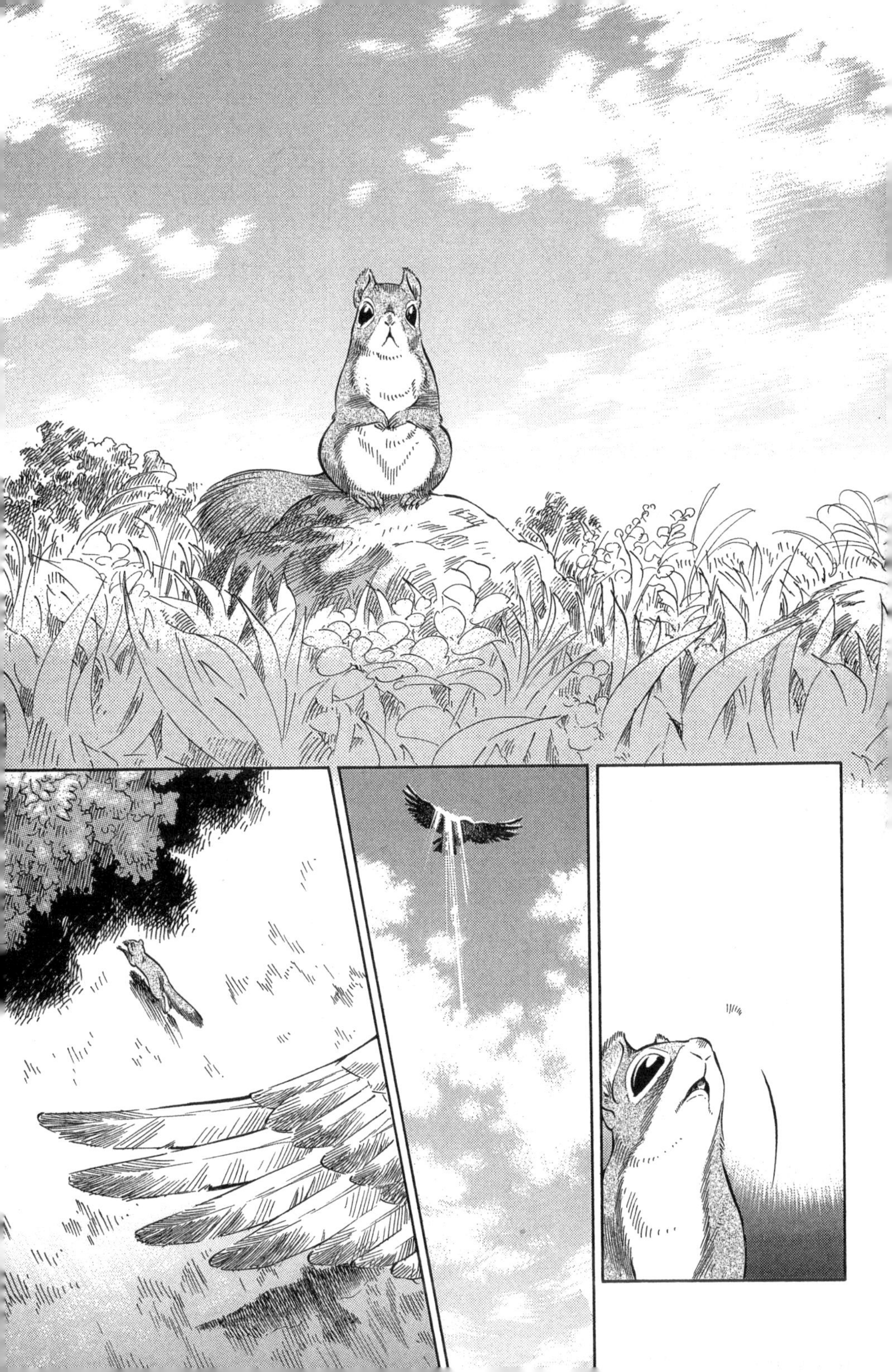

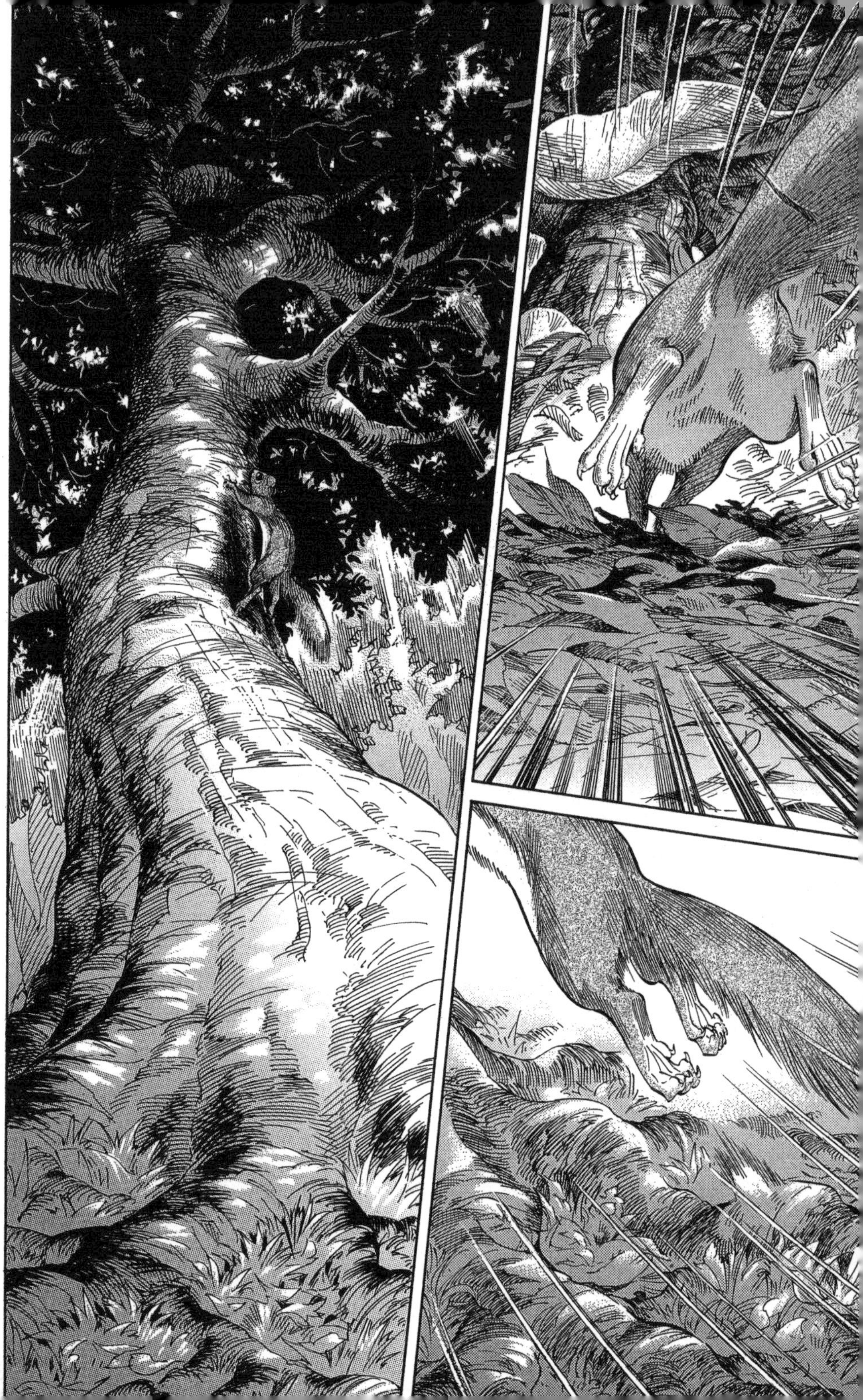

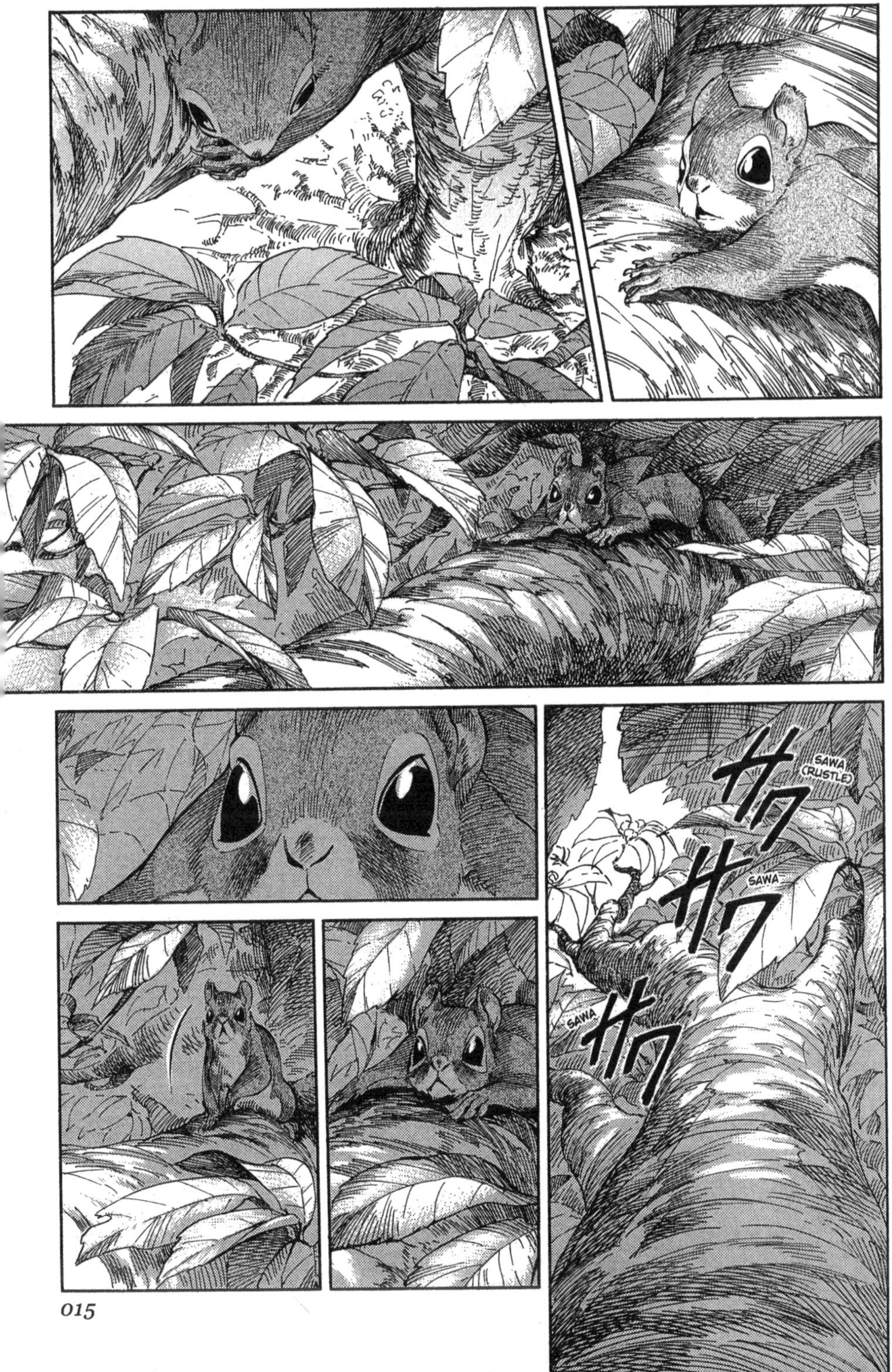
SAWA (RUSTLE)
SAWA
SAWA

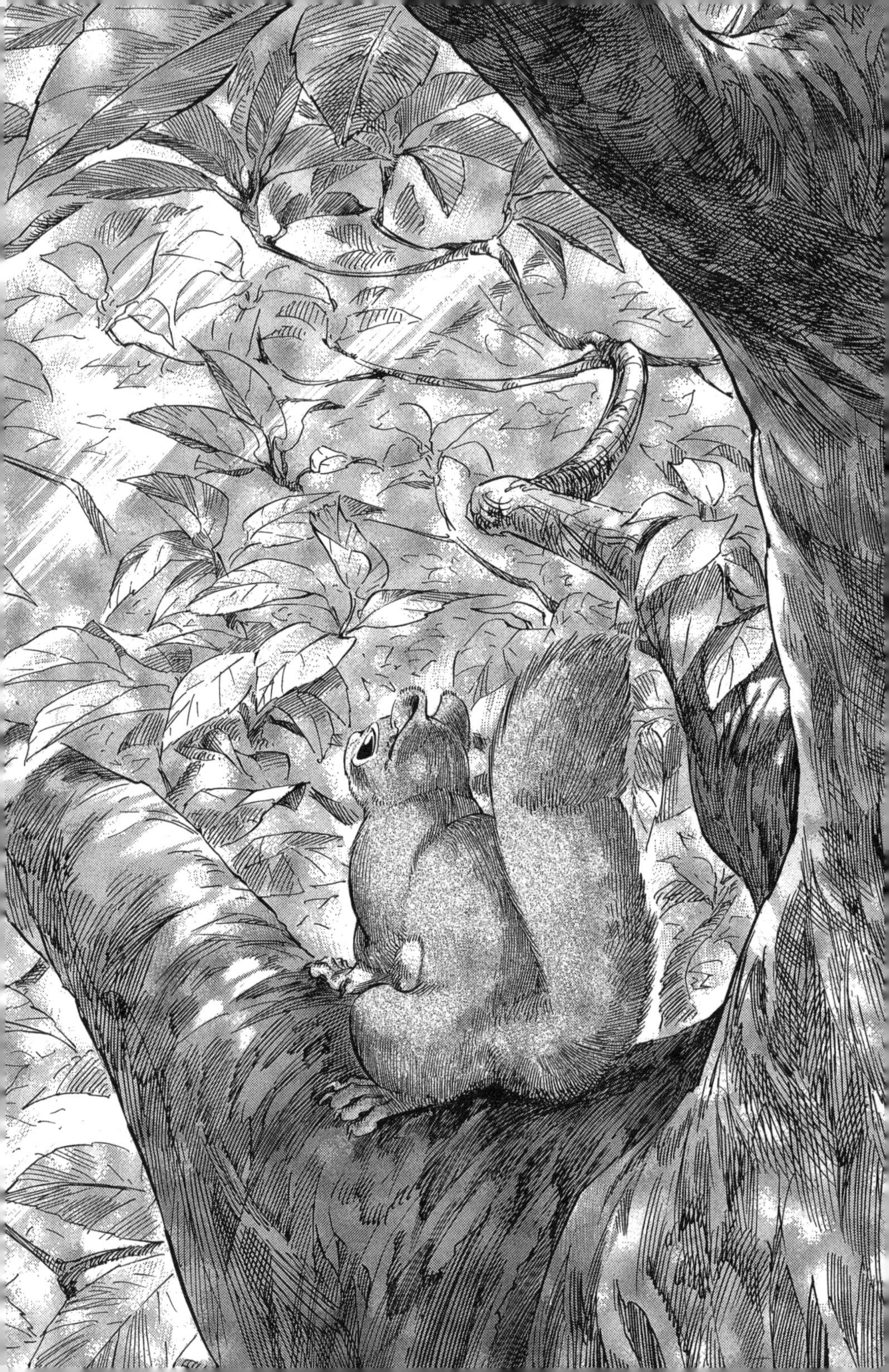

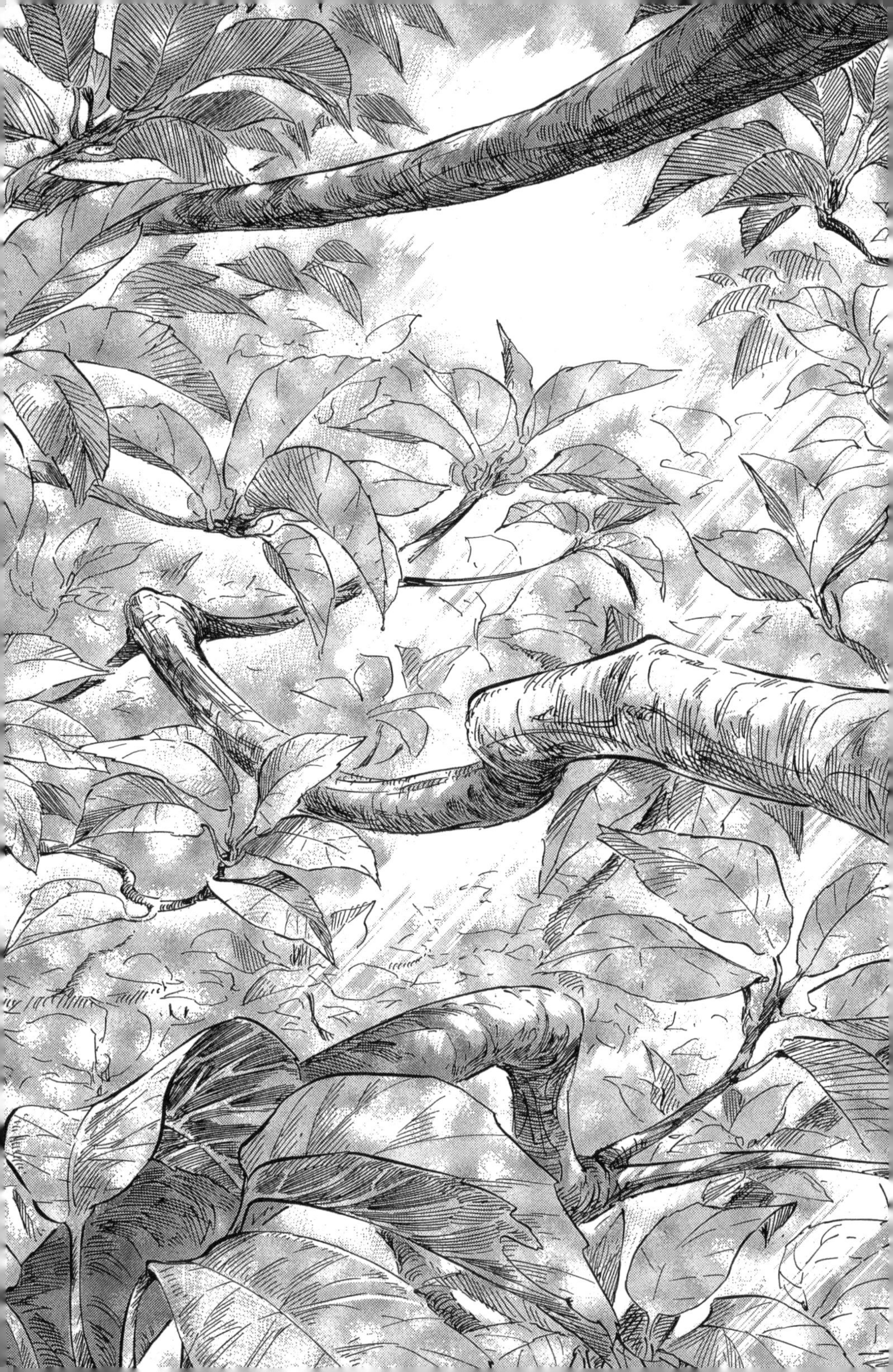

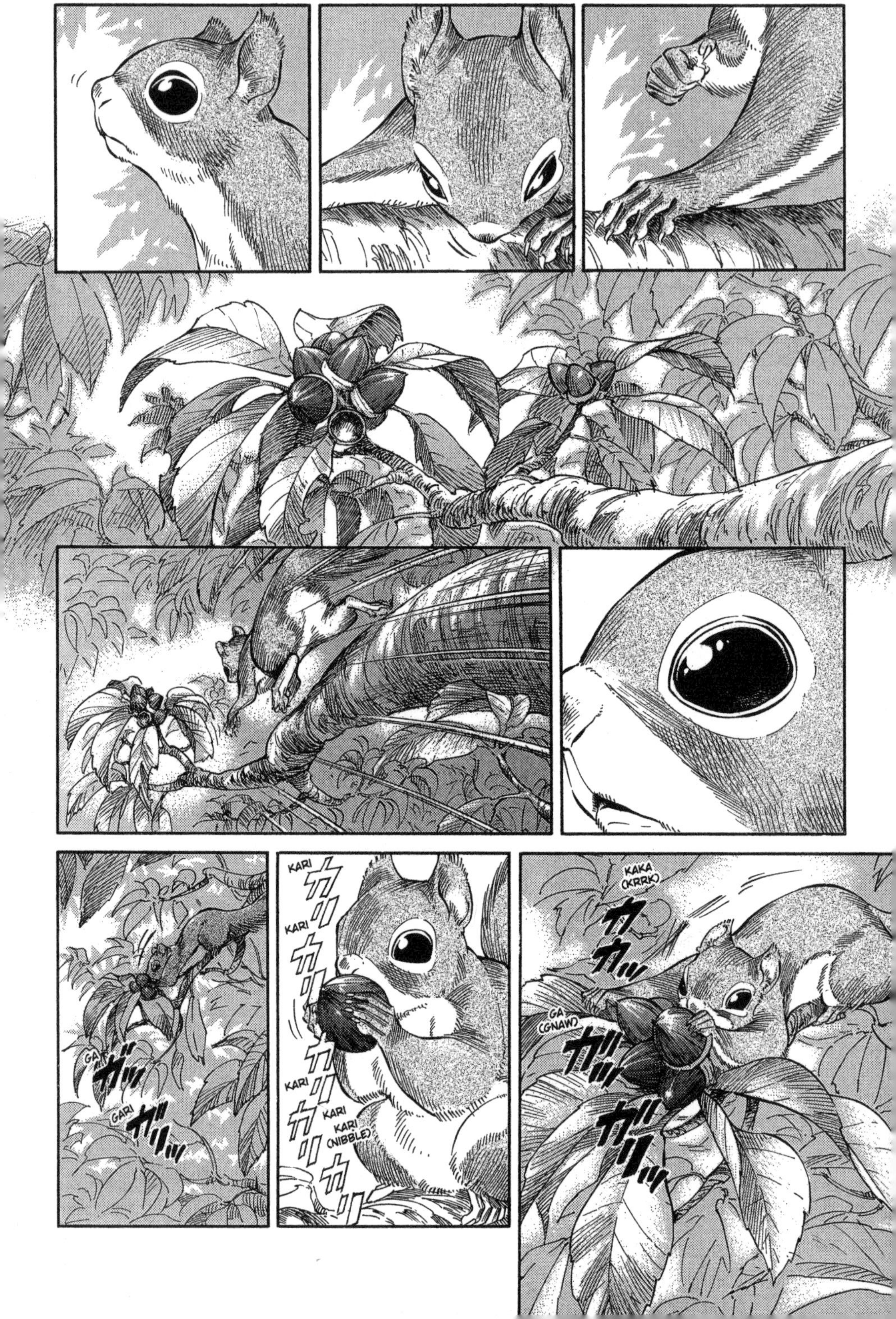
KAKA (KRRK)
GA (GNAW)
KARI
KARI
KARI
KARI
KARI (NIBBLE)
GA
GARI

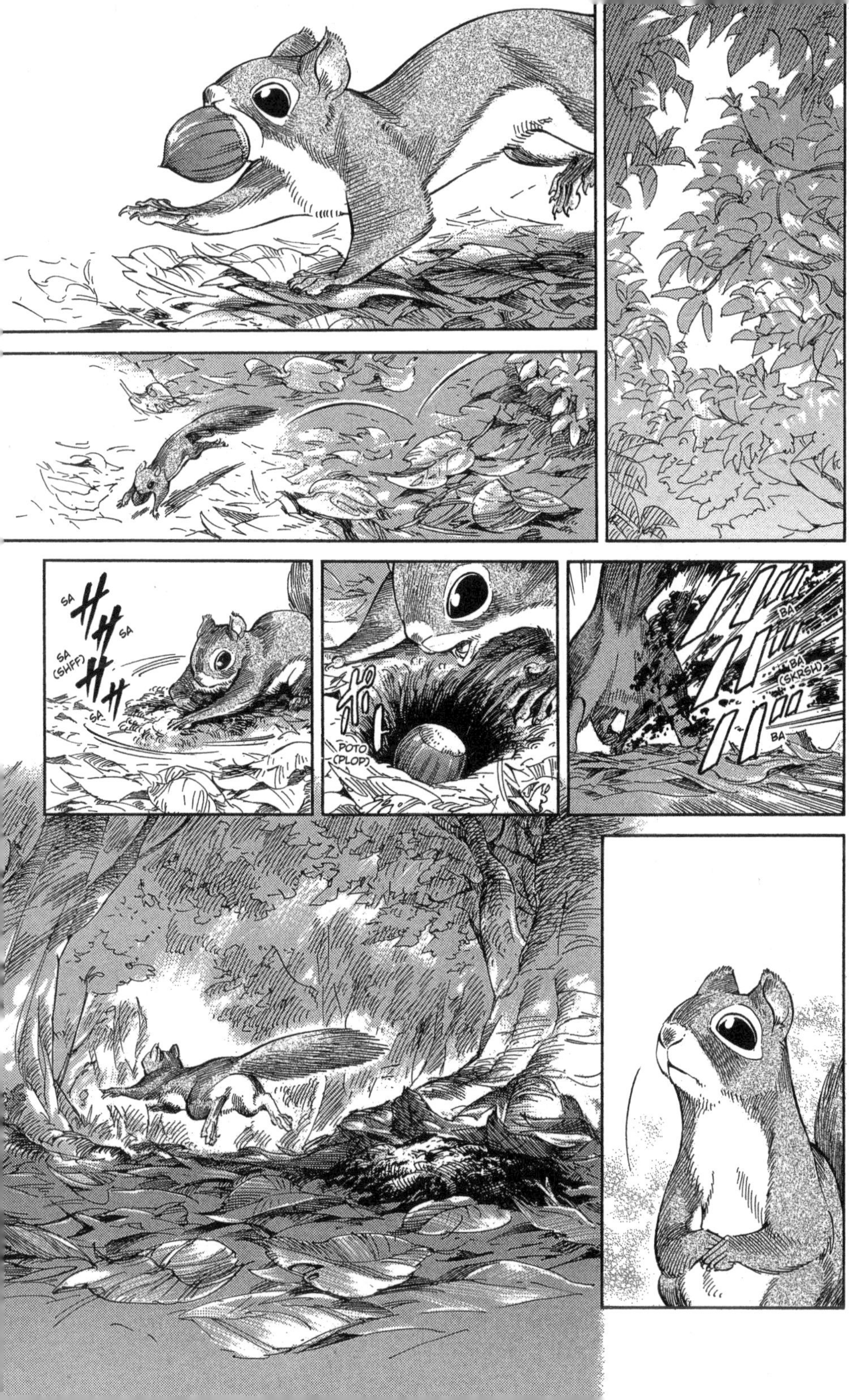
BA
BA
(SKRSH)
BA
POTO
(PLOP)
SA
SA
SA
(SHFF)
SA

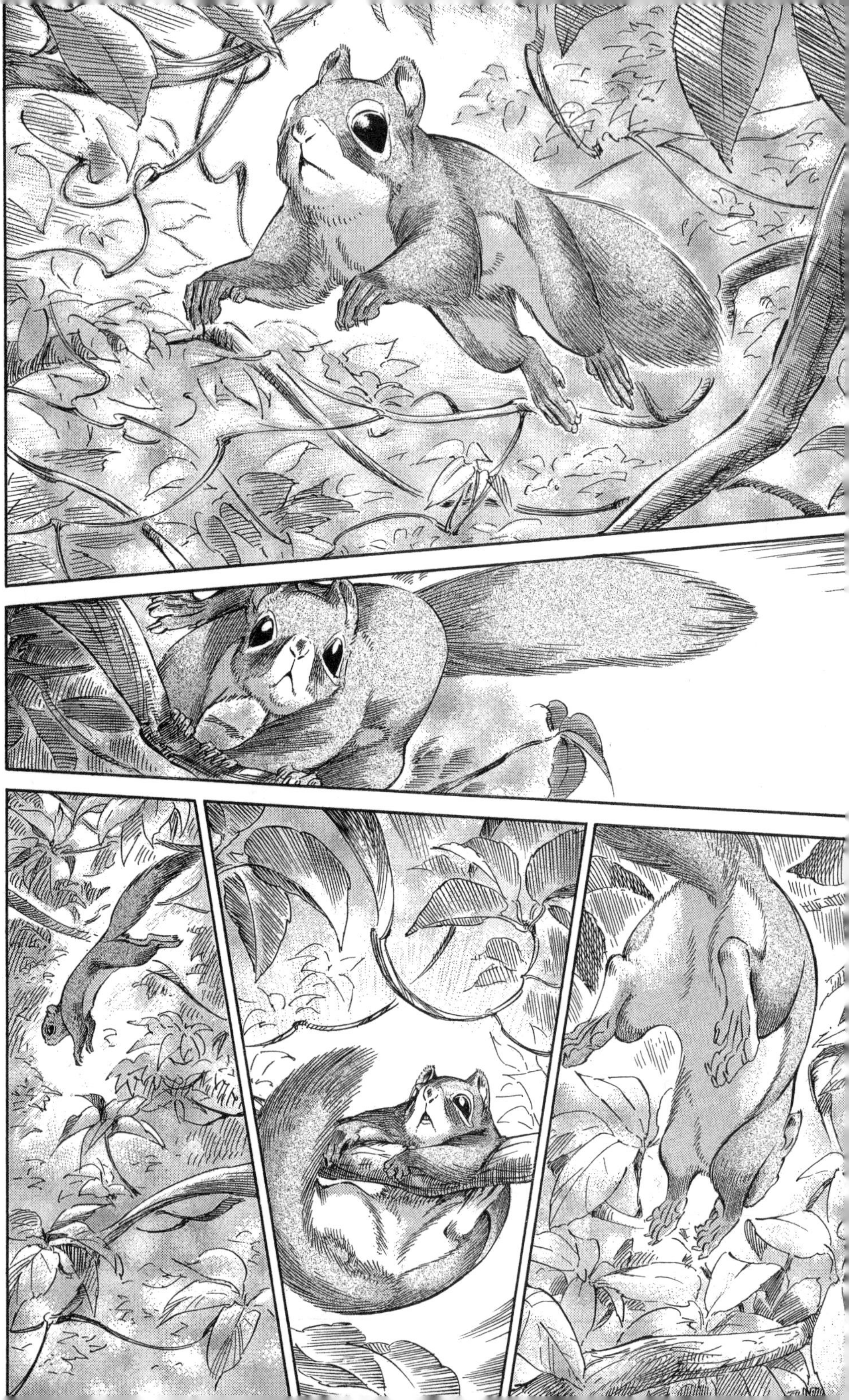

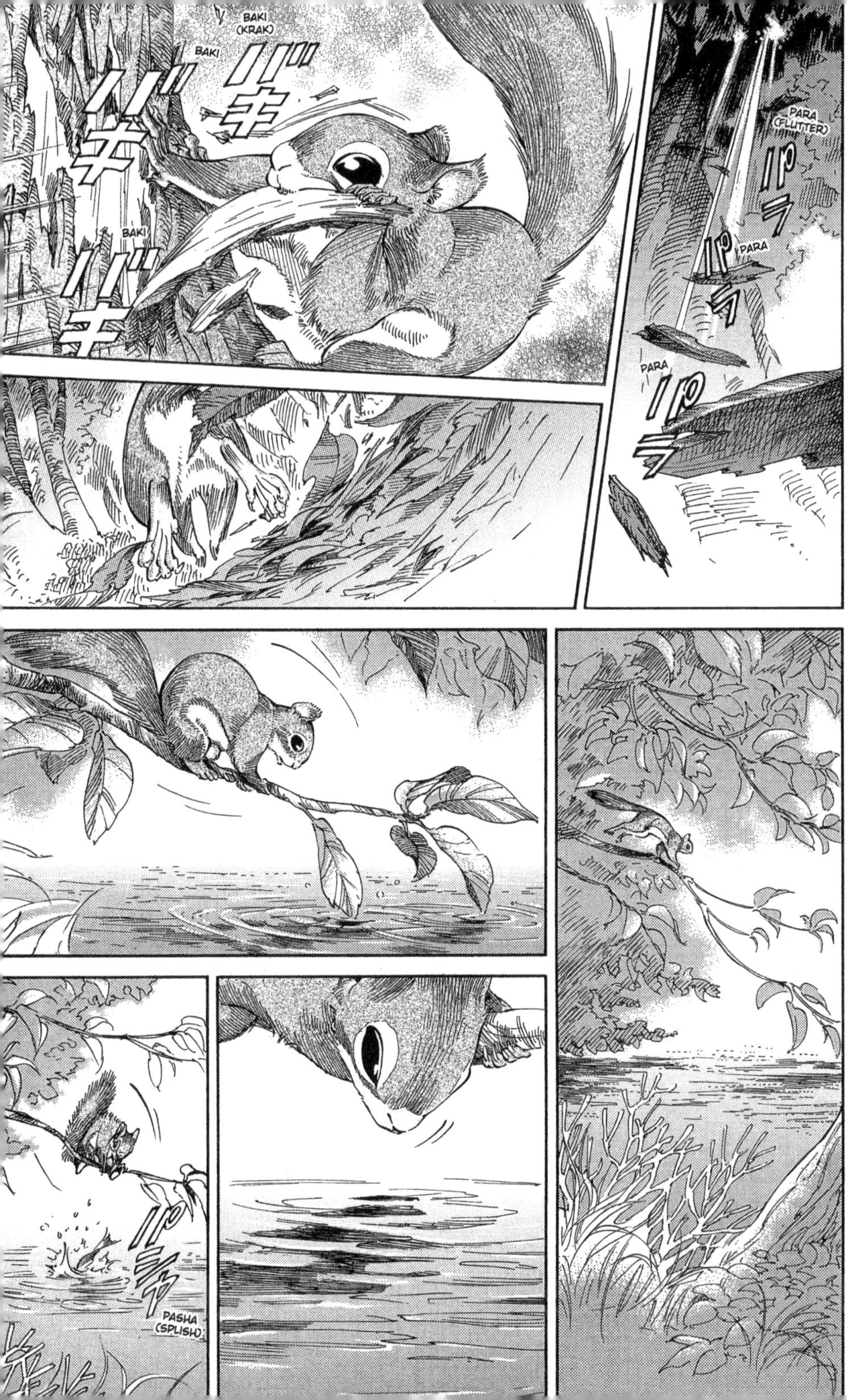
PARA (FLUTTER)
パラ
PARA
パラ
PARA
パラ
BAKI (KRAK)
バキ
BAKI
バキ
BAKI
バキ
パシャ
PASHA (SPLISH)

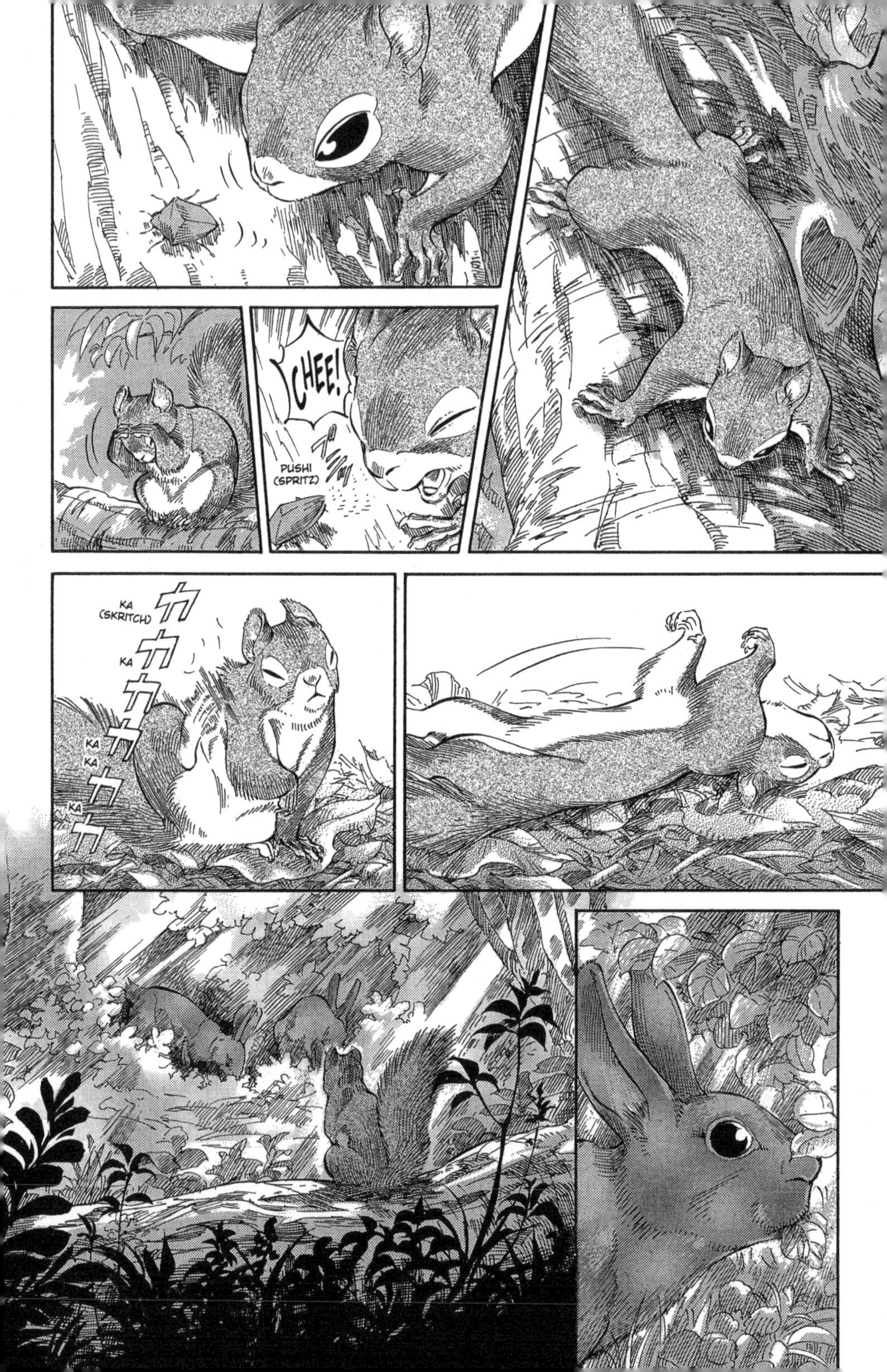
CHEE!
PUSHI (SPRITZ)
KA (SKRITCH)
カ
KA
カ
カ
KA
KA
カ
カ
KA
カ

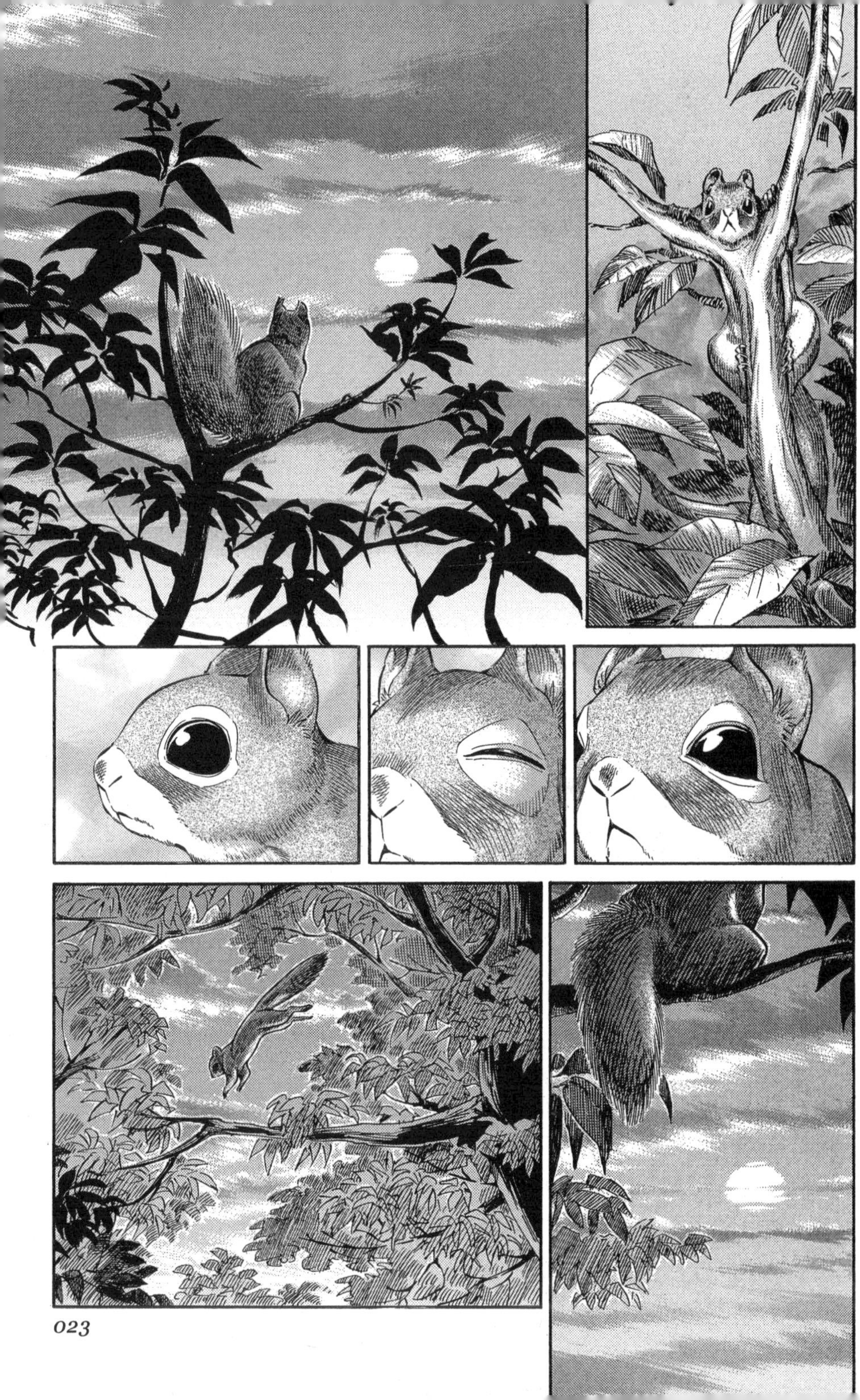

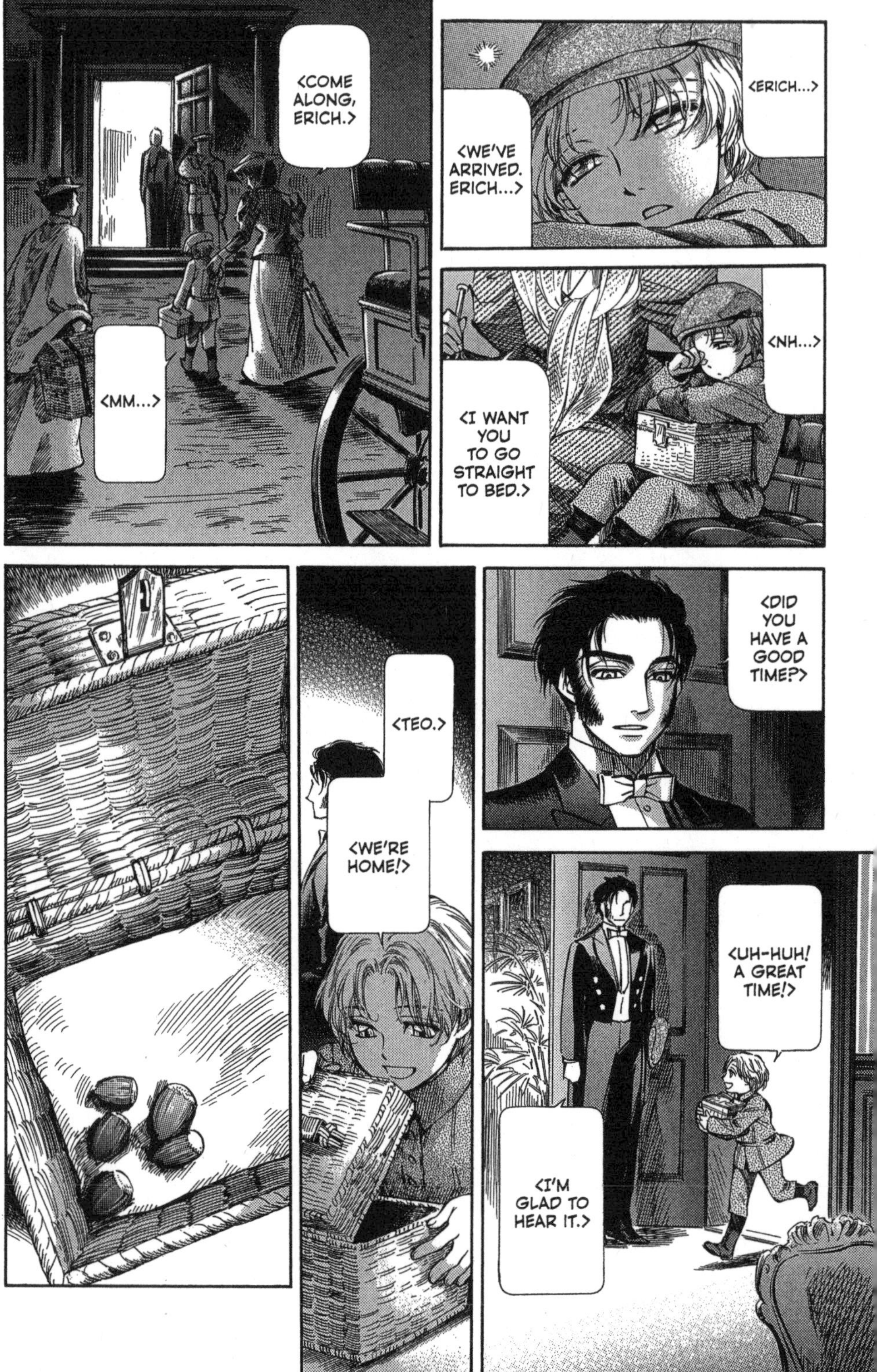
<ERICH...>
<WE'VE ARRIVED. ERICH...>
<NH...>
<I WANT YOU TO GO STRAIGHT TO BED.>
<COME ALONG, ERICH.>
<MM...>
<DID YOU HAVE A GOOD TIME?>
<UH-HUH! A GREAT TIME!>
<I'M GLAD TO HEAR IT.>
<TEO.>
<WE'RE HOME!>

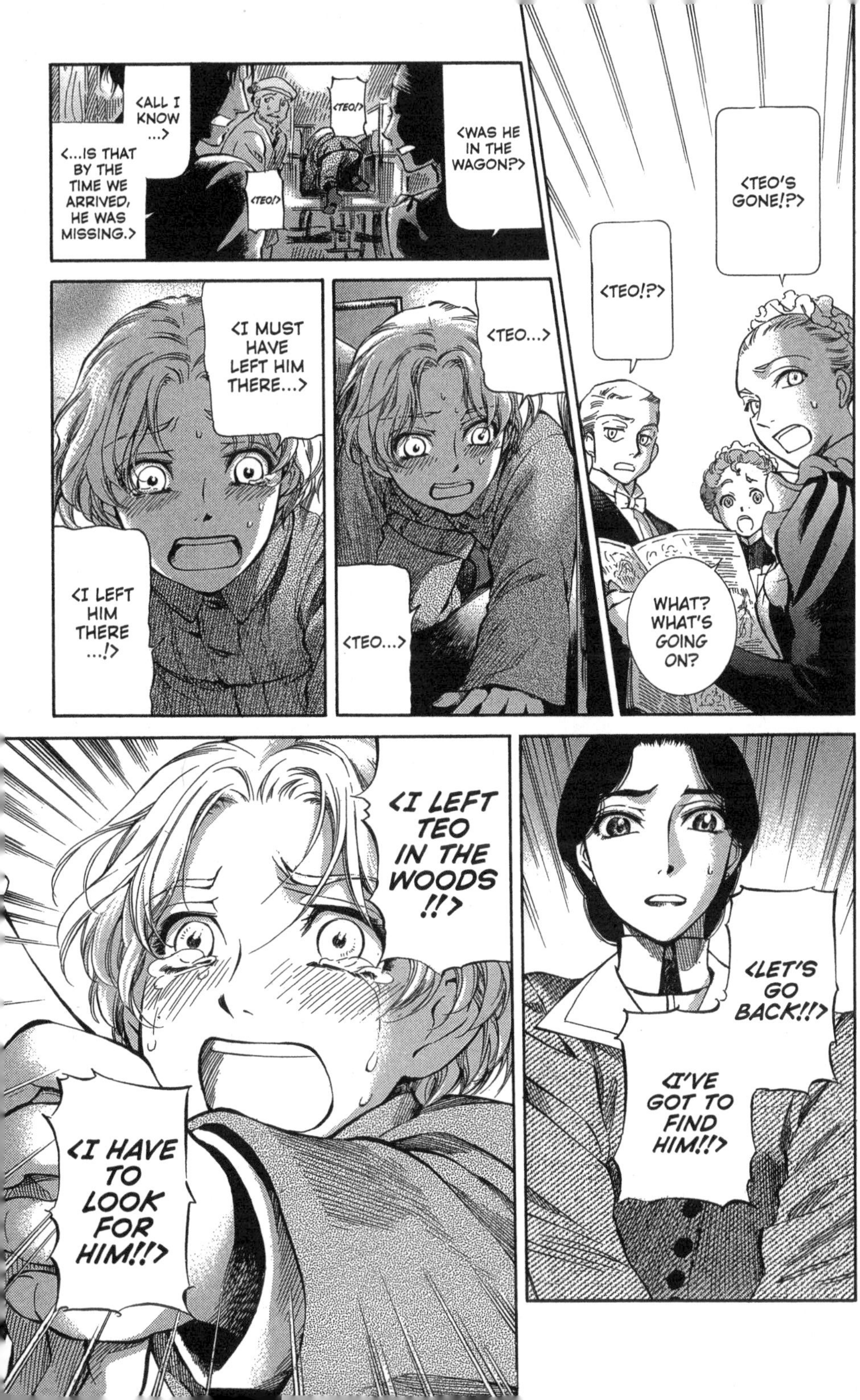
<TEO'S GONE!?>
<TEO!?>
WHAT? WHAT'S GOING ON?
<WAS HE IN THE WAGON?>
<TEO!?>
<ALL I KNOW ...>
<TEO!?>
<...IS THAT BY THE TIME WE ARRIVED, HE WAS MISSING.>
<TEO...>
<TEO...>
<I MUST HAVE LEFT HIM THERE...>
<I LEFT HIM THERE ...!>
<LET'S GO BACK!!>
<I'VE GOT TO FIND HIM!!>
<I LEFT TEO IN THE WOODS!!>
<I HAVE TO LOOK FOR HIM!!>

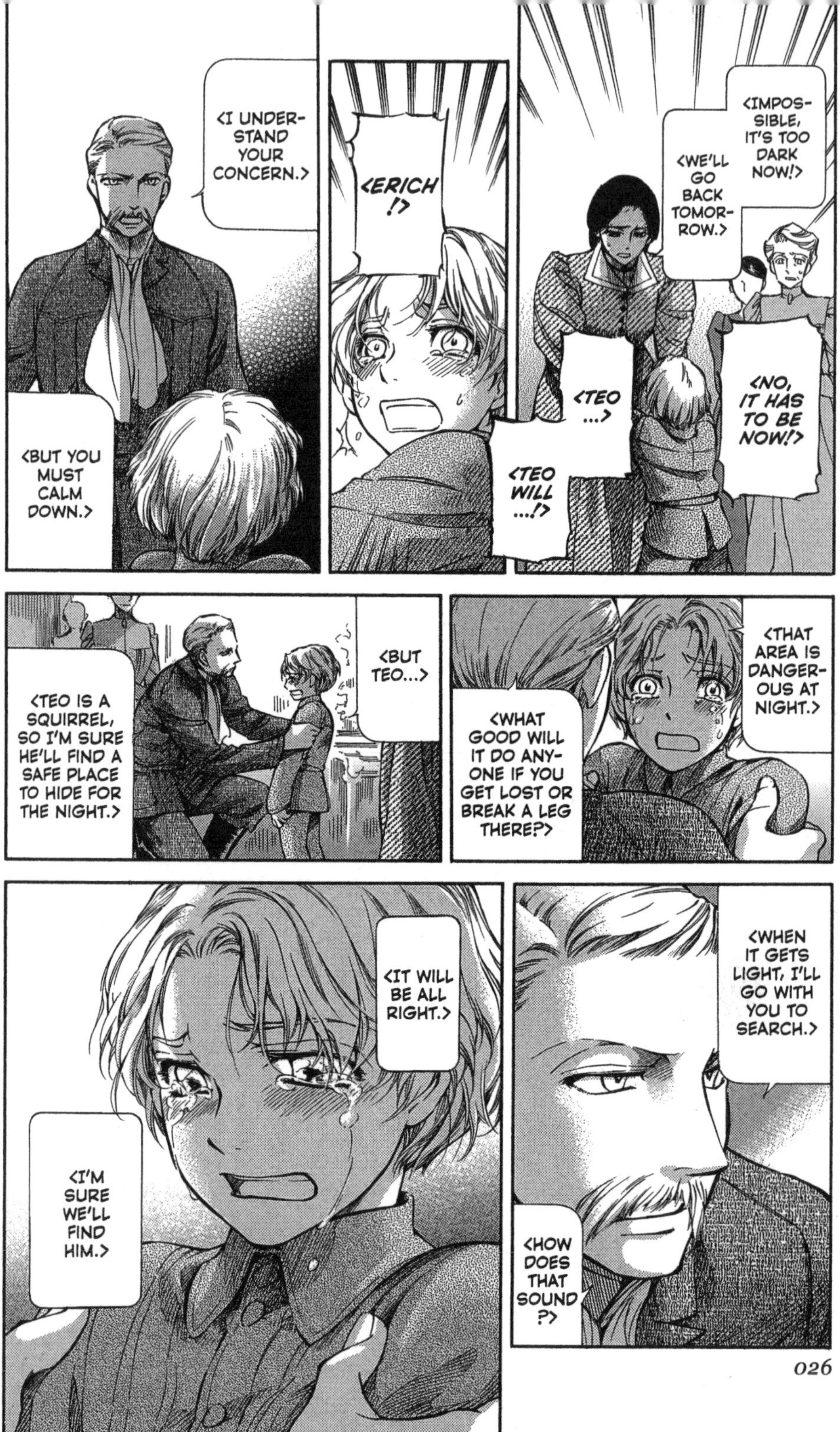
<IMPOSSIBLE, IT'S TOO DARK NOW!>
<WE'LL GO BACK TOMORROW.>
<NO, IT HAS TO BE NOW!>
<TEO ...>
<TEO WILL ...!>
<ERICH!?>
<I UNDERSTAND YOUR CONCERN.>
<BUT YOU MUST CALM DOWN.>
<THAT AREA IS DANGEROUS AT NIGHT.>
<WHAT GOOD WILL IT DO ANYONE IF YOU GET LOST OR BREAK A LEG THERE?>
<BUT TEO...>
<TEO IS A SQUIRREL, SO I'M SURE HE'LL FIND A SAFE PLACE TO HIDE FOR THE NIGHT.>
<WHEN IT GETS LIGHT, I'LL GO WITH YOU TO SEARCH.>
<HOW DOES THAT SOUND?>
<IT WILL BE ALL RIGHT.>
<I'M SURE WE'LL FIND HIM.>

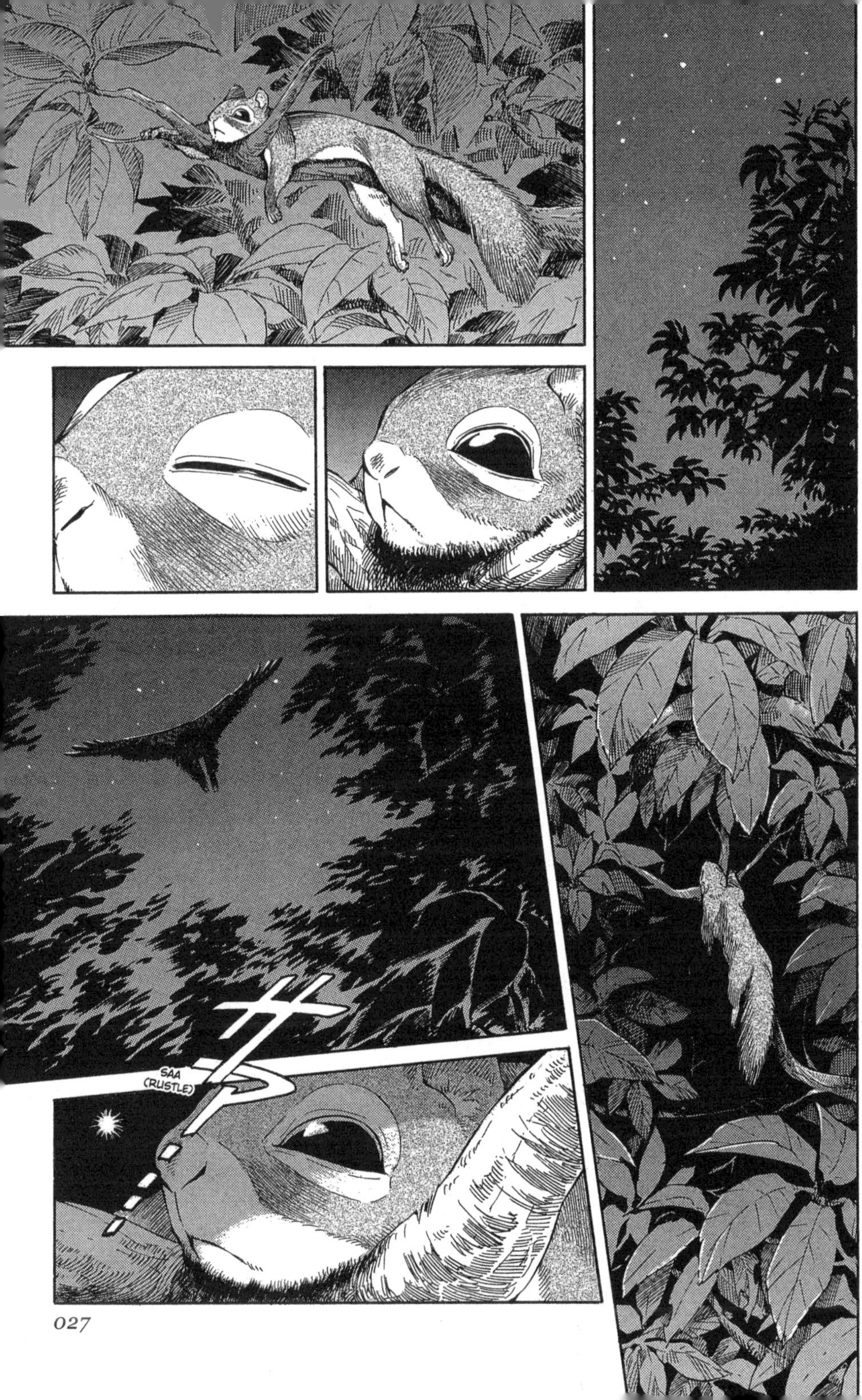
SAA
(RUSTLE)

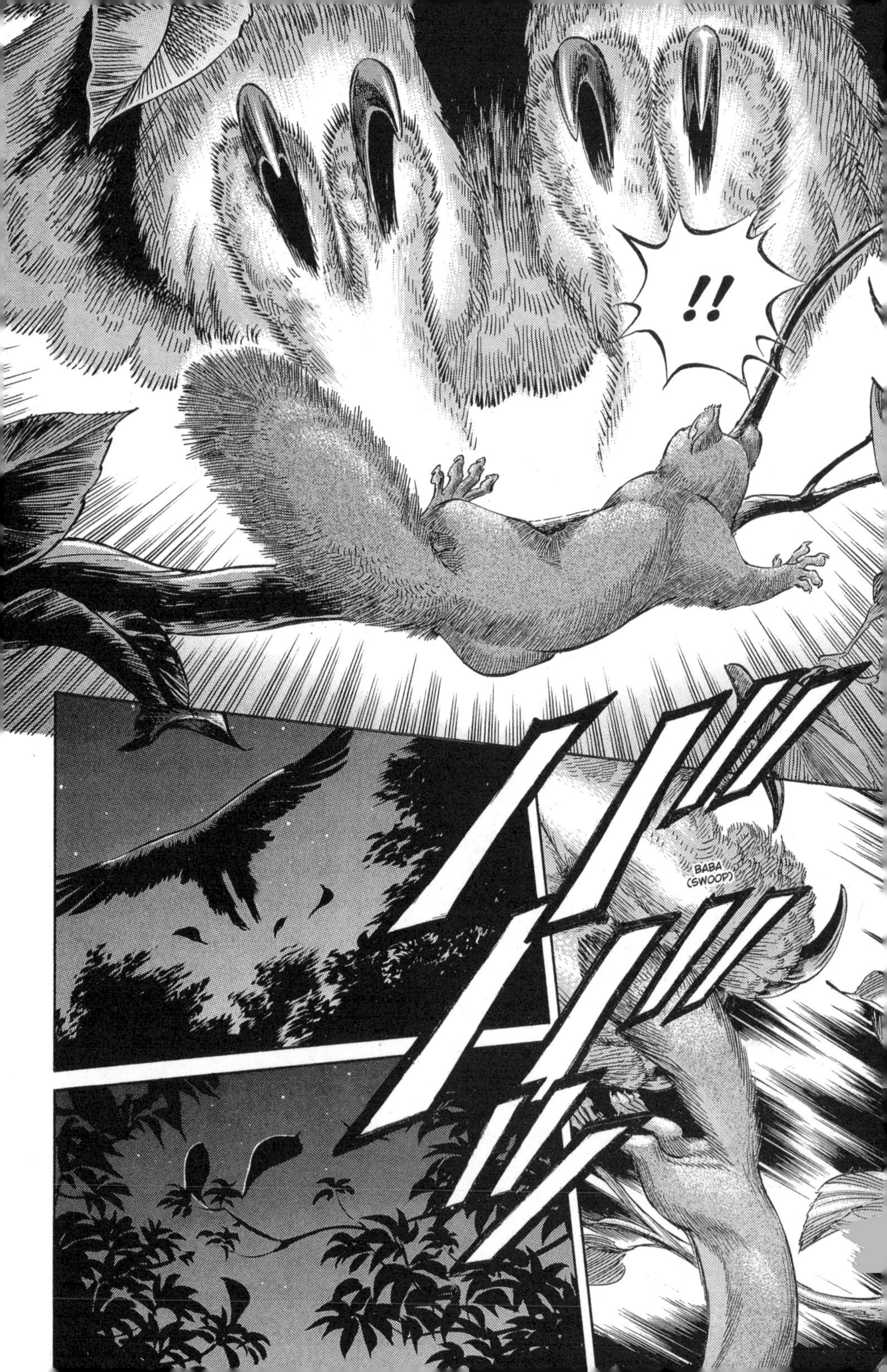
!!
BABA
(SWOOP)

HFF!
HFF!

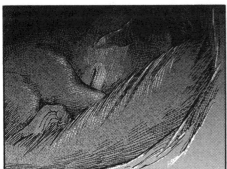
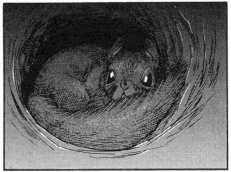

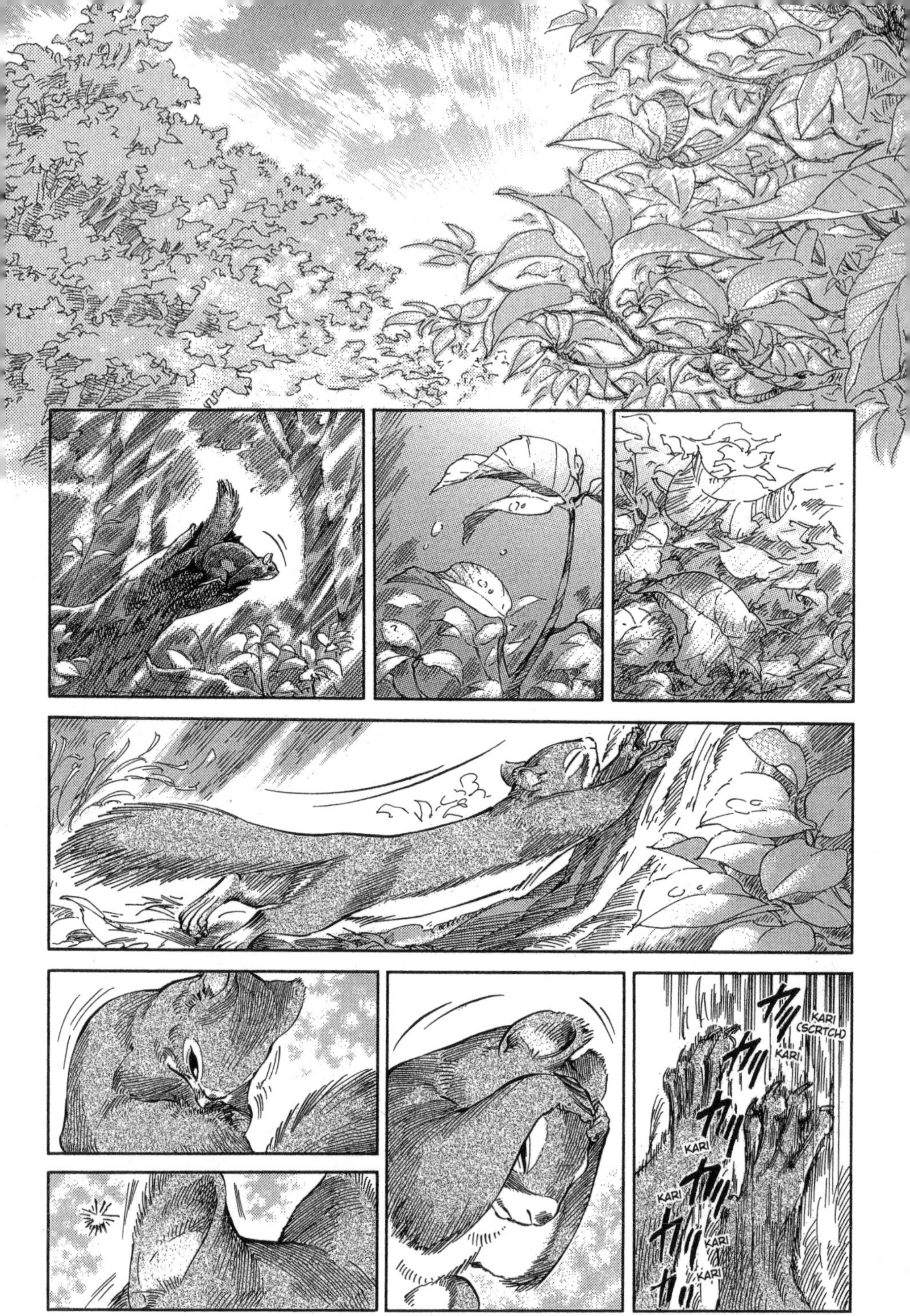
KARI (SCRTCH)
KARI
KARI
KARI
KARI
KARI

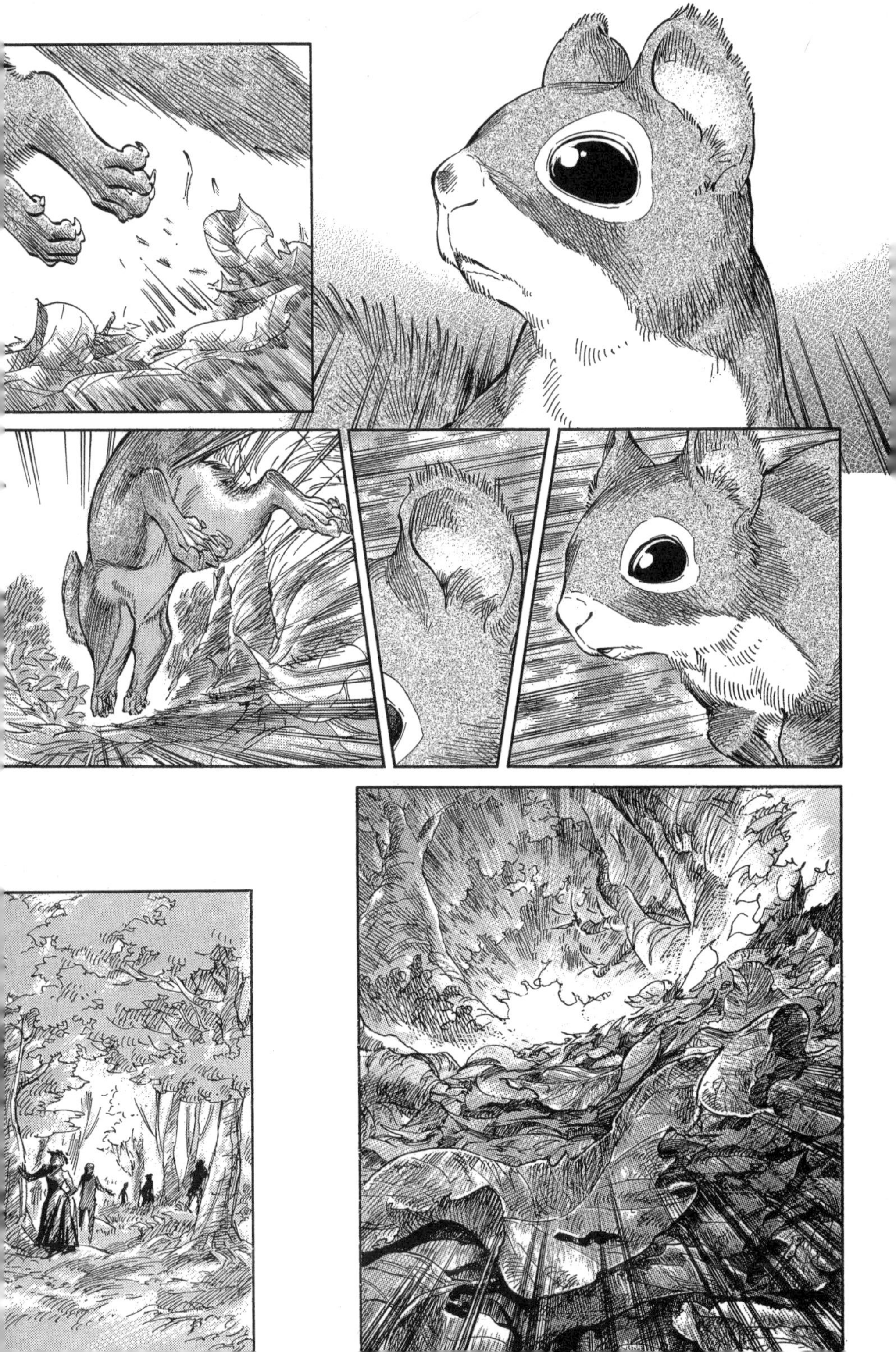

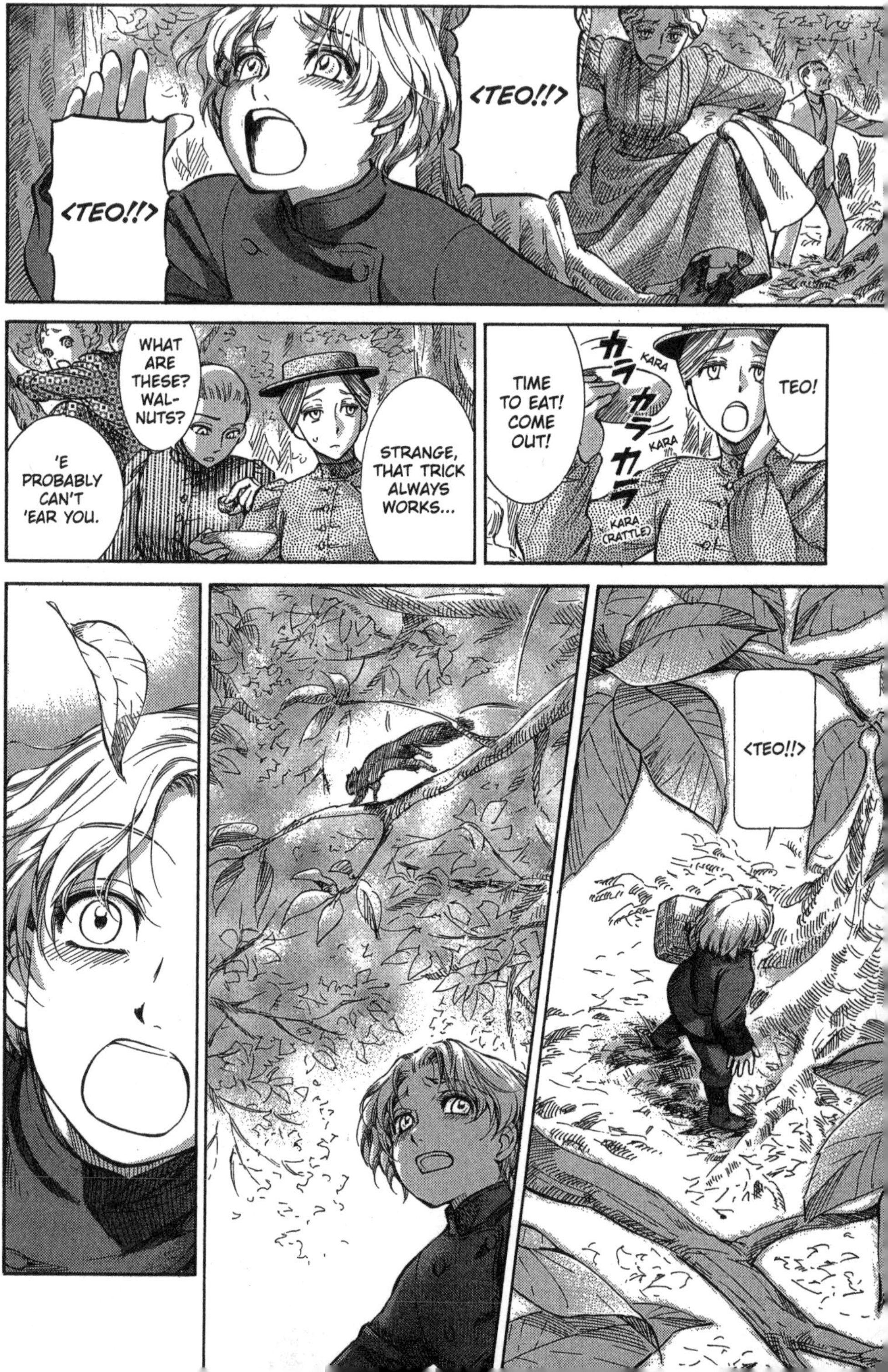
<TEO!!>
<TEO!!>
TEO!
カラ KARA
TIME TO EAT! COME OUT!
カラ KARA
カラ KARA (RATTLE)
STRANGE, THAT TRICK ALWAYS WORKS...
WHAT ARE THESE? WAL-NUTS?
'E PROBABLY CAN'T 'EAR YOU.
<TEO!!>

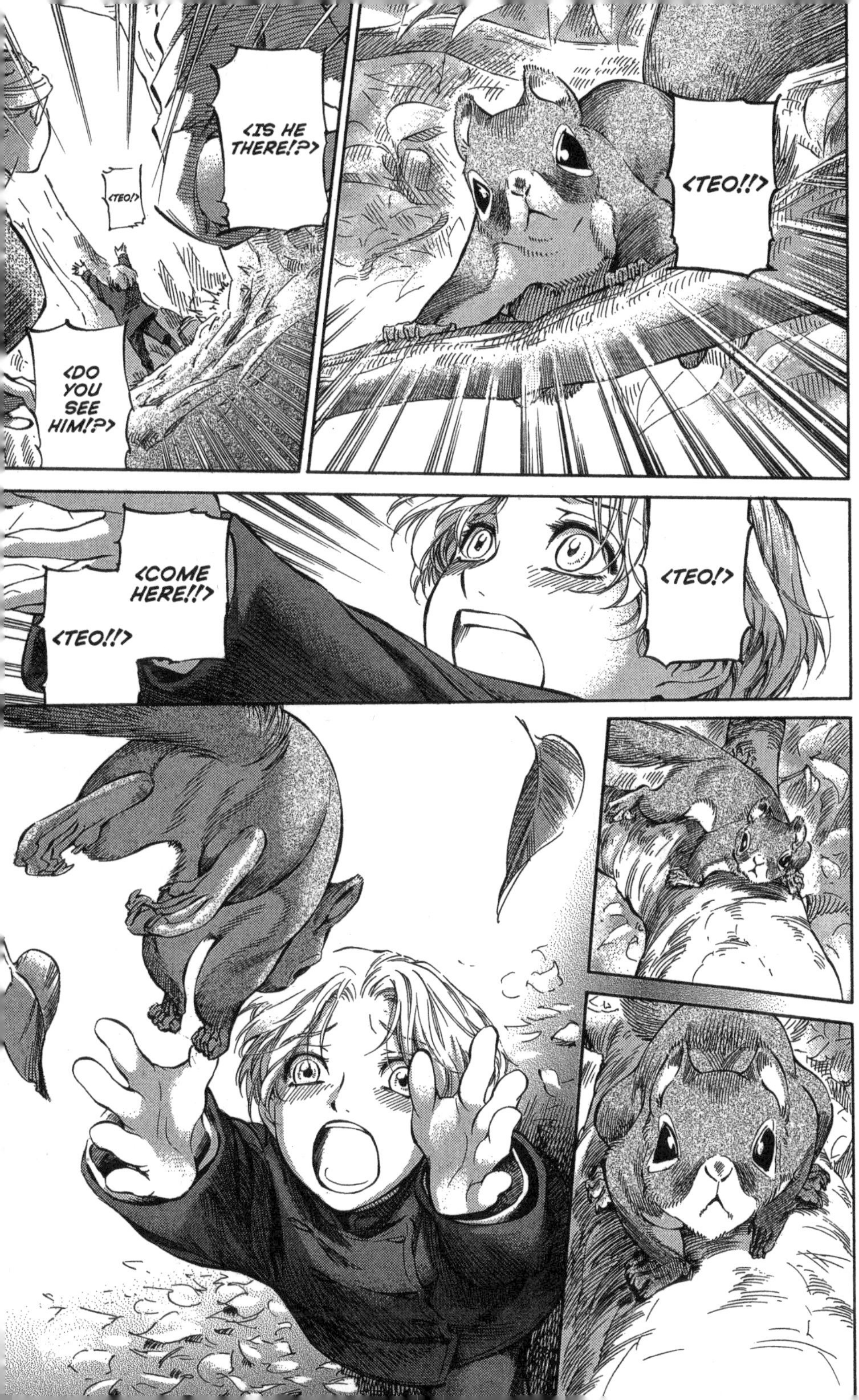
<TEO!!>
<IS HE THERE!?>
<TEO!>
<DO YOU SEE HIM!?>
<TEO!>
<COME HERE!!>
<TEO!!>

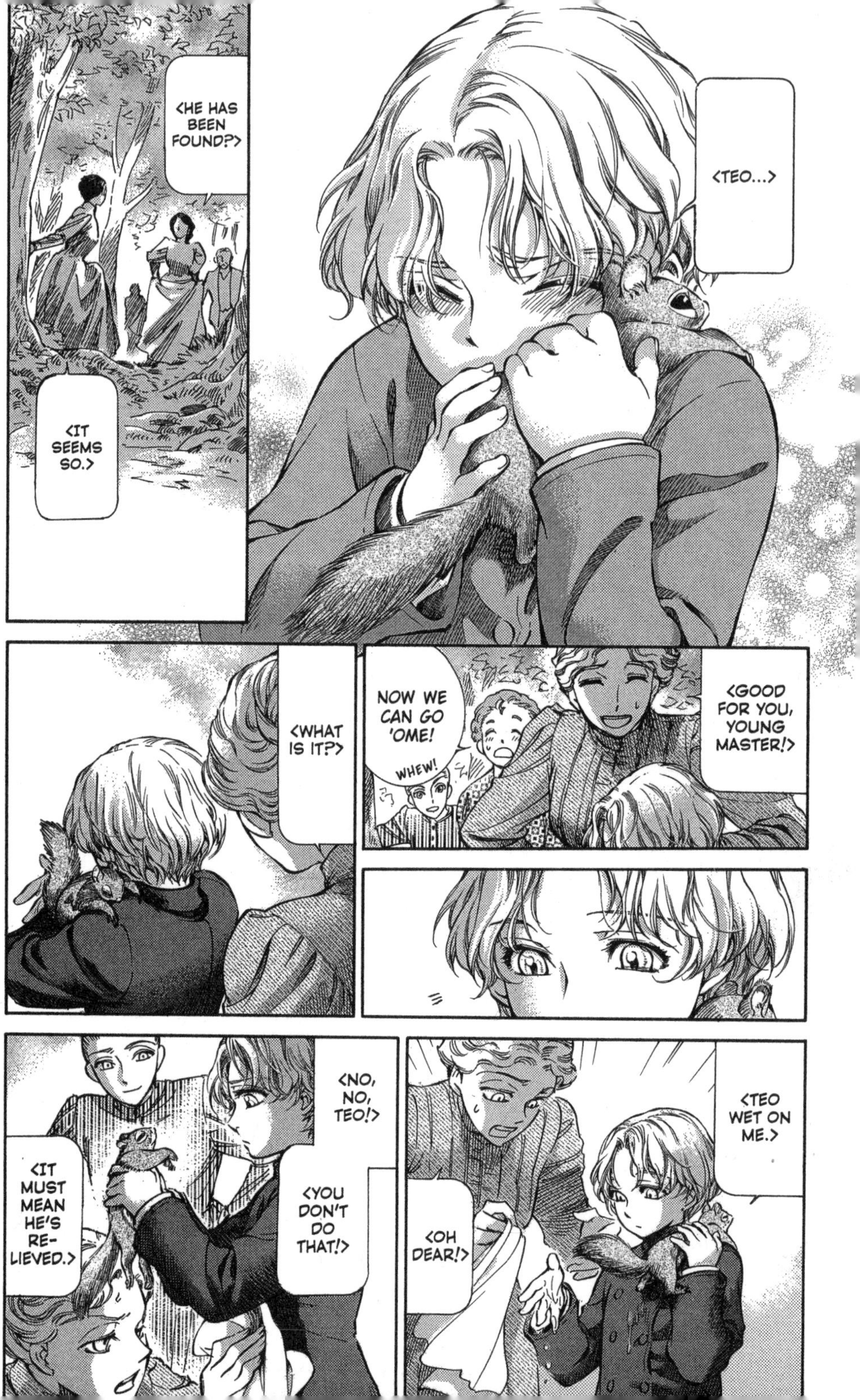
<TEO...>
<HE HAS BEEN FOUND?>
<IT SEEMS SO.>
<GOOD FOR YOU, YOUNG MASTER!>
NOW WE CAN GO 'OME!
WHEW!
<WHAT IS IT?>
<TEO WET ON ME.>
<OH DEAR!>
<NO, NO, TEO!>
<YOU DON'T DO THAT!>
<IT MUST MEAN HE'S RE-LIEVED.>

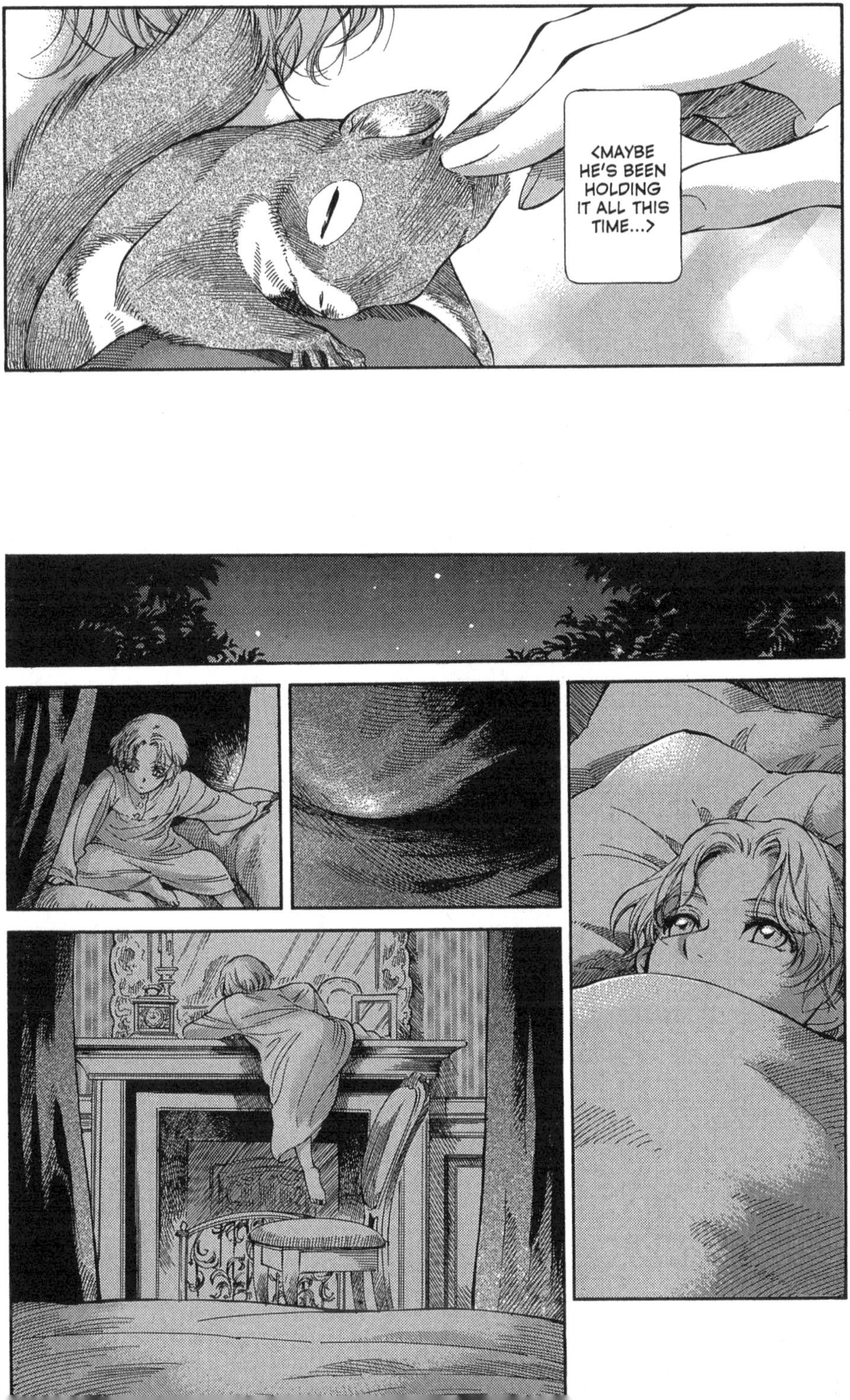
<MAYBE HE'S BEEN HOLDING IT ALL THIS TIME...>

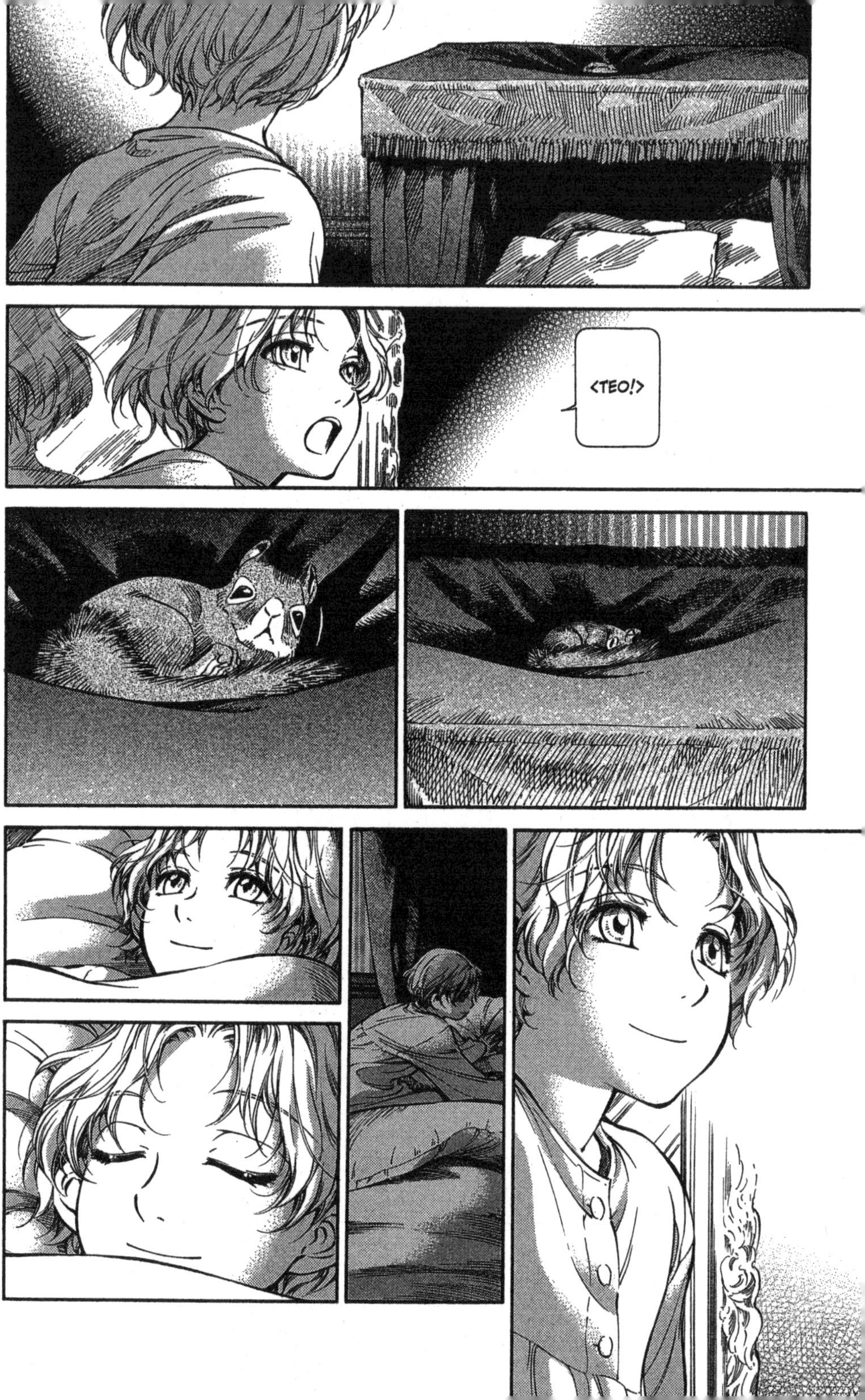
<TEO!>

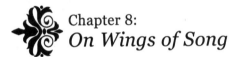

Chapter 8:
On Wings of Song

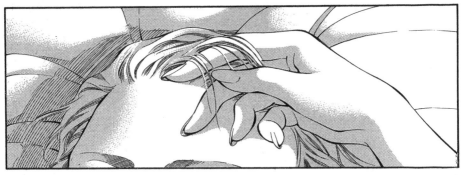

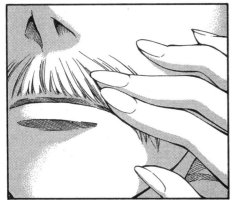

〈……〉

Chapter 8: *On Wings of Song*

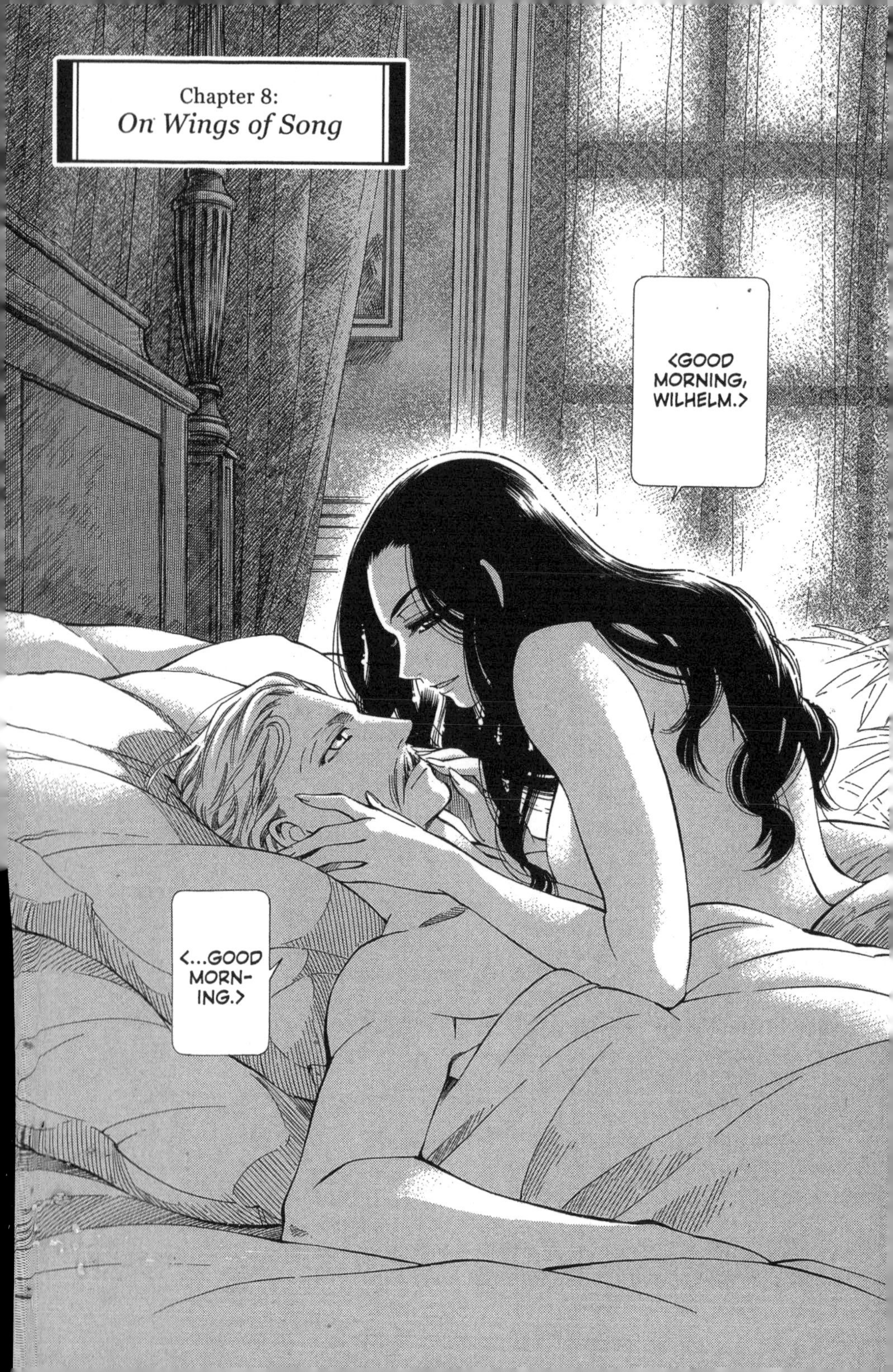

<GOOD MORNING, WILHELM.>
<...GOOD MORNING.>

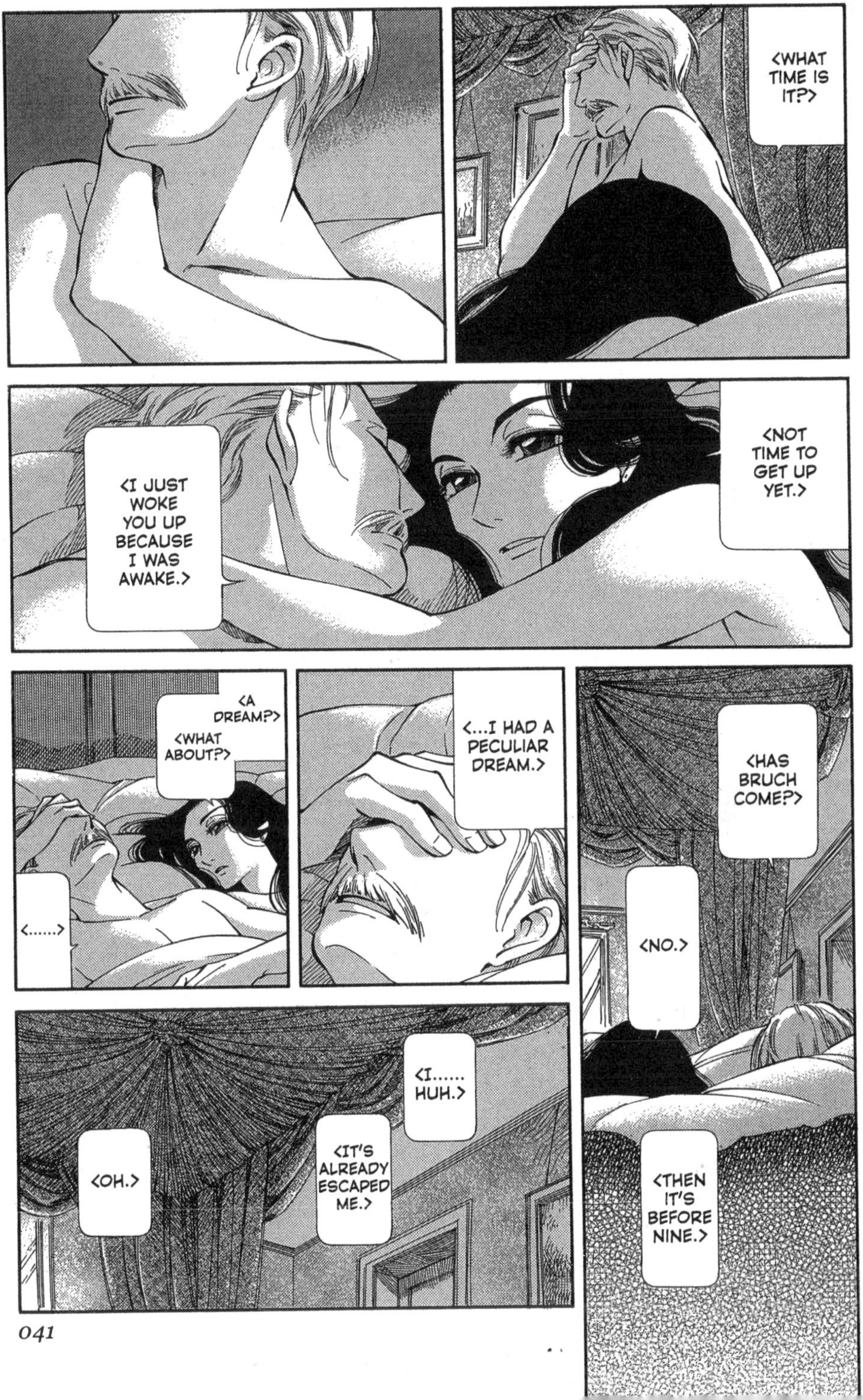
<WHAT TIME IS IT?>
<NOT TIME TO GET UP YET.>
<I JUST WOKE YOU UP BECAUSE I WAS AWAKE.>
<HAS BRUCH COME?>
<NO.>
<THEN IT'S BEFORE NINE.>
<...I HAD A PECULIAR DREAM.>
<A DREAM?>
<WHAT ABOUT?>
<......>
<I...... HUH.>
<IT'S ALREADY ESCAPED ME.>
<OH.>

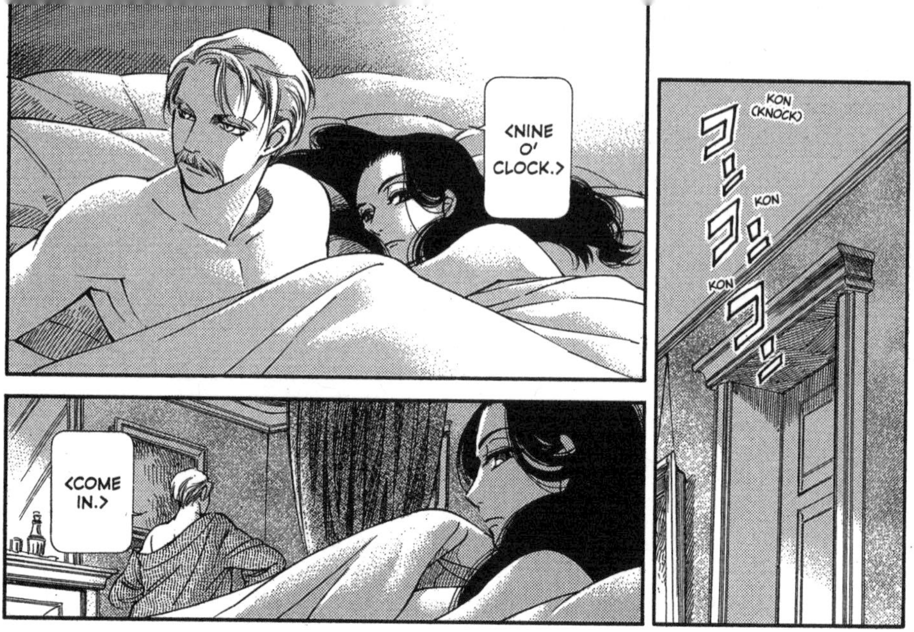
KON (KNOCK)
KON
KON
<NINE O' CLOCK.>
<COME IN.>

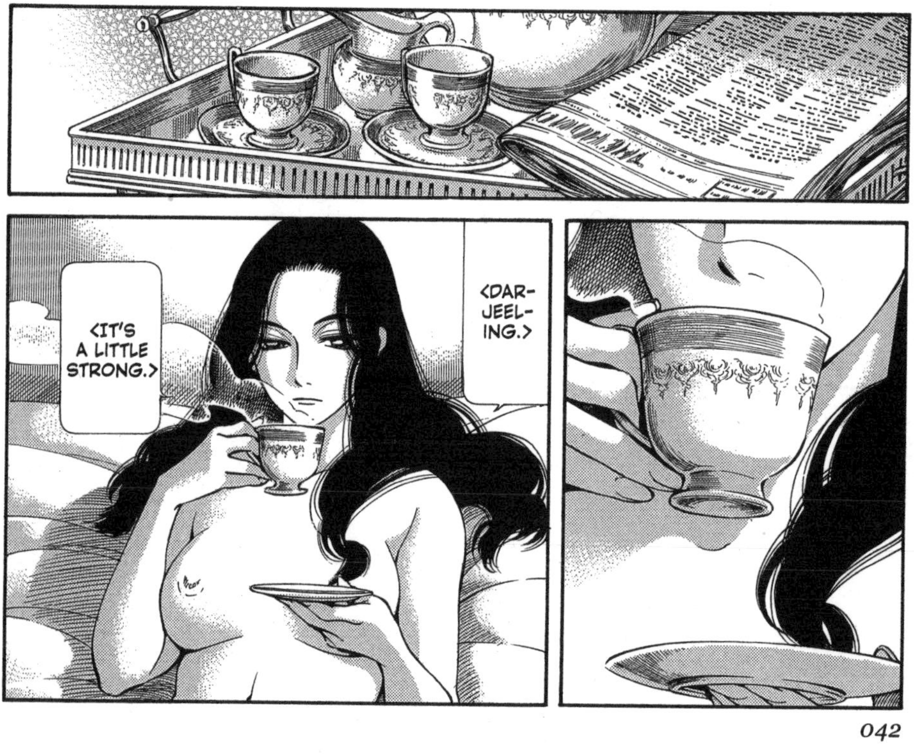
<DAR-JEEL-ING.>
<IT'S A LITTLE STRONG.>

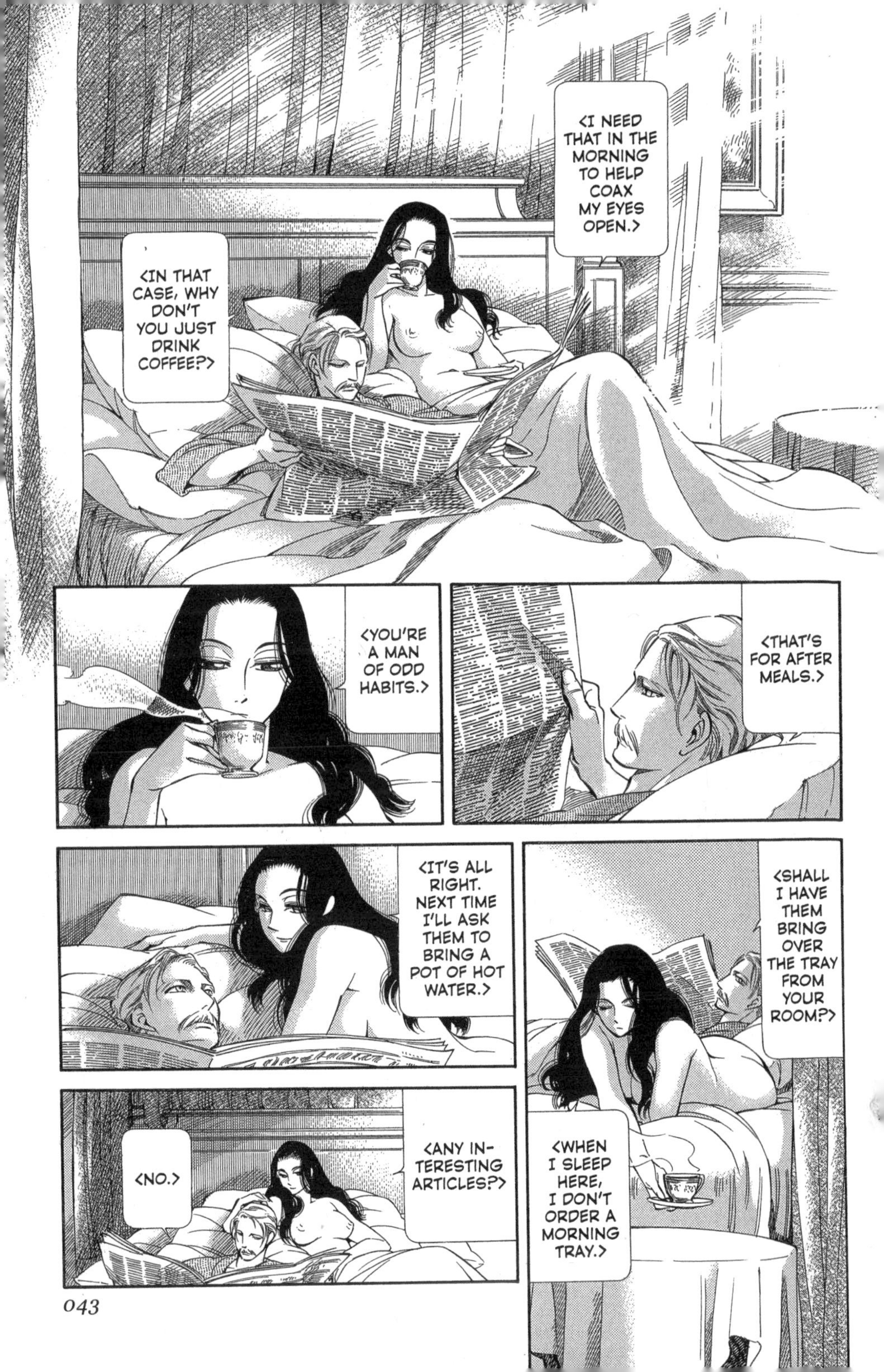
<I NEED THAT IN THE MORNING TO HELP COAX MY EYES OPEN.>
<IN THAT CASE, WHY DON'T YOU JUST DRINK COFFEE?>
<THAT'S FOR AFTER MEALS.>
<YOU'RE A MAN OF ODD HABITS.>
<SHALL I HAVE THEM BRING OVER THE TRAY FROM YOUR ROOM?>
<WHEN I SLEEP HERE, I DON'T ORDER A MORNING TRAY.>
<IT'S ALL RIGHT. NEXT TIME I'LL ASK THEM TO BRING A POT OF HOT WATER.>
<ANY IN-TERESTING ARTICLES?>
<NO.>

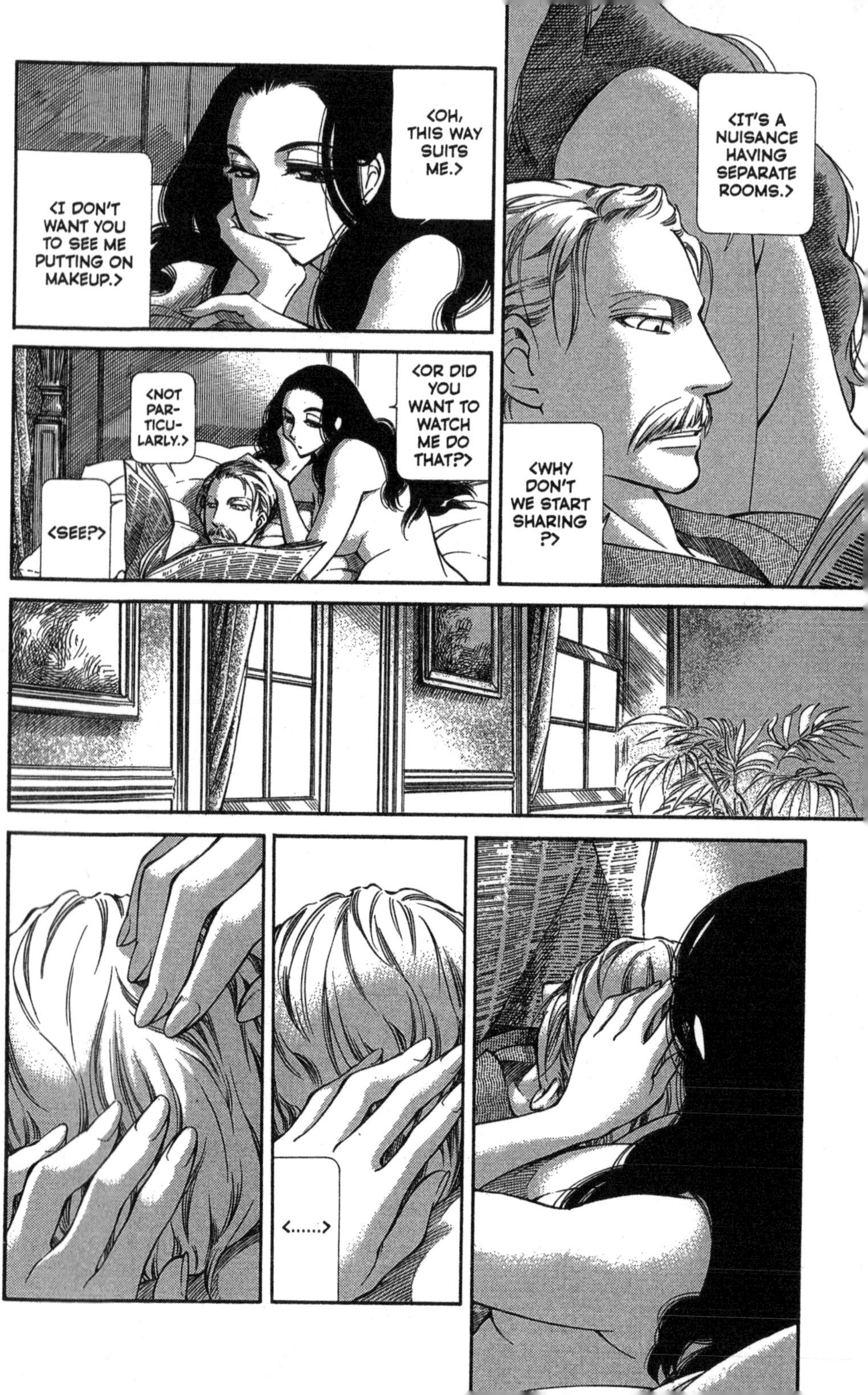
<IT'S A NUISANCE HAVING SEPARATE ROOMS.>
<WHY DON'T WE START SHARING?>
<OH, THIS WAY SUITS ME.>
<I DON'T WANT YOU TO SEE ME PUTTING ON MAKEUP.>
<OR DID YOU WANT TO WATCH ME DO THAT?>
<NOT PARTICULARLY.>
<SEE?>
<......>

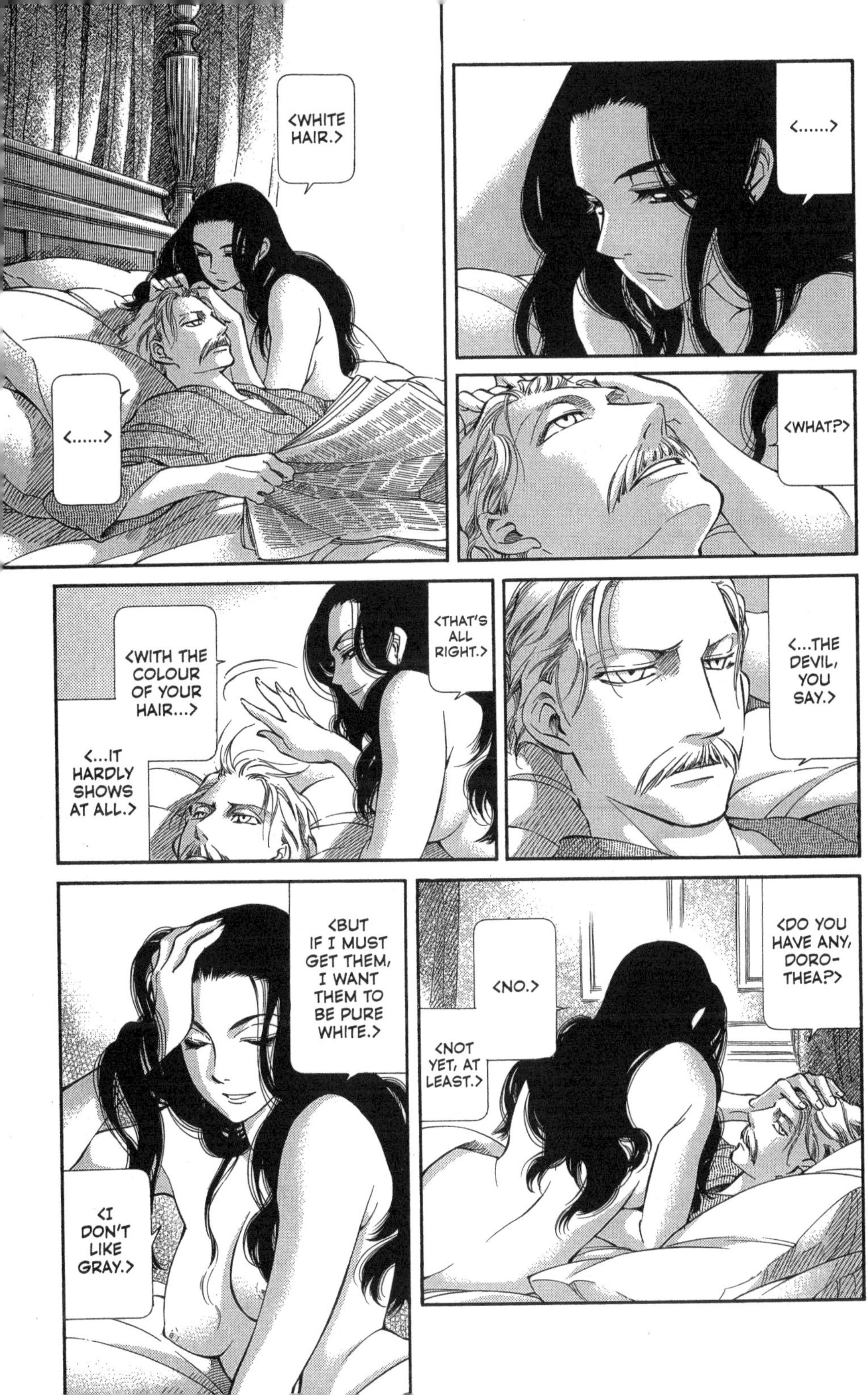
<......>
<WHAT?>
<WHITE HAIR.>
<......>
<...THE DEVIL, YOU SAY.>
<THAT'S ALL RIGHT.>
<WITH THE COLOUR OF YOUR HAIR...>
<...IT HARDLY SHOWS AT ALL.>
<DO YOU HAVE ANY, DORO-THEA?>
<NO.>
<NOT YET, AT LEAST.>
<BUT IF I MUST GET THEM, I WANT THEM TO BE PURE WHITE.>
<I DON'T LIKE GRAY.>

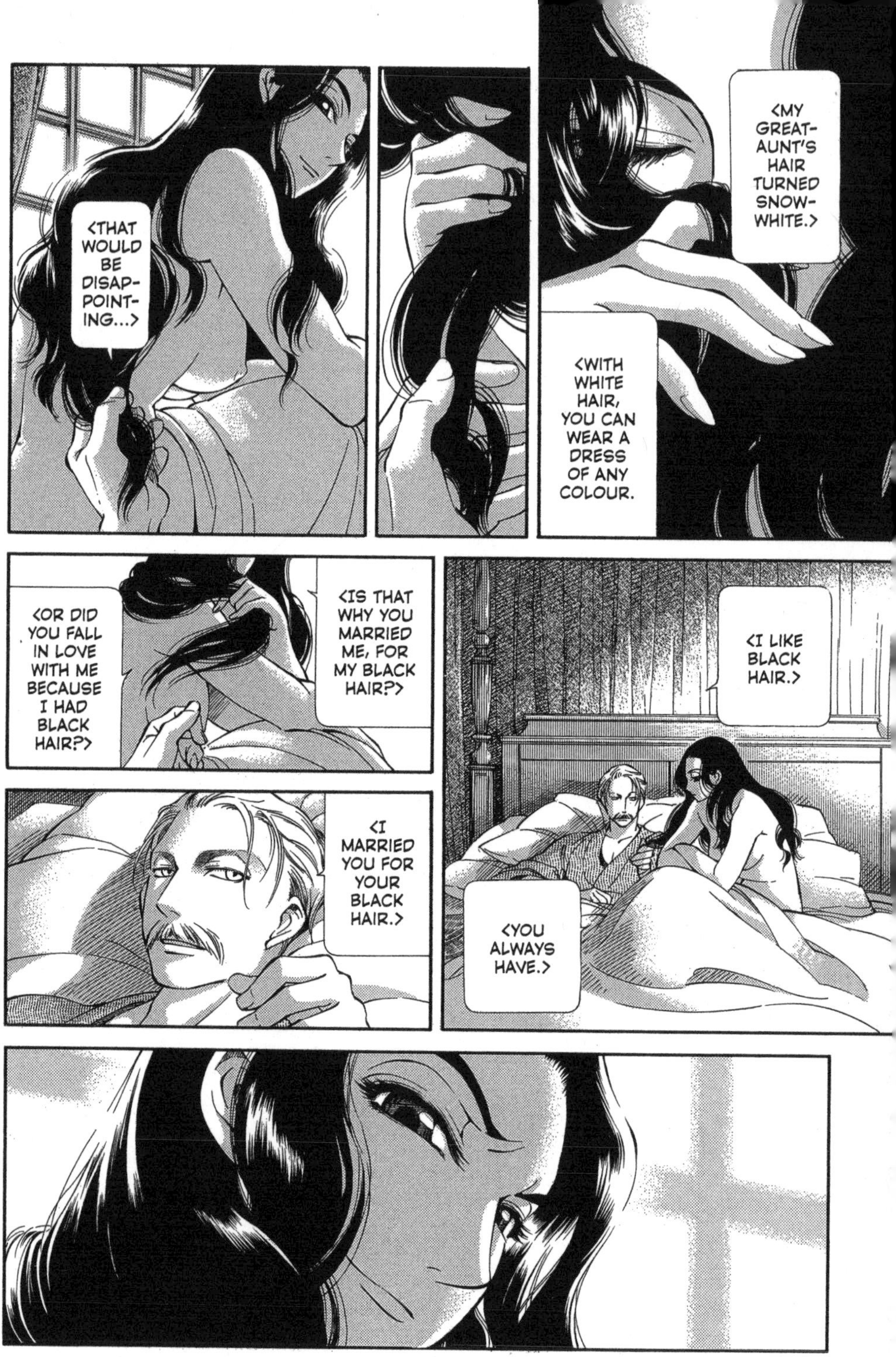
<MY GREAT-AUNT'S HAIR TURNED SNOW-WHITE.>
<WITH WHITE HAIR, YOU CAN WEAR A DRESS OF ANY COLOUR.
<THAT WOULD BE DISAPPOINTING...>
<I LIKE BLACK HAIR.>
<YOU ALWAYS HAVE.>
<IS THAT WHY YOU MARRIED ME, FOR MY BLACK HAIR?>
<OR DID YOU FALL IN LOVE WITH ME BECAUSE I HAD BLACK HAIR?>
<I MARRIED YOU FOR YOUR BLACK HAIR.>

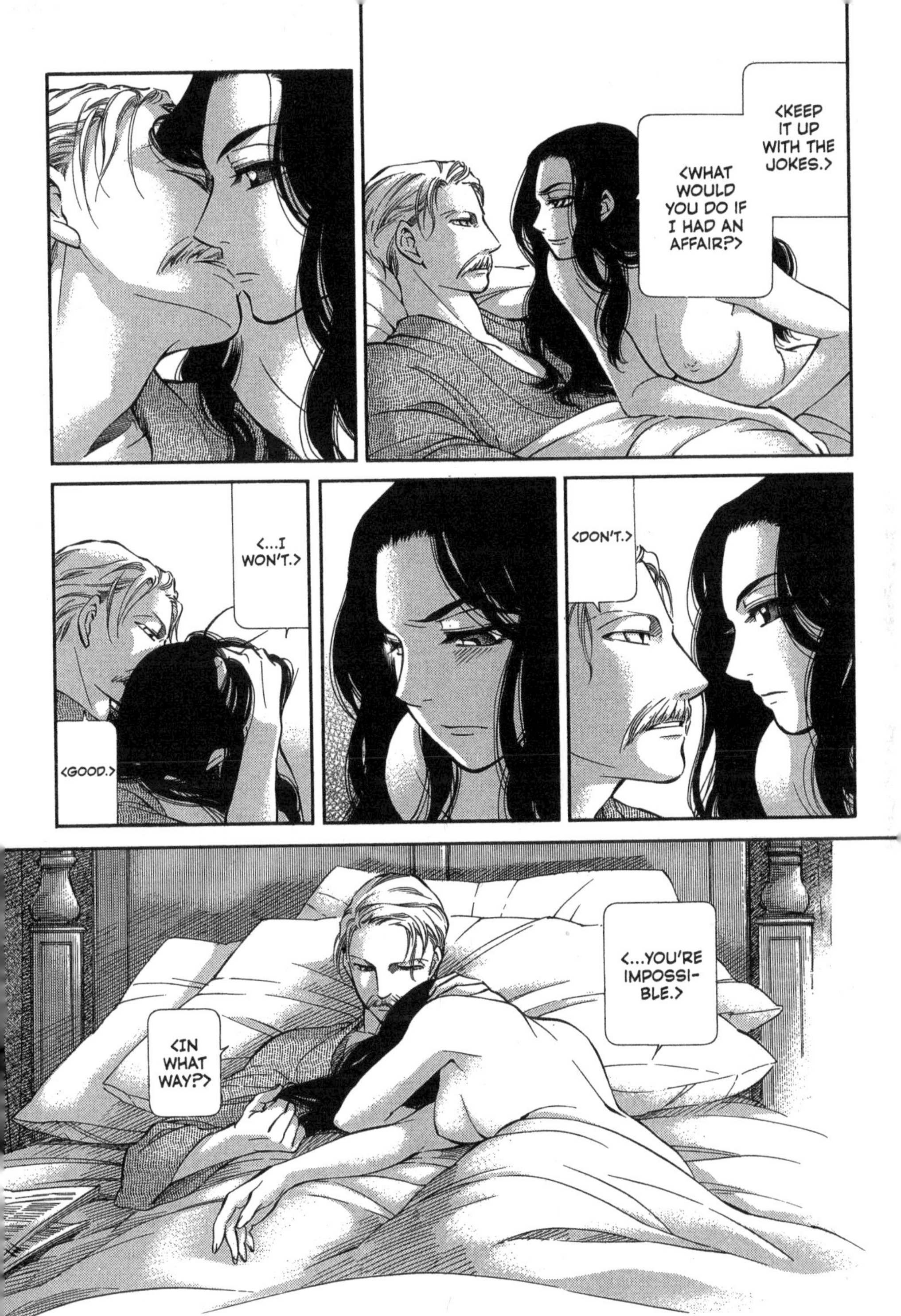
<KEEP IT UP WITH THE JOKES.>
<WHAT WOULD YOU DO IF I HAD AN AFFAIR?>
<DON'T.>
<...I WON'T.>
<GOOD.>
<...YOU'RE IMPOSSI-BLE.>
<IN WHAT WAY?>

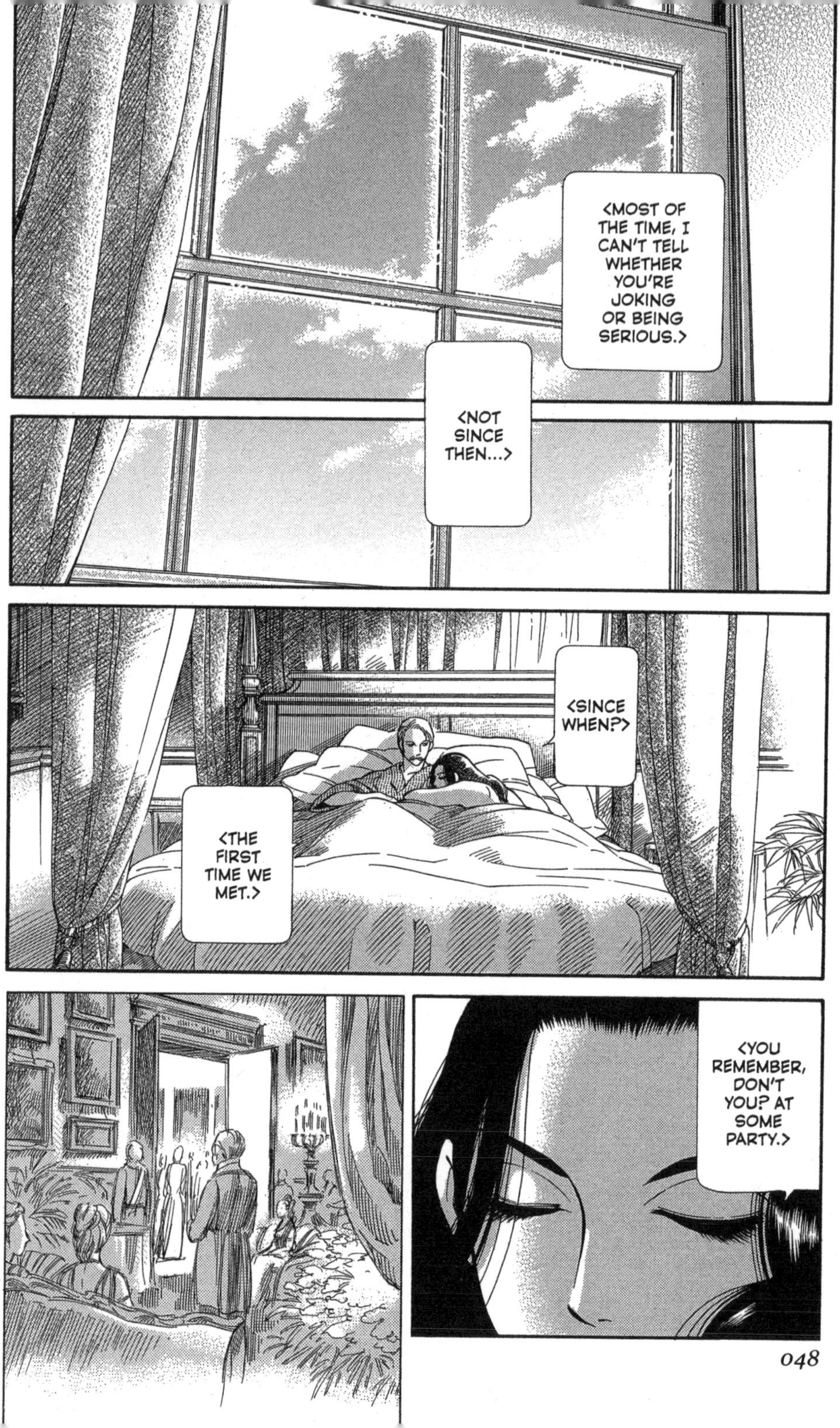
<MOST OF THE TIME, I CAN'T TELL WHETHER YOU'RE JOKING OR BEING SERIOUS.>
<NOT SINCE THEN...>
<SINCE WHEN?>
<THE FIRST TIME WE MET.>
<YOU REMEMBER, DON'T YOU? AT SOME PARTY.>

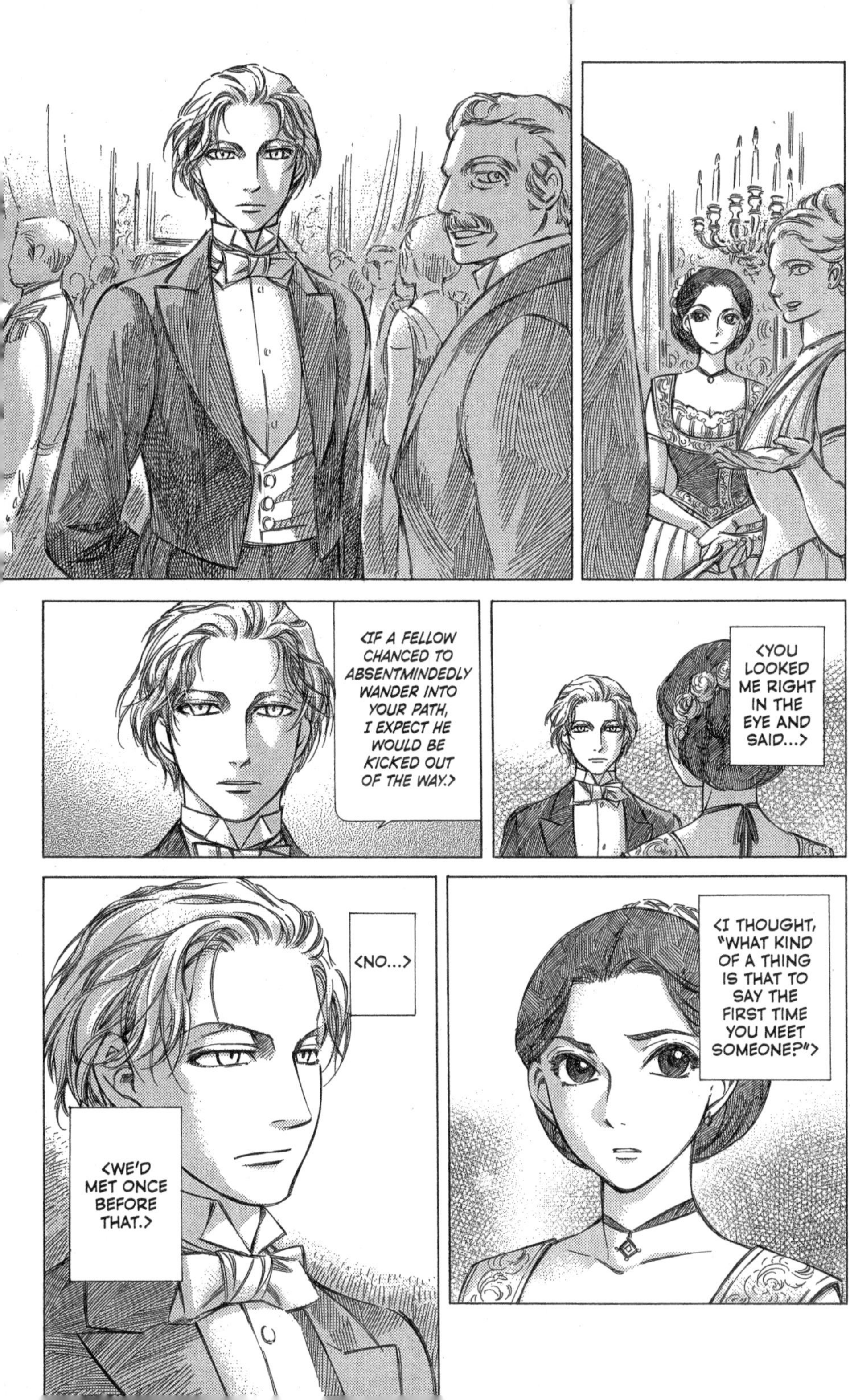
<YOU LOOKED ME RIGHT IN THE EYE AND SAID...>
<IF A FELLOW CHANCED TO ABSENTMINDEDLY WANDER INTO YOUR PATH, I EXPECT HE WOULD BE KICKED OUT OF THE WAY.>
<I THOUGHT, "WHAT KIND OF A THING IS THAT TO SAY THE FIRST TIME YOU MEET SOMEONE?">
<NO...>
<WE'D MET ONCE BEFORE THAT.>

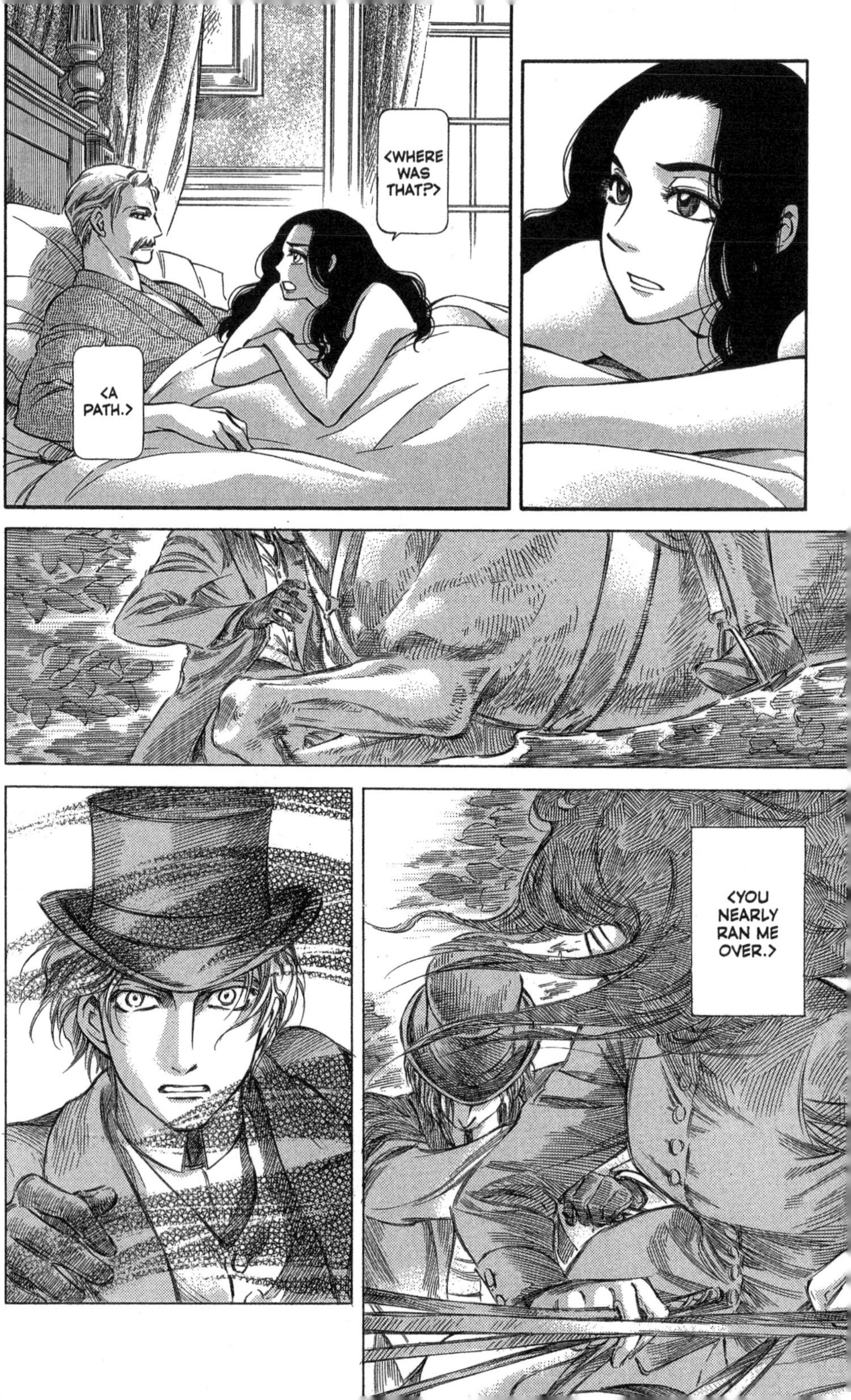
<WHERE WAS THAT?>
<A PATH.>
<YOU NEARLY RAN ME OVER.>

‹I'M SORRY!›

‹STRADDLING A MAN'S SADDLE WITH YOUR HAIR UNBOUND...›

‹...I THOUGHT TO MYSELF, "WHAT A ROUGH YOUNG WOMAN."›

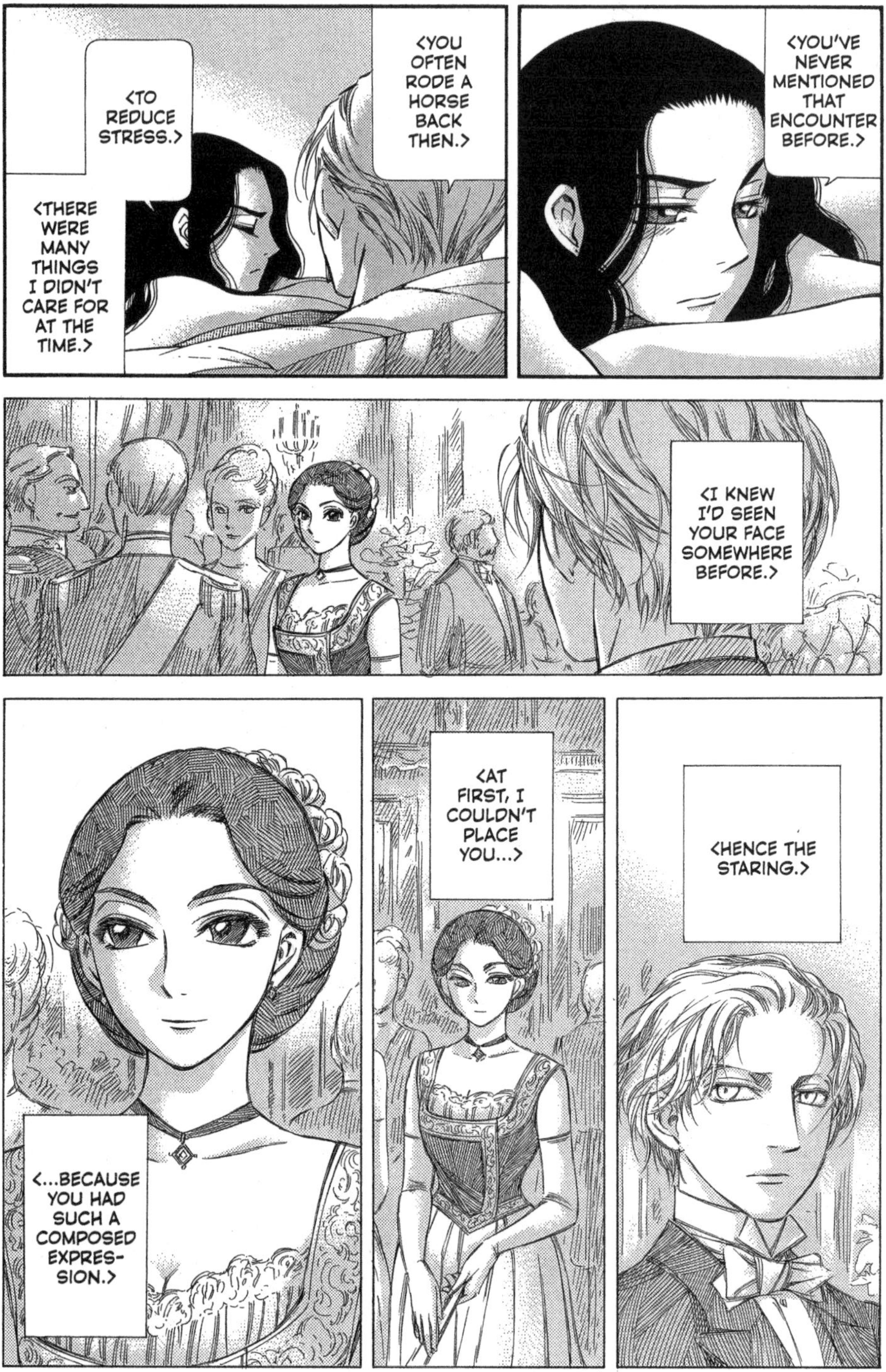
<YOU'VE NEVER MENTIONED THAT ENCOUNTER BEFORE.>
<YOU OFTEN RODE A HORSE BACK THEN.>
<TO REDUCE STRESS.>
<THERE WERE MANY THINGS I DIDN'T CARE FOR AT THE TIME.>
<I KNEW I'D SEEN YOUR FACE SOMEWHERE BEFORE.>
<HENCE THE STARING.>
<AT FIRST, I COULDN'T PLACE YOU...>
<...BECAUSE YOU HAD SUCH A COMPOSED EXPRES-SION.>

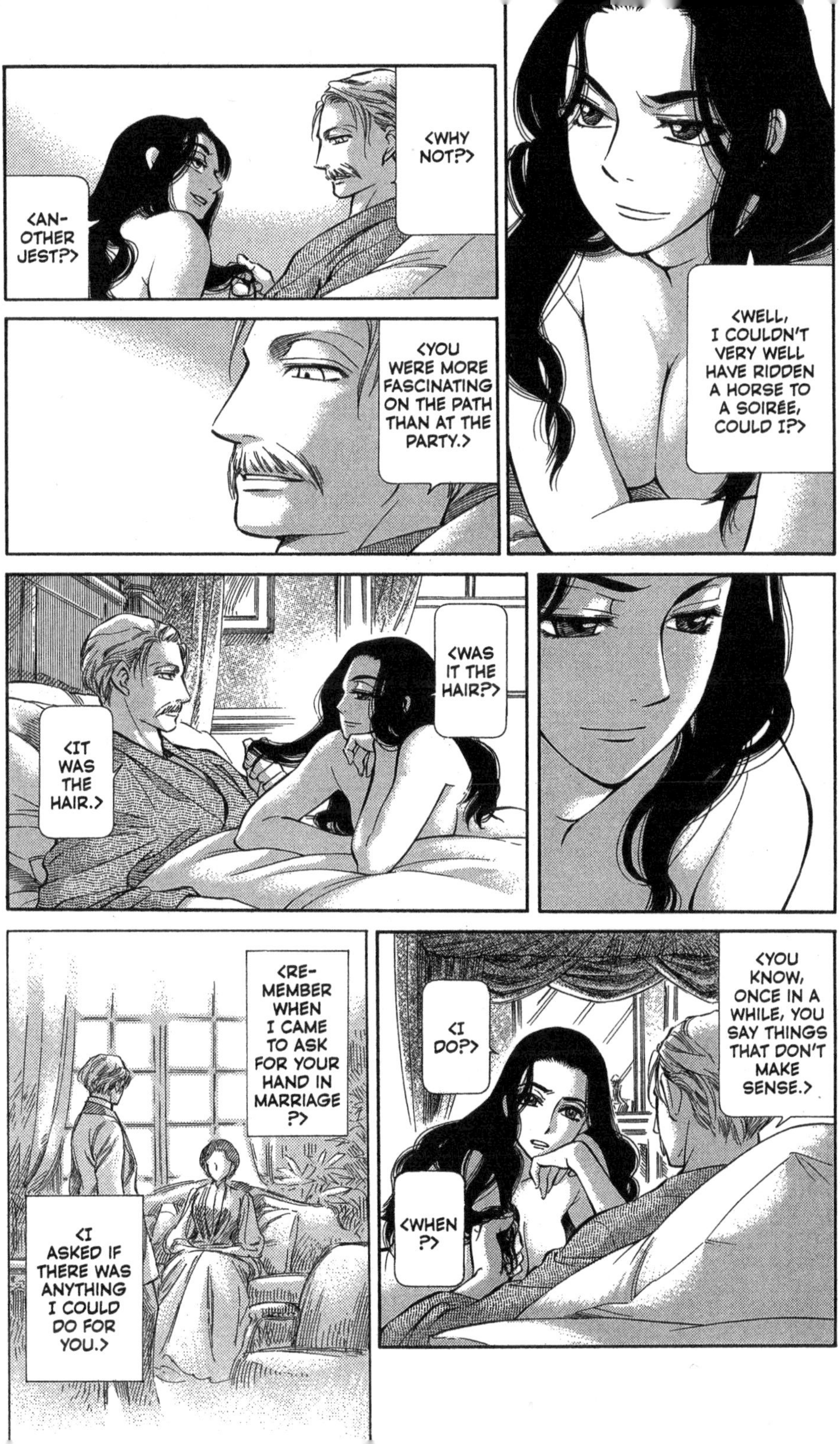
<WELL, I COULDN'T VERY WELL HAVE RIDDEN A HORSE TO A SOIRÉE, COULD I?>
<WHY NOT?>
<AN-OTHER JEST?>
<YOU WERE MORE FASCINATING ON THE PATH THAN AT THE PARTY.>
<WAS IT THE HAIR?>
<IT WAS THE HAIR.>
<YOU KNOW, ONCE IN A WHILE, YOU SAY THINGS THAT DON'T MAKE SENSE.>
<I DO?>
<WHEN?>
<RE-MEMBER WHEN I CAME TO ASK FOR YOUR HAND IN MARRIAGE?>
<I ASKED IF THERE WAS ANYTHING I COULD DO FOR YOU.>

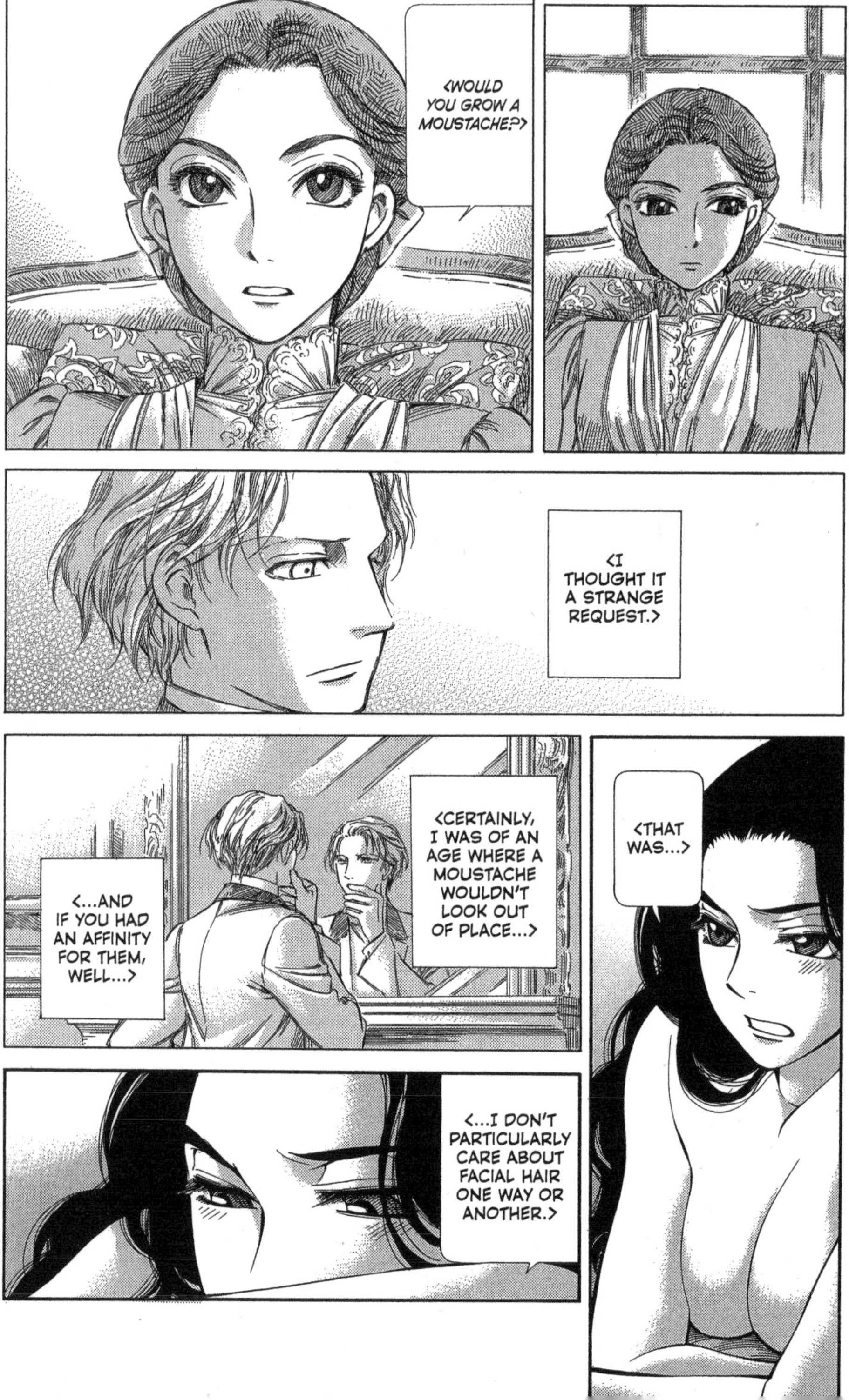
<WOULD YOU GROW A MOUSTACHE?>
<I THOUGHT IT A STRANGE REQUEST.>
<THAT WAS...>
<CERTAINLY, I WAS OF AN AGE WHERE A MOUSTACHE WOULDN'T LOOK OUT OF PLACE...>
<...AND IF YOU HAD AN AFFINITY FOR THEM, WELL...>
<...I DON'T PARTICULARLY CARE ABOUT FACIAL HAIR ONE WAY OR ANOTHER.>

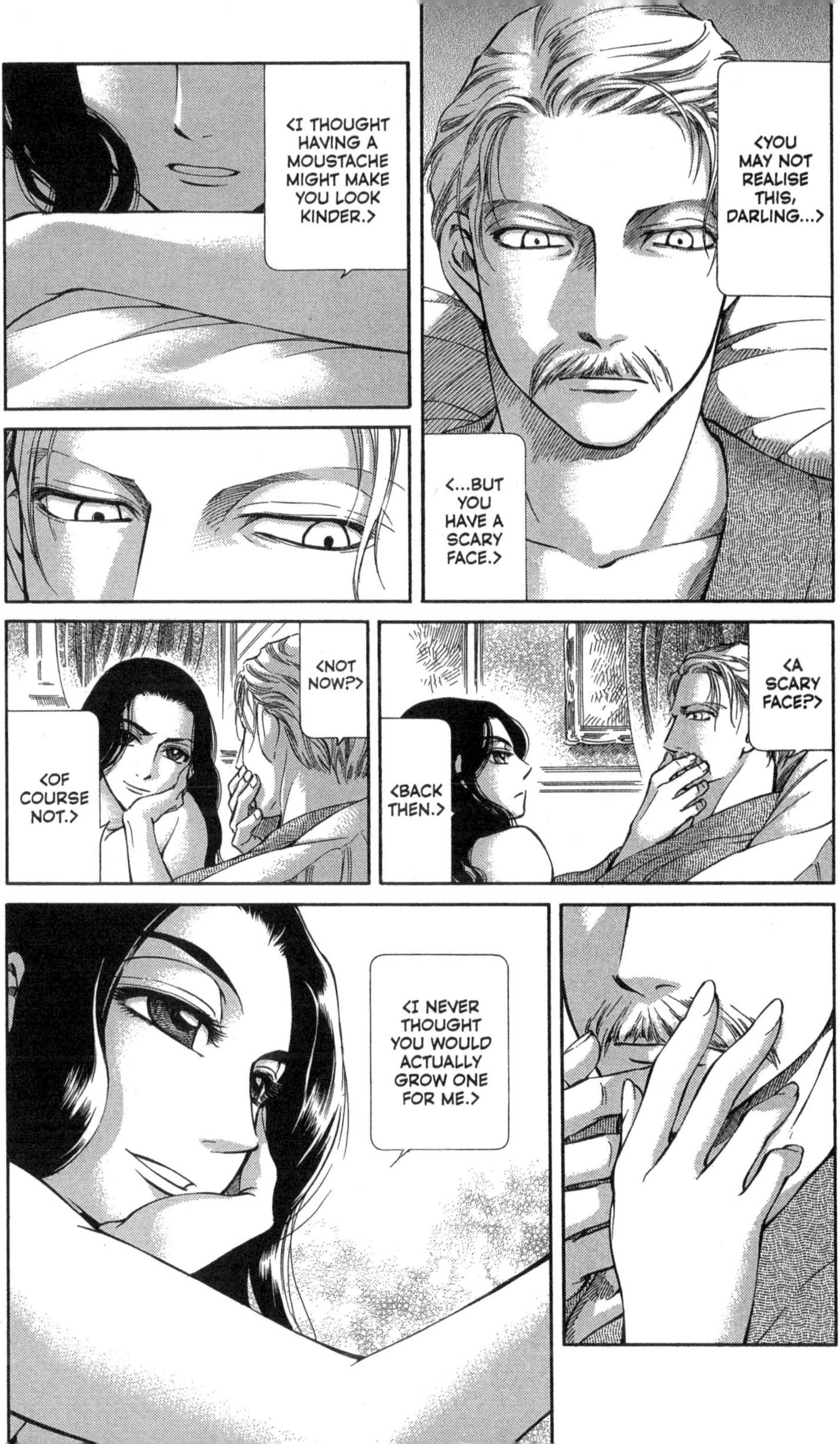
<YOU MAY NOT REALISE THIS, DARLING...>
<...BUT YOU HAVE A SCARY FACE.>
<I THOUGHT HAVING A MOUSTACHE MIGHT MAKE YOU LOOK KINDER.>
<A SCARY FACE?>
<BACK THEN.>
<NOT NOW?>
<OF COURSE NOT.>
<I NEVER THOUGHT YOU WOULD ACTUALLY GROW ONE FOR ME.>

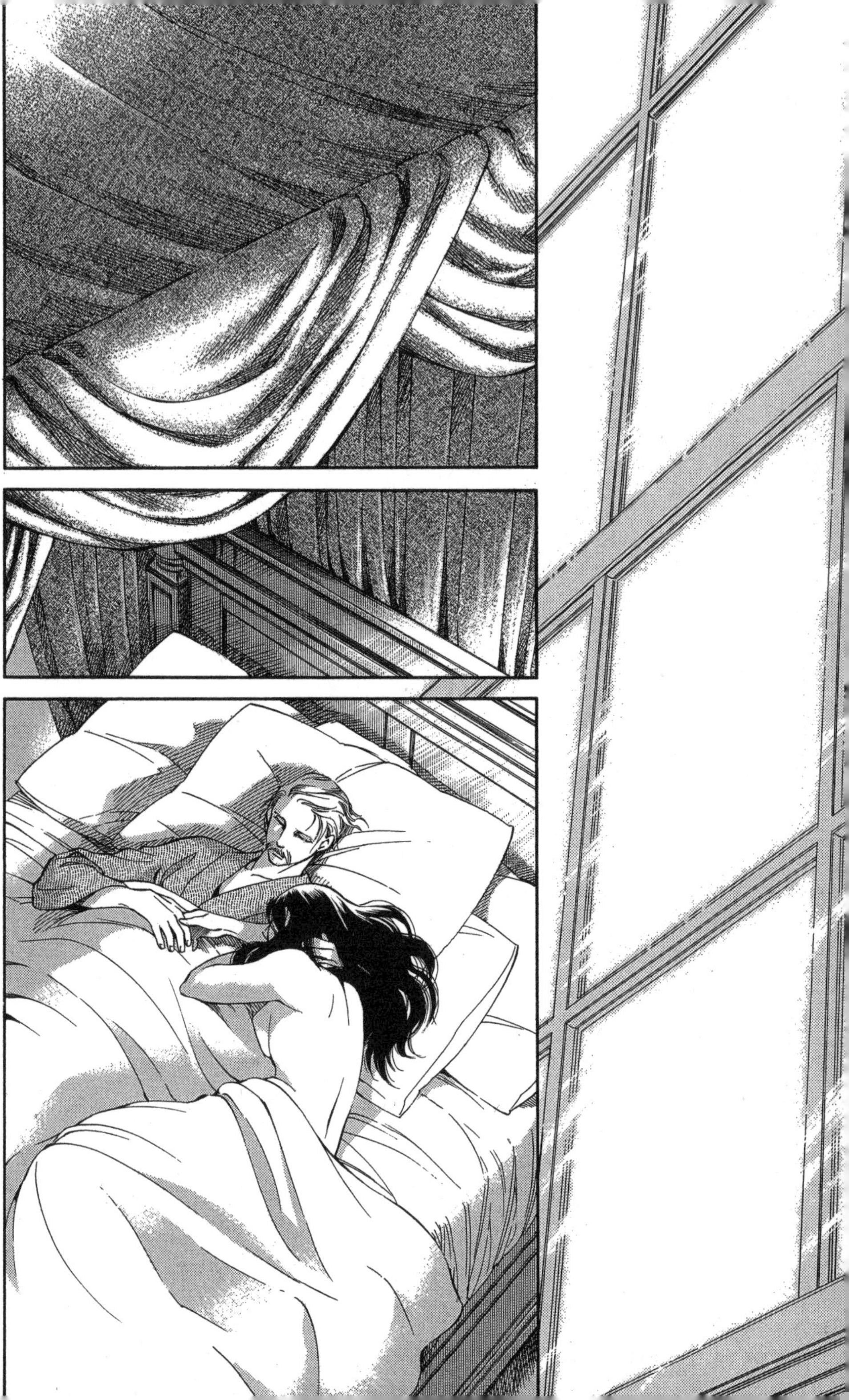

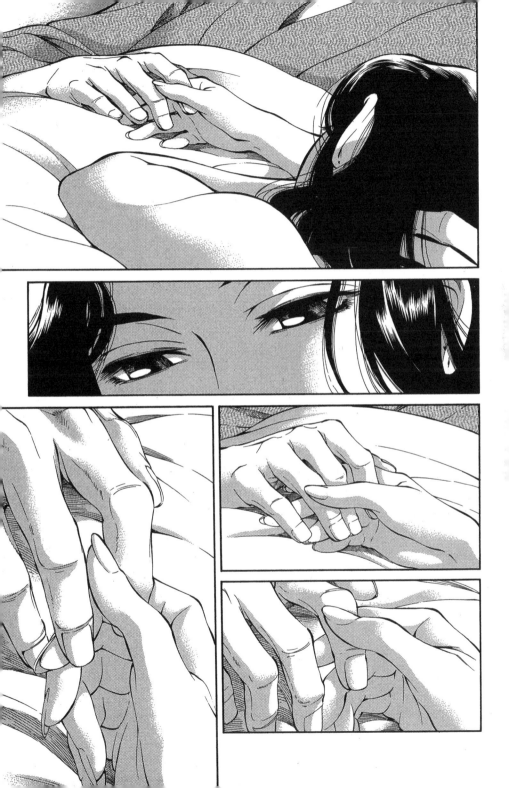

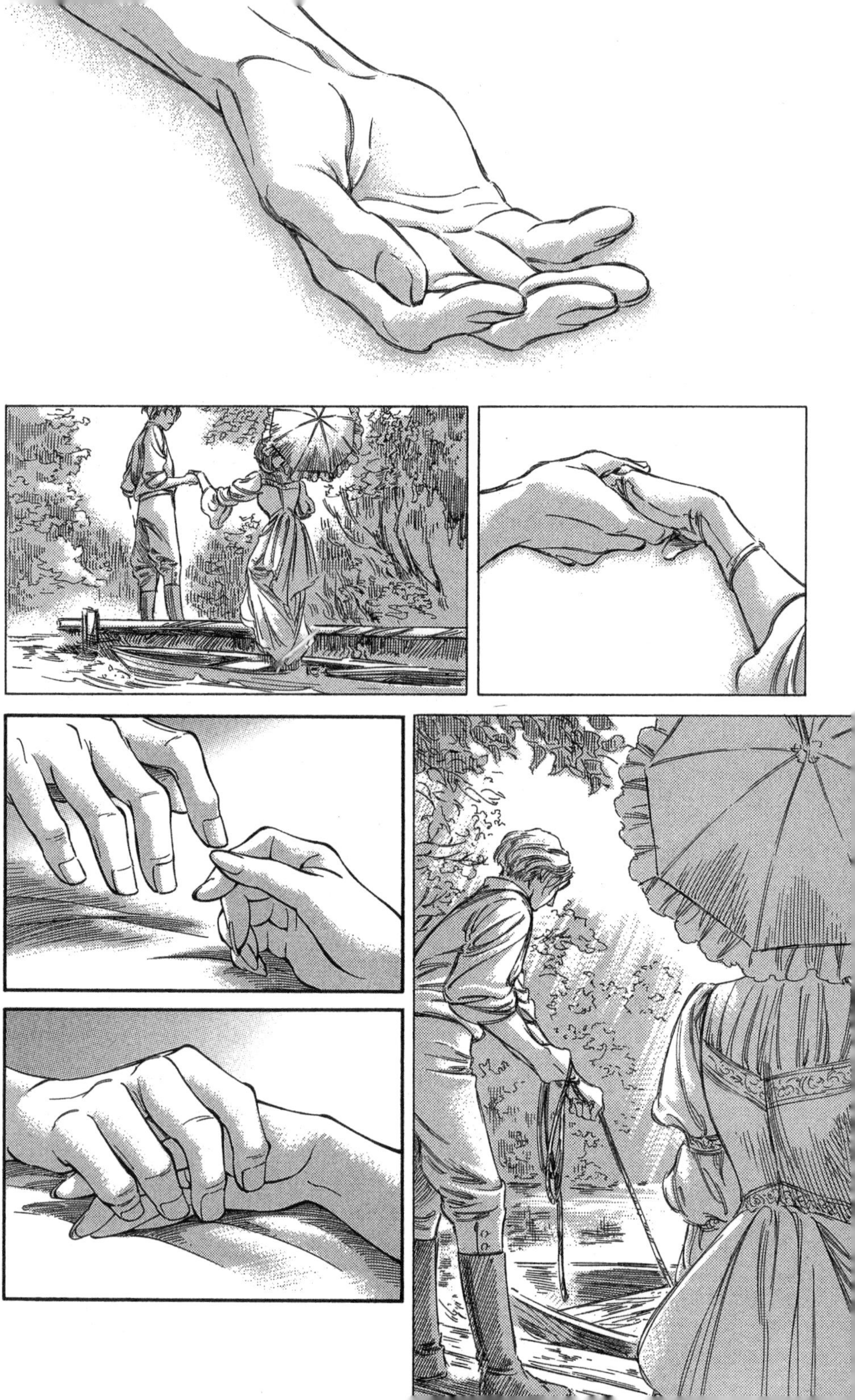

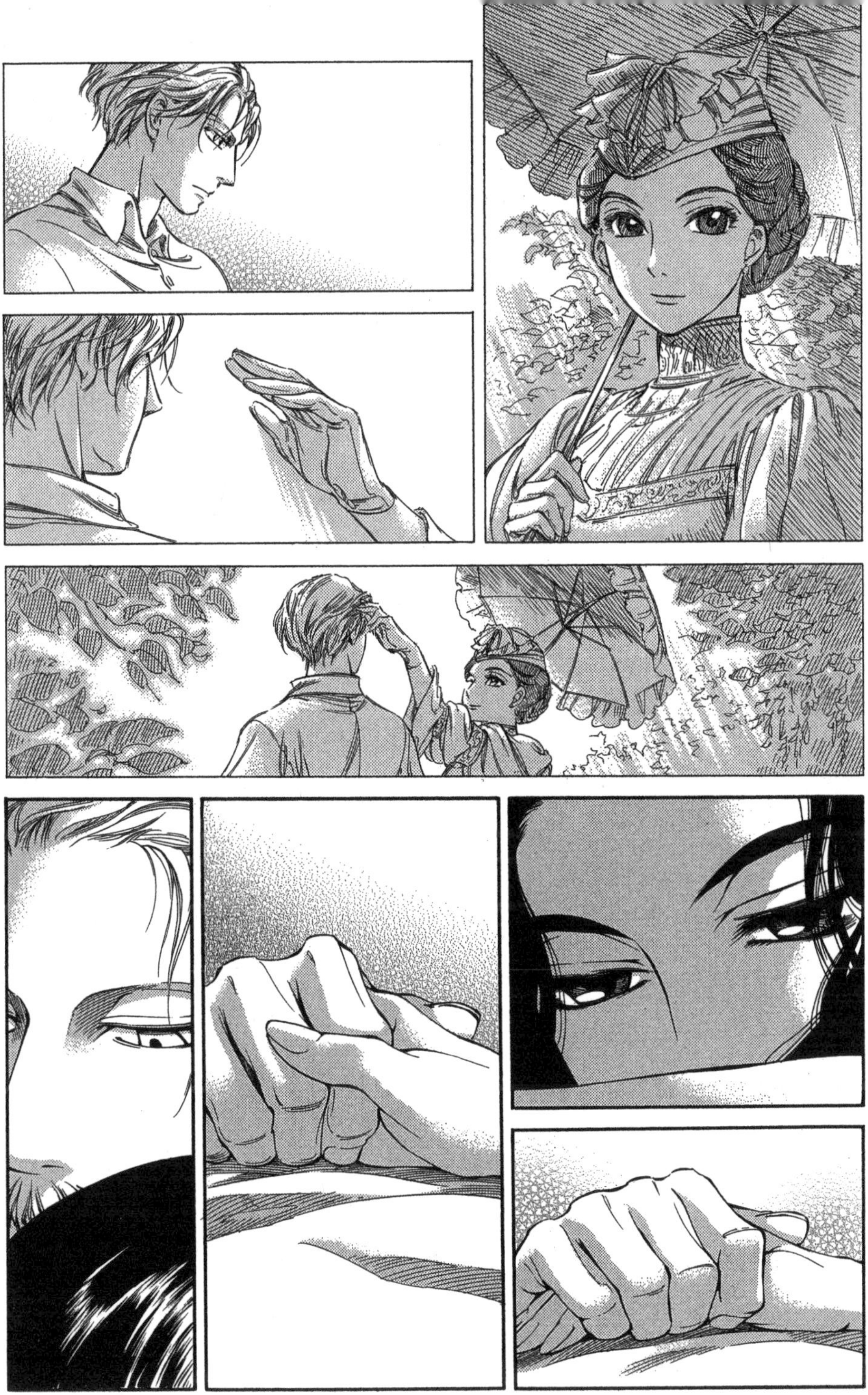

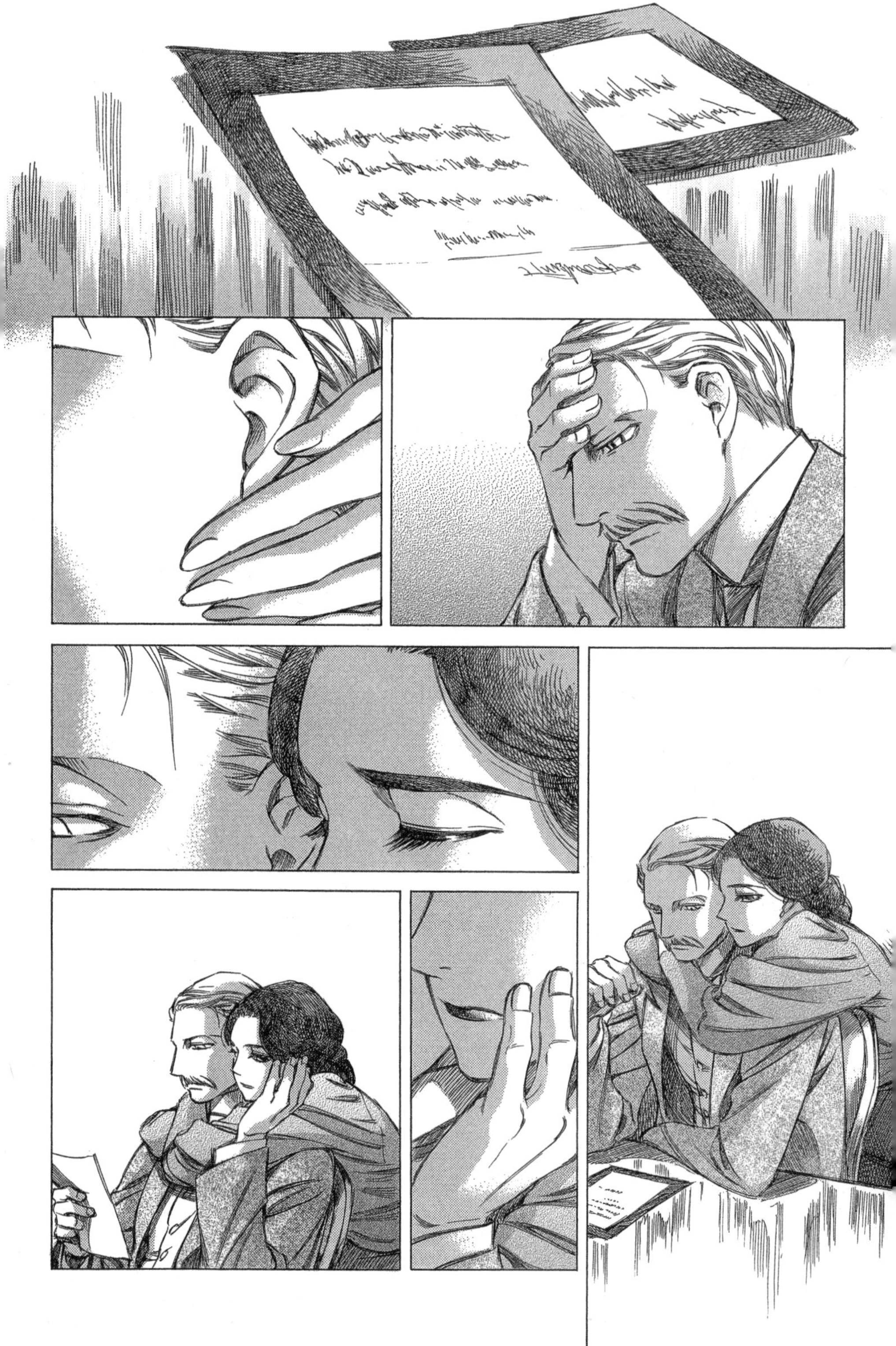

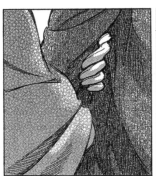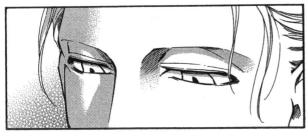

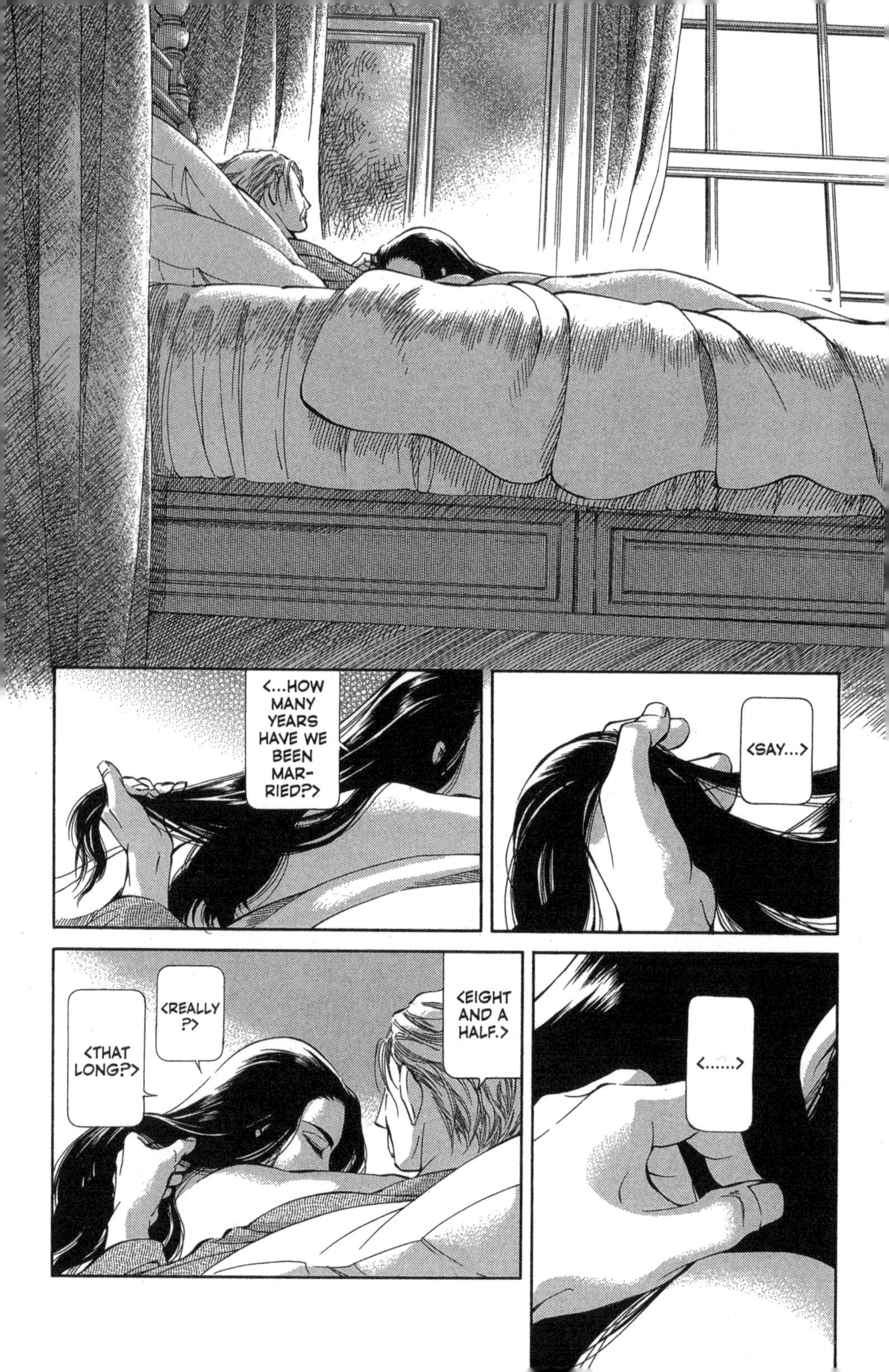
<SAY...>
<...HOW MANY YEARS HAVE WE BEEN MARRIED?>
<......>
<EIGHT AND A HALF.>
<REALLY?>
<THAT LONG?>

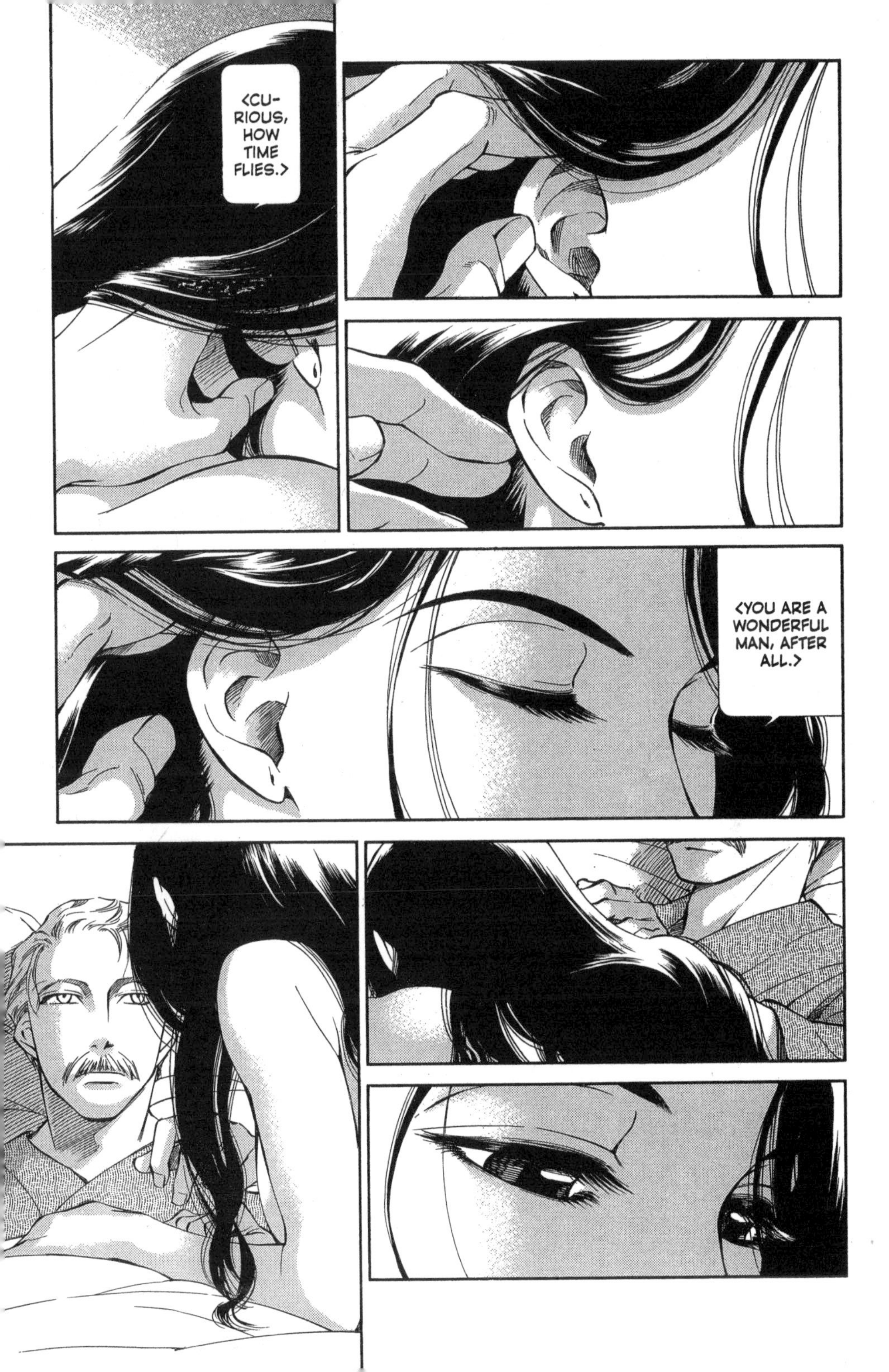
<CU-RIOUS, HOW TIME FLIES.>
<YOU ARE A WONDERFUL MAN, AFTER ALL.>

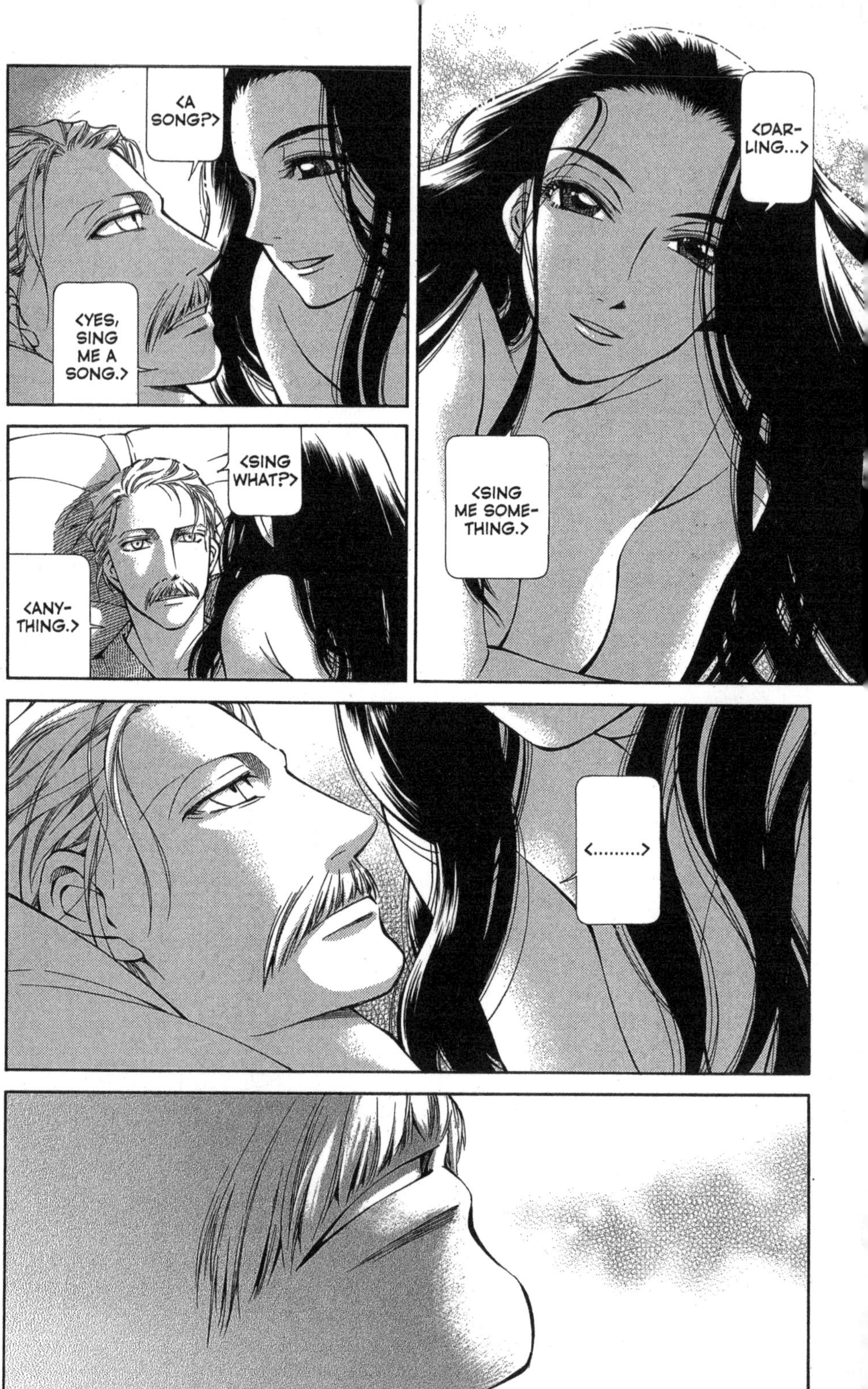
<DAR-LING...>
<SING ME SOME-THING.>
<A SONG?>
<YES, SING ME A SONG.>
<SING WHAT?>
<ANY-THING.>
<.........>

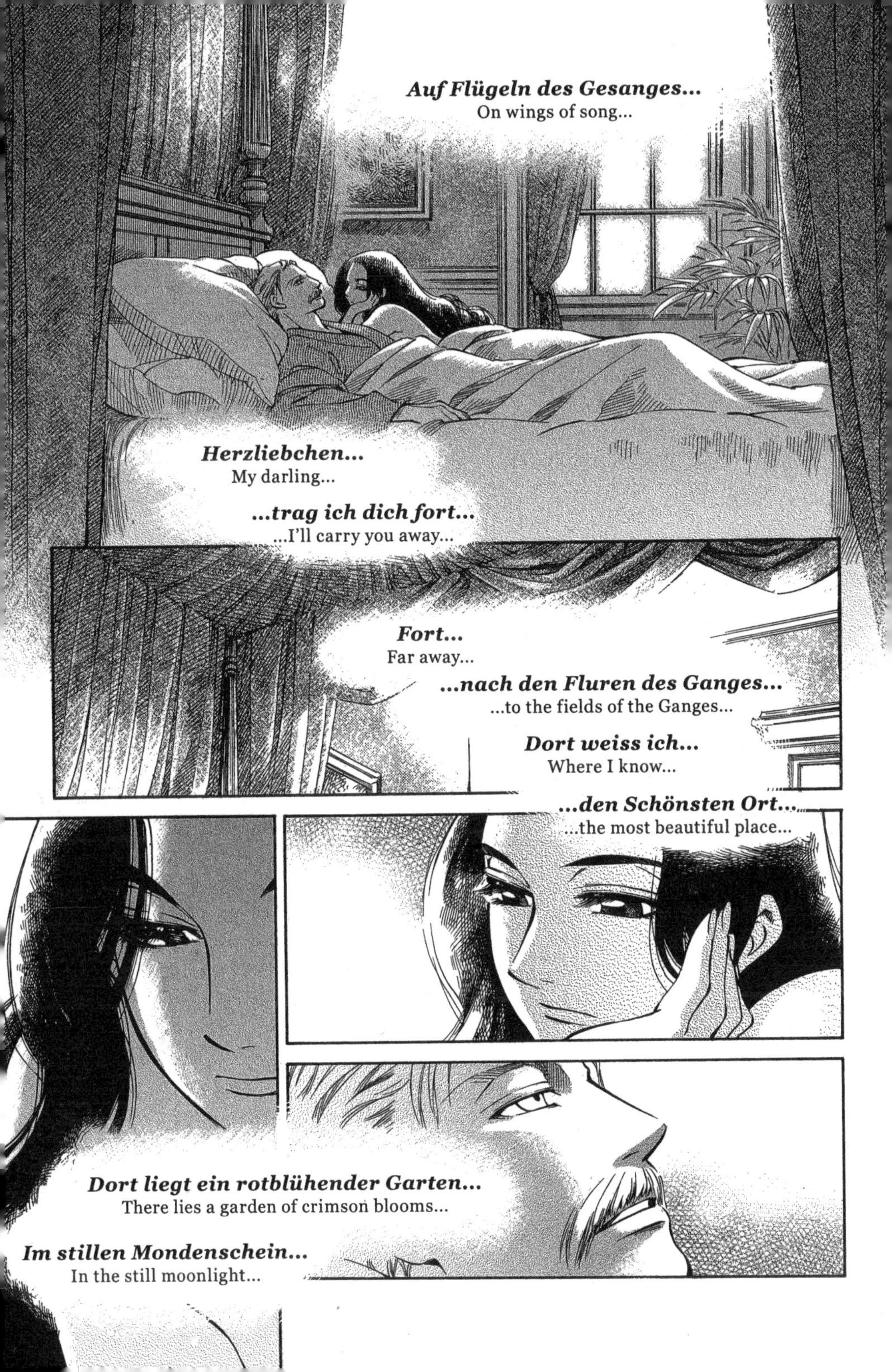

Auf Flügeln des Gesanges...
On wings of song...
Herzliebchen...
My darling...
...trag ich dich fort...
...I'll carry you away...
Fort...
Far away...
...nach den Fluren des Ganges...
...to the fields of the Ganges...
Dort weiss ich...
Where I know...
...den Schönsten Ort...
...the most beautiful place...
Dort liegt ein rotblühender Garten...
There lies a garden of crimson blooms...
Im stillen Mondenschein...
In the still moonlight...

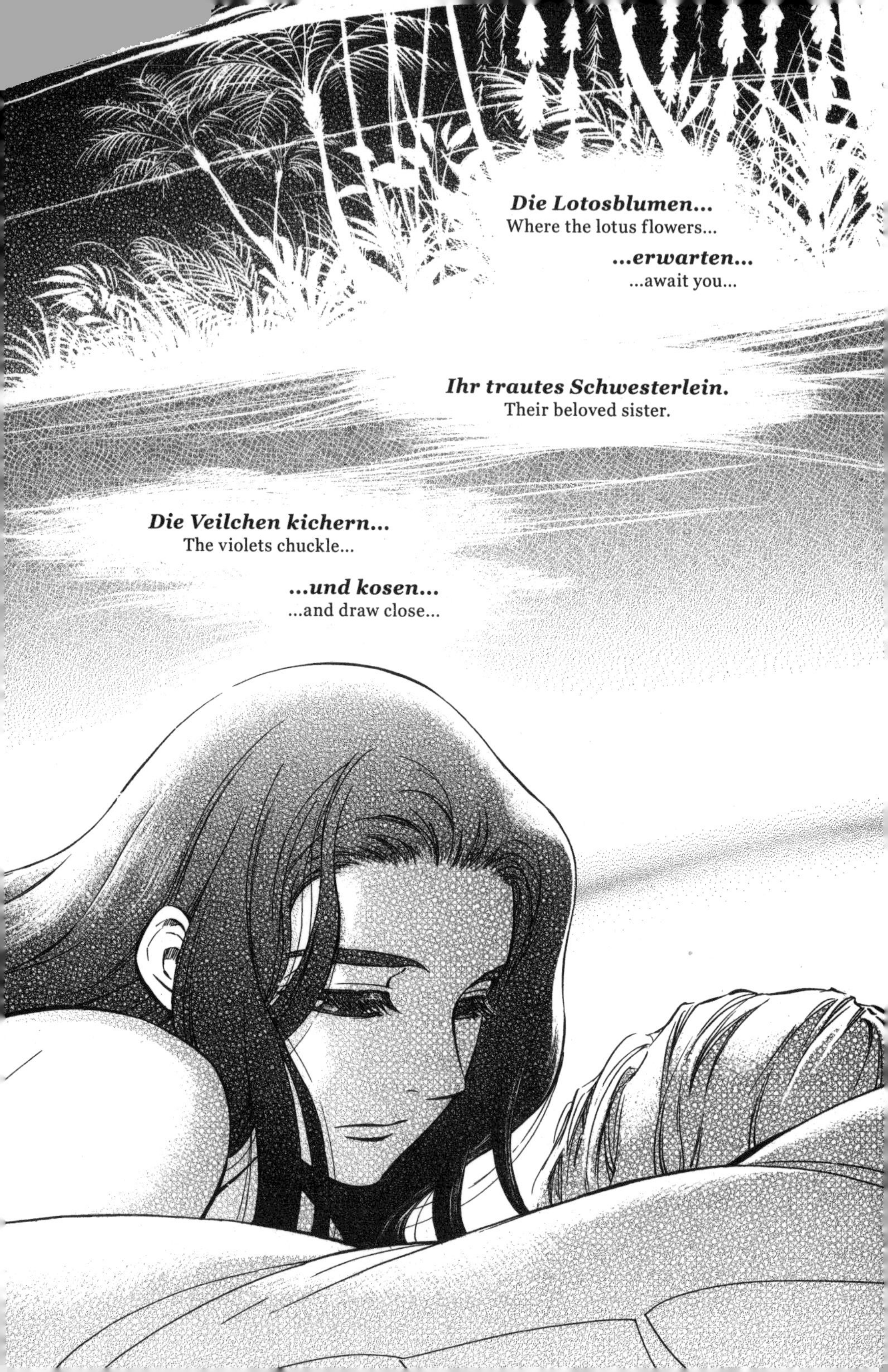

Die Lotosblumen...
Where the lotus flowers...
...erwarten...
...await you...
Ihr trautes Schwesterlein.
Their beloved sister.
Die Veilchen kichern...
The violets chuckle...
...und kosen...
...and draw close...

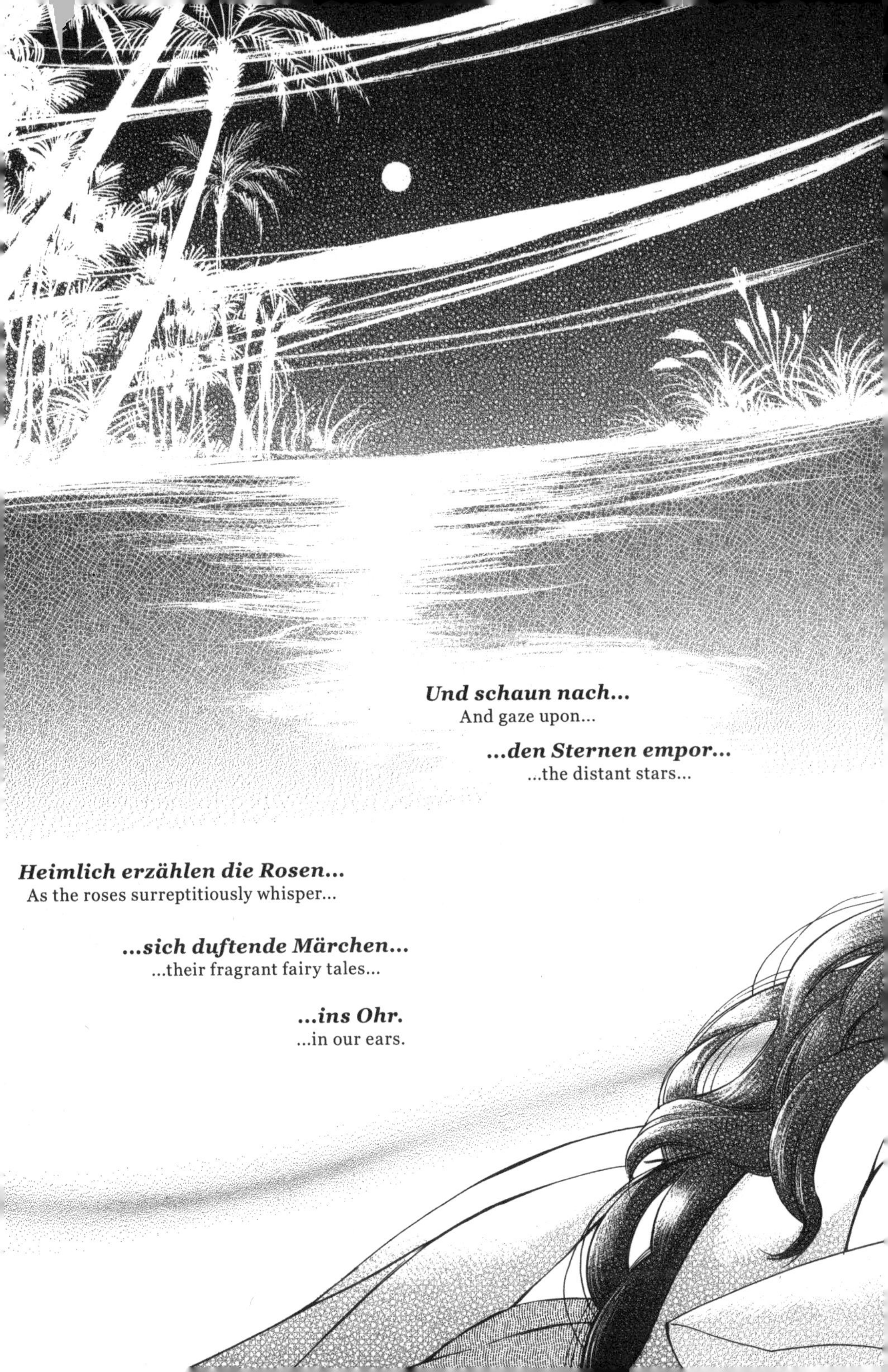
Und schaun nach...
And gaze upon...
...den Sternen empor...
...the distant stars...
Heimlich erzählen die Rosen...
As the roses surreptitiously whisper...
...sich duftende Märchen...
...their fragrant fairy tales...
...ins Ohr.
...in our ears.

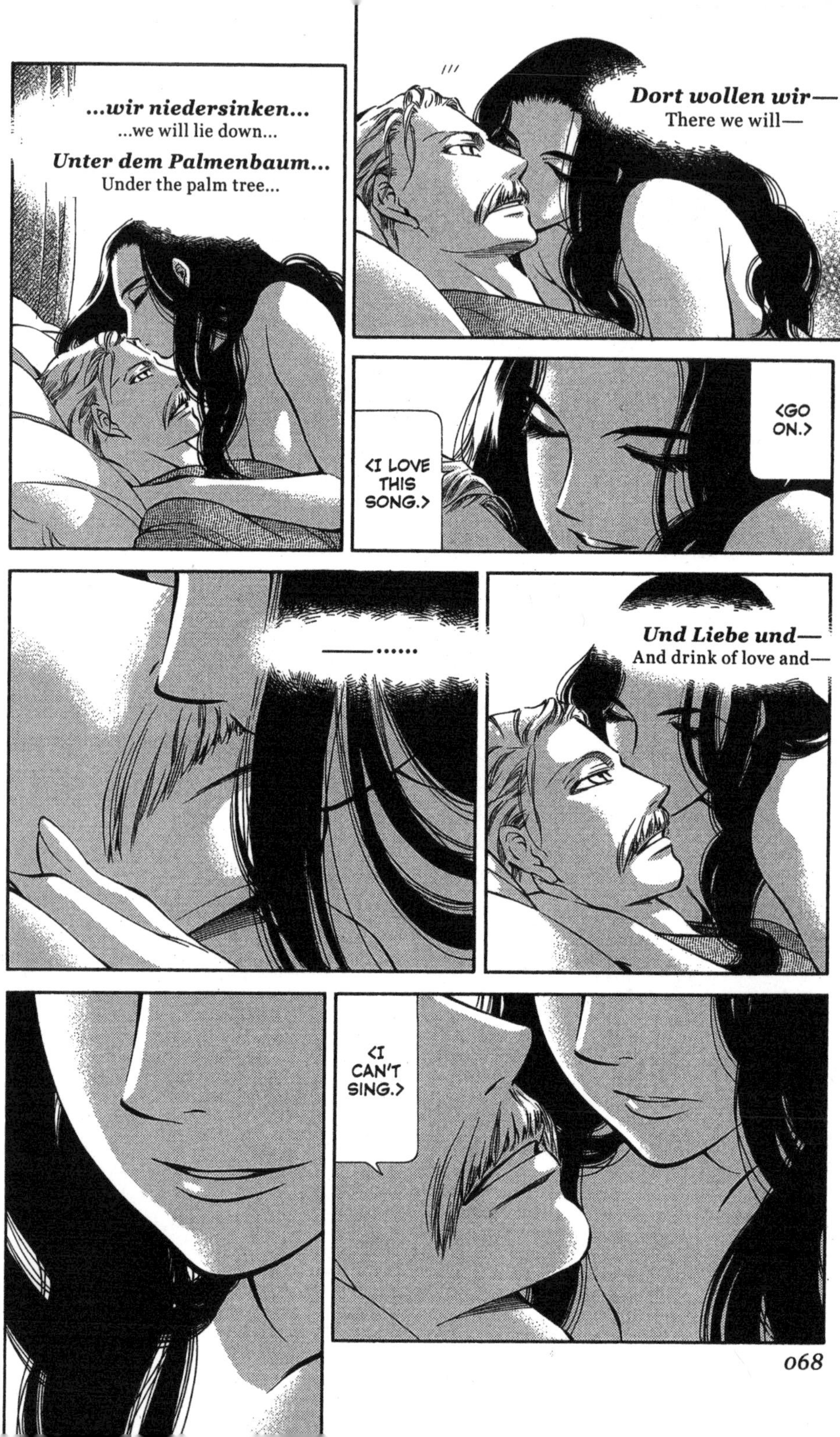
Dort wollen wir—
There we will—
<GO ON.>
<I LOVE THIS SONG.>
...wir niedersinken...
...we will lie down...
Unter dem Palmenbaum...
Under the palm tree...
Und Liebe und—
And drink of love and—
——......
<I CAN'T SING.>

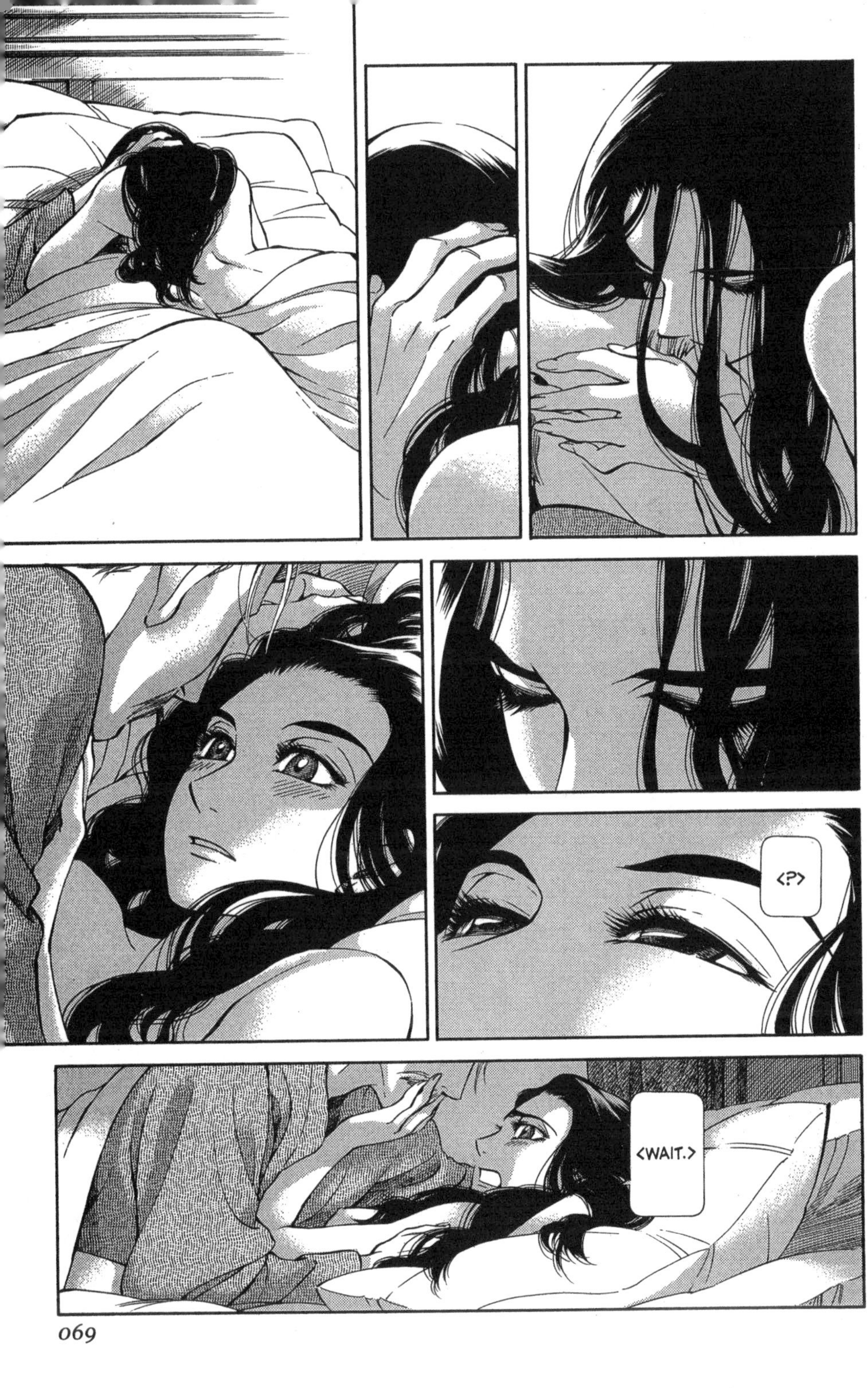
<?>
<WAIT.>

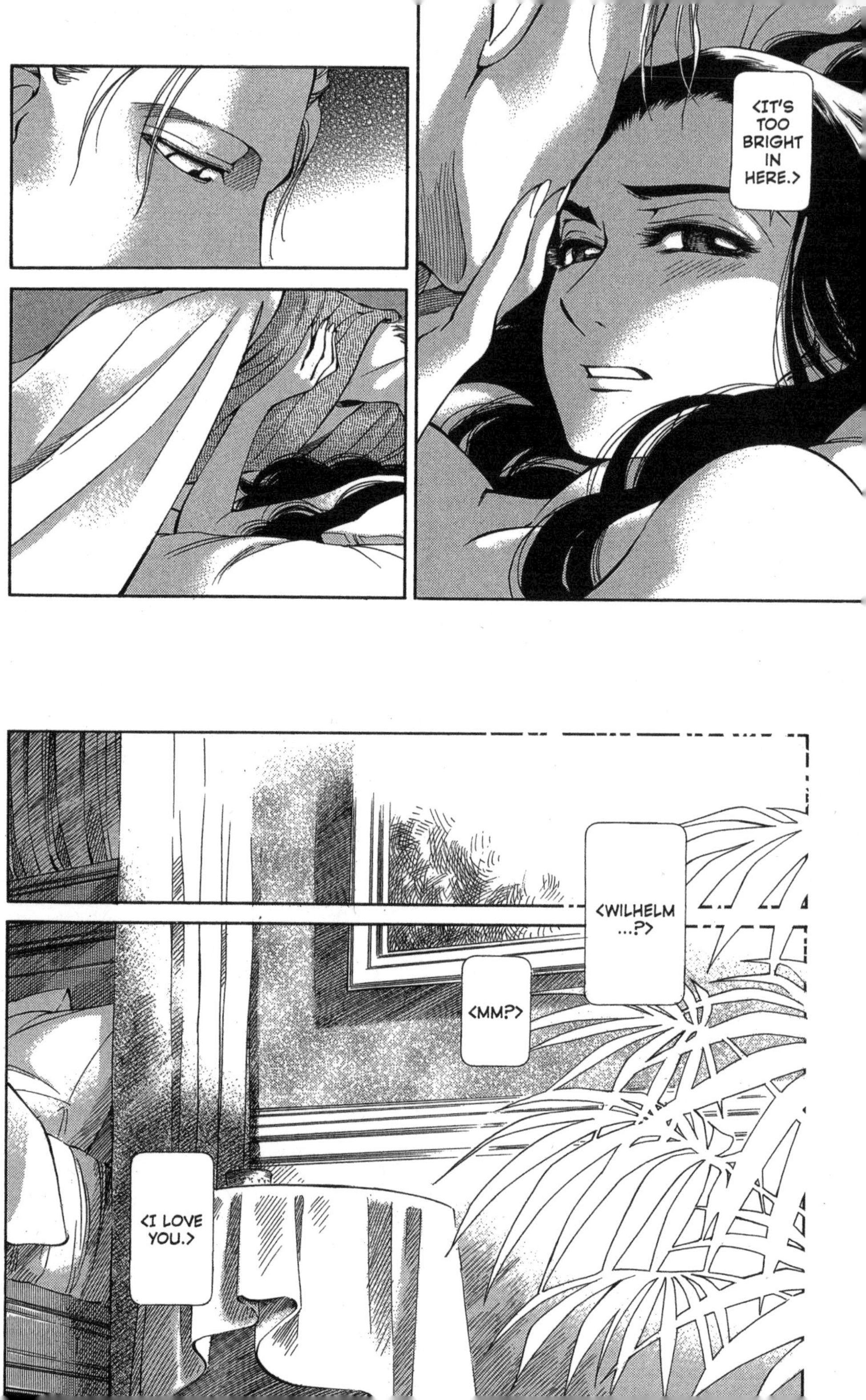
<IT'S TOO BRIGHT IN HERE.>
<WILHELM ...?>
<MM?>
<I LOVE YOU.>

Chapter 9:
Friendship

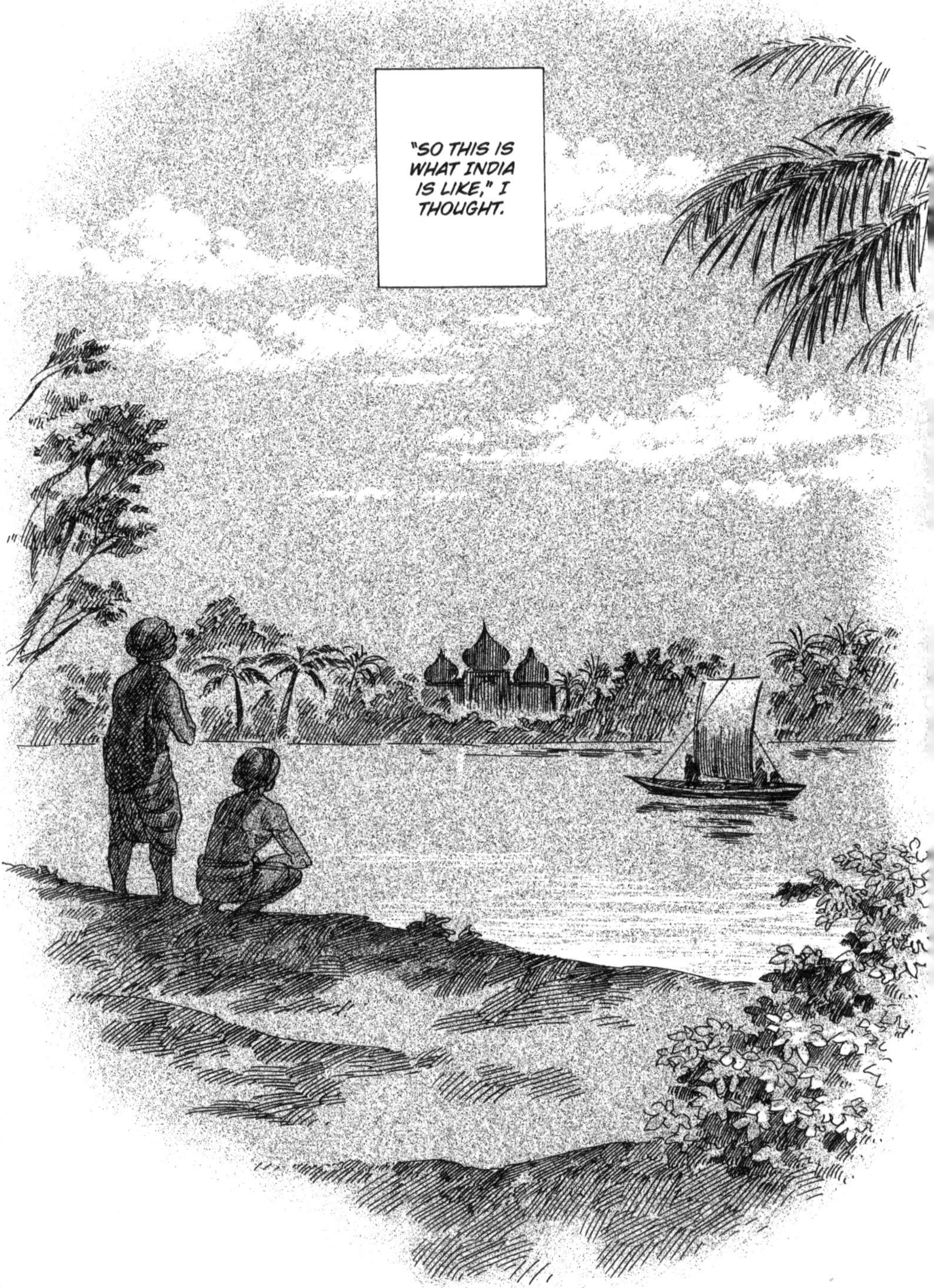
"SO THIS IS WHAT INDIA IS LIKE," I THOUGHT.

Chapter 9: *Friendship*

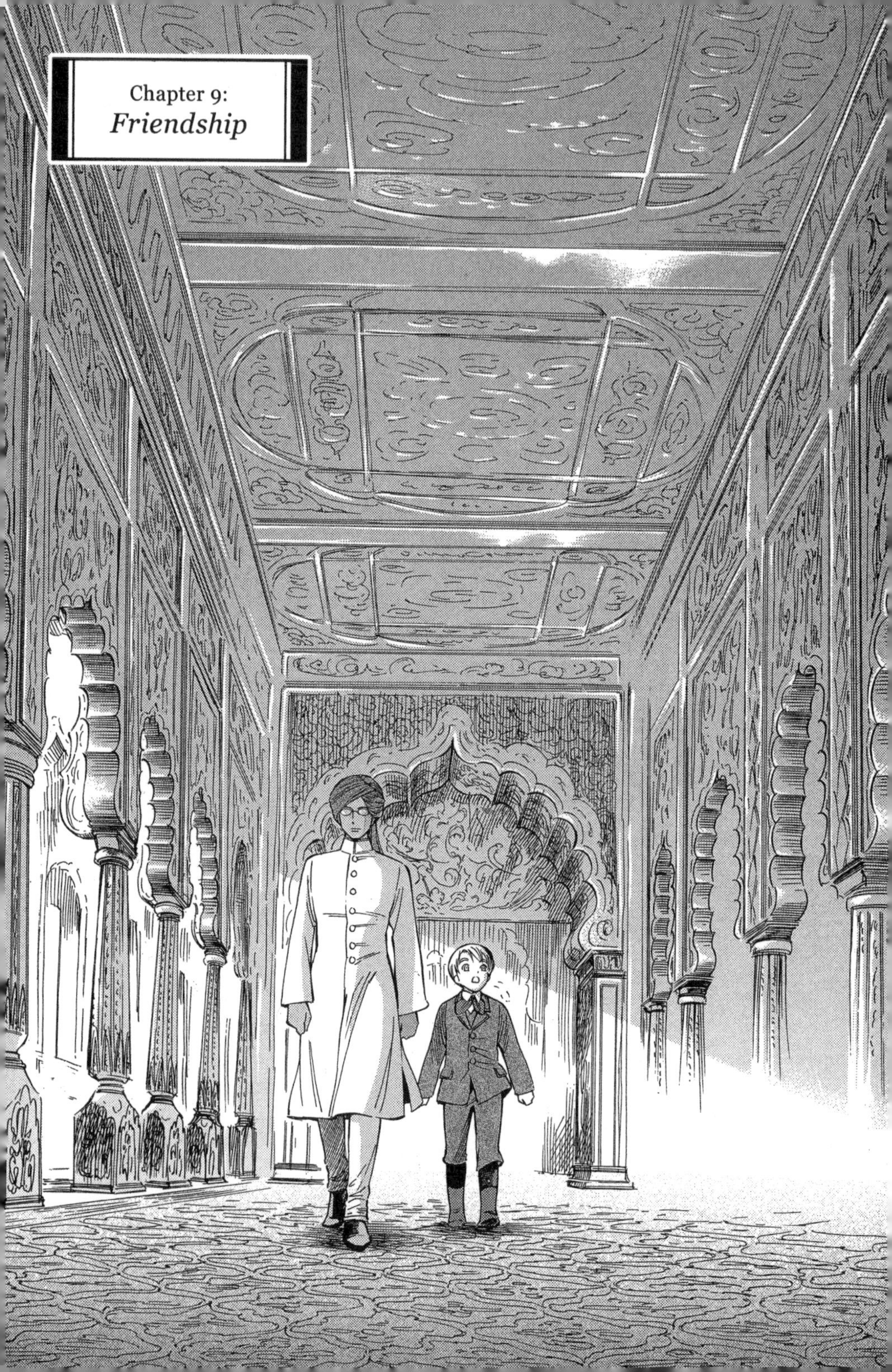

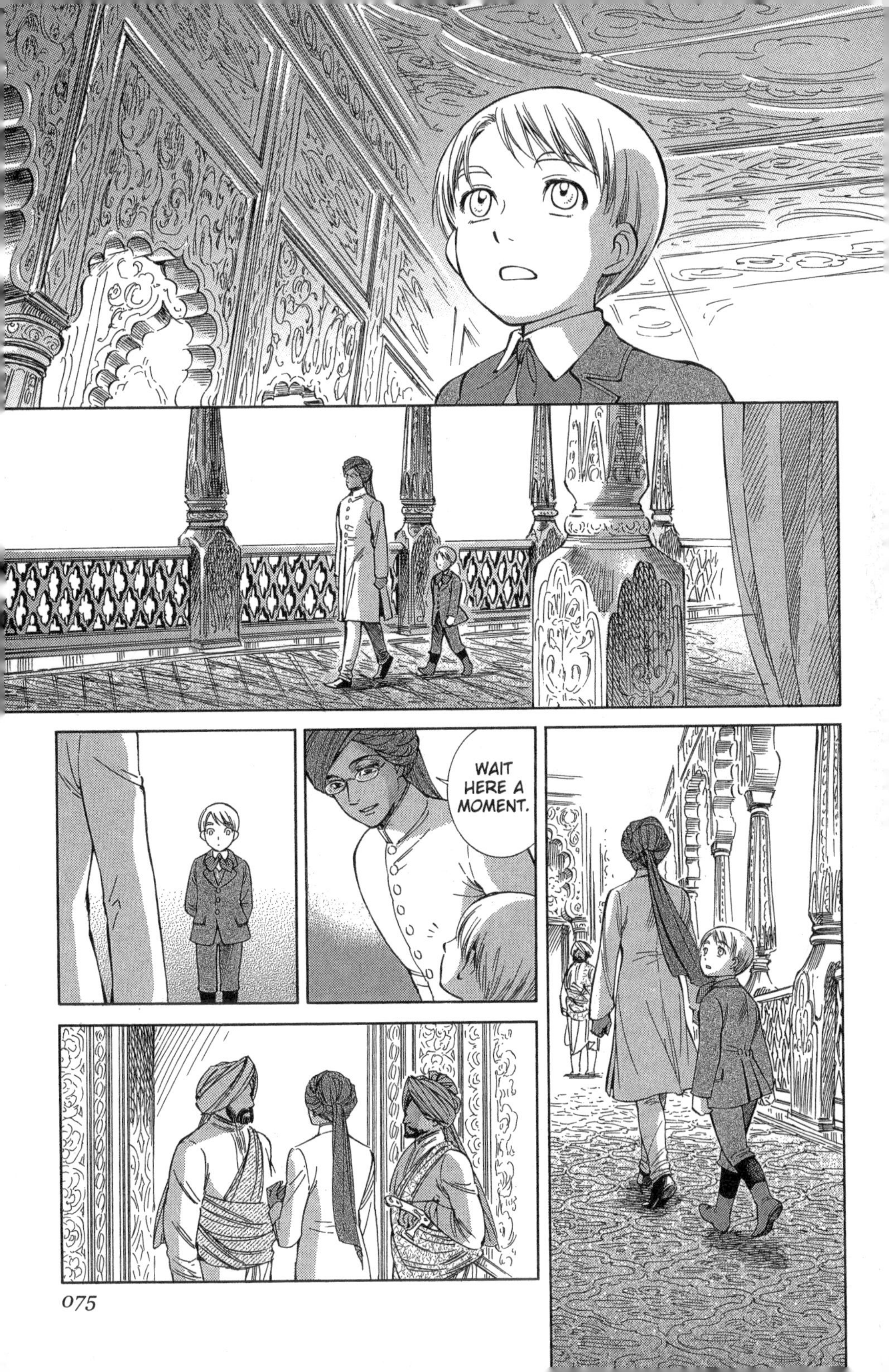
WAIT HERE A MOMENT.

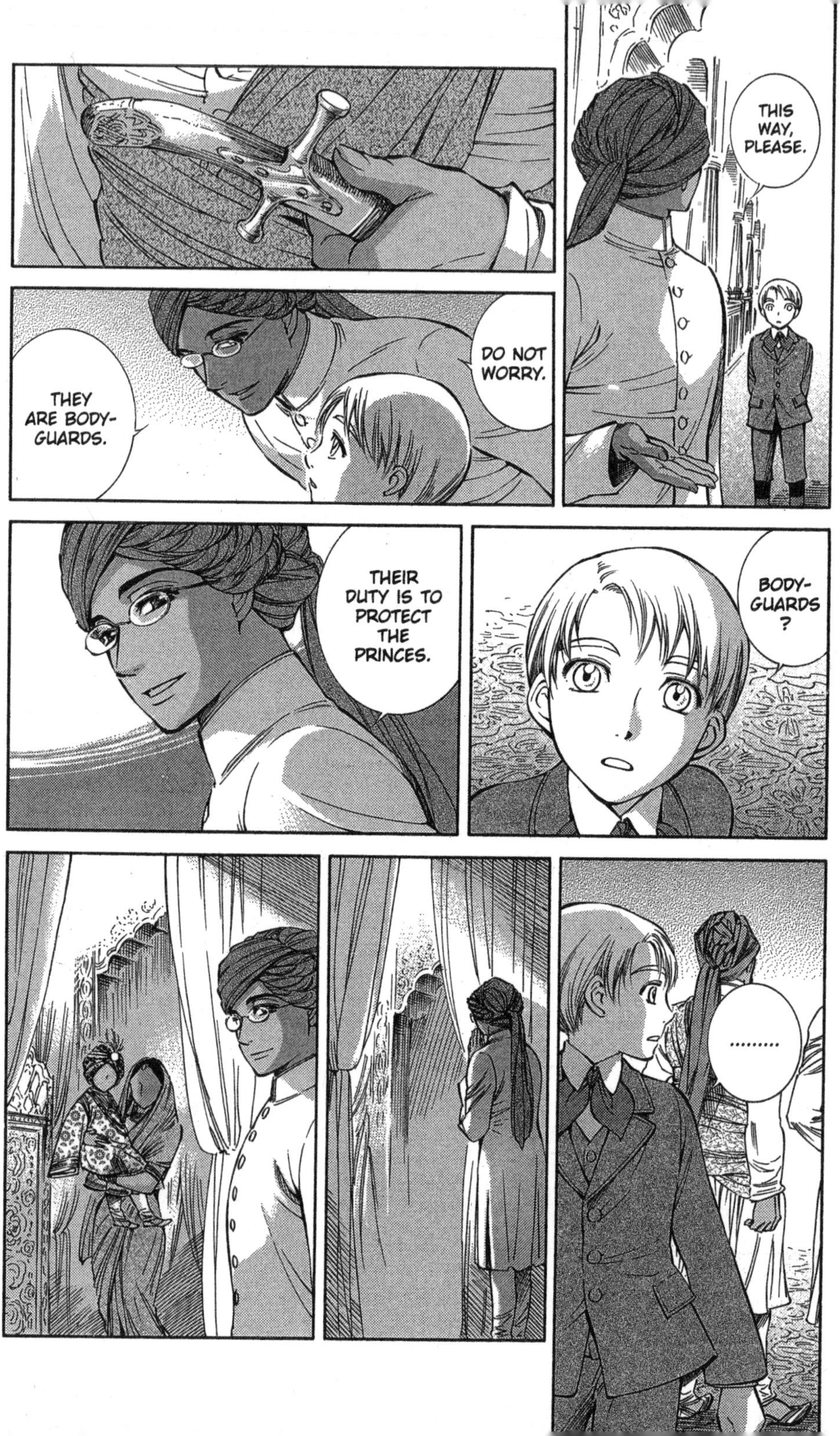
THIS WAY, PLEASE.
DO NOT WORRY.
THEY ARE BODY-GUARDS.
BODY-GUARDS?
THEIR DUTY IS TO PROTECT THE PRINCES.
....

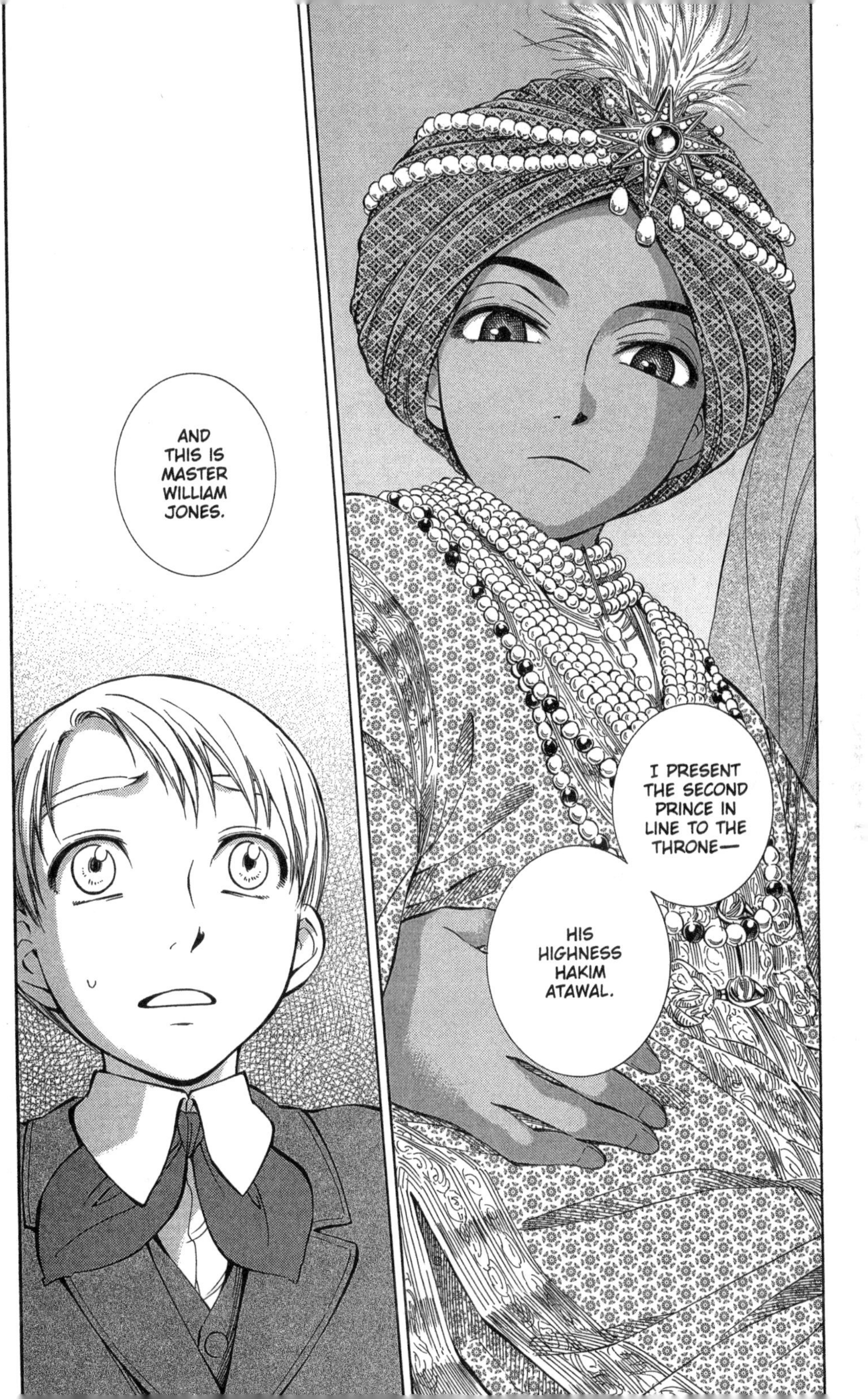
I PRESENT THE SECOND PRINCE IN LINE TO THE THRONE—
HIS HIGHNESS HAKIM ATAWAL.
AND THIS IS MASTER WILLIAM JONES.

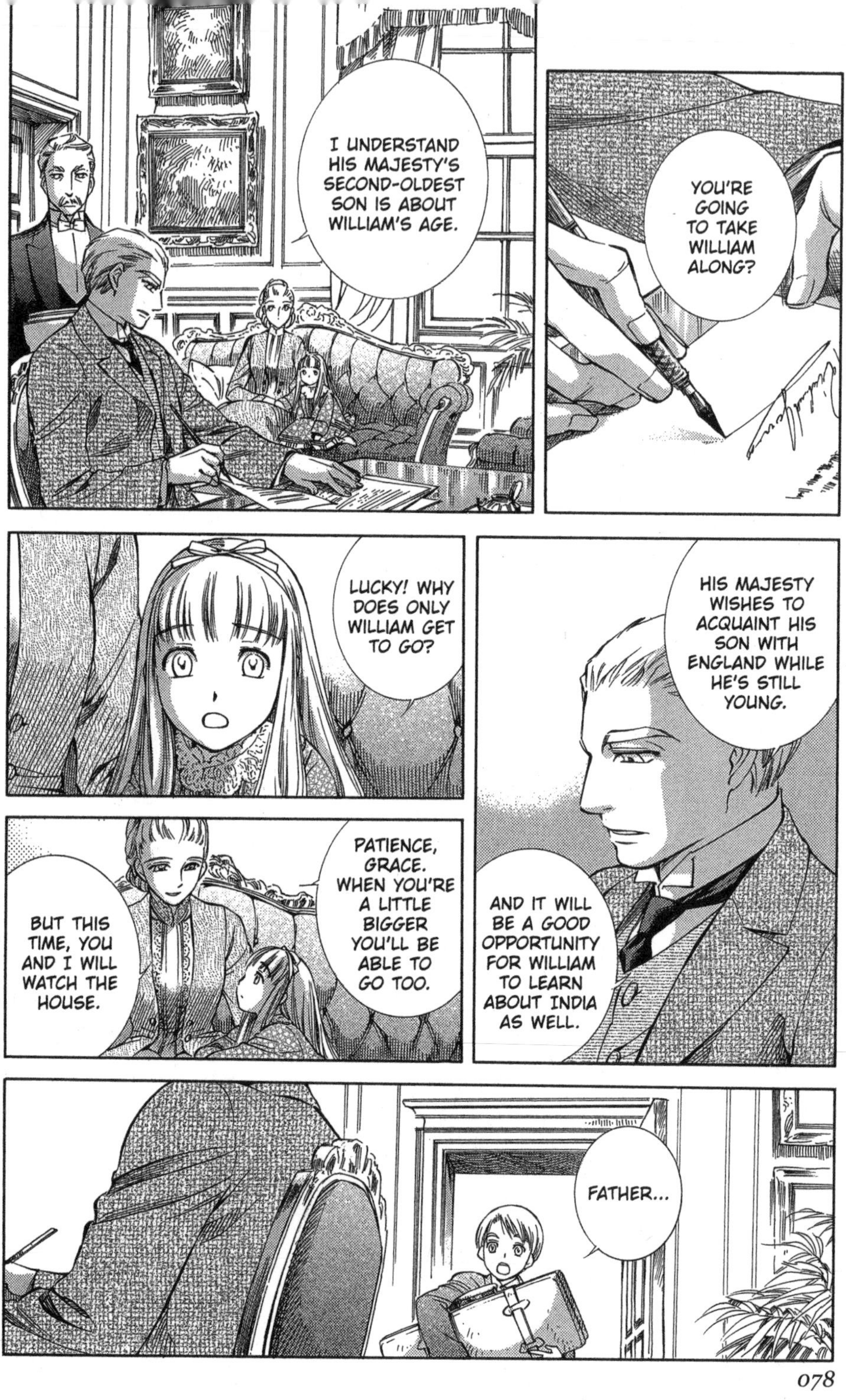
YOU'RE GOING TO TAKE WILLIAM ALONG?
I UNDERSTAND HIS MAJESTY'S SECOND-OLDEST SON IS ABOUT WILLIAM'S AGE.
HIS MAJESTY WISHES TO ACQUAINT HIS SON WITH ENGLAND WHILE HE'S STILL YOUNG.
AND IT WILL BE A GOOD OPPORTUNITY FOR WILLIAM TO LEARN ABOUT INDIA AS WELL.
LUCKY! WHY DOES ONLY WILLIAM GET TO GO?
PATIENCE, GRACE. WHEN YOU'RE A LITTLE BIGGER YOU'LL BE ABLE TO GO TOO.
BUT THIS TIME, YOU AND I WILL WATCH THE HOUSE.
FATHER...

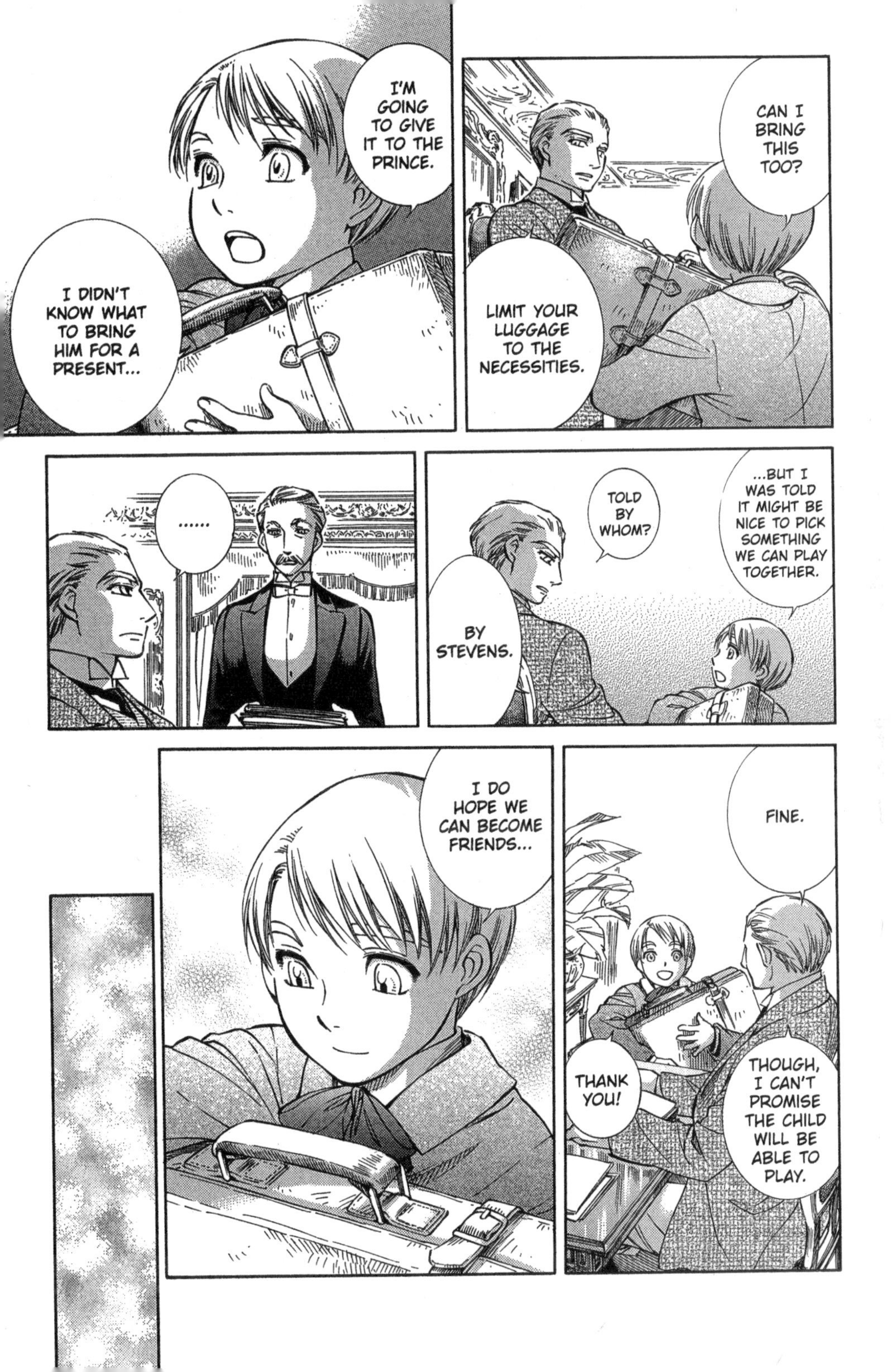
CAN I BRING THIS TOO?
LIMIT YOUR LUGGAGE TO THE NECESSITIES.
I'M GOING TO GIVE IT TO THE PRINCE.
I DIDN'T KNOW WHAT TO BRING HIM FOR A PRESENT...
...BUT I WAS TOLD IT MIGHT BE NICE TO PICK SOMETHING WE CAN PLAY TOGETHER.
TOLD BY WHOM?
BY STEVENS.
......
FINE.
THOUGH, I CAN'T PROMISE THE CHILD WILL BE ABLE TO PLAY.
THANK YOU!
I DO HOPE WE CAN BECOME FRIENDS...

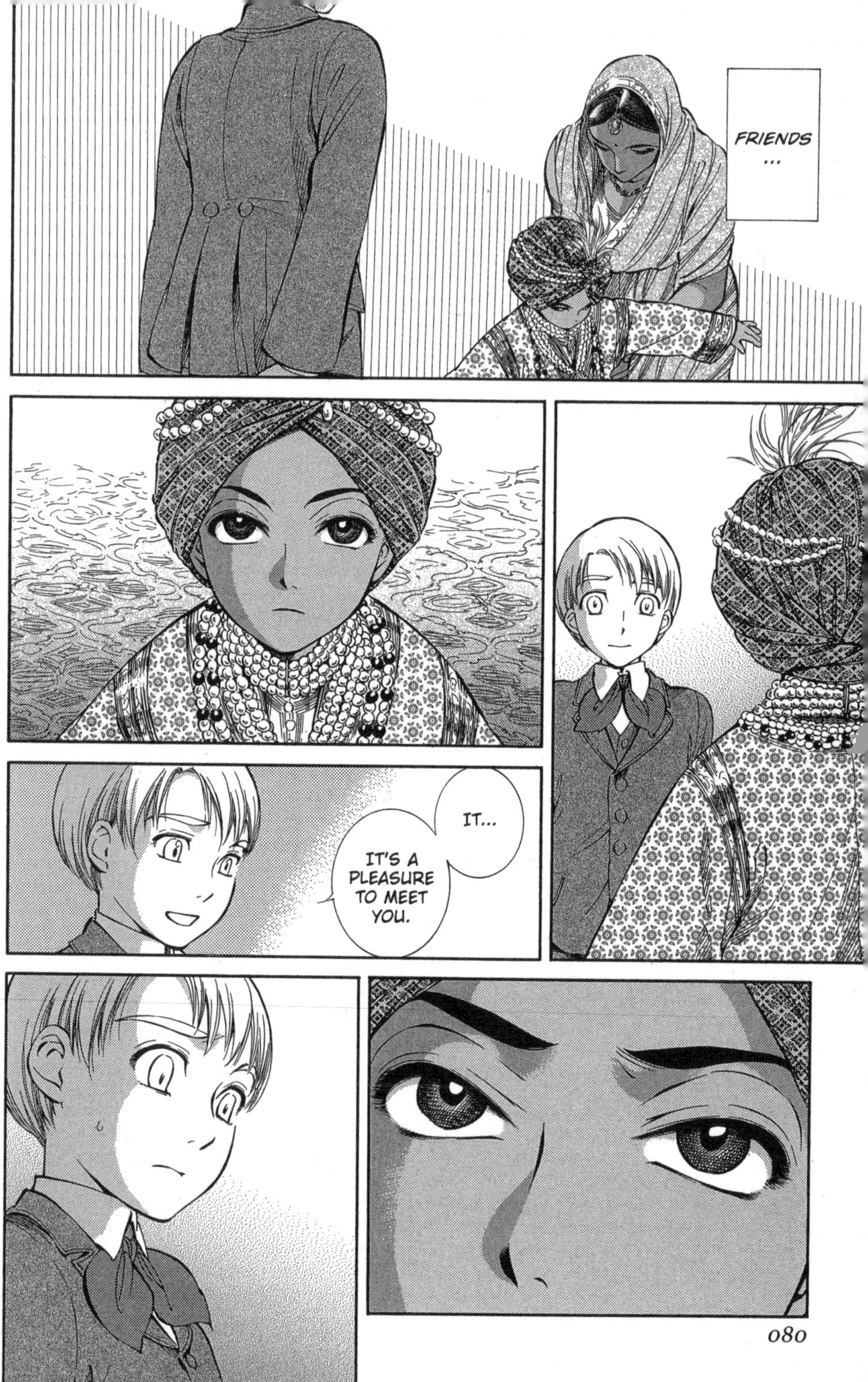
FRIENDS ...
IT...
IT'S A PLEASURE TO MEET YOU.

HE SPOKE...

OH.

THE PRINCE ASKED ME WHAT YOU SAID.

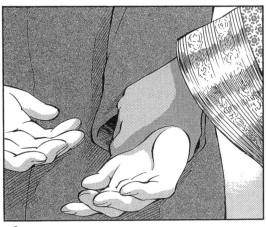

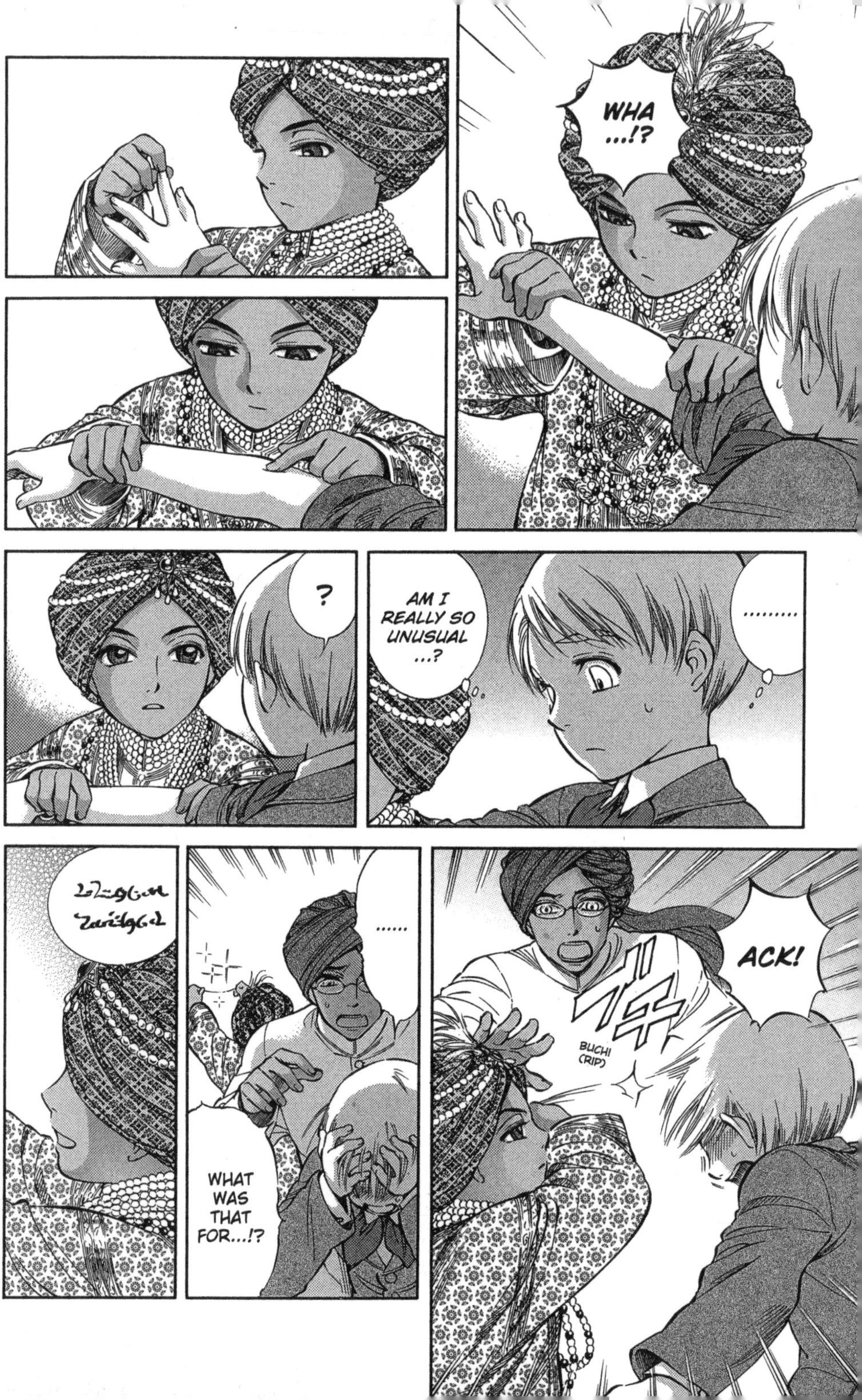
WHA ...!?
....
AM I REALLY SO UNUSUAL ...?
?
ACK!
BUCHI (RIP)
......
WHAT WAS THAT FOR...!?

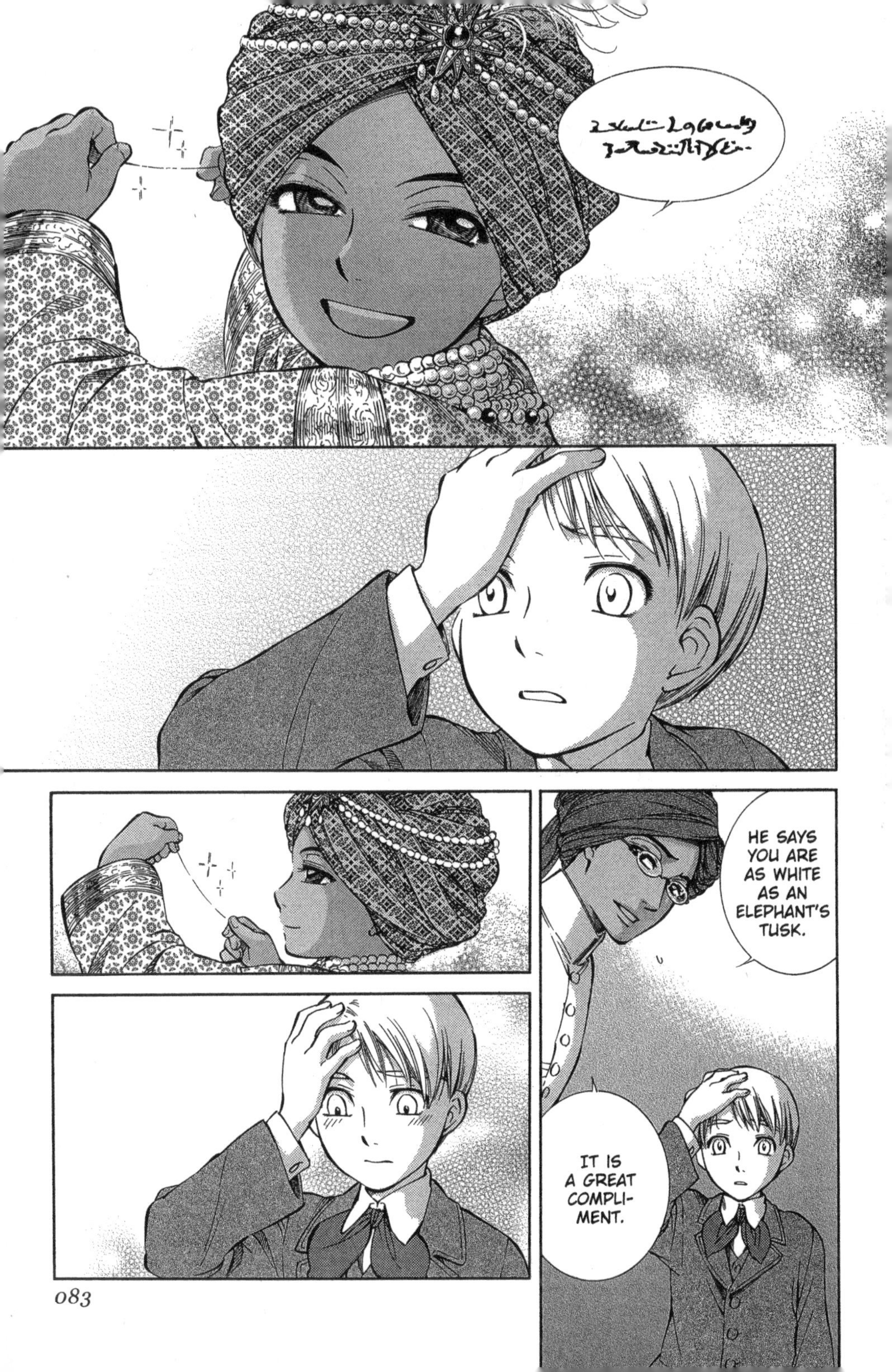
HE SAYS YOU ARE AS WHITE AS AN ELEPHANT'S TUSK.
IT IS A GREAT COMPLIMENT.

YOUR FABRICS ARE IMMENSELY POPULAR IN ENGLAND AS WELL.

OUR LAST SHIPMENT...

THE GAME IS CALLED "TENNIS"...

HAVE YOU EVER PLAYED...

NO.

YOU HAVEN'T.

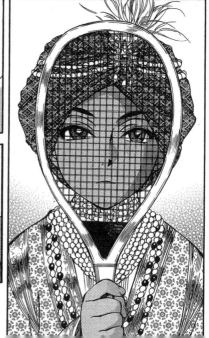

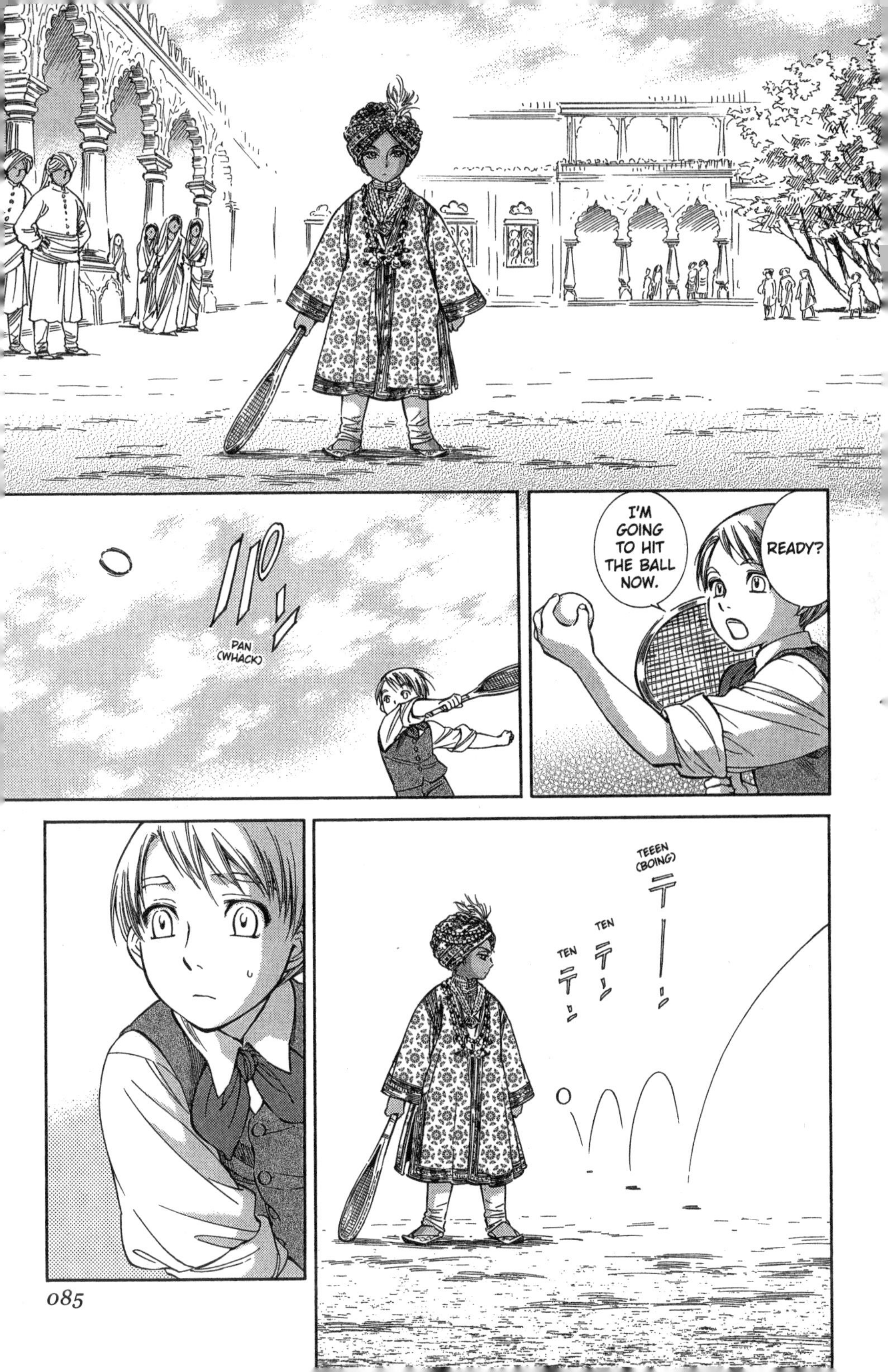
READY?
I'M GOING TO HIT THE BALL NOW.
PAN (WHACK)
TEEEN (BOING)
TEN
TEN

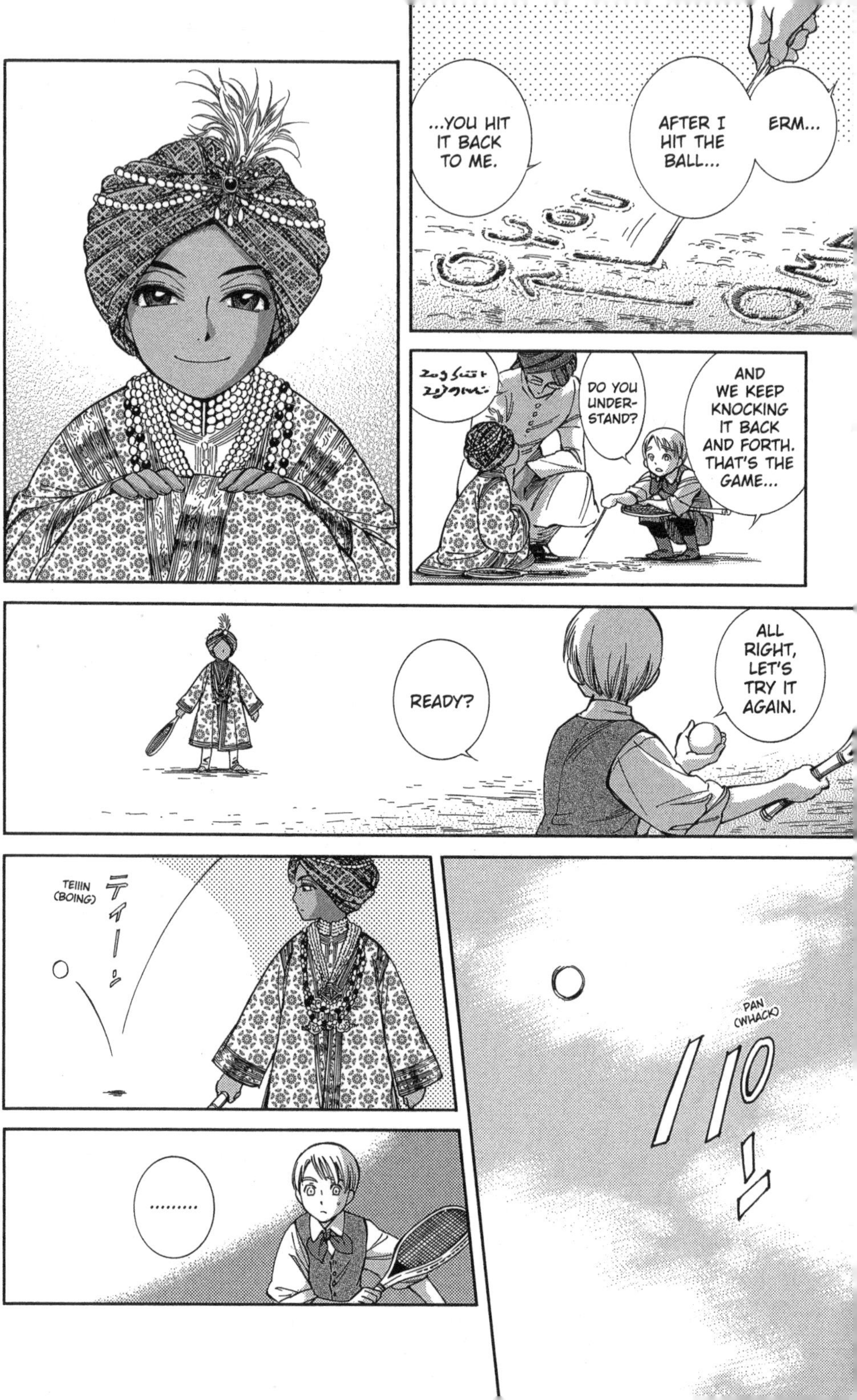
ERM...
AFTER I HIT THE BALL...
...YOU HIT IT BACK TO ME.
AND WE KEEP KNOCKING IT BACK AND FORTH. THAT'S THE GAME...
DO YOU UNDERSTAND?
ALL RIGHT, LET'S TRY IT AGAIN.
READY?
PAN (WHACK)
TEIIIN (BOING)
....

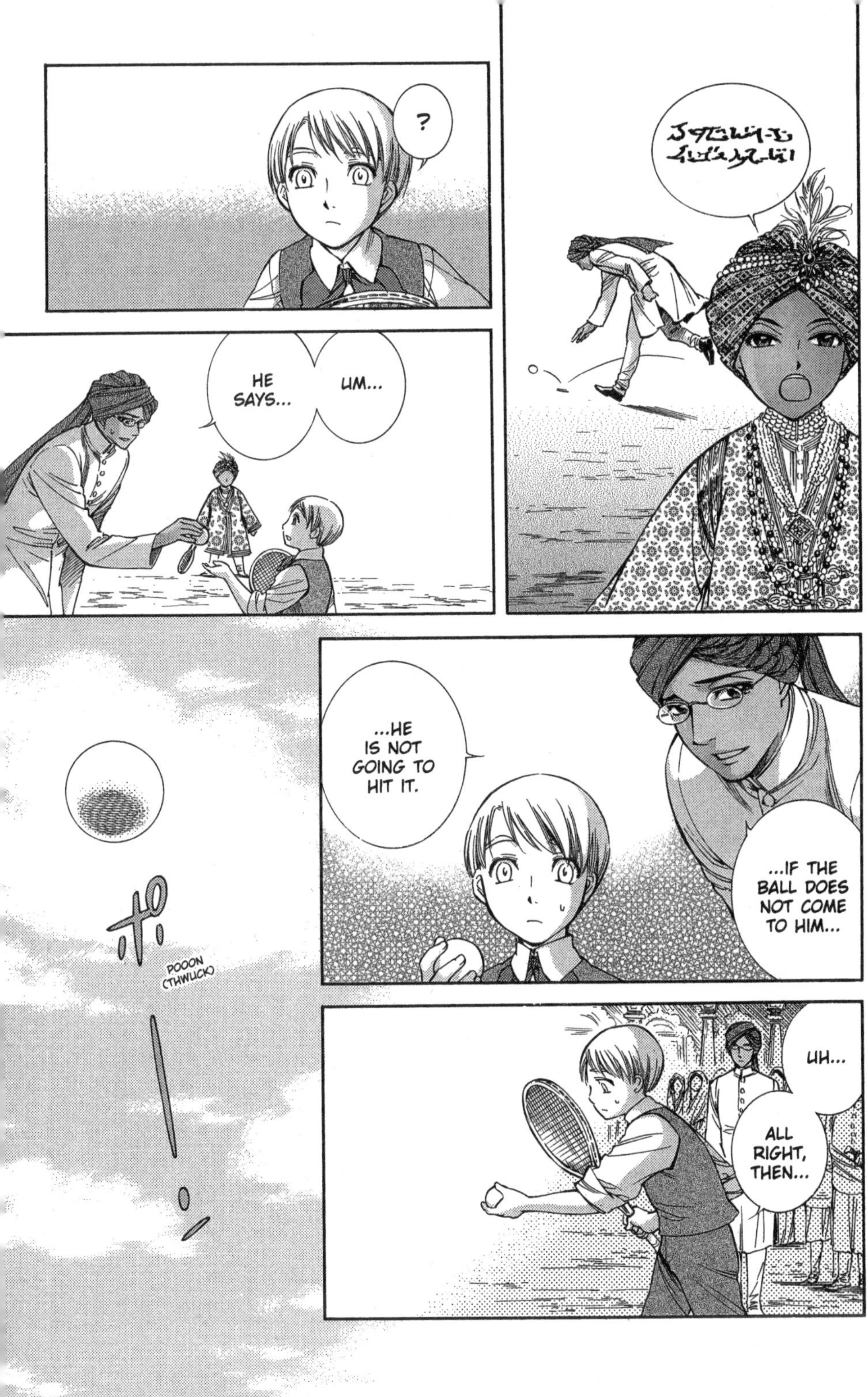
?
UM...
HE SAYS...
...IF THE BALL DOES NOT COME TO HIM...
...HE IS NOT GOING TO HIT IT.
UH...
ALL RIGHT, THEN...
POOON (THWUCK)

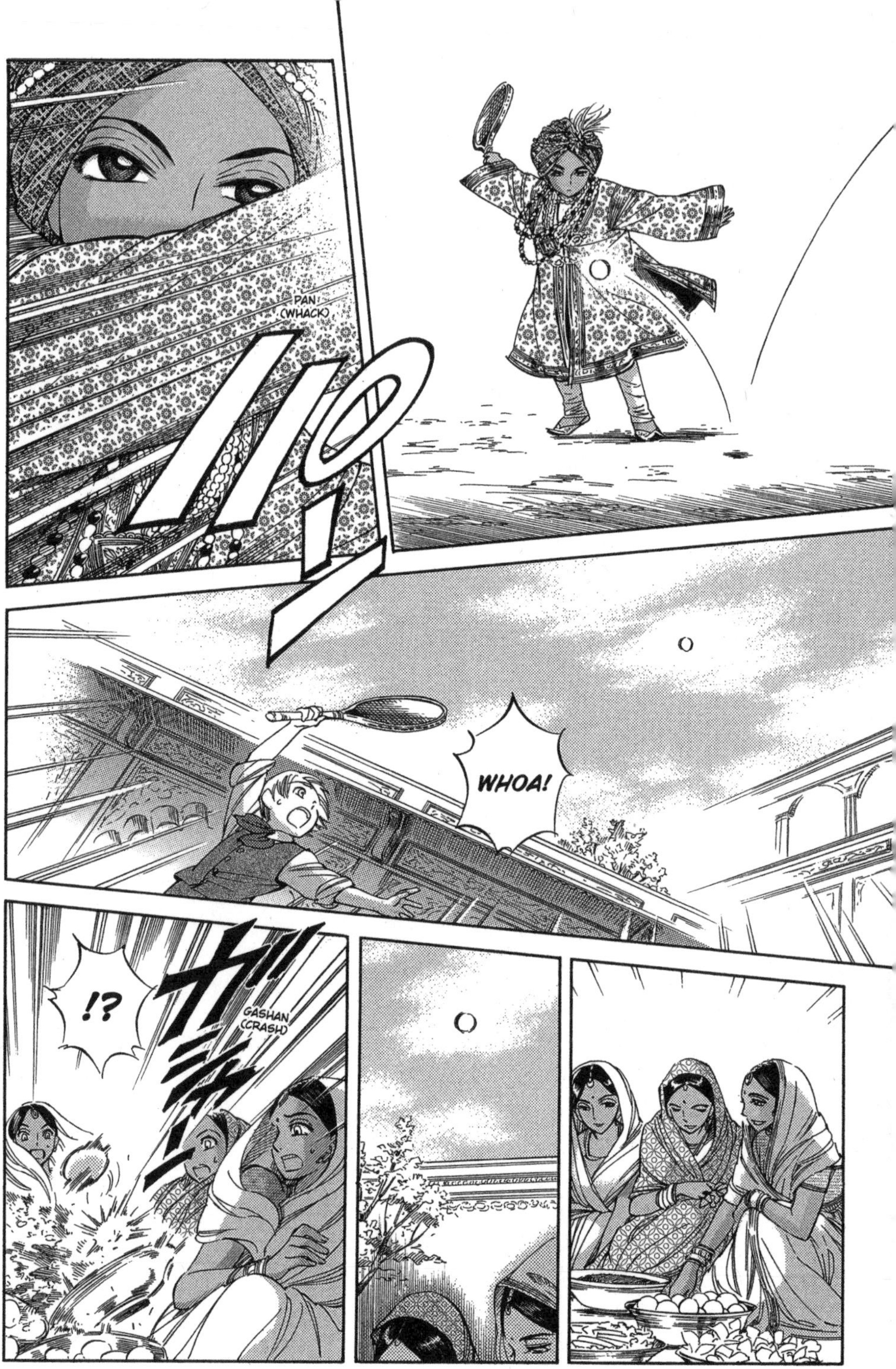
PAN
(WHACK)
WHOA!
GASHAN
(CRASH)
!?

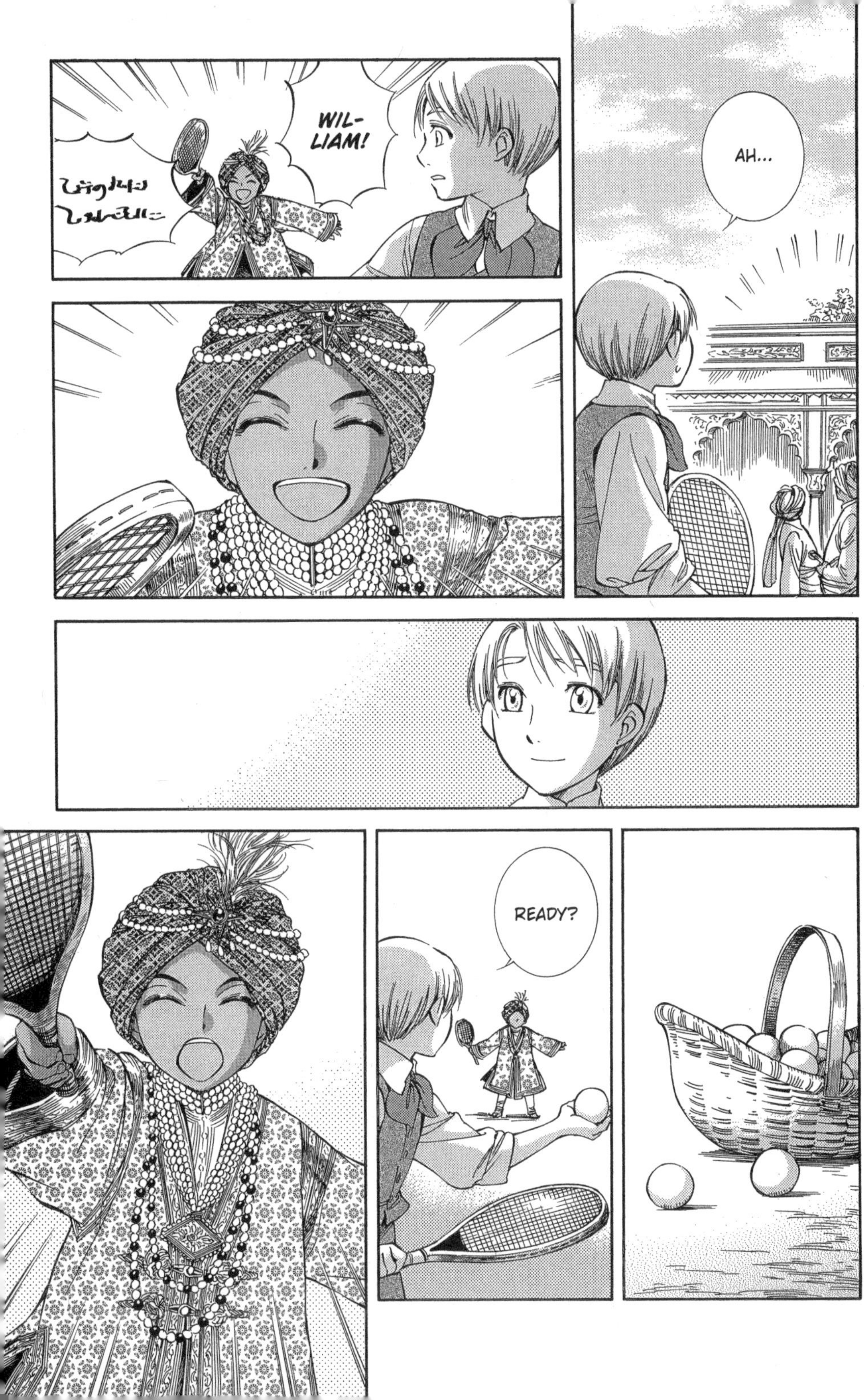
AH...
WIL-
LIAM!
READY?

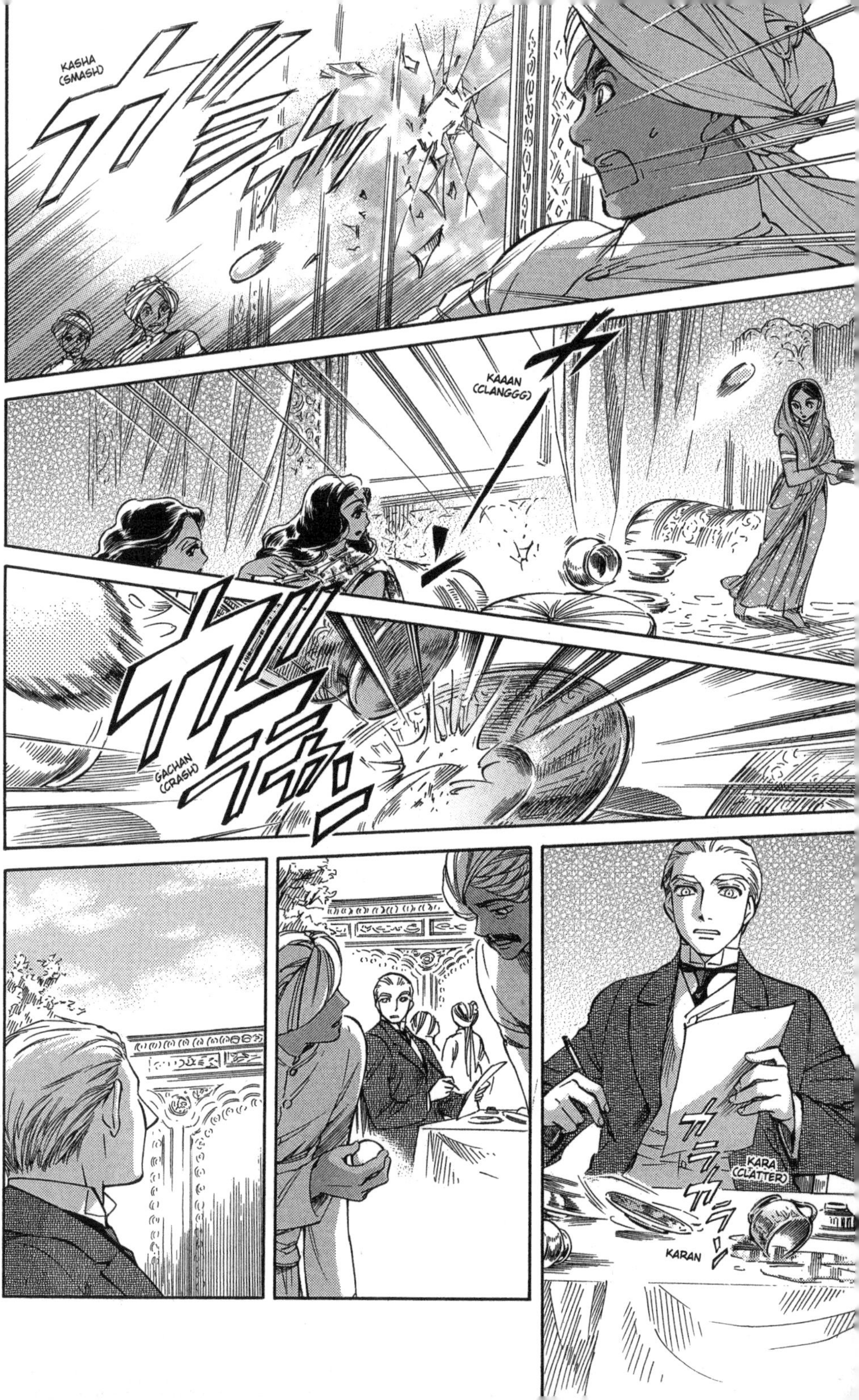
KASHA (SMASH)
KAAAN (CLANGGG)
GACHAN (CRASH)
KARA (CLATTER)
KARAN

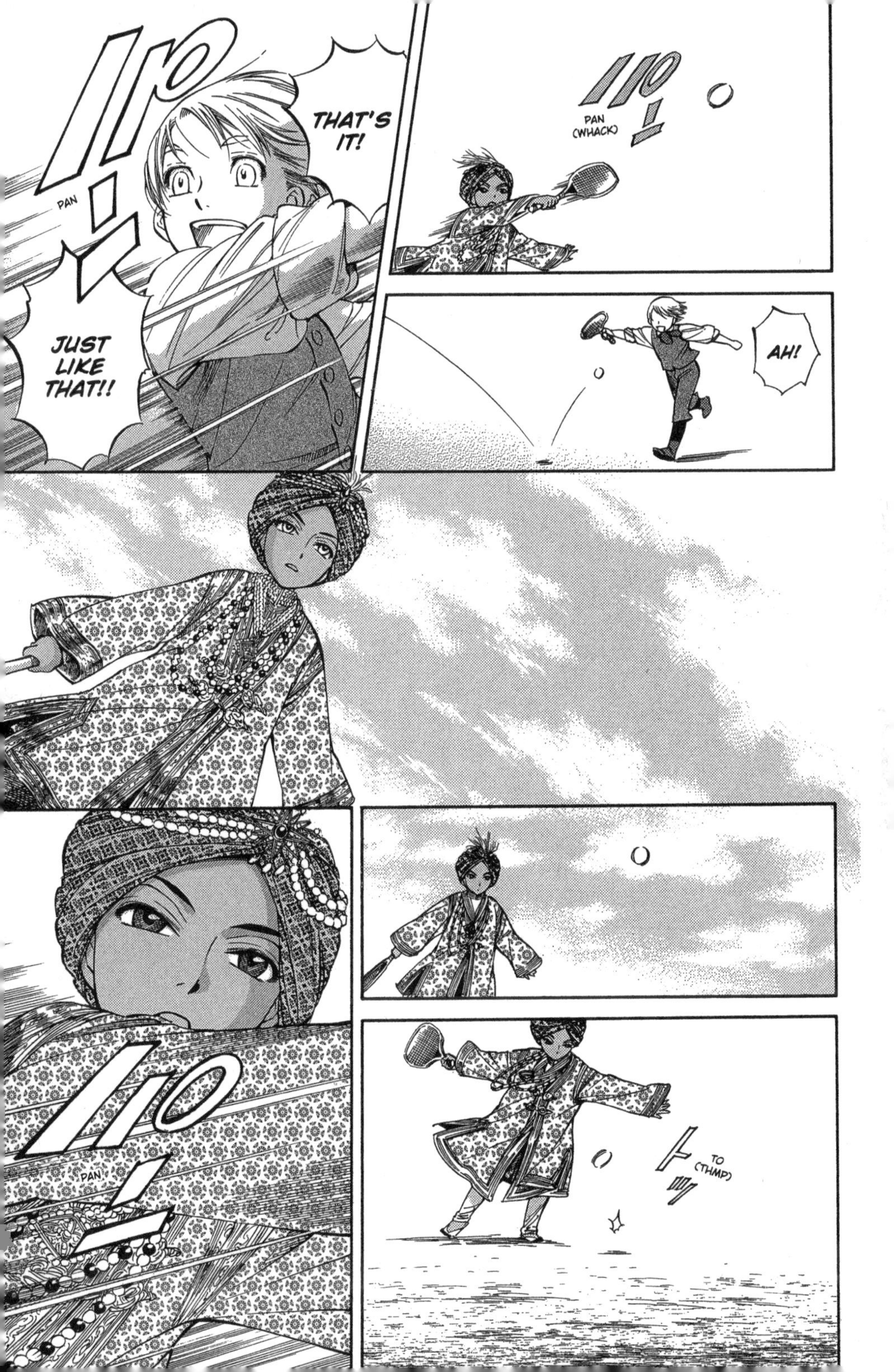
PAN (WHACK)
AH!
THAT'S IT!
PAN
JUST LIKE THAT!!
TO (THMP)
PAN

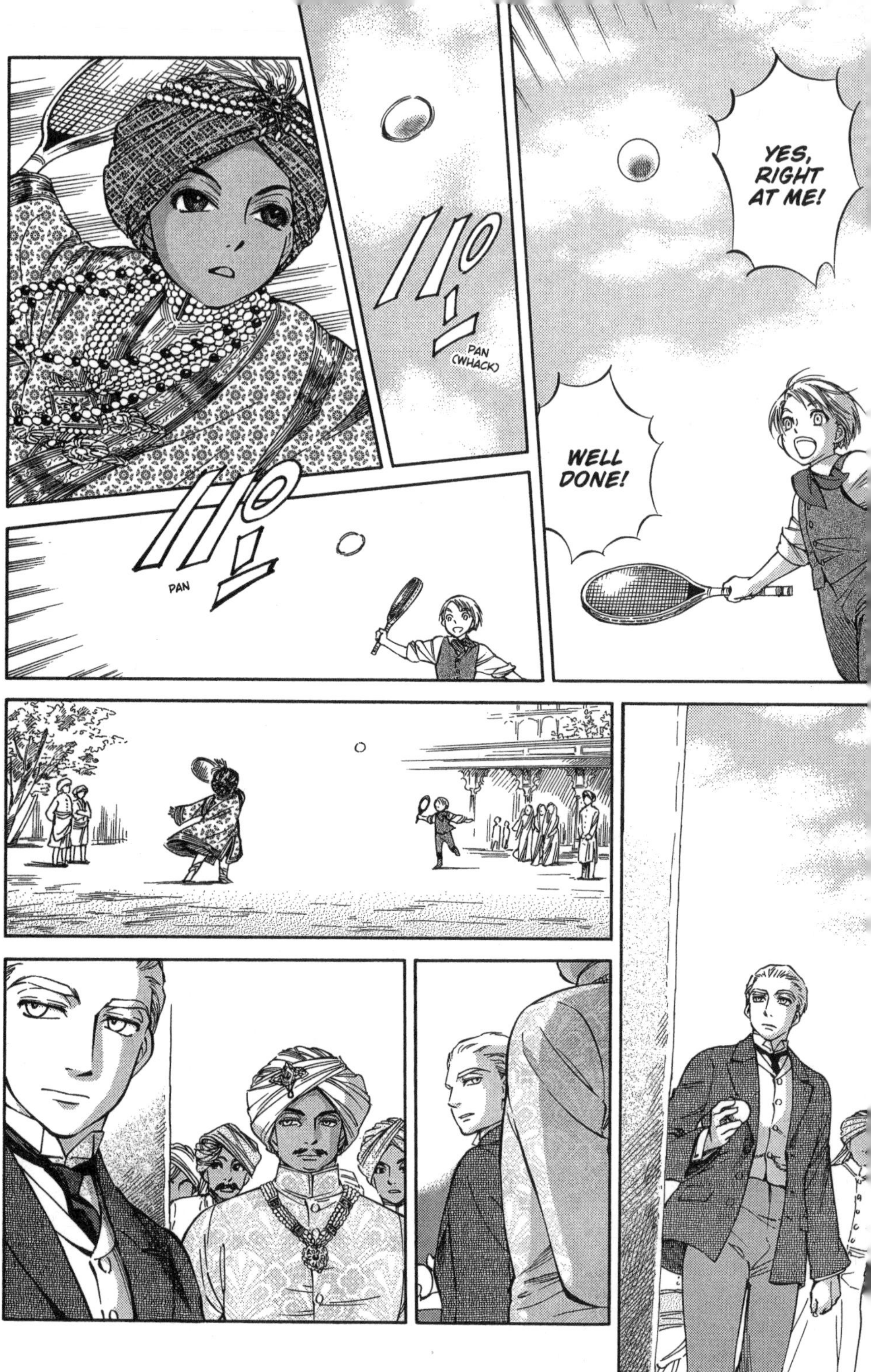

YES, RIGHT AT ME!
PAN (WHACK)
WELL DONE!
PAN

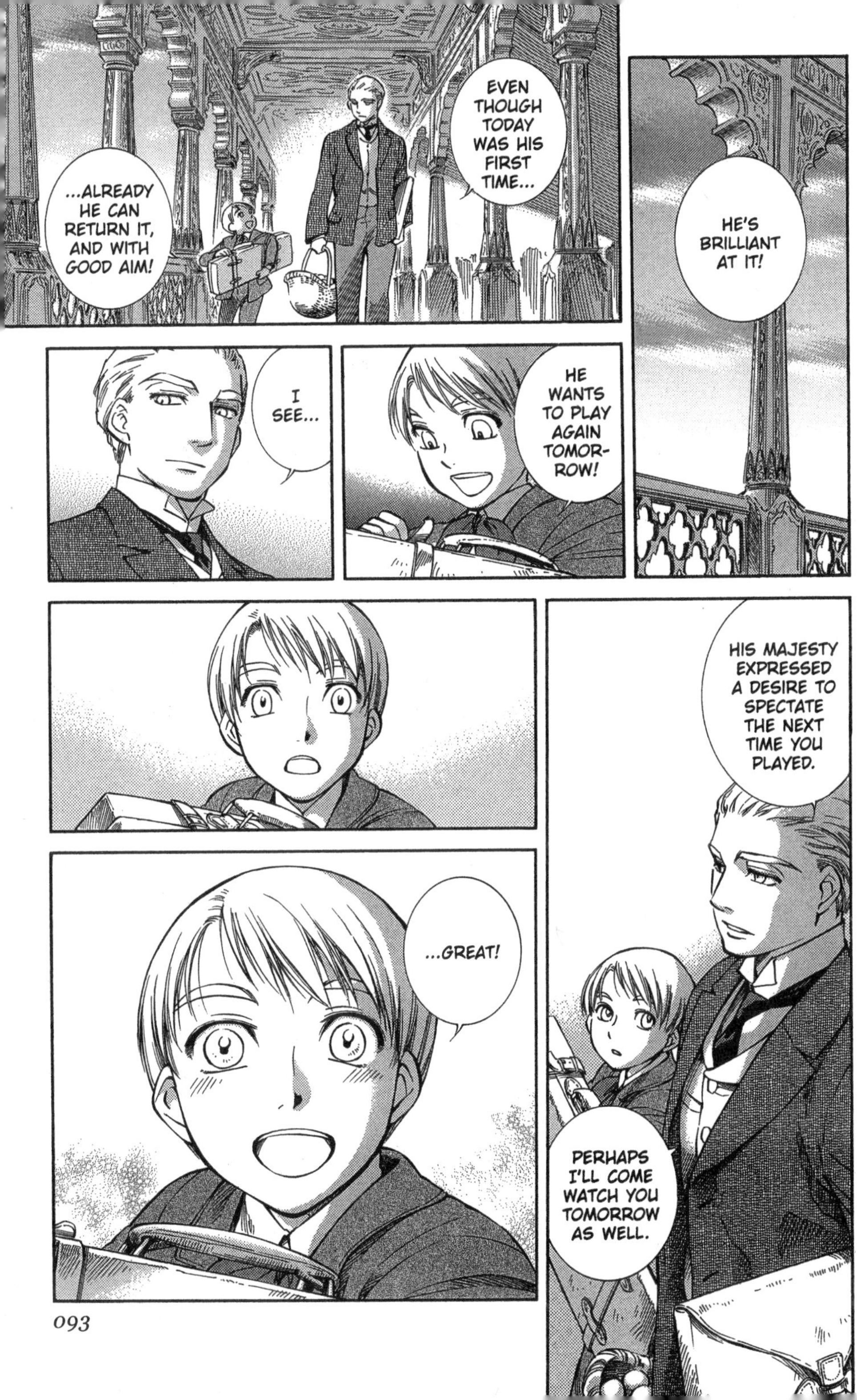
EVEN THOUGH TODAY WAS HIS FIRST TIME...
...ALREADY HE CAN RETURN IT, AND WITH GOOD AIM!
HE'S BRILLIANT AT IT!
HE WANTS TO PLAY AGAIN TOMOR-ROW!
I SEE...
HIS MAJESTY EXPRESSED A DESIRE TO SPECTATE THE NEXT TIME YOU PLAYED.
PERHAPS I'LL COME WATCH YOU TOMORROW AS WELL.
...GREAT!

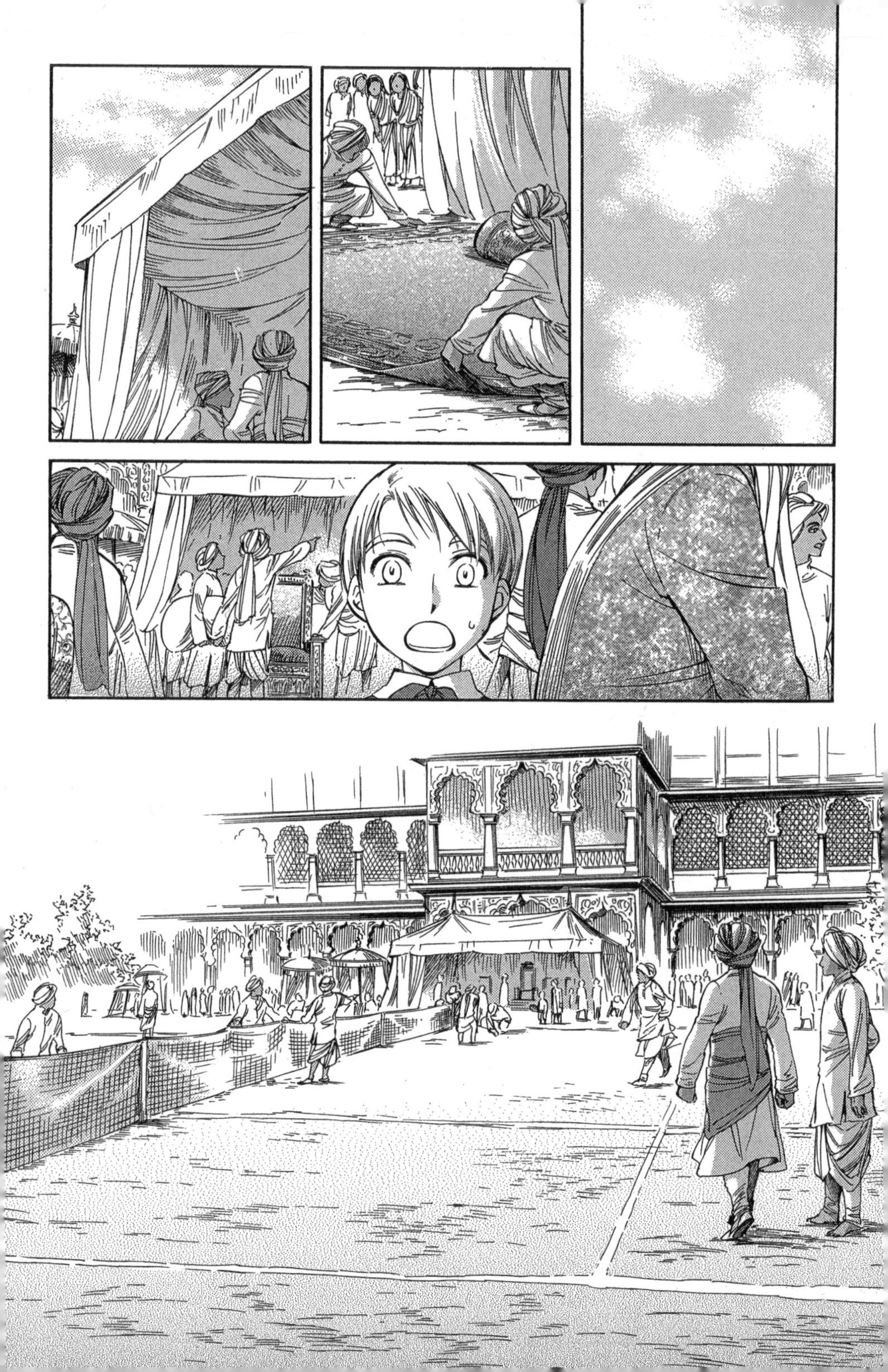

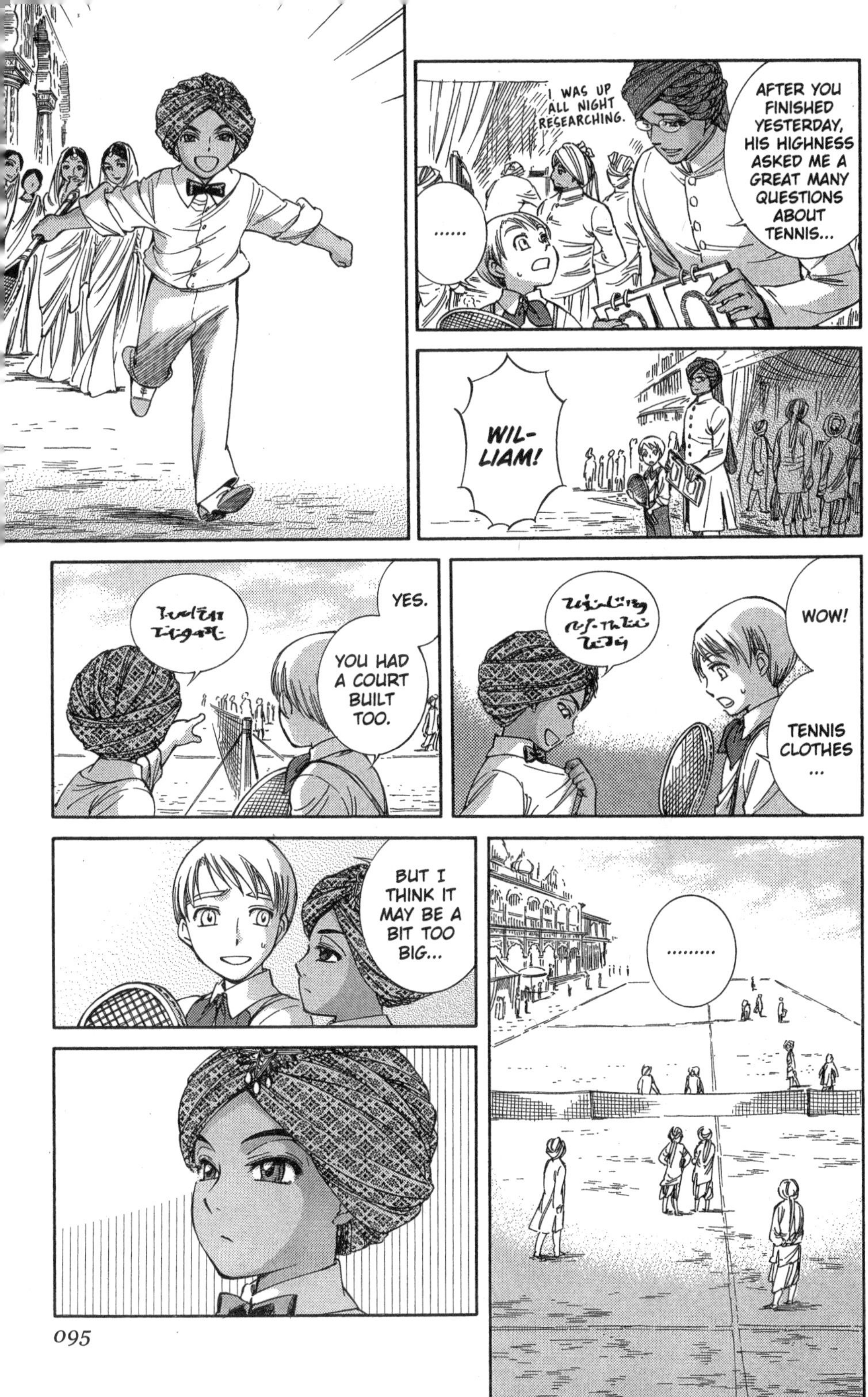
AFTER YOU FINISHED YESTERDAY, HIS HIGHNESS ASKED ME A GREAT MANY QUESTIONS ABOUT TENNIS...
I WAS UP ALL NIGHT RESEARCHING.
......
WIL-LIAM!
WOW!
TENNIS CLOTHES ...
YES.
YOU HAD A COURT BUILT TOO.
....
BUT I THINK IT MAY BE A BIT TOO BIG...

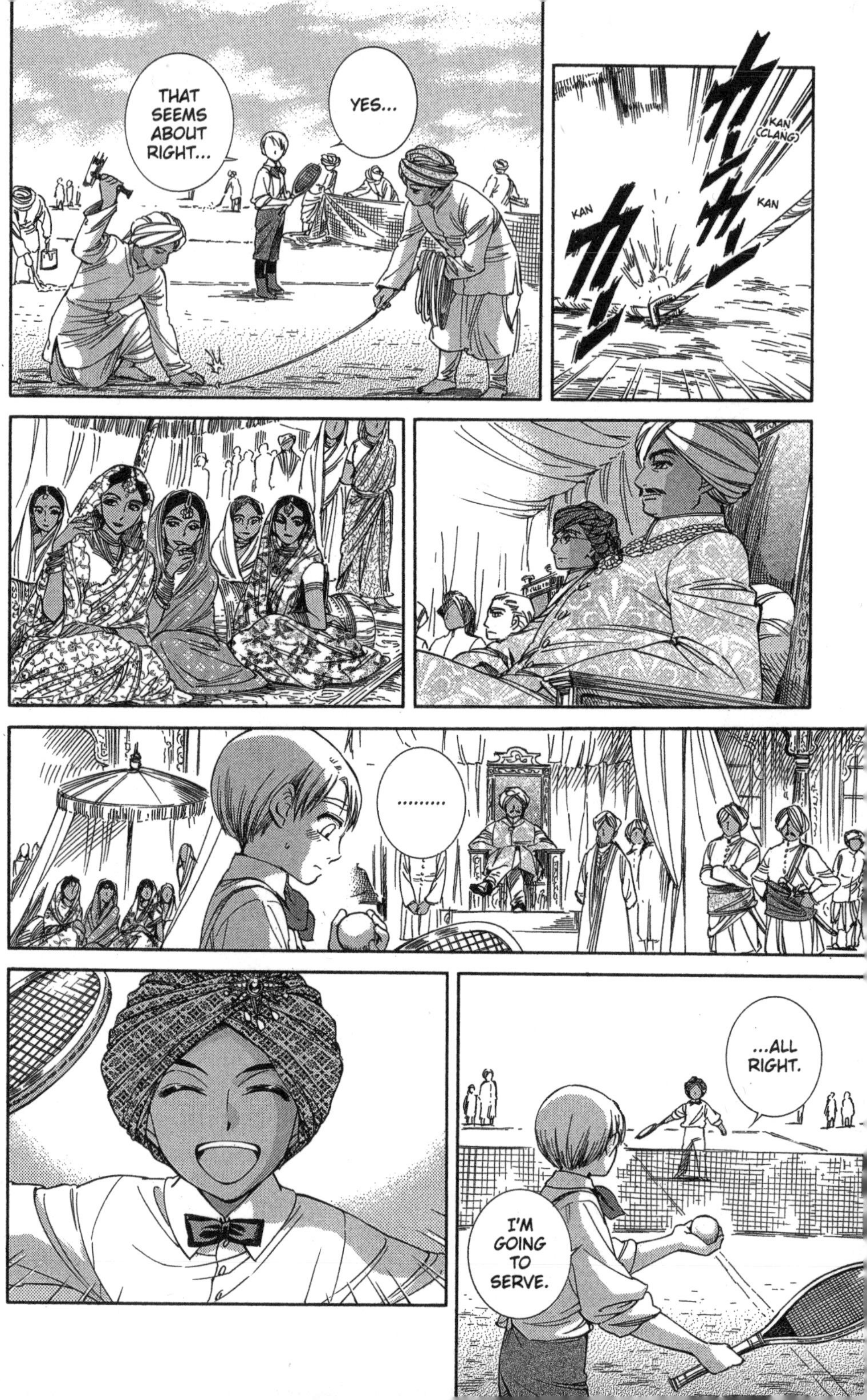
KAN (CLANG)
KAN
KAN
YES...
THAT SEEMS ABOUT RIGHT...
....
...ALL RIGHT.
I'M GOING TO SERVE.

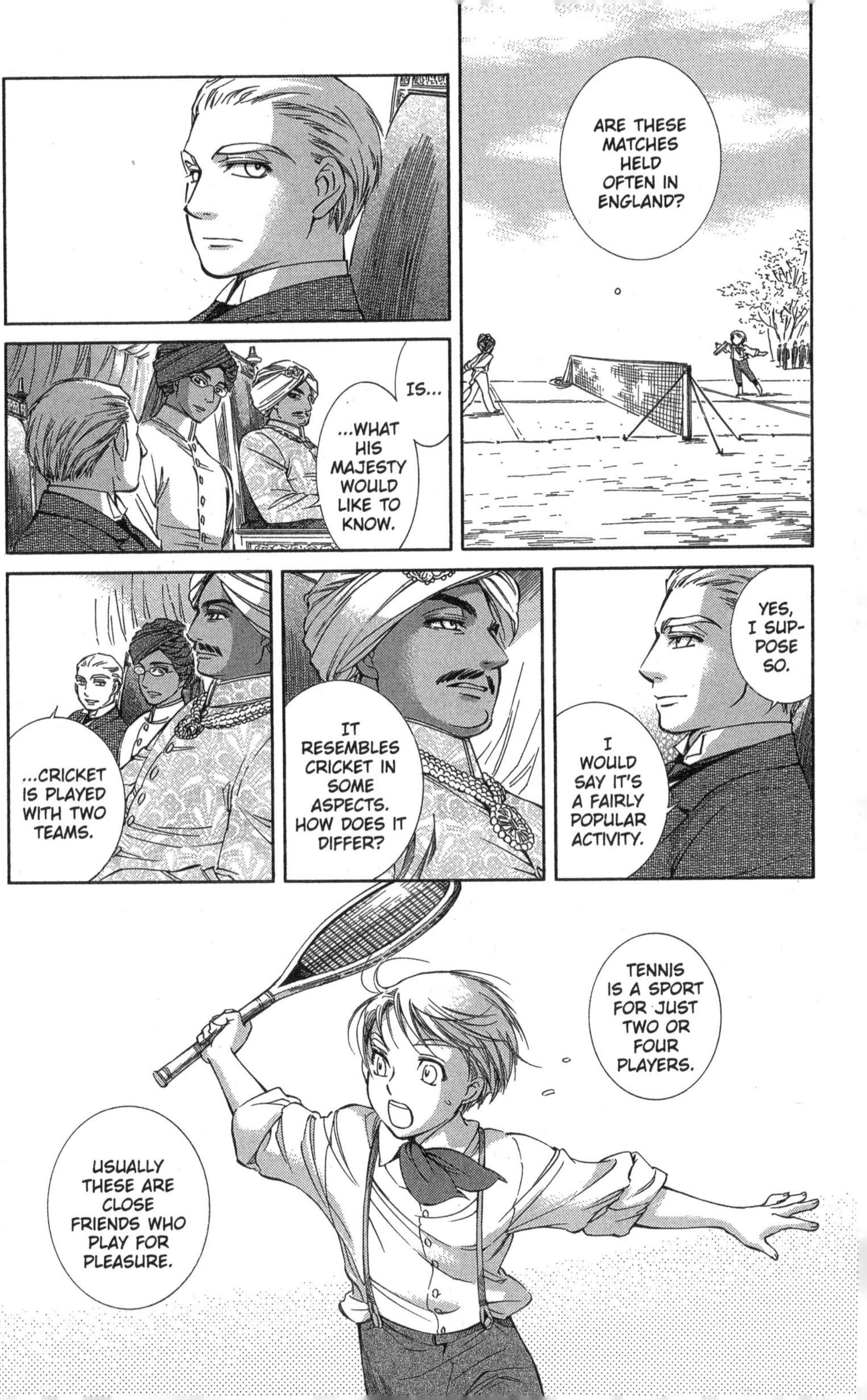
ARE THESE MATCHES HELD OFTEN IN ENGLAND?
IS...
...WHAT HIS MAJESTY WOULD LIKE TO KNOW.
YES, I SUP-POSE SO.
I WOULD SAY IT'S A FAIRLY POPULAR ACTIVITY.
IT RESEMBLES CRICKET IN SOME ASPECTS. HOW DOES IT DIFFER?
...CRICKET IS PLAYED WITH TWO TEAMS.
TENNIS IS A SPORT FOR JUST TWO OR FOUR PLAYERS.
USUALLY THESE ARE CLOSE FRIENDS WHO PLAY FOR PLEASURE.

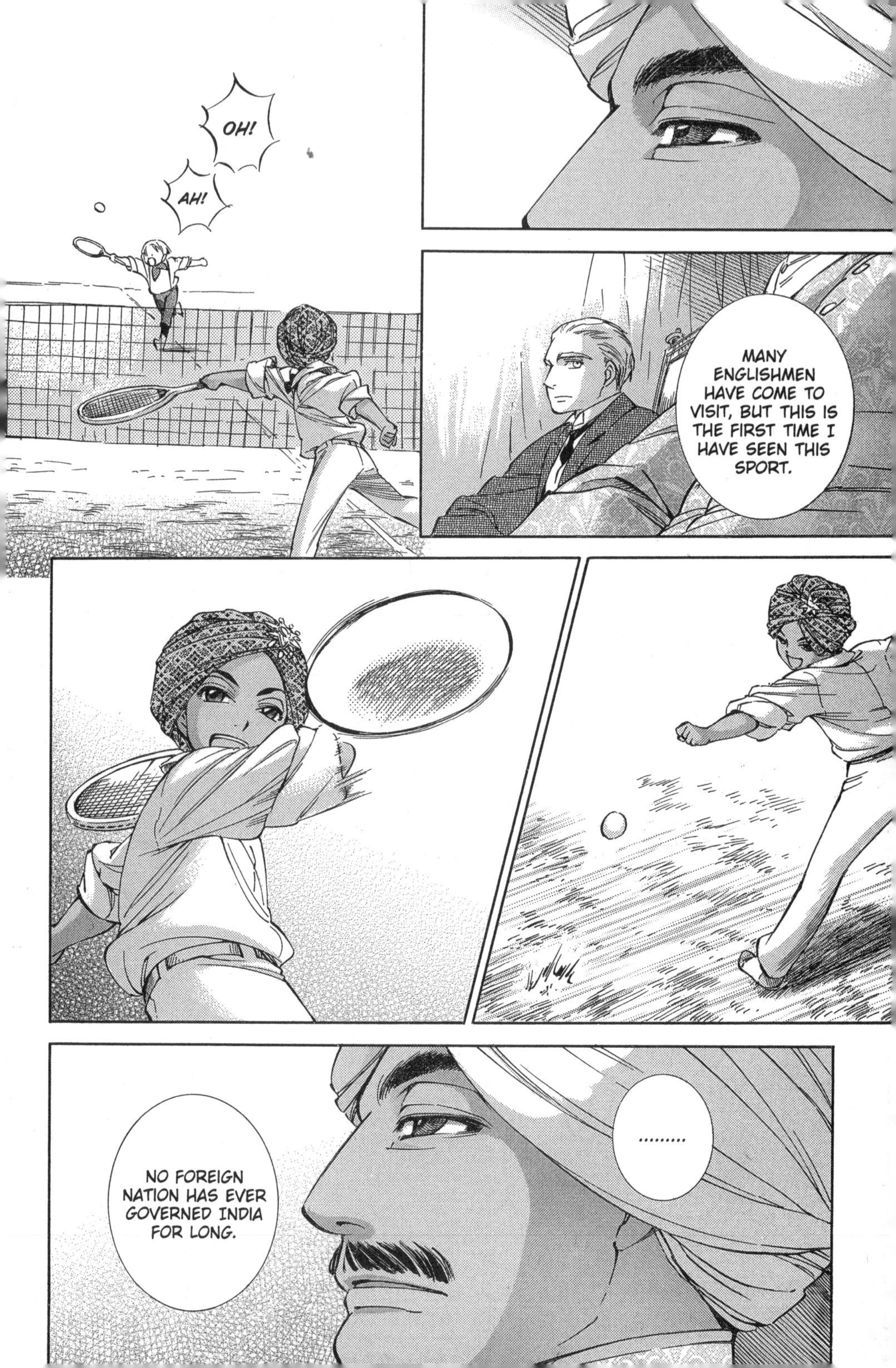
MANY ENGLISHMEN HAVE COME TO VISIT, BUT THIS IS THE FIRST TIME I HAVE SEEN THIS SPORT.
OH!
AH!
....
NO FOREIGN NATION HAS EVER GOVERNED INDIA FOR LONG.

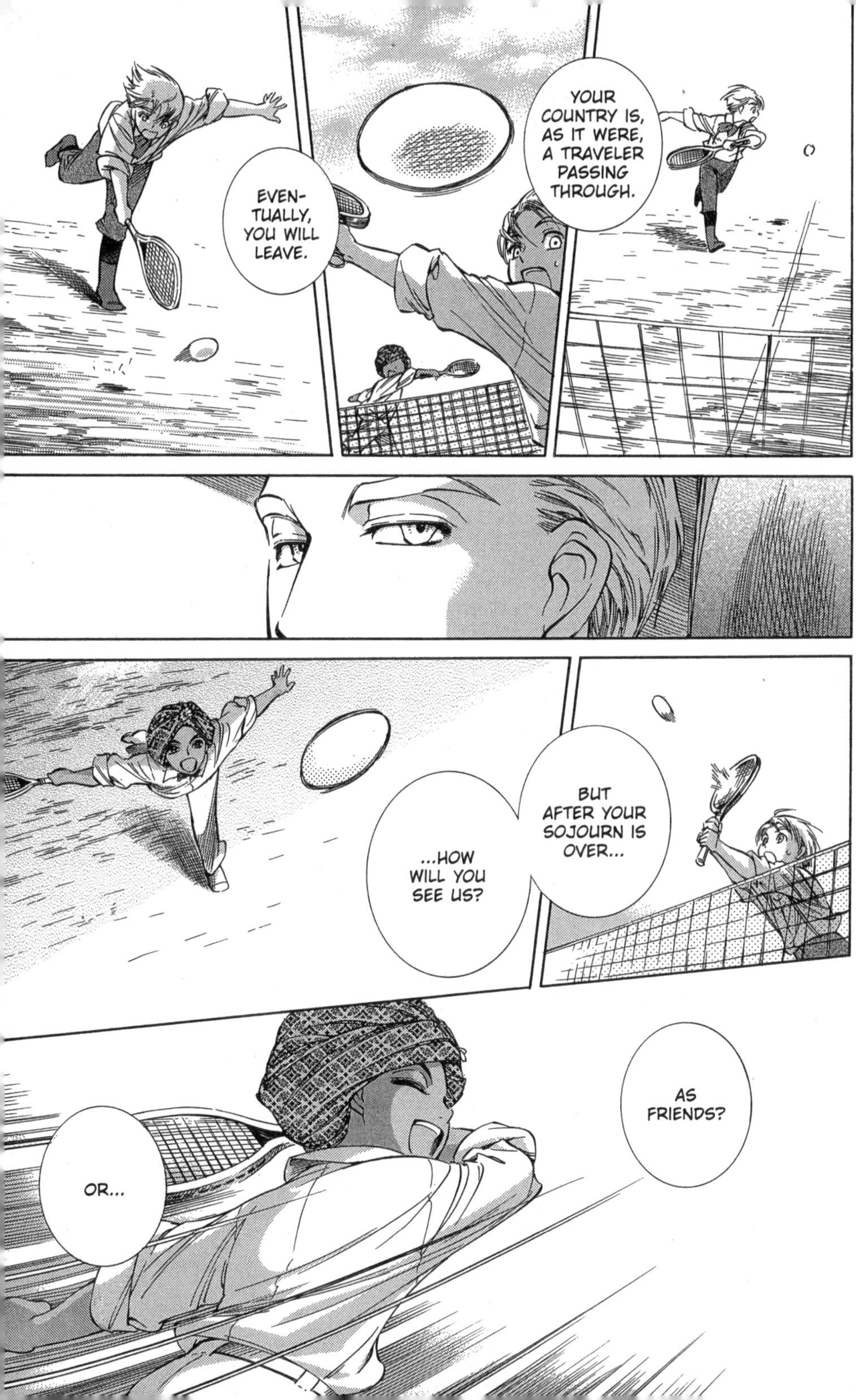
YOUR COUNTRY IS, AS IT WERE, A TRAVELER PASSING THROUGH.
EVEN-TUALLY, YOU WILL LEAVE.
BUT AFTER YOUR SOJOURN IS OVER...
...HOW WILL YOU SEE US?
AS FRIENDS?
OR...

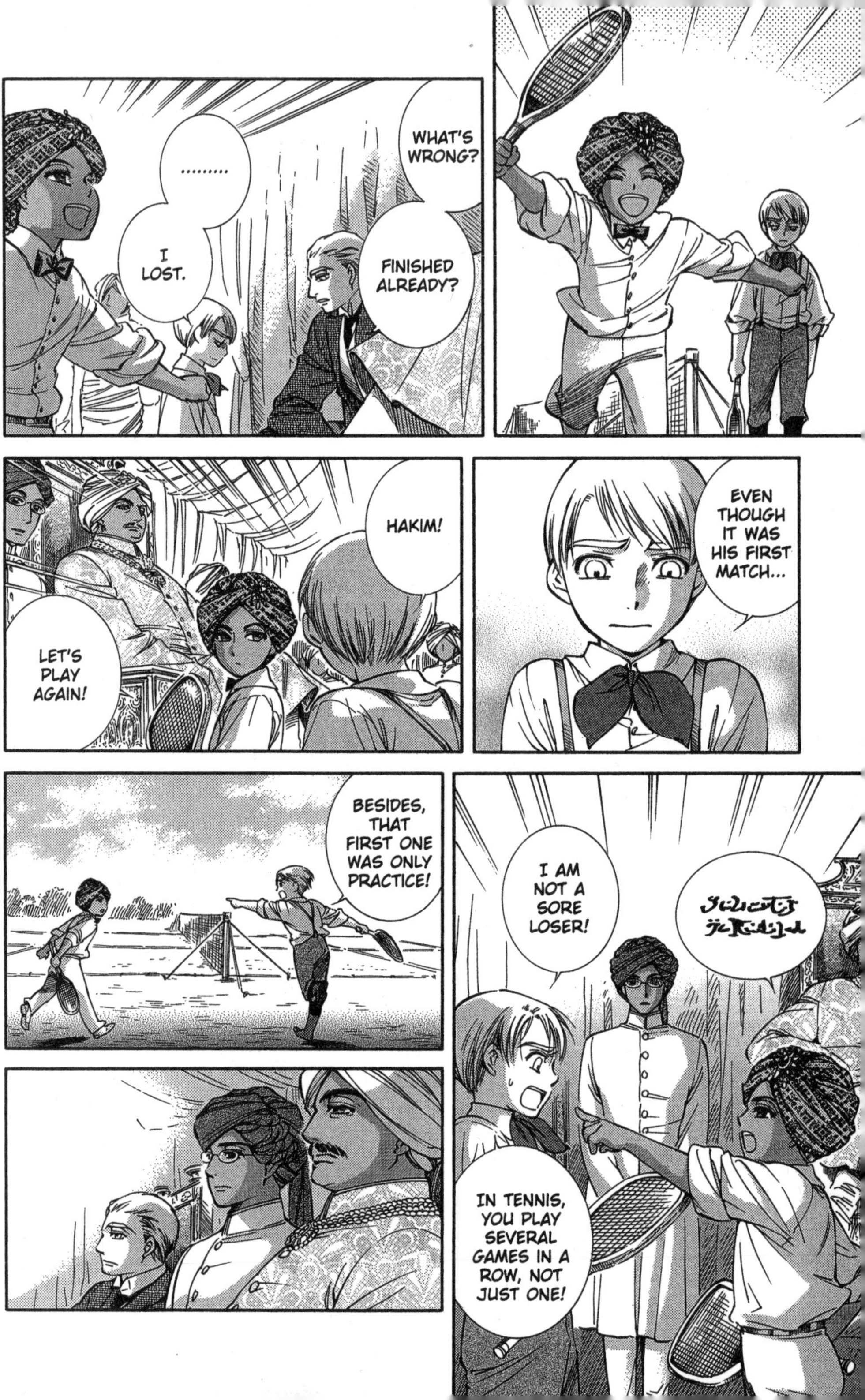
WHAT'S WRONG?
FINISHED ALREADY?
....
I LOST.
EVEN THOUGH IT WAS HIS FIRST MATCH...
HAKIM!
LET'S PLAY AGAIN!
I AM NOT A SORE LOSER!
IN TENNIS, YOU PLAY SEVERAL GAMES IN A ROW, NOT JUST ONE!
BESIDES, THAT FIRST ONE WAS ONLY PRACTICE!

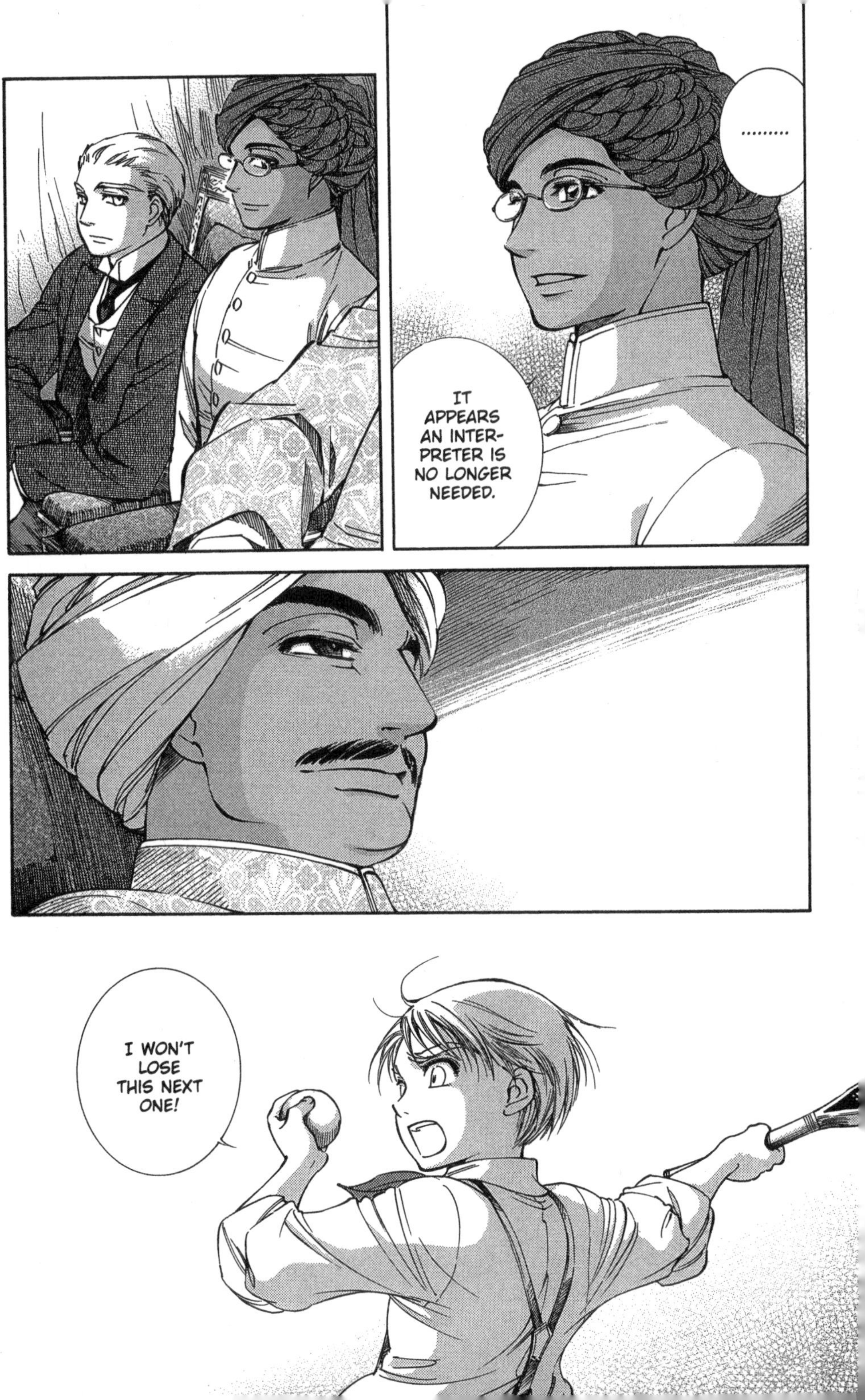
....
IT APPEARS AN INTERPRETER IS NO LONGER NEEDED.
I WON'T LOSE THIS NEXT ONE!

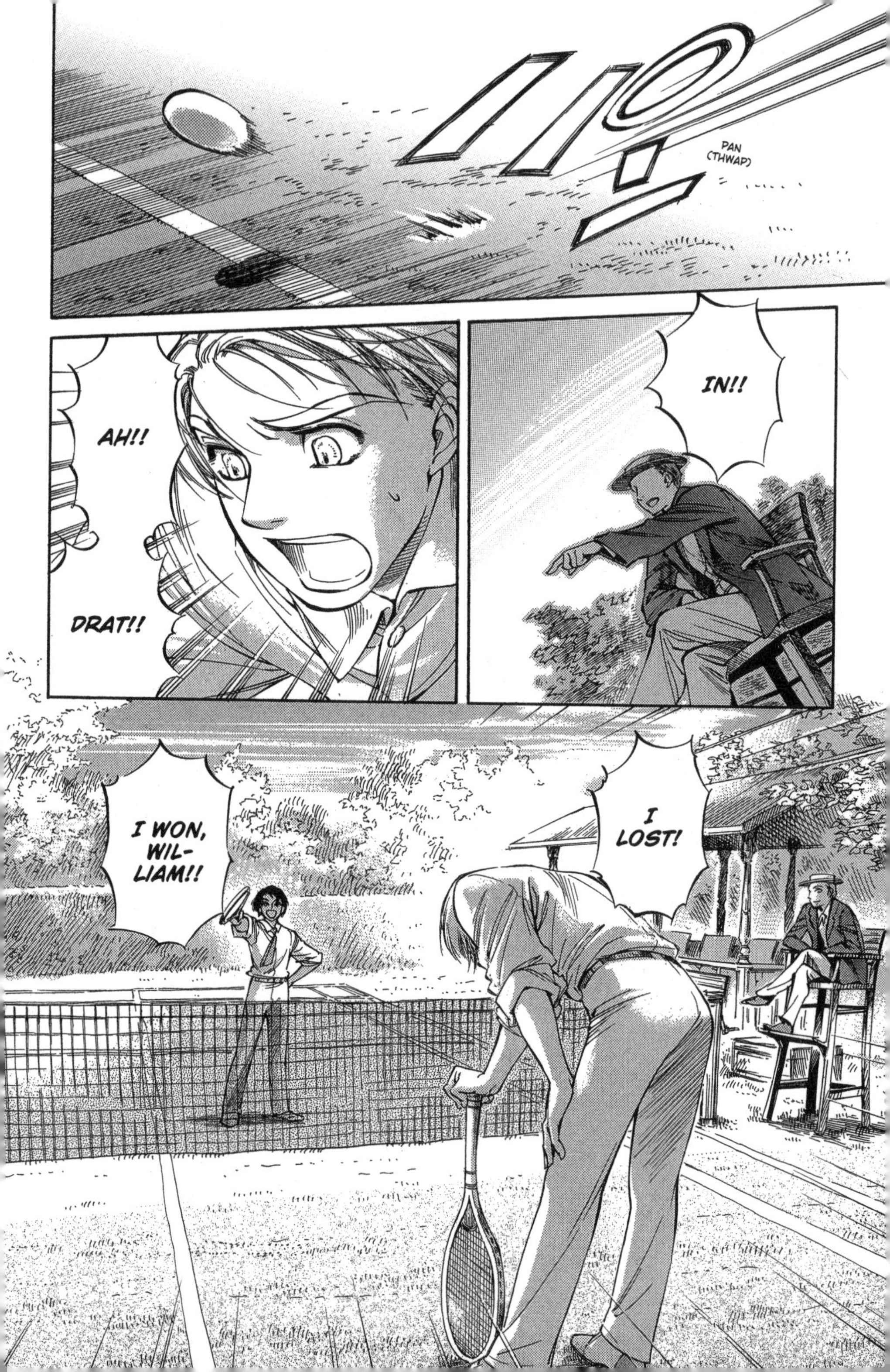
PAN
(THWAP)
IN!!
AH!!
DRAT!!
I LOST!
I WON, WIL-LIAM!!

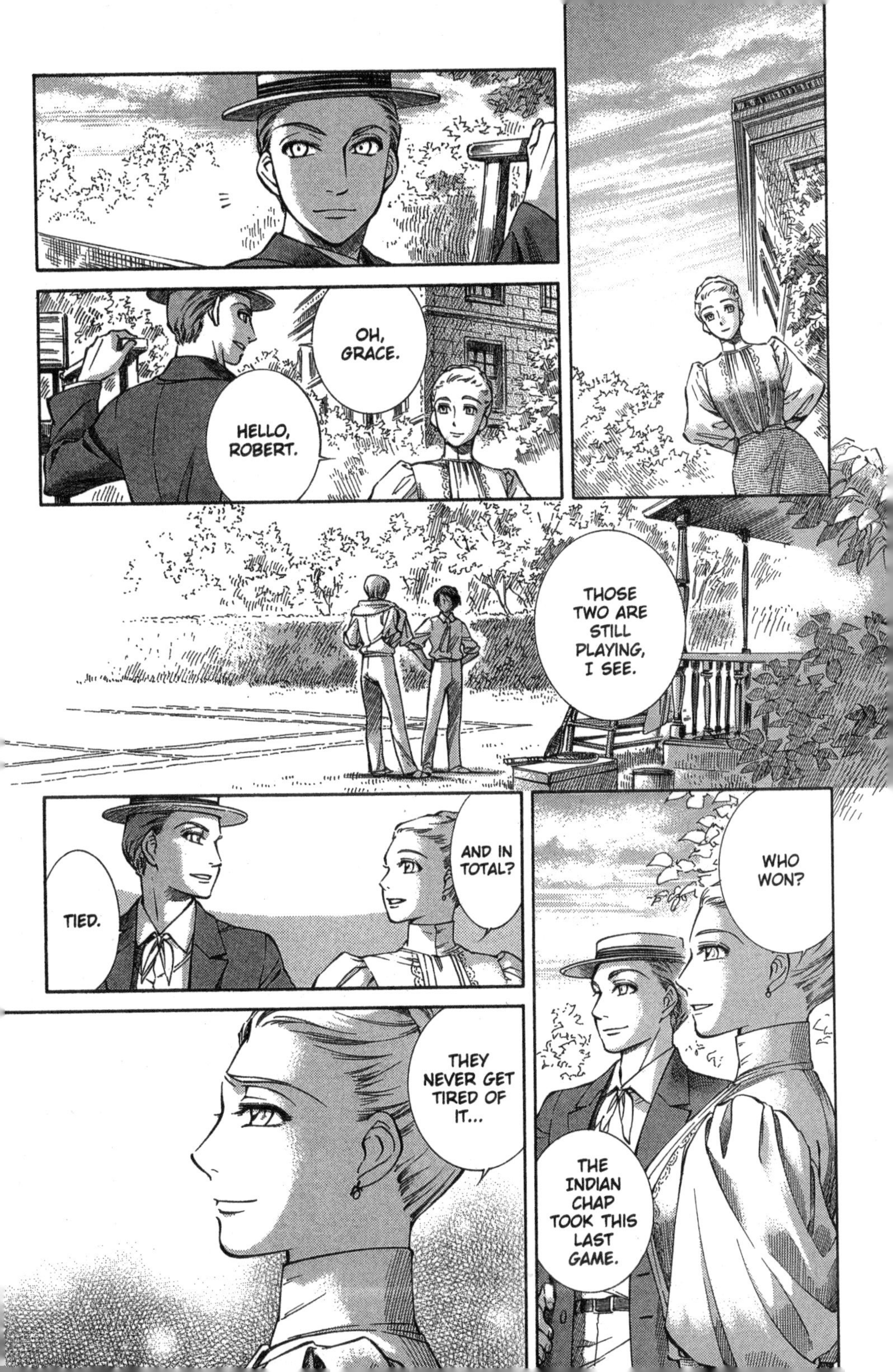
OH, GRACE.
HELLO, ROBERT.
THOSE TWO ARE STILL PLAYING, I SEE.
WHO WON?
THE INDIAN CHAP TOOK THIS LAST GAME.
AND IN TOTAL?
TIED.
THEY NEVER GET TIRED OF IT...

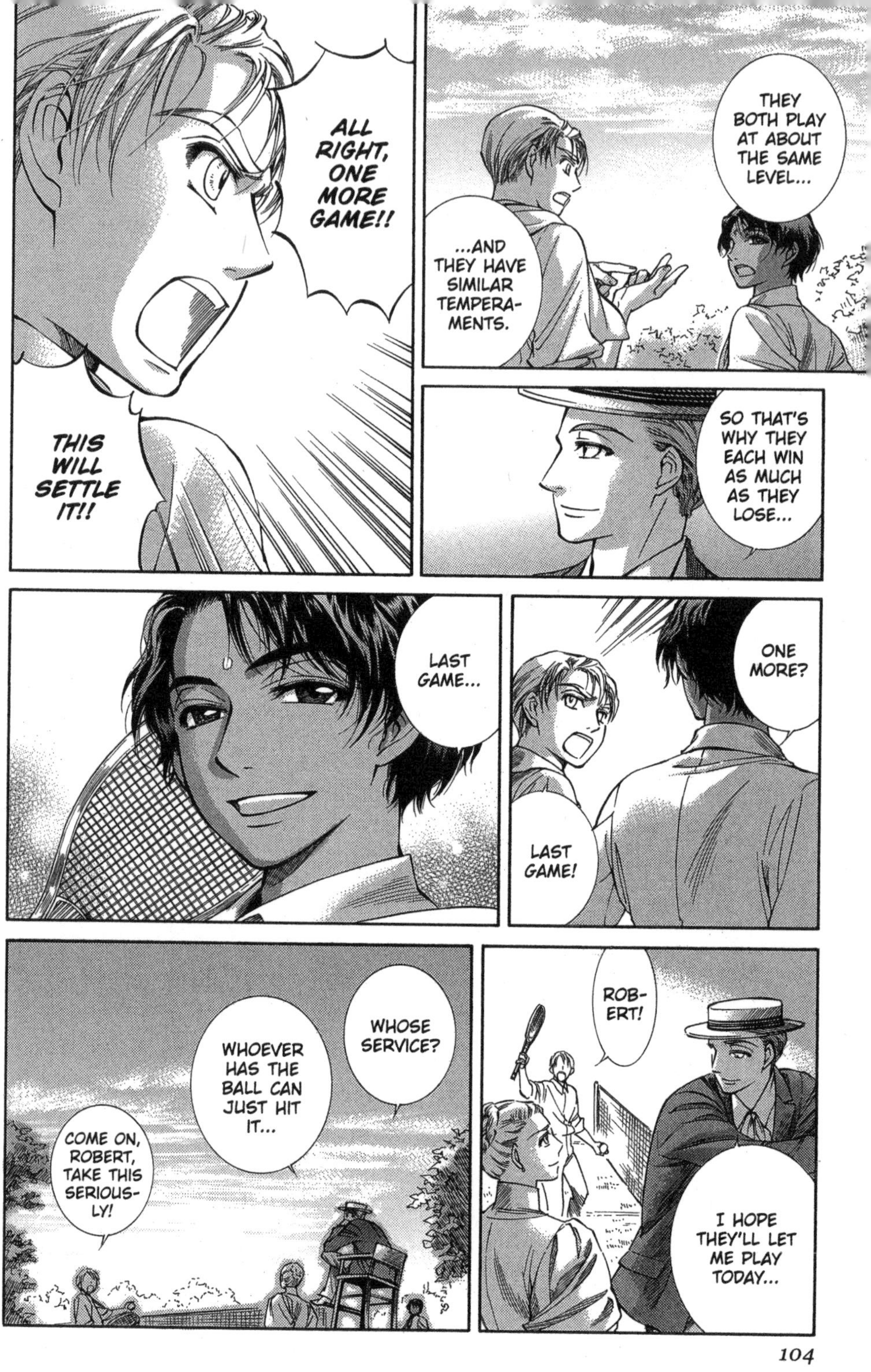
THEY BOTH PLAY AT ABOUT THE SAME LEVEL...
...AND THEY HAVE SIMILAR TEMPERA-MENTS.
SO THAT'S WHY THEY EACH WIN AS MUCH AS THEY LOSE...
ALL RIGHT, ONE MORE GAME!!
THIS WILL SETTLE IT!!
ONE MORE?
LAST GAME!
LAST GAME...
ROB-ERT!
I HOPE THEY'LL LET ME PLAY TODAY...
WHOSE SERVICE?
WHOEVER HAS THE BALL CAN JUST HIT IT...
COME ON, ROBERT, TAKE THIS SERIOUS-LY!

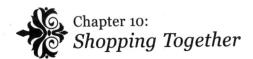 Chapter 10:
Shopping Together

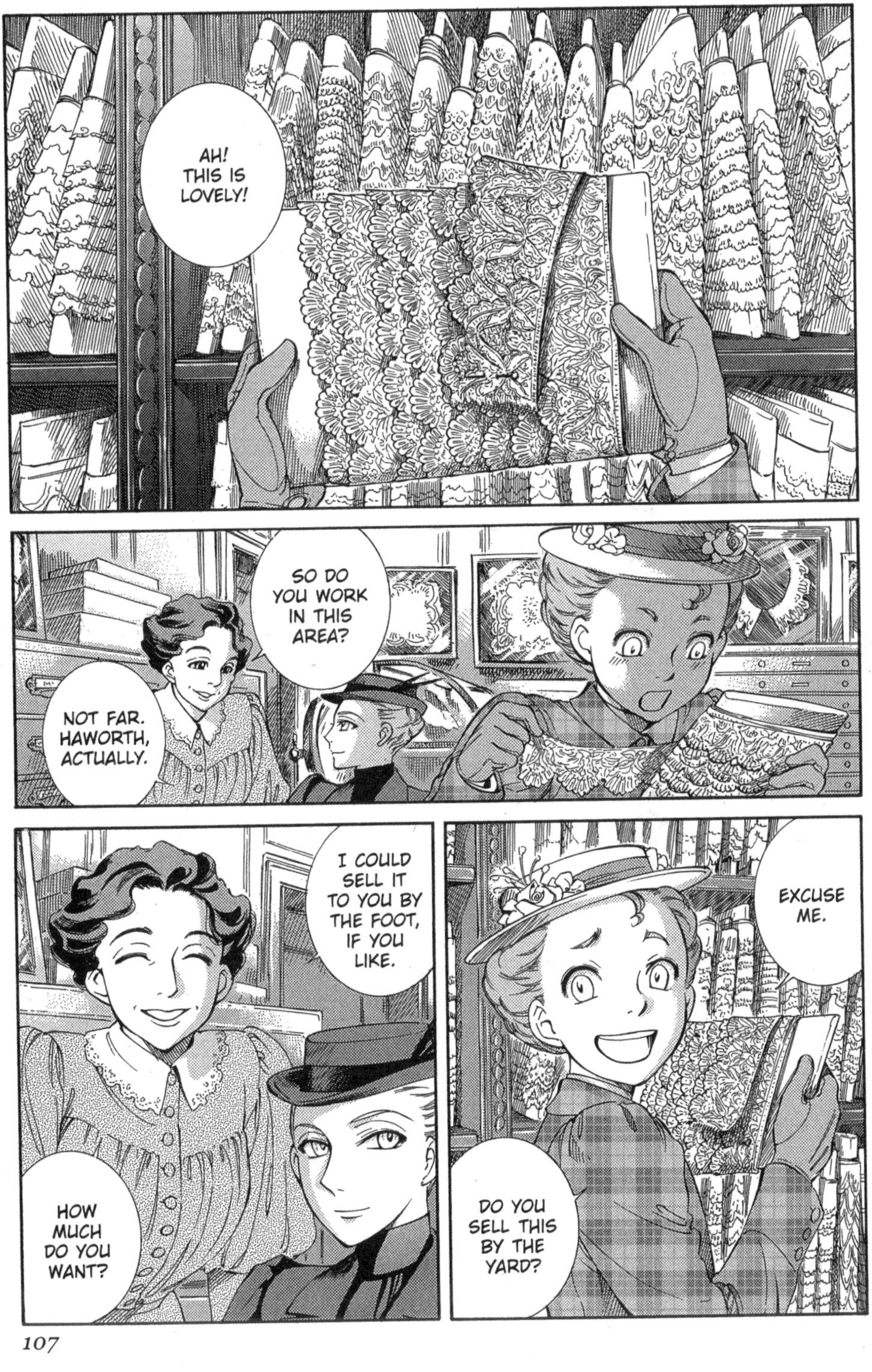
AH! THIS IS LOVELY!
SO DO YOU WORK IN THIS AREA?
NOT FAR. HAWORTH, ACTUALLY.
EXCUSE ME.
DO YOU SELL THIS BY THE YARD?
I COULD SELL IT TO YOU BY THE FOOT, IF YOU LIKE.
HOW MUCH DO YOU WANT?

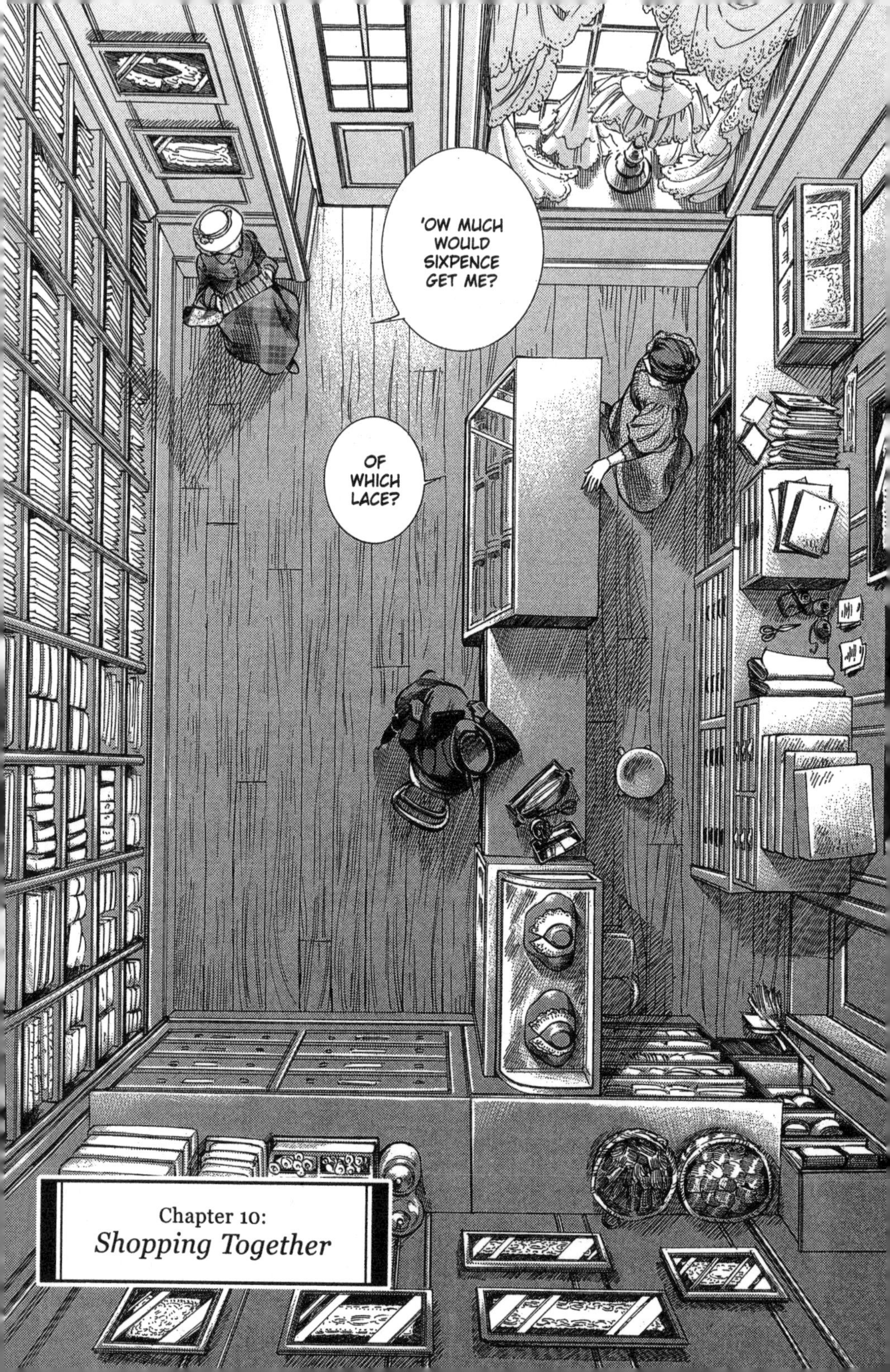
'OW MUCH WOULD SIXPENCE GET ME?
OF WHICH LACE?

Chapter 10: *Shopping Together*

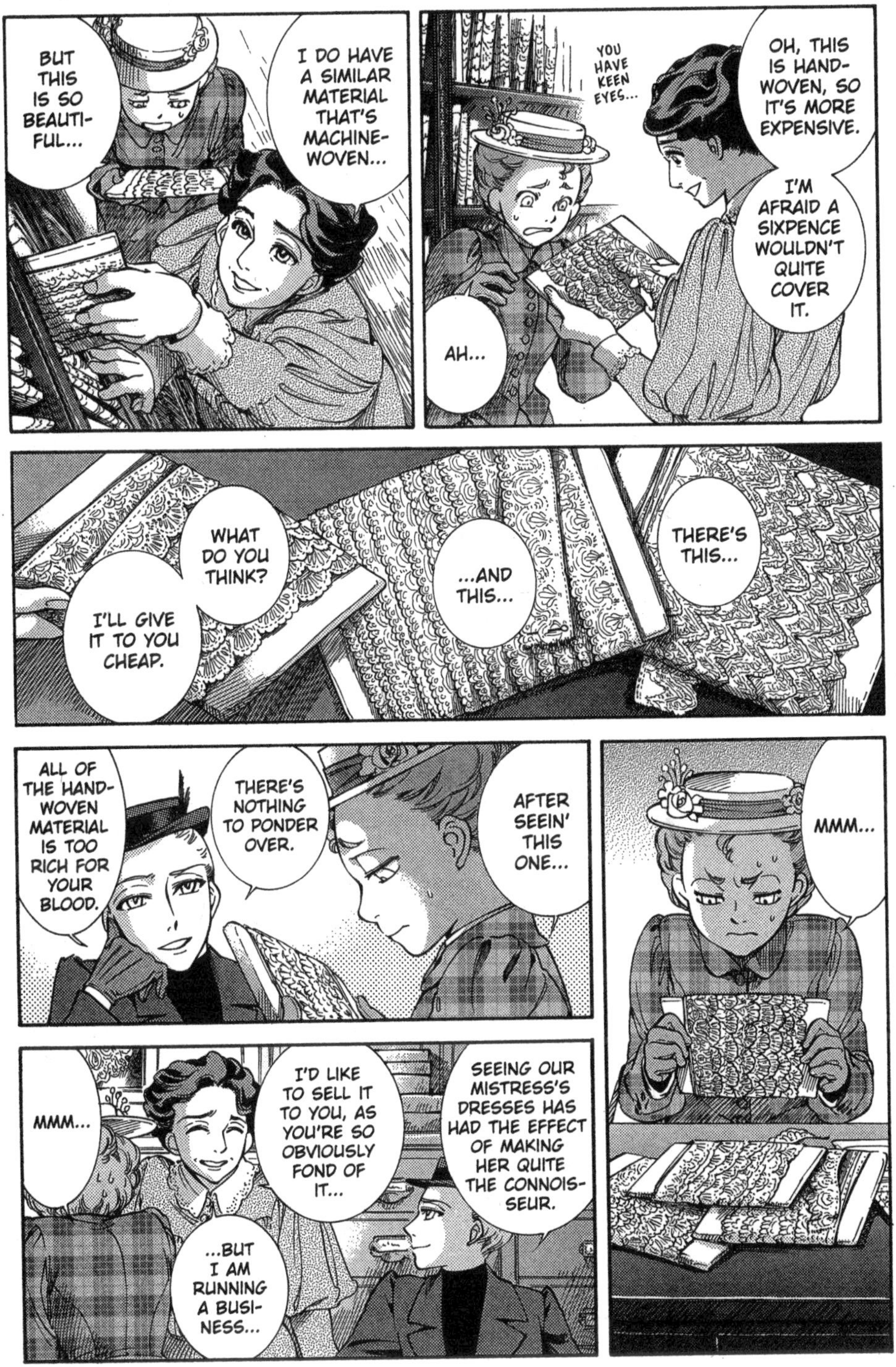
OH, THIS IS HAND-WOVEN, SO IT'S MORE EXPENSIVE.
I'M AFRAID A SIXPENCE WOULDN'T QUITE COVER IT.
YOU HAVE KEEN EYES...
AH...
I DO HAVE A SIMILAR MATERIAL THAT'S MACHINE-WOVEN...
BUT THIS IS SO BEAUTIFUL...
THERE'S THIS...
...AND THIS...
WHAT DO YOU THINK?
I'LL GIVE IT TO YOU CHEAP.
MMM...
AFTER SEEIN' THIS ONE...
THERE'S NOTHING TO PONDER OVER.
ALL OF THE HAND-WOVEN MATERIAL IS TOO RICH FOR YOUR BLOOD.
SEEING OUR MISTRESS'S DRESSES HAS HAD THE EFFECT OF MAKING HER QUITE THE CONNOISSEUR.
I'D LIKE TO SELL IT TO YOU, AS YOU'RE SO OBVIOUSLY FOND OF IT...
...BUT I AM RUNNING A BUSINESS...
MMM...

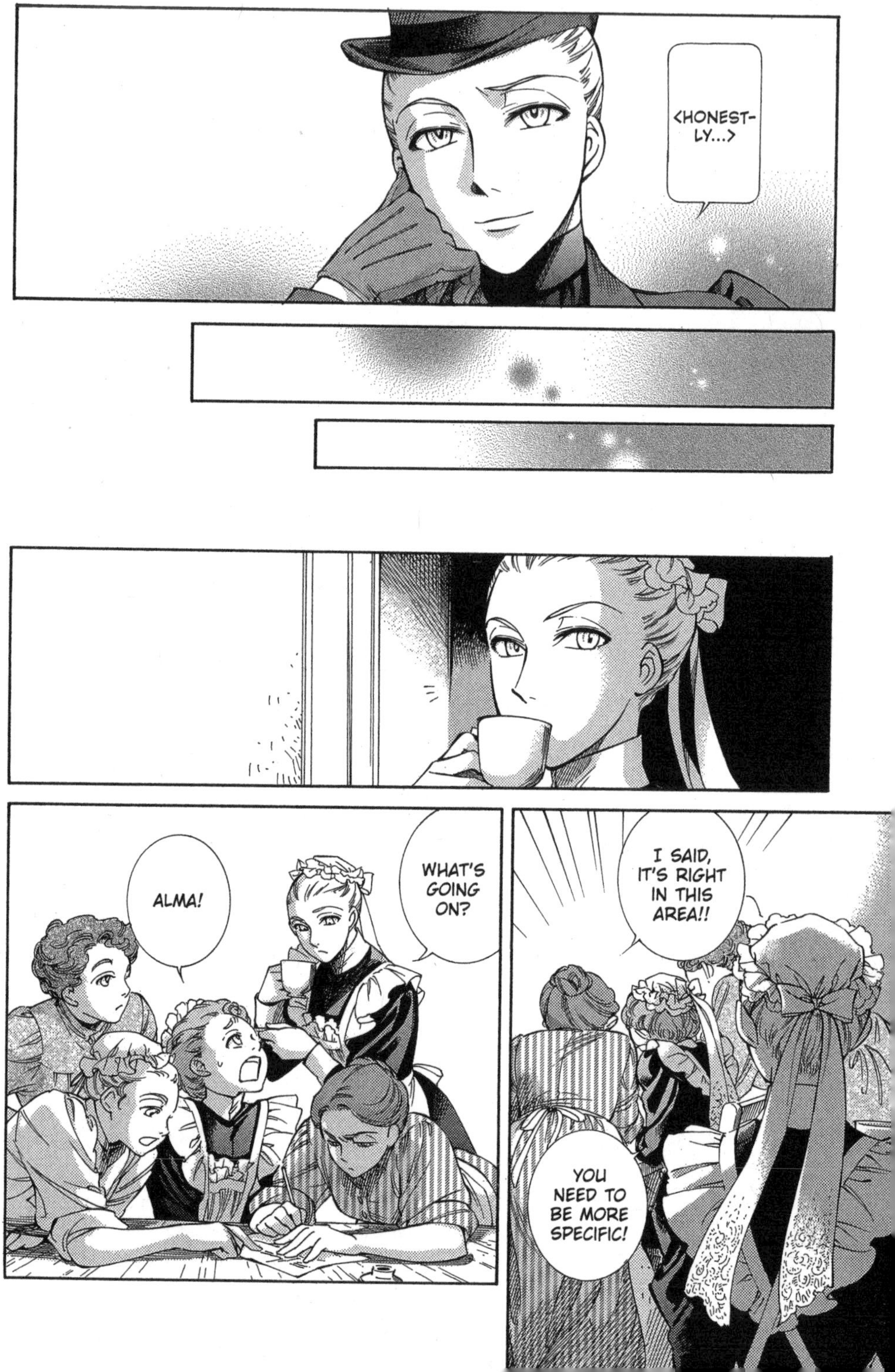
<HONEST-LY...>
I SAID, IT'S RIGHT IN THIS AREA!!
YOU NEED TO BE MORE SPECIFIC!
WHAT'S GOING ON?
ALMA!

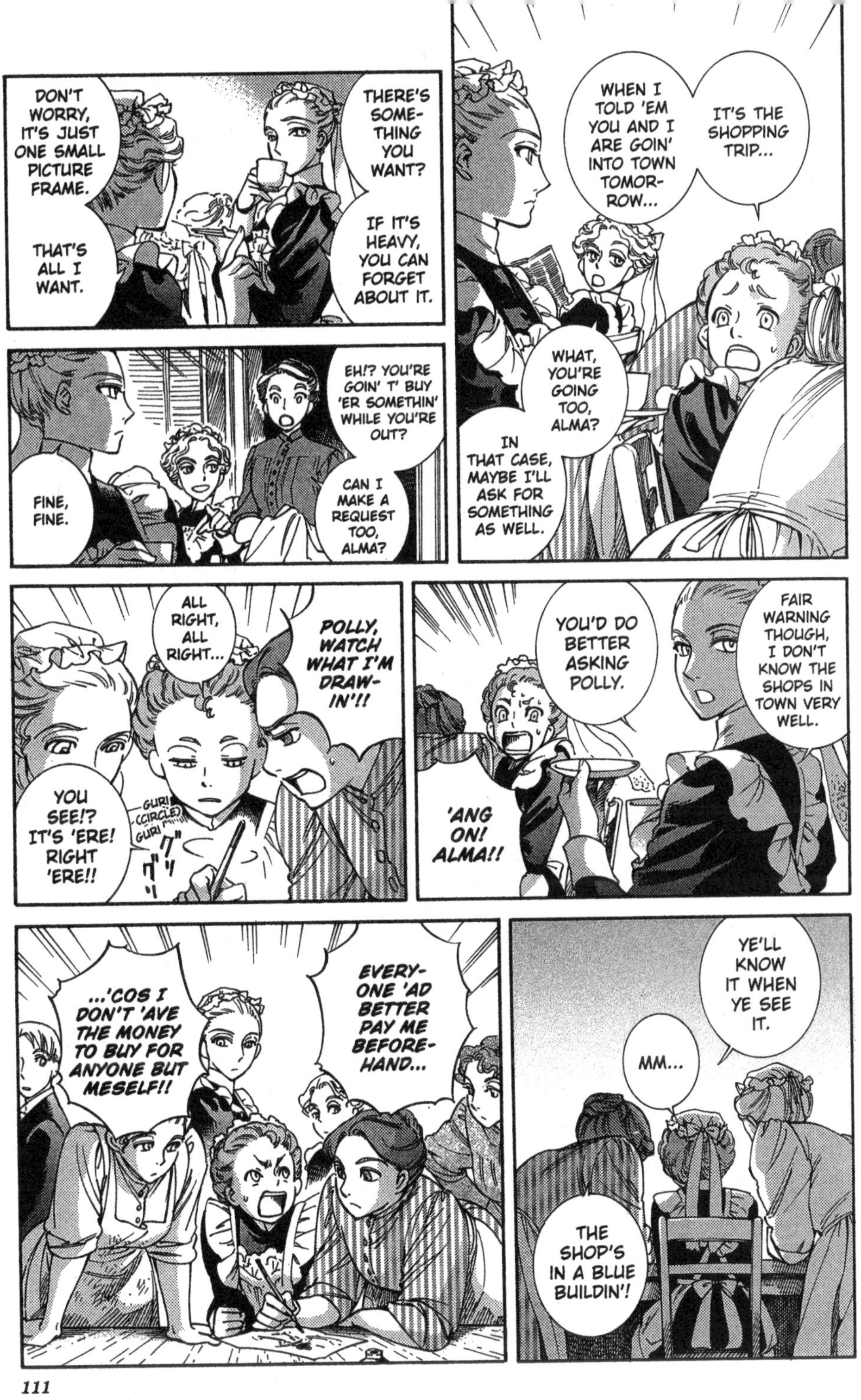
IT'S THE SHOPPING TRIP...
WHEN I TOLD 'EM YOU AND I ARE GOIN' INTO TOWN TOMORROW...
WHAT, YOU'RE GOING TOO, ALMA?
IN THAT CASE, MAYBE I'LL ASK FOR SOMETHING AS WELL.
THERE'S SOMETHING YOU WANT?
IF IT'S HEAVY, YOU CAN FORGET ABOUT IT.
DON'T WORRY, IT'S JUST ONE SMALL PICTURE FRAME.
THAT'S ALL I WANT.
EH!? YOU'RE GOIN' T' BUY 'ER SOMETHIN' WHILE YOU'RE OUT?
CAN I MAKE A REQUEST TOO, ALMA?
FINE, FINE.
FAIR WARNING THOUGH, I DON'T KNOW THE SHOPS IN TOWN VERY WELL.
YOU'D DO BETTER ASKING POLLY.
'ANG ON! ALMA!!
POLLY, WATCH WHAT I'M DRAWIN'!!
ALL RIGHT, ALL RIGHT...
YOU SEE!? IT'S 'ERE! RIGHT 'ERE!!
GURI (CIRCLE) GURI
YE'LL KNOW IT WHEN YE SEE IT.
MM...
THE SHOP'S IN A BLUE BUILDIN'!
EVERYONE 'AD BETTER PAY ME BEFOREHAND...
...'COS I DON'T 'AVE THE MONEY TO BUY FOR ANYONE BUT MESELF!!

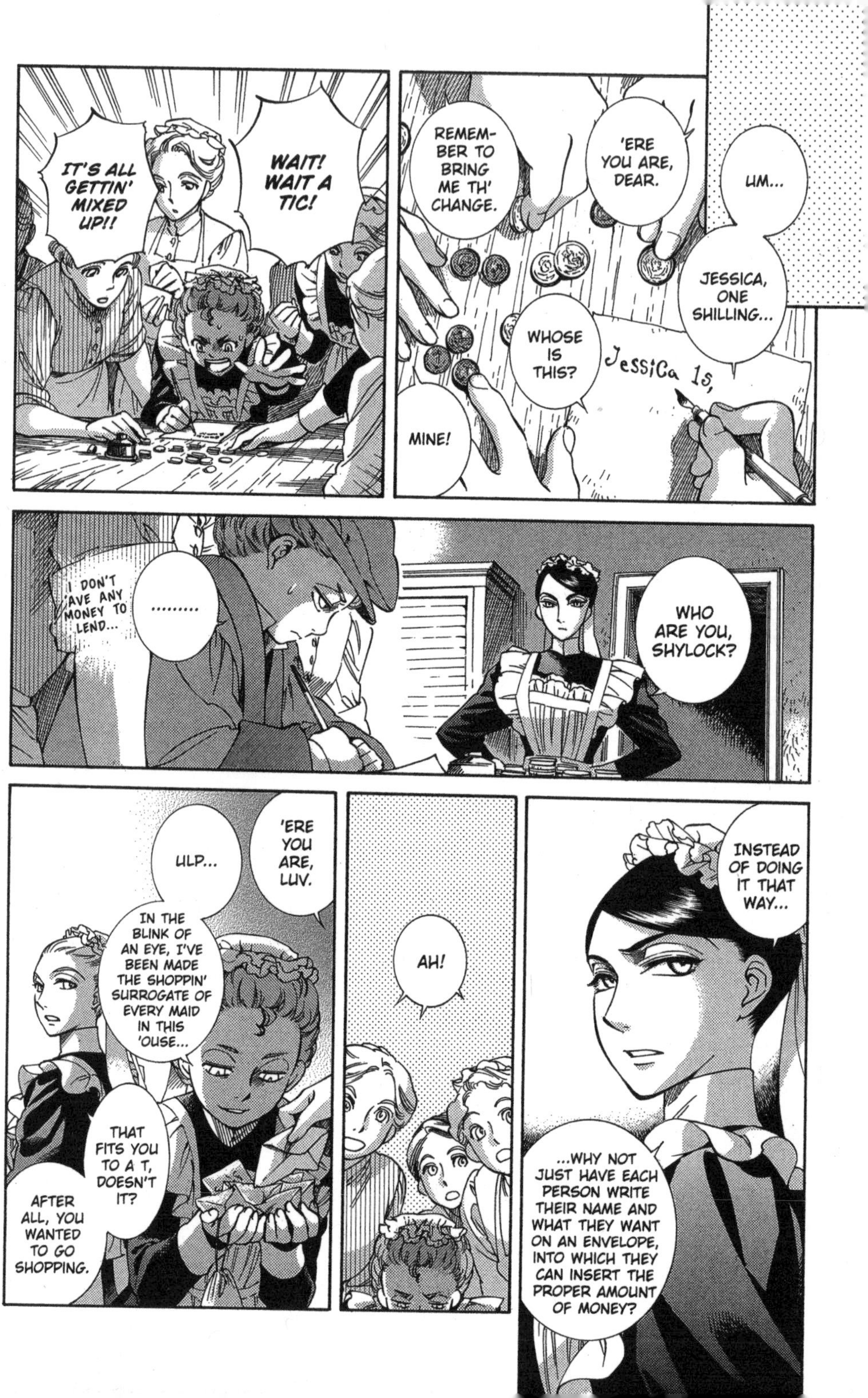
UM...
JESSICA, ONE SHILLING...
'ERE YOU ARE, DEAR.
REMEMBER TO BRING ME TH' CHANGE.
Jessica 1s,
WHOSE IS THIS?
MINE!
WAIT! WAIT A TIC!
IT'S ALL GETTIN' MIXED UP!!
WHO ARE YOU, SHYLOCK?
....
I DON'T 'AVE ANY MONEY TO LEND...
INSTEAD OF DOING IT THAT WAY...
...WHY NOT JUST HAVE EACH PERSON WRITE THEIR NAME AND WHAT THEY WANT ON AN ENVELOPE, INTO WHICH THEY CAN INSERT THE PROPER AMOUNT OF MONEY?
AH!
'ERE YOU ARE, LUV.
ULP...
IN THE BLINK OF AN EYE, I'VE BEEN MADE THE SHOPPIN' SURROGATE OF EVERY MAID IN THIS 'OUSE...
THAT FITS YOU TO A T, DOESN'T IT?
AFTER ALL, YOU WANTED TO GO SHOPPING.

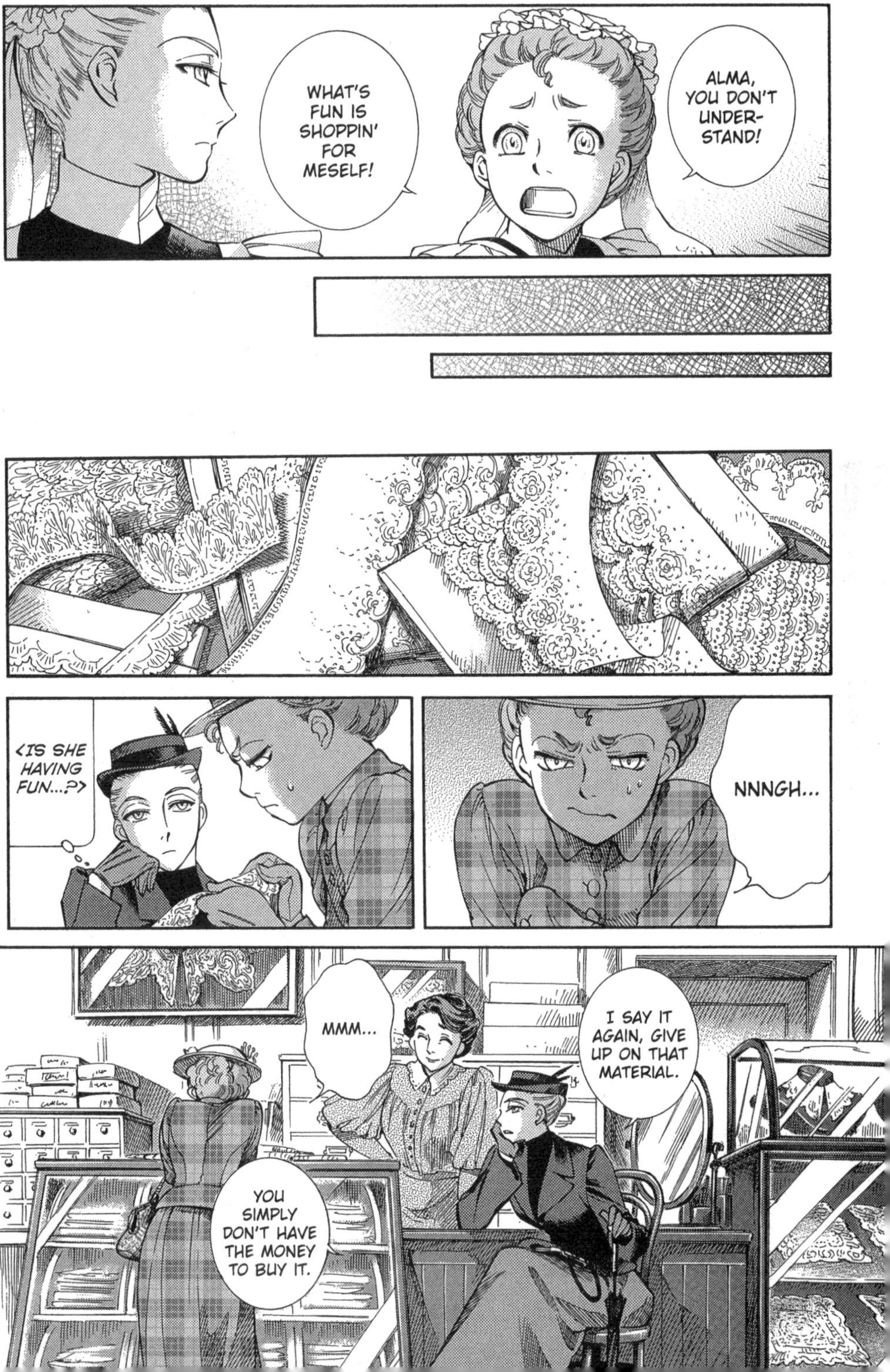
ALMA, YOU DON'T UNDER-STAND!
WHAT'S FUN IS SHOPPIN' FOR MESELF!
NNNGH...
<IS SHE HAVING FUN...?>
I SAY IT AGAIN, GIVE UP ON THAT MATERIAL.
MMM...
YOU SIMPLY DON'T HAVE THE MONEY TO BUY IT.

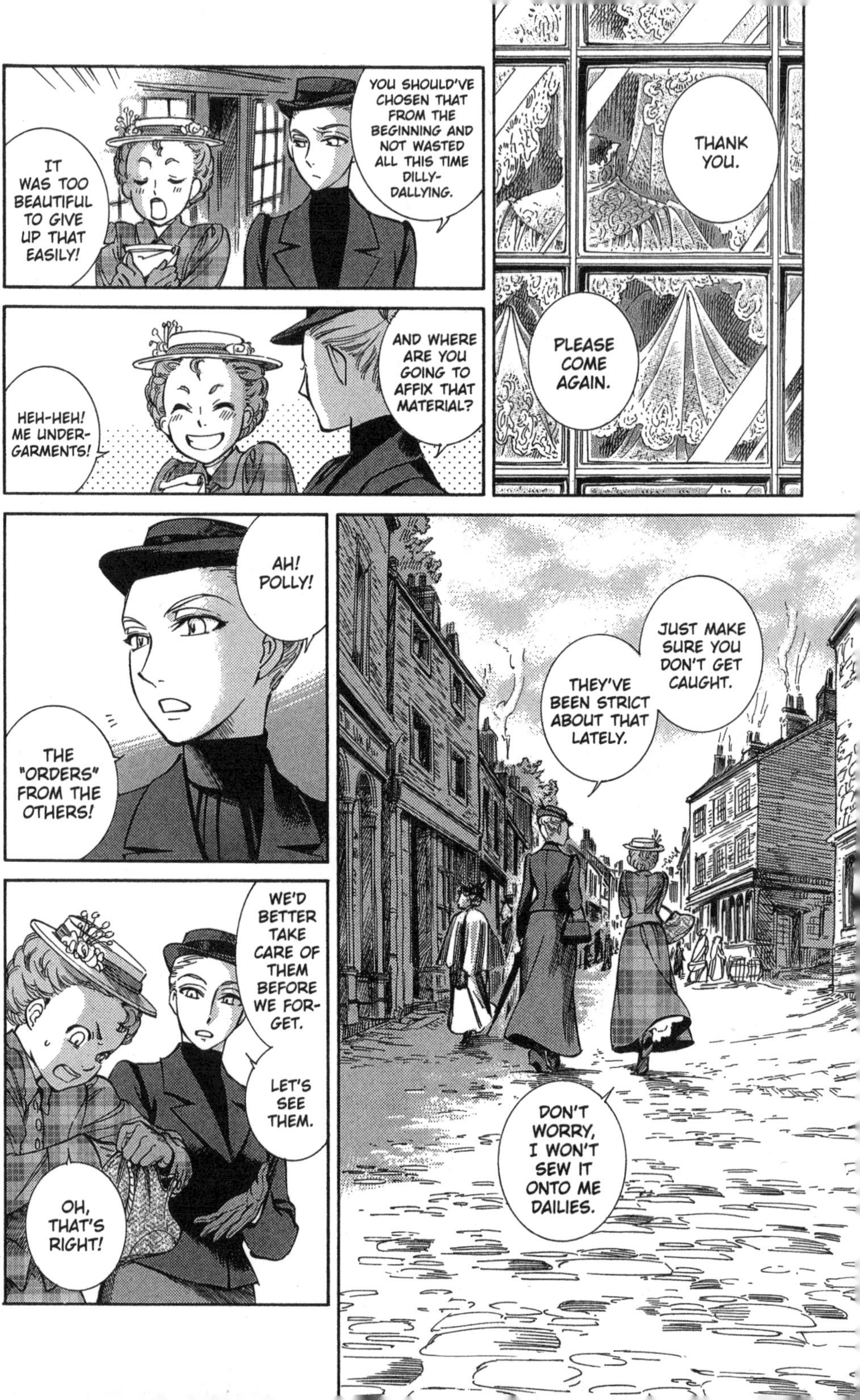
THANK YOU.
PLEASE COME AGAIN.
YOU SHOULD'VE CHOSEN THAT FROM THE BEGINNING AND NOT WASTED ALL THIS TIME DILLY-DALLYING.
IT WAS TOO BEAUTIFUL TO GIVE UP THAT EASILY!
AND WHERE ARE YOU GOING TO AFFIX THAT MATERIAL?
HEH-HEH! ME UNDER-GARMENTS!
JUST MAKE SURE YOU DON'T GET CAUGHT.
THEY'VE BEEN STRICT ABOUT THAT LATELY.
DON'T WORRY, I WON'T SEW IT ONTO ME DAILIES.
AH! POLLY!
THE "ORDERS" FROM THE OTHERS!
WE'D BETTER TAKE CARE OF THEM BEFORE WE FOR-GET.
LET'S SEE THEM.
OH, THAT'S RIGHT!

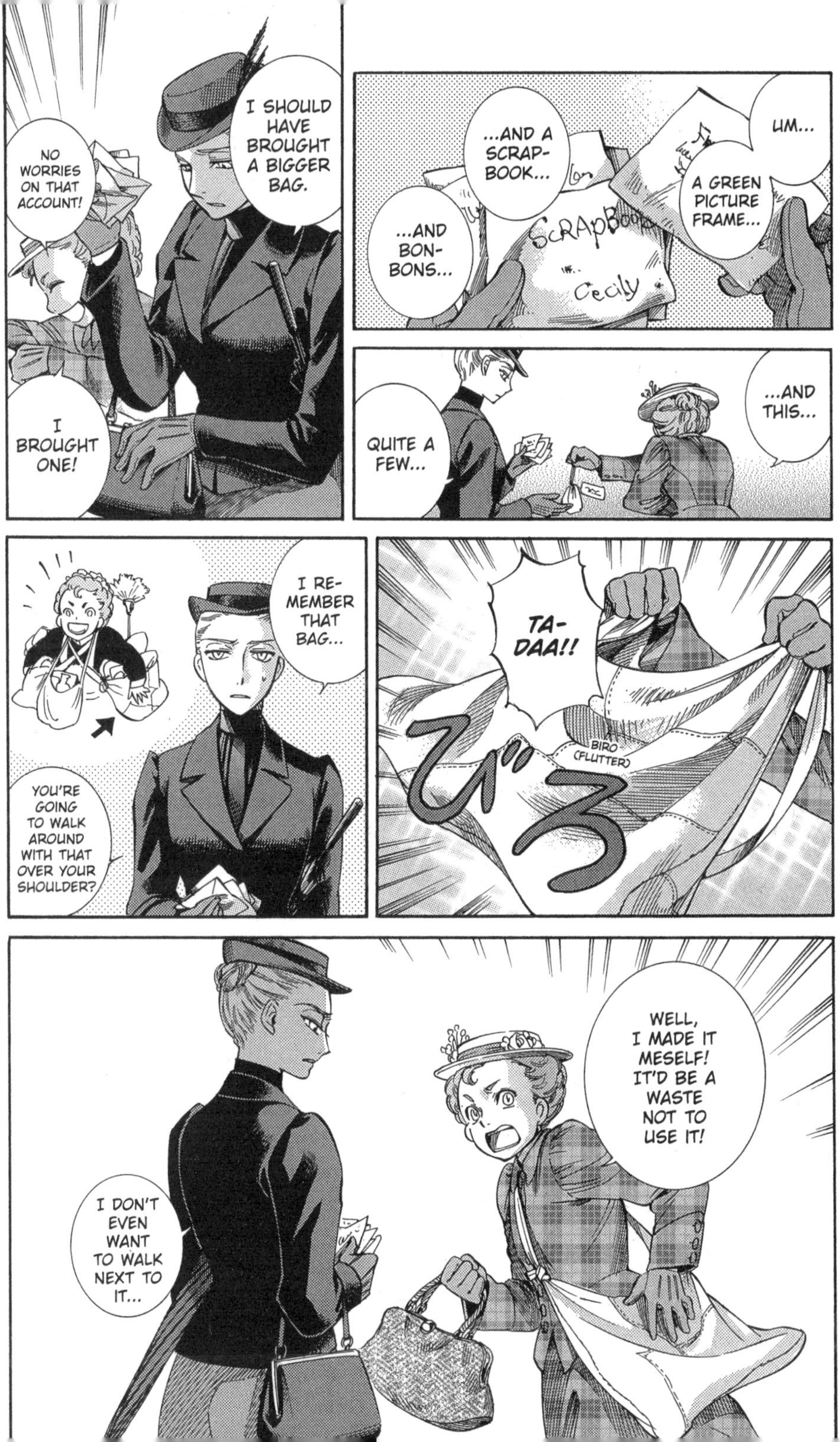
UM...
A GREEN PICTURE FRAME...
...AND A SCRAP-BOOK...
...AND BON-BONS...
Cecily
...AND THIS...
QUITE A FEW...
I SHOULD HAVE BROUGHT A BIGGER BAG.
NO WORRIES ON THAT ACCOUNT!
I BROUGHT ONE!
TA-DAA!!
びろ
BIRO (FLUTTER)
I RE-MEMBER THAT BAG...
YOU'RE GOING TO WALK AROUND WITH THAT OVER YOUR SHOULDER?
WELL, I MADE IT MESELF! IT'D BE A WASTE NOT TO USE IT!
I DON'T EVEN WANT TO WALK NEXT TO IT...

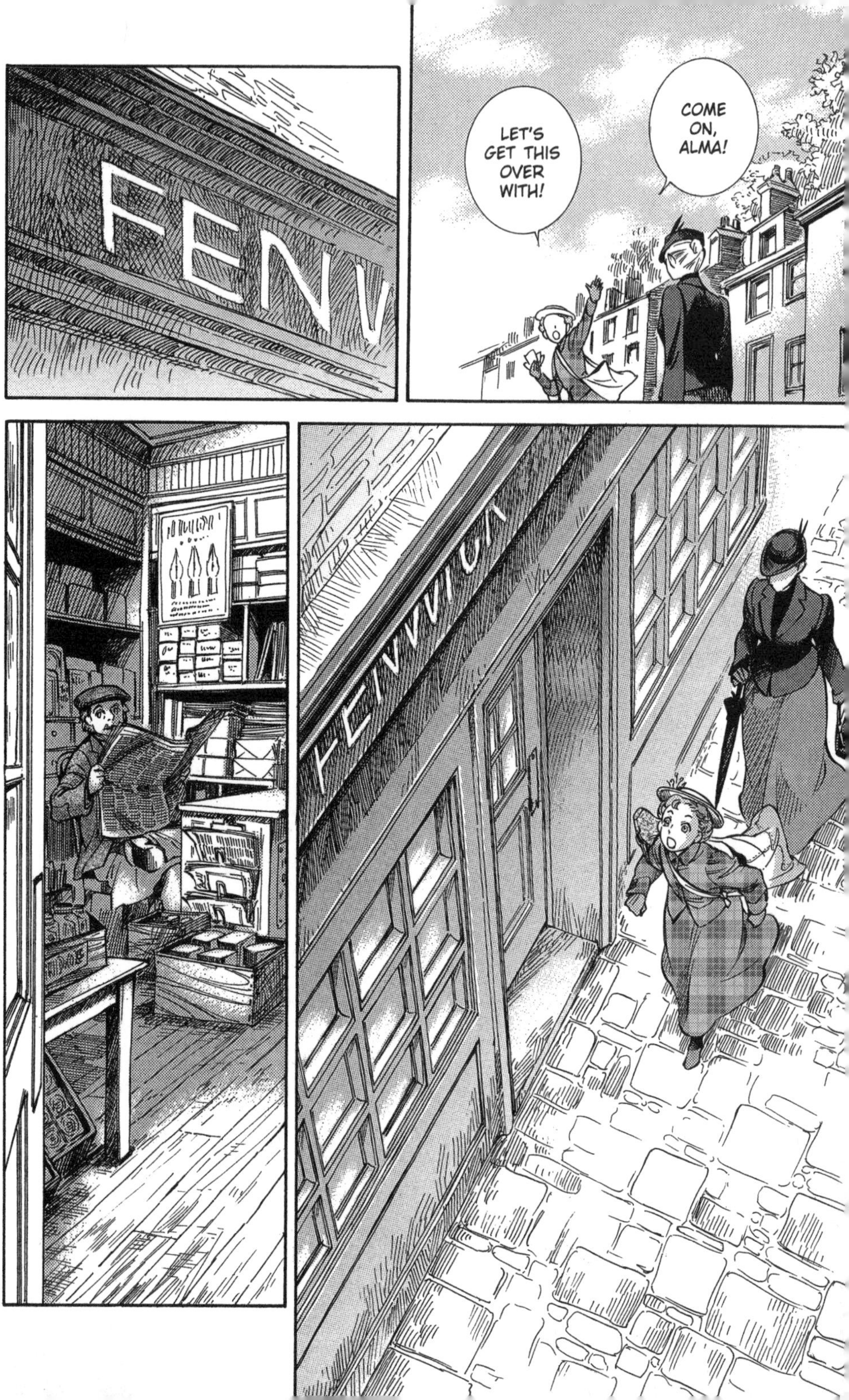
COME ON, ALMA!
LET'S GET THIS OVER WITH!

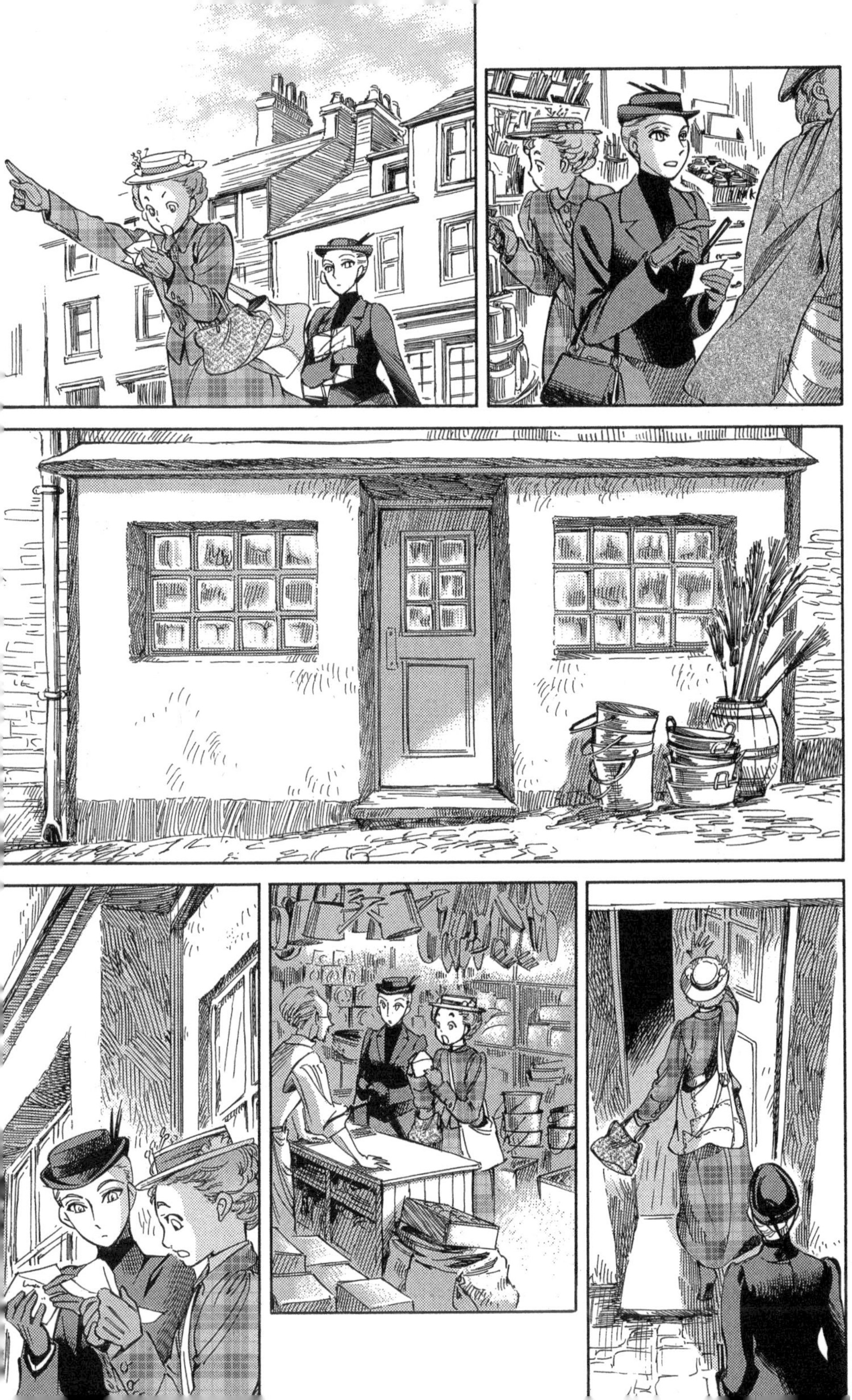

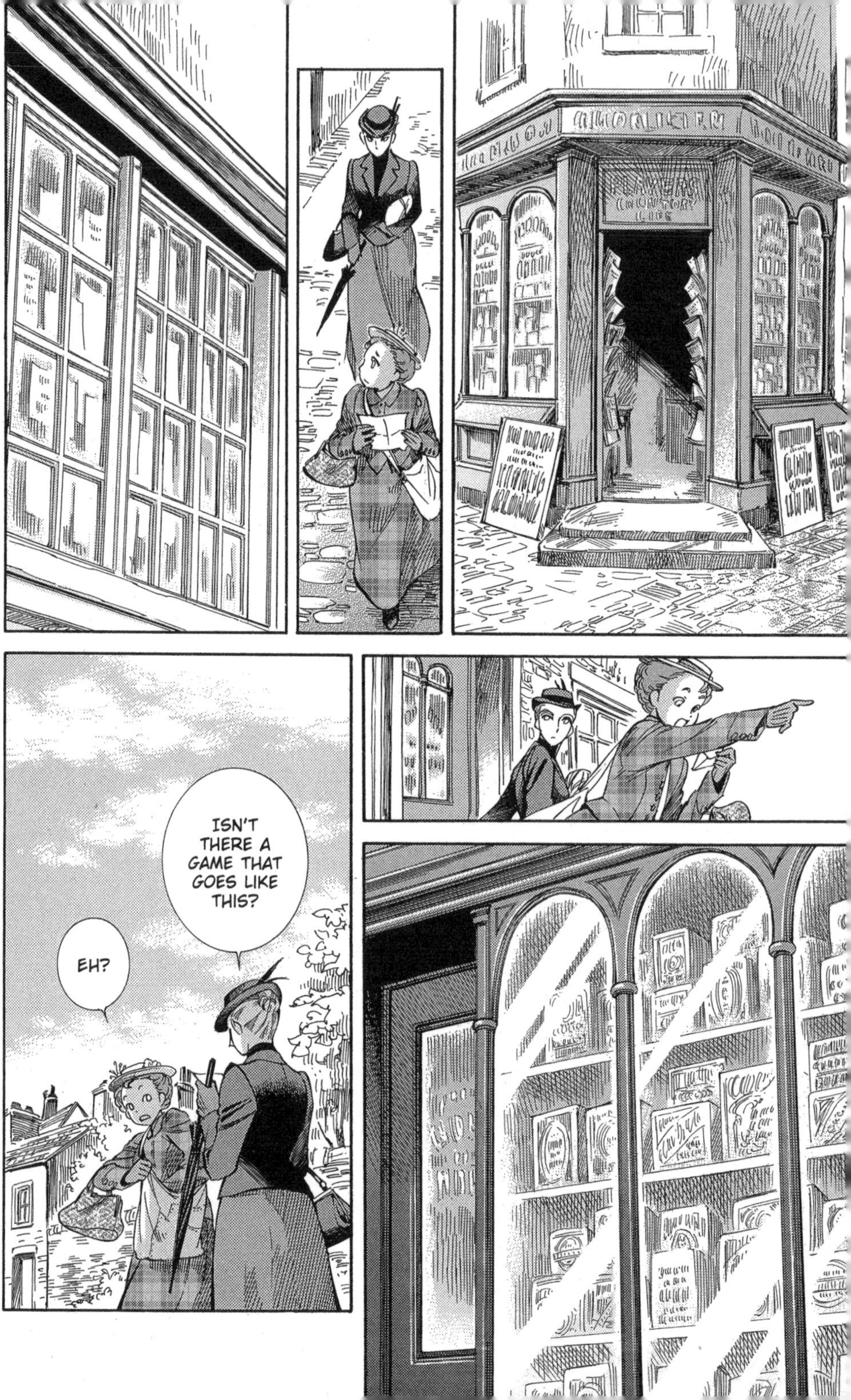
ISN'T THERE A GAME THAT GOES LIKE THIS?
EH?

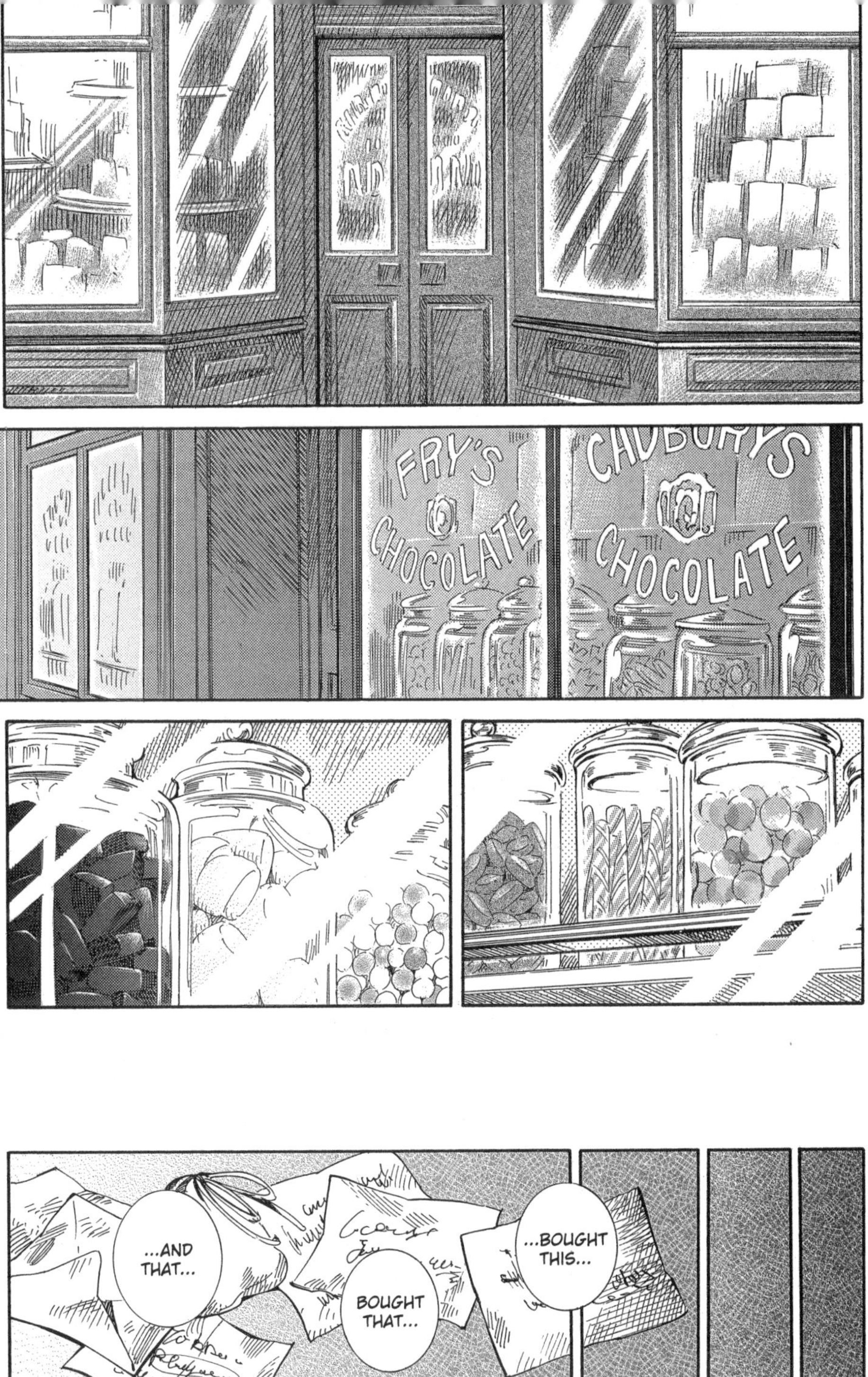
CADBURYS CHOCOLATE
FRY'S CHOCOLATE
...BOUGHT THIS...
BOUGHT THAT...
...AND THAT...

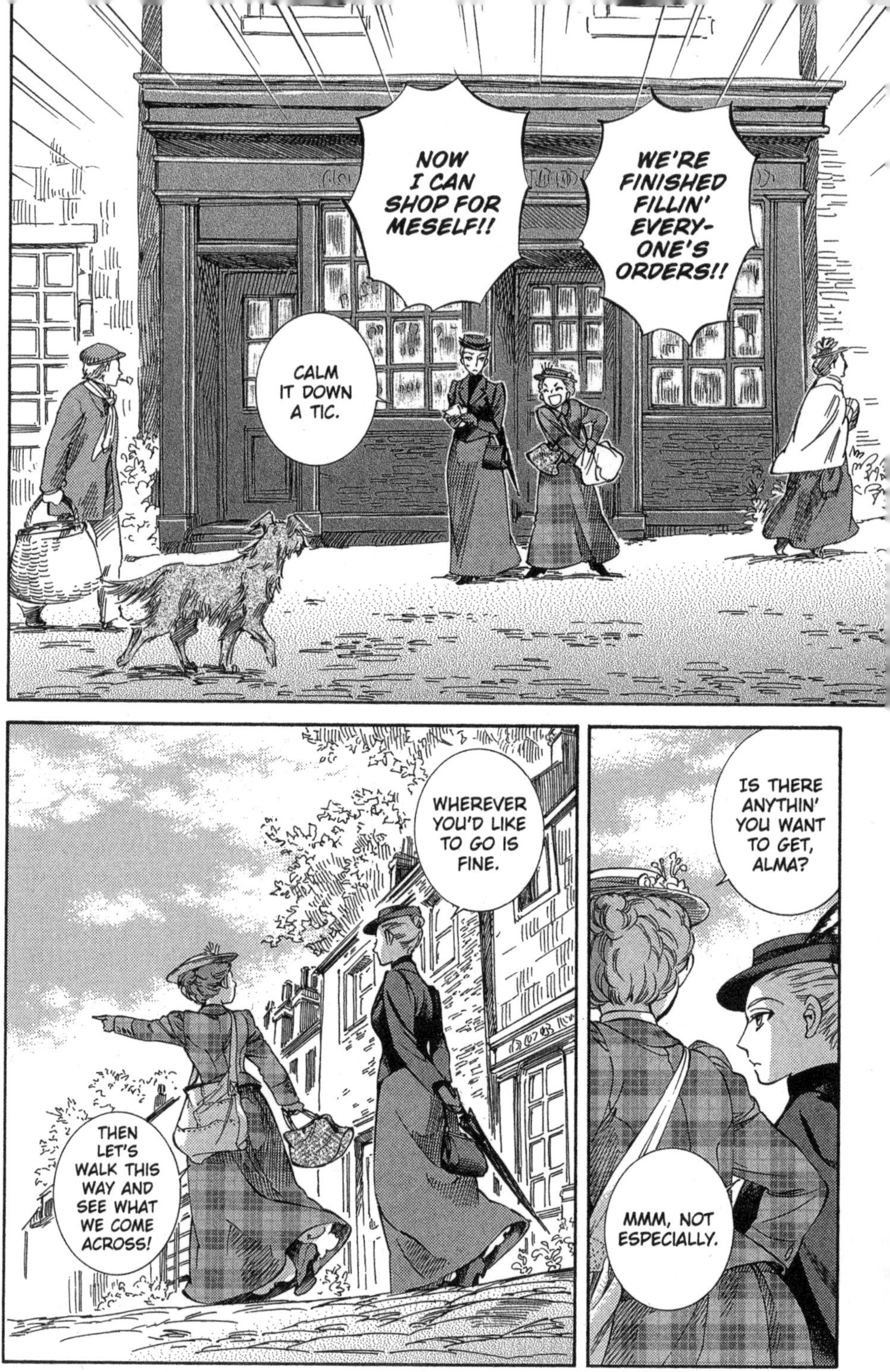
WE'RE FINISHED FILLIN' EVERY-ONE'S ORDERS!!
NOW I CAN SHOP FOR MESELF!!
CALM IT DOWN A TIC.
IS THERE ANYTHIN' YOU WANT TO GET, ALMA?
MMM, NOT ESPECIALLY.
WHEREVER YOU'D LIKE TO GO IS FINE.
THEN LET'S WALK THIS WAY AND SEE WHAT WE COME ACROSS!

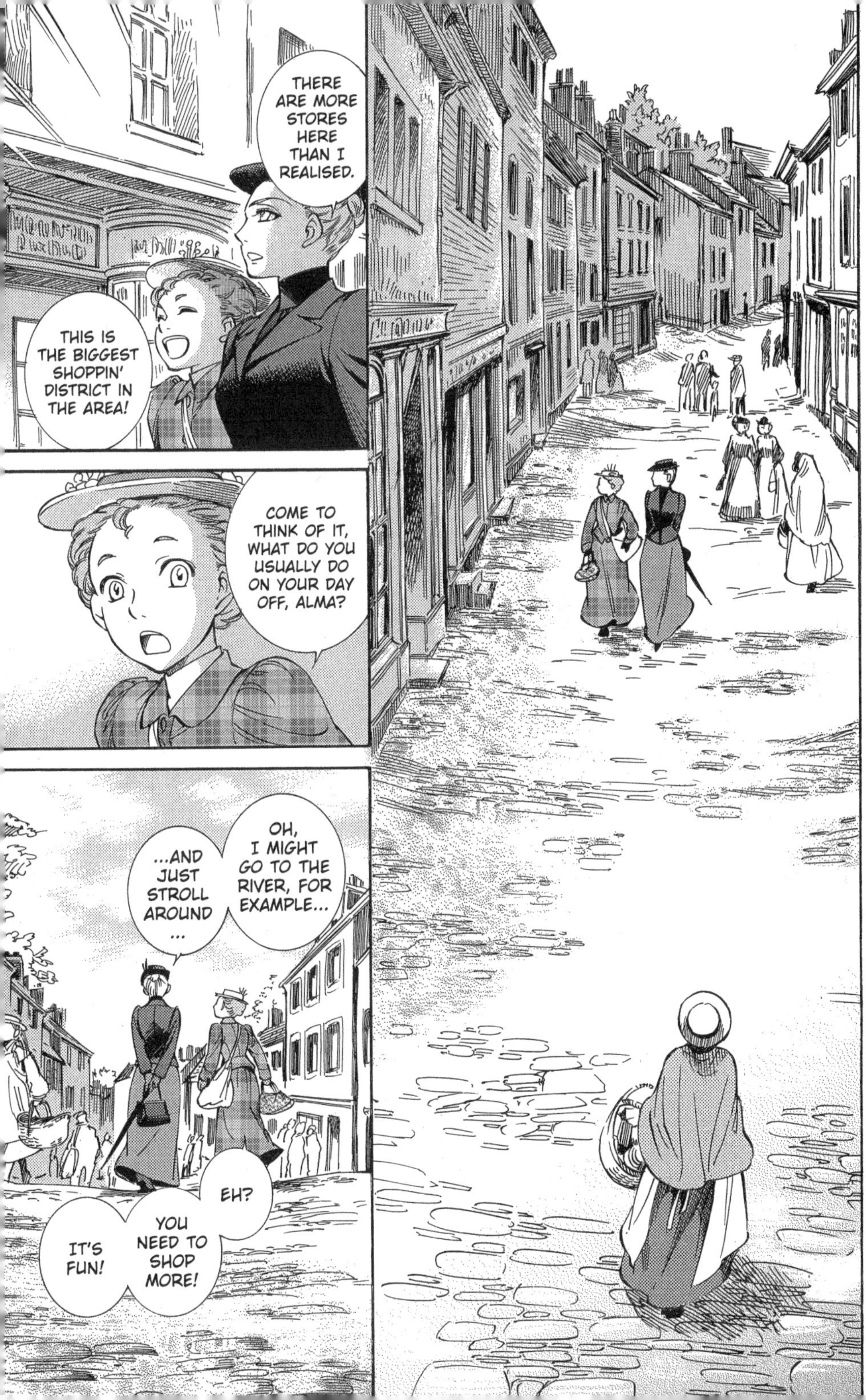
THERE ARE MORE STORES HERE THAN I REALISED.
THIS IS THE BIGGEST SHOPPIN' DISTRICT IN THE AREA!
COME TO THINK OF IT, WHAT DO YOU USUALLY DO ON YOUR DAY OFF, ALMA?
OH, I MIGHT GO TO THE RIVER, FOR EXAMPLE...
...AND JUST STROLL AROUND ...
EH?
YOU NEED TO SHOP MORE!
IT'S FUN!

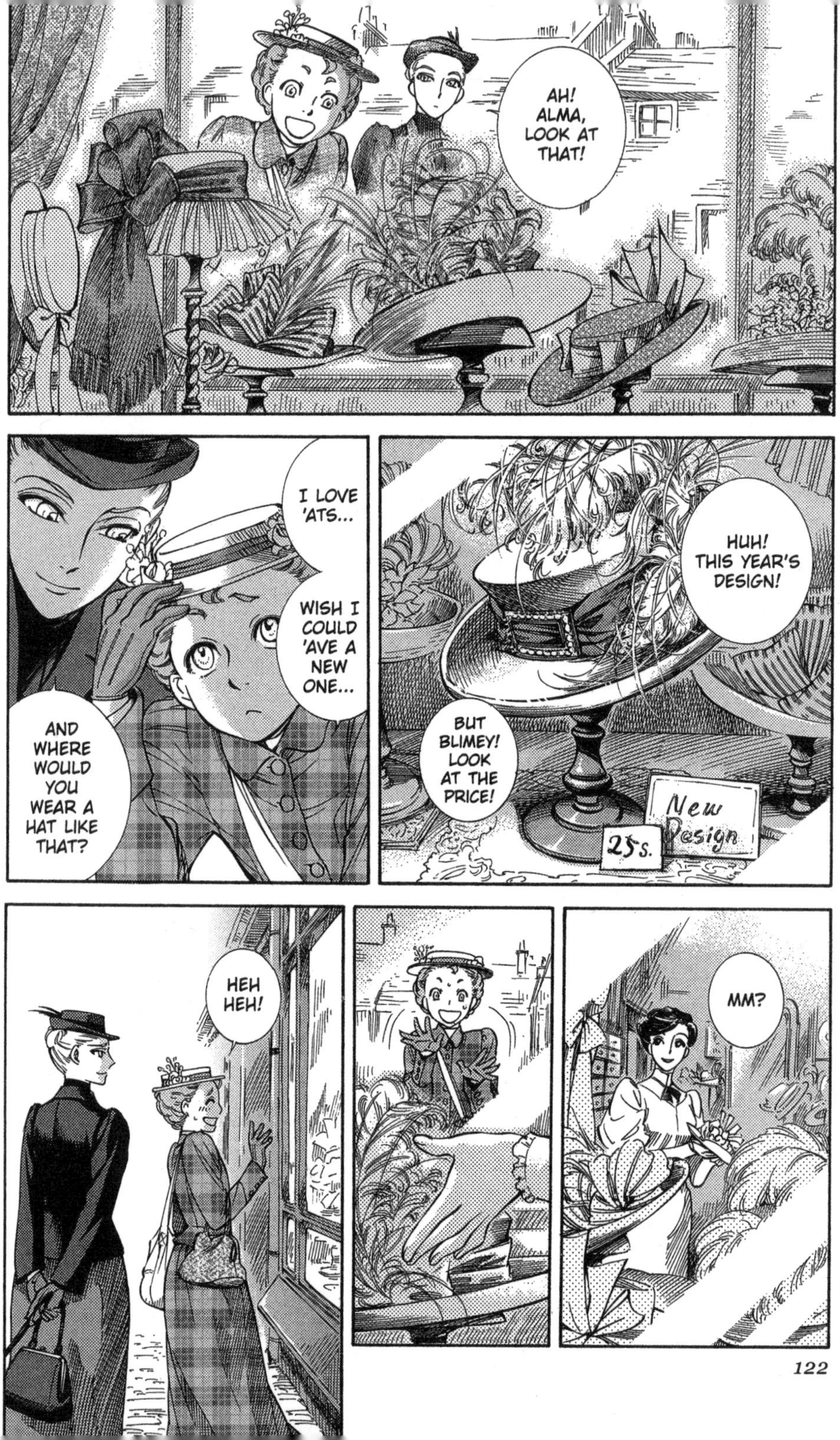
AH! ALMA, LOOK AT THAT!
HUH! THIS YEAR'S DESIGN!
BUT BLIMEY! LOOK AT THE PRICE!
25s.
New Design
I LOVE 'ATS...
WISH I COULD 'AVE A NEW ONE...
AND WHERE WOULD YOU WEAR A HAT LIKE THAT?
MM?
HEH HEH!

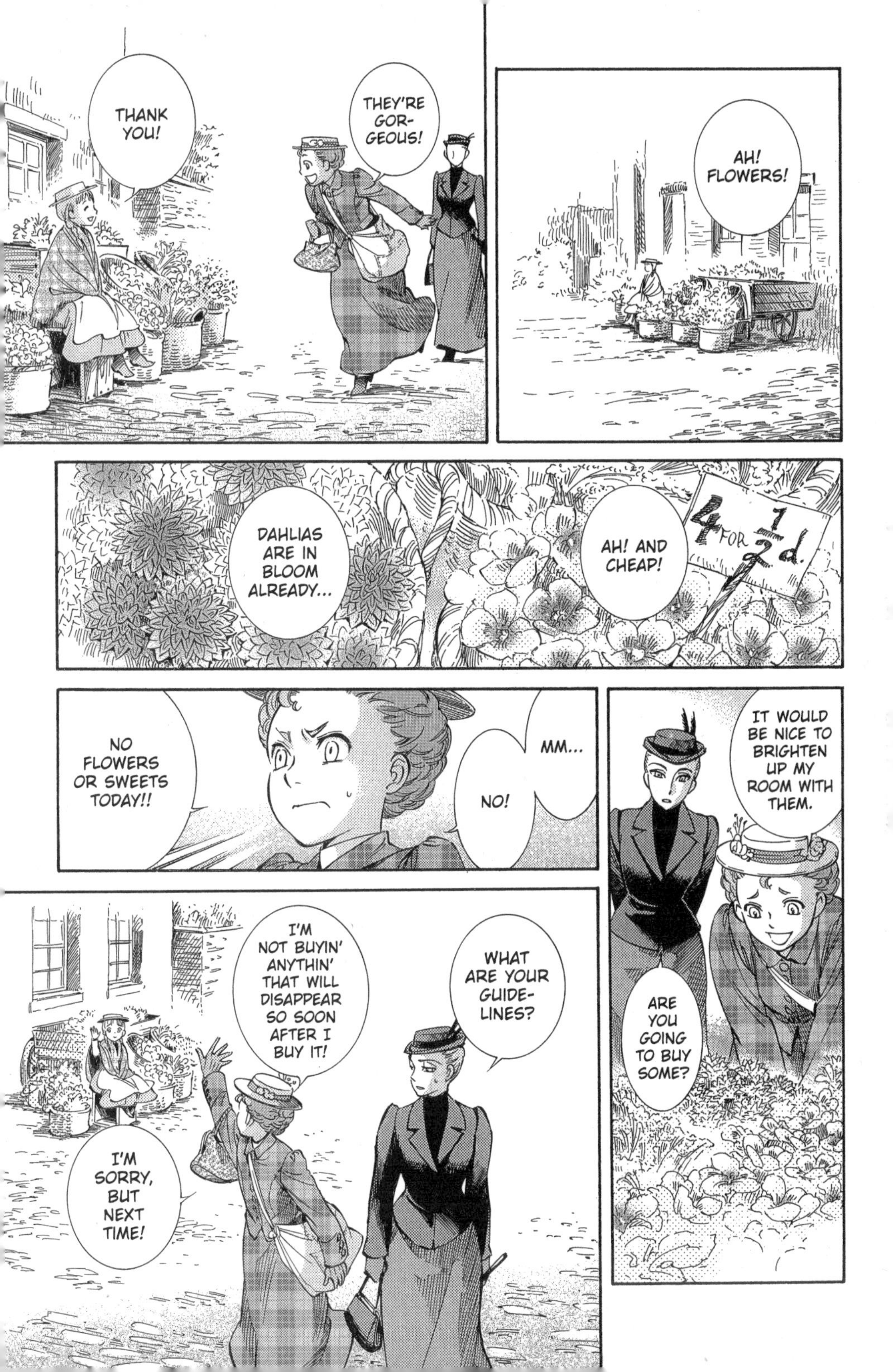
AH! FLOWERS!
THEY'RE GOR-GEOUS!
THANK YOU!
AH! AND CHEAP!
4 FOR 1/2d.
DAHLIAS ARE IN BLOOM ALREADY...
IT WOULD BE NICE TO BRIGHTEN UP MY ROOM WITH THEM.
ARE YOU GOING TO BUY SOME?
MM...
NO!
NO FLOWERS OR SWEETS TODAY!!
WHAT ARE YOUR GUIDE-LINES?
I'M NOT BUYIN' ANYTHIN' THAT WILL DISAPPEAR SO SOON AFTER I BUY IT!
I'M SORRY, BUT NEXT TIME!

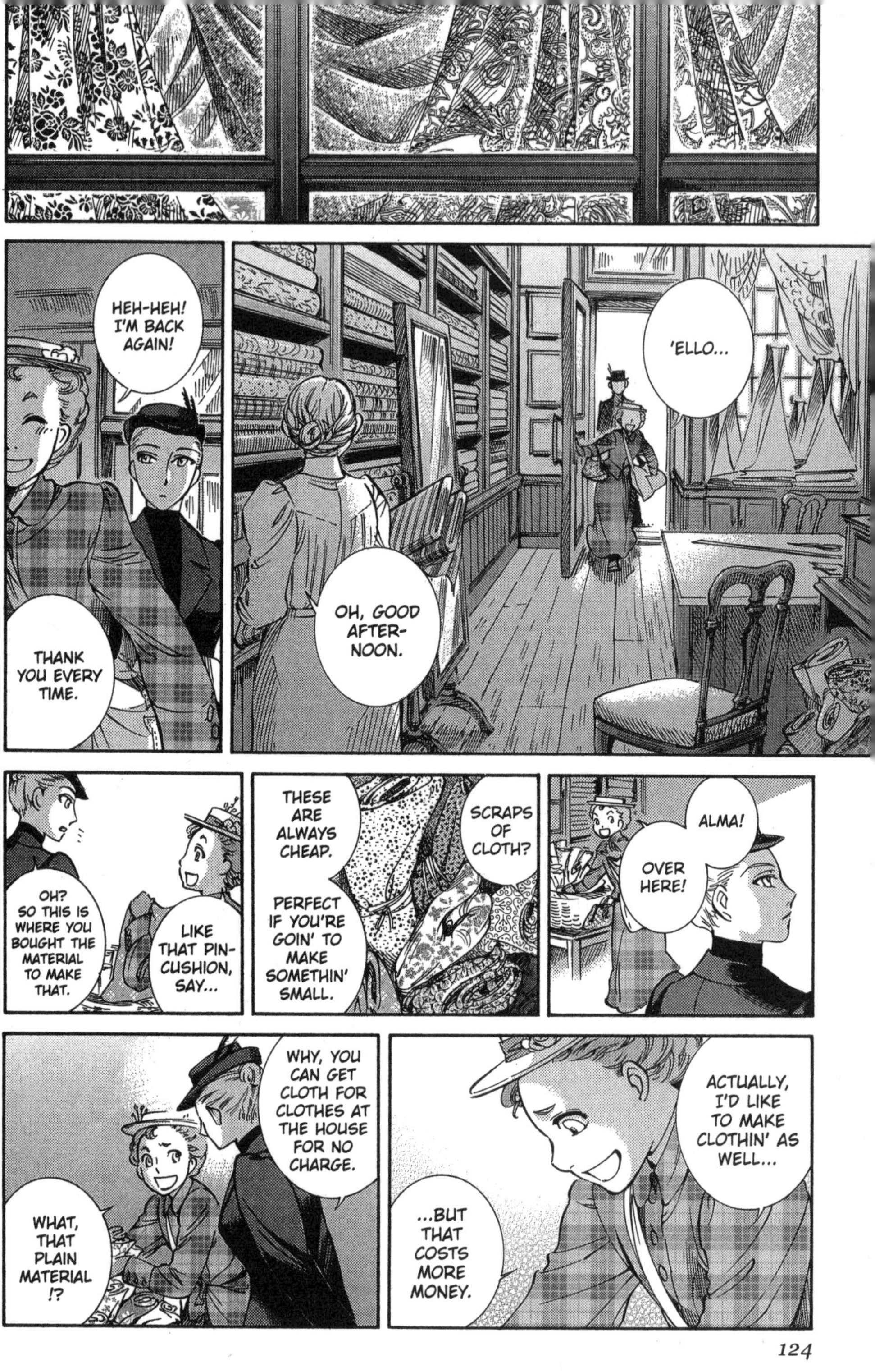
'ELLO...
OH, GOOD AFTERNOON.
HEH-HEH! I'M BACK AGAIN!
THANK YOU EVERY TIME.
ALMA!
OVER HERE!
SCRAPS OF CLOTH?
THESE ARE ALWAYS CHEAP.
PERFECT IF YOU'RE GOIN' TO MAKE SOMETHIN' SMALL.
LIKE THAT PIN-CUSHION, SAY...
OH? SO THIS IS WHERE YOU BOUGHT THE MATERIAL TO MAKE THAT.
ACTUALLY, I'D LIKE TO MAKE CLOTHIN' AS WELL...
...BUT THAT COSTS MORE MONEY.
WHY, YOU CAN GET CLOTH FOR CLOTHES AT THE HOUSE FOR NO CHARGE.
WHAT, THAT PLAIN MATERIAL!?

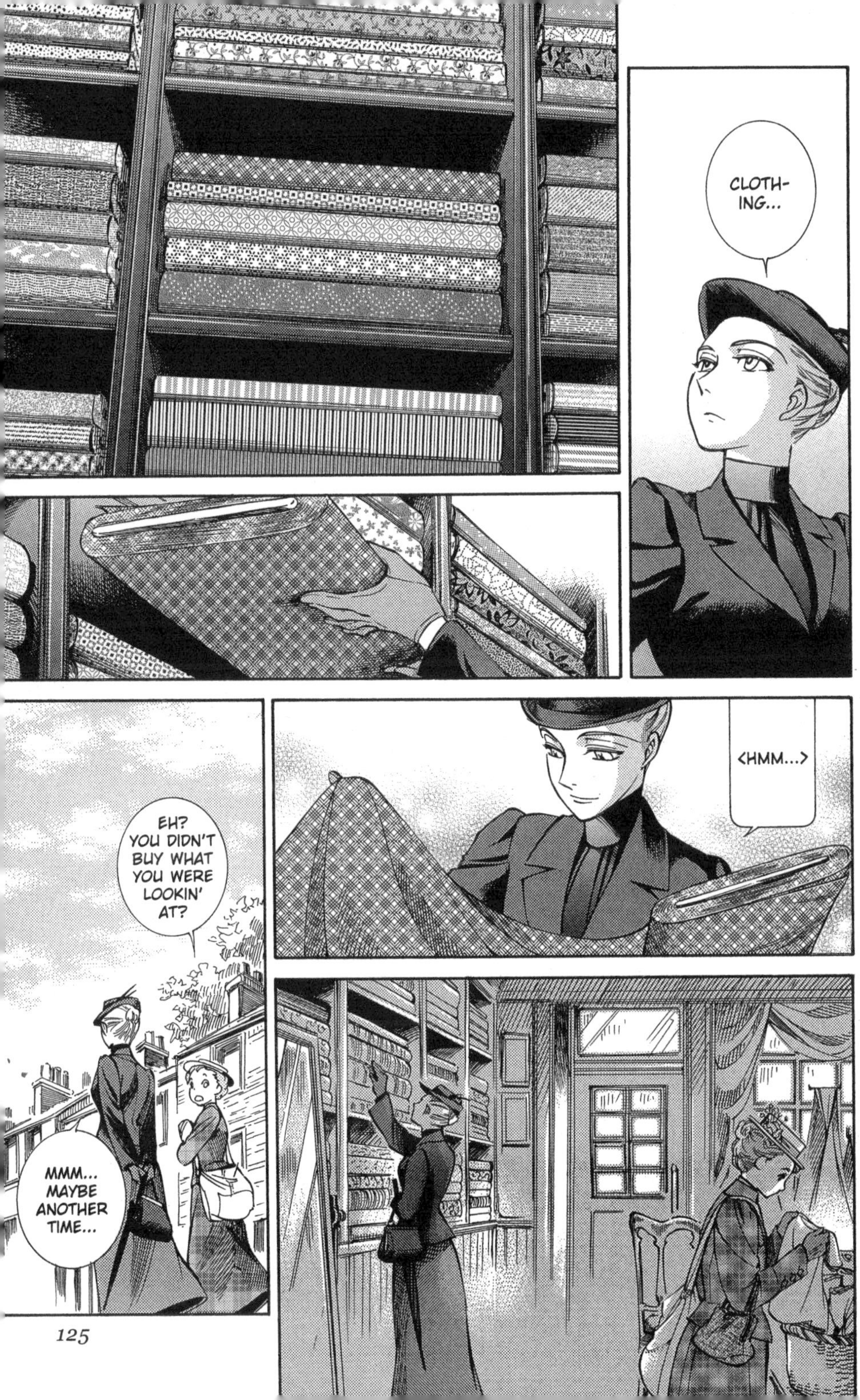
CLOTH-ING...
<HMM...>
EH? YOU DIDN'T BUY WHAT YOU WERE LOOKIN' AT?
MMM... MAYBE ANOTHER TIME...

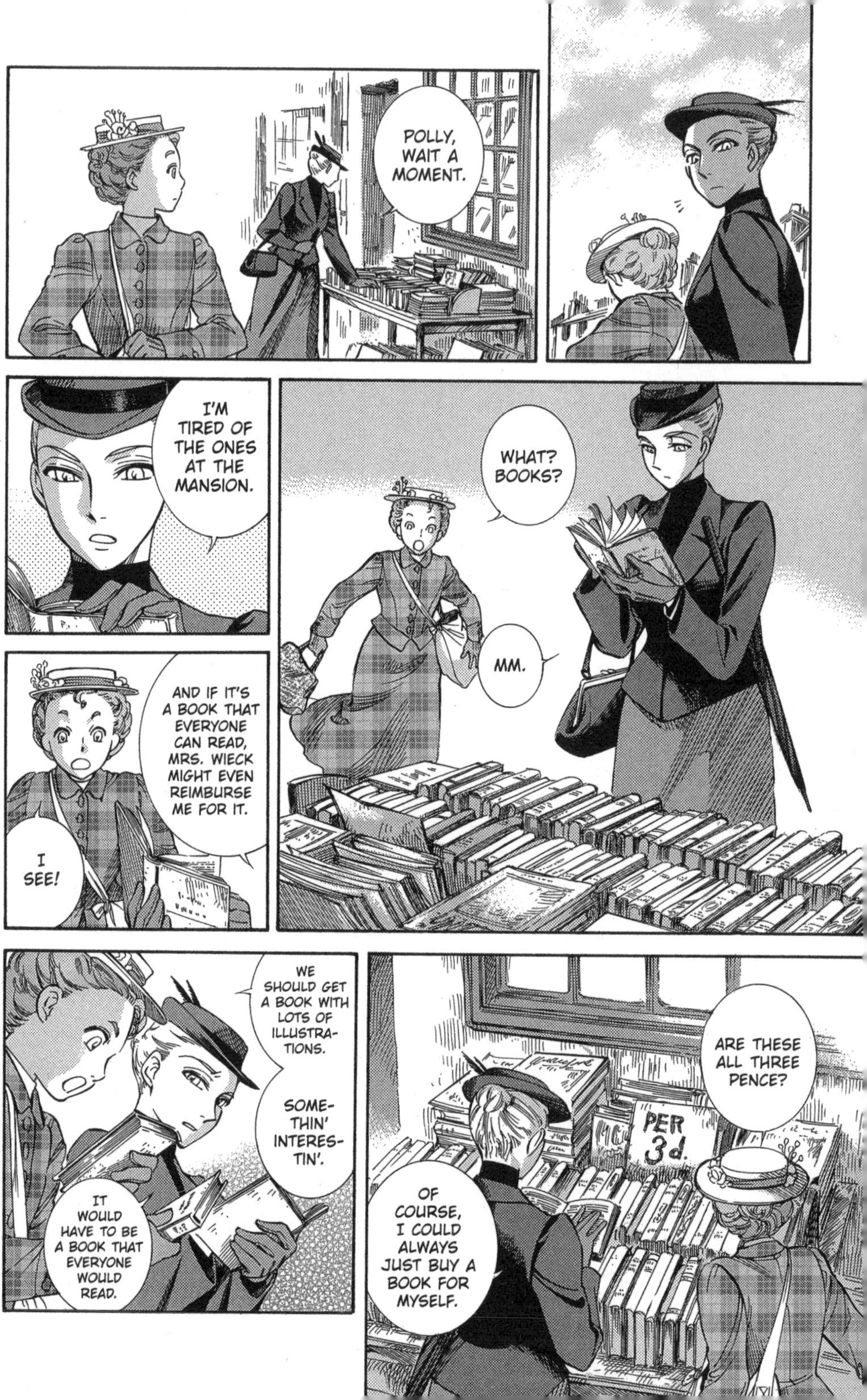
POLLY, WAIT A MOMENT.
WHAT? BOOKS?
MM.
I'M TIRED OF THE ONES AT THE MANSION.
AND IF IT'S A BOOK THAT EVERYONE CAN READ, MRS. WIECK MIGHT EVEN REIMBURSE ME FOR IT.
I SEE!
ARE THESE ALL THREE PENCE?
PER 3d.
OF COURSE, I COULD ALWAYS JUST BUY A BOOK FOR MYSELF.
WE SHOULD GET A BOOK WITH LOTS OF ILLUSTRATIONS.
SOMETHIN' INTERESTIN'.
IT WOULD HAVE TO BE A BOOK THAT EVERYONE WOULD READ.

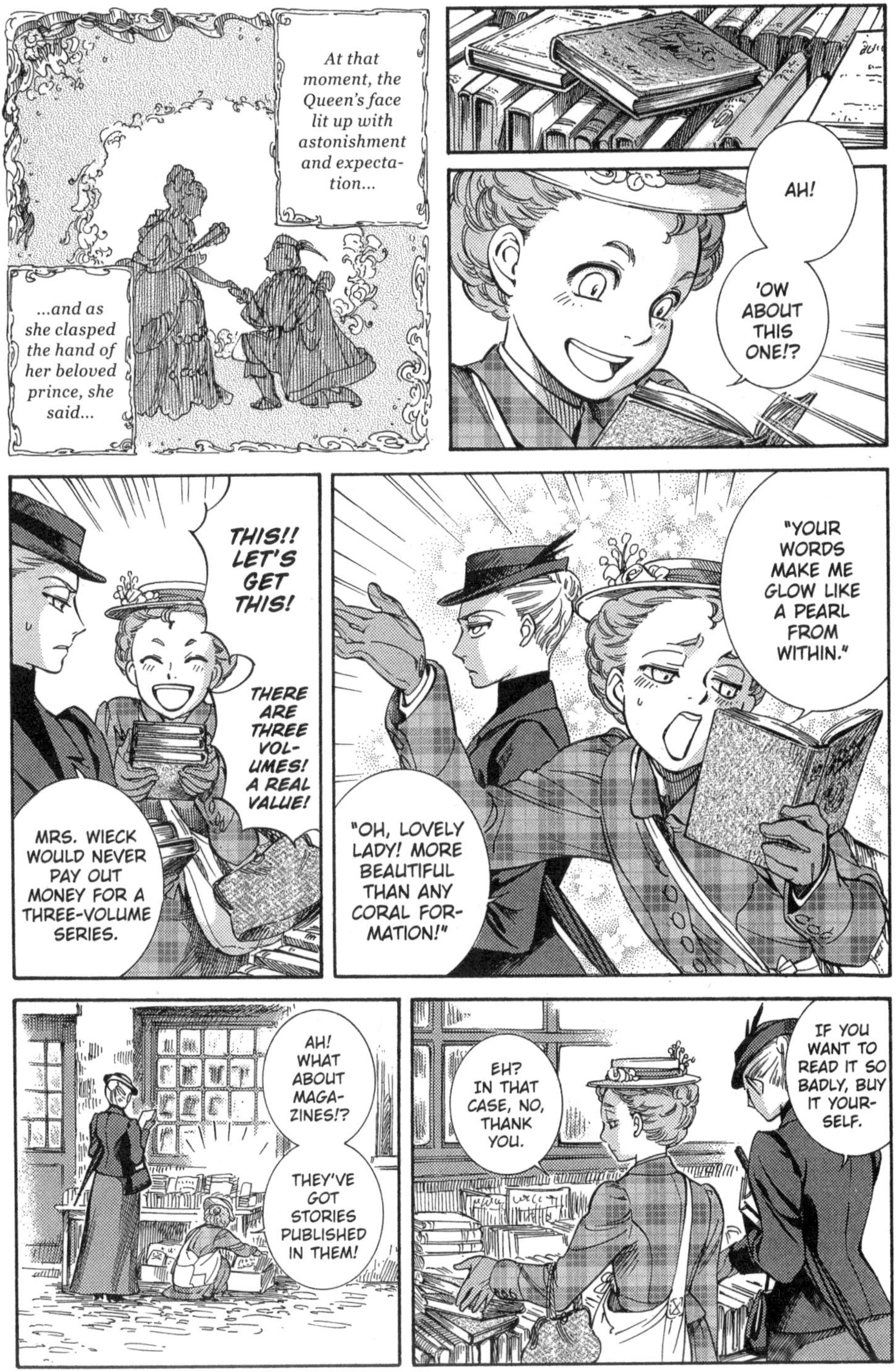

AH!
'OW ABOUT THIS ONE!?
At that moment, the Queen's face lit up with astonishment and expectation...
...and as she clasped the hand of her beloved prince, she said...
"YOUR WORDS MAKE ME GLOW LIKE A PEARL FROM WITHIN."
"OH, LOVELY LADY! MORE BEAUTIFUL THAN ANY CORAL FORMATION!"
THIS!! LET'S GET THIS!
THERE ARE THREE VOLUMES! A REAL VALUE!
MRS. WIECK WOULD NEVER PAY OUT MONEY FOR A THREE-VOLUME SERIES.
IF YOU WANT TO READ IT SO BADLY, BUY IT YOURSELF.
EH? IN THAT CASE, NO, THANK YOU.
AH! WHAT ABOUT MAGAZINES!?
THEY'VE GOT STORIES PUBLISHED IN THEM!

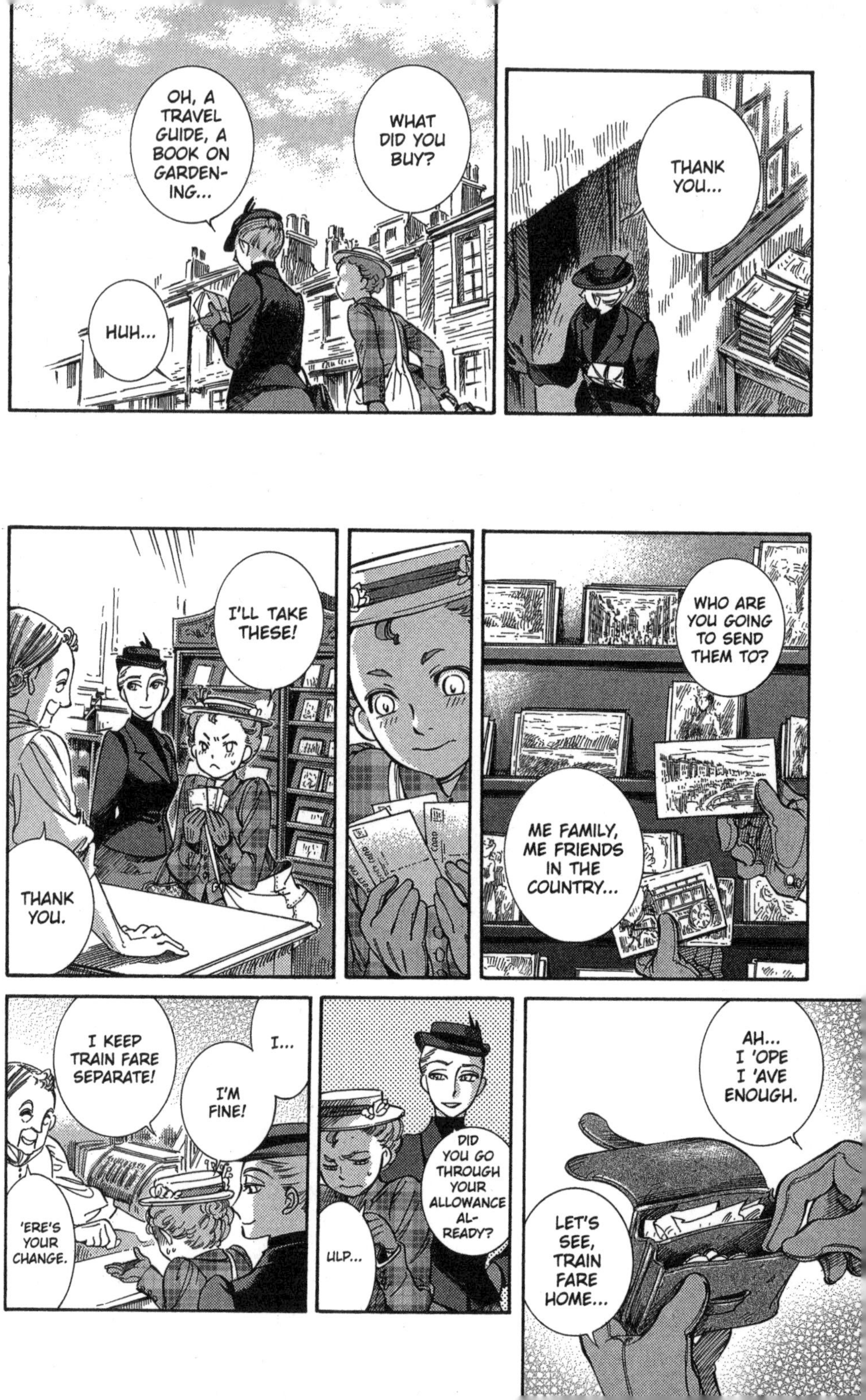
THANK YOU...
WHAT DID YOU BUY?
OH, A TRAVEL GUIDE, A BOOK ON GARDEN-ING...
HUH...
WHO ARE YOU GOING TO SEND THEM TO?
ME FAMILY, ME FRIENDS IN THE COUNTRY...
I'LL TAKE THESE!
THANK YOU.
AH... I 'OPE I 'AVE ENOUGH.
LET'S SEE, TRAIN FARE HOME...
DID YOU GO THROUGH YOUR ALLOWANCE AL-READY?
ULP...
I...
I'M FINE!
I KEEP TRAIN FARE SEPARATE!
'ERE'S YOUR CHANGE.

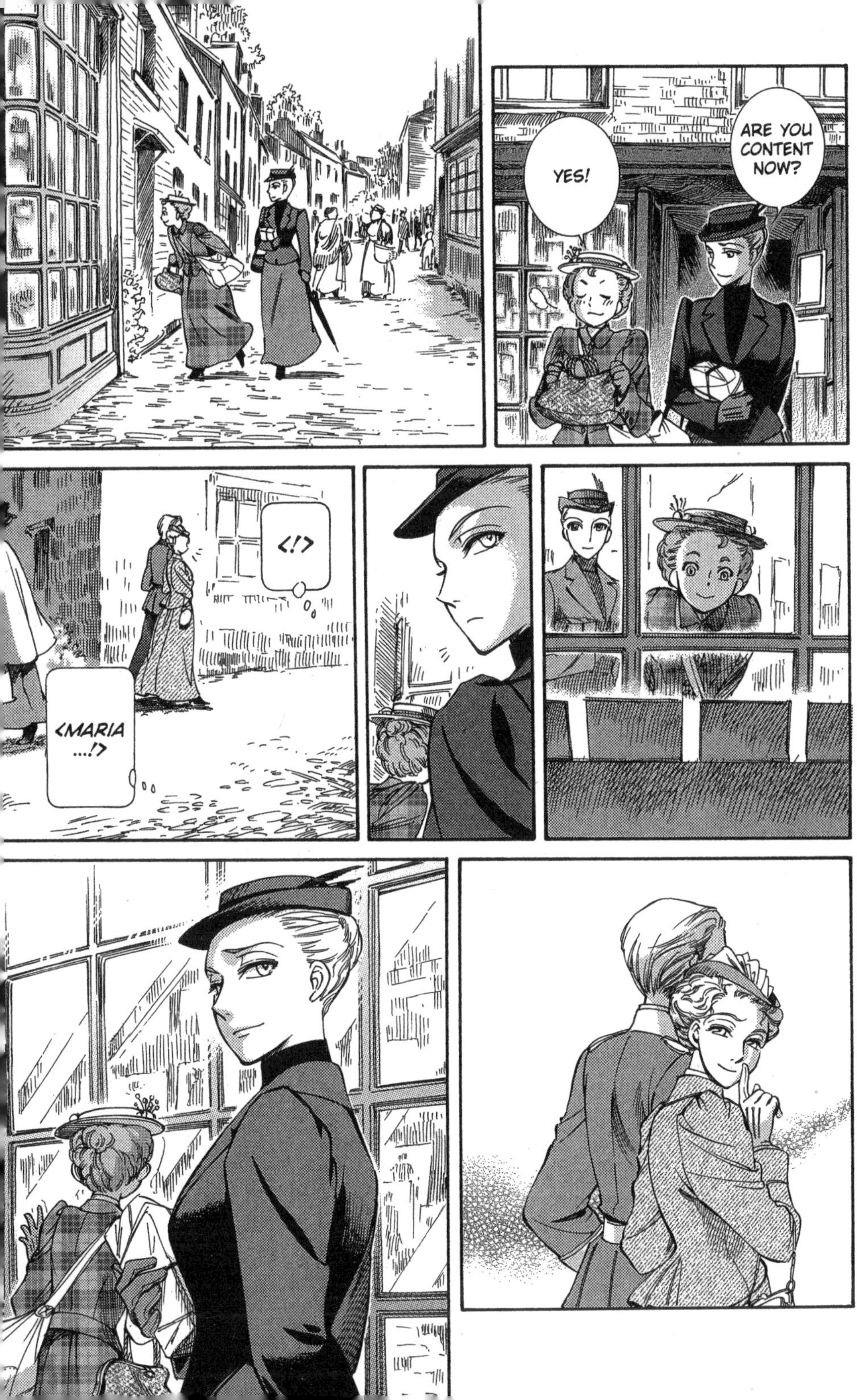
ARE YOU CONTENT NOW?
YES!
<!?>
<MARIA ...!?>

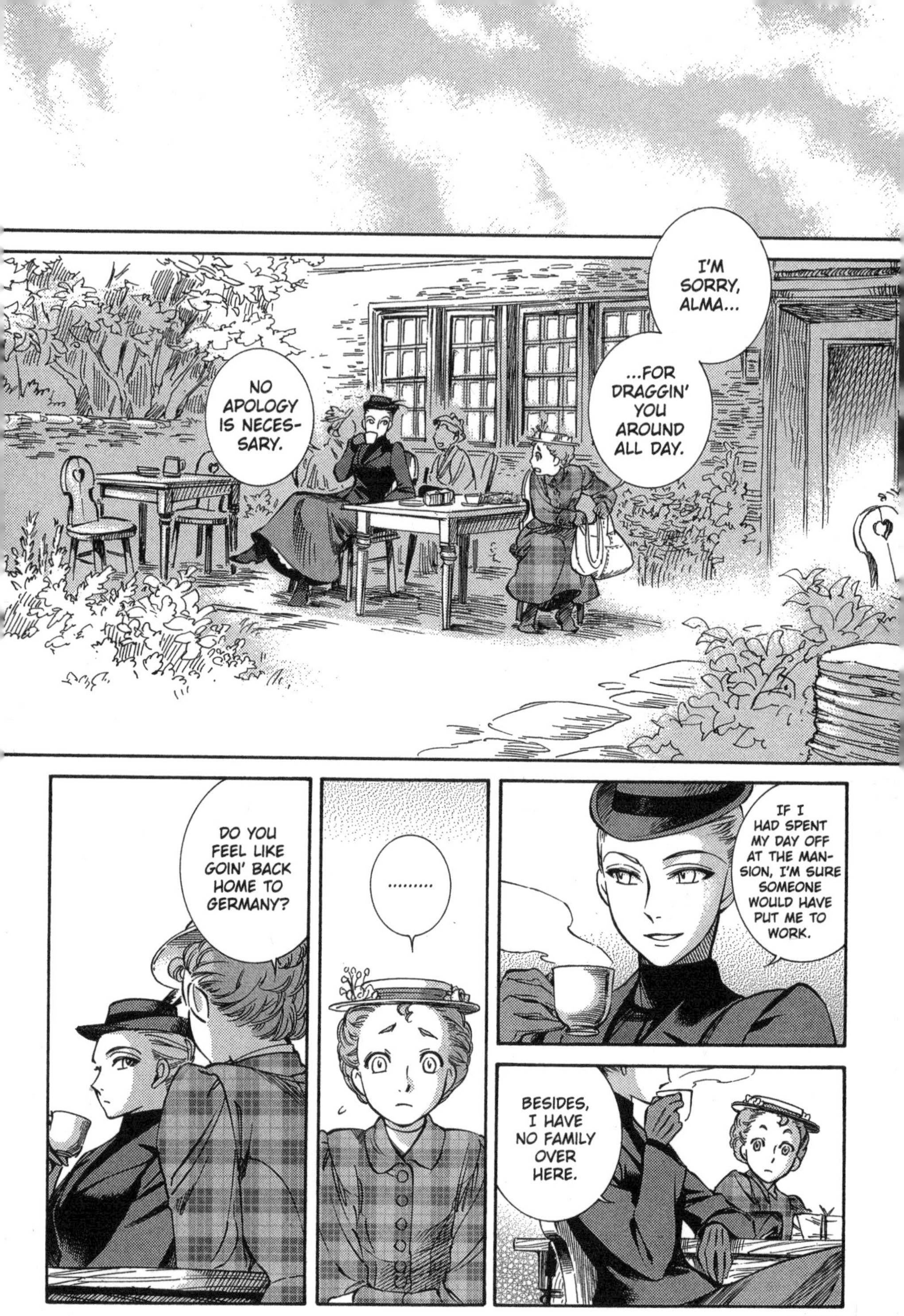
I'M SORRY, ALMA...
...FOR DRAGGIN' YOU AROUND ALL DAY.
NO APOLOGY IS NECES-SARY.
IF I HAD SPENT MY DAY OFF AT THE MAN-SION, I'M SURE SOMEONE WOULD HAVE PUT ME TO WORK.
BESIDES, I HAVE NO FAMILY OVER HERE.
....
DO YOU FEEL LIKE GOIN' BACK HOME TO GERMANY?

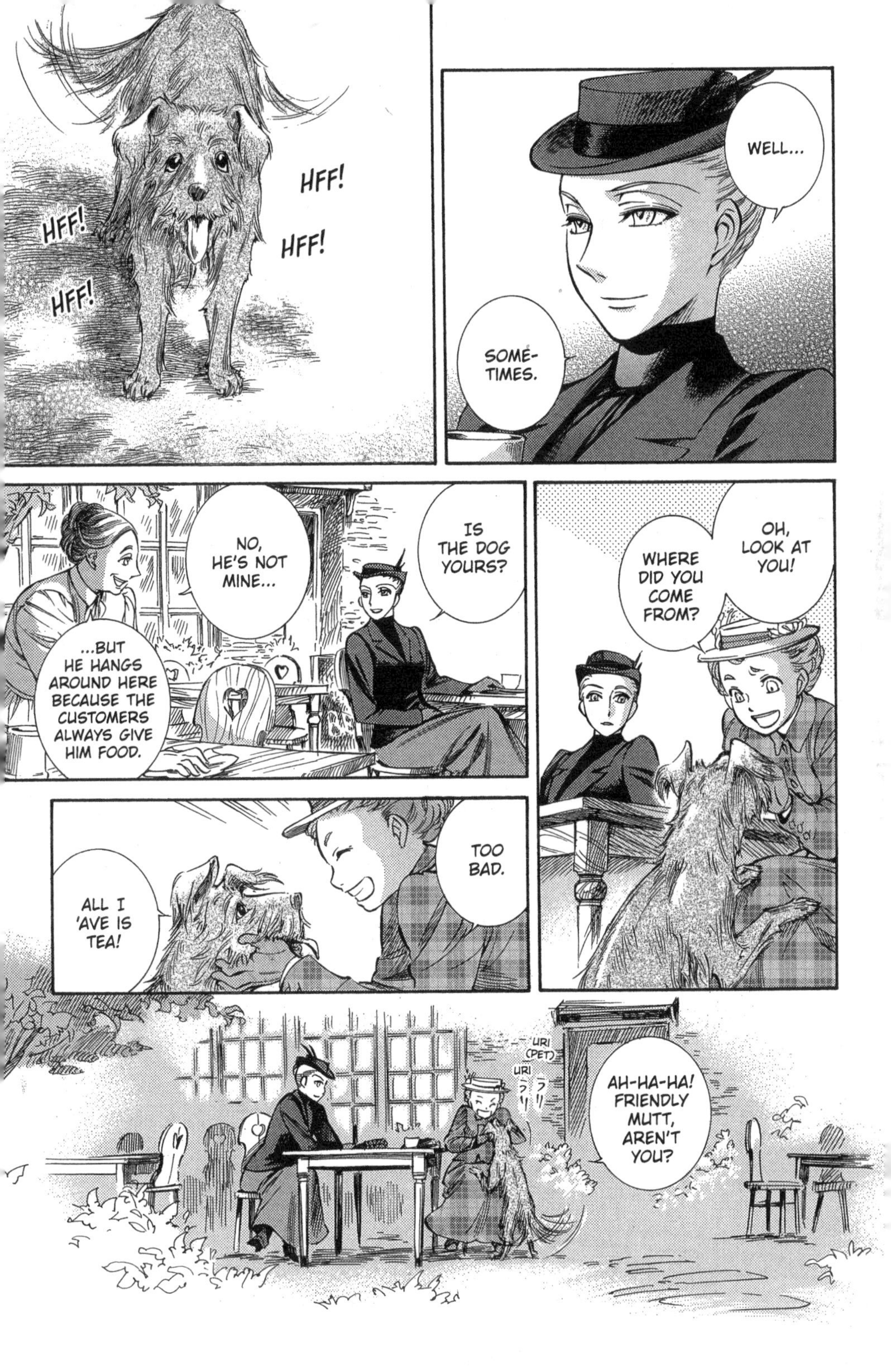

WELL...
SOME-TIMES.
HFF!
HFF!
HFF!
HFF!
OH, LOOK AT YOU!
WHERE DID YOU COME FROM?
IS THE DOG YOURS?
NO, HE'S NOT MINE...
...BUT HE HANGS AROUND HERE BECAUSE THE CUSTOMERS ALWAYS GIVE HIM FOOD.
TOO BAD.
ALL I 'AVE IS TEA!
URI (PET)
ウリ
URI
ウリ
AH-HA-HA! FRIENDLY MUTT, AREN'T YOU?

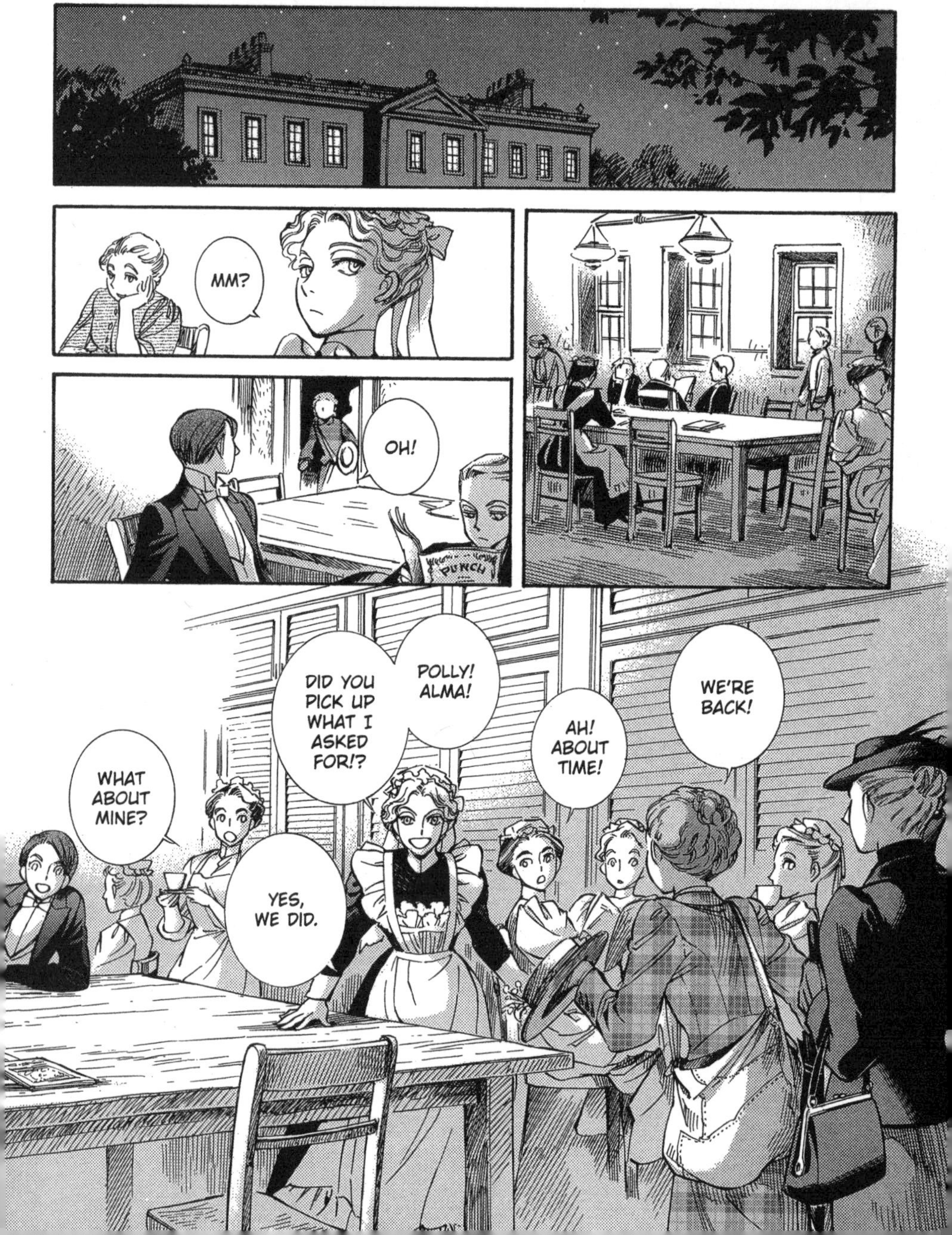
MM?
OH!
PUNCH
WE'RE BACK!
AH! ABOUT TIME!
POLLY! ALMA!
DID YOU PICK UP WHAT I ASKED FOR!?
WHAT ABOUT MINE?
YES, WE DID.

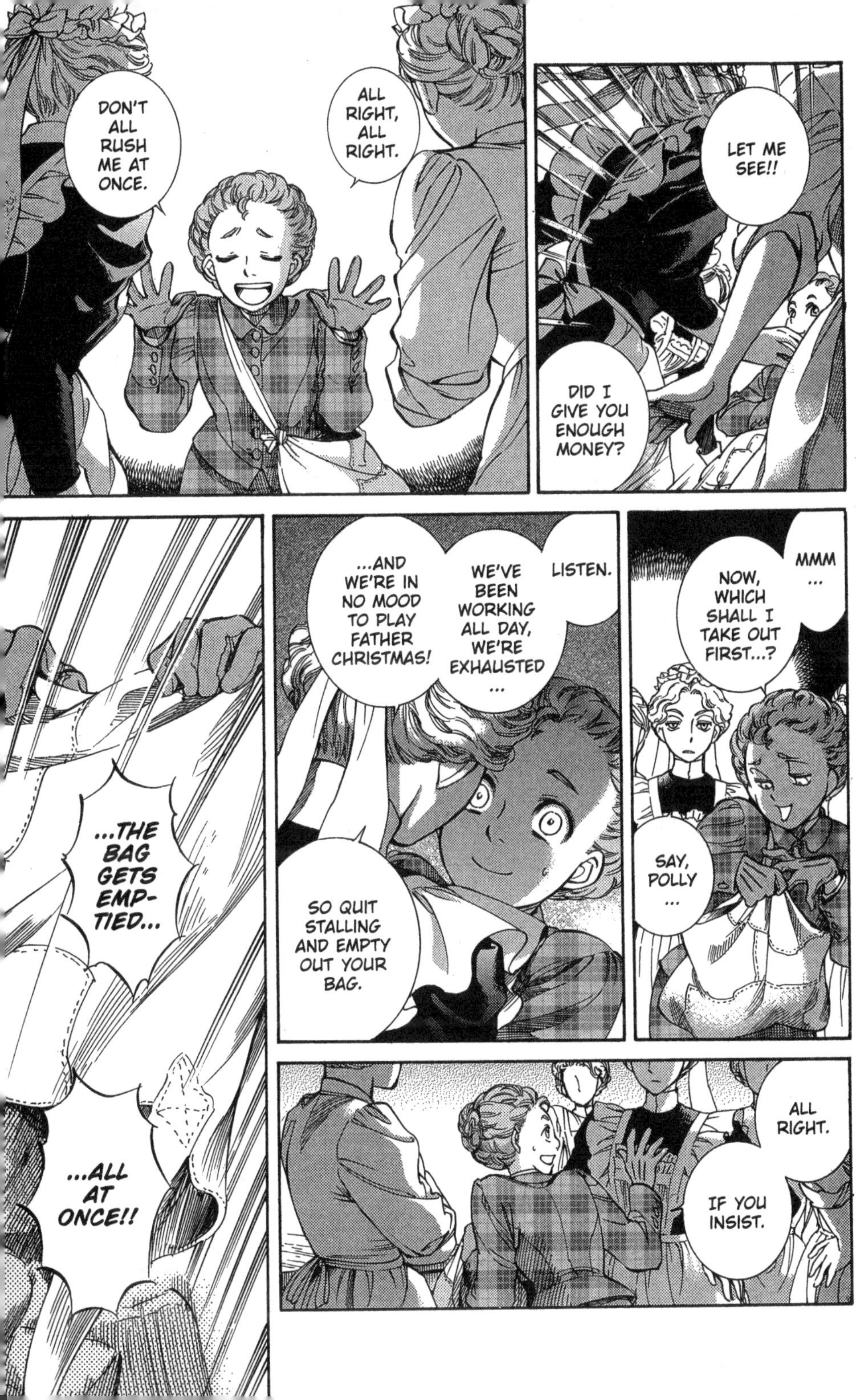
LET ME SEE!!
DID I GIVE YOU ENOUGH MONEY?
ALL RIGHT, ALL RIGHT.
DON'T ALL RUSH ME AT ONCE.
MMM...
NOW, WHICH SHALL I TAKE OUT FIRST...?
SAY, POLLY...
LISTEN.
WE'VE BEEN WORKING ALL DAY, WE'RE EXHAUSTED...
...AND WE'RE IN NO MOOD TO PLAY FATHER CHRISTMAS!
SO QUIT STALLING AND EMPTY OUT YOUR BAG.
ALL RIGHT.
IF YOU INSIST.
...THE BAG GETS EMPTIED...
...ALL AT ONCE!!

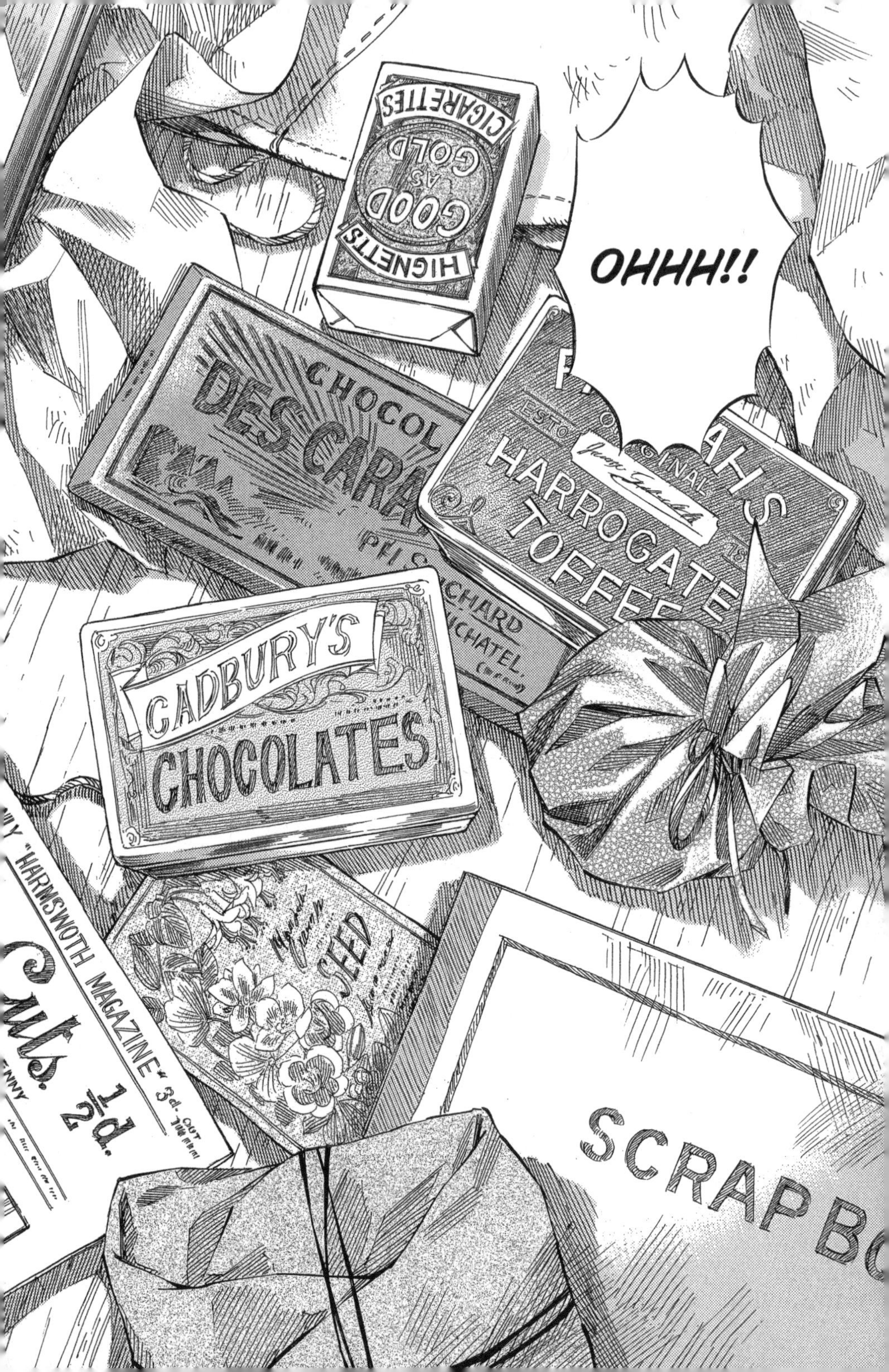
OHHHH!!
CADBURY'S
CHOCOLATES
HARROGATE
"HARMSWOTH MAGAZINE"
SEED

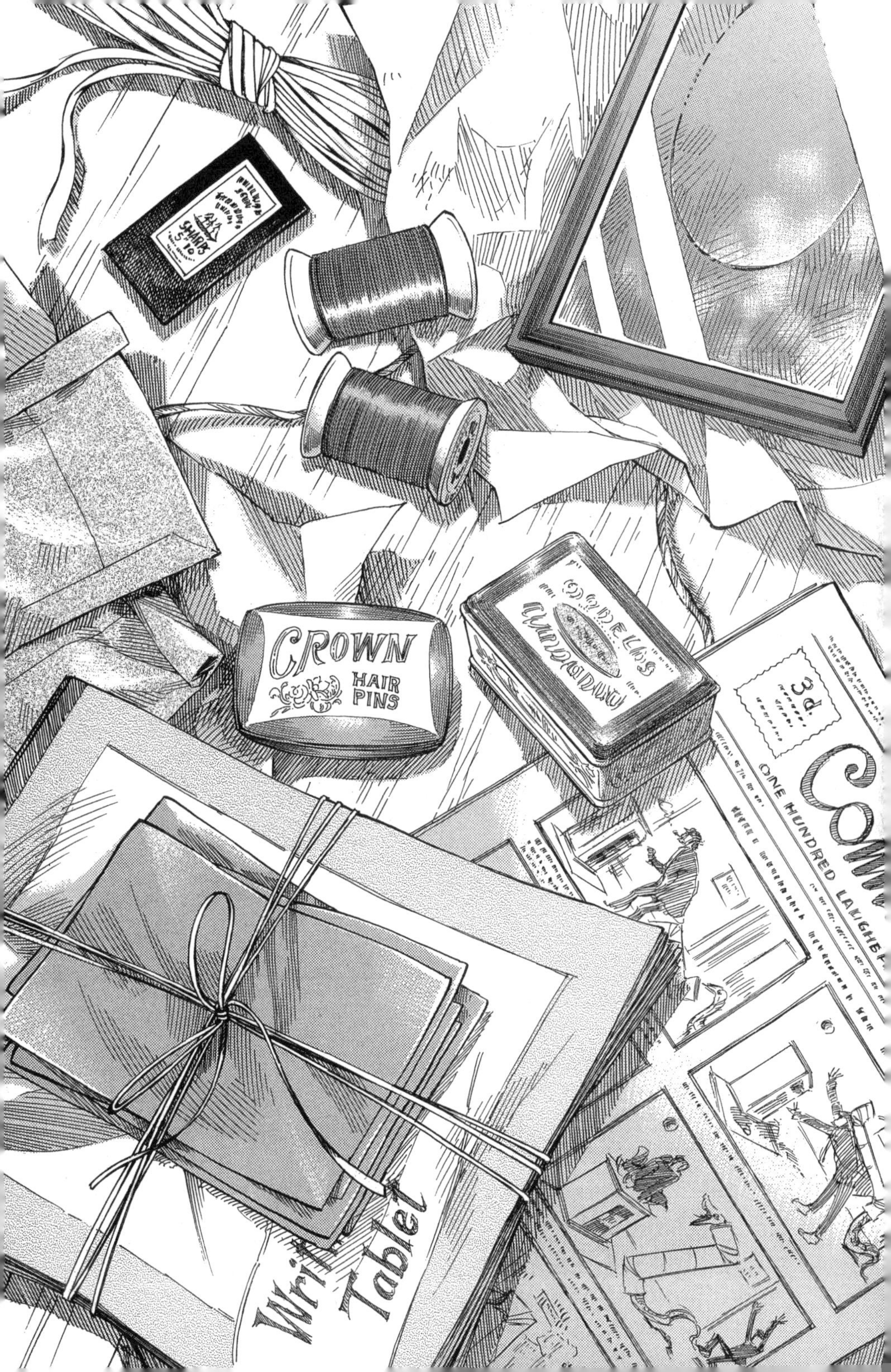
CROWN
HAIR
PINS
3d.
ONE HUNDRED LAUGHTER
Writ
Tablet

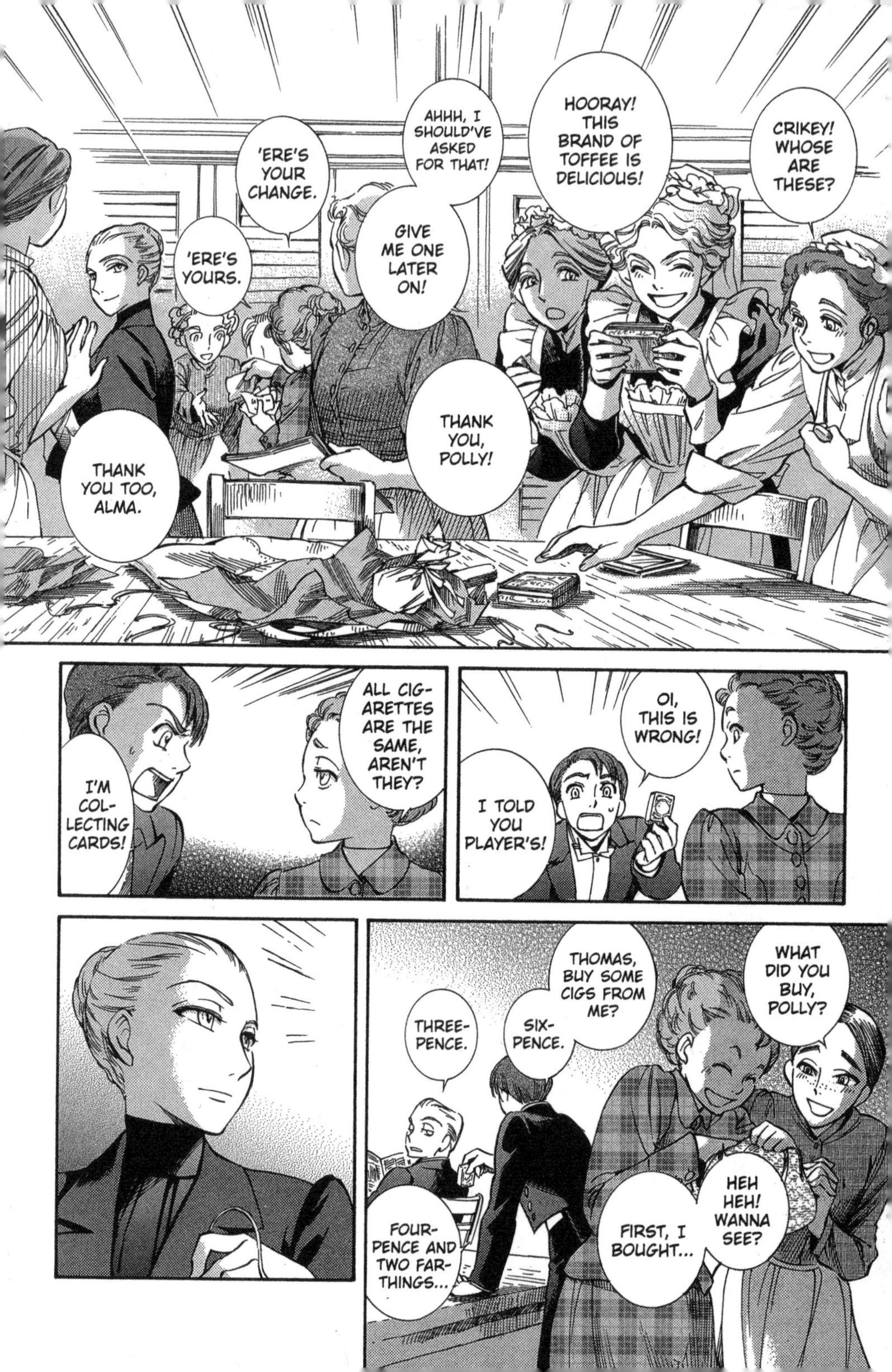
CRIKEY! WHOSE ARE THESE?
HOORAY! THIS BRAND OF TOFFEE IS DELICIOUS!
AHHH, I SHOULD'VE ASKED FOR THAT!
GIVE ME ONE LATER ON!
'ERE'S YOUR CHANGE.
'ERE'S YOURS.
THANK YOU, POLLY!
THANK YOU TOO, ALMA.
OI, THIS IS WRONG!
I TOLD YOU PLAYER'S!
ALL CIGARETTES ARE THE SAME, AREN'T THEY?
I'M COLLECTING CARDS!
WHAT DID YOU BUY, POLLY?
THOMAS, BUY SOME CIGS FROM ME?
SIXPENCE.
THREEPENCE.
HEH HEH! WANNA SEE?
FIRST, I BOUGHT...
FOURPENCE AND TWO FARTHINGS...

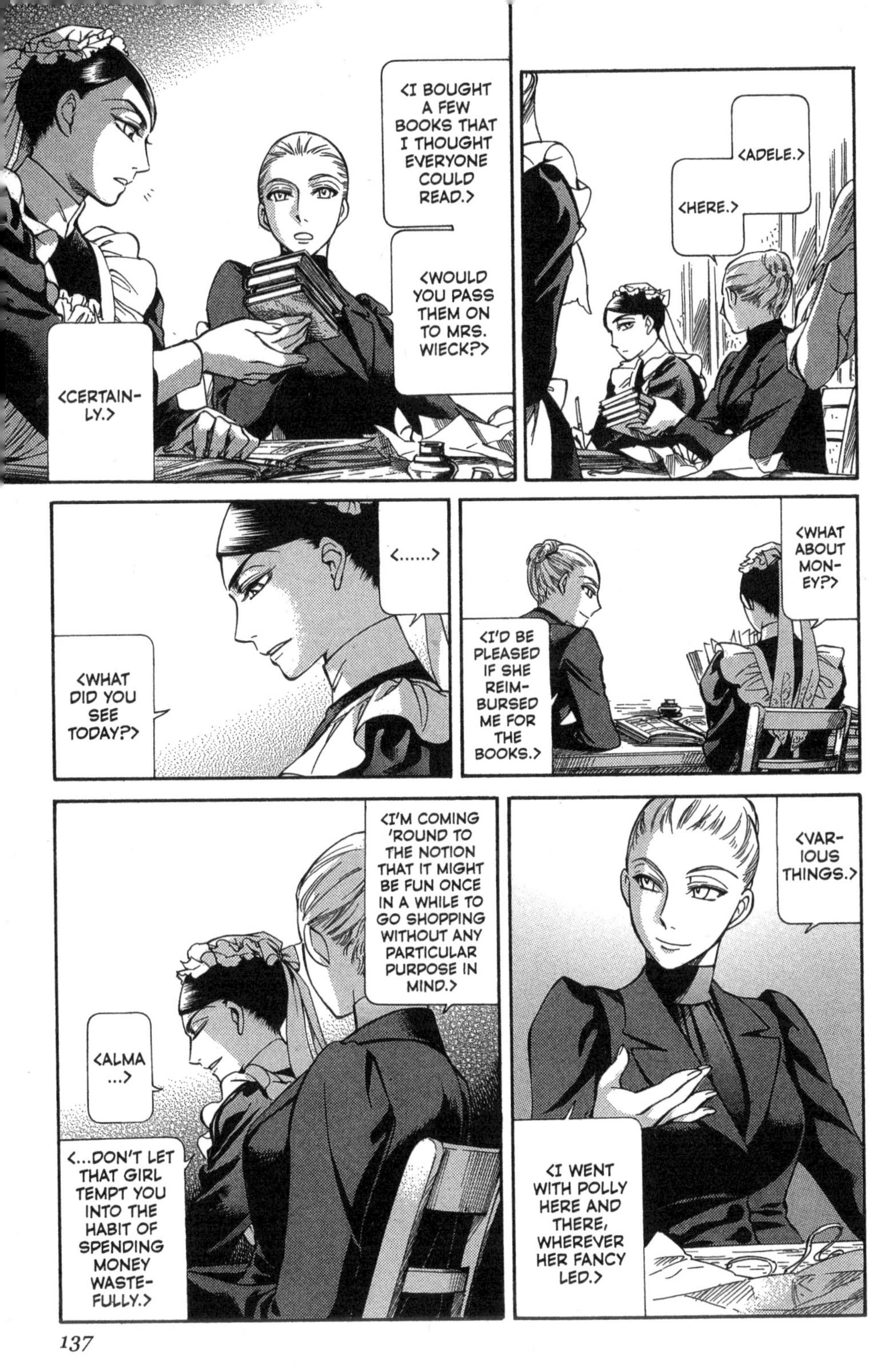

<ADELE.>
<HERE.>
<I BOUGHT A FEW BOOKS THAT I THOUGHT EVERYONE COULD READ.>
<WOULD YOU PASS THEM ON TO MRS. WIECK?>
<CERTAINLY.>
<WHAT ABOUT MONEY?>
<I'D BE PLEASED IF SHE REIMBURSED ME FOR THE BOOKS.>
<......>
<WHAT DID YOU SEE TODAY?>
<VARIOUS THINGS.>
<I WENT WITH POLLY HERE AND THERE, WHEREVER HER FANCY LED.>
<I'M COMING 'ROUND TO THE NOTION THAT IT MIGHT BE FUN ONCE IN A WHILE TO GO SHOPPING WITHOUT ANY PARTICULAR PURPOSE IN MIND.>
<ALMA ...>
<...DON'T LET THAT GIRL TEMPT YOU INTO THE HABIT OF SPENDING MONEY WASTEFULLY.>

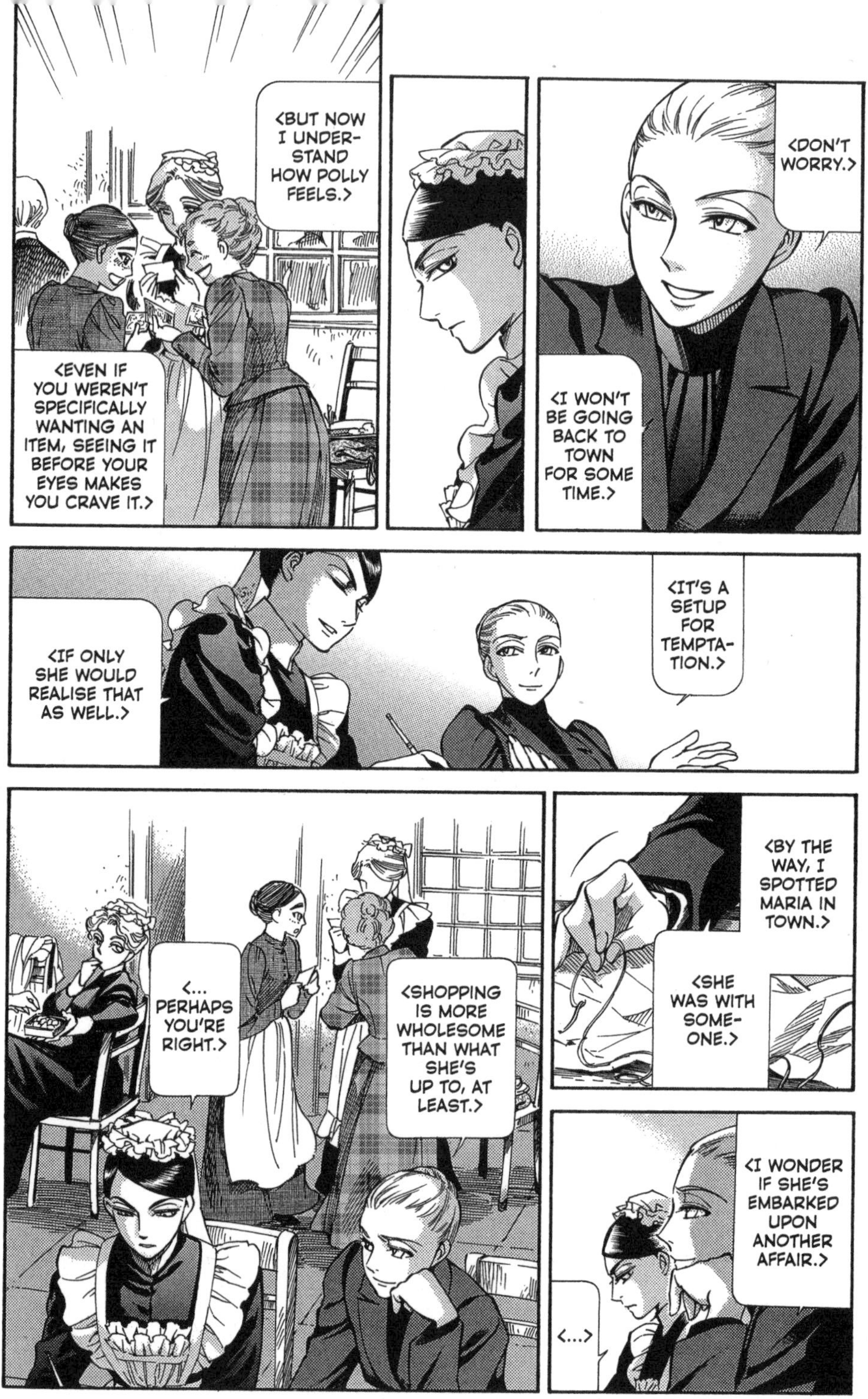
<DON'T WORRY.>
<I WON'T BE GOING BACK TO TOWN FOR SOME TIME.>
<BUT NOW I UNDERSTAND HOW POLLY FEELS.>
<EVEN IF YOU WEREN'T SPECIFICALLY WANTING AN ITEM, SEEING IT BEFORE YOUR EYES MAKES YOU CRAVE IT.>
<IT'S A SETUP FOR TEMPTATION.>
<IF ONLY SHE WOULD REALISE THAT AS WELL.>
<BY THE WAY, I SPOTTED MARIA IN TOWN.>
<SHE WAS WITH SOME-ONE.>
<I WONDER IF SHE'S EMBARKED UPON ANOTHER AFFAIR.>
<...>
<SHOPPING IS MORE WHOLESOME THAN WHAT SHE'S UP TO, AT LEAST.>
<... PERHAPS YOU'RE RIGHT.>

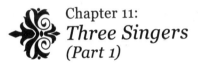

Chapter 11:
Three Singers
(Part 1)

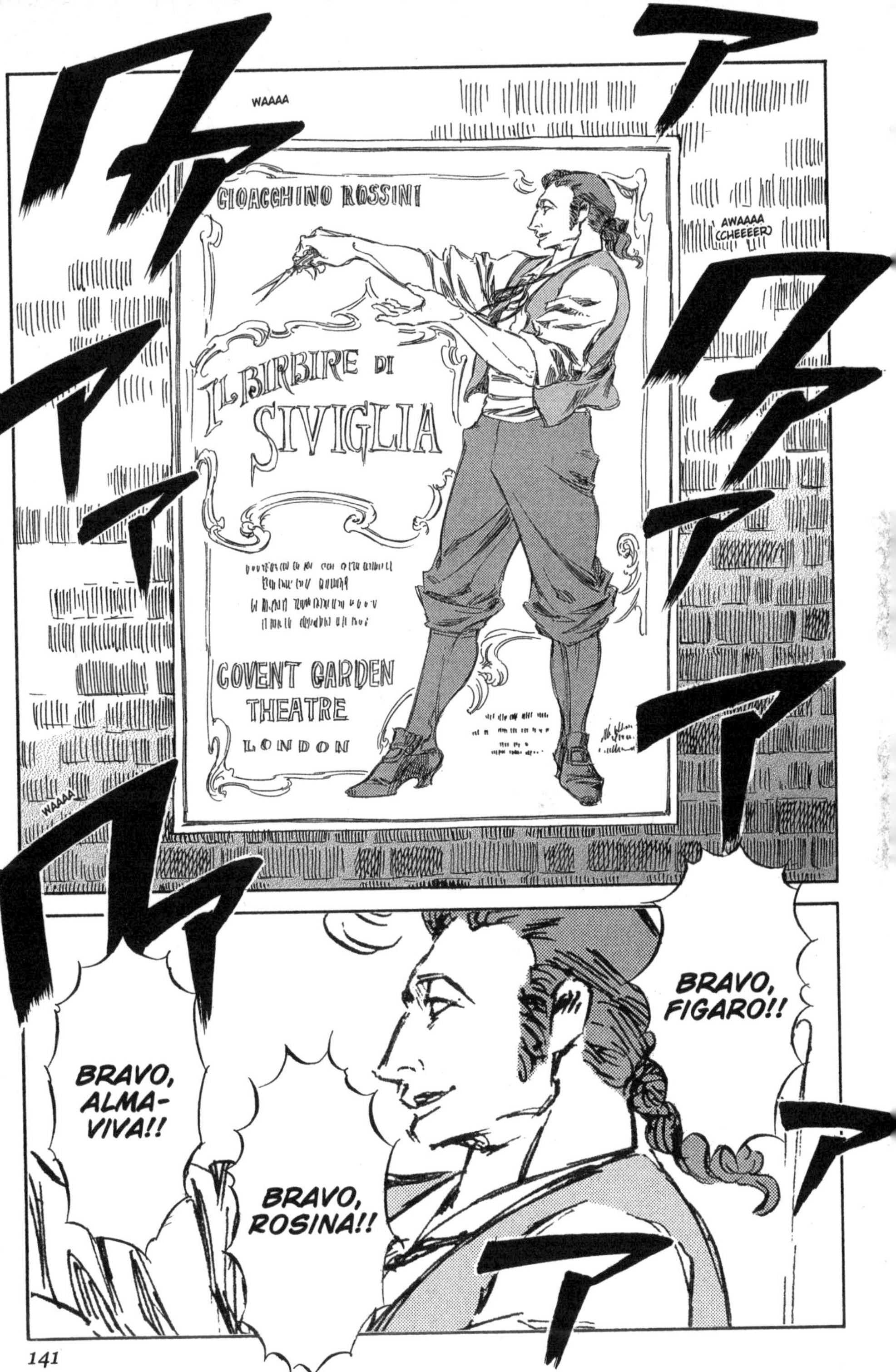
WAAAA
AWAAAA (CHEEEER)
GIOACCHINO ROSSINI
IL BIRBIRE DI SIVIGLIA
COVENT GARDEN THEATRE
LONDON
WAAAA
BRAVO, FIGARO!!
BRAVO, ROSINA!!
BRAVO, ALMA-VIVA!!

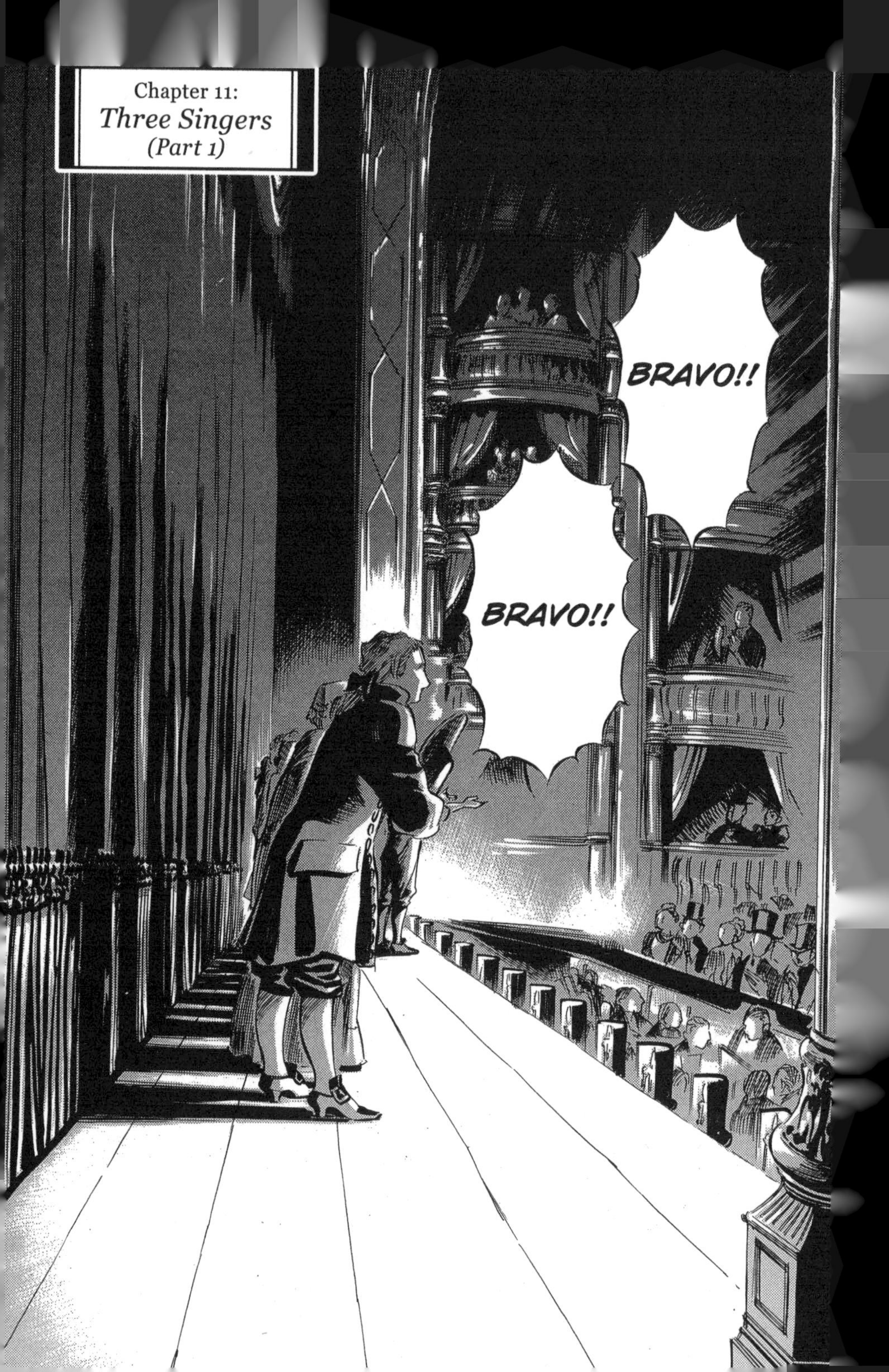
Chapter 11:
Three Singers
(Part 1)
BRAVO!!
BRAVO!!

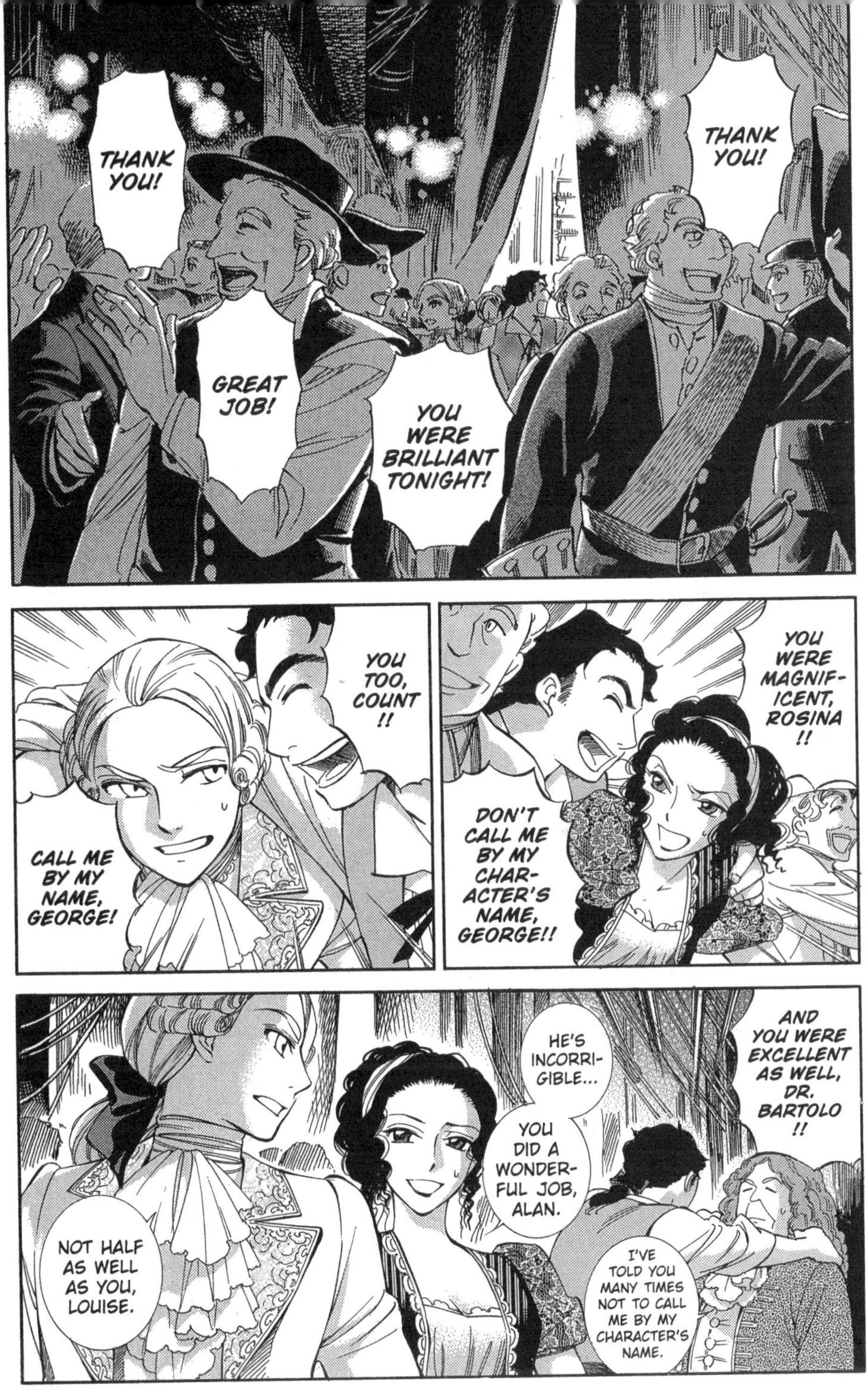
THANK YOU!
YOU WERE BRILLIANT TONIGHT!
THANK YOU!
GREAT JOB!
YOU WERE MAGNIFICENT, ROSINA!!
DON'T CALL ME BY MY CHARACTER'S NAME, GEORGE!!
YOU TOO, COUNT!!
CALL ME BY MY NAME, GEORGE!
AND YOU WERE EXCELLENT AS WELL, DR. BARTOLO!!
I'VE TOLD YOU MANY TIMES NOT TO CALL ME BY MY CHARACTER'S NAME.
HE'S INCORRIGIBLE...
YOU DID A WONDERFUL JOB, ALAN.
NOT HALF AS WELL AS YOU, LOUISE.

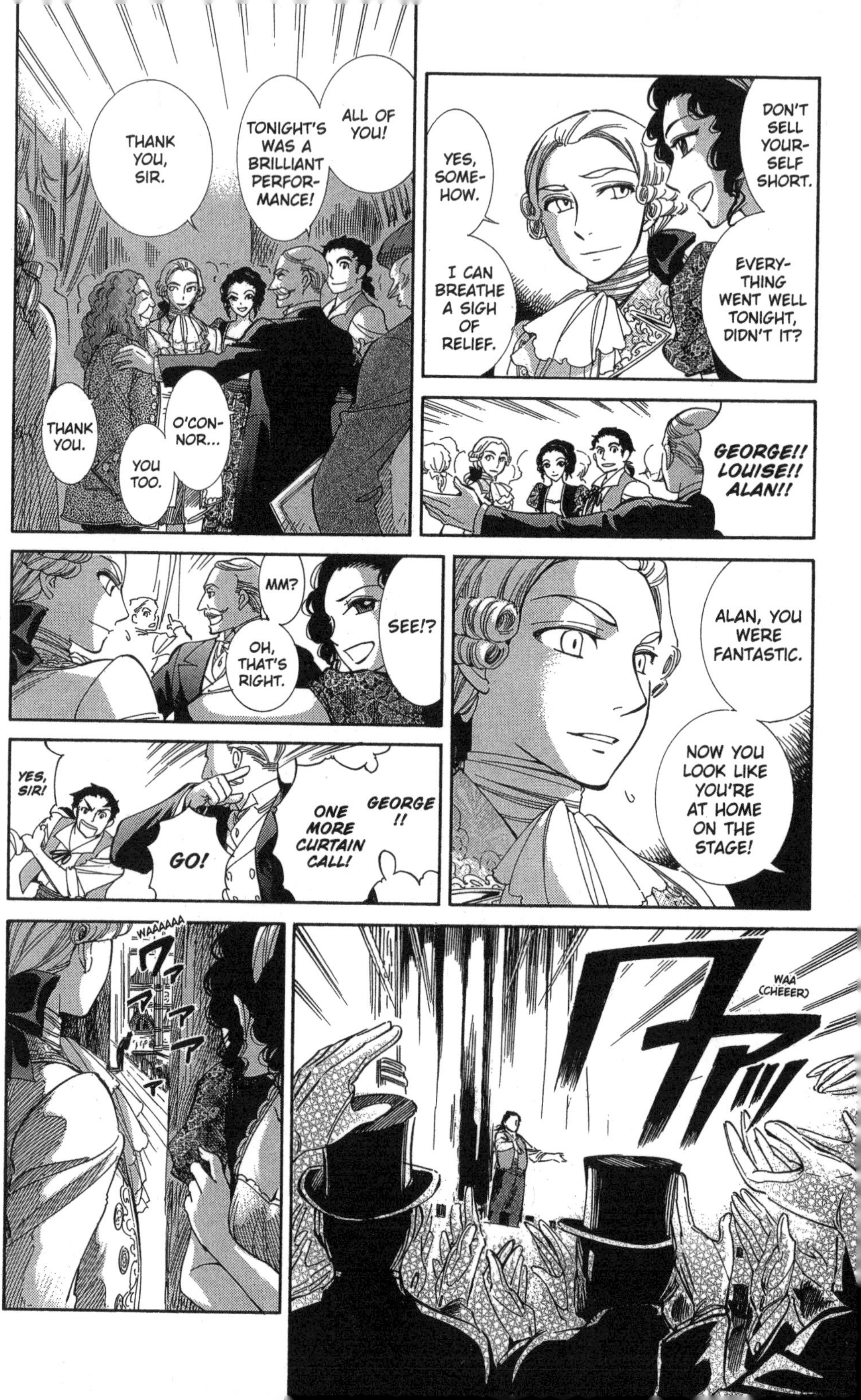
EVERY-THING WENT WELL TONIGHT, DIDN'T IT?
YES, SOME-HOW.
I CAN BREATHE A SIGH OF RELIEF.
DON'T SELL YOUR-SELF SHORT.
GEORGE!! LOUISE!! ALAN!!
ALL OF YOU!
TONIGHT'S WAS A BRILLIANT PERFOR-MANCE!
THANK YOU, SIR.
O'CON-NOR...
YOU TOO.
THANK YOU.
ALAN, YOU WERE FANTASTIC.
NOW YOU LOOK LIKE YOU'RE AT HOME ON THE STAGE!
SEE!?
MM?
OH, THAT'S RIGHT.
GEORGE !!
ONE MORE CURTAIN CALL!
GO!
YES, SIR!
WAA (CHEEER)
WAAAAAA

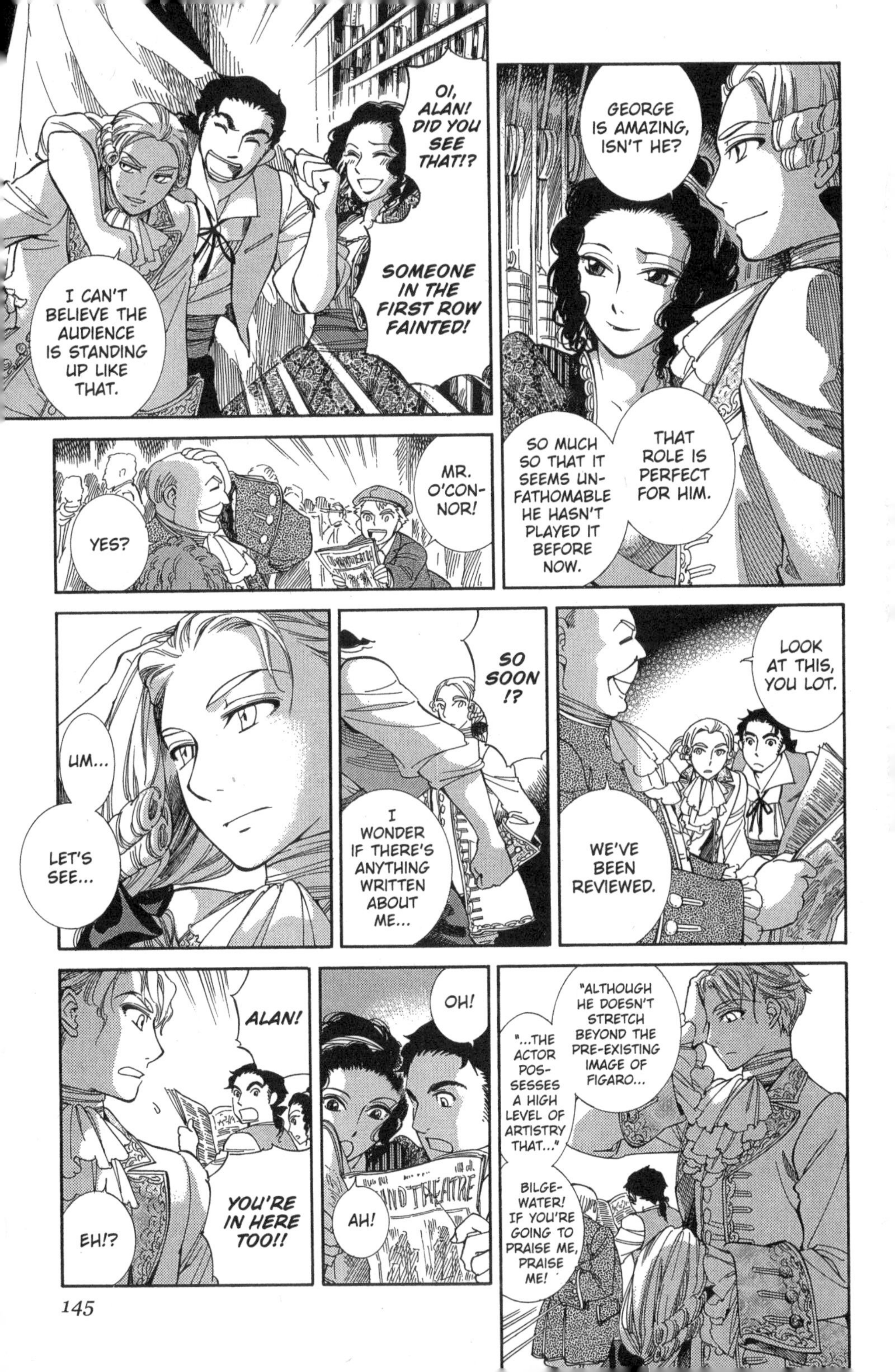
GEORGE IS AMAZING, ISN'T HE?
THAT ROLE IS PERFECT FOR HIM.
SO MUCH SO THAT IT SEEMS UN-FATHOMABLE HE HASN'T PLAYED IT BEFORE NOW.
OI, ALAN! DID YOU SEE THAT!?
SOMEONE IN THE FIRST ROW FAINTED!
I CAN'T BELIEVE THE AUDIENCE IS STANDING UP LIKE THAT.
MR. O'CON-NOR!
YES?
LOOK AT THIS, YOU LOT.
WE'VE BEEN REVIEWED.
SO SOON !?
I WONDER IF THERE'S ANYTHING WRITTEN ABOUT ME...
UM...
LET'S SEE...
"ALTHOUGH HE DOESN'T STRETCH BEYOND THE PRE-EXISTING IMAGE OF FIGARO...
"...THE ACTOR POS-SESSES A HIGH LEVEL OF ARTISTRY THAT..."
BILGE-WATER! IF YOU'RE GOING TO PRAISE ME, PRAISE ME!
OH!
AH!
ALAN!
YOU'RE IN HERE TOO!!
EH!?

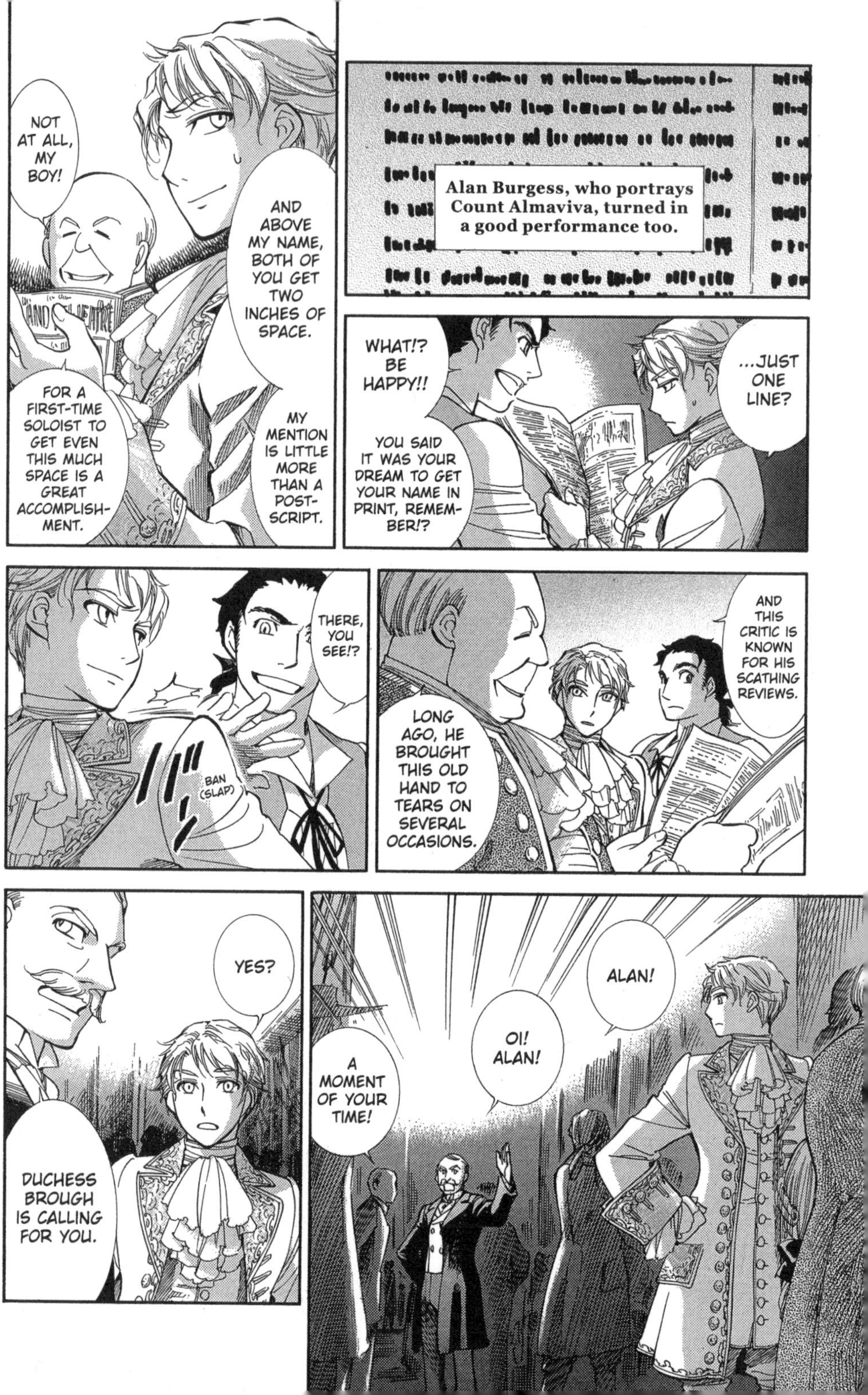

Alan Burgess, who portrays Count Almaviva, turned in a good performance too.
...JUST ONE LINE?
WHAT!? BE HAPPY!!
YOU SAID IT WAS YOUR DREAM TO GET YOUR NAME IN PRINT, REMEMBER!?
AND ABOVE MY NAME, BOTH OF YOU GET TWO INCHES OF SPACE.
MY MENTION IS LITTLE MORE THAN A POST-SCRIPT.
NOT AT ALL, MY BOY!
FOR A FIRST-TIME SOLOIST TO GET EVEN THIS MUCH SPACE IS A GREAT ACCOMPLISHMENT.
AND THIS CRITIC IS KNOWN FOR HIS SCATHING REVIEWS.
LONG AGO, HE BROUGHT THIS OLD HAND TO TEARS ON SEVERAL OCCASIONS.
THERE, YOU SEE!?
BAN (SLAP)
ALAN!
OI! ALAN!
A MOMENT OF YOUR TIME!
YES?
DUCHESS BROUGH IS CALLING FOR YOU.

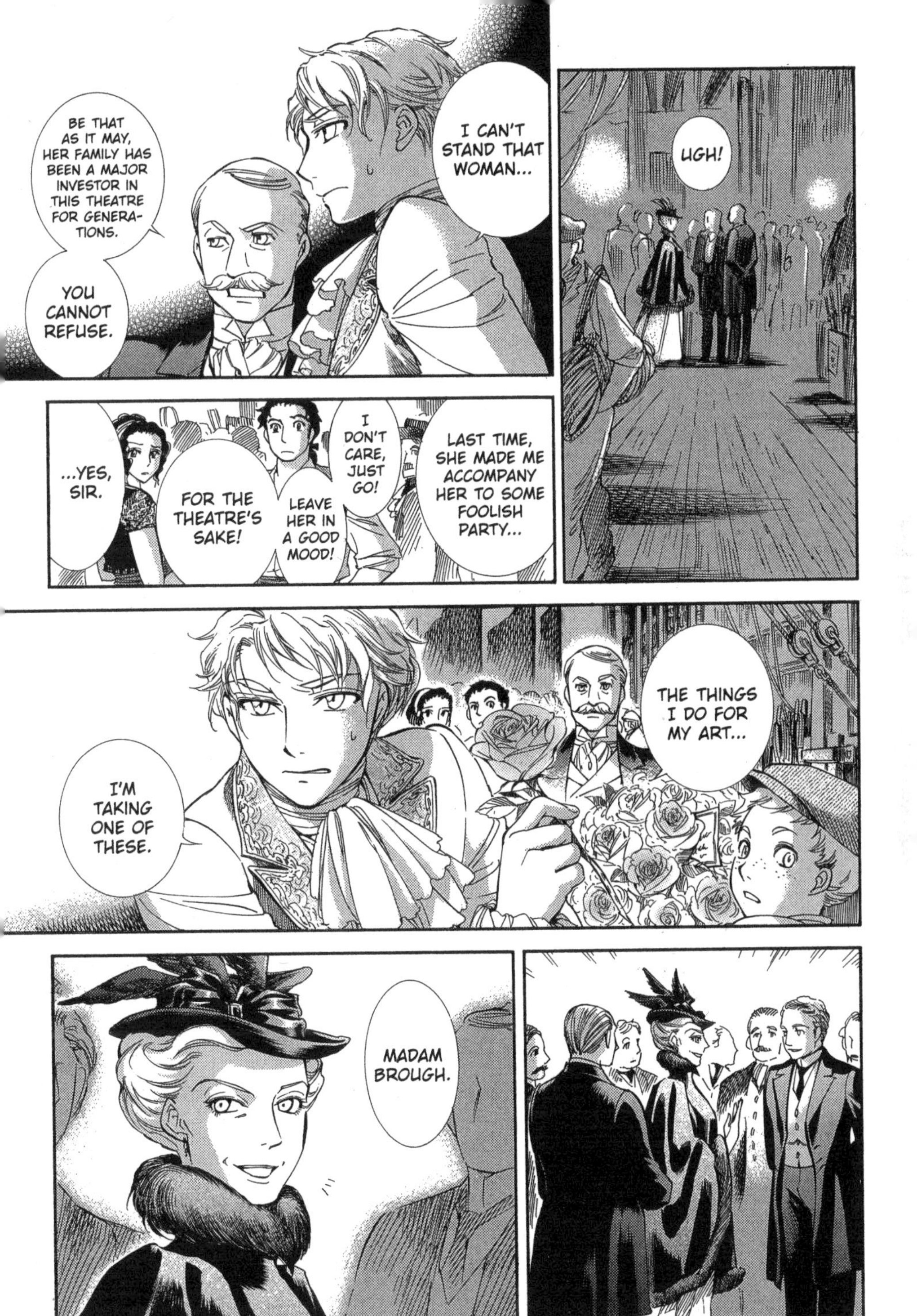
UGH!
I CAN'T STAND THAT WOMAN...
BE THAT AS IT MAY, HER FAMILY HAS BEEN A MAJOR INVESTOR IN THIS THEATRE FOR GENERATIONS.
YOU CANNOT REFUSE.
LAST TIME, SHE MADE ME ACCOMPANY HER TO SOME FOOLISH PARTY...
I DON'T CARE, JUST GO!
LEAVE HER IN A GOOD MOOD!
FOR THE THEATRE'S SAKE!
...YES, SIR.
THE THINGS I DO FOR MY ART...
I'M TAKING ONE OF THESE.
MADAM BROUGH.

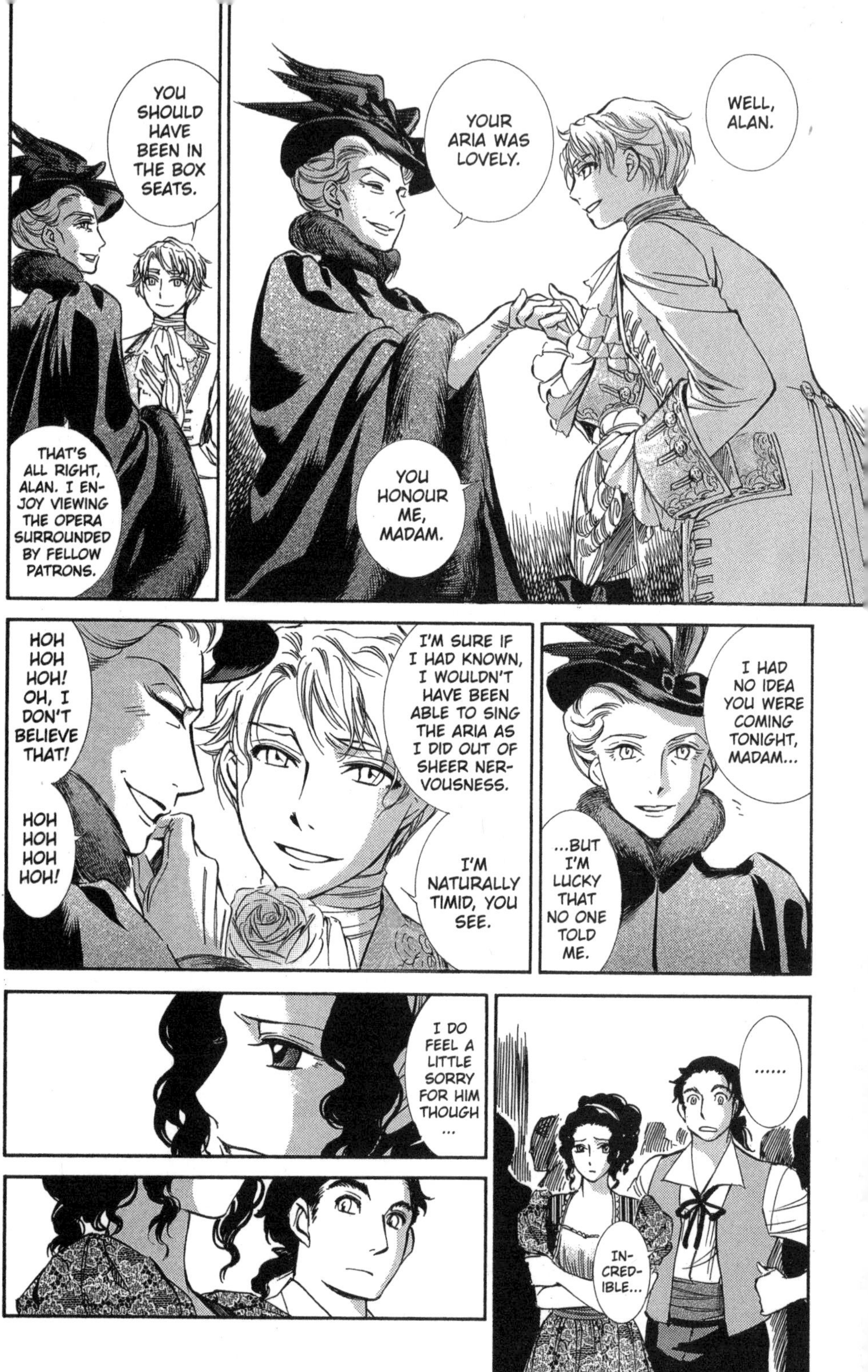
WELL, ALAN.
YOUR ARIA WAS LOVELY.
YOU HONOUR ME, MADAM.
YOU SHOULD HAVE BEEN IN THE BOX SEATS.
THAT'S ALL RIGHT, ALAN. I ENJOY VIEWING THE OPERA SURROUNDED BY FELLOW PATRONS.
I HAD NO IDEA YOU WERE COMING TONIGHT, MADAM...
...BUT I'M LUCKY THAT NO ONE TOLD ME.
I'M SURE IF I HAD KNOWN, I WOULDN'T HAVE BEEN ABLE TO SING THE ARIA AS I DID OUT OF SHEER NERVOUSNESS.
I'M NATURALLY TIMID, YOU SEE.
HOH HOH HOH! OH, I DON'T BELIEVE THAT!
HOH HOH HOH HOH!
......
INCREDIBLE...
I DO FEEL A LITTLE SORRY FOR HIM THOUGH...

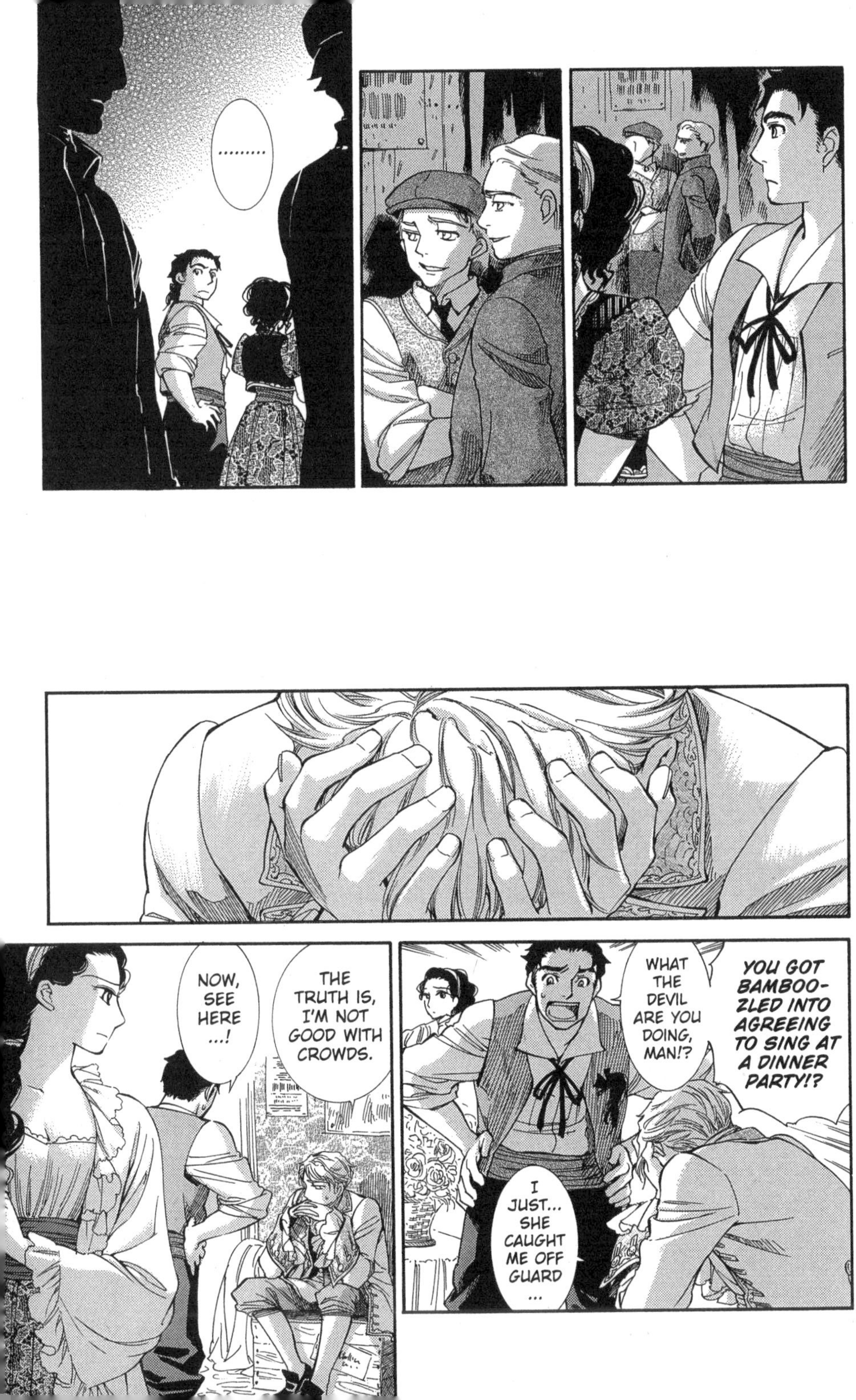
....
YOU GOT BAMBOOZLED INTO AGREEING TO SING AT A DINNER PARTY!?
WHAT THE DEVIL ARE YOU DOING, MAN!?
I JUST... SHE CAUGHT ME OFF GUARD ...
THE TRUTH IS, I'M NOT GOOD WITH CROWDS.
NOW, SEE HERE ...!

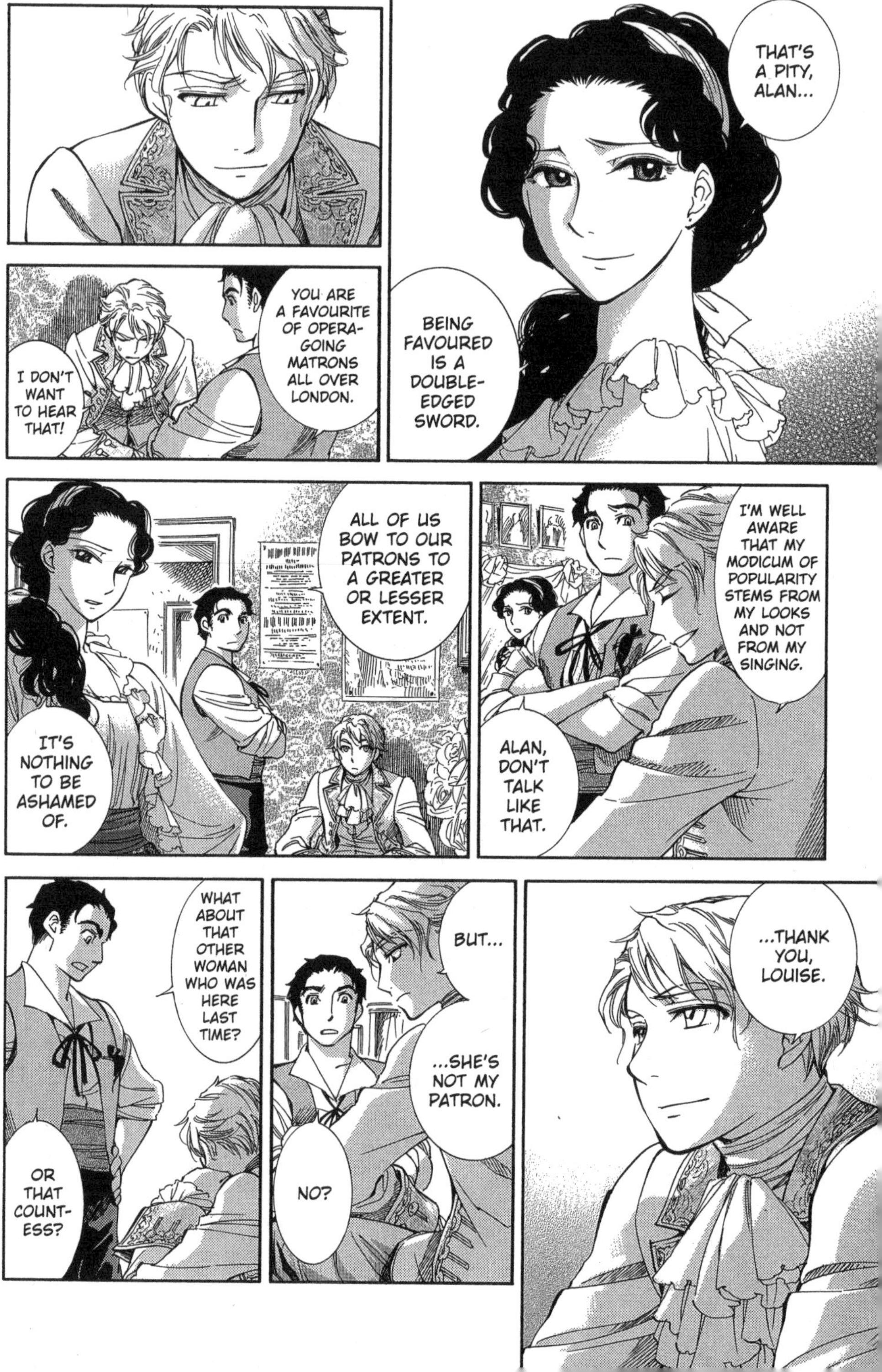

THAT'S A PITY, ALAN...
BEING FAVOURED IS A DOUBLE-EDGED SWORD.
YOU ARE A FAVOURITE OF OPERA-GOING MATRONS ALL OVER LONDON.
I DON'T WANT TO HEAR THAT!
I'M WELL AWARE THAT MY MODICUM OF POPULARITY STEMS FROM MY LOOKS AND NOT FROM MY SINGING.
ALAN, DON'T TALK LIKE THAT.
ALL OF US BOW TO OUR PATRONS TO A GREATER OR LESSER EXTENT.
IT'S NOTHING TO BE ASHAMED OF.
...THANK YOU, LOUISE.
BUT...
...SHE'S NOT MY PATRON.
NO?
WHAT ABOUT THAT OTHER WOMAN WHO WAS HERE LAST TIME?
OR THAT COUNT-ESS?

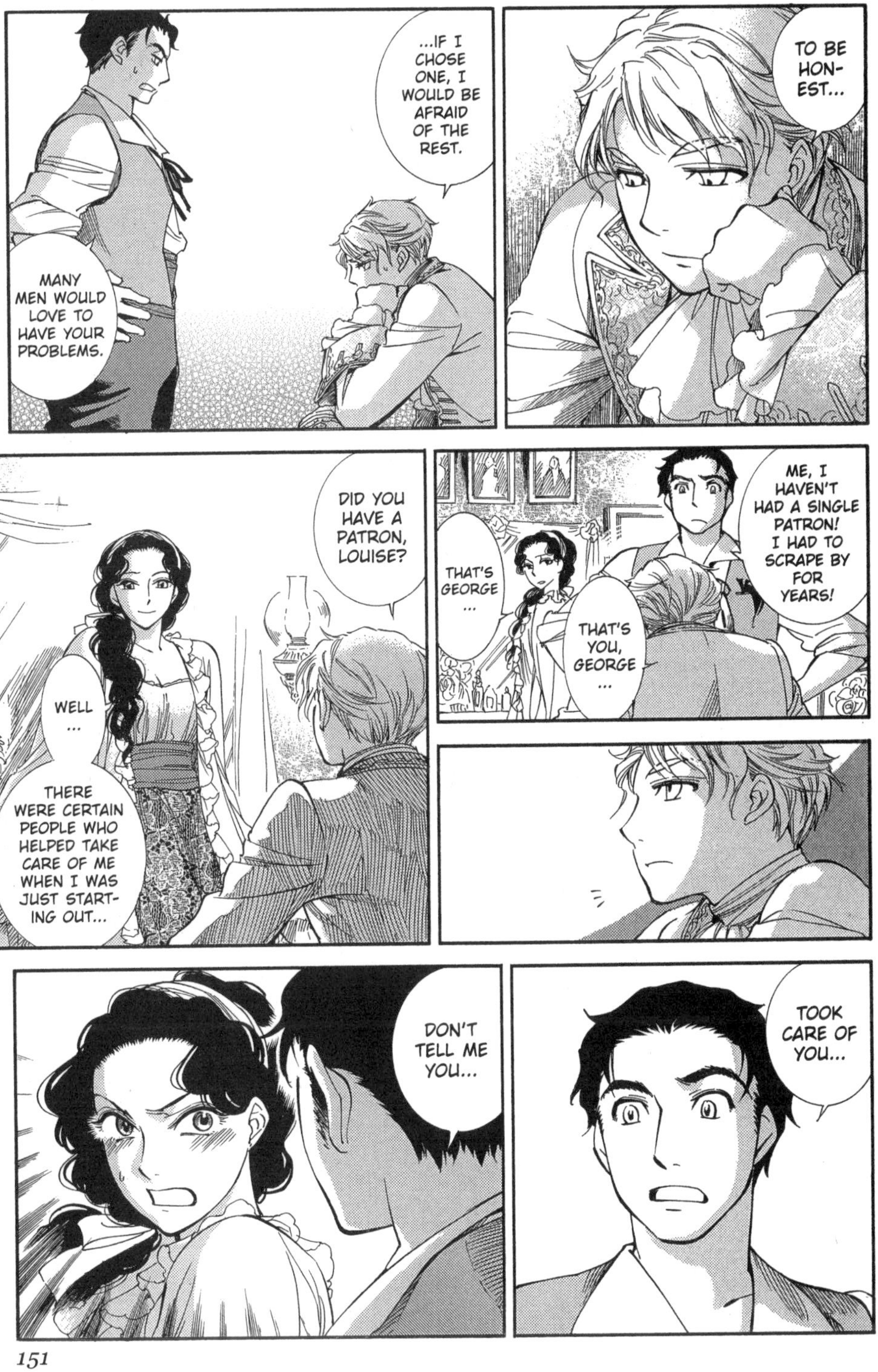
TO BE HON-EST...
...IF I CHOSE ONE, I WOULD BE AFRAID OF THE REST.
MANY MEN WOULD LOVE TO HAVE YOUR PROBLEMS.
ME, I HAVEN'T HAD A SINGLE PATRON! I HAD TO SCRAPE BY FOR YEARS!
THAT'S YOU, GEORGE...
THAT'S GEORGE...
DID YOU HAVE A PATRON, LOUISE?
WELL...
THERE WERE CERTAIN PEOPLE WHO HELPED TAKE CARE OF ME WHEN I WAS JUST START-ING OUT...
TOOK CARE OF YOU...
DON'T TELL ME YOU...

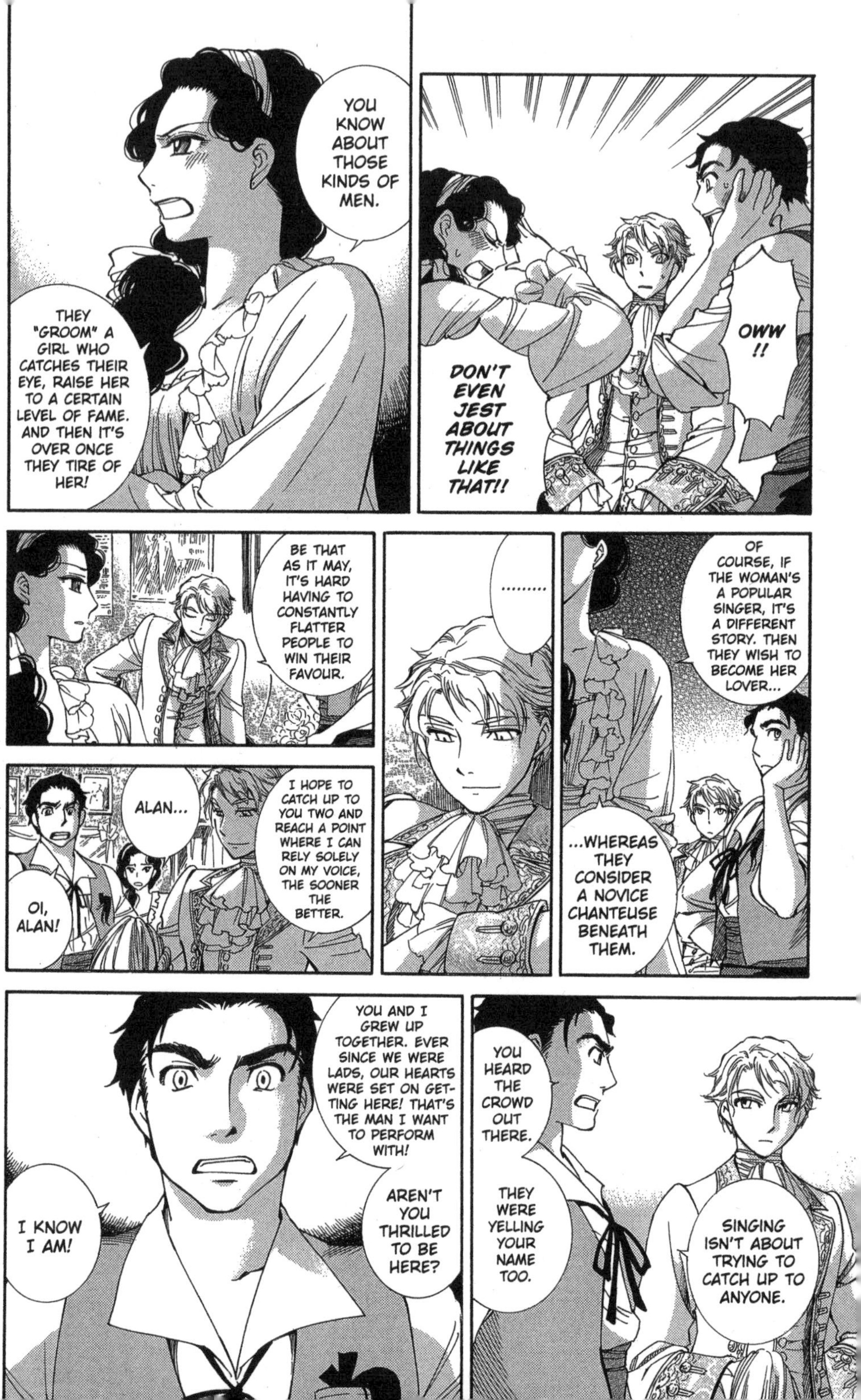
OWW !!
DON'T EVEN JEST ABOUT THINGS LIKE THAT!!
YOU KNOW ABOUT THOSE KINDS OF MEN.
THEY "GROOM" A GIRL WHO CATCHES THEIR EYE, RAISE HER TO A CERTAIN LEVEL OF FAME. AND THEN IT'S OVER ONCE THEY TIRE OF HER!
OF COURSE, IF THE WOMAN'S A POPULAR SINGER, IT'S A DIFFERENT STORY. THEN THEY WISH TO BECOME HER LOVER...
...WHEREAS THEY CONSIDER A NOVICE CHANTEUSE BENEATH THEM.
....
BE THAT AS IT MAY, IT'S HARD HAVING TO CONSTANTLY FLATTER PEOPLE TO WIN THEIR FAVOUR.
I HOPE TO CATCH UP TO YOU TWO AND REACH A POINT WHERE I CAN RELY SOLELY ON MY VOICE, THE SOONER THE BETTER.
ALAN...
OI, ALAN!
YOU HEARD THE CROWD OUT THERE.
THEY WERE YELLING YOUR NAME TOO.
SINGING ISN'T ABOUT TRYING TO CATCH UP TO ANYONE.
YOU AND I GREW UP TOGETHER. EVER SINCE WE WERE LADS, OUR HEARTS WERE SET ON GETTING HERE! THAT'S THE MAN I WANT TO PERFORM WITH!
AREN'T YOU THRILLED TO BE HERE?
I KNOW I AM!

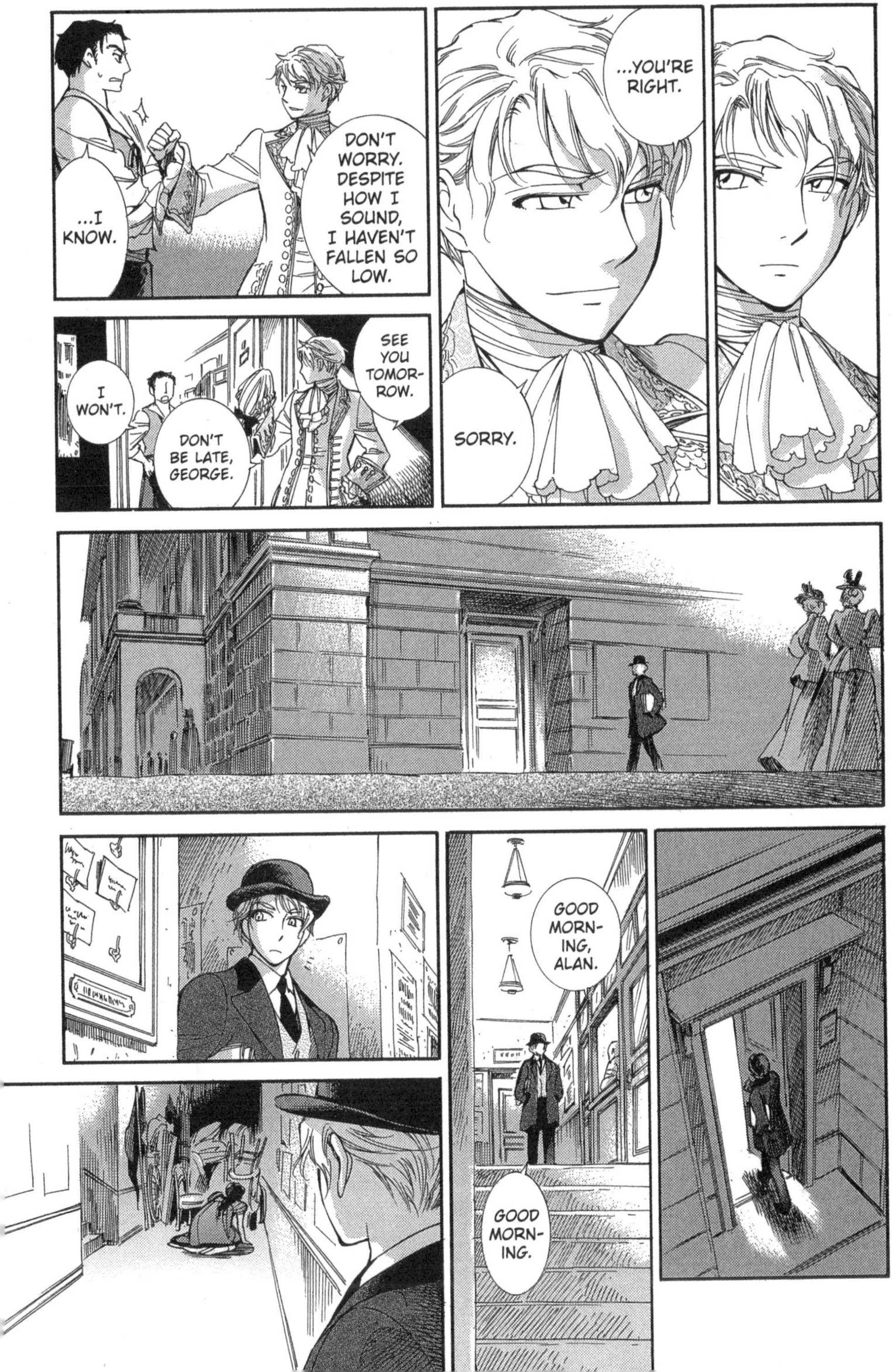
...YOU'RE RIGHT.
SORRY.
DON'T WORRY. DESPITE HOW I SOUND, I HAVEN'T FALLEN SO LOW.
...I KNOW.
SEE YOU TOMORROW.
DON'T BE LATE, GEORGE.
I WON'T.
GOOD MORNING, ALAN.
GOOD MORNING.

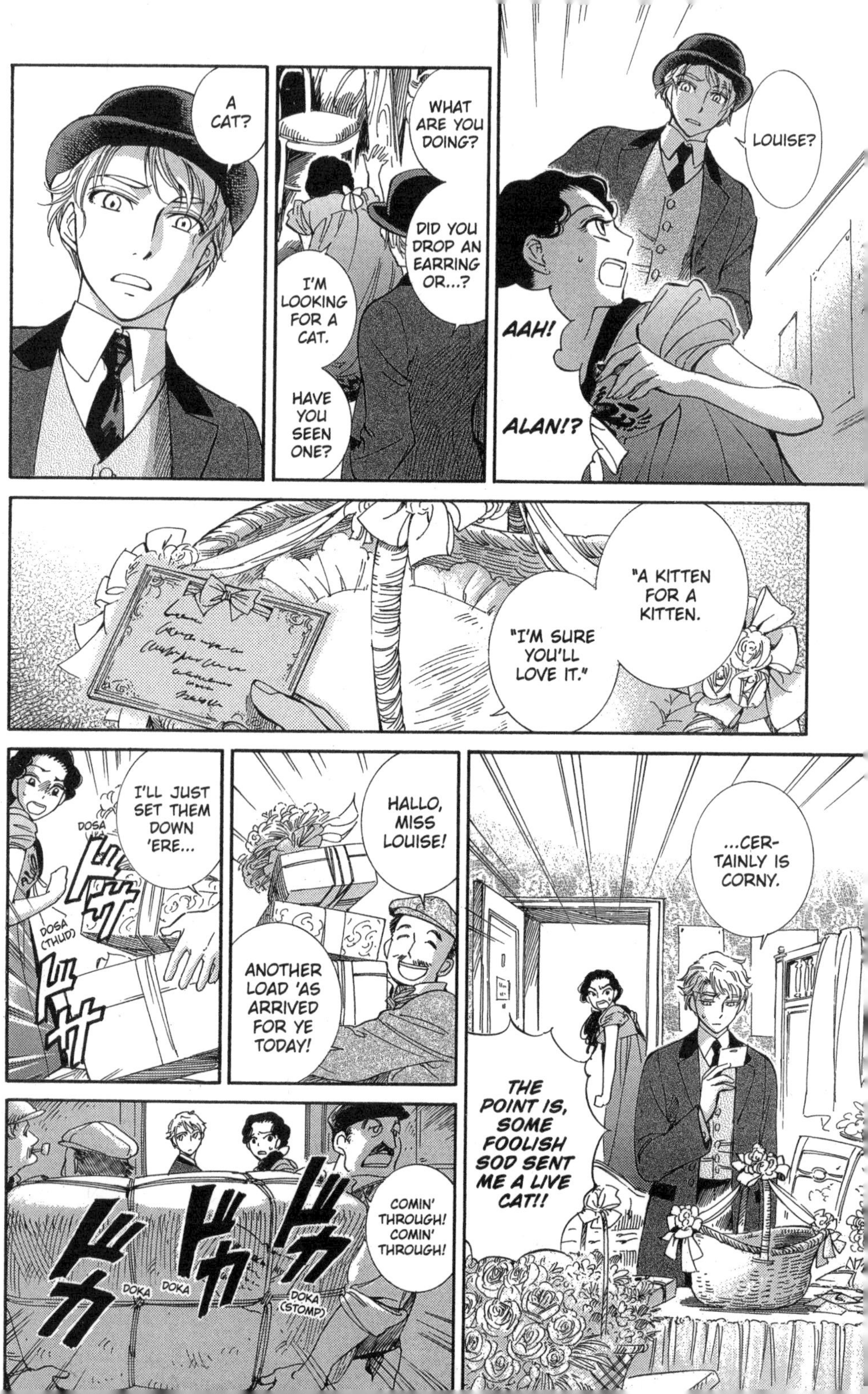
LOUISE?
AAH!
ALAN!?
WHAT ARE YOU DOING?
DID YOU DROP AN EARRING OR...?
I'M LOOKING FOR A CAT.
HAVE YOU SEEN ONE?
A CAT?
"A KITTEN FOR A KITTEN.
"I'M SURE YOU'LL LOVE IT."
...CER-TAINLY IS CORNY.
THE POINT IS, SOME FOOLISH SOD SENT ME A LIVE CAT!!
HALLO, MISS LOUISE!
ANOTHER LOAD 'AS ARRIVED FOR YE TODAY!
I'LL JUST SET THEM DOWN 'ERE...
DOSA
DOSA (THUD)
COMIN' THROUGH! COMIN' THROUGH!
DOKA (STOMP)
DOKA
DOKA

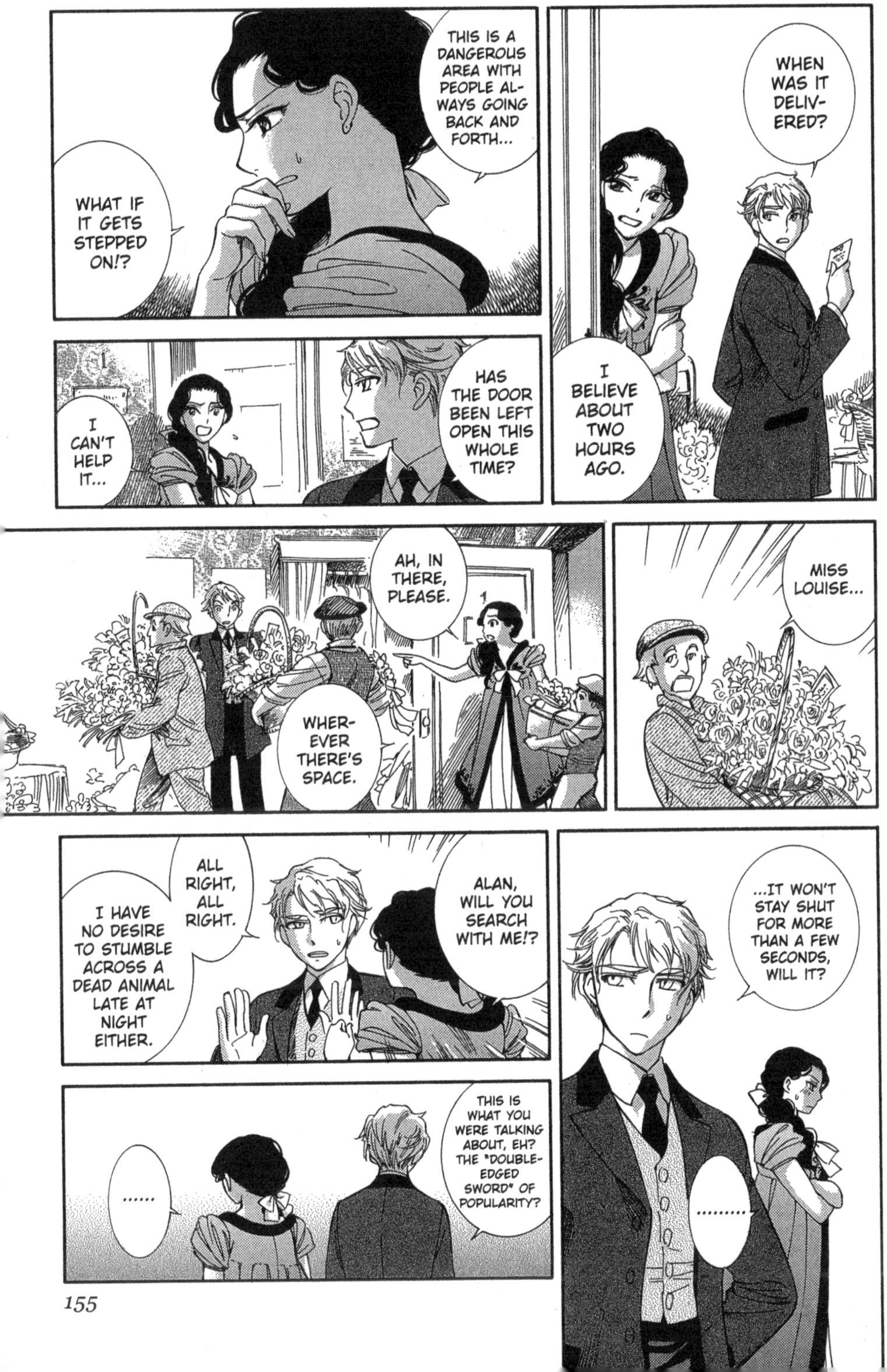
WHEN WAS IT DELIVERED?
I BELIEVE ABOUT TWO HOURS AGO.
THIS IS A DANGEROUS AREA WITH PEOPLE ALWAYS GOING BACK AND FORTH...
WHAT IF IT GETS STEPPED ON!?
HAS THE DOOR BEEN LEFT OPEN THIS WHOLE TIME?
I CAN'T HELP IT...
MISS LOUISE...
AH, IN THERE, PLEASE.
WHEREVER THERE'S SPACE.
...IT WON'T STAY SHUT FOR MORE THAN A FEW SECONDS, WILL IT?
....
ALAN, WILL YOU SEARCH WITH ME!?
ALL RIGHT, ALL RIGHT.
I HAVE NO DESIRE TO STUMBLE ACROSS A DEAD ANIMAL LATE AT NIGHT EITHER.
THIS IS WHAT YOU WERE TALKING ABOUT, EH? THE "DOUBLE-EDGED SWORD" OF POPULARITY?
......

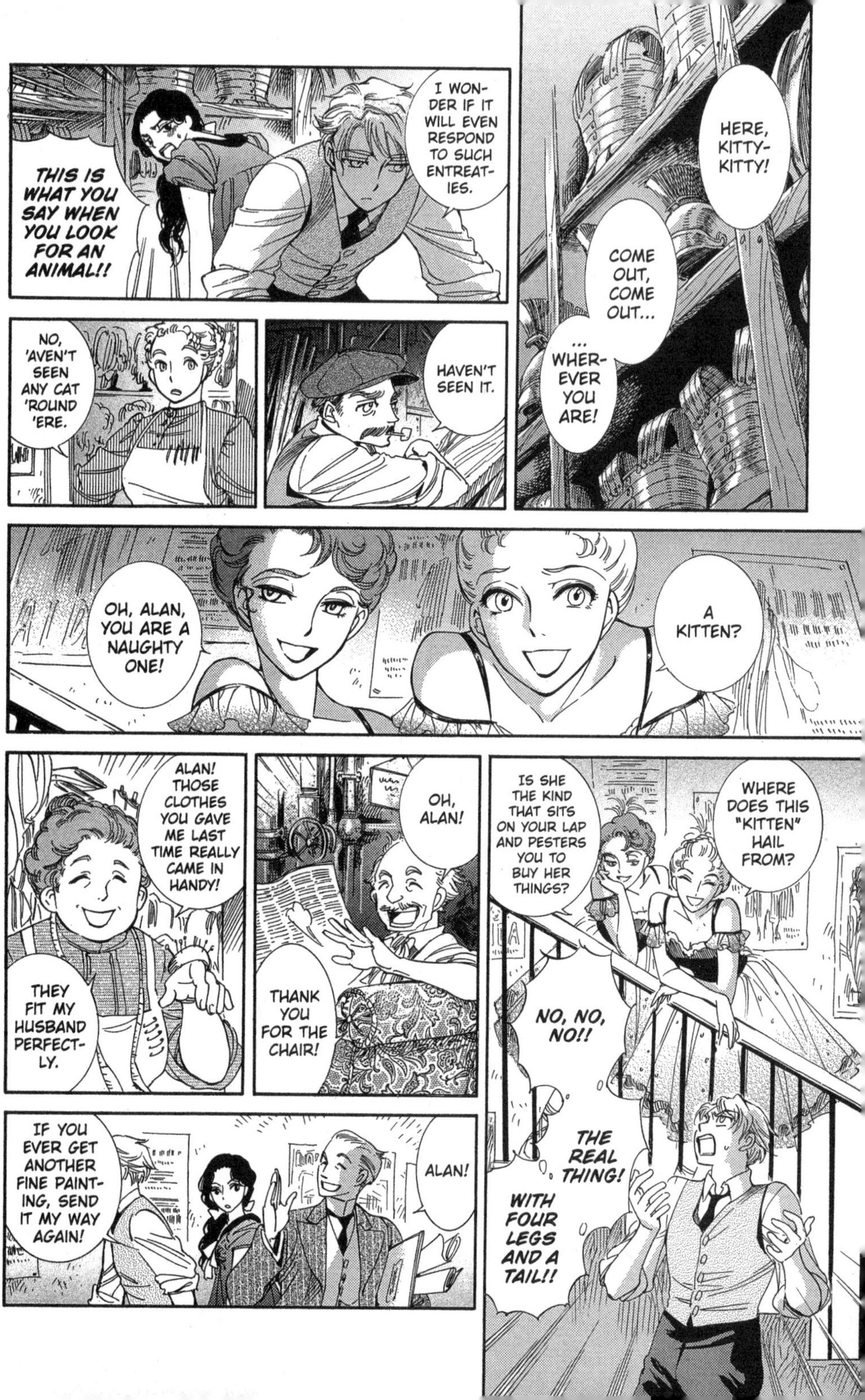
HERE, KITTY-KITTY!
COME OUT, COME OUT...
...WHEREVER YOU ARE!
I WONDER IF IT WILL EVEN RESPOND TO SUCH ENTREATIES.
THIS IS WHAT YOU SAY WHEN YOU LOOK FOR AN ANIMAL!!
HAVEN'T SEEN IT.
NO, 'AVEN'T SEEN ANY CAT 'ROUND 'ERE.
A KITTEN?
OH, ALAN, YOU ARE A NAUGHTY ONE!
WHERE DOES THIS "KITTEN" HAIL FROM?
IS SHE THE KIND THAT SITS ON YOUR LAP AND PESTERS YOU TO BUY HER THINGS?
NO, NO, NO!!
THE REAL THING!
WITH FOUR LEGS AND A TAIL!!
OH, ALAN!
THANK YOU FOR THE CHAIR!
ALAN! THOSE CLOTHES YOU GAVE ME LAST TIME REALLY CAME IN HANDY!
THEY FIT MY HUSBAND PERFECTLY.
ALAN!
IF YOU EVER GET ANOTHER FINE PAINTING, SEND IT MY WAY AGAIN!

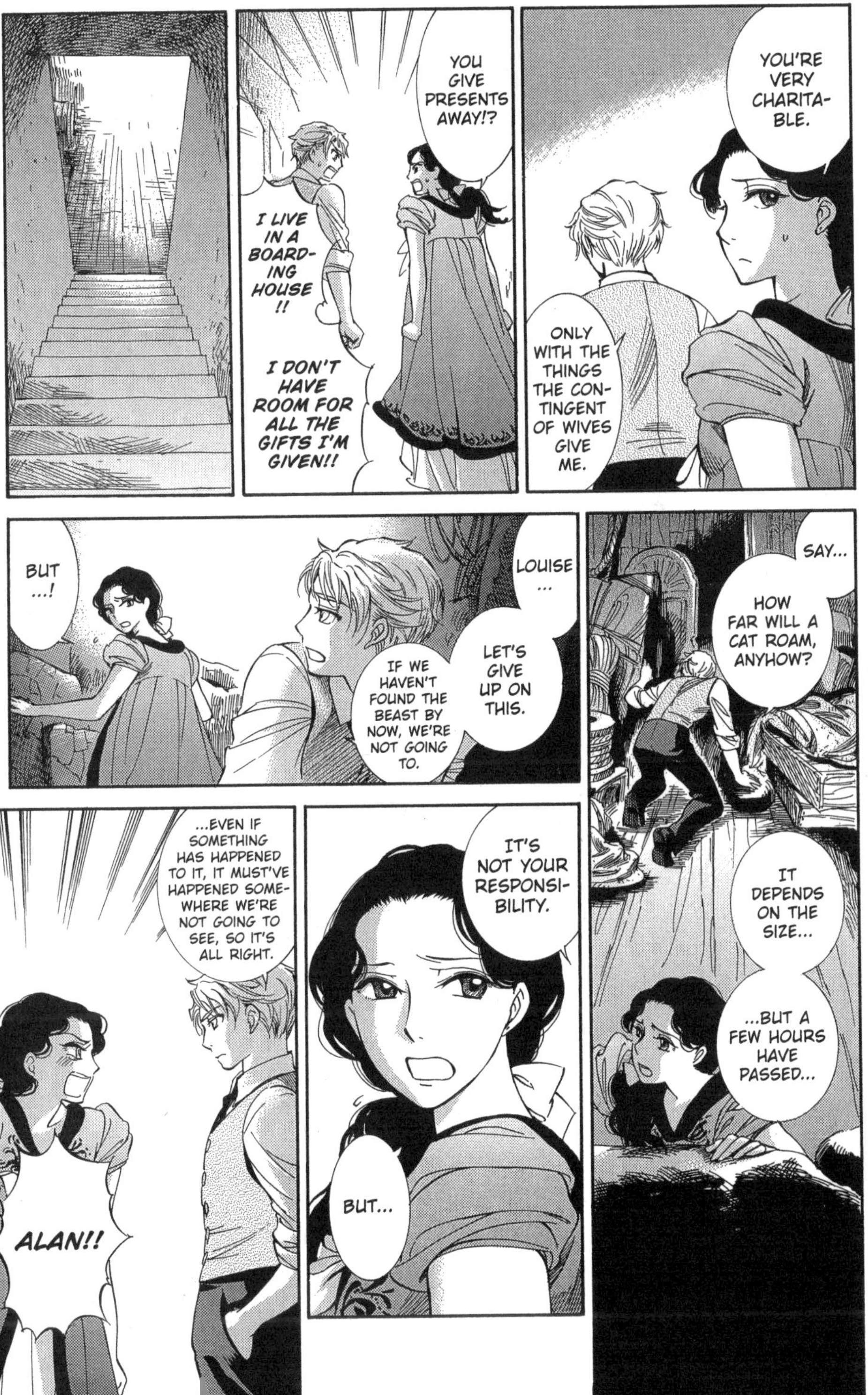
YOU'RE VERY CHARITA-BLE.
ONLY WITH THE THINGS THE CON-TINGENT OF WIVES GIVE ME.
YOU GIVE PRESENTS AWAY!?
I LIVE IN A BOARD-ING HOUSE !!
I DON'T HAVE ROOM FOR ALL THE GIFTS I'M GIVEN!!
SAY...
HOW FAR WILL A CAT ROAM, ANYHOW?
IT DEPENDS ON THE SIZE...
...BUT A FEW HOURS HAVE PASSED...
LOUISE ...
LET'S GIVE UP ON THIS.
IF WE HAVEN'T FOUND THE BEAST BY NOW, WE'RE NOT GOING TO.
BUT ...!
IT'S NOT YOUR RESPONSI-BILITY.
BUT...
...EVEN IF SOMETHING HAS HAPPENED TO IT, IT MUST'VE HAPPENED SOME-WHERE WE'RE NOT GOING TO SEE, SO IT'S ALL RIGHT.
ALAN!!

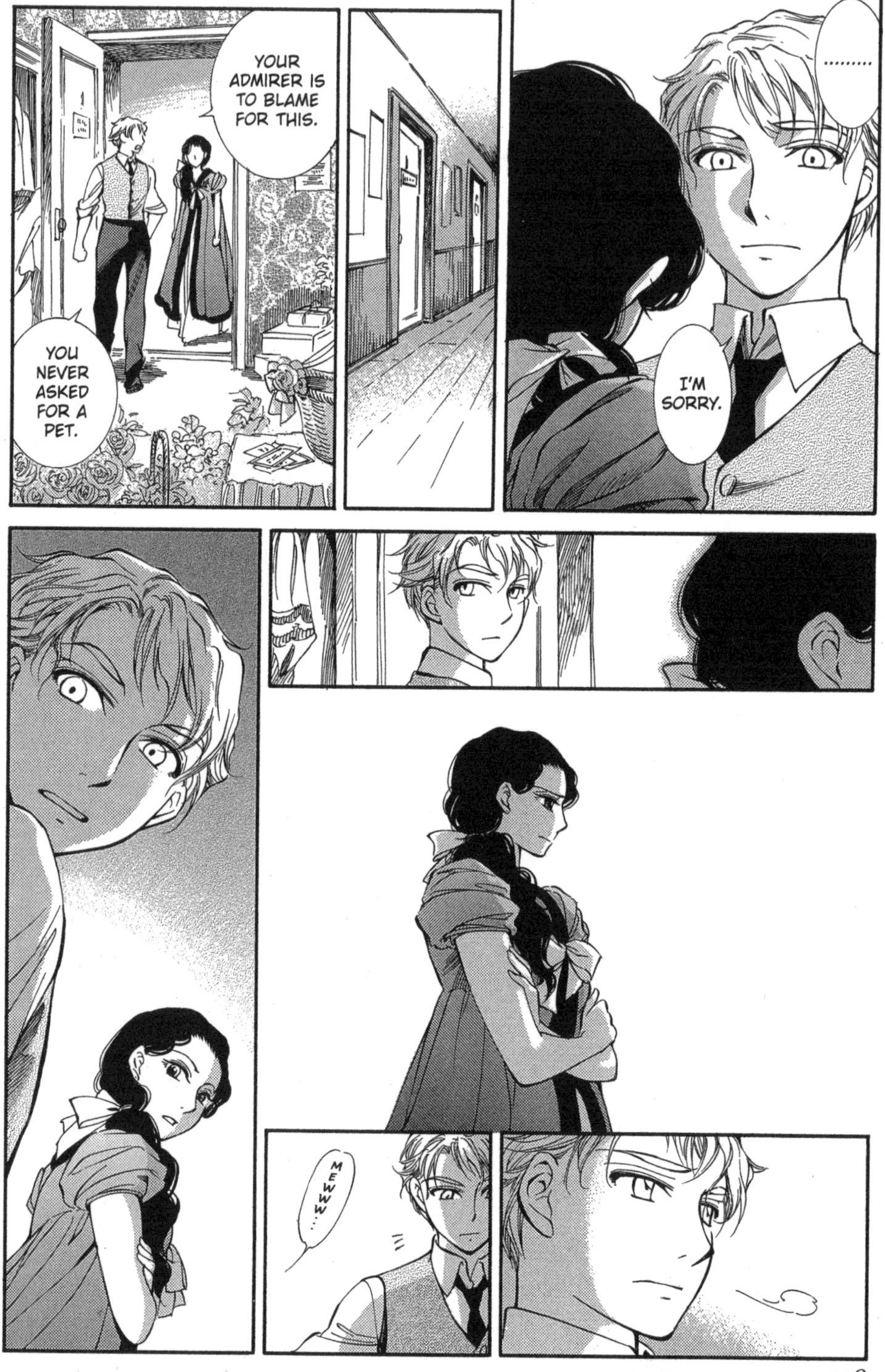
....
I'M SORRY.
YOUR ADMIRER IS TO BLAME FOR THIS.
YOU NEVER ASKED FOR A PET.
MEWWW...

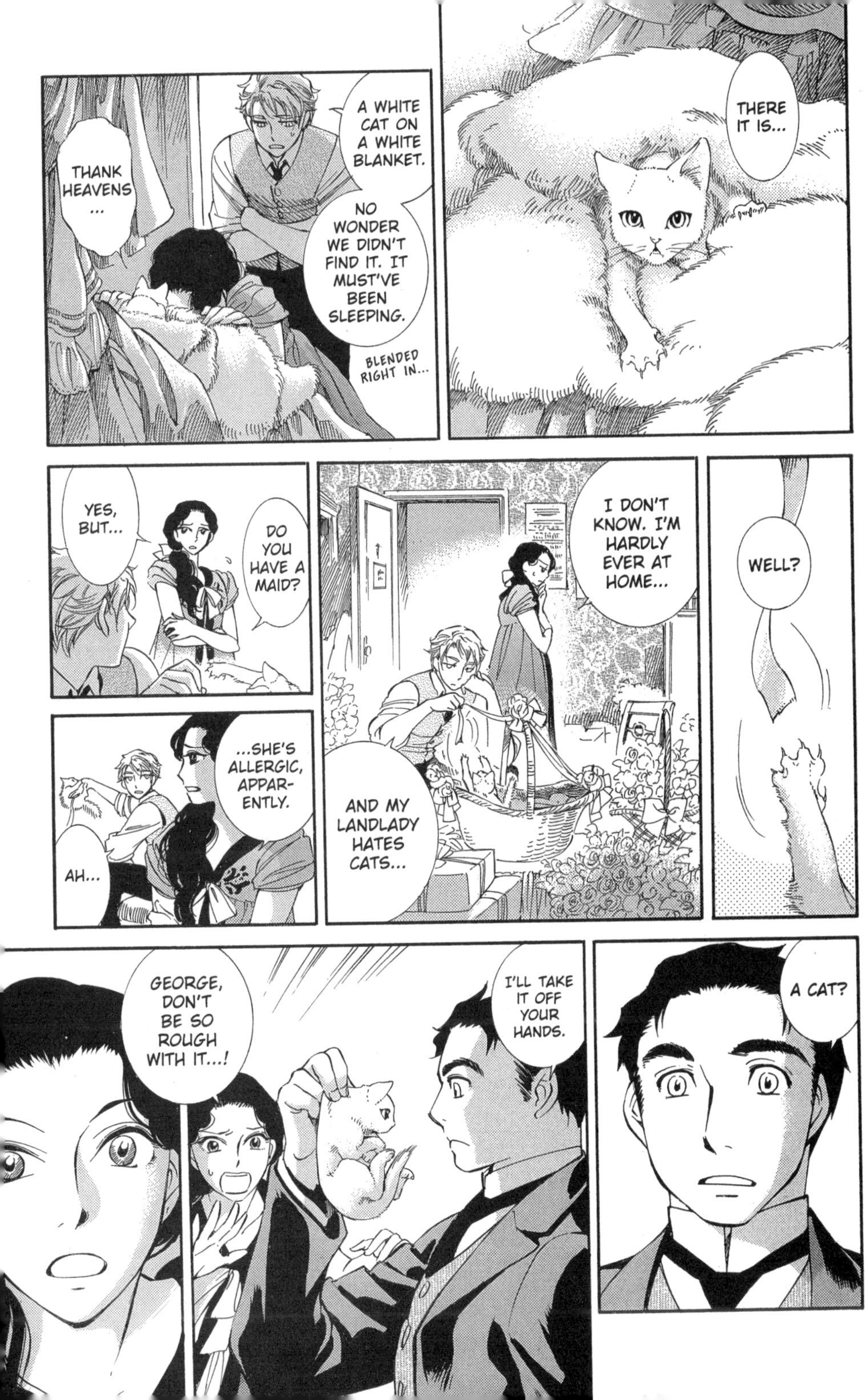
THERE IT IS...
A WHITE CAT ON A WHITE BLANKET.
NO WONDER WE DIDN'T FIND IT. IT MUST'VE BEEN SLEEPING.
BLENDED RIGHT IN...
THANK HEAVENS ...
WELL?
I DON'T KNOW. I'M HARDLY EVER AT HOME...
AND MY LANDLADY HATES CATS...
DO YOU HAVE A MAID?
YES, BUT...
...SHE'S ALLERGIC, APPARENTLY.
AH...
A CAT?
I'LL TAKE IT OFF YOUR HANDS.
GEORGE, DON'T BE SO ROUGH WITH IT...!

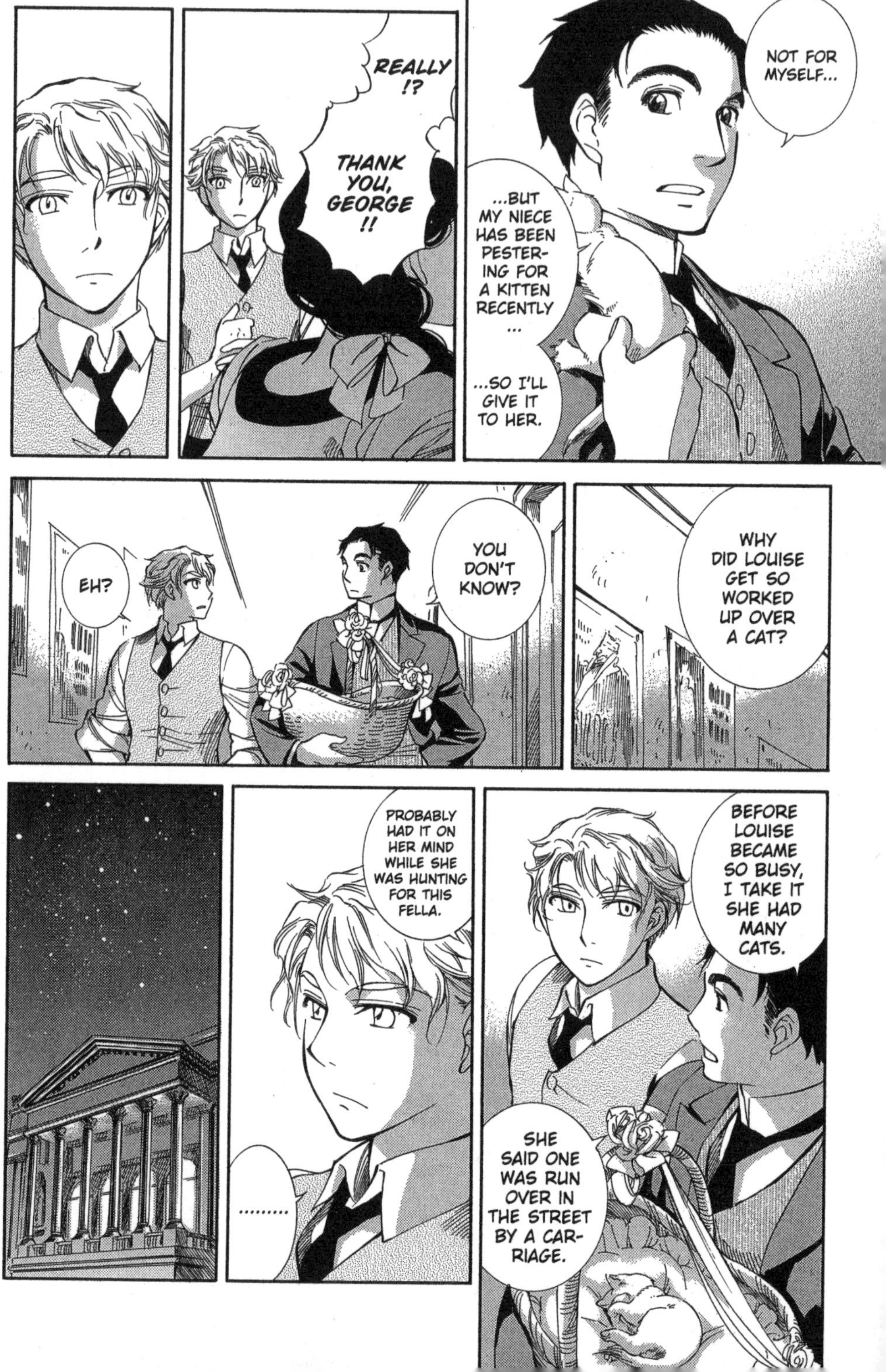
NOT FOR MYSELF...
...BUT MY NIECE HAS BEEN PESTER-ING FOR A KITTEN RECENTLY ...
...SO I'LL GIVE IT TO HER.
REALLY !?
THANK YOU, GEORGE !!
WHY DID LOUISE GET SO WORKED UP OVER A CAT?
YOU DON'T KNOW?
EH?
BEFORE LOUISE BECAME SO BUSY, I TAKE IT SHE HAD MANY CATS.
SHE SAID ONE WAS RUN OVER IN THE STREET BY A CAR-RIAGE.
PROBABLY HAD IT ON HER MIND WHILE SHE WAS HUNTING FOR THIS FELLA.
....

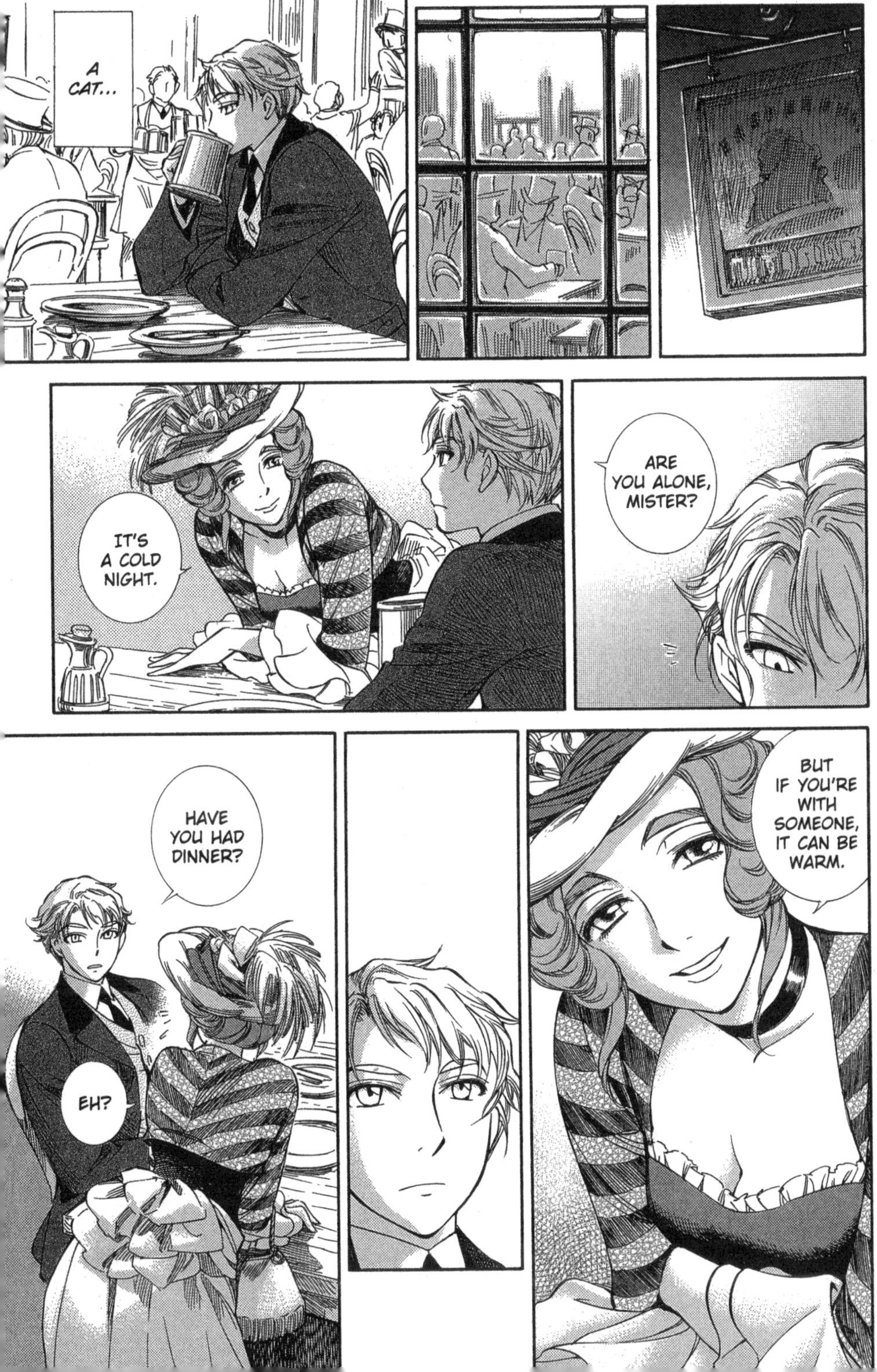
A CAT...
ARE YOU ALONE, MISTER?
IT'S A COLD NIGHT.
BUT IF YOU'RE WITH SOMEONE, IT CAN BE WARM.
HAVE YOU HAD DINNER?
EH?

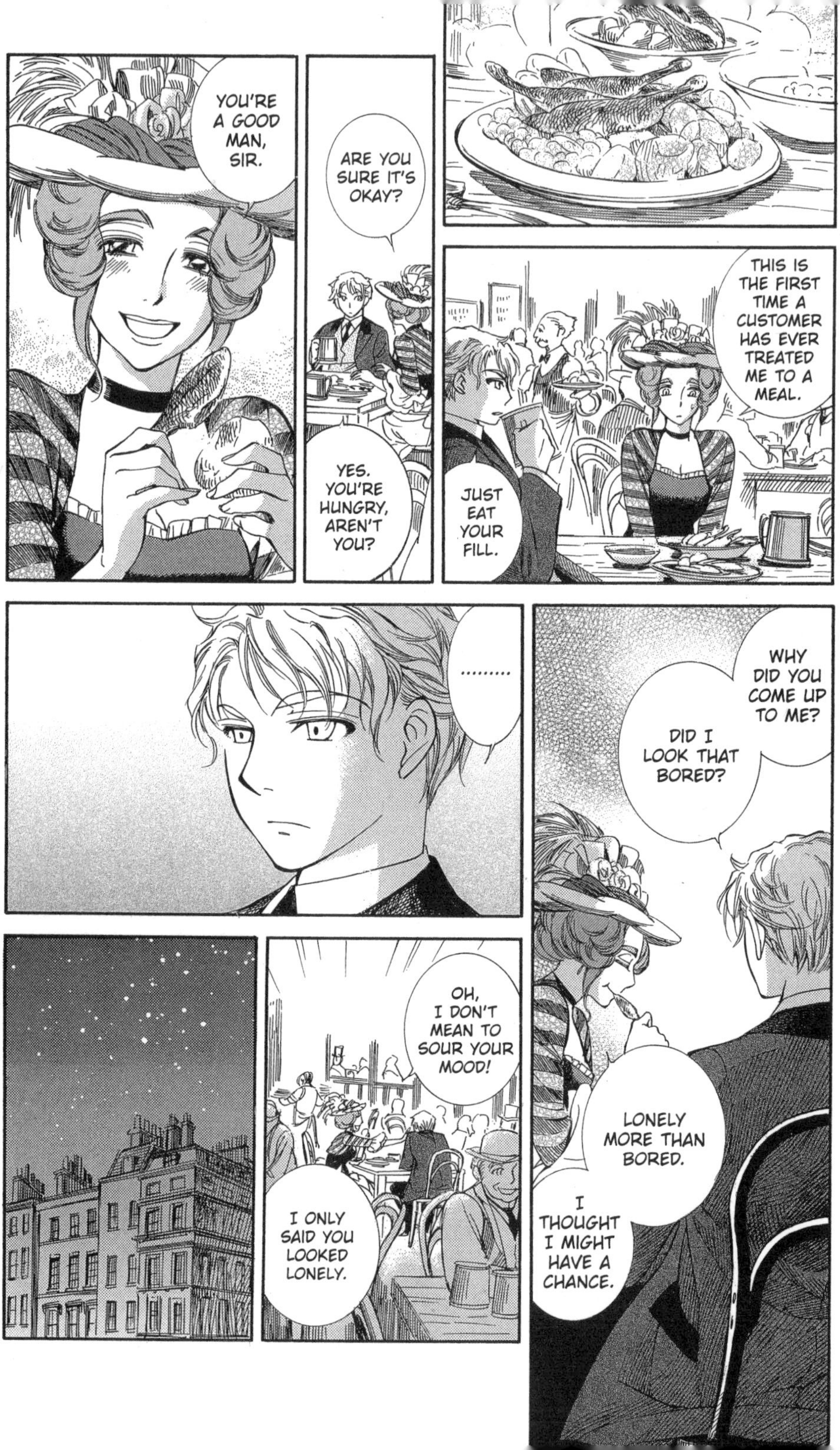
THIS IS THE FIRST TIME A CUSTOMER HAS EVER TREATED ME TO A MEAL.
JUST EAT YOUR FILL.
ARE YOU SURE IT'S OKAY?
YES. YOU'RE HUNGRY, AREN'T YOU?
YOU'RE A GOOD MAN, SIR.
WHY DID YOU COME UP TO ME?
DID I LOOK THAT BORED?
LONELY MORE THAN BORED.
I THOUGHT I MIGHT HAVE A CHANCE.
....
OH, I DON'T MEAN TO SOUR YOUR MOOD!
I ONLY SAID YOU LOOKED LONELY.

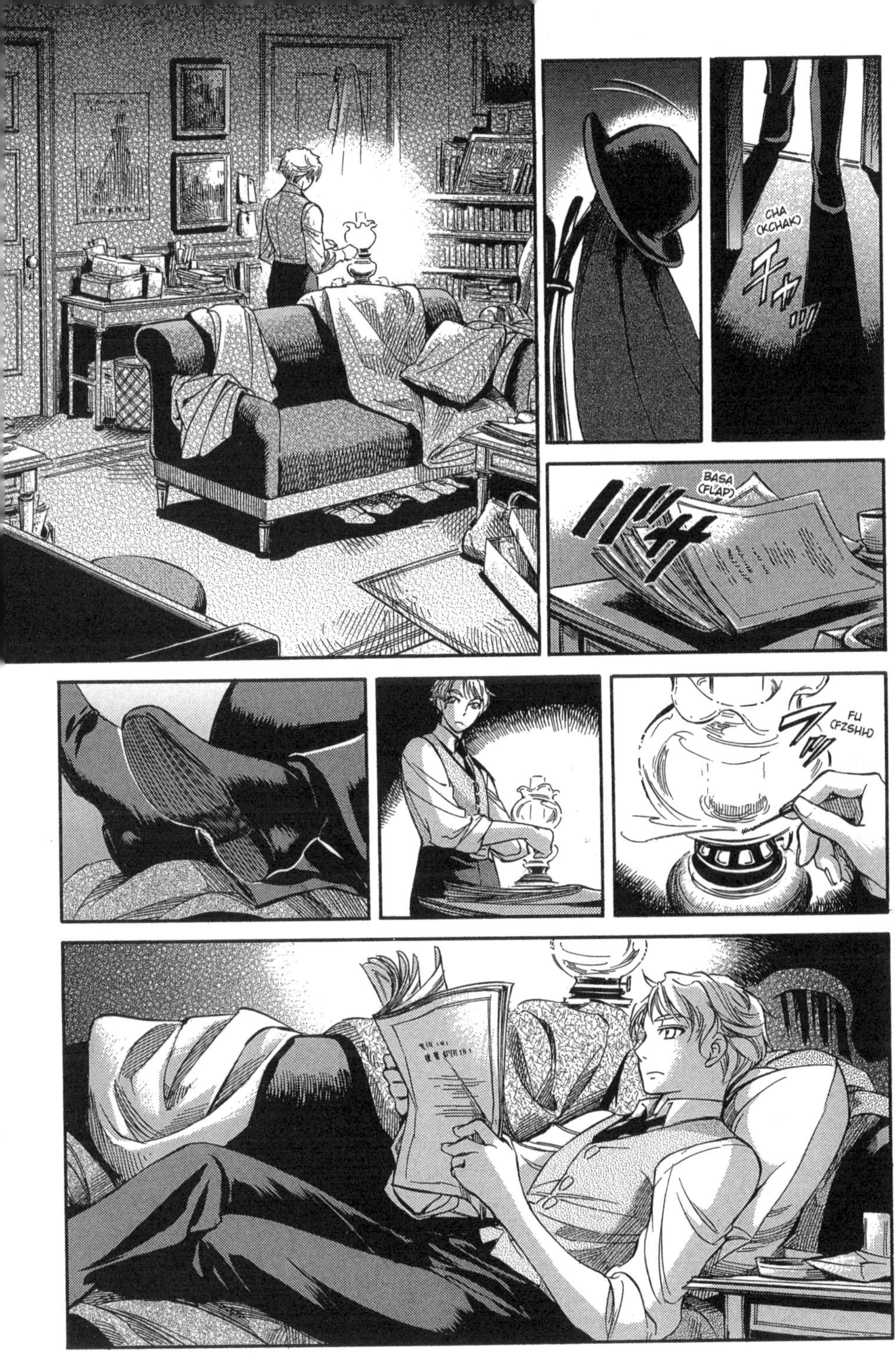
CHA (KCHAK)
チャッ
BASA (FLAP)
バサッ
FU (FZSHH)
フッ

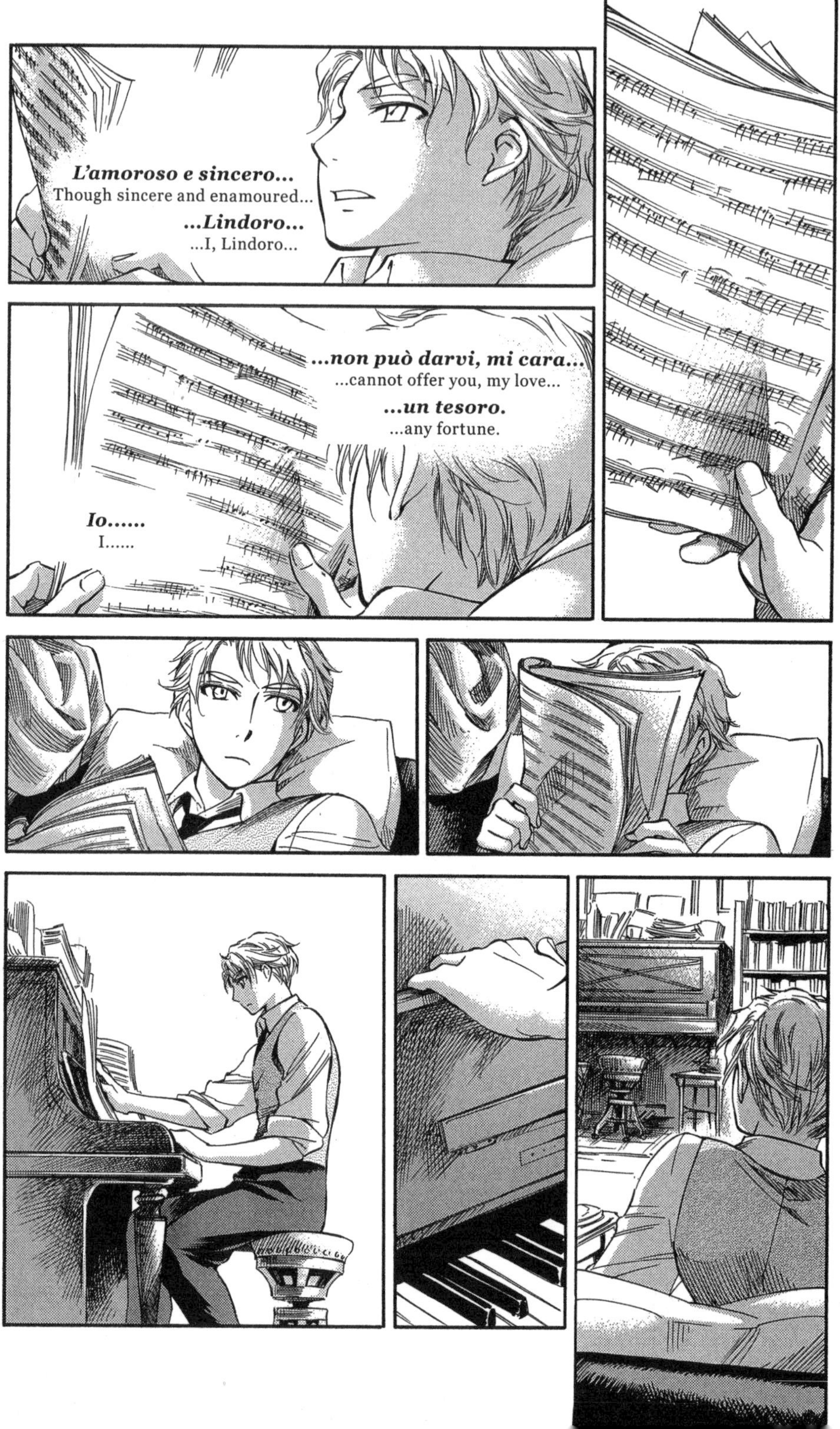
L'amoroso e sincero...
Though sincere and enamoured...
...Lindoro...
...I, Lindoro...
...non può darvi, mi cara...
...cannot offer you, my love...
...un tesoro.
...any fortune.
Io......
I......

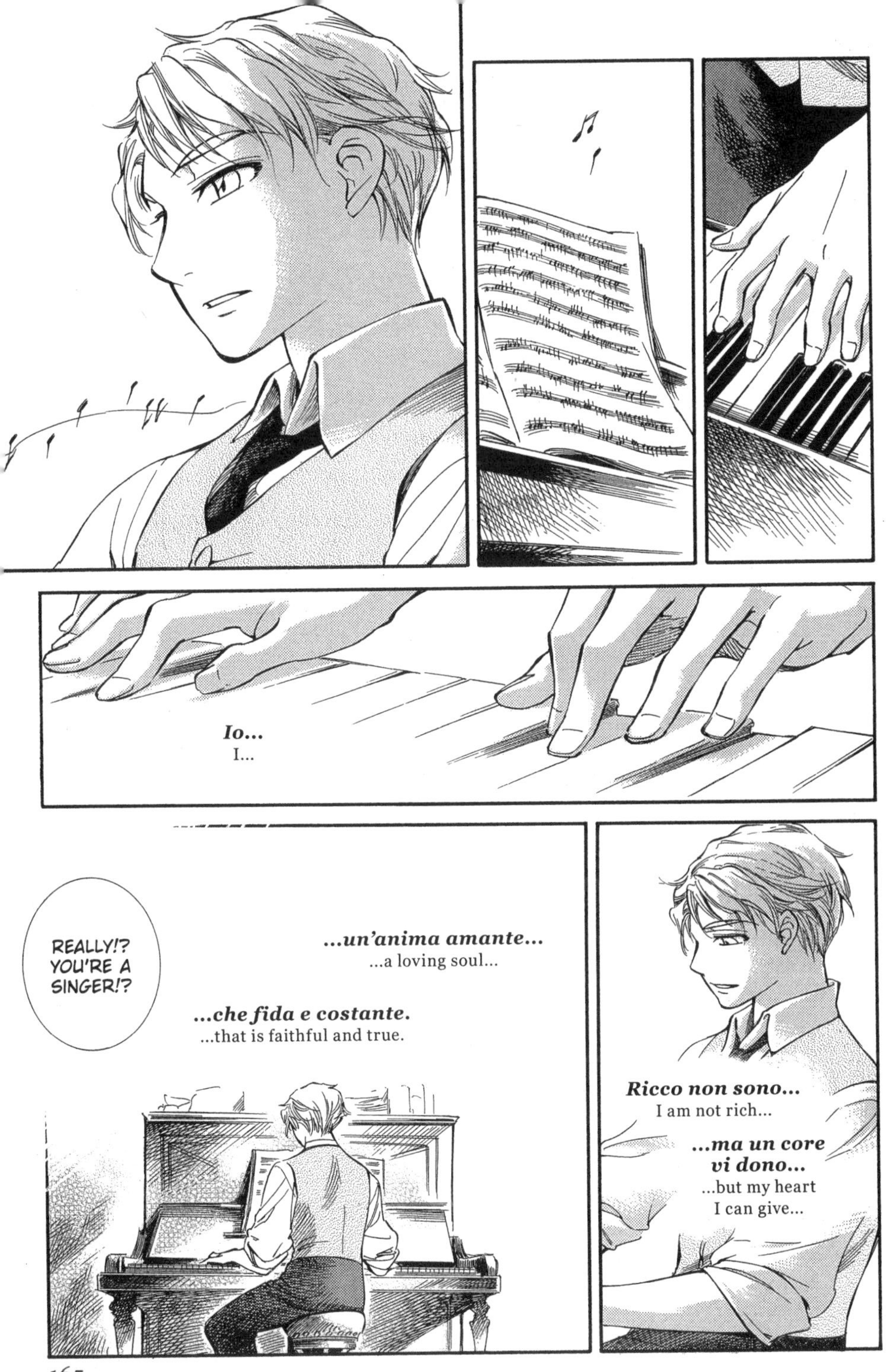
Io...
I...
Ricco non sono...
I am not rich...
...ma un core vi dono...
...but my heart I can give...
...un'anima amante...
...a loving soul...
...che fida e costante.
...that is faithful and true.
REALLY!? YOU'RE A SINGER!?

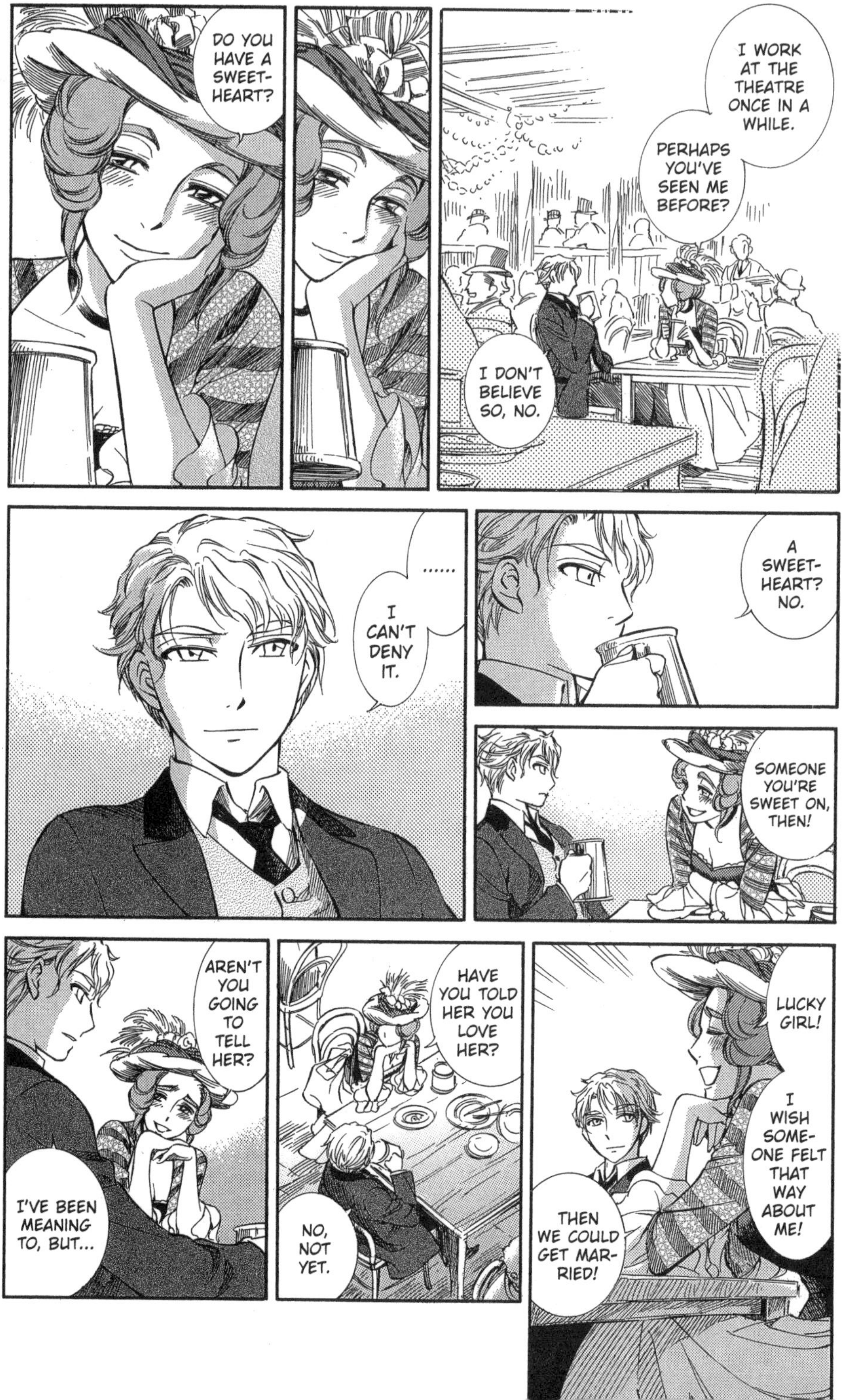
I WORK AT THE THEATRE ONCE IN A WHILE.
PERHAPS YOU'VE SEEN ME BEFORE?
I DON'T BELIEVE SO, NO.
DO YOU HAVE A SWEET-HEART?
A SWEET-HEART? NO.
SOMEONE YOU'RE SWEET ON, THEN!
......
I CAN'T DENY IT.
LUCKY GIRL!
I WISH SOME-ONE FELT THAT WAY ABOUT ME!
THEN WE COULD GET MAR-RIED!
HAVE YOU TOLD HER YOU LOVE HER?
NO, NOT YET.
AREN'T YOU GOING TO TELL HER?
I'VE BEEN MEANING TO, BUT...

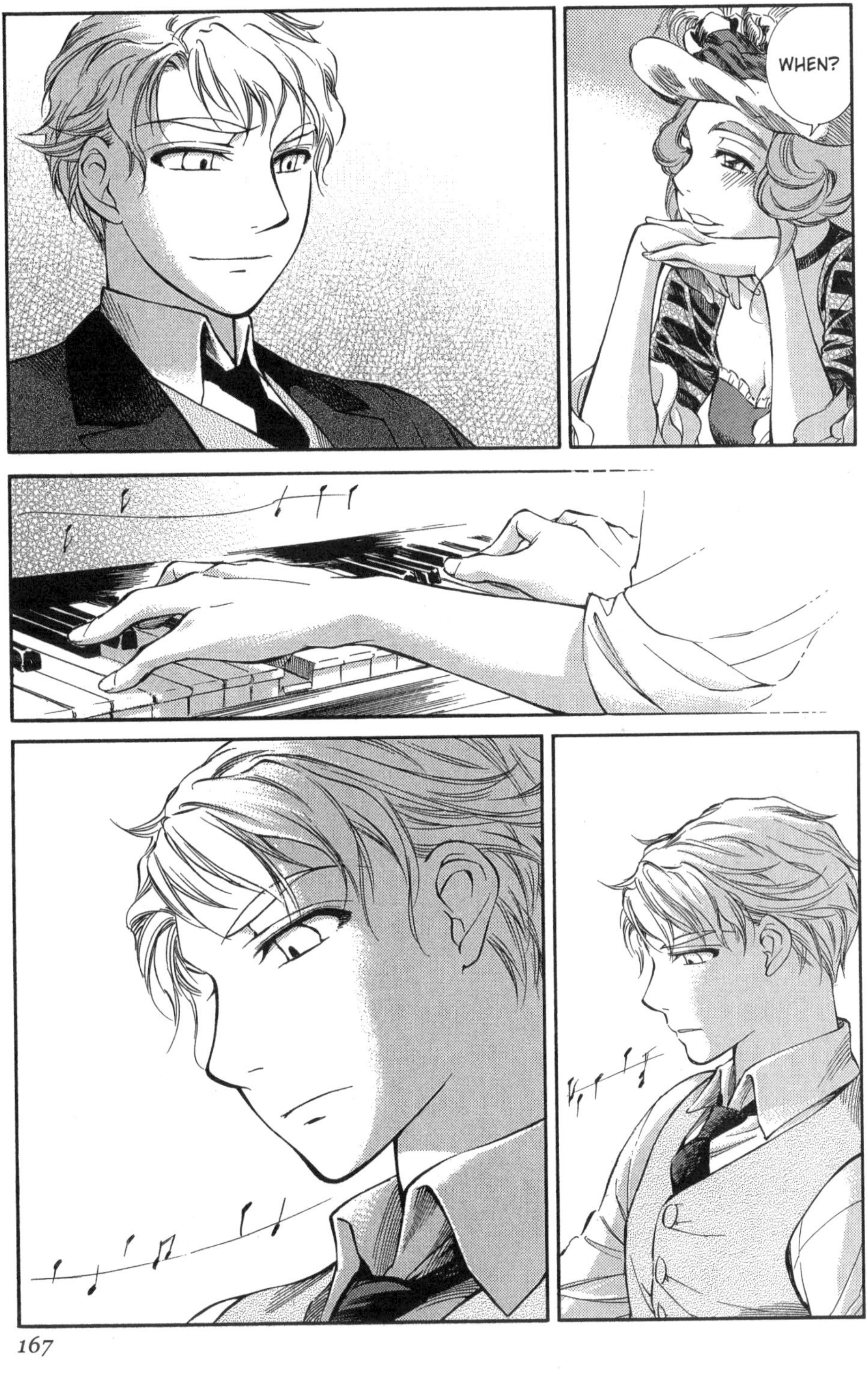
WHEN?

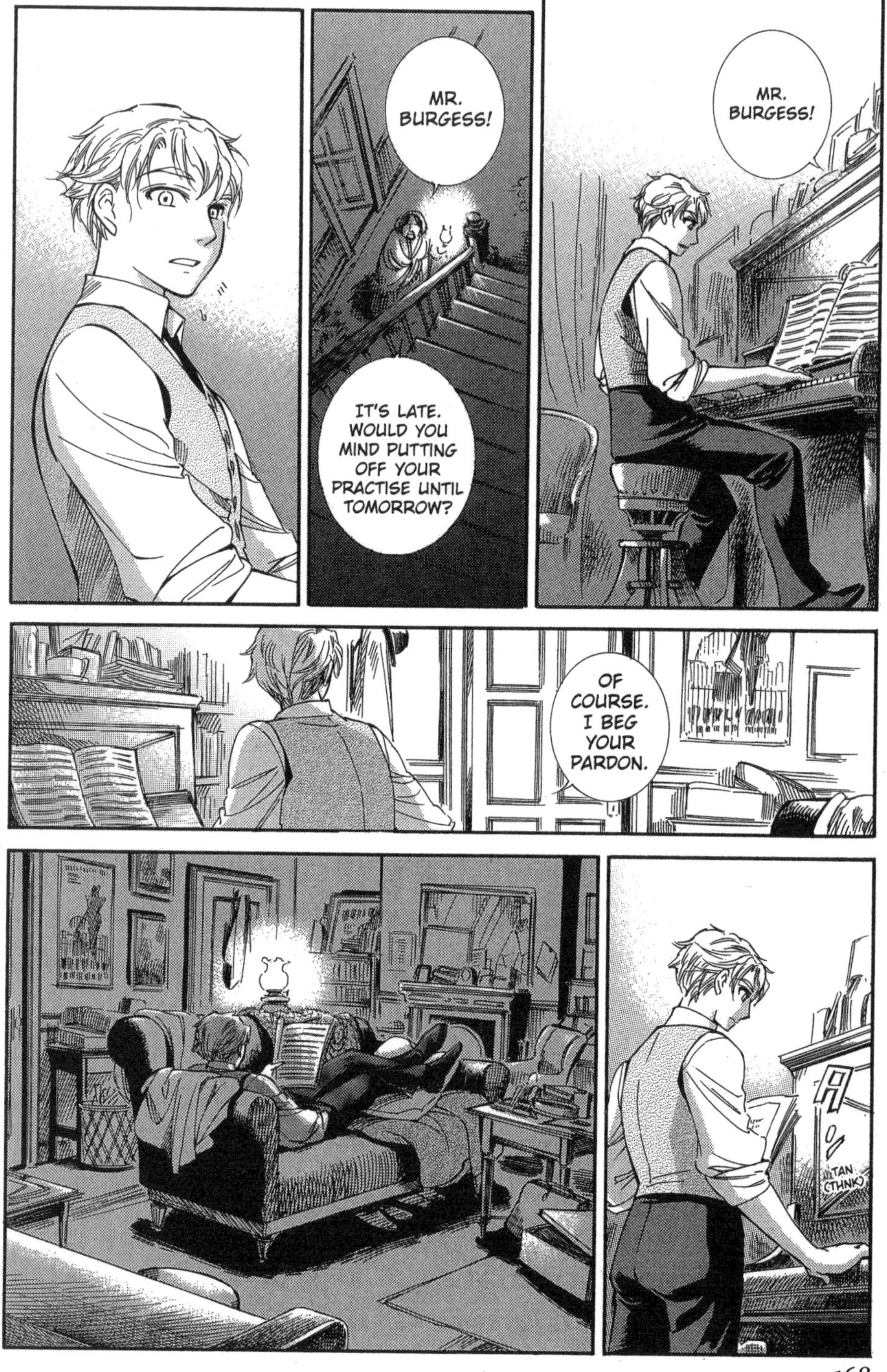
MR. BURGESS!
MR. BURGESS!
IT'S LATE. WOULD YOU MIND PUTTING OFF YOUR PRACTISE UNTIL TOMORROW?
OF COURSE. I BEG YOUR PARDON.
TAN (THNK)

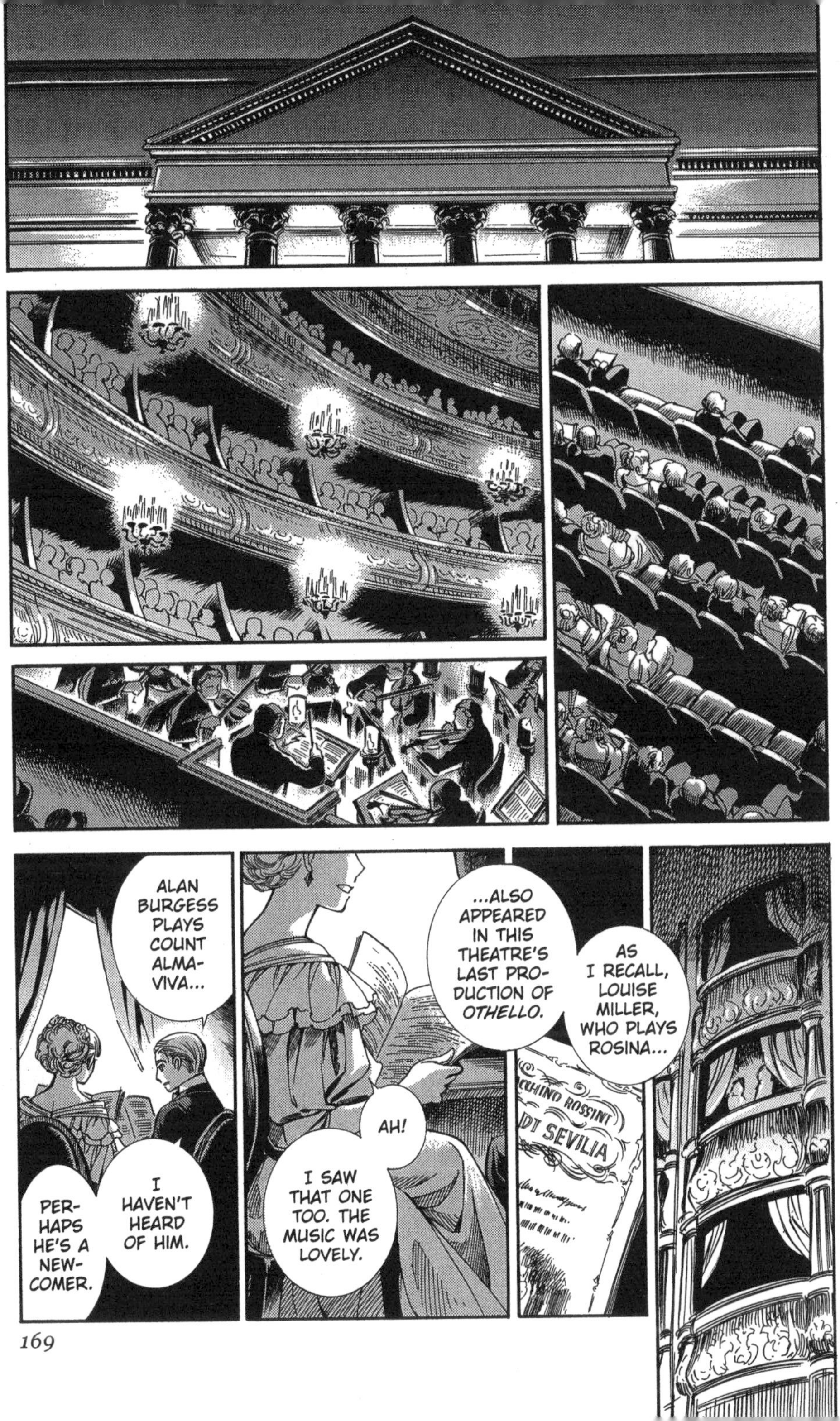
AS I RECALL, LOUISE MILLER, WHO PLAYS ROSINA...
...ALSO APPEARED IN THIS THEATRE'S LAST PRODUCTION OF *OTHELLO*.
ROSSINI
DI SEVILIA
AH!
I SAW THAT ONE TOO. THE MUSIC WAS LOVELY.
ALAN BURGESS PLAYS COUNT ALMA-VIVA...
I HAVEN'T HEARD OF HIM.
PER-HAPS HE'S A NEW-COMER.

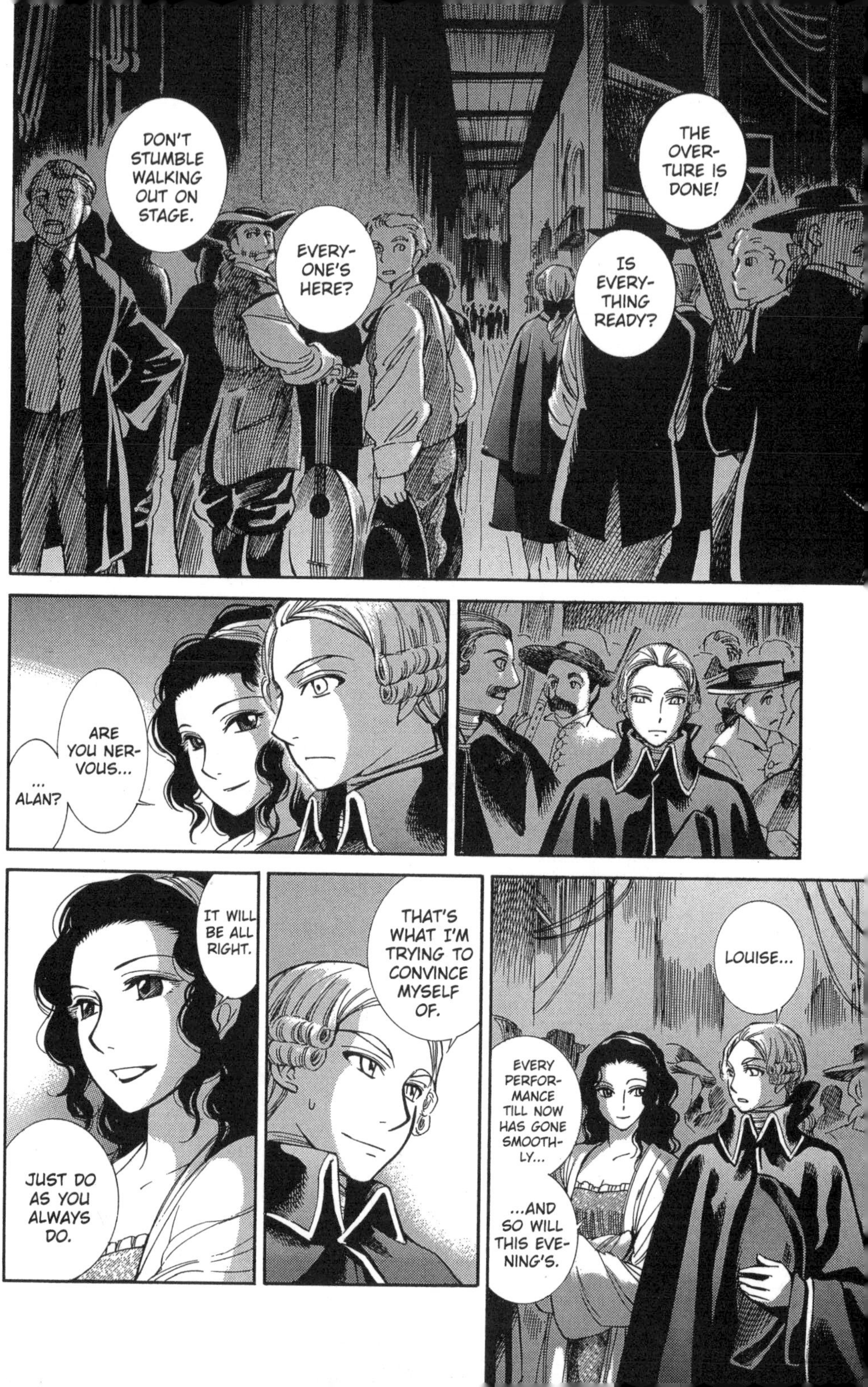
THE OVERTURE IS DONE!
IS EVERYTHING READY?
EVERYONE'S HERE?
DON'T STUMBLE WALKING OUT ON STAGE.
ARE YOU NERVOUS...
...ALAN?
LOUISE...
EVERY PERFORMANCE TILL NOW HAS GONE SMOOTHLY...
...AND SO WILL THIS EVENING'S.
THAT'S WHAT I'M TRYING TO CONVINCE MYSELF OF.
IT WILL BE ALL RIGHT.
JUST DO AS YOU ALWAYS DO.

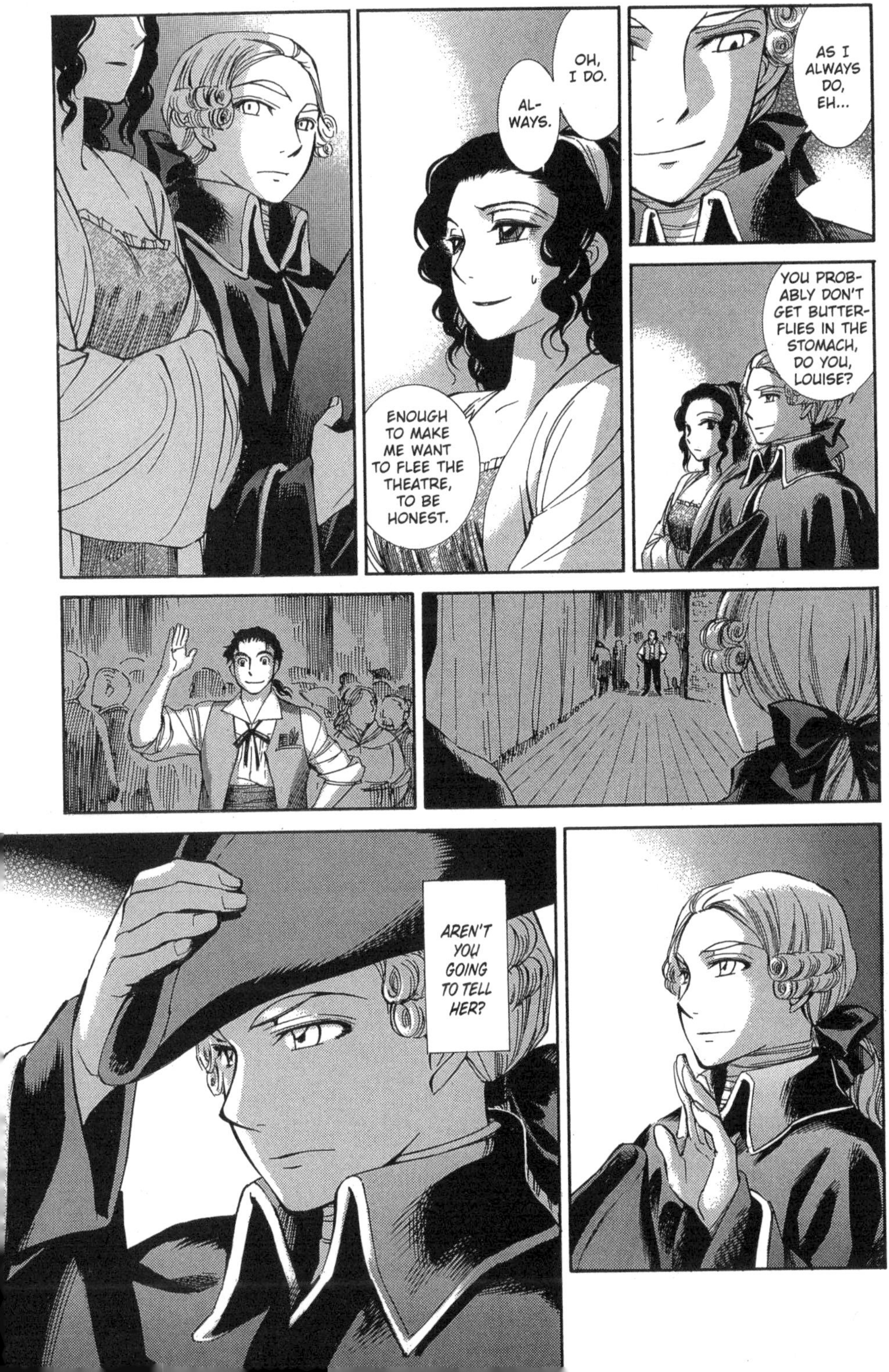
AS I ALWAYS DO, EH...
YOU PROBABLY DON'T GET BUTTERFLIES IN THE STOMACH, DO YOU, LOUISE?
OH, I DO.
ALWAYS.
ENOUGH TO MAKE ME WANT TO FLEE THE THEATRE, TO BE HONEST.
AREN'T YOU GOING TO TELL HER?

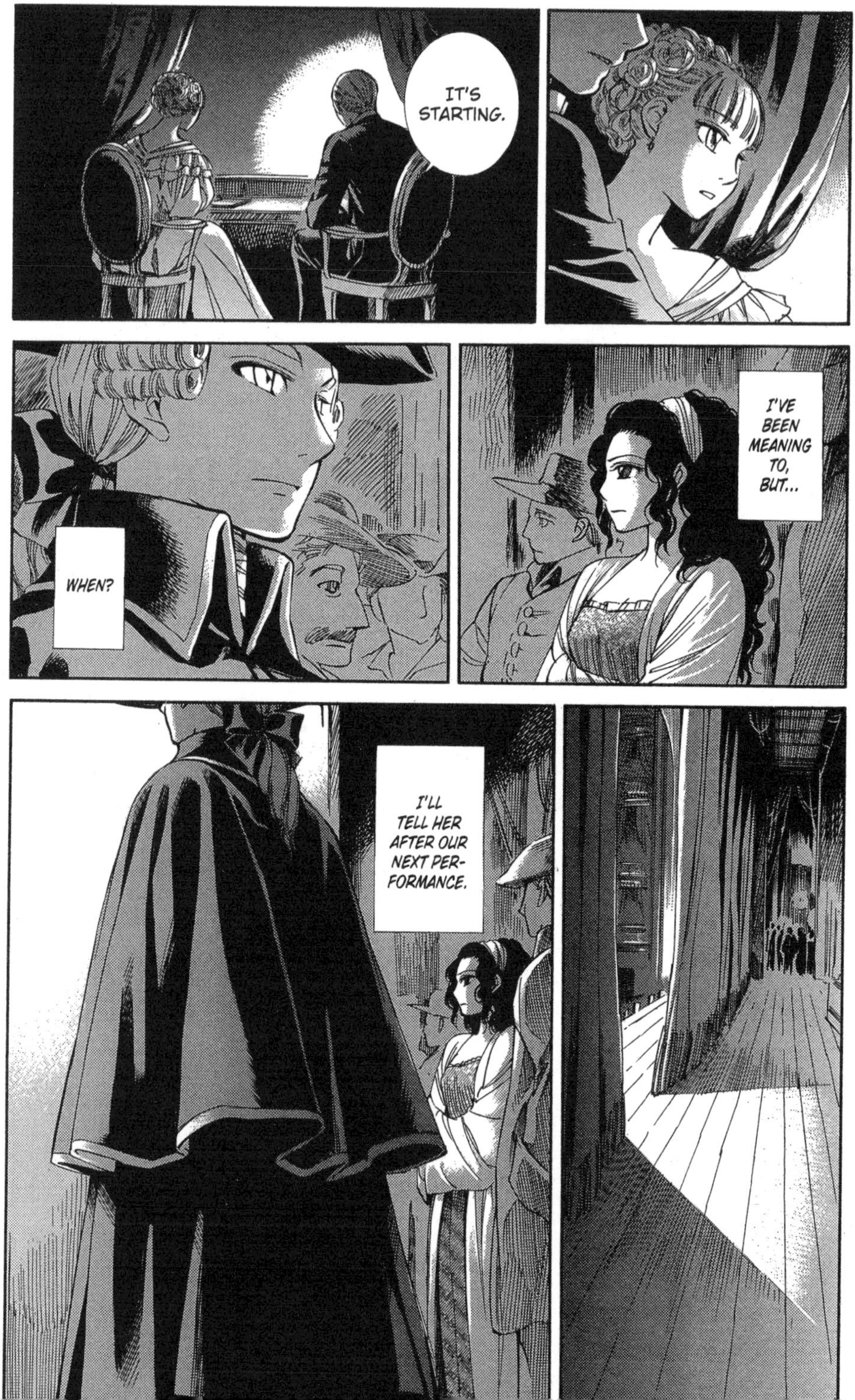
IT'S STARTING.
I'VE BEEN MEANING TO, BUT...
WHEN?
I'LL TELL HER AFTER OUR NEXT PER-FORMANCE.

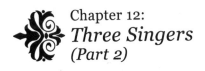

Chapter 12:
Three Singers
(Part 2)

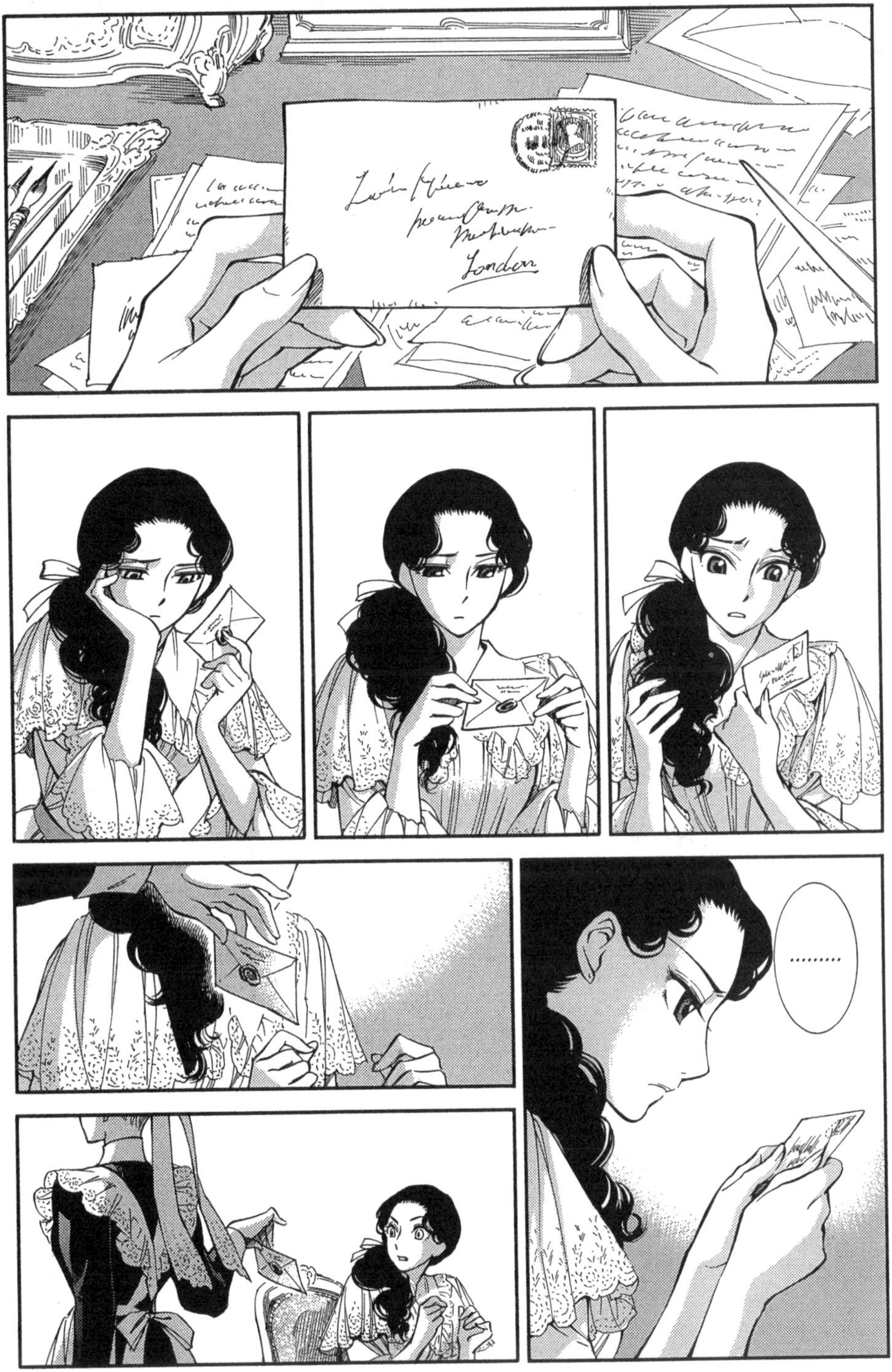
London
....

Chapter 12: *Three Singers* (Part 2)

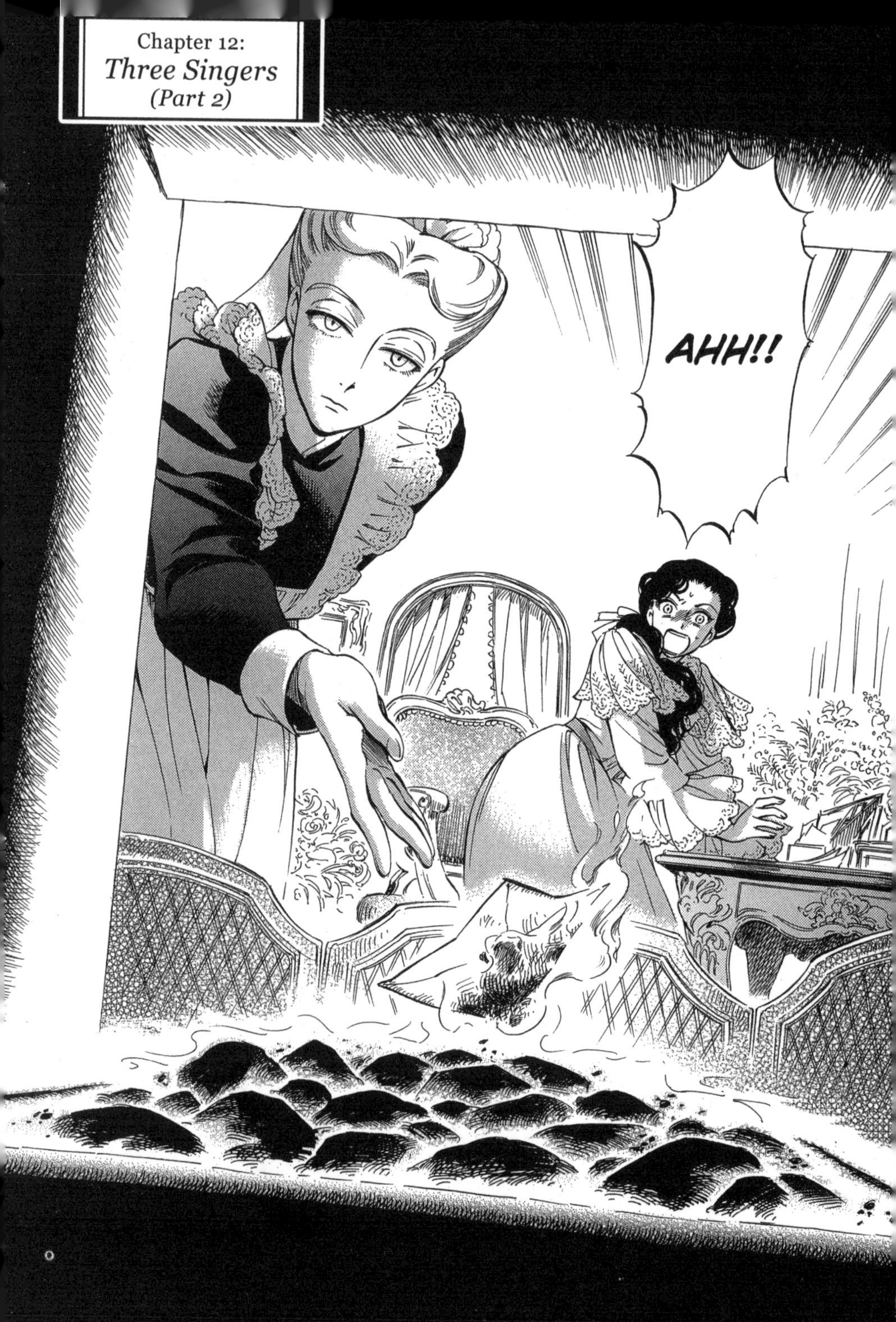

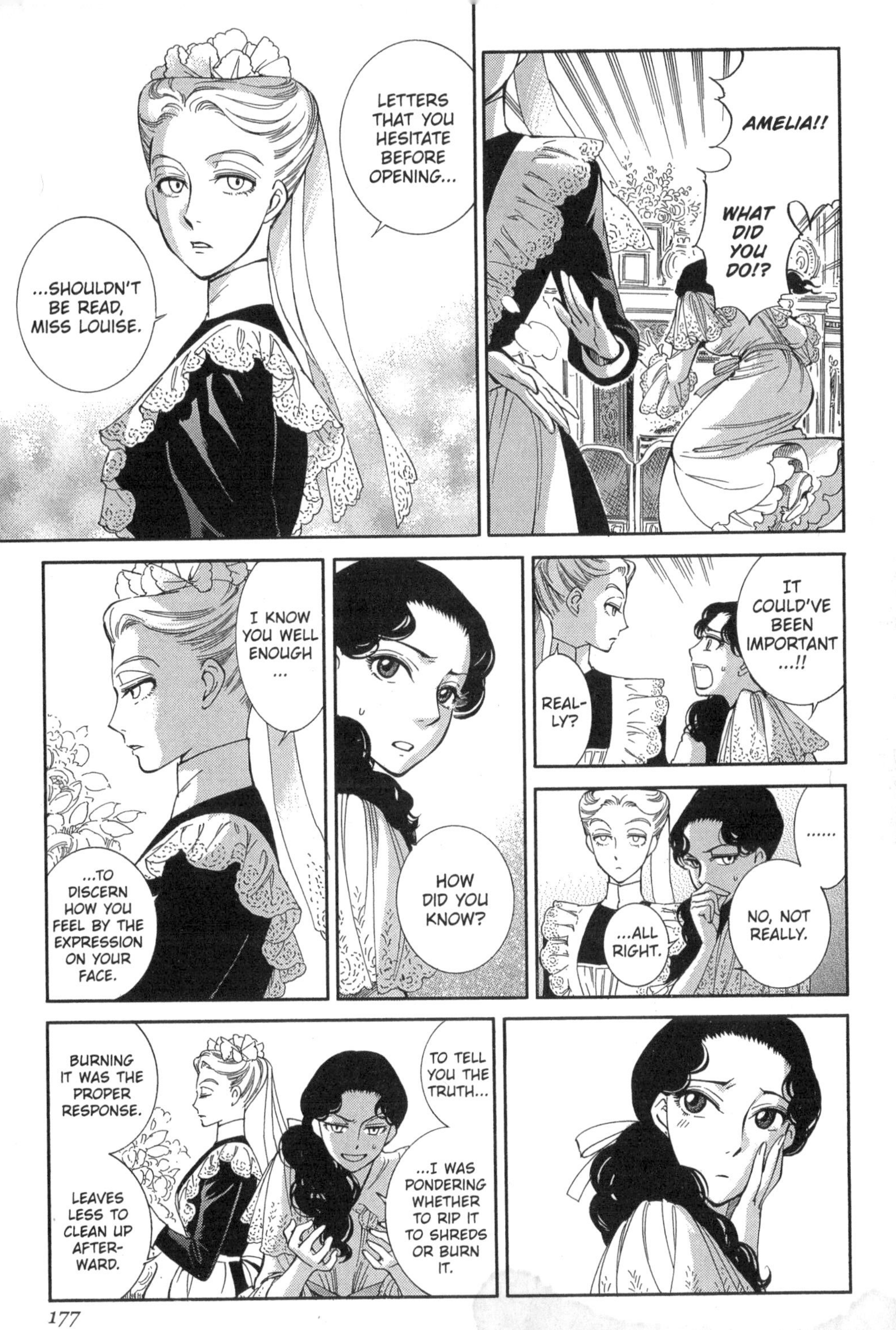
AMELIA!!
WHAT DID YOU DO!?
LETTERS THAT YOU HESITATE BEFORE OPENING...
...SHOULDN'T BE READ, MISS LOUISE.
IT COULD'VE BEEN IMPORTANT...!!
REAL-LY?
......
NO, NOT REALLY.
...ALL RIGHT.
HOW DID YOU KNOW?
I KNOW YOU WELL ENOUGH...
...TO DISCERN HOW YOU FEEL BY THE EXPRESSION ON YOUR FACE.
TO TELL YOU THE TRUTH...
...I WAS PONDERING WHETHER TO RIP IT TO SHREDS OR BURN IT.
BURNING IT WAS THE PROPER RESPONSE.
LEAVES LESS TO CLEAN UP AFTER-WARD.

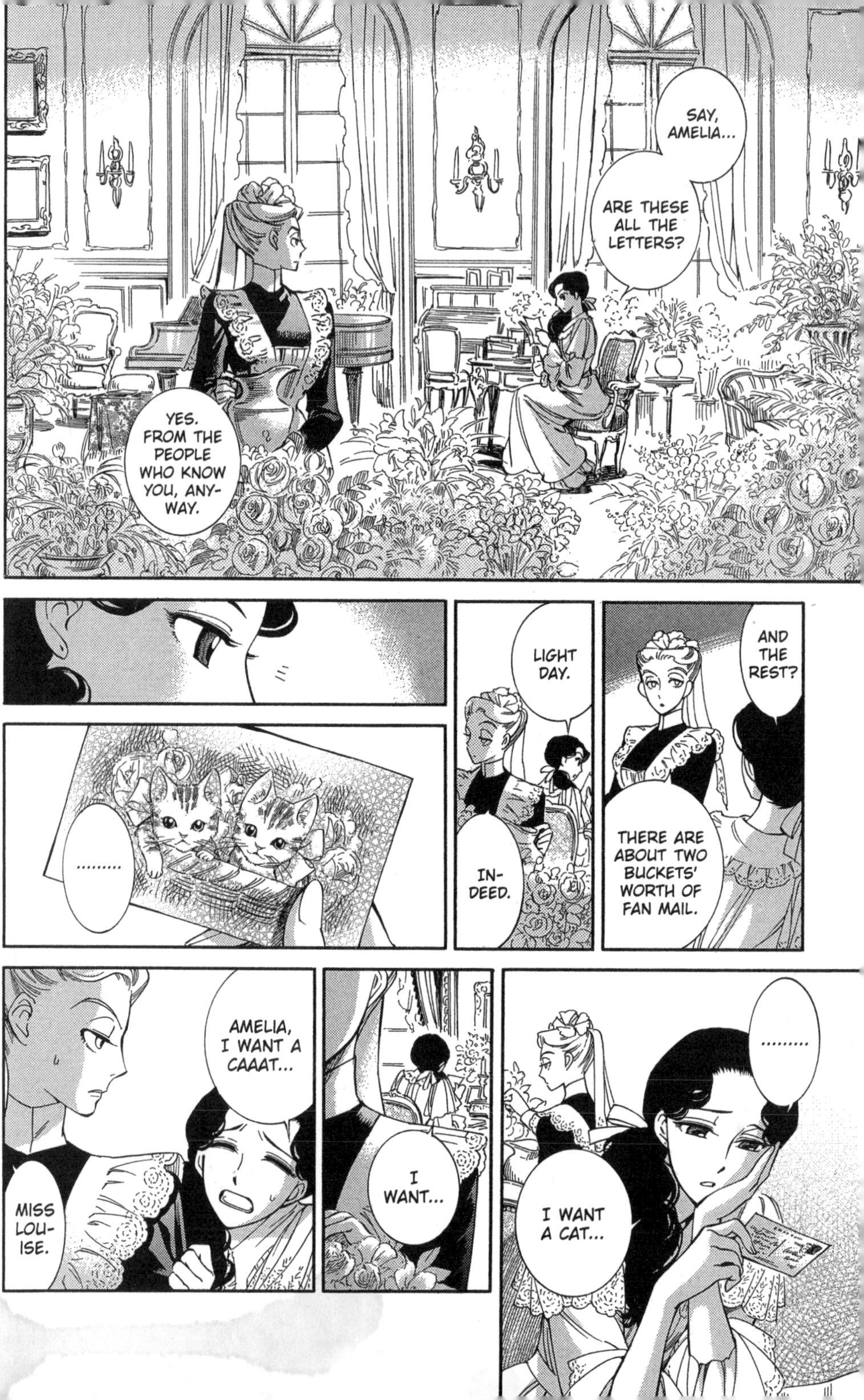
SAY, AMELIA...
ARE THESE ALL THE LETTERS?
YES. FROM THE PEOPLE WHO KNOW YOU, ANYWAY.
AND THE REST?
THERE ARE ABOUT TWO BUCKETS' WORTH OF FAN MAIL.
LIGHT DAY.
INDEED.
....
....
I WANT A CAT...
I WANT...
AMELIA, I WANT A CAAAT...
MISS LOUISE.

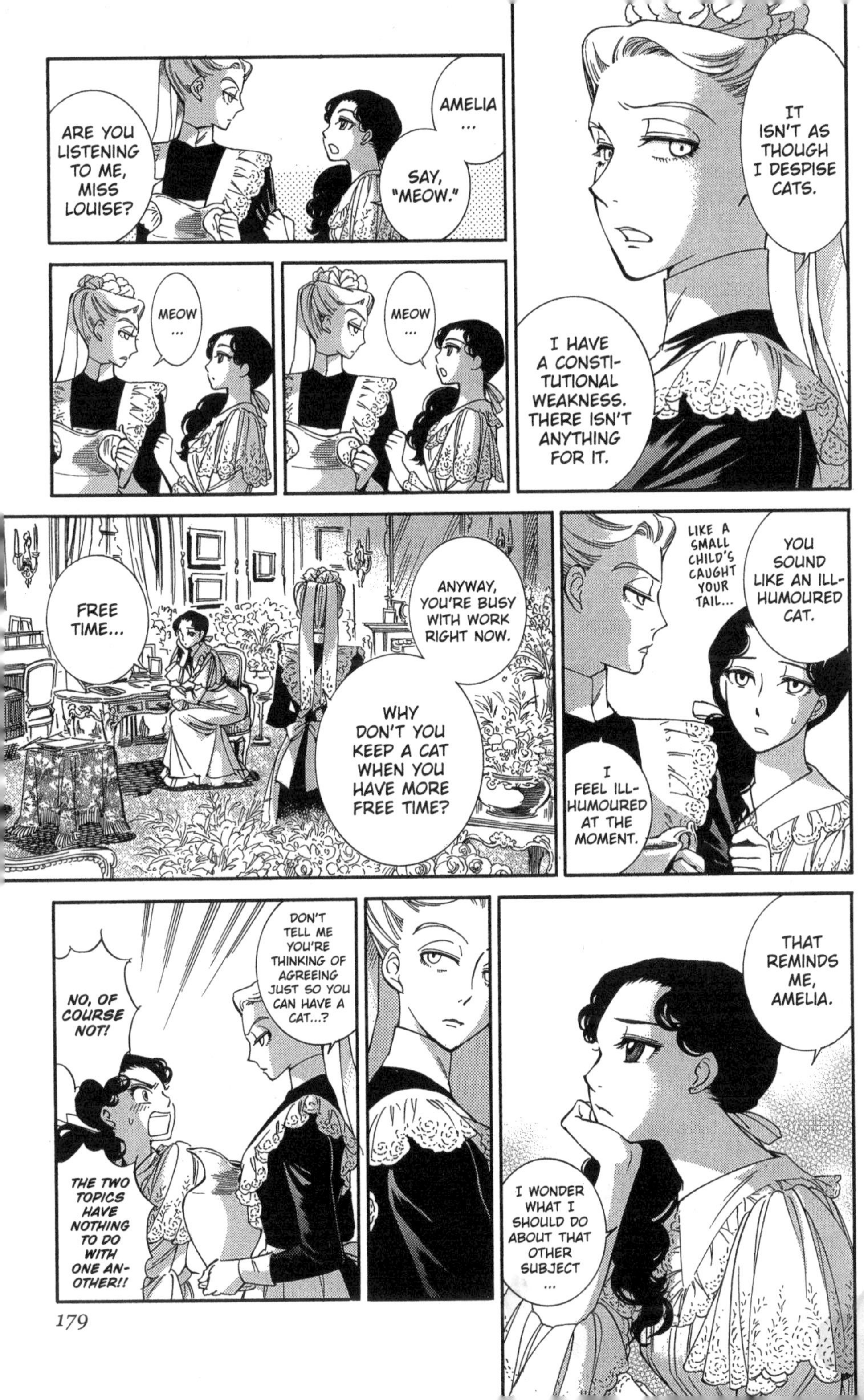
IT ISN'T AS THOUGH I DESPISE CATS.
I HAVE A CONSTITUTIONAL WEAKNESS. THERE ISN'T ANYTHING FOR IT.
AMELIA ...
SAY, "MEOW."
ARE YOU LISTENING TO ME, MISS LOUISE?
MEOW ...
MEOW ...
YOU SOUND LIKE AN ILL-HUMOURED CAT.
LIKE A SMALL CHILD'S CAUGHT YOUR TAIL...
I FEEL ILL-HUMOURED AT THE MOMENT.
ANYWAY, YOU'RE BUSY WITH WORK RIGHT NOW.
WHY DON'T YOU KEEP A CAT WHEN YOU HAVE MORE FREE TIME?
FREE TIME...
THAT REMINDS ME, AMELIA.
I WONDER WHAT I SHOULD DO ABOUT THAT OTHER SUBJECT ...
DON'T TELL ME YOU'RE THINKING OF AGREEING JUST SO YOU CAN HAVE A CAT...?
NO, OF COURSE NOT!
THE TWO TOPICS HAVE NOTHING TO DO WITH ONE ANOTHER!!

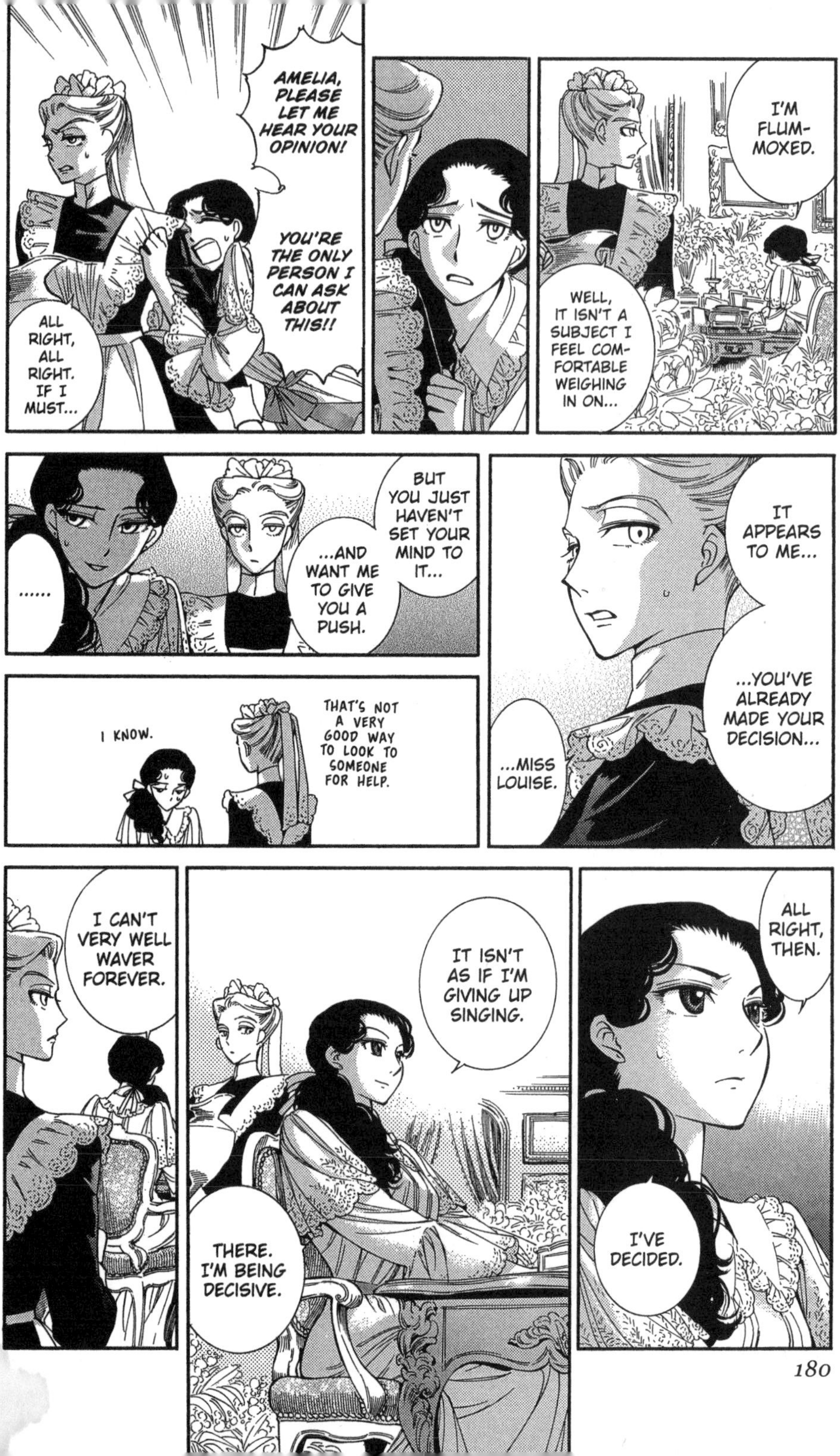
I'M FLUM-MOXED.
WELL, IT ISN'T A SUBJECT I FEEL COM-FORTABLE WEIGHING IN ON...
AMELIA, PLEASE LET ME HEAR YOUR OPINION!
YOU'RE THE ONLY PERSON I CAN ASK ABOUT THIS!!
ALL RIGHT, ALL RIGHT. IF I MUST...
IT APPEARS TO ME...
...YOU'VE ALREADY MADE YOUR DECISION...
...MISS LOUISE.
BUT YOU JUST HAVEN'T SET YOUR MIND TO IT...
...AND WANT ME TO GIVE YOU A PUSH.
......
THAT'S NOT A VERY GOOD WAY TO LOOK TO SOMEONE FOR HELP.
I KNOW.
ALL RIGHT, THEN.
I'VE DECIDED.
IT ISN'T AS IF I'M GIVING UP SINGING.
THERE. I'M BEING DECISIVE.
I CAN'T VERY WELL WAVER FOREVER.

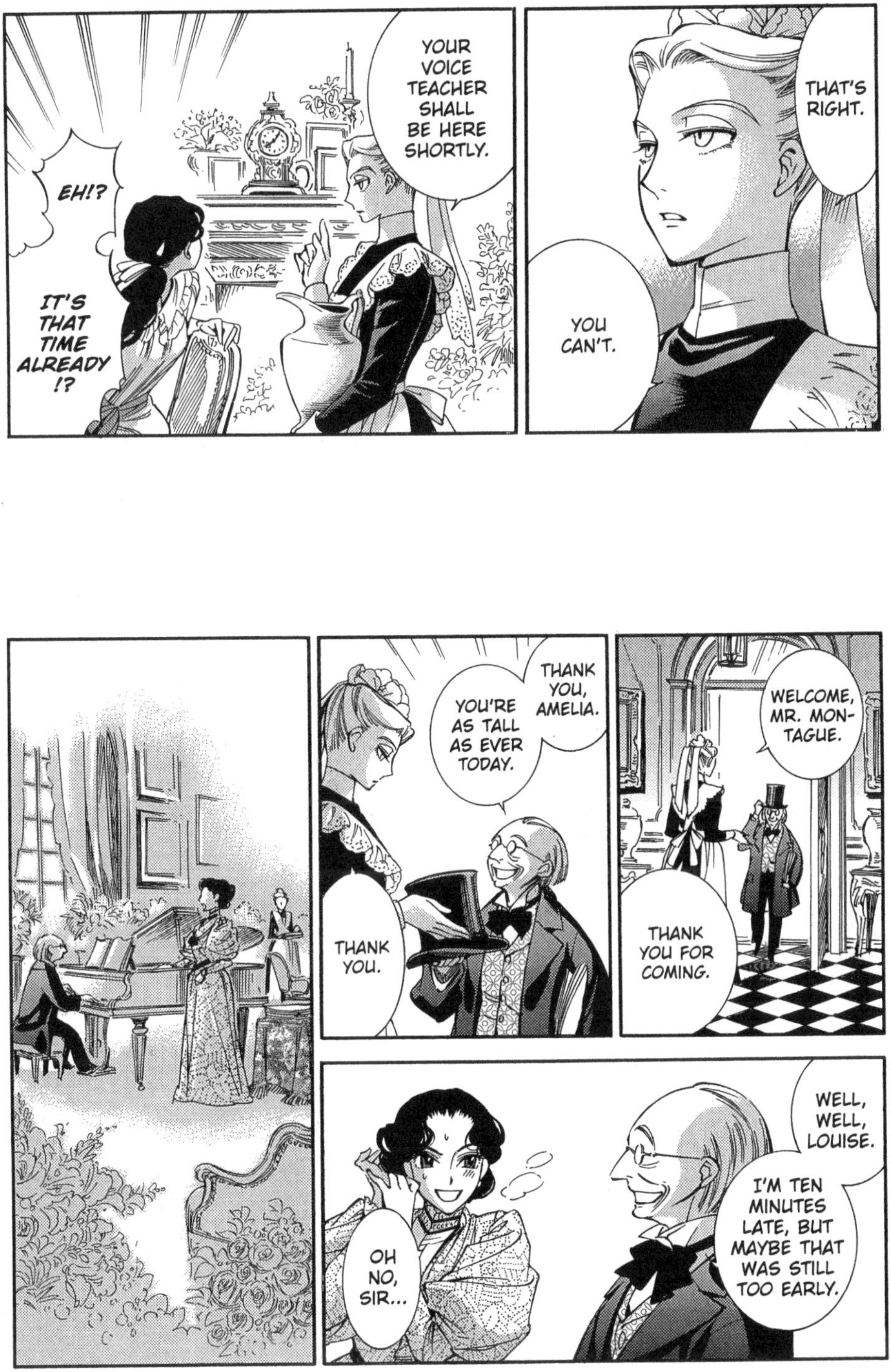
THAT'S RIGHT.
YOU CAN'T.
YOUR VOICE TEACHER SHALL BE HERE SHORTLY.
EH!?
IT'S THAT TIME ALREADY !?
WELCOME, MR. MON-TAGUE.
THANK YOU FOR COMING.
THANK YOU, AMELIA.
YOU'RE AS TALL AS EVER TODAY.
THANK YOU.
WELL, WELL, LOUISE.
I'M TEN MINUTES LATE, BUT MAYBE THAT WAS STILL TOO EARLY.
OH NO, SIR...

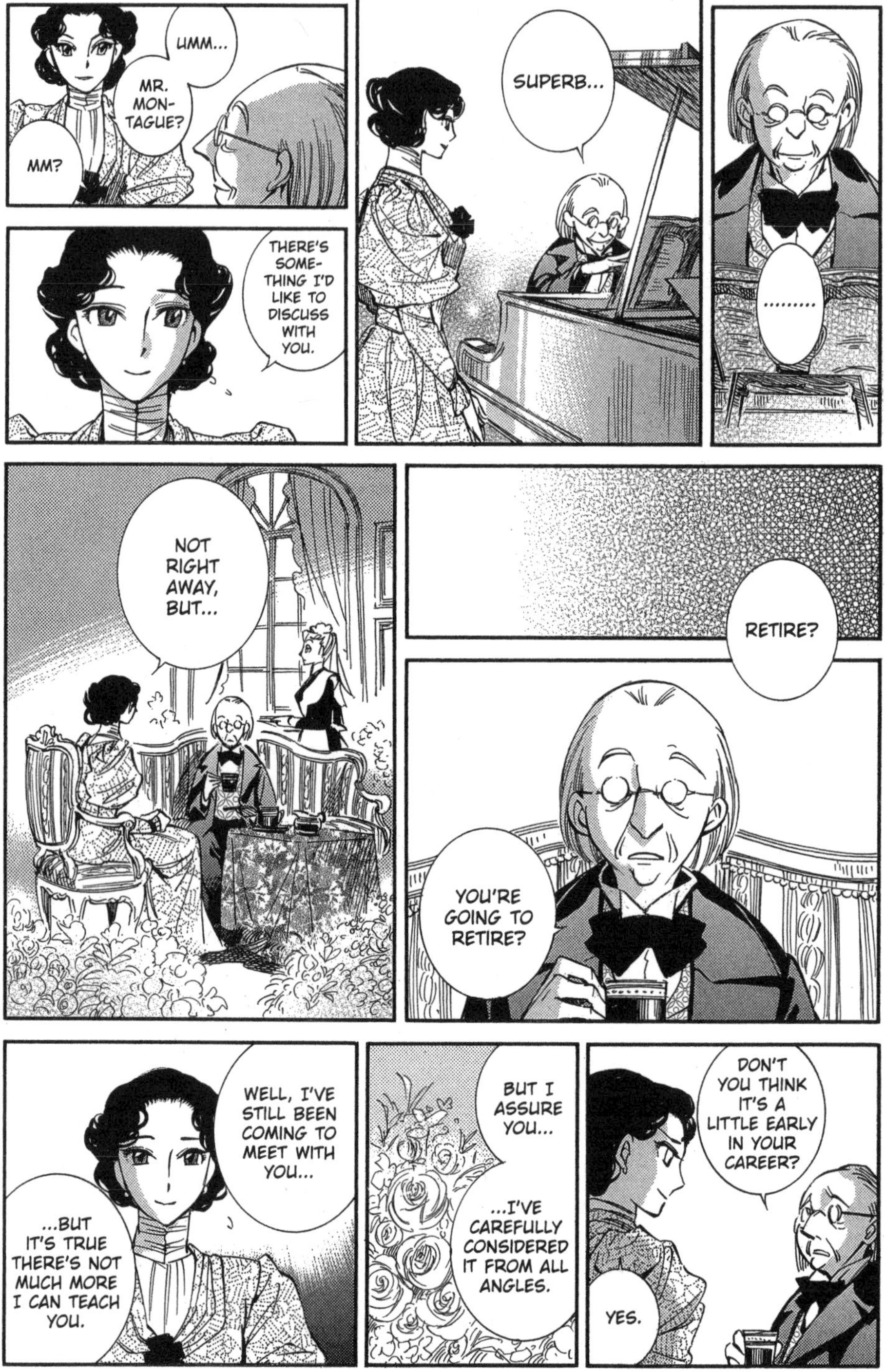
....
SUPERB...
UMM...
MR. MONTAGUE?
MM?
THERE'S SOMETHING I'D LIKE TO DISCUSS WITH YOU.
RETIRE?
YOU'RE GOING TO RETIRE?
NOT RIGHT AWAY, BUT...
DON'T YOU THINK IT'S A LITTLE EARLY IN YOUR CAREER?
YES.
BUT I ASSURE YOU...
...I'VE CAREFULLY CONSIDERED IT FROM ALL ANGLES.
WELL, I'VE STILL BEEN COMING TO MEET WITH YOU...
...BUT IT'S TRUE THERE'S NOT MUCH MORE I CAN TEACH YOU.

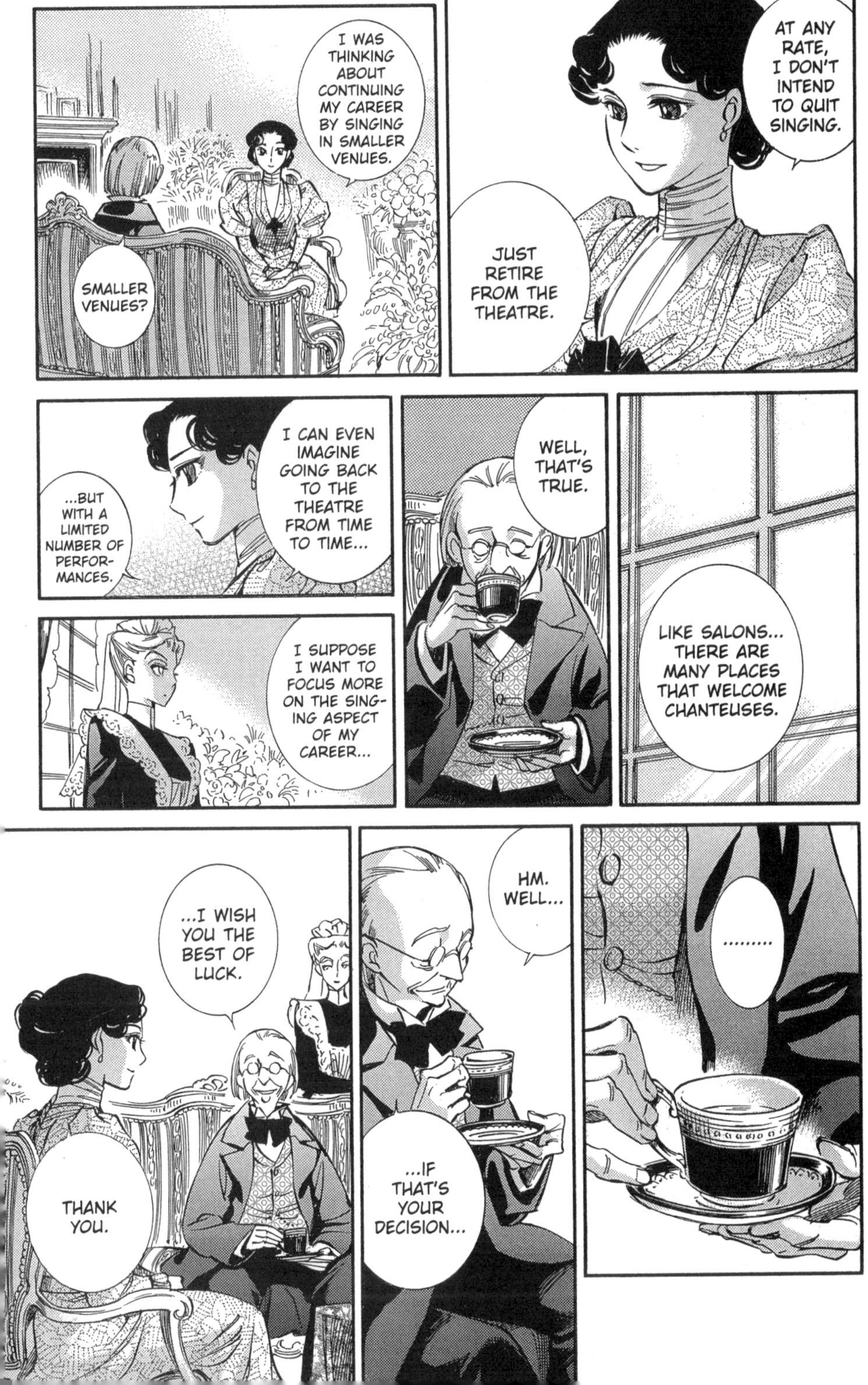
AT ANY RATE, I DON'T INTEND TO QUIT SINGING.
JUST RETIRE FROM THE THEATRE.
I WAS THINKING ABOUT CONTINUING MY CAREER BY SINGING IN SMALLER VENUES.
SMALLER VENUES?
LIKE SALONS... THERE ARE MANY PLACES THAT WELCOME CHANTEUSES.
WELL, THAT'S TRUE.
I CAN EVEN IMAGINE GOING BACK TO THE THEATRE FROM TIME TO TIME...
...BUT WITH A LIMITED NUMBER OF PERFOR-MANCES.
I SUPPOSE I WANT TO FOCUS MORE ON THE SING-ING ASPECT OF MY CAREER...
....
HM. WELL...
...IF THAT'S YOUR DECISION...
...I WISH YOU THE BEST OF LUCK.
THANK YOU.

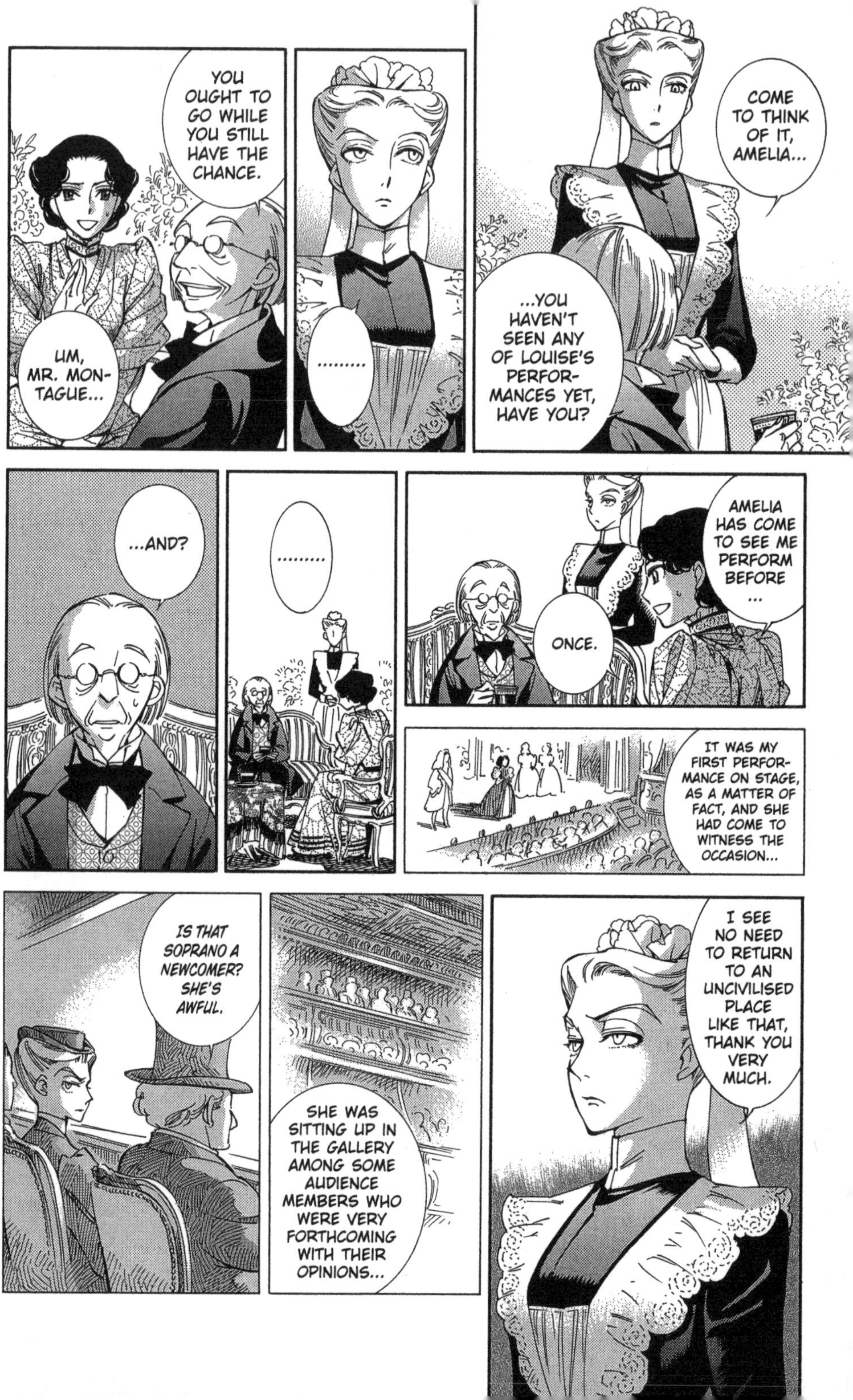
COME TO THINK OF IT, AMELIA...
...YOU HAVEN'T SEEN ANY OF LOUISE'S PERFORMANCES YET, HAVE YOU?
....
YOU OUGHT TO GO WHILE YOU STILL HAVE THE CHANCE.
UM, MR. MONTAGUE...
AMELIA HAS COME TO SEE ME PERFORM BEFORE ...
ONCE.
IT WAS MY FIRST PERFORMANCE ON STAGE, AS A MATTER OF FACT, AND SHE HAD COME TO WITNESS THE OCCASION...
....
...AND?
I SEE NO NEED TO RETURN TO AN UNCIVILISED PLACE LIKE THAT, THANK YOU VERY MUCH.
SHE WAS SITTING UP IN THE GALLERY AMONG SOME AUDIENCE MEMBERS WHO WERE VERY FORTHCOMING WITH THEIR OPINIONS...
IS THAT SOPRANO A NEWCOMER? SHE'S AWFUL.

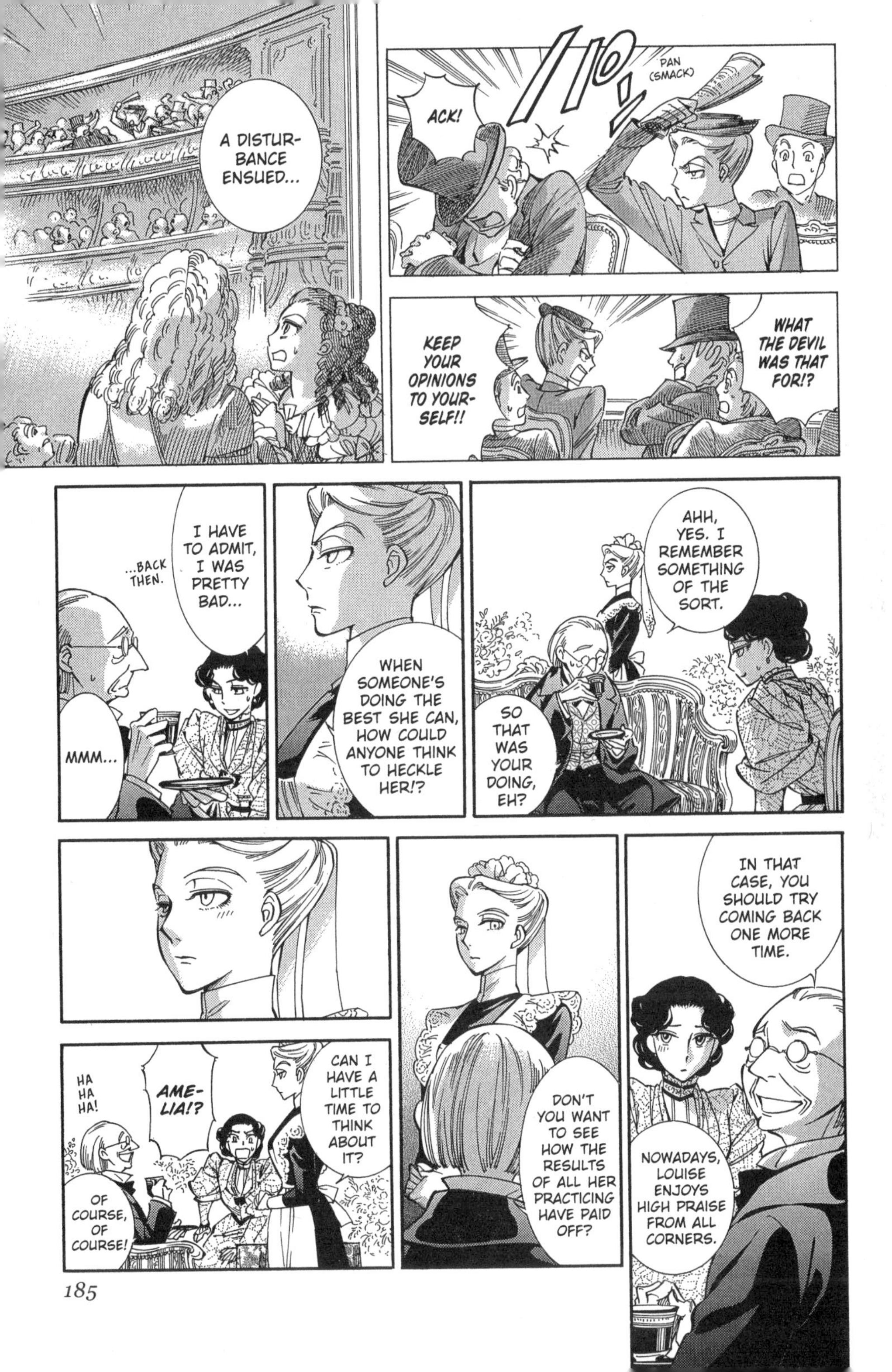
PAN
(SMACK)
ACK!
WHAT THE DEVIL WAS THAT FOR!?
KEEP YOUR OPINIONS TO YOURSELF!!
A DISTURBANCE ENSUED...
AHH, YES. I REMEMBER SOMETHING OF THE SORT.
SO THAT WAS YOUR DOING, EH?
WHEN SOMEONE'S DOING THE BEST SHE CAN, HOW COULD ANYONE THINK TO HECKLE HER!?
I HAVE TO ADMIT, I WAS PRETTY BAD...
...BACK THEN.
MMM...
IN THAT CASE, YOU SHOULD TRY COMING BACK ONE MORE TIME.
NOWADAYS, LOUISE ENJOYS HIGH PRAISE FROM ALL CORNERS.
DON'T YOU WANT TO SEE HOW THE RESULTS OF ALL HER PRACTICING HAVE PAID OFF?
CAN I HAVE A LITTLE TIME TO THINK ABOUT IT?
AME-LIA!?
HA HA HA!
OF COURSE, OF COURSE!

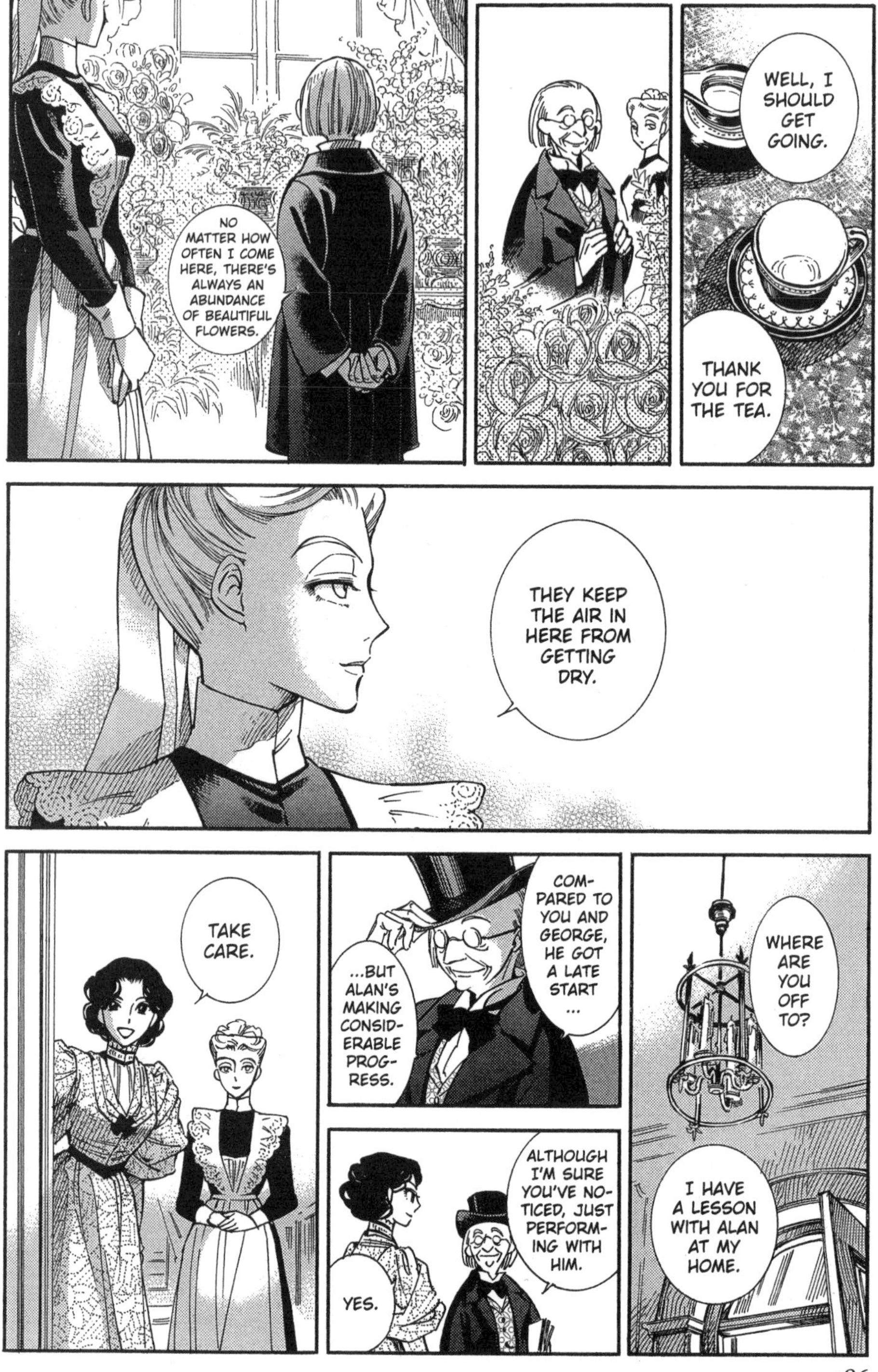
WELL, I SHOULD GET GOING.
THANK YOU FOR THE TEA.
NO MATTER HOW OFTEN I COME HERE, THERE'S ALWAYS AN ABUNDANCE OF BEAUTIFUL FLOWERS.
THEY KEEP THE AIR IN HERE FROM GETTING DRY.
WHERE ARE YOU OFF TO?
I HAVE A LESSON WITH ALAN AT MY HOME.
COMPARED TO YOU AND GEORGE, HE GOT A LATE START...
...BUT ALAN'S MAKING CONSIDERABLE PROGRESS.
ALTHOUGH I'M SURE YOU'VE NOTICED, JUST PERFORMING WITH HIM.
YES.
TAKE CARE.

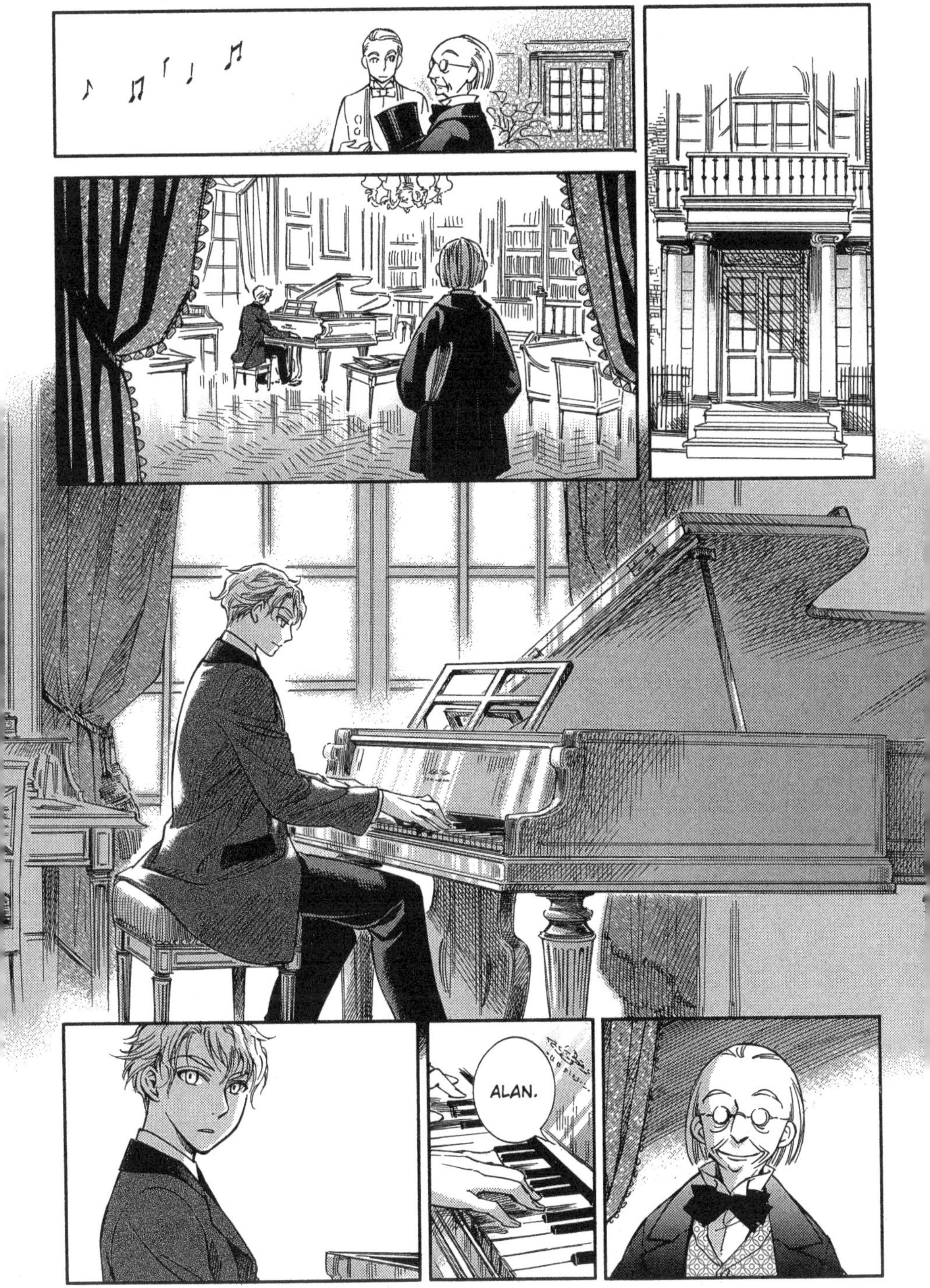
ALAN.

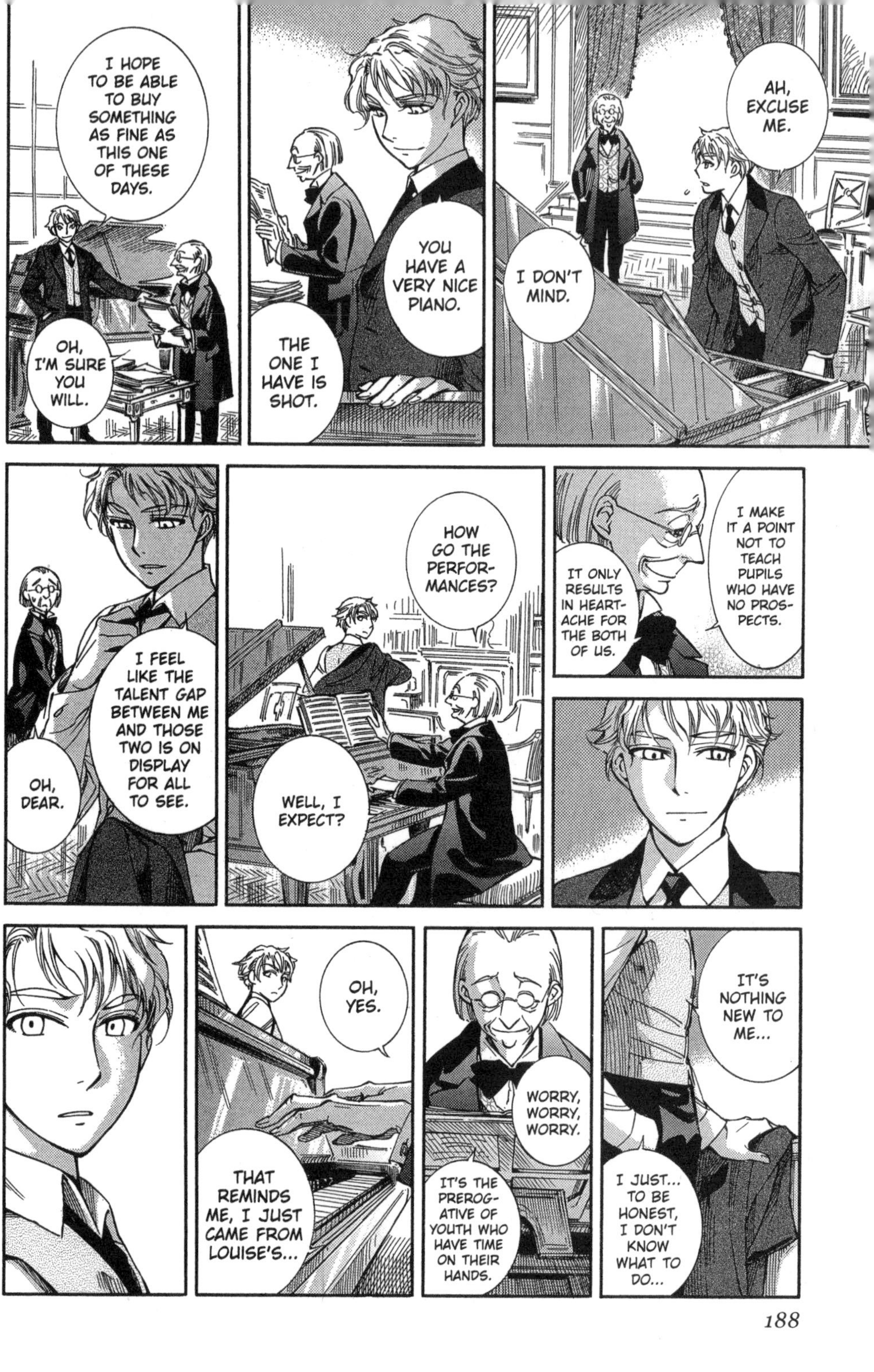
AH, EXCUSE ME.
I DON'T MIND.
YOU HAVE A VERY NICE PIANO.
THE ONE I HAVE IS SHOT.
I HOPE TO BE ABLE TO BUY SOMETHING AS FINE AS THIS ONE OF THESE DAYS.
OH, I'M SURE YOU WILL.
I MAKE IT A POINT NOT TO TEACH PUPILS WHO HAVE NO PROSPECTS.
IT ONLY RESULTS IN HEARTACHE FOR THE BOTH OF US.
HOW GO THE PERFORMANCES?
WELL, I EXPECT?
I FEEL LIKE THE TALENT GAP BETWEEN ME AND THOSE TWO IS ON DISPLAY FOR ALL TO SEE.
OH, DEAR.
IT'S NOTHING NEW TO ME...
I JUST... TO BE HONEST, I DON'T KNOW WHAT TO DO...
WORRY, WORRY, WORRY.
IT'S THE PREROGATIVE OF YOUTH WHO HAVE TIME ON THEIR HANDS.
OH, YES.
THAT REMINDS ME, I JUST CAME FROM LOUISE'S...

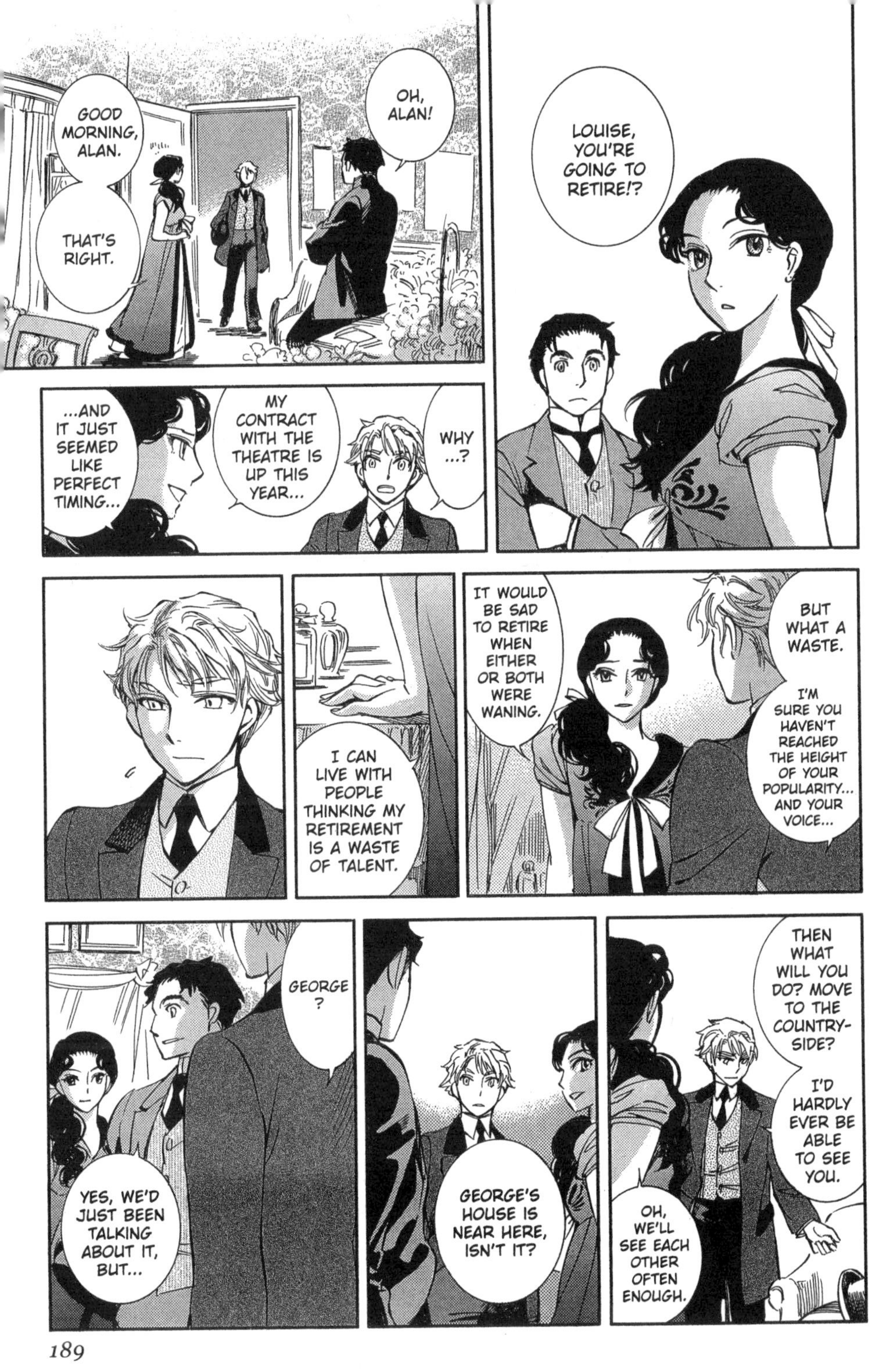
LOUISE, YOU'RE GOING TO RETIRE!?
OH, ALAN!
GOOD MORNING, ALAN.
THAT'S RIGHT.
WHY ...?
MY CONTRACT WITH THE THEATRE IS UP THIS YEAR...
...AND IT JUST SEEMED LIKE PERFECT TIMING...
BUT WHAT A WASTE.
I'M SURE YOU HAVEN'T REACHED THE HEIGHT OF YOUR POPULARITY... AND YOUR VOICE...
IT WOULD BE SAD TO RETIRE WHEN EITHER OR BOTH WERE WANING.
I CAN LIVE WITH PEOPLE THINKING MY RETIREMENT IS A WASTE OF TALENT.
THEN WHAT WILL YOU DO? MOVE TO THE COUNTRY-SIDE?
I'D HARDLY EVER BE ABLE TO SEE YOU.
OH, WE'LL SEE EACH OTHER OFTEN ENOUGH.
GEORGE'S HOUSE IS NEAR HERE, ISN'T IT?
GEORGE?
YES, WE'D JUST BEEN TALKING ABOUT IT, BUT...

GOOD MORNING, ALAN.

THAT'S RIGHT.

OH, ALAN!

LOUISE, YOU'RE GOING TO RETIRE!?

...AND IT JUST SEEMED LIKE PERFECT TIMING...

MY CONTRACT WITH THE THEATRE IS UP THIS YEAR...

WHY ...?

I CAN LIVE WITH PEOPLE THINKING MY RETIREMENT IS A WASTE OF TALENT.

IT WOULD BE SAD TO RETIRE WHEN EITHER OR BOTH WERE WANING.

BUT WHAT A WASTE.

I'M SURE YOU HAVEN'T REACHED THE HEIGHT OF YOUR POPULARITY... AND YOUR VOICE...

GEORGE?

YES, WE'D JUST BEEN TALKING ABOUT IT, BUT...

GEORGE'S HOUSE IS NEAR HERE, ISN'T IT?

THEN WHAT WILL YOU DO? MOVE TO THE COUNTRYSIDE?

I'D HARDLY EVER BE ABLE TO SEE YOU.

OH, WE'LL SEE EACH OTHER OFTEN ENOUGH.

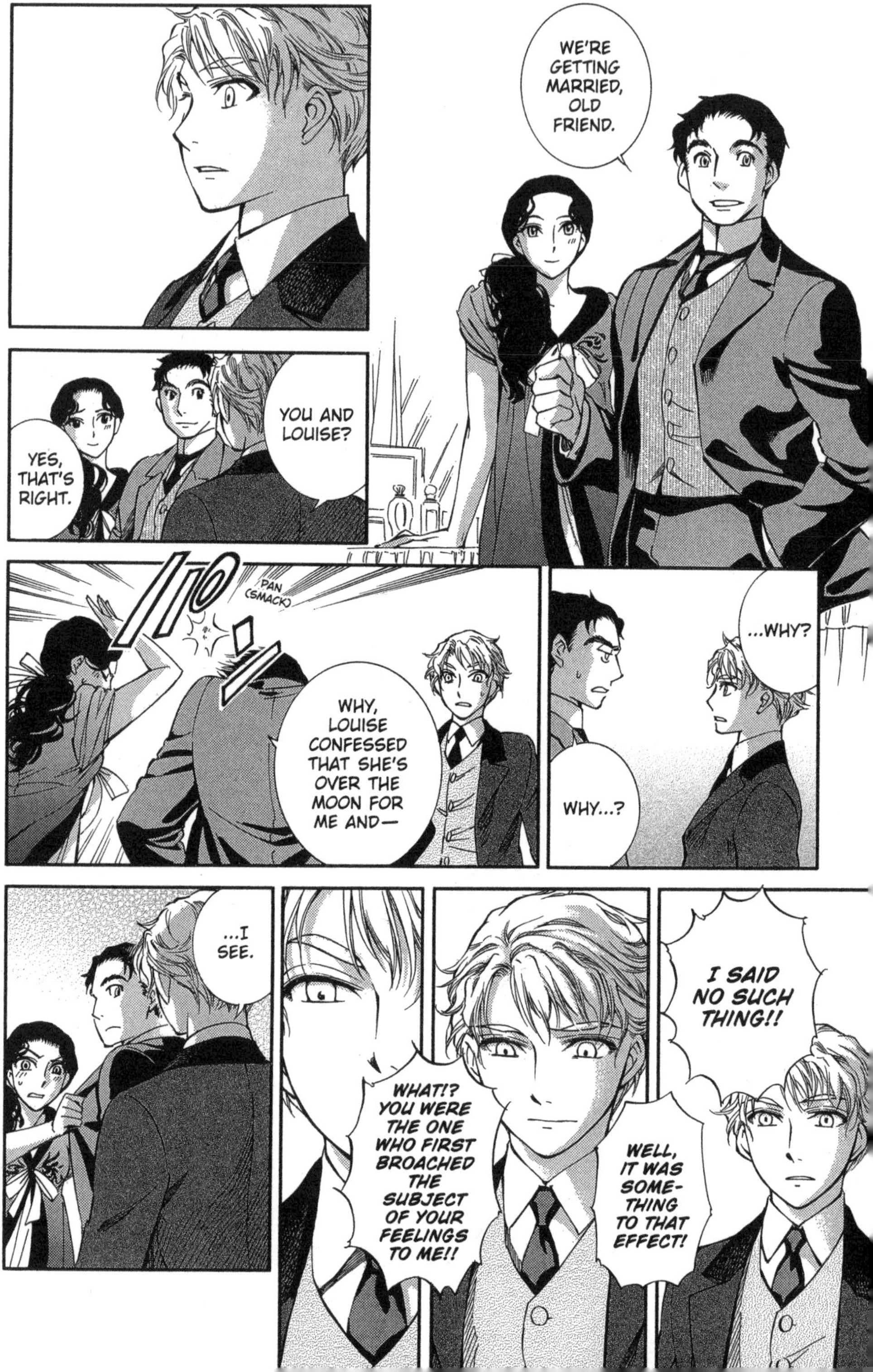
WE'RE GETTING MARRIED, OLD FRIEND.
YOU AND LOUISE?
YES, THAT'S RIGHT.
...WHY?
WHY...?
PAN (SMACK)
WHY, LOUISE CONFESSED THAT SHE'S OVER THE MOON FOR ME AND—
I SAID NO SUCH THING!!
WELL, IT WAS SOME-THING TO THAT EFFECT!
WHAT!? YOU WERE THE ONE WHO FIRST BROACHED THE SUBJECT OF YOUR FEELINGS TO ME!!
...I SEE.

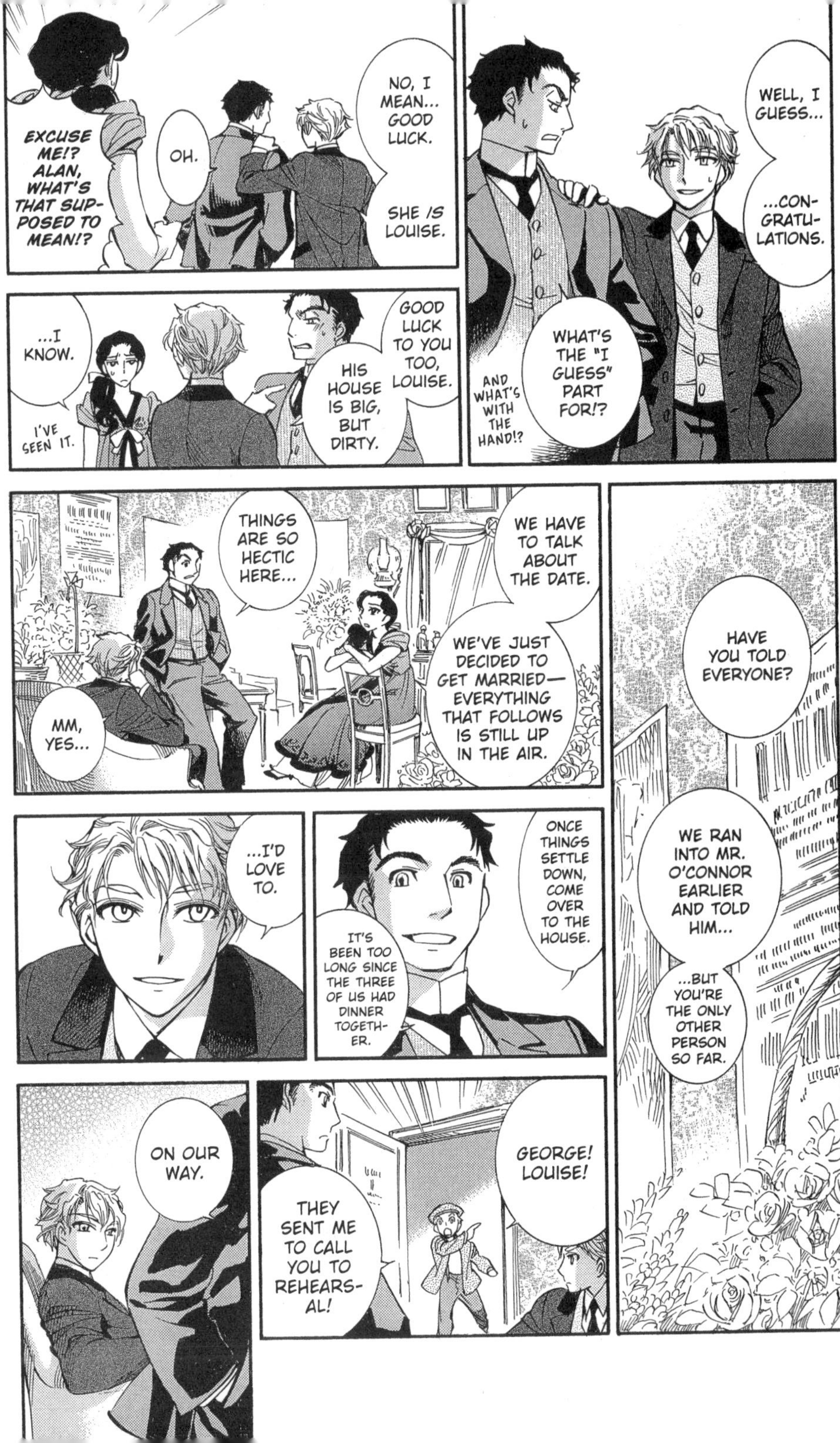
WELL, I GUESS...
...CONGRATULATIONS.
WHAT'S THE "I GUESS" PART FOR!?
AND WHAT'S WITH THE HAND!?
NO, I MEAN... GOOD LUCK.
SHE IS LOUISE.
OH.
EXCUSE ME!? ALAN, WHAT'S THAT SUPPOSED TO MEAN!?
GOOD LUCK TO YOU TOO, LOUISE.
HIS HOUSE IS BIG, BUT DIRTY.
...I KNOW.
I'VE SEEN IT.
HAVE YOU TOLD EVERYONE?
WE RAN INTO MR. O'CONNOR EARLIER AND TOLD HIM...
...BUT YOU'RE THE ONLY OTHER PERSON SO FAR.
WE HAVE TO TALK ABOUT THE DATE.
THINGS ARE SO HECTIC HERE...
WE'VE JUST DECIDED TO GET MARRIED— EVERYTHING THAT FOLLOWS IS STILL UP IN THE AIR.
MM, YES...
ONCE THINGS SETTLE DOWN, COME OVER TO THE HOUSE.
IT'S BEEN TOO LONG SINCE THE THREE OF US HAD DINNER TOGETHER.
...I'D LOVE TO.
GEORGE! LOUISE!
THEY SENT ME TO CALL YOU TO REHEARSAL!
ON OUR WAY.

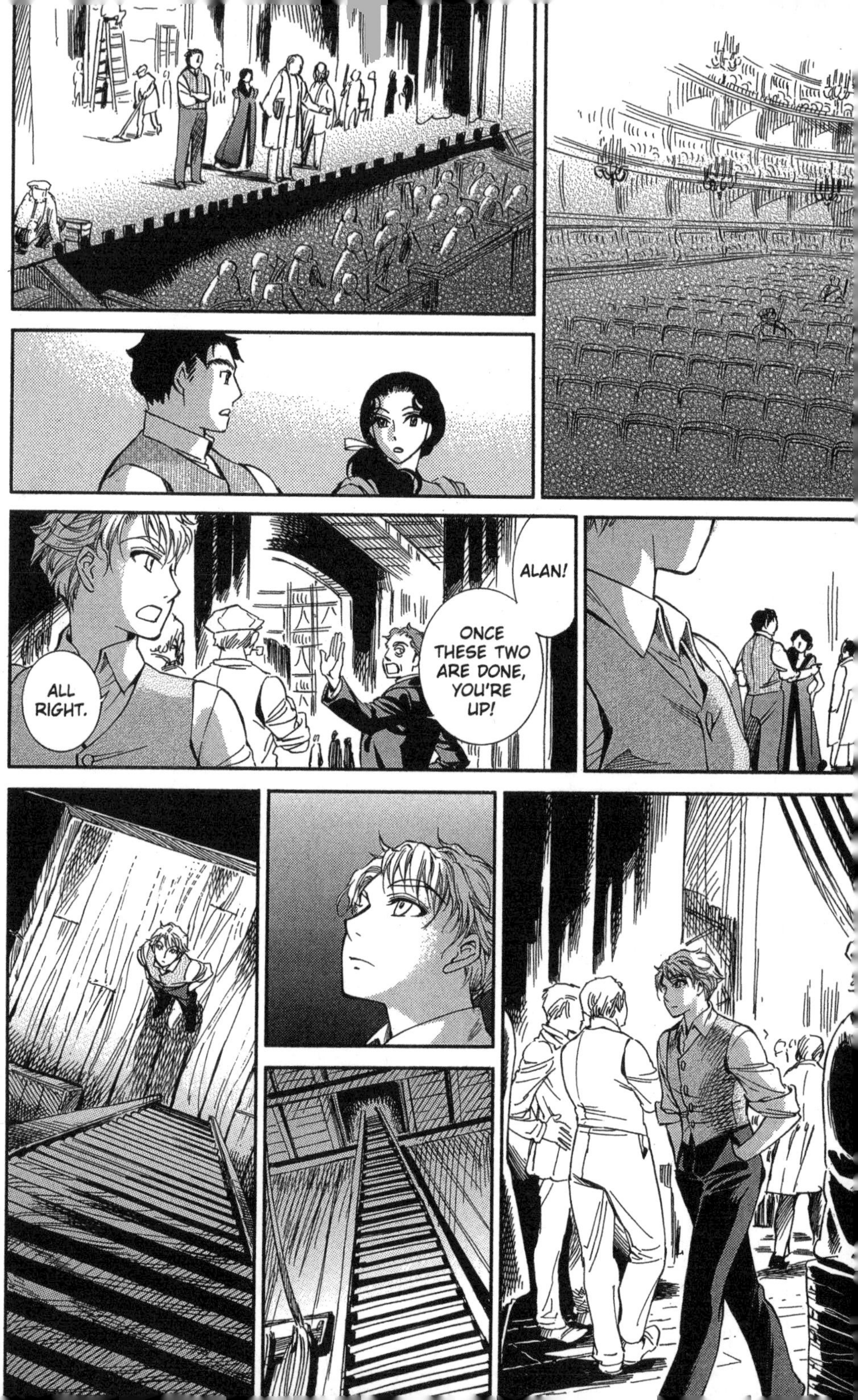
ALAN!
ONCE THESE TWO ARE DONE, YOU'RE UP!
ALL RIGHT.

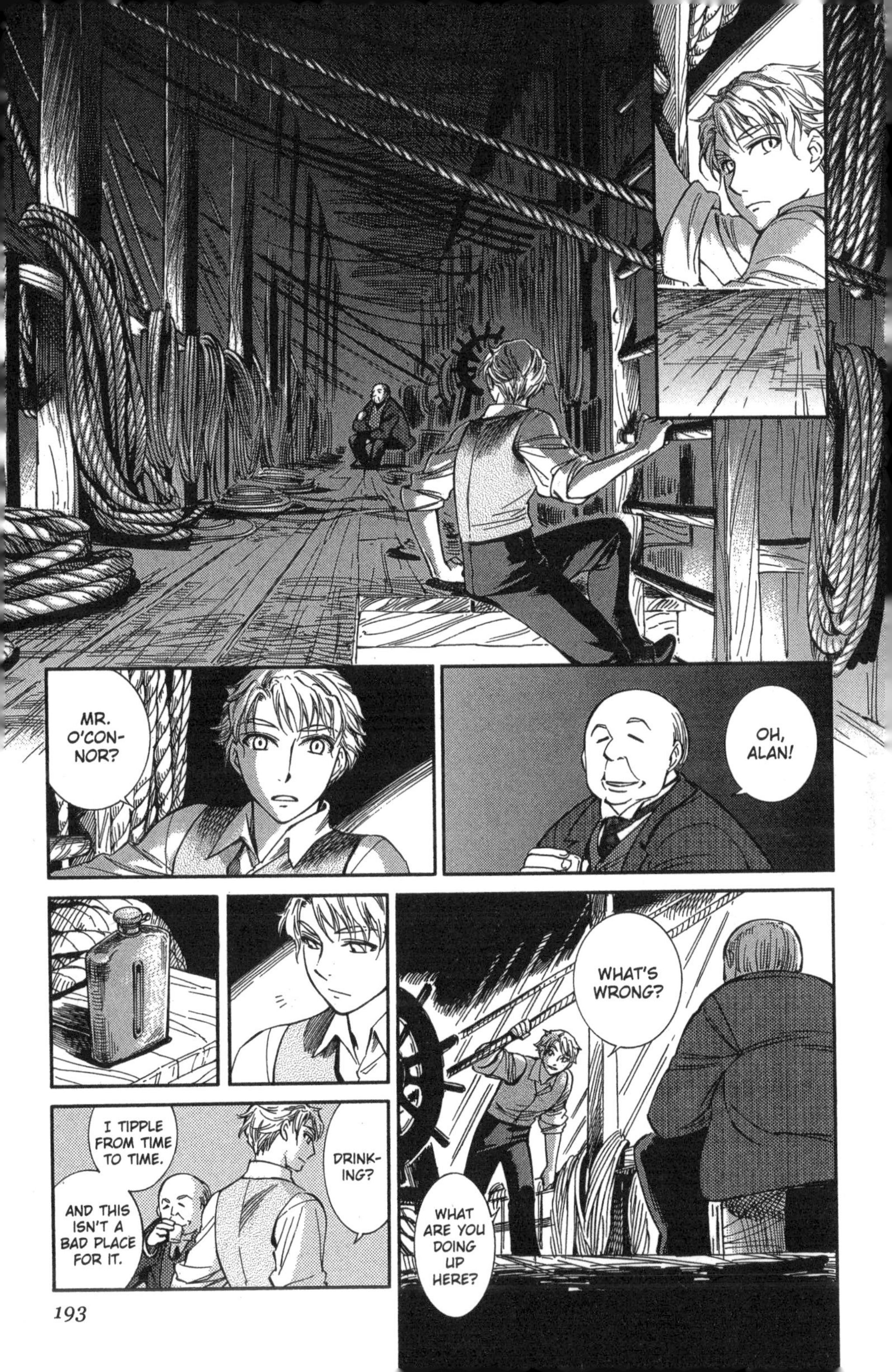
OH, ALAN!
MR. O'CON-NOR?
WHAT'S WRONG?
WHAT ARE YOU DOING UP HERE?
DRINK-ING?
I TIPPLE FROM TIME TO TIME.
AND THIS ISN'T A BAD PLACE FOR IT.

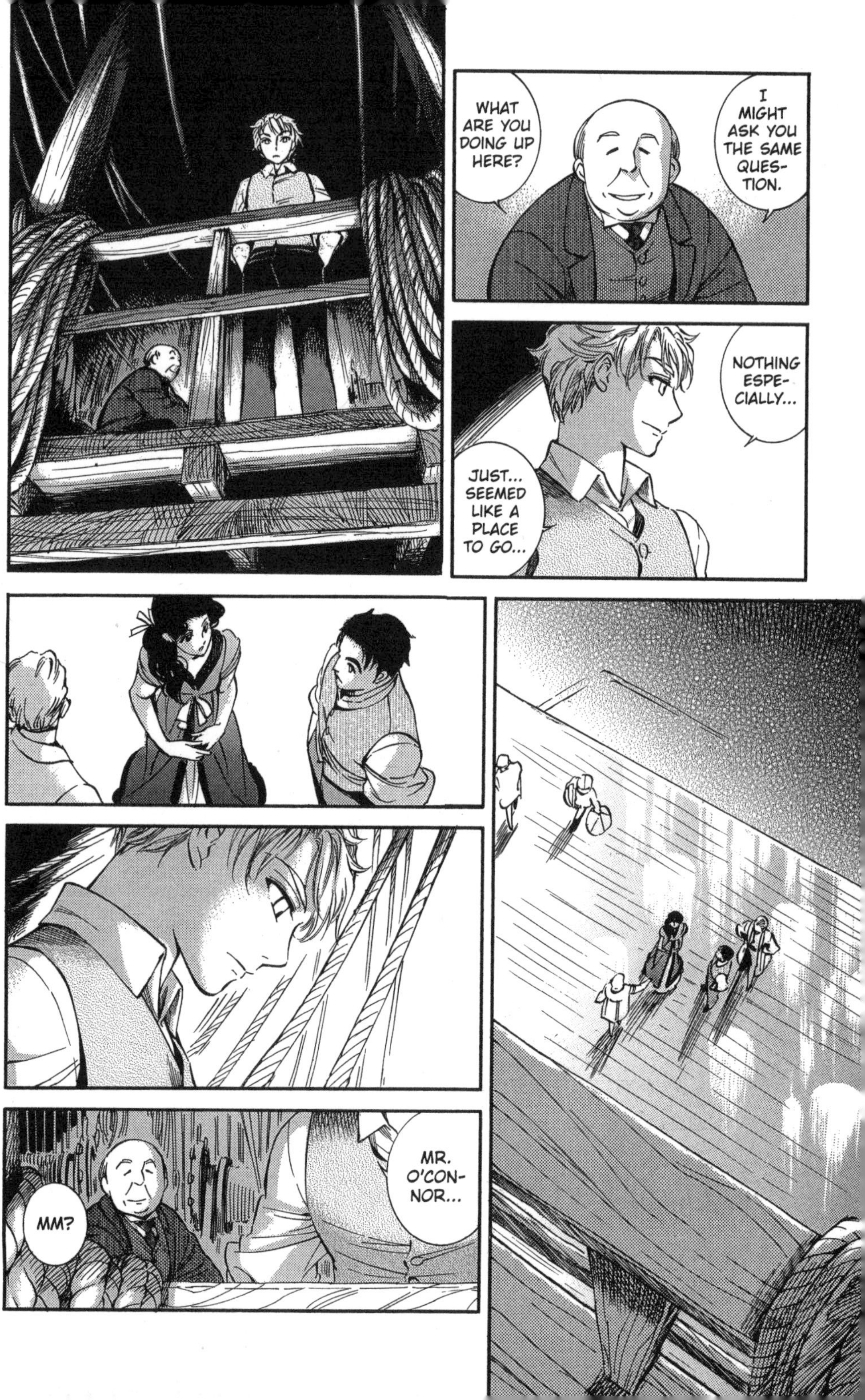
WHAT ARE YOU DOING UP HERE?
I MIGHT ASK YOU THE SAME QUES-TION.
NOTHING ESPE-CIALLY...
JUST... SEEMED LIKE A PLACE TO GO...
MR. O'CON-NOR...
MM?

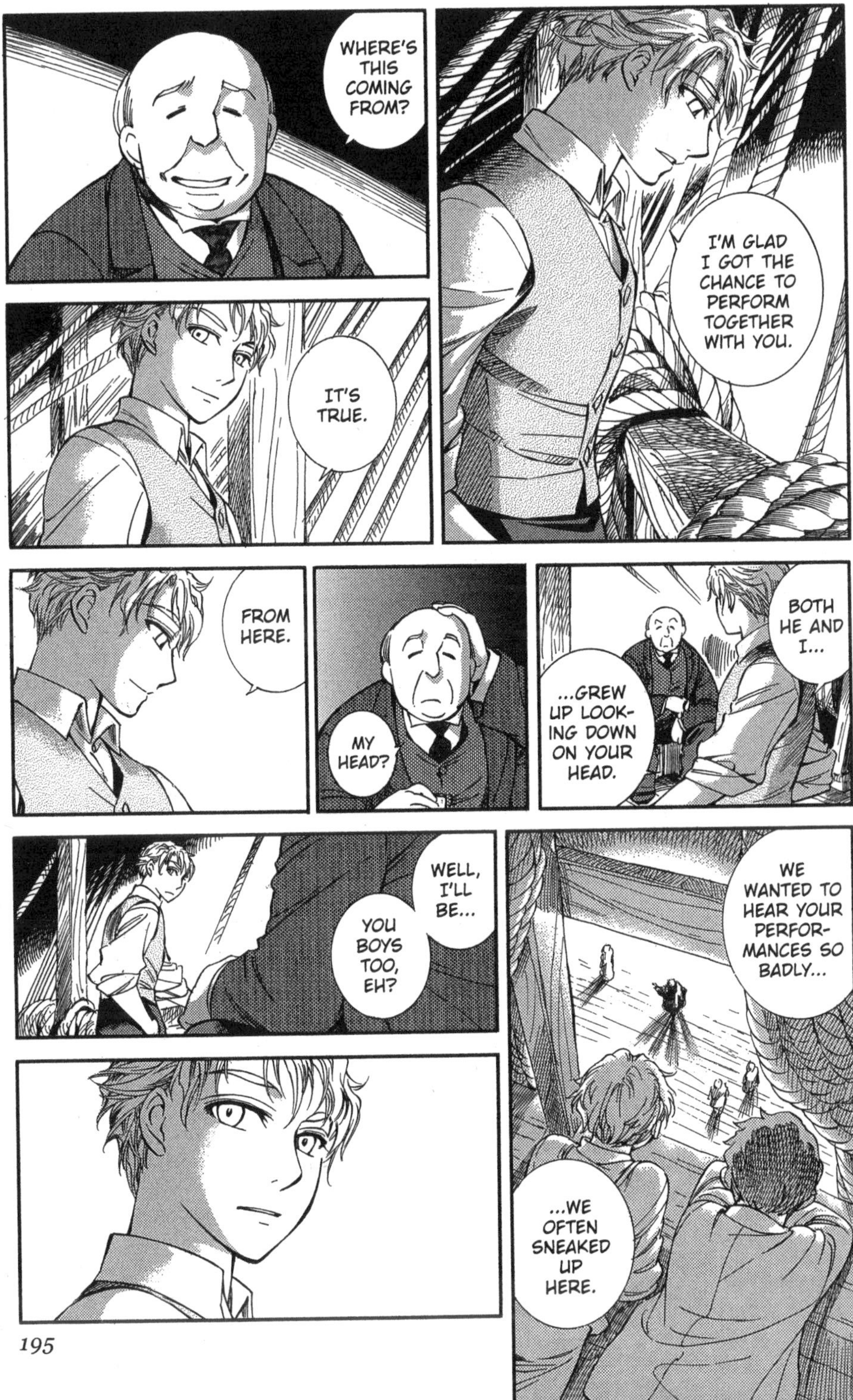
I'M GLAD I GOT THE CHANCE TO PERFORM TOGETHER WITH YOU.
WHERE'S THIS COMING FROM?
IT'S TRUE.
BOTH HE AND I...
...GREW UP LOOKING DOWN ON YOUR HEAD.
MY HEAD?
FROM HERE.
WE WANTED TO HEAR YOUR PERFORMANCES SO BADLY...
...WE OFTEN SNEAKED UP HERE.
WELL, I'LL BE...
YOU BOYS TOO, EH?

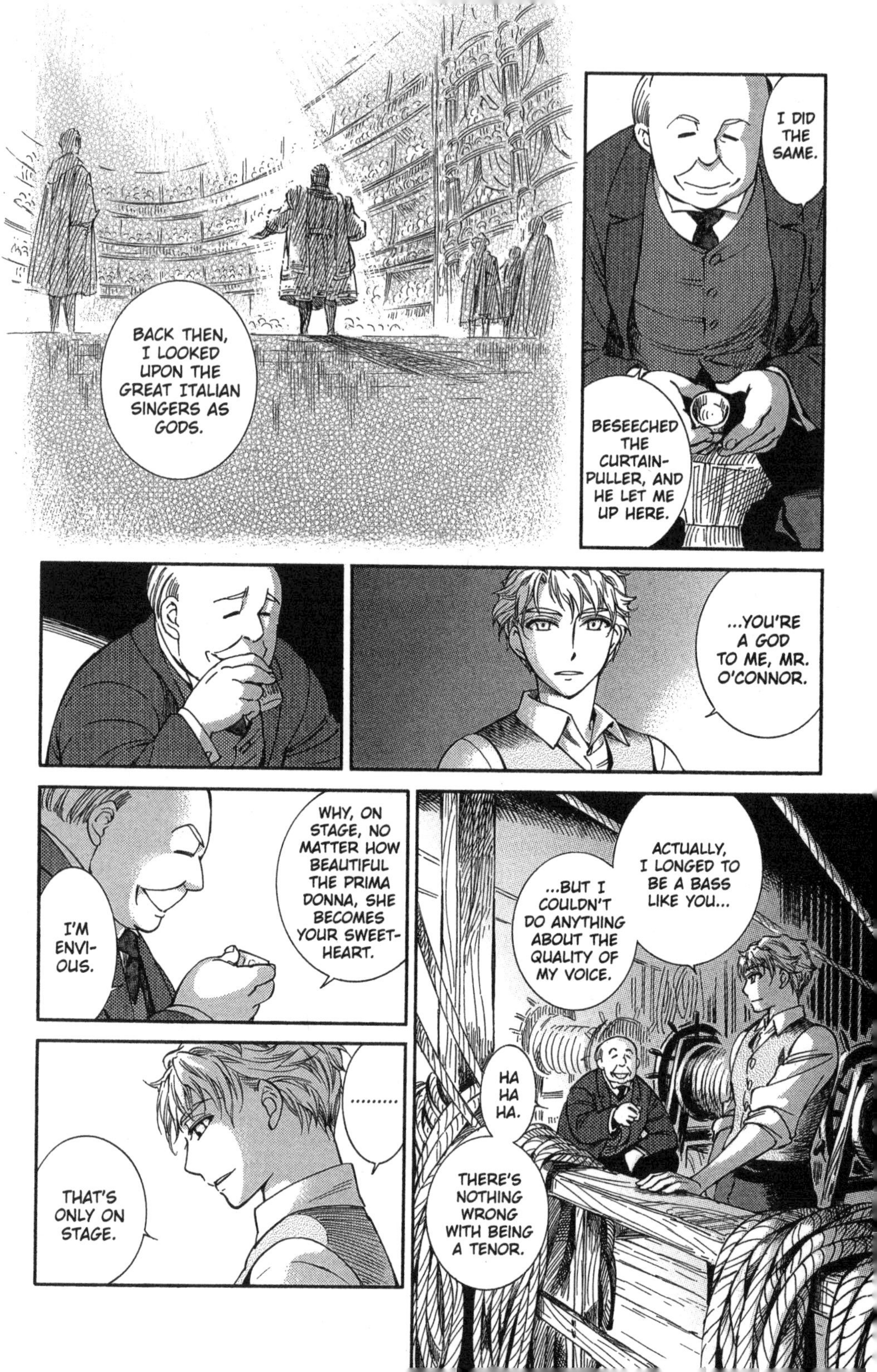
I DID THE SAME.
BESEECHED THE CURTAIN-PULLER, AND HE LET ME UP HERE.
BACK THEN, I LOOKED UPON THE GREAT ITALIAN SINGERS AS GODS.
...YOU'RE A GOD TO ME, MR. O'CONNOR.
ACTUALLY, I LONGED TO BE A BASS LIKE YOU...
...BUT I COULDN'T DO ANYTHING ABOUT THE QUALITY OF MY VOICE.
HA HA HA.
THERE'S NOTHING WRONG WITH BEING A TENOR.
WHY, ON STAGE, NO MATTER HOW BEAUTIFUL THE PRIMA DONNA, SHE BECOMES YOUR SWEET-HEART.
I'M ENVI-OUS.
....
THAT'S ONLY ON STAGE.

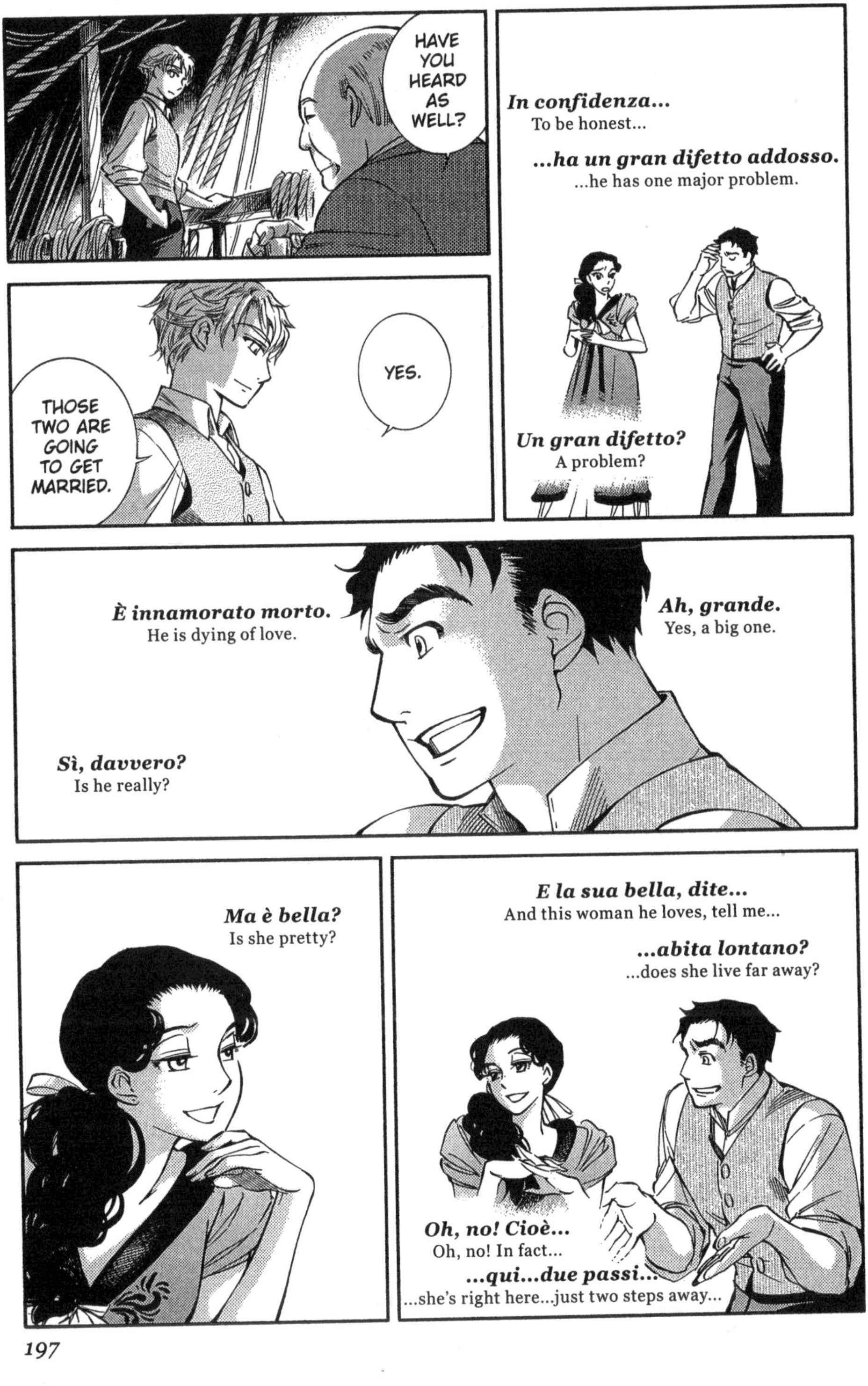
In confidenza...
To be honest...
...ha un gran difetto addosso.
...he has one major problem.
Un gran difetto?
A problem?
HAVE YOU HEARD AS WELL?
YES.
THOSE TWO ARE GOING TO GET MARRIED.
Ah, grande.
Yes, a big one.
È innamorato morto.
He is dying of love.
Sì, davvero?
Is he really?
E la sua bella, dite...
And this woman he loves, tell me...
...abita lontano?
...does she live far away?
Oh, no! Cioè...
Oh, no! In fact...
...qui...due passi...
...she's right here...just two steps away...
Ma è bella?
Is she pretty?

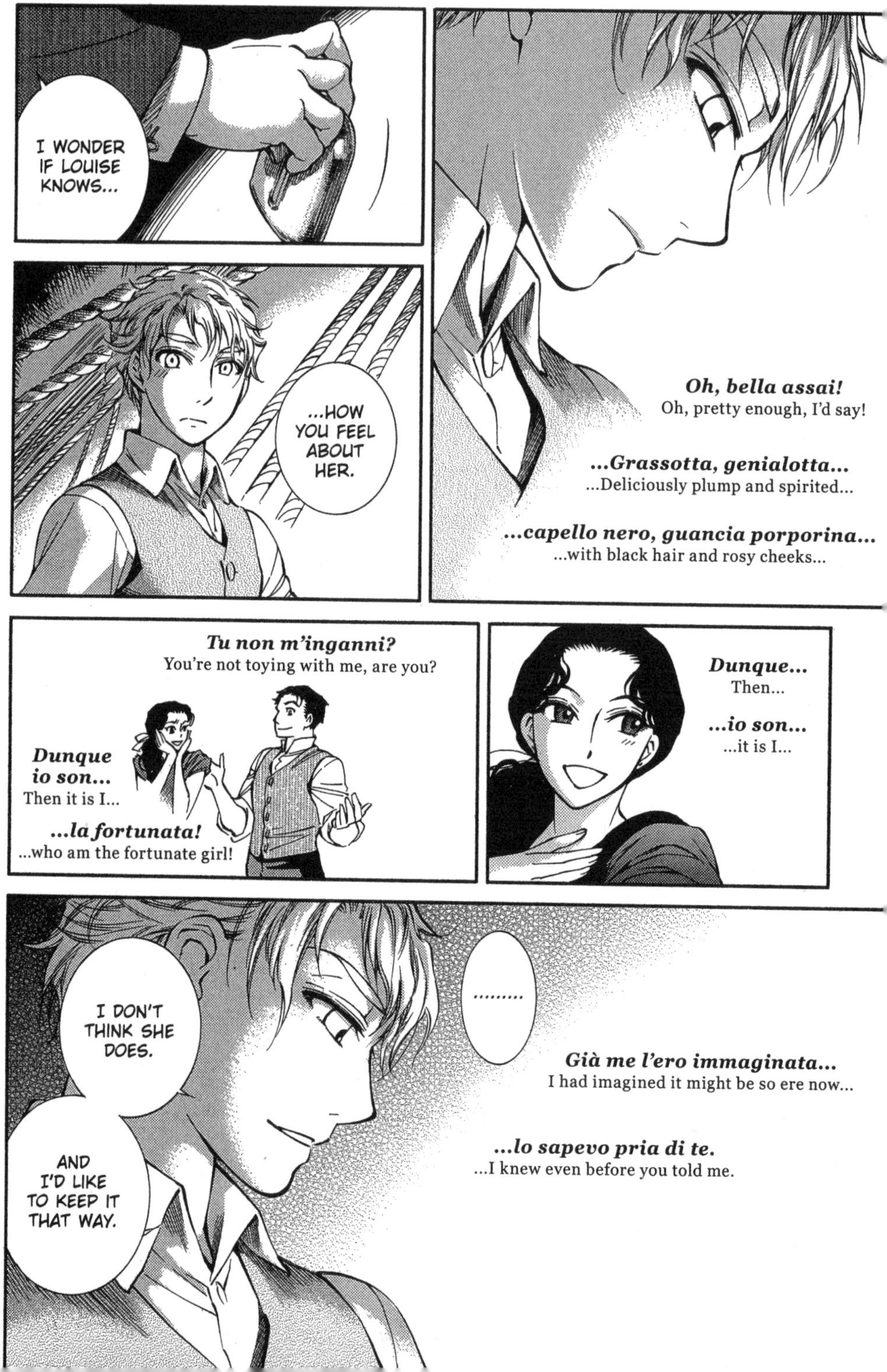
Oh, bella assai!
Oh, pretty enough, I'd say!
...Grassotta, genialotta...
...Deliciously plump and spirited...
...capello nero, guancia porporina...
...with black hair and rosy cheeks...
I WONDER IF LOUISE KNOWS...
...HOW YOU FEEL ABOUT HER.
Dunque...
Then...
...io son...
...it is I...
Tu non m'inganni?
You're not toying with me, are you?
Dunque io son...
Then it is I...
...la fortunata!
...who am the fortunate girl!
....
Già me l'ero immaginata...
I had imagined it might be so ere now...
...lo sapevo pria di te.
...I knew even before you told me.
I DON'T THINK SHE DOES.
AND I'D LIKE TO KEEP IT THAT WAY.

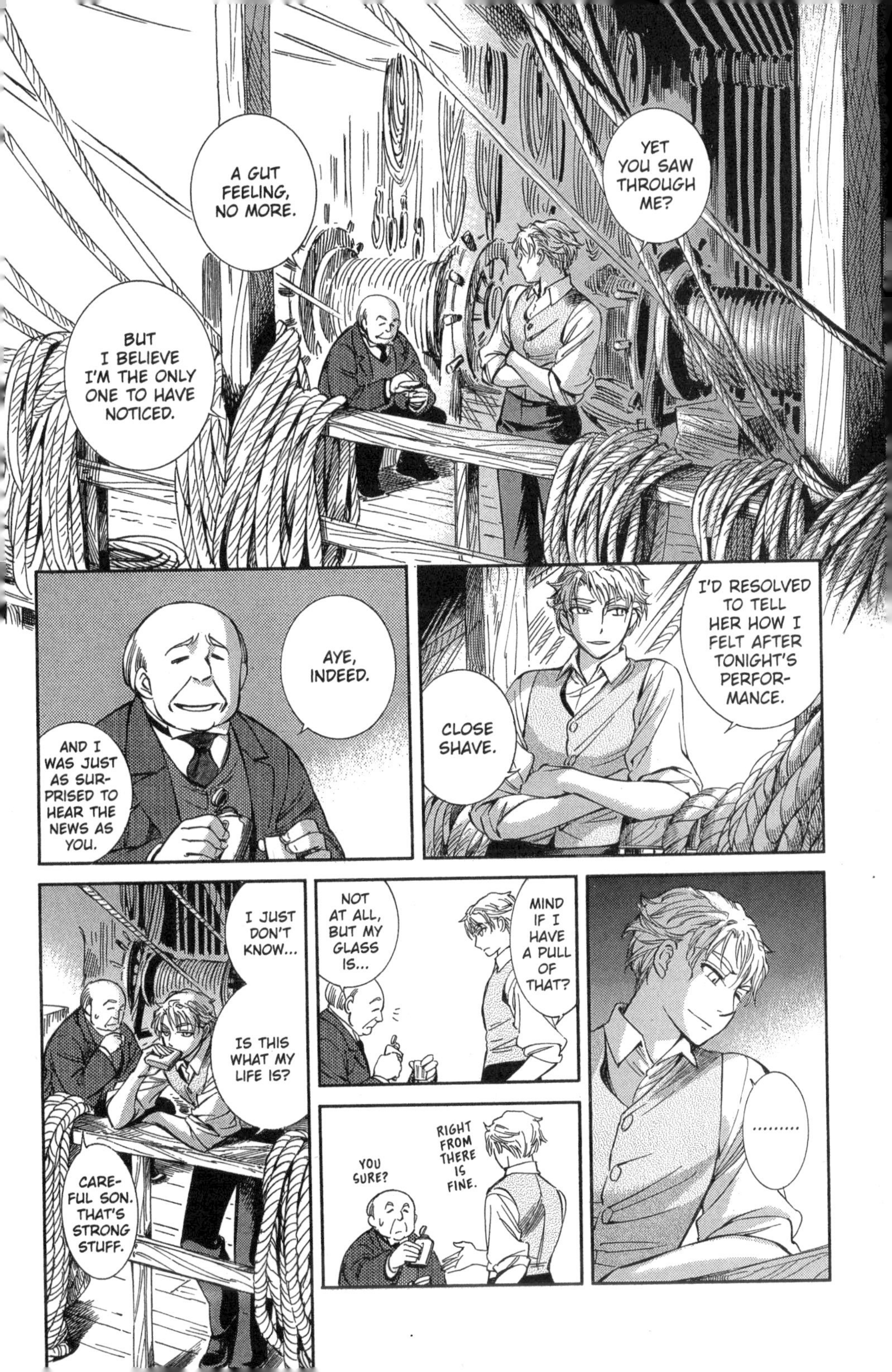
YET YOU SAW THROUGH ME?
A GUT FEELING, NO MORE.
BUT I BELIEVE I'M THE ONLY ONE TO HAVE NOTICED.
I'D RESOLVED TO TELL HER HOW I FELT AFTER TONIGHT'S PERFORMANCE.
CLOSE SHAVE.
AYE, INDEED.
AND I WAS JUST AS SURPRISED TO HEAR THE NEWS AS YOU.
....
MIND IF I HAVE A PULL OF THAT?
NOT AT ALL, BUT MY GLASS IS...
RIGHT FROM THERE IS FINE.
YOU SURE?
I JUST DON'T KNOW...
IS THIS WHAT MY LIFE IS?
CAREFUL SON. THAT'S STRONG STUFF.

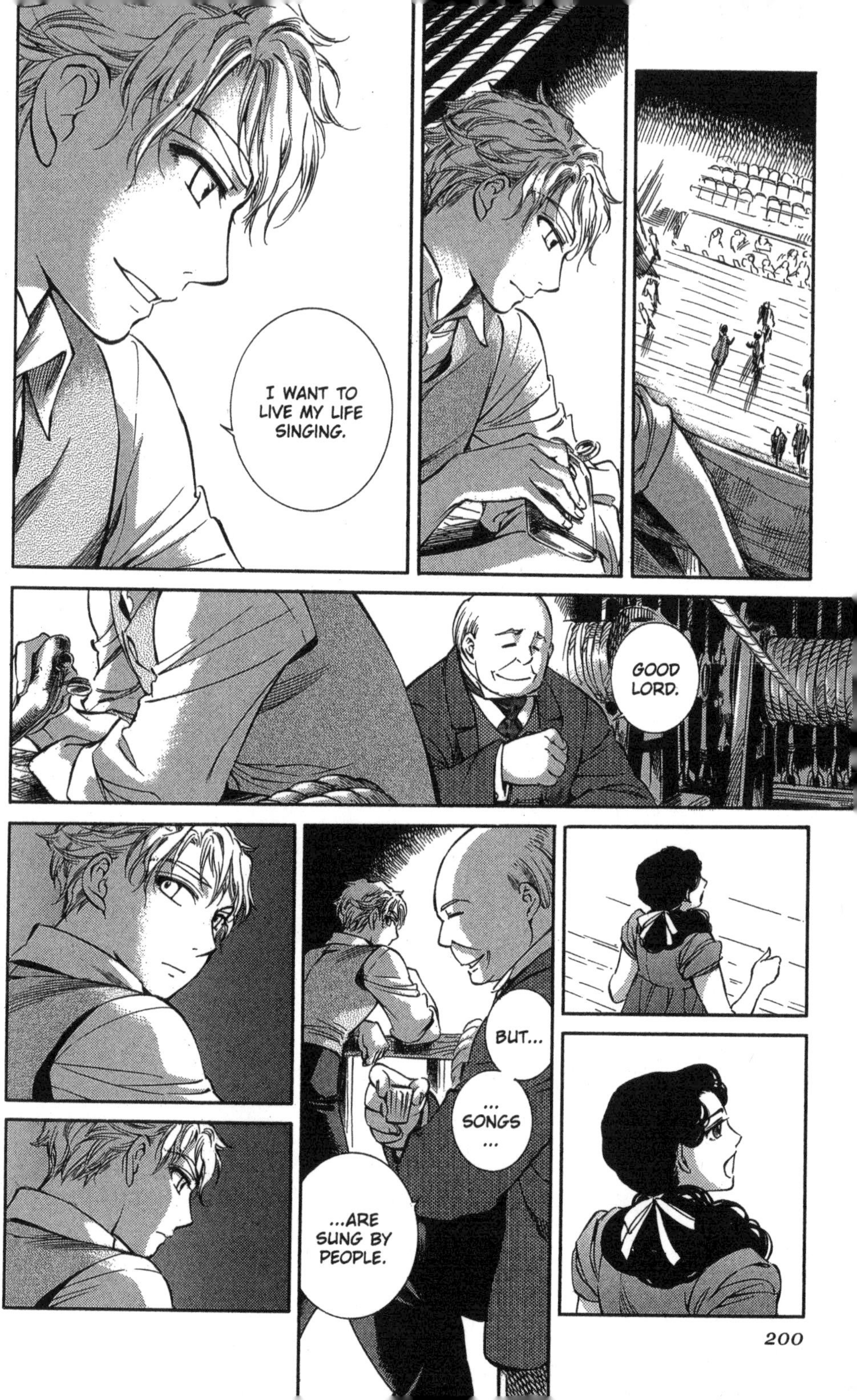
I WANT TO LIVE MY LIFE SINGING.
GOOD LORD.
BUT...
... SONGS ...
...ARE SUNG BY PEOPLE.

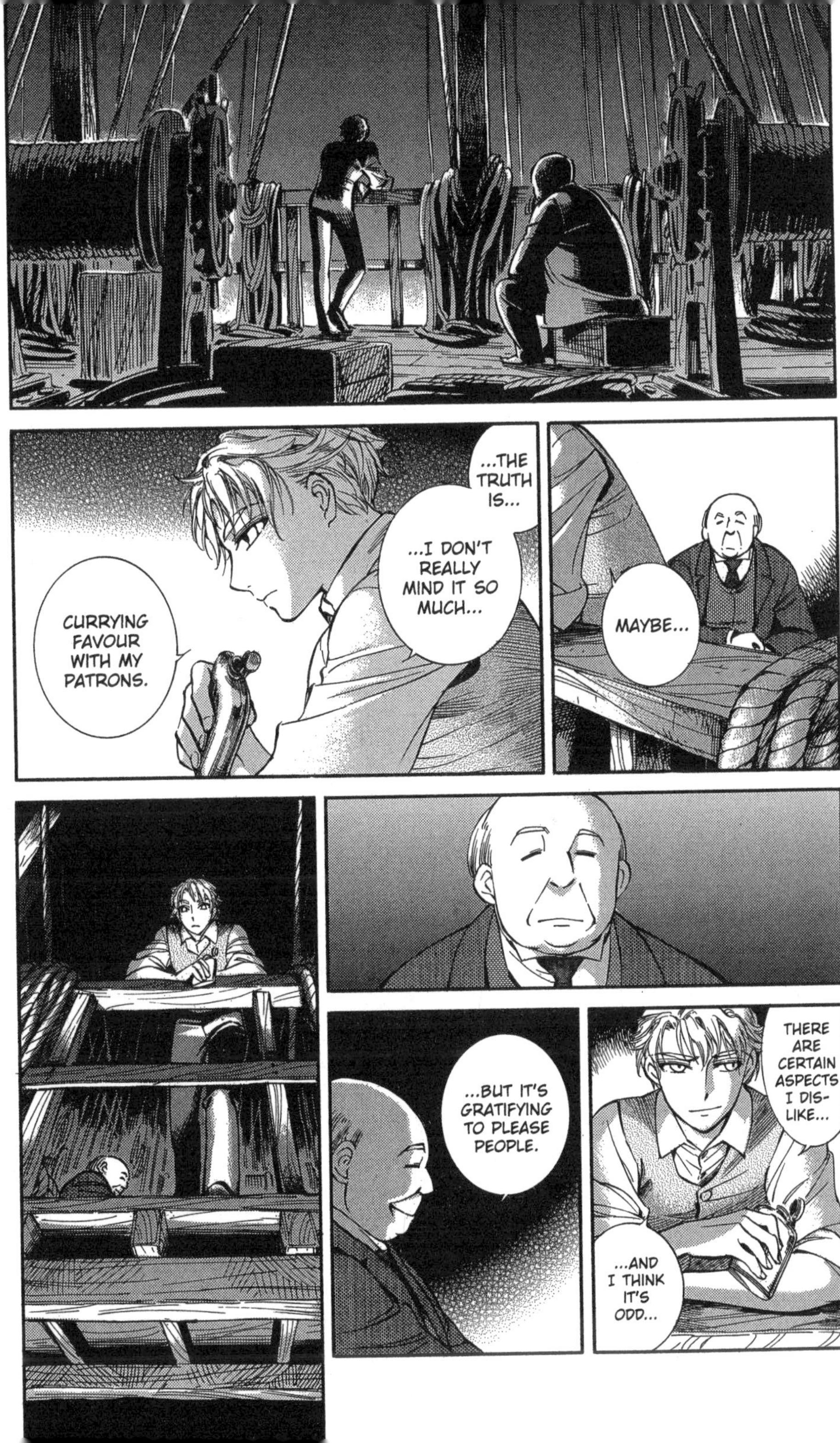
MAYBE...
...THE TRUTH IS...
...I DON'T REALLY MIND IT SO MUCH...
CURRYING FAVOUR WITH MY PATRONS.
THERE ARE CERTAIN ASPECTS I DIS-LIKE...
...AND I THINK IT'S ODD...
...BUT IT'S GRATIFYING TO PLEASE PEOPLE.

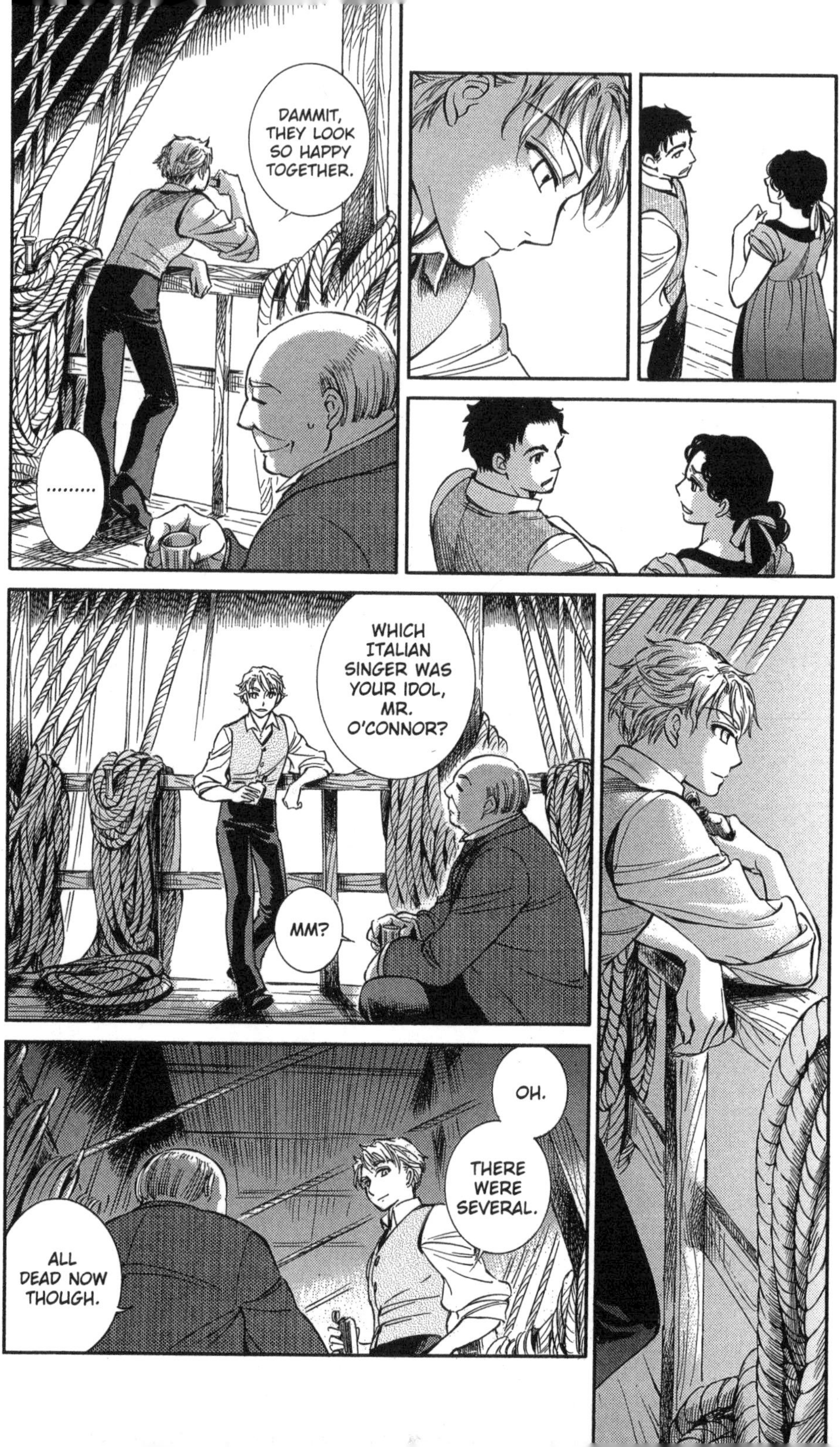
DAMMIT, THEY LOOK SO HAPPY TOGETHER.
....
WHICH ITALIAN SINGER WAS YOUR IDOL, MR. O'CONNOR?
MM?
OH.
THERE WERE SEVERAL.
ALL DEAD NOW THOUGH.

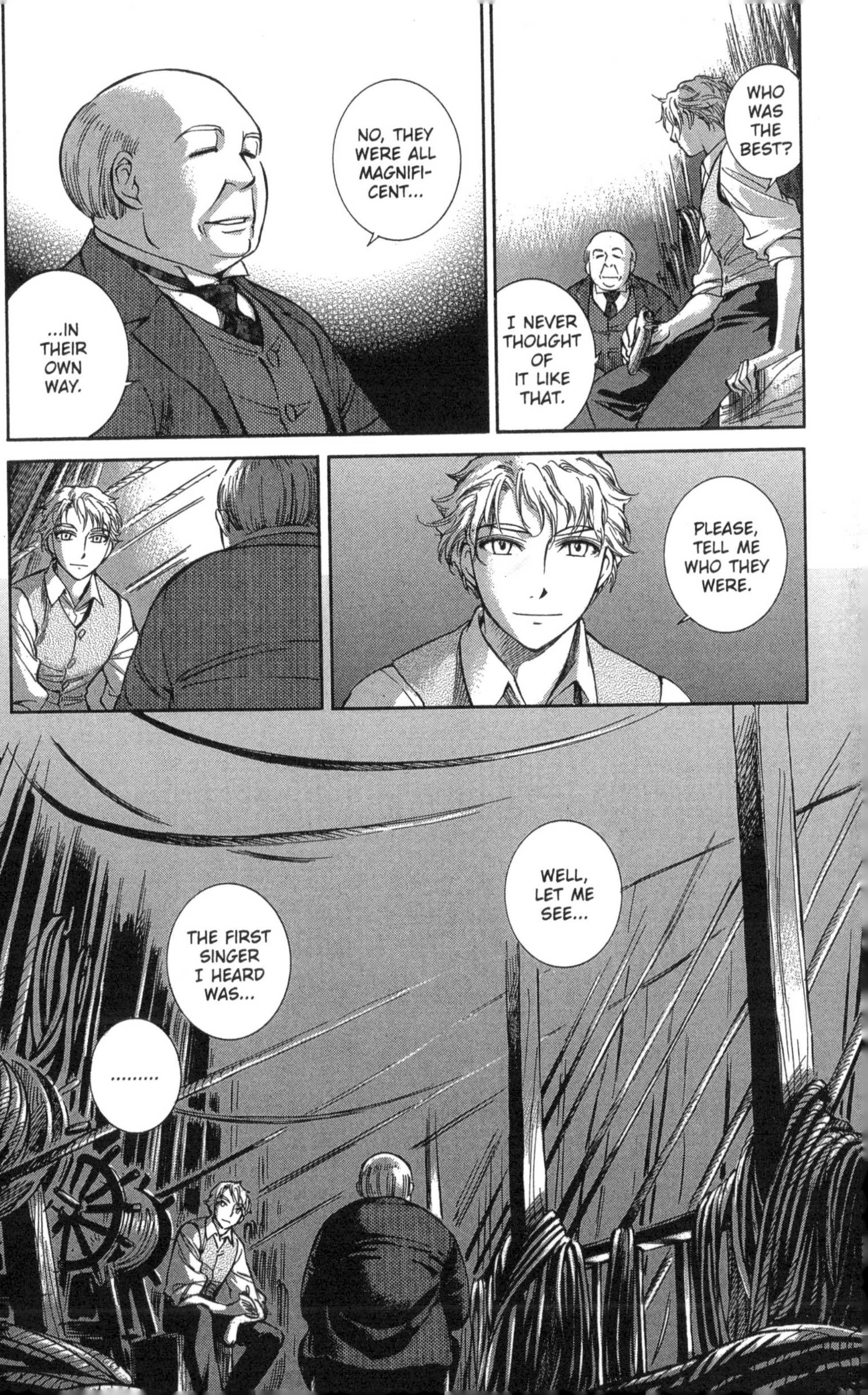
WHO WAS THE BEST?
I NEVER THOUGHT OF IT LIKE THAT.
NO, THEY WERE ALL MAGNIFICENT...
...IN THEIR OWN WAY.
PLEASE, TELL ME WHO THEY WERE.
WELL, LET ME SEE...
THE FIRST SINGER I HEARD WAS...
....

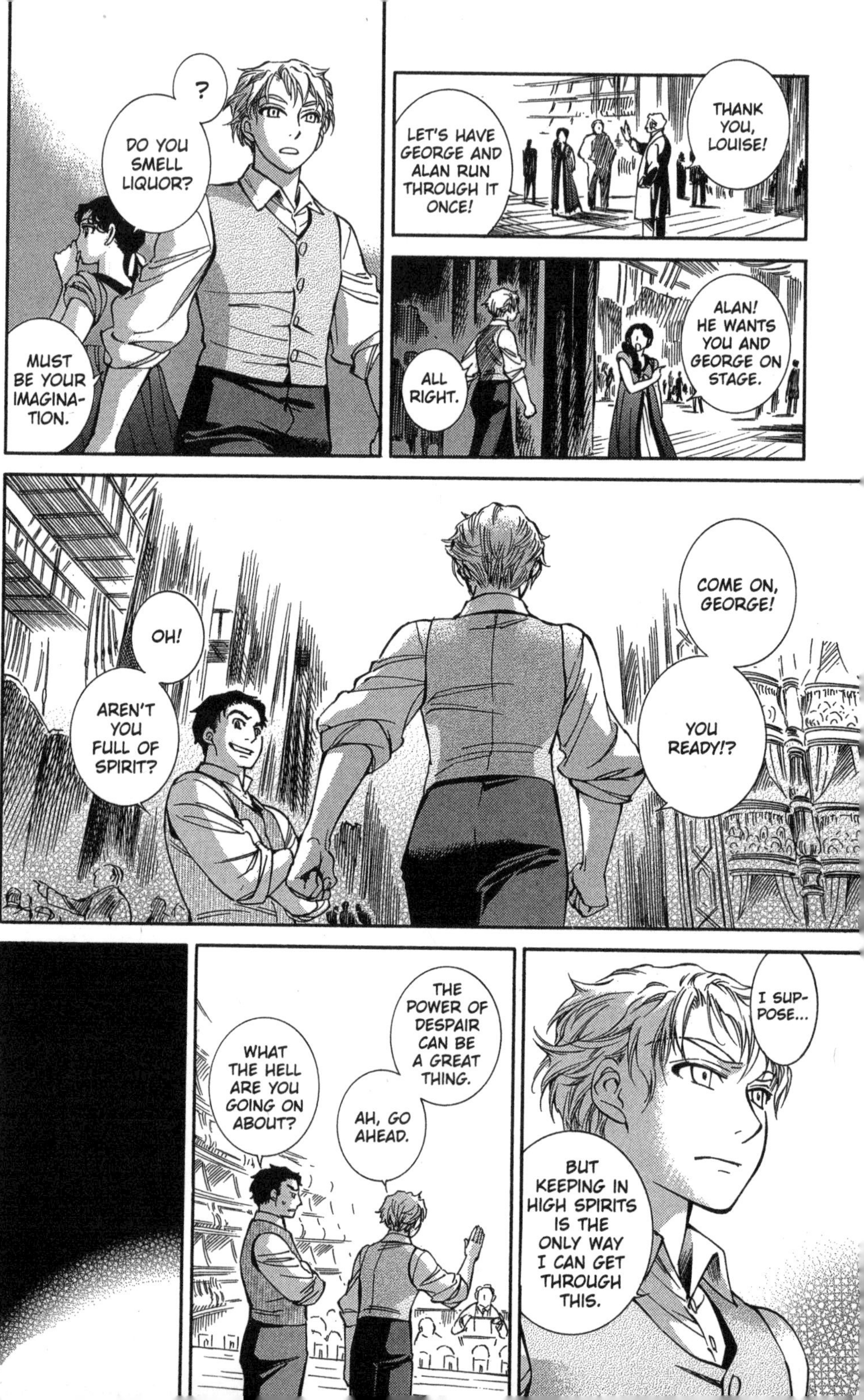

THANK YOU, LOUISE!
LET'S HAVE GEORGE AND ALAN RUN THROUGH IT ONCE!
ALAN! HE WANTS YOU AND GEORGE ON STAGE.
ALL RIGHT.
?
DO YOU SMELL LIQUOR?
MUST BE YOUR IMAGINA-TION.
COME ON, GEORGE!
YOU READY!?
OH!
AREN'T YOU FULL OF SPIRIT?
I SUP-POSE...
BUT KEEPING IN HIGH SPIRITS IS THE ONLY WAY I CAN GET THROUGH THIS.
THE POWER OF DESPAIR CAN BE A GREAT THING.
WHAT THE HELL ARE YOU GOING ON ABOUT?
AH, GO AHEAD.

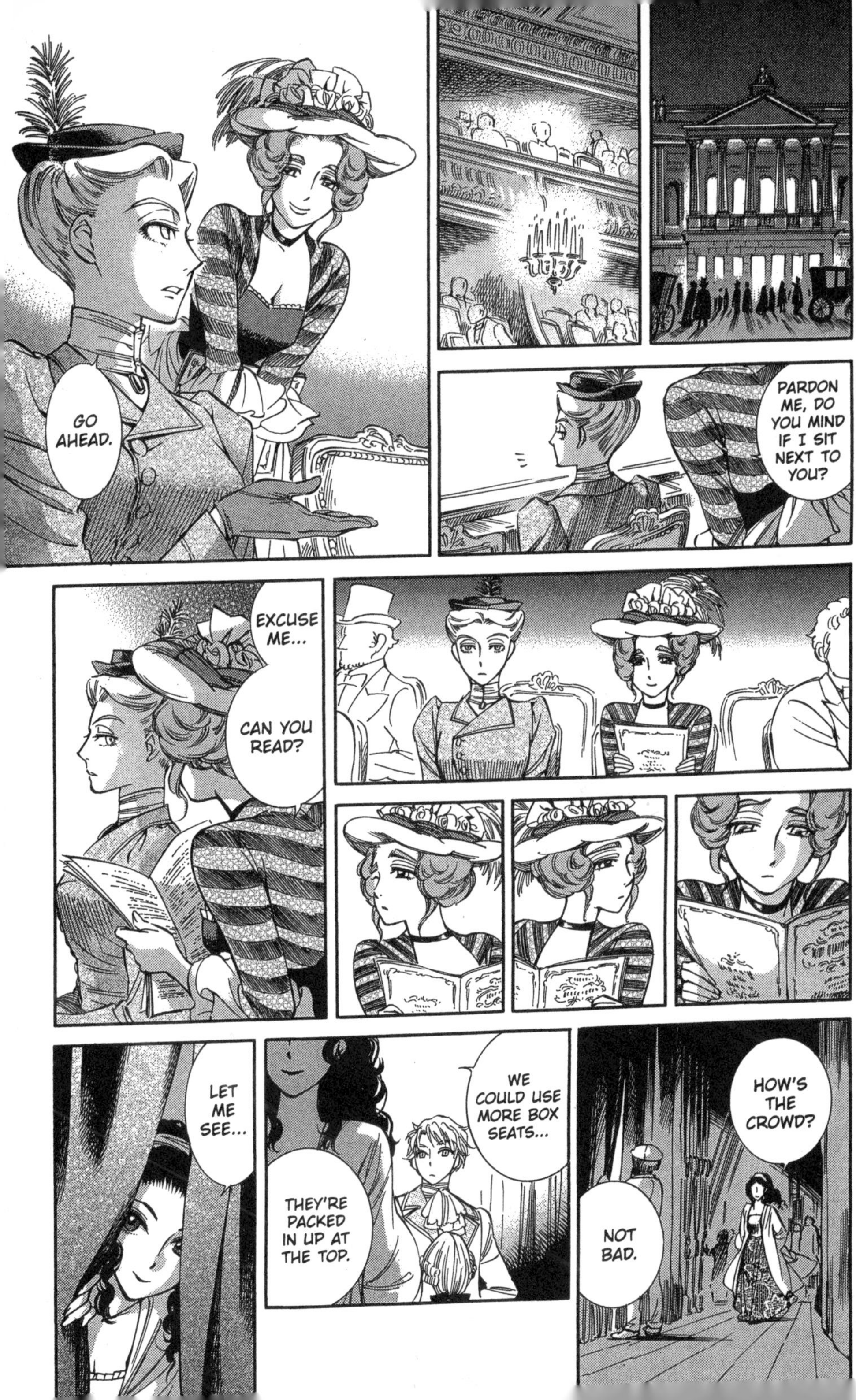
PARDON ME, DO YOU MIND IF I SIT NEXT TO YOU?
GO AHEAD.
EXCUSE ME...
CAN YOU READ?
HOW'S THE CROWD?
NOT BAD.
WE COULD USE MORE BOX SEATS...
THEY'RE PACKED IN UP AT THE TOP.
LET ME SEE...

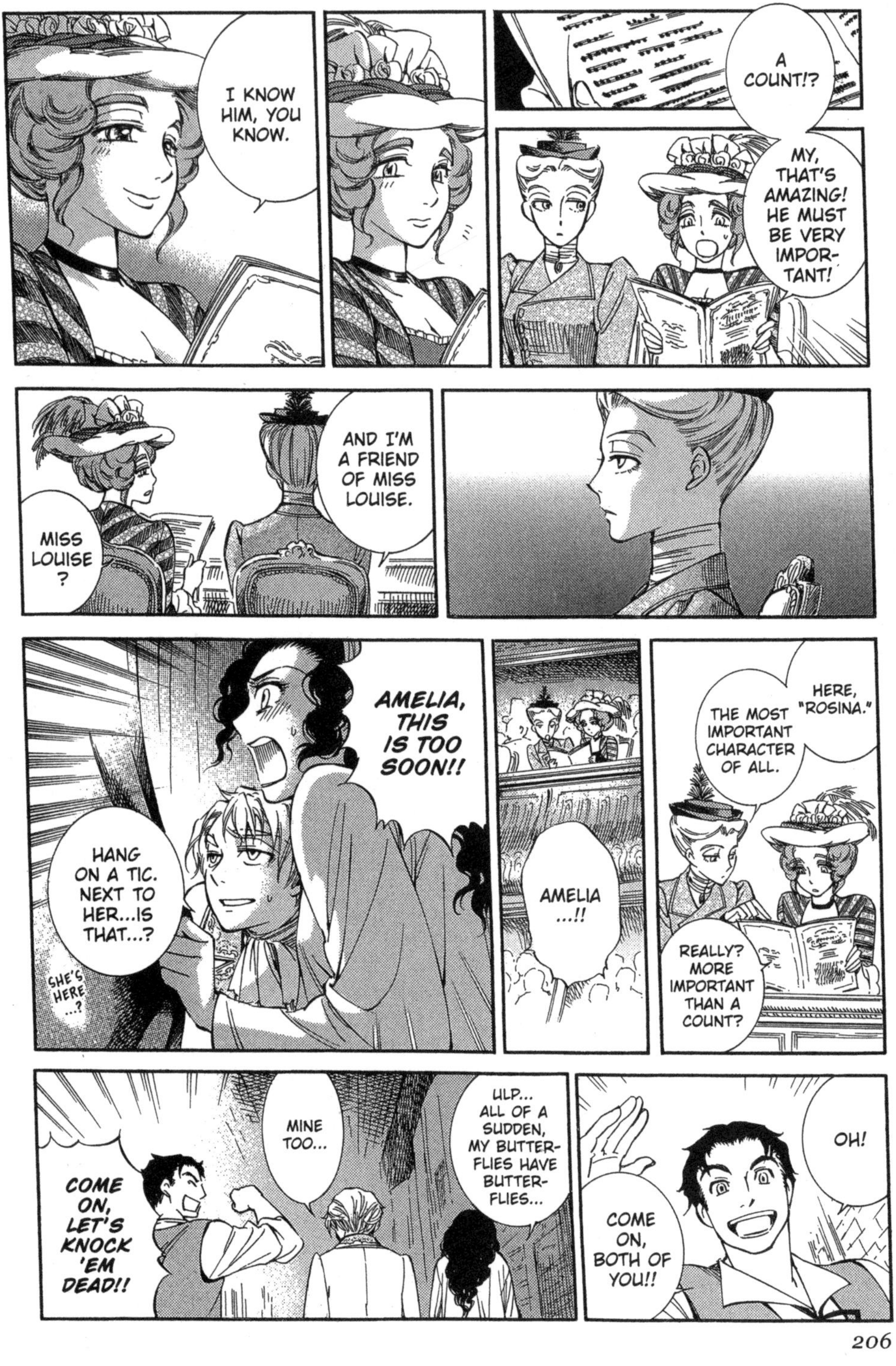
A COUNT!?
MY, THAT'S AMAZING! HE MUST BE VERY IMPORTANT!
I KNOW HIM, YOU KNOW.
AND I'M A FRIEND OF MISS LOUISE.
MISS LOUISE ?
HERE, "ROSINA."
THE MOST IMPORTANT CHARACTER OF ALL.
REALLY? MORE IMPORTANT THAN A COUNT?
AMELIA ...!!
AMELIA, THIS IS TOO SOON!!
HANG ON A TIC. NEXT TO HER...IS THAT...?
SHE'S HERE ...?
OH!
COME ON, BOTH OF YOU!!
ULP... ALL OF A SUDDEN, MY BUTTERFLIES HAVE BUTTERFLIES...
MINE TOO...
COME ON, LET'S KNOCK 'EM DEAD!!

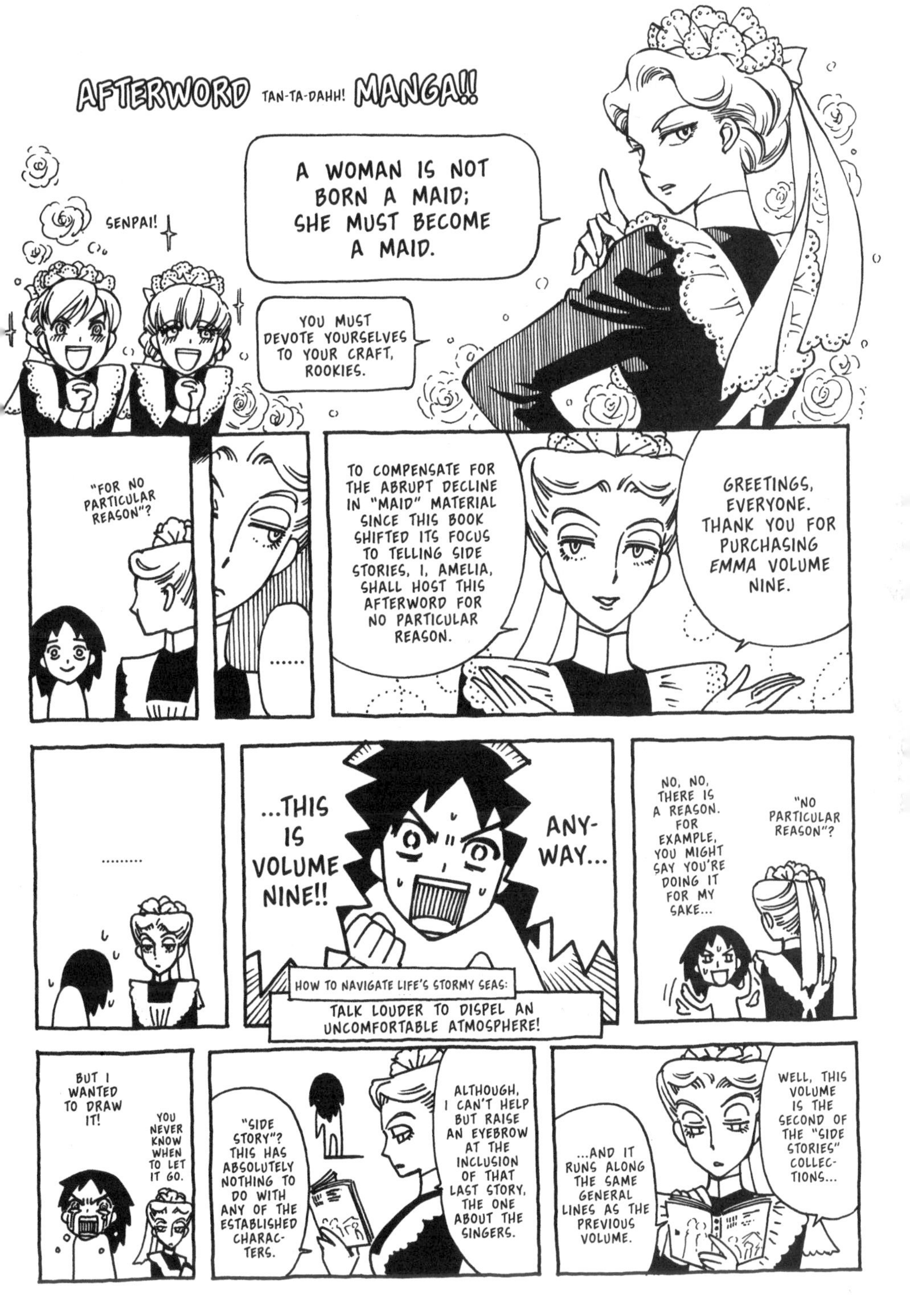
AFTERWORD TAN-TA-DAHH! MANGA!!
A WOMAN IS NOT BORN A MAID; SHE MUST BECOME A MAID.
YOU MUST DEVOTE YOURSELVES TO YOUR CRAFT, ROOKIES.
SENPAI!
GREETINGS, EVERYONE. THANK YOU FOR PURCHASING EMMA VOLUME NINE.
TO COMPENSATE FOR THE ABRUPT DECLINE IN "MAID" MATERIAL SINCE THIS BOOK SHIFTED ITS FOCUS TO TELLING SIDE STORIES, I, AMELIA, SHALL HOST THIS AFTERWORD FOR NO PARTICULAR REASON.
......
"FOR NO PARTICULAR REASON"?
"NO PARTICULAR REASON"?
NO, NO, THERE IS A REASON. FOR EXAMPLE, YOU MIGHT SAY YOU'RE DOING IT FOR MY SAKE...
ANY-WAY...
...THIS IS VOLUME NINE!!
HOW TO NAVIGATE LIFE'S STORMY SEAS:
TALK LOUDER TO DISPEL AN UNCOMFORTABLE ATMOSPHERE!
....
WELL, THIS VOLUME IS THE SECOND OF THE "SIDE STORIES" COLLEC-TIONS...
...AND IT RUNS ALONG THE SAME GENERAL LINES AS THE PREVIOUS VOLUME.
ALTHOUGH, I CAN'T HELP BUT RAISE AN EYEBROW AT THE INCLUSION OF THAT LAST STORY, THE ONE ABOUT THE SINGERS.
"SIDE STORY"? THIS HAS ABSOLUTELY NOTHING TO DO WITH ANY OF THE ESTABLISHED CHARAC-TERS.
BUT I WANTED TO DRAW IT!
YOU NEVER KNOW WHEN TO LET IT GO.

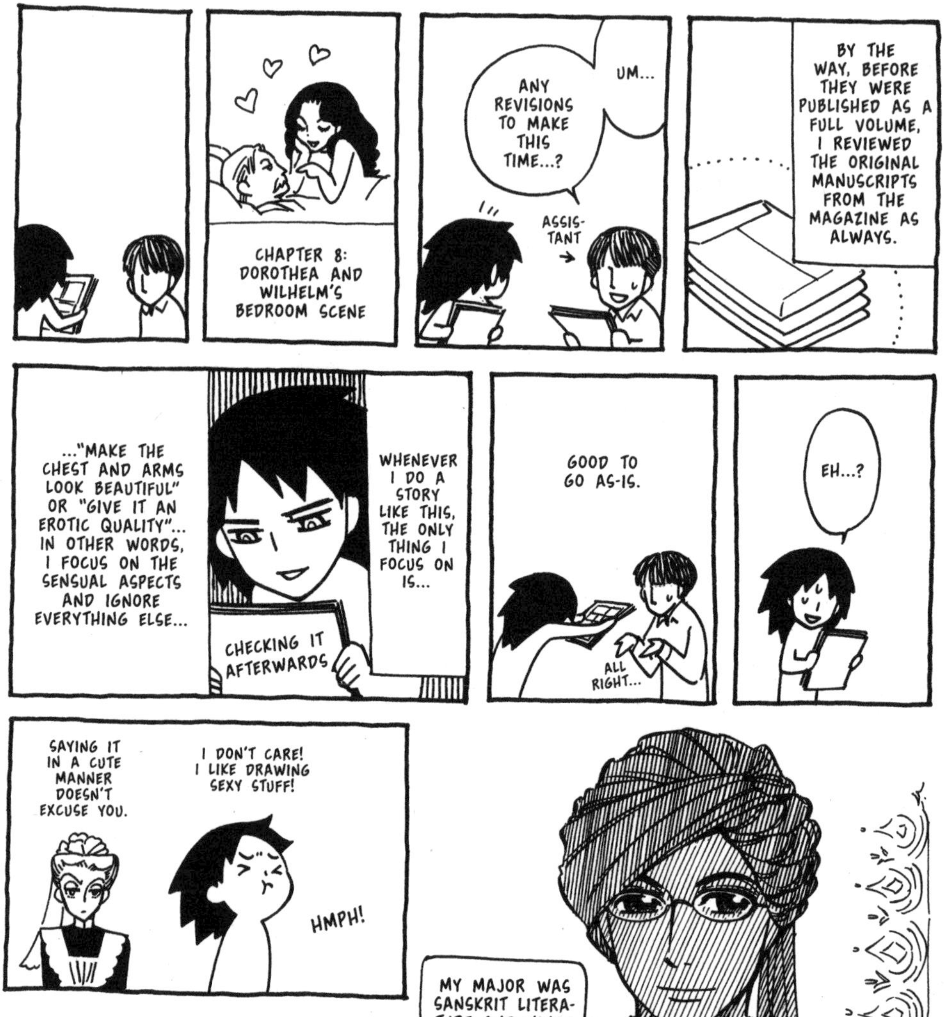
BY THE WAY, BEFORE THEY WERE PUBLISHED AS A FULL VOLUME, I REVIEWED THE ORIGINAL MANUSCRIPTS FROM THE MAGAZINE AS ALWAYS.
UM...
ANY REVISIONS TO MAKE THIS TIME...?
ASSIS-TANT
CHAPTER 8: DOROTHEA AND WILHELM'S BEDROOM SCENE
EH...?
GOOD TO GO AS-IS.
ALL RIGHT...
WHENEVER I DO A STORY LIKE THIS, THE ONLY THING I FOCUS ON IS...
CHECKING IT AFTERWARDS
..."MAKE THE CHEST AND ARMS LOOK BEAUTIFUL" OR "GIVE IT AN EROTIC QUALITY"... IN OTHER WORDS, I FOCUS ON THE SENSUAL ASPECTS AND IGNORE EVERYTHING ELSE...
I DON'T CARE! I LIKE DRAWING SEXY STUFF!
HMPH!
SAYING IT IN A CUTE MANNER DOESN'T EXCUSE YOU.

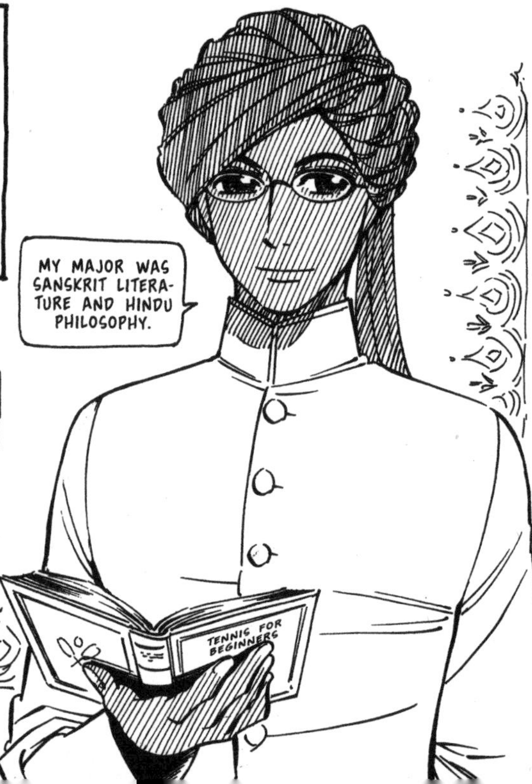
MY MAJOR WAS SANSKRIT LITERA-TURE AND HINDU PHILOSOPHY.
TENNIS FOR BEGINNERS

SUBASH CHANDRA (26)

I CAME UP WITH HIS NAME BUT DIDN'T GET A CHANCE TO USE IT IN THE STORY. AFTER GRADUATING FROM UNIVERSITY IN BENGAL, HE WAS HIRED AS AN INTERPRETER BY HAKIM'S FATHER...IS WHAT I IMAGINE.

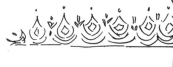

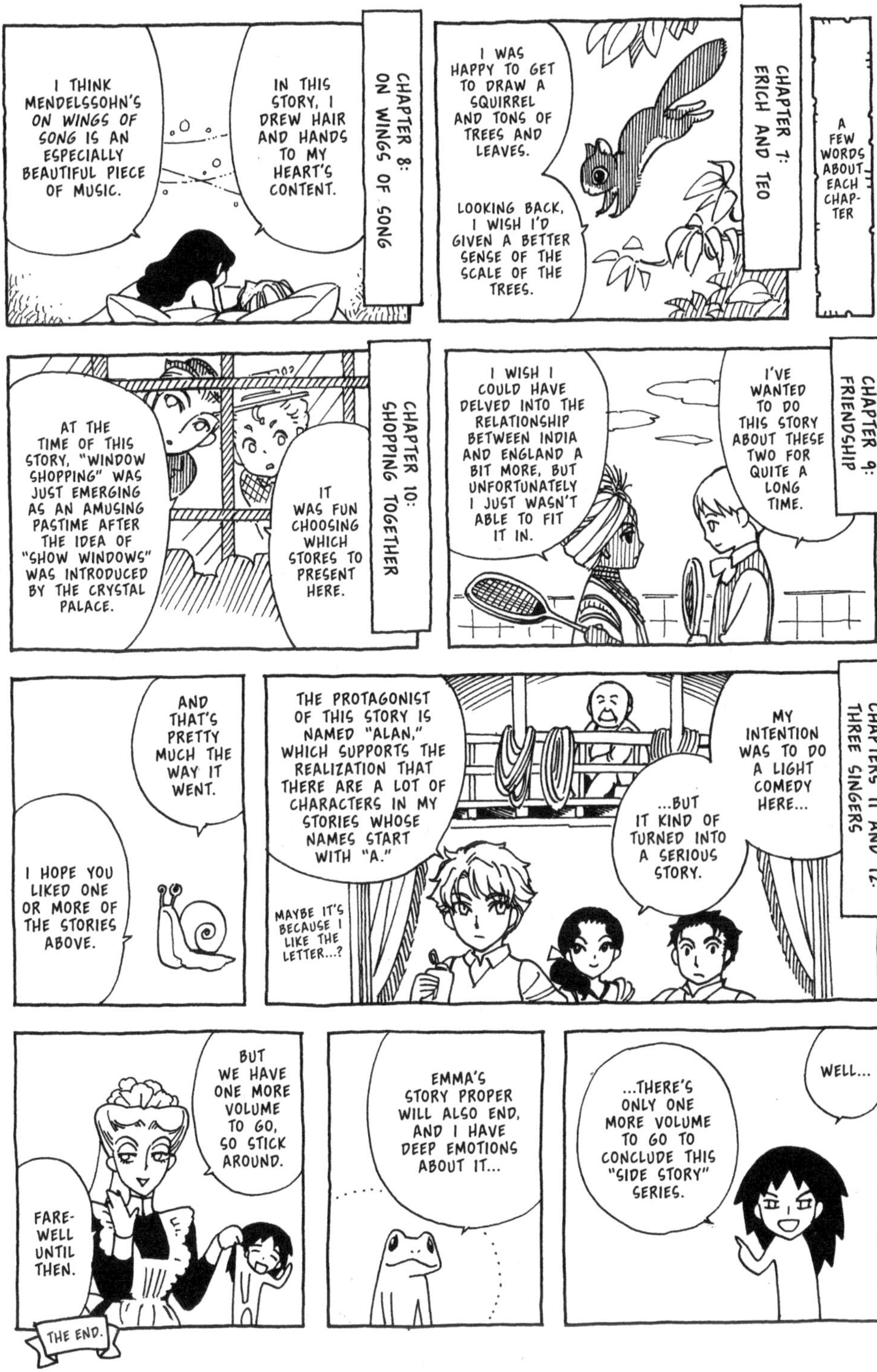
A FEW WORDS ABOUT EACH CHAPTER
CHAPTER 7: ERICH AND TEO
I WAS HAPPY TO GET TO DRAW A SQUIRREL AND TONS OF TREES AND LEAVES.
LOOKING BACK, I WISH I'D GIVEN A BETTER SENSE OF THE SCALE OF THE TREES.
CHAPTER 8: ON WINGS OF SONG
IN THIS STORY, I DREW HAIR AND HANDS TO MY HEART'S CONTENT.
I THINK MENDELSSOHN'S ON WINGS OF SONG IS AN ESPECIALLY BEAUTIFUL PIECE OF MUSIC.
CHAPTER 9: FRIENDSHIP
I'VE WANTED TO DO THIS STORY ABOUT THESE TWO FOR QUITE A LONG TIME.
I WISH I COULD HAVE DELVED INTO THE RELATIONSHIP BETWEEN INDIA AND ENGLAND A BIT MORE, BUT UNFORTUNATELY I JUST WASN'T ABLE TO FIT IT IN.
CHAPTER 10: SHOPPING TOGETHER
IT WAS FUN CHOOSING WHICH STORES TO PRESENT HERE.
AT THE TIME OF THIS STORY, "WINDOW SHOPPING" WAS JUST EMERGING AS AN AMUSING PASTIME AFTER THE IDEA OF "SHOW WINDOWS" WAS INTRODUCED BY THE CRYSTAL PALACE.
CHAPTERS 11 AND 12: THREE SINGERS
MY INTENTION WAS TO DO A LIGHT COMEDY HERE...
...BUT IT KIND OF TURNED INTO A SERIOUS STORY.
THE PROTAGONIST OF THIS STORY IS NAMED "ALAN," WHICH SUPPORTS THE REALIZATION THAT THERE ARE A LOT OF CHARACTERS IN MY STORIES WHOSE NAMES START WITH "A."
MAYBE IT'S BECAUSE I LIKE THE LETTER...?
AND THAT'S PRETTY MUCH THE WAY IT WENT.
I HOPE YOU LIKED ONE OR MORE OF THE STORIES ABOVE.
WELL...
...THERE'S ONLY ONE MORE VOLUME TO GO TO CONCLUDE THIS "SIDE STORY" SERIES.
EMMA'S STORY PROPER WILL ALSO END, AND I HAVE DEEP EMOTIONS ABOUT IT...
BUT WE HAVE ONE MORE VOLUME TO GO, SO STICK AROUND.
FARE-WELL UNTIL THEN.
THE END.

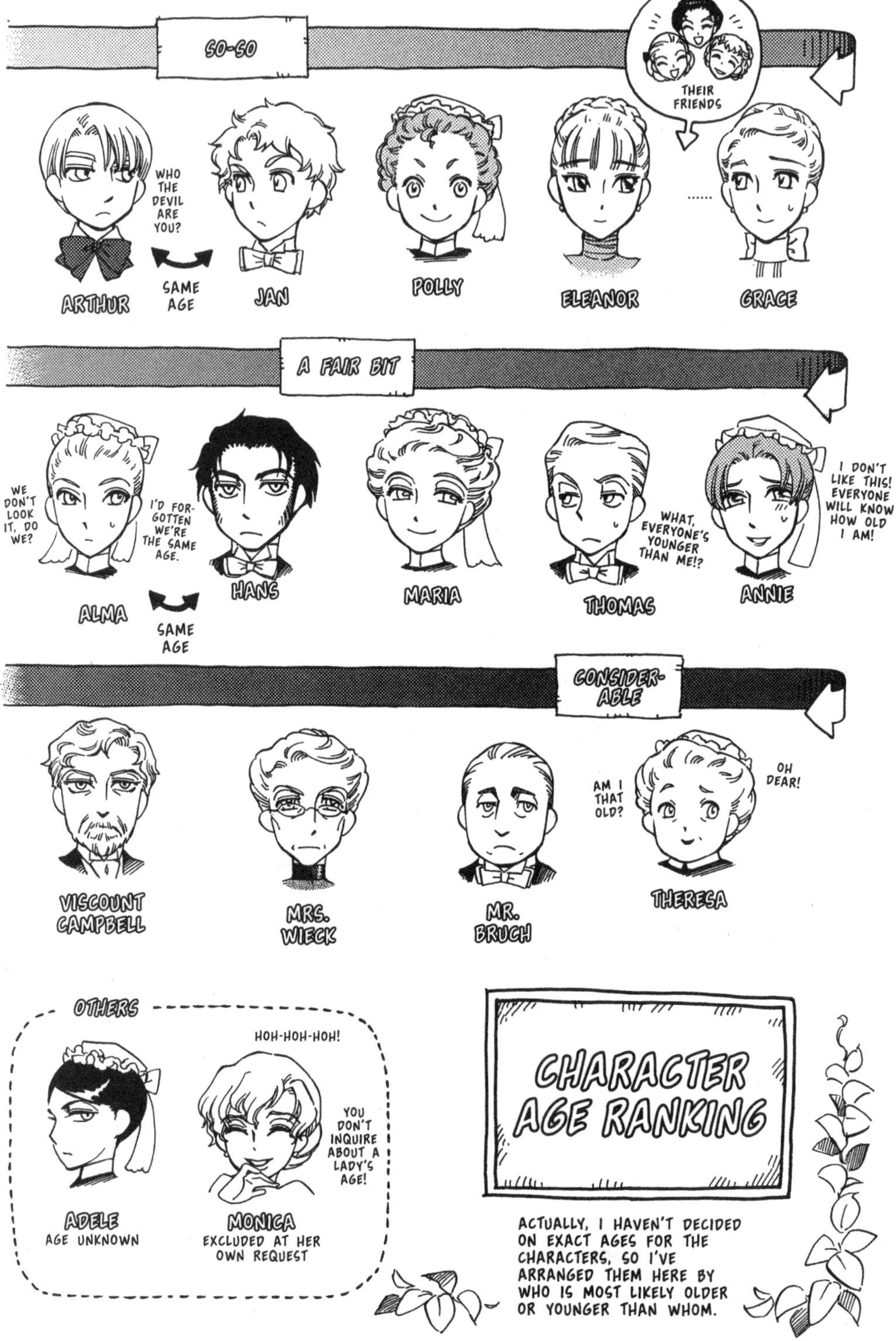
CHARACTER AGE RANKING
ACTUALLY, I HAVEN'T DECIDED ON EXACT AGES FOR THE CHARACTERS, SO I'VE ARRANGED THEM HERE BY WHO IS MOST LIKELY OLDER OR YOUNGER THAN WHOM.
SO-SO
THEIR FRIENDS
GRACE
......
ELEANOR
POLLY
JAN
WHO THE DEVIL ARE YOU?
SAME AGE
ARTHUR
A FAIR BIT
I DON'T LIKE THIS! EVERYONE WILL KNOW HOW OLD I AM!
ANNIE
WHAT, EVERYONE'S YOUNGER THAN ME!?
THOMAS
MARIA
I'D FORGOTTEN WE'RE THE SAME AGE.
HANS
SAME AGE
WE DON'T LOOK IT, DO WE?
ALMA
CONSIDERABLE
OH DEAR!
AM I THAT OLD?
THERESA
MR. BRUCH
MRS. WIECK
VISCOUNT CAMPBELL
OTHERS
HOH-HOH-HOH!
YOU DON'T INQUIRE ABOUT A LADY'S AGE!
MONICA
EXCLUDED AT HER OWN REQUEST
ADELE
AGE UNKNOWN

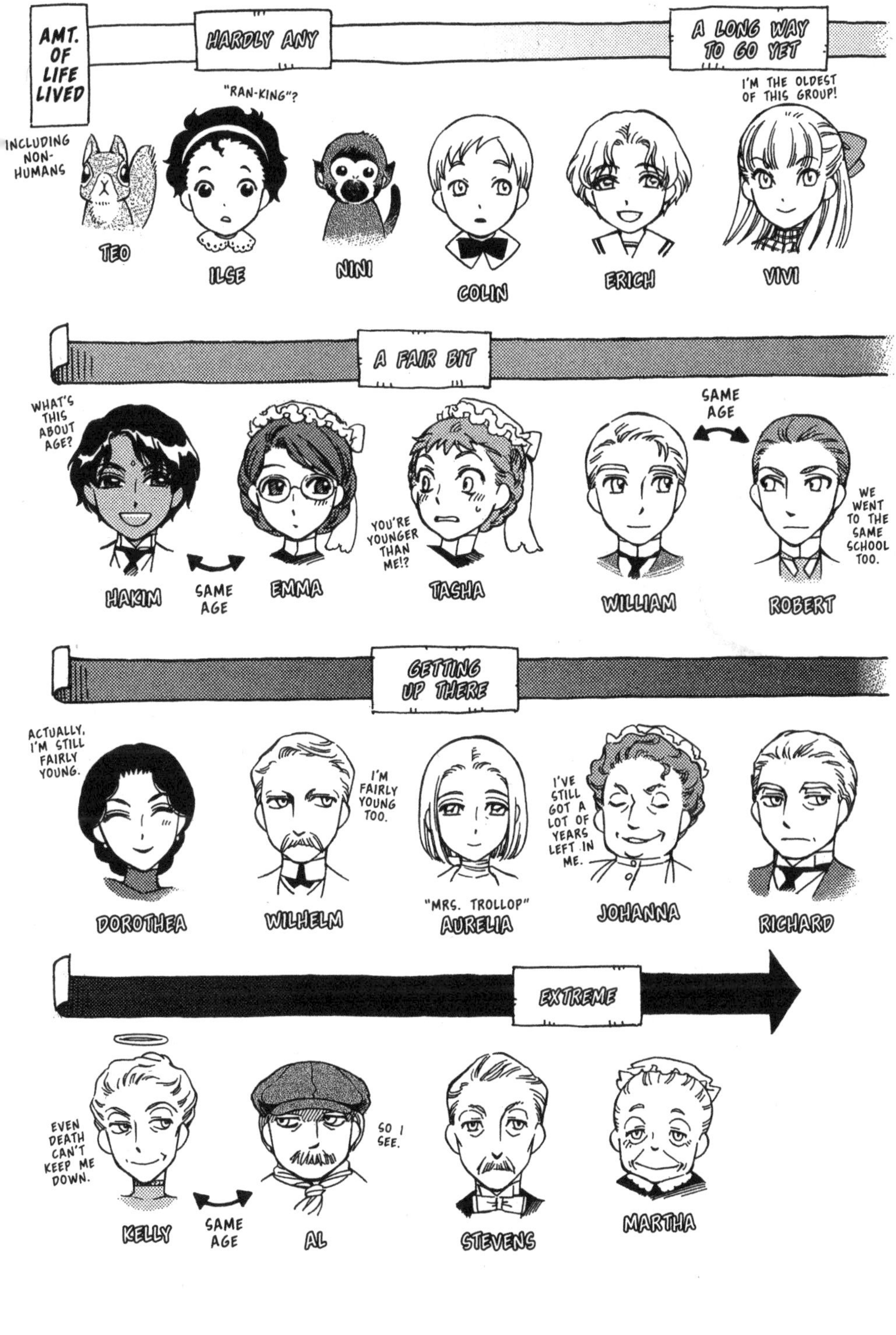
AMT. OF LIFE LIVED
HARDLY ANY
A LONG WAY TO GO YET
INCLUDING NON-HUMANS
TEO
"RAN-KING"?
ILSE
NINI
COLIN
ERICH
I'M THE OLDEST OF THIS GROUP!
VIVI
A FAIR BIT
WHAT'S THIS ABOUT AGE?
HAKIM
SAME AGE
EMMA
YOU'RE YOUNGER THAN ME!?
TASHA
SAME AGE
WILLIAM
WE WENT TO THE SAME SCHOOL TOO.
ROBERT
GETTING UP THERE
ACTUALLY, I'M STILL FAIRLY YOUNG.
DOROTHEA
I'M FAIRLY YOUNG TOO.
WILHELM
"MRS. TROLLOP"
AURELIA
I'VE STILL GOT A LOT OF YEARS LEFT IN ME.
JOHANNA
RICHARD
EXTREME
EVEN DEATH CAN'T KEEP ME DOWN.
KELLY
SAME AGE
SO I SEE.
AL
STEVENS
MARTHA

Emma

Chapter 13:
The Bicycle

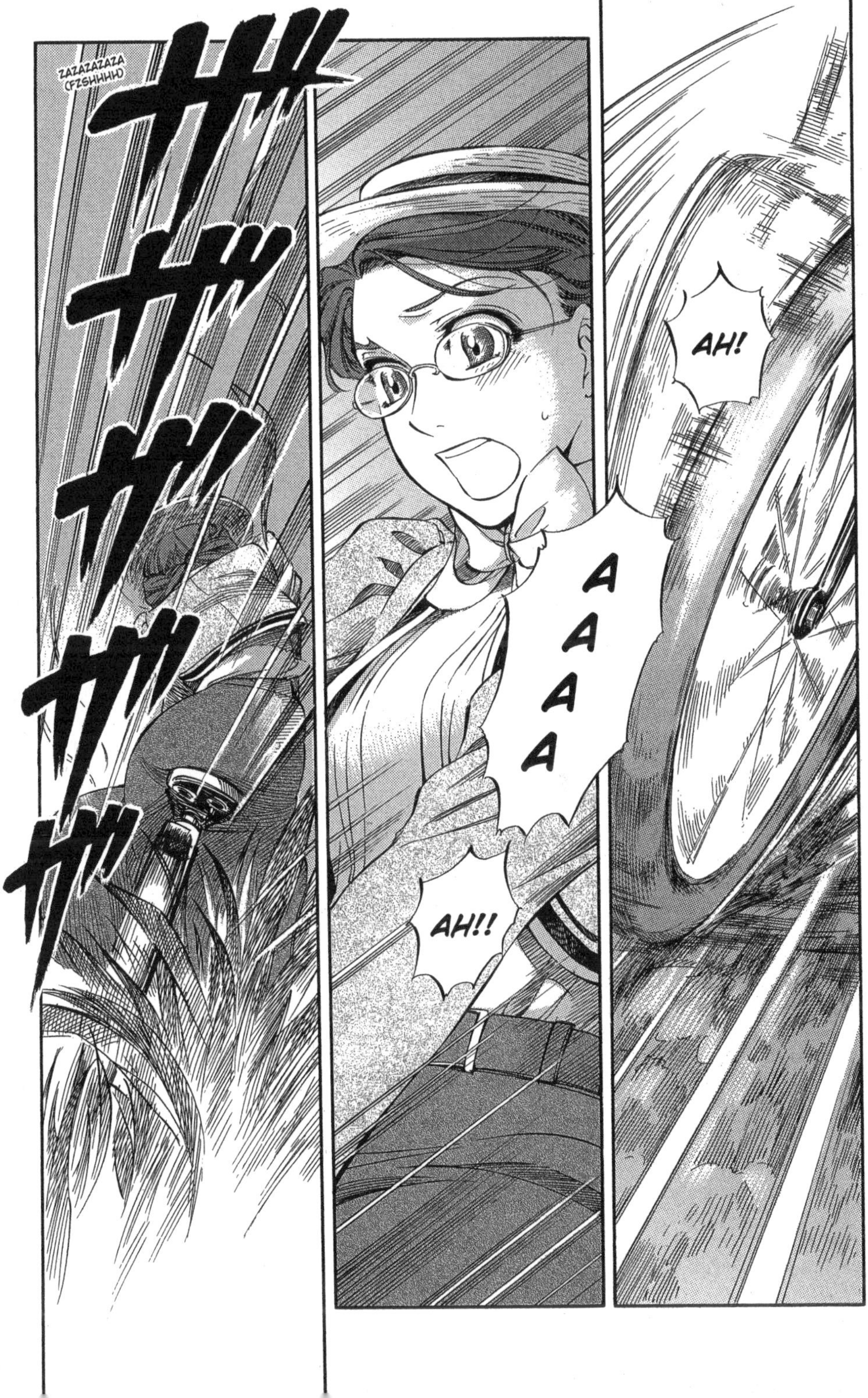
AH!
AAAAA
AH!!
ZAZAZAZAZA
(FZSHHHH)

Chapter 13:
The Bicycle

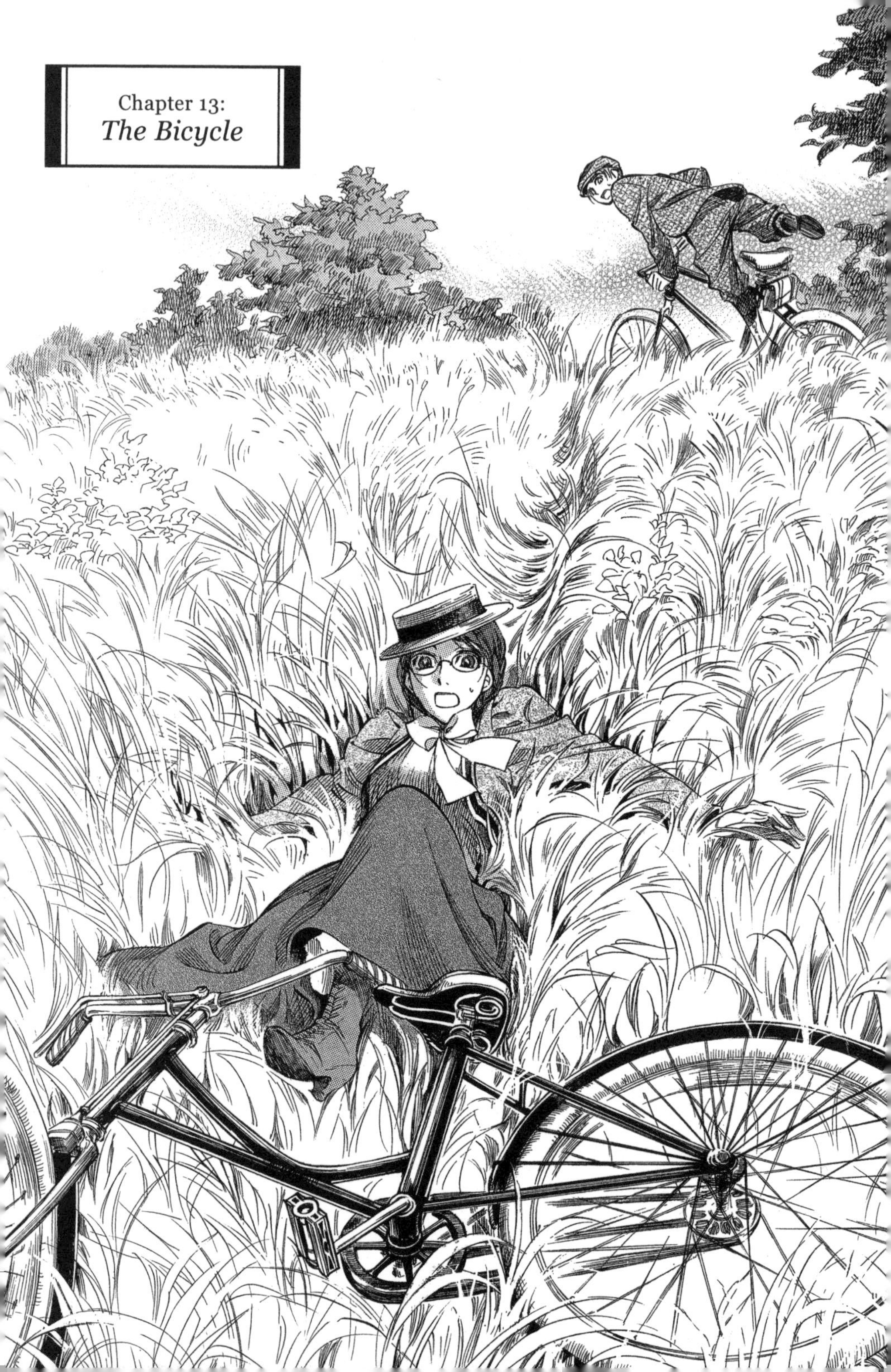

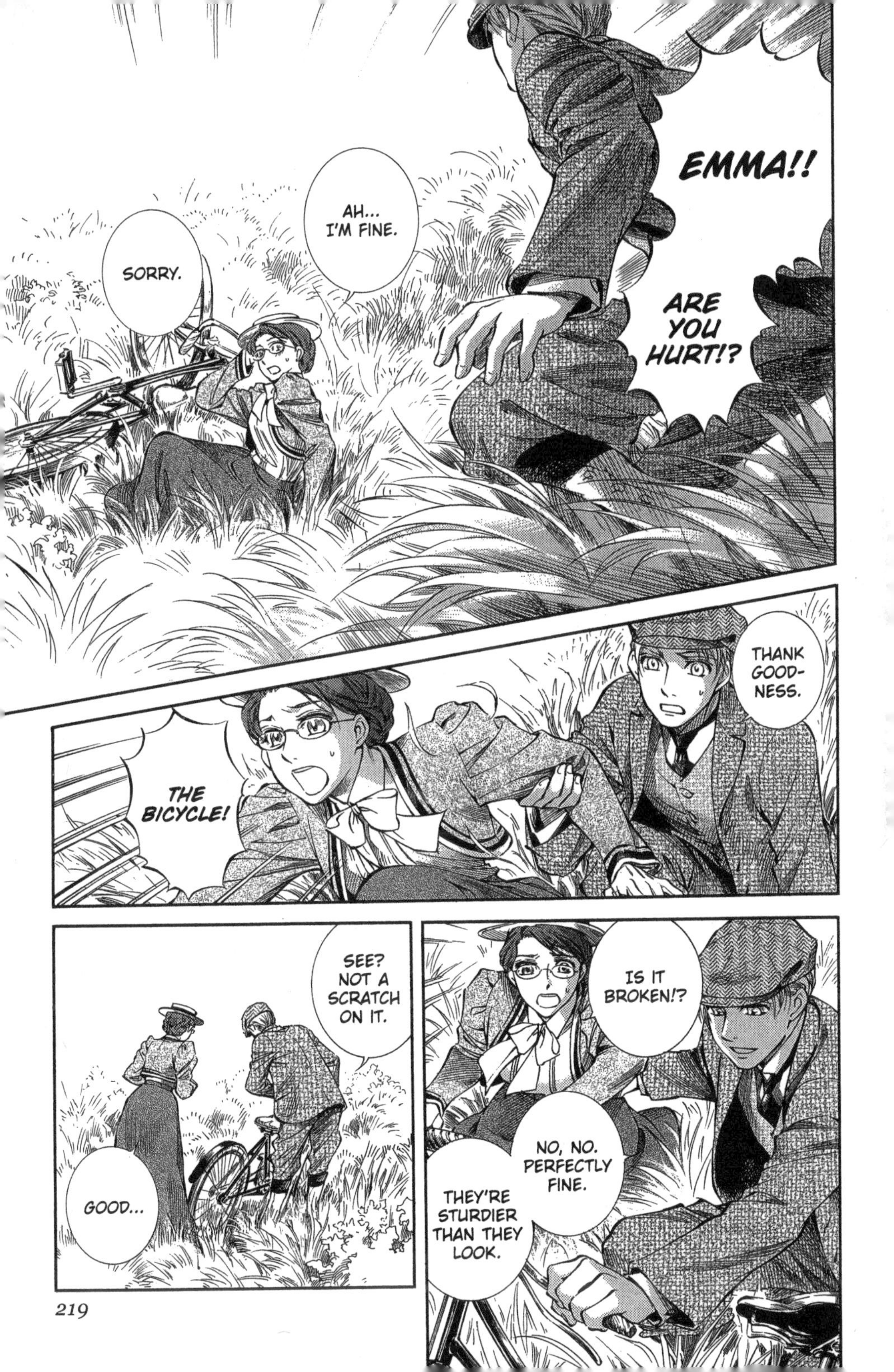
EMMA!!
ARE YOU HURT!?
AH... I'M FINE.
SORRY.
THANK GOOD-NESS.
THE BICYCLE!
IS IT BROKEN!?
NO, NO. PERFECTLY FINE.
THEY'RE STURDIER THAN THEY LOOK.
SEE? NOT A SCRATCH ON IT.
GOOD...

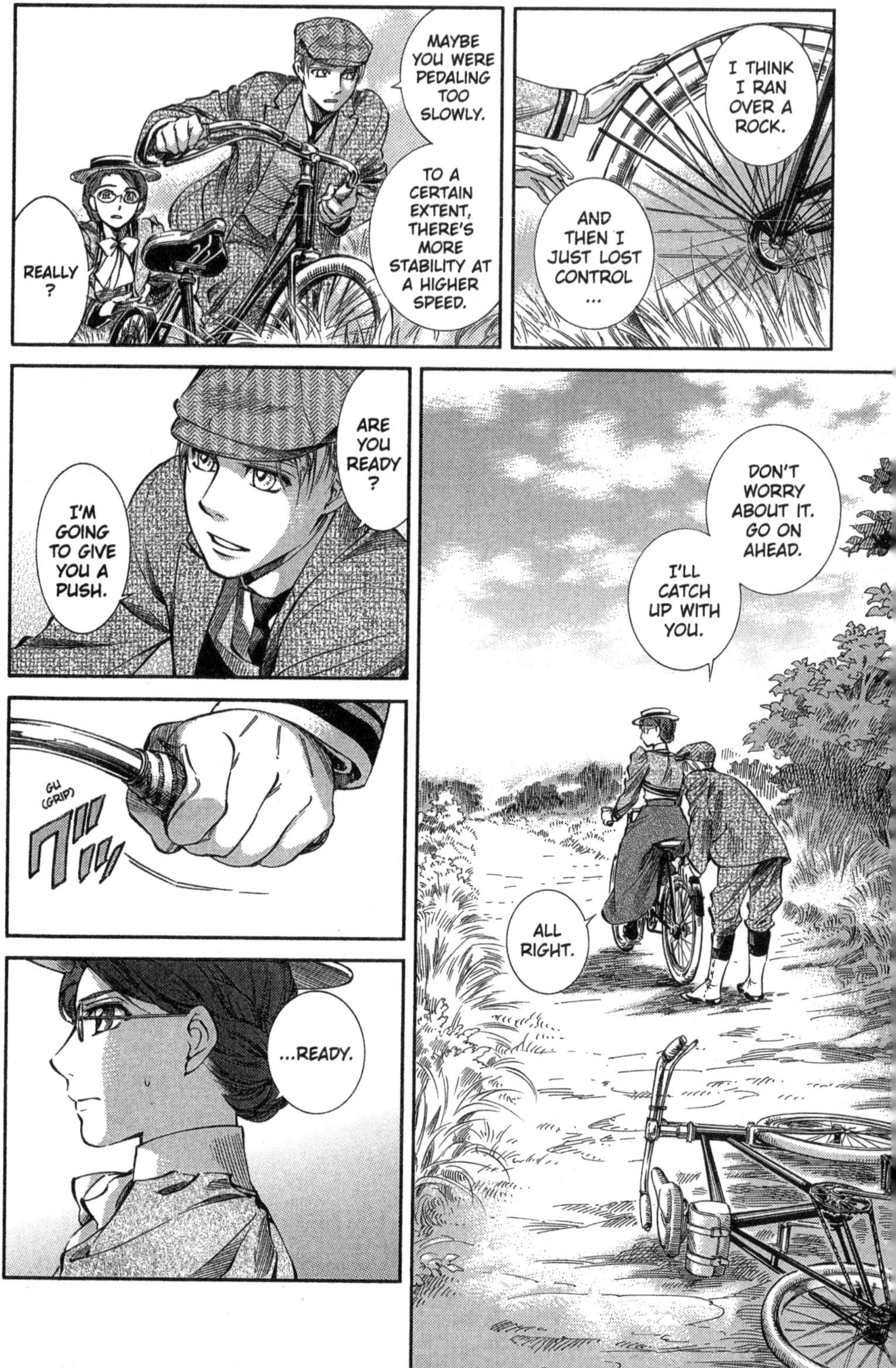
I THINK I RAN OVER A ROCK.
AND THEN I JUST LOST CONTROL ...
MAYBE YOU WERE PEDALING TOO SLOWLY.
TO A CERTAIN EXTENT, THERE'S MORE STABILITY AT A HIGHER SPEED.
REALLY ?
DON'T WORRY ABOUT IT. GO ON AHEAD.
I'LL CATCH UP WITH YOU.
ALL RIGHT.
ARE YOU READY ?
I'M GOING TO GIVE YOU A PUSH.
GU (GRIP)
...READY.

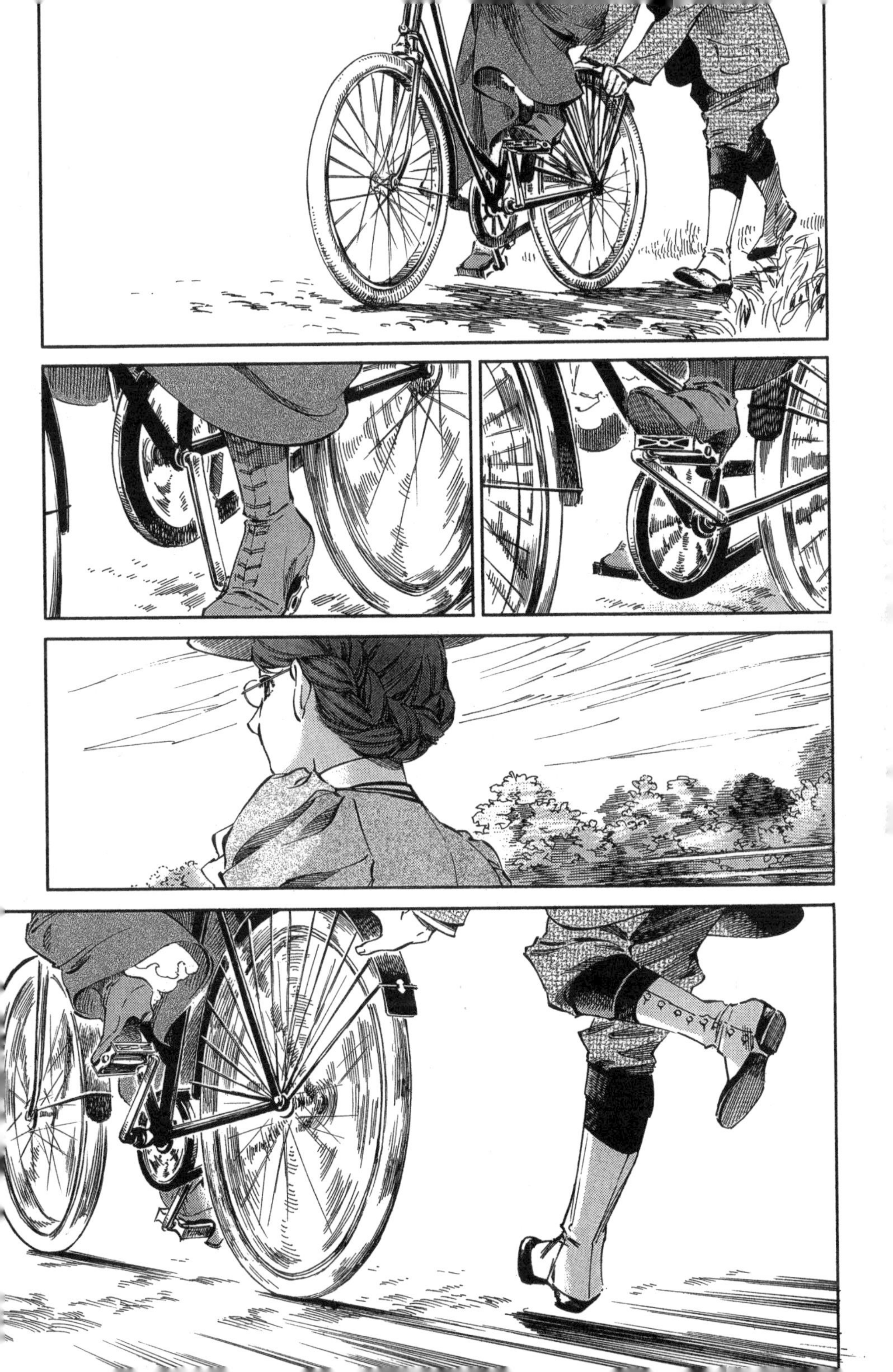

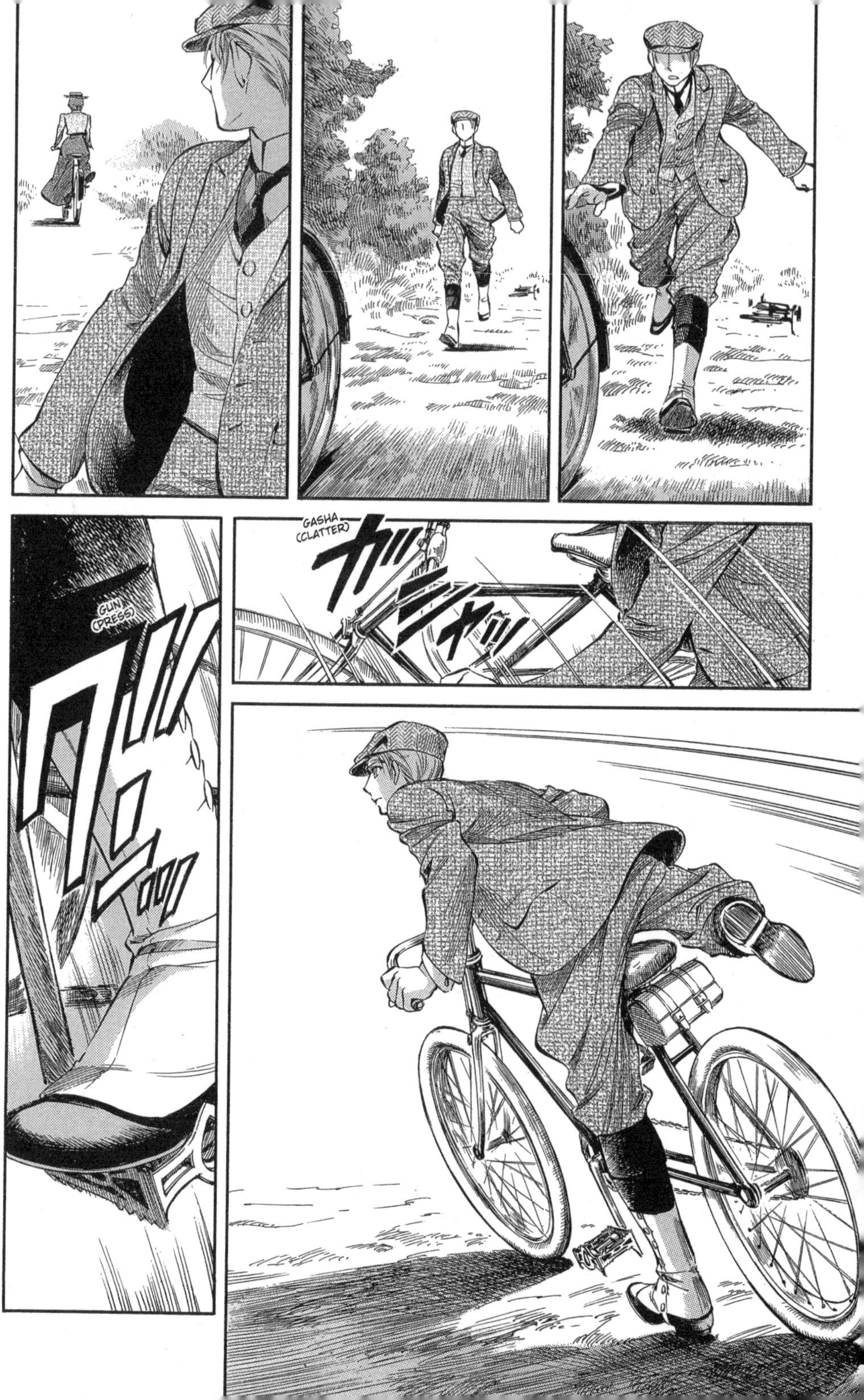
GASHA (CLATTER)
GUN (PRESS)

I KNOW HIM, YOU KNOW.

A COUNT!?

MY, THAT'S AMAZING! HE MUST BE VERY IMPORTANT!

AND I'M A FRIEND OF MISS LOUISE.

MISS LOUISE?

AMELIA, THIS IS TOO SOON!!

HANG ON A TIC. NEXT TO HER...IS THAT...?

SHE'S HERE...?

AMELIA ...!!

HERE, "ROSINA." THE MOST IMPORTANT CHARACTER OF ALL.

REALLY? MORE IMPORTANT THAN A COUNT?

MINE TOO...

ULP... ALL OF A SUDDEN, MY BUTTERFLIES HAVE BUTTERFLIES...

COME ON, LET'S KNOCK 'EM DEAD!!

OH!

COME ON, BOTH OF YOU!!

GO AHEAD.

PARDON ME, DO YOU MIND IF I SIT NEXT TO YOU?

EXCUSE ME...

CAN YOU READ?

LET ME SEE...

WE COULD USE MORE BOX SEATS...

THEY'RE PACKED IN UP AT THE TOP.

HOW'S THE CROWD?

NOT BAD.

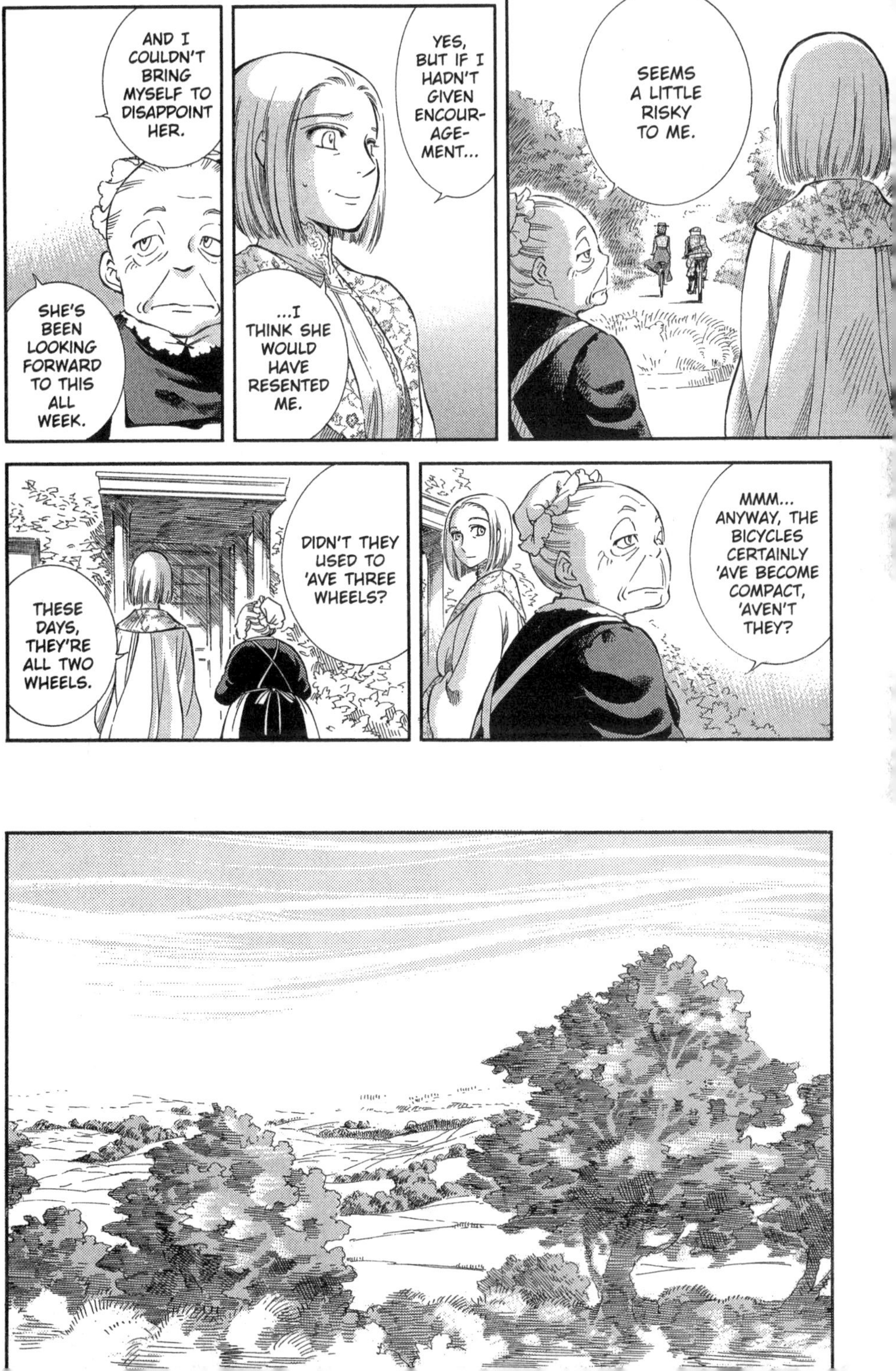
SEEMS A LITTLE RISKY TO ME.
YES, BUT IF I HADN'T GIVEN ENCOURAGEMENT...
...I THINK SHE WOULD HAVE RESENTED ME.
AND I COULDN'T BRING MYSELF TO DISAPPOINT HER.
SHE'S BEEN LOOKING FORWARD TO THIS ALL WEEK.
MMM... ANYWAY, THE BICYCLES CERTAINLY 'AVE BECOME COMPACT, 'AVEN'T THEY?
DIDN'T THEY USED TO 'AVE THREE WHEELS?
THESE DAYS, THEY'RE ALL TWO WHEELS.

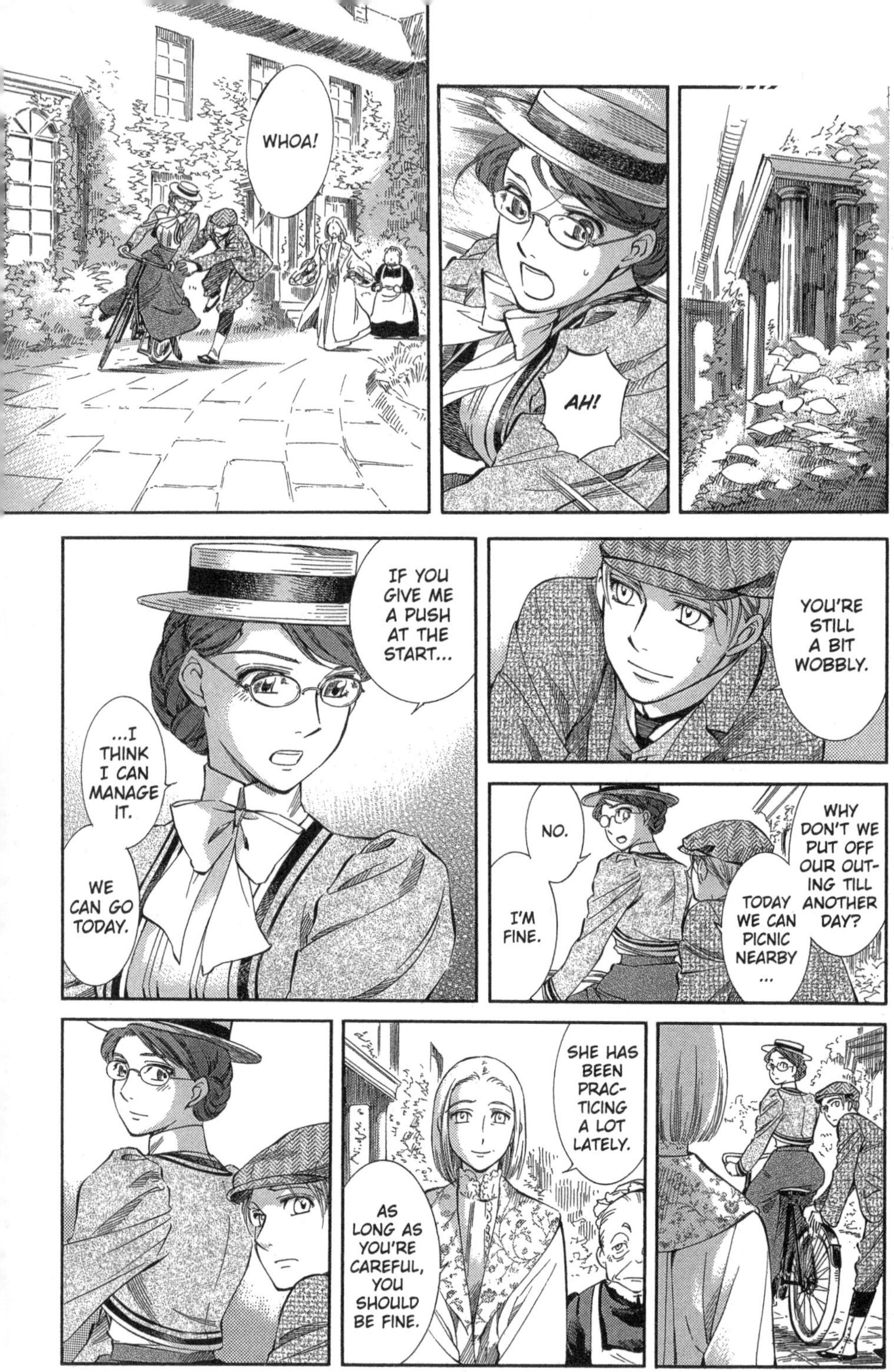
AH!
WHOA!
YOU'RE STILL A BIT WOBBLY.
WHY DON'T WE PUT OFF OUR OUT-ING TILL ANOTHER DAY?
TODAY WE CAN PICNIC NEARBY...
NO.
I'M FINE.
IF YOU GIVE ME A PUSH AT THE START...
...I THINK I CAN MANAGE IT.
WE CAN GO TODAY.
SHE HAS BEEN PRAC-TICING A LOT LATELY.
AS LONG AS YOU'RE CAREFUL, YOU SHOULD BE FINE.

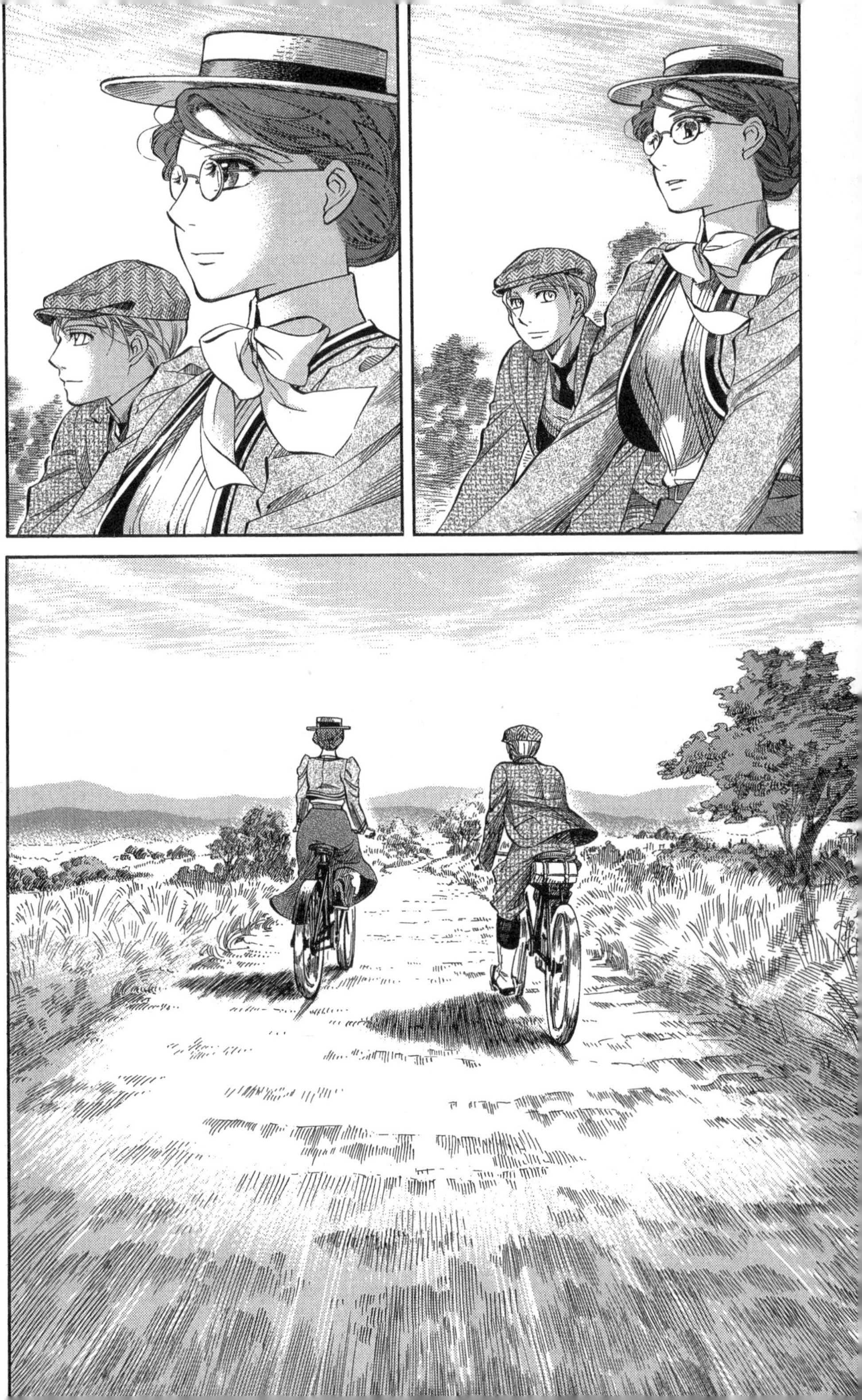

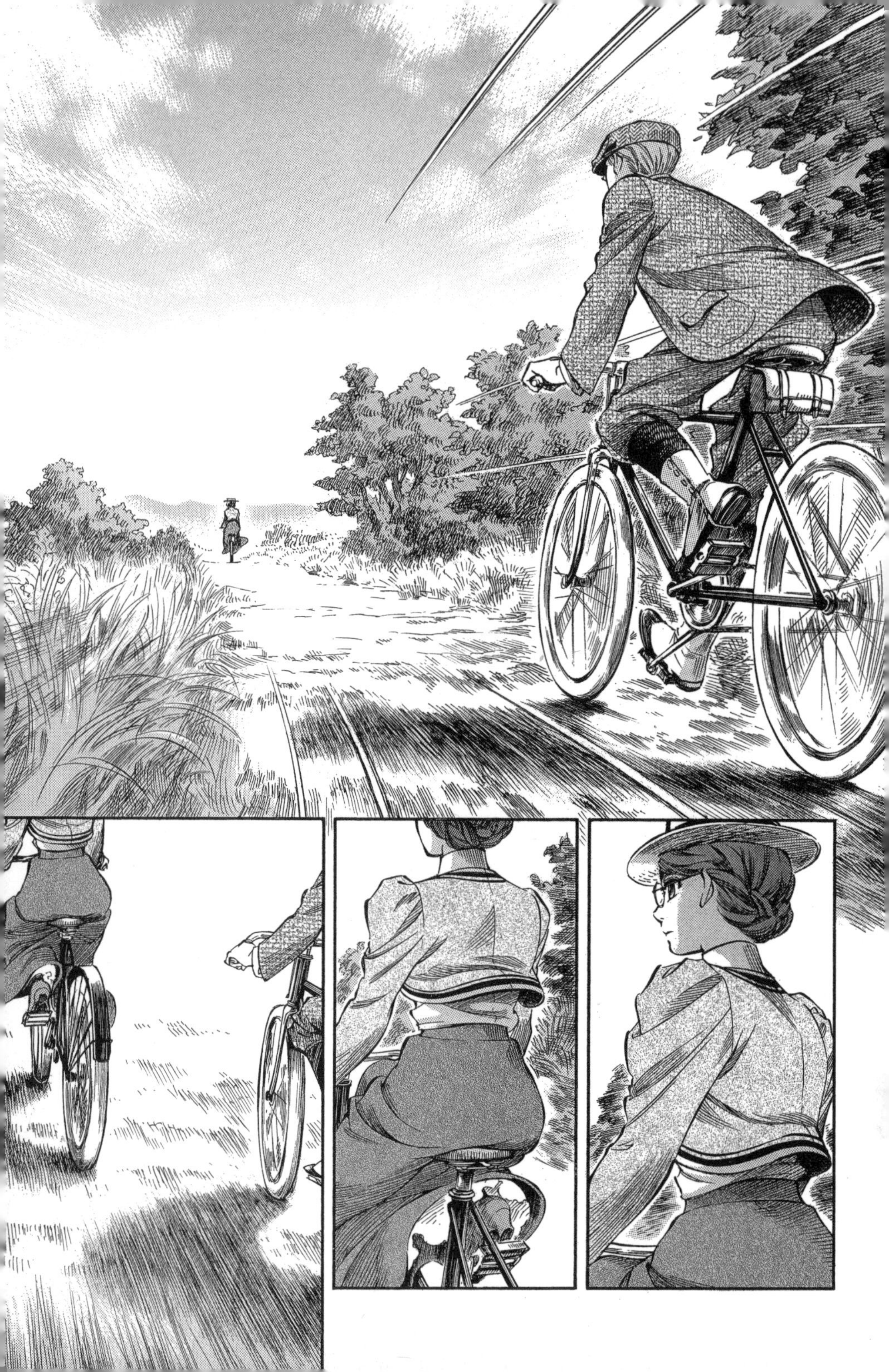

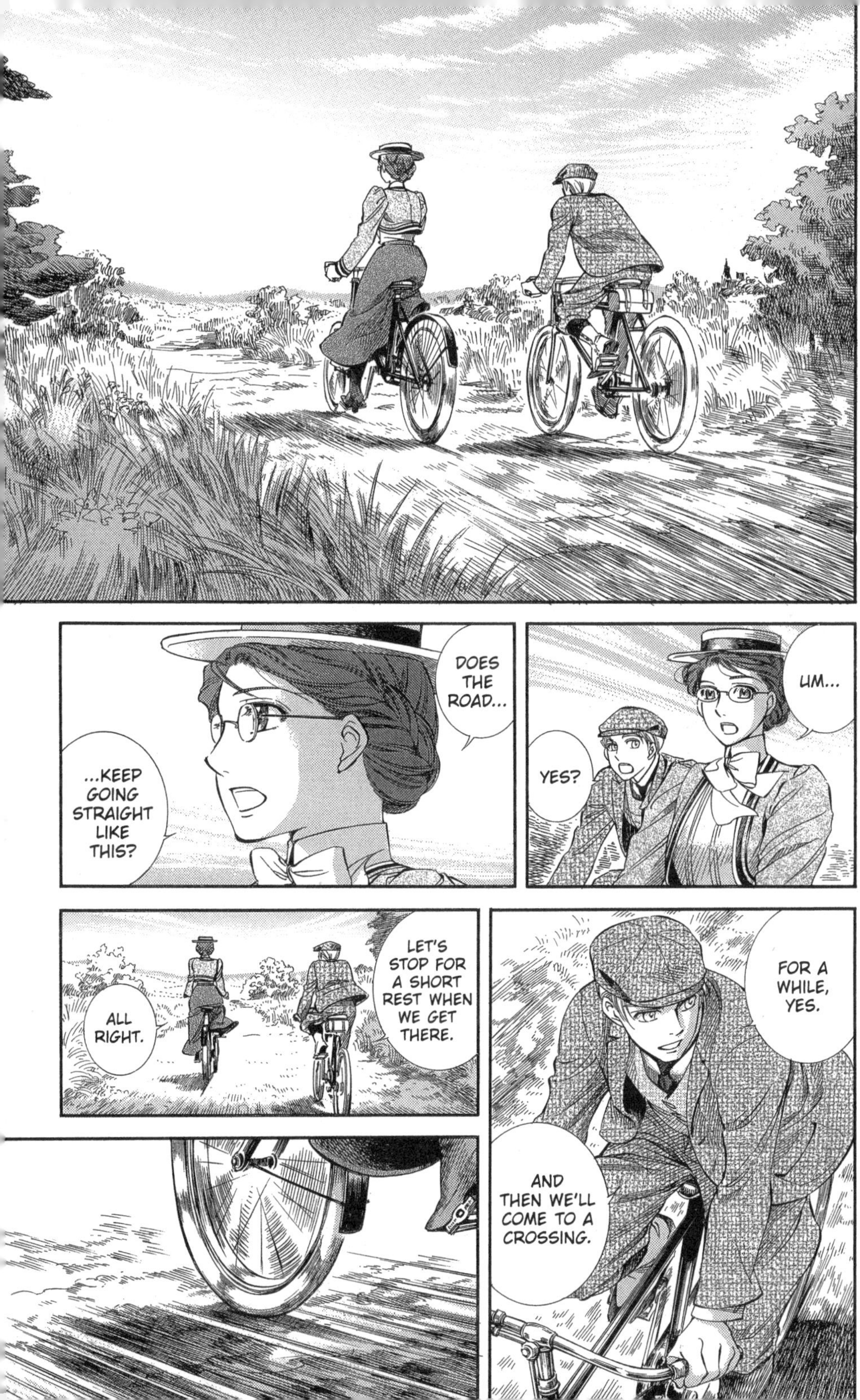
UM...
YES?
DOES THE ROAD...
...KEEP GOING STRAIGHT LIKE THIS?
FOR A WHILE, YES.
AND THEN WE'LL COME TO A CROSSING.
LET'S STOP FOR A SHORT REST WHEN WE GET THERE.
ALL RIGHT.

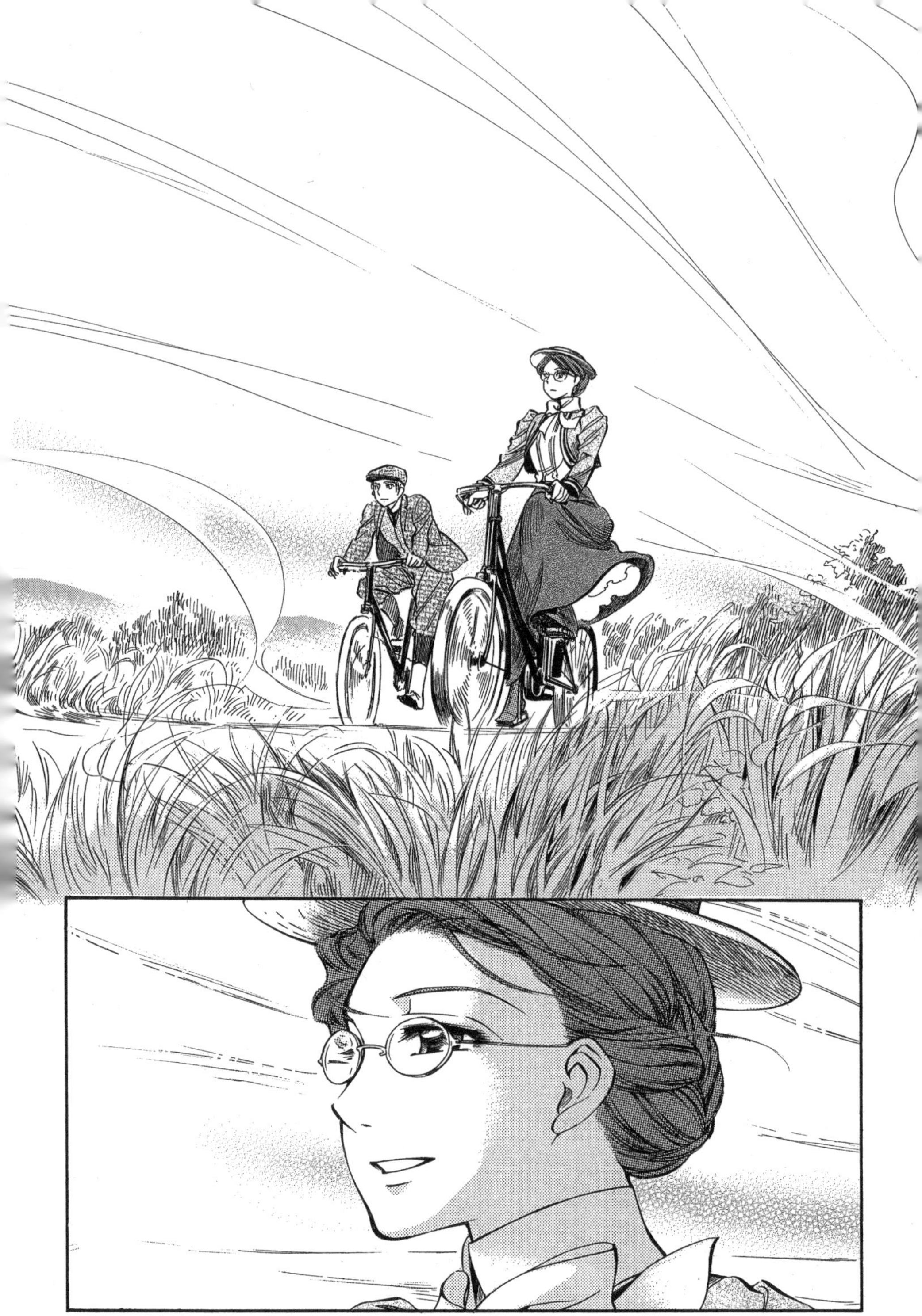

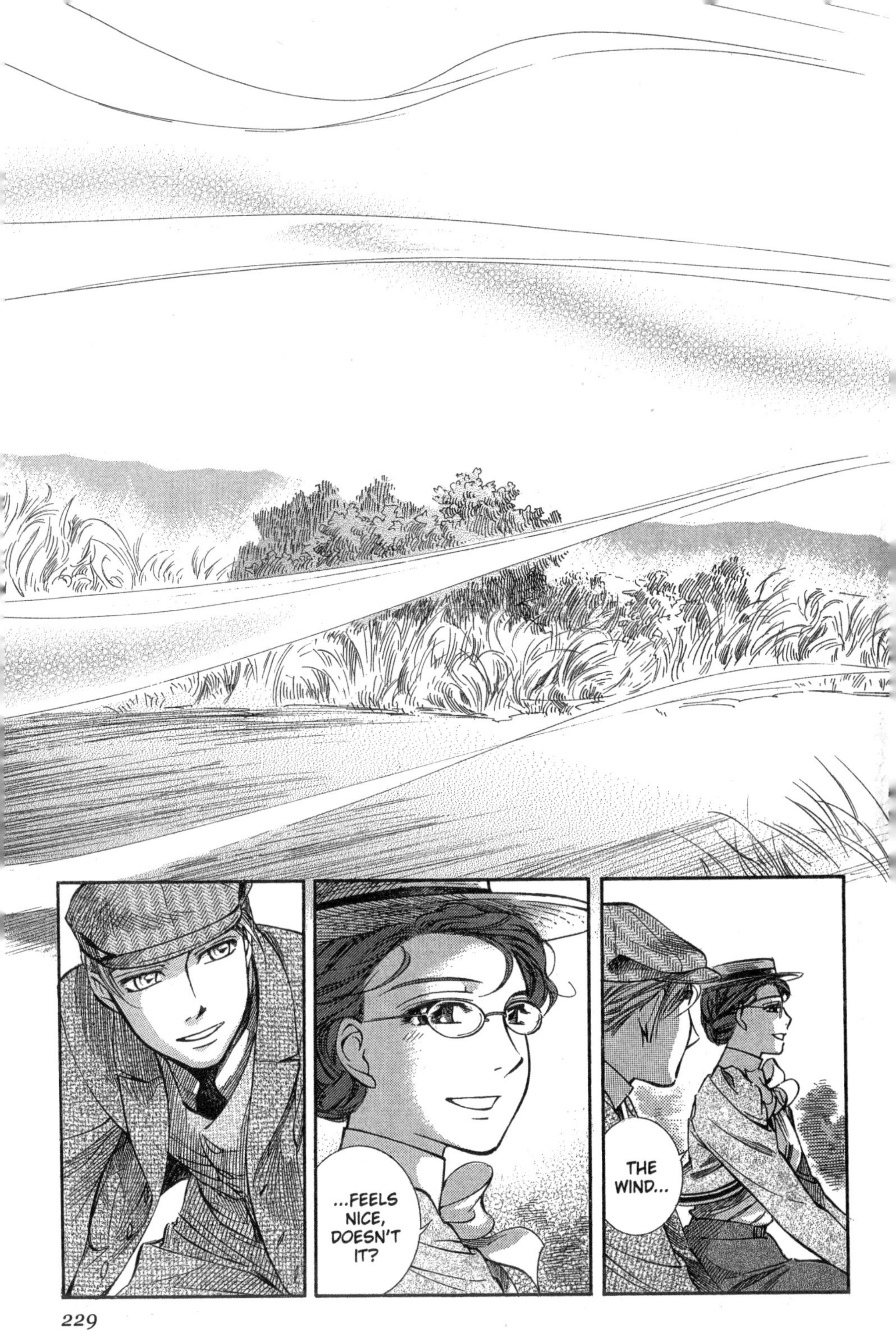
THE WIND...
...FEELS NICE, DOESN'T IT?

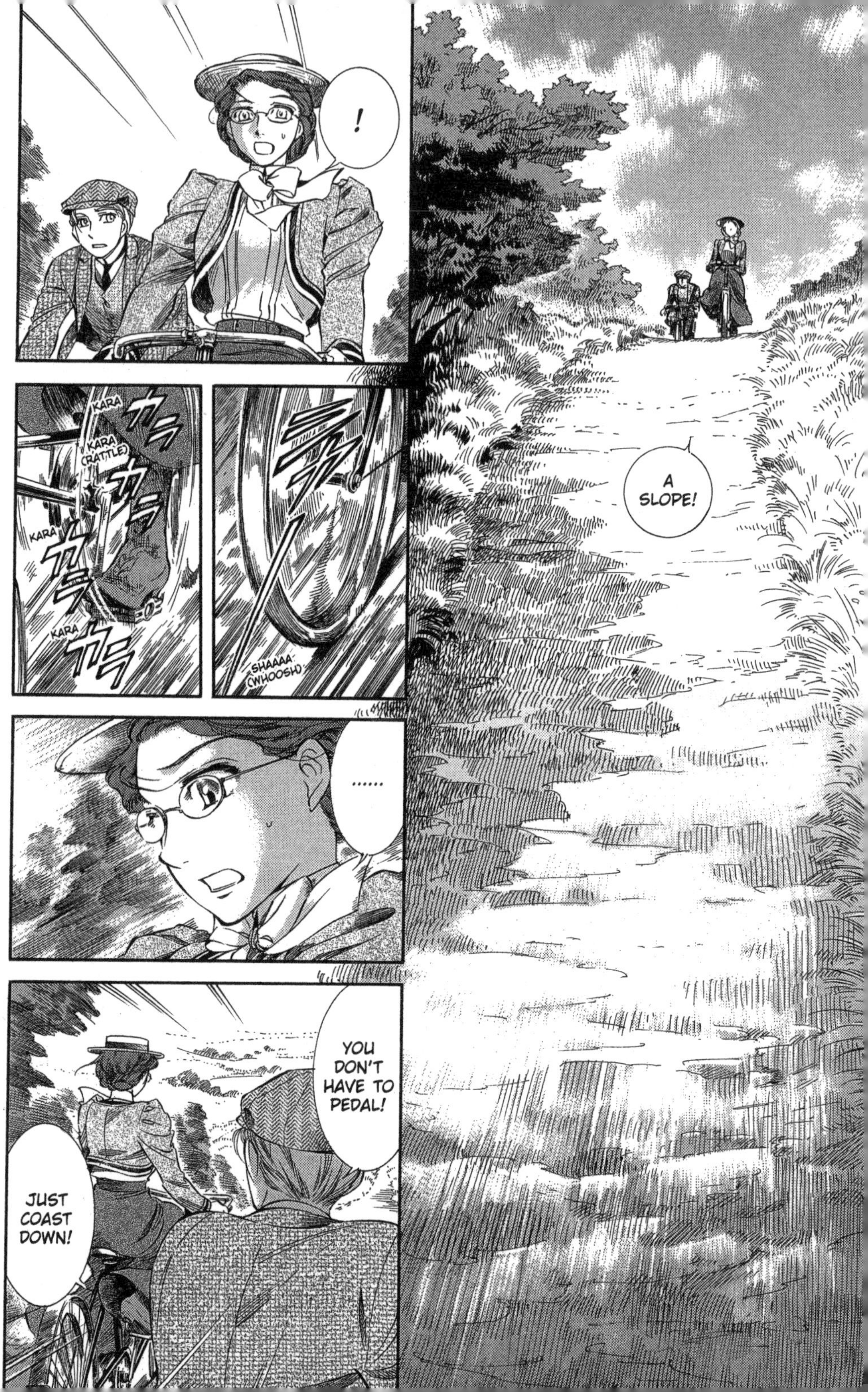
A SLOPE!
!
SHAAAA (WHOOSH)
KARA
KARA (RATTLE)
KARA
KARA
......
YOU DON'T HAVE TO PEDAL!
JUST COAST DOWN!

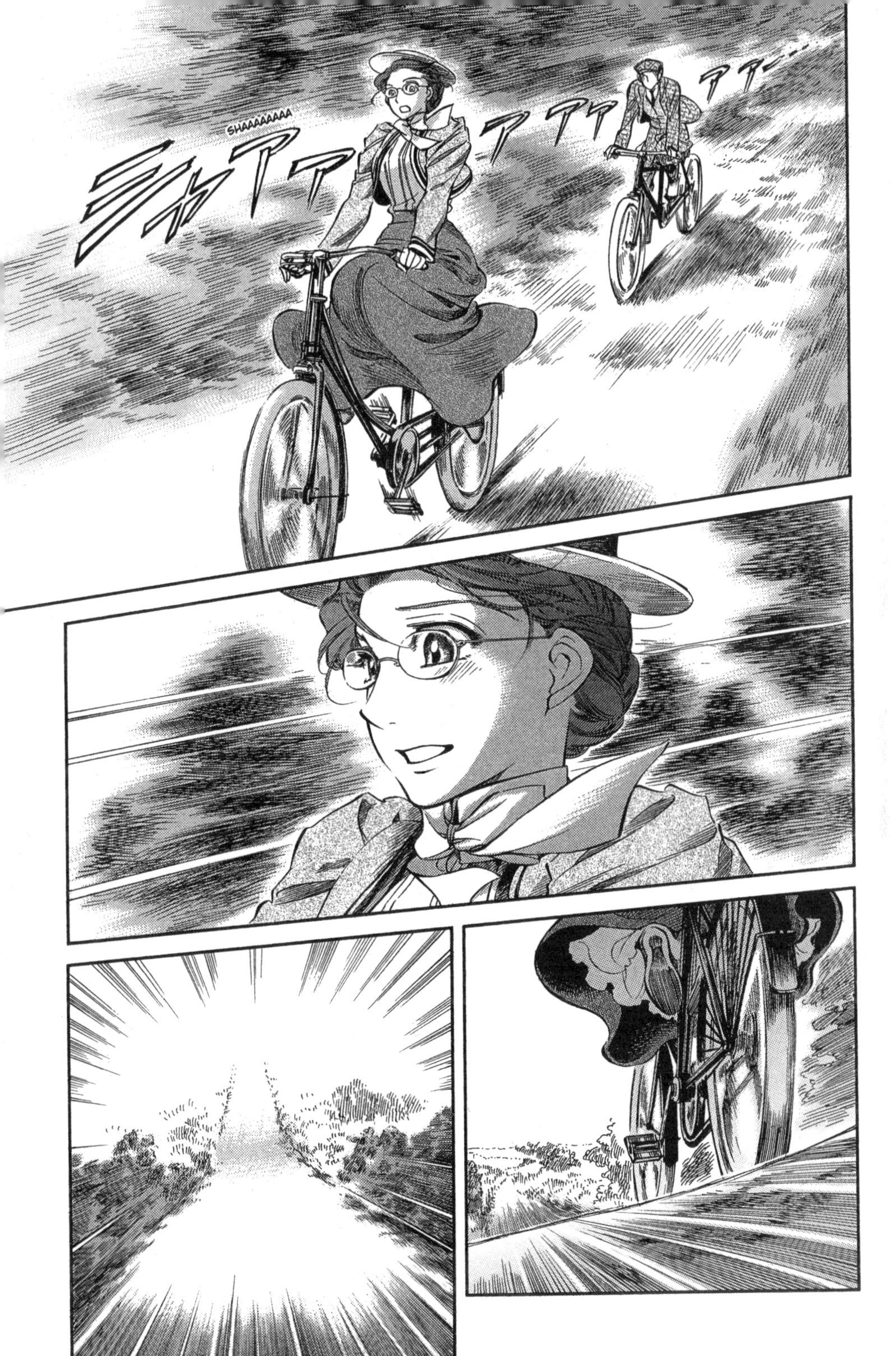
SHAAAAAAAA

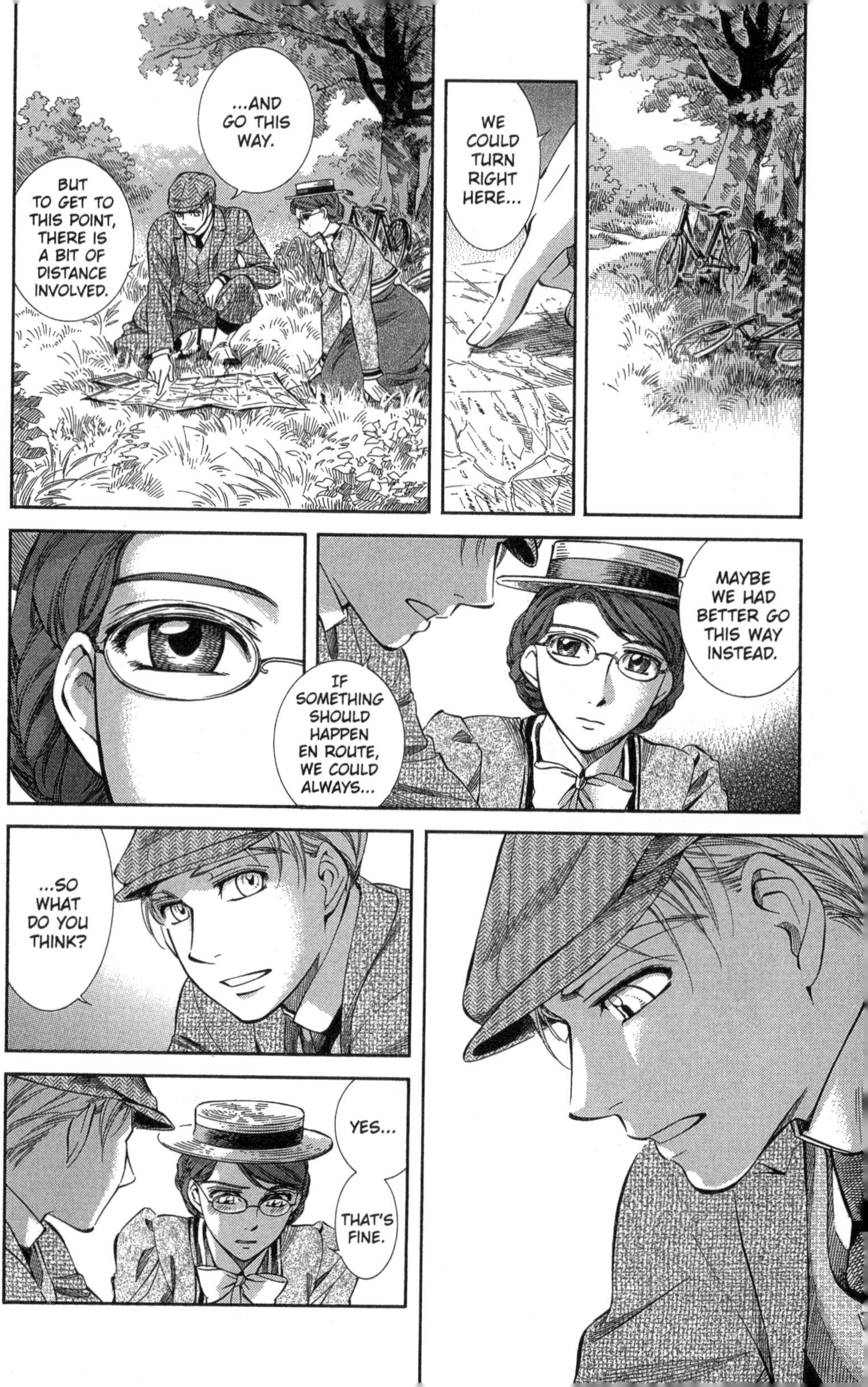
WE COULD TURN RIGHT HERE...
...AND GO THIS WAY.
BUT TO GET TO THIS POINT, THERE IS A BIT OF DISTANCE INVOLVED.
MAYBE WE HAD BETTER GO THIS WAY INSTEAD.
IF SOMETHING SHOULD HAPPEN EN ROUTE, WE COULD ALWAYS...
...SO WHAT DO YOU THINK?
YES...
THAT'S FINE.

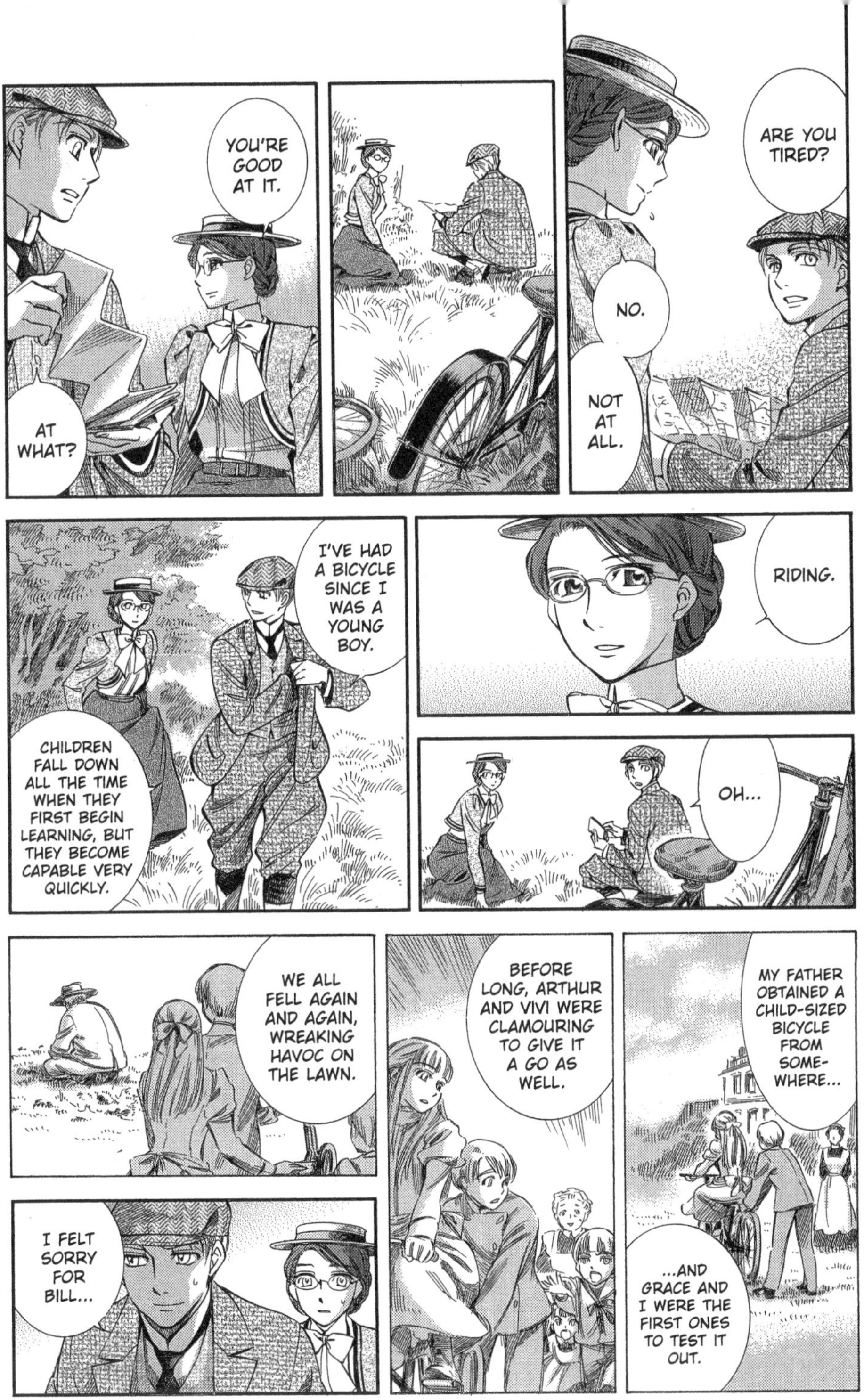
ARE YOU TIRED?
NO.
NOT AT ALL.
YOU'RE GOOD AT IT.
AT WHAT?
RIDING.
OH...
I'VE HAD A BICYCLE SINCE I WAS A YOUNG BOY.
CHILDREN FALL DOWN ALL THE TIME WHEN THEY FIRST BEGIN LEARNING, BUT THEY BECOME CAPABLE VERY QUICKLY.
MY FATHER OBTAINED A CHILD-SIZED BICYCLE FROM SOME-WHERE...
...AND GRACE AND I WERE THE FIRST ONES TO TEST IT OUT.
BEFORE LONG, ARTHUR AND VIVI WERE CLAMOURING TO GIVE IT A GO AS WELL.
WE ALL FELL AGAIN AND AGAIN, WREAKING HAVOC ON THE LAWN.
I FELT SORRY FOR BILL...

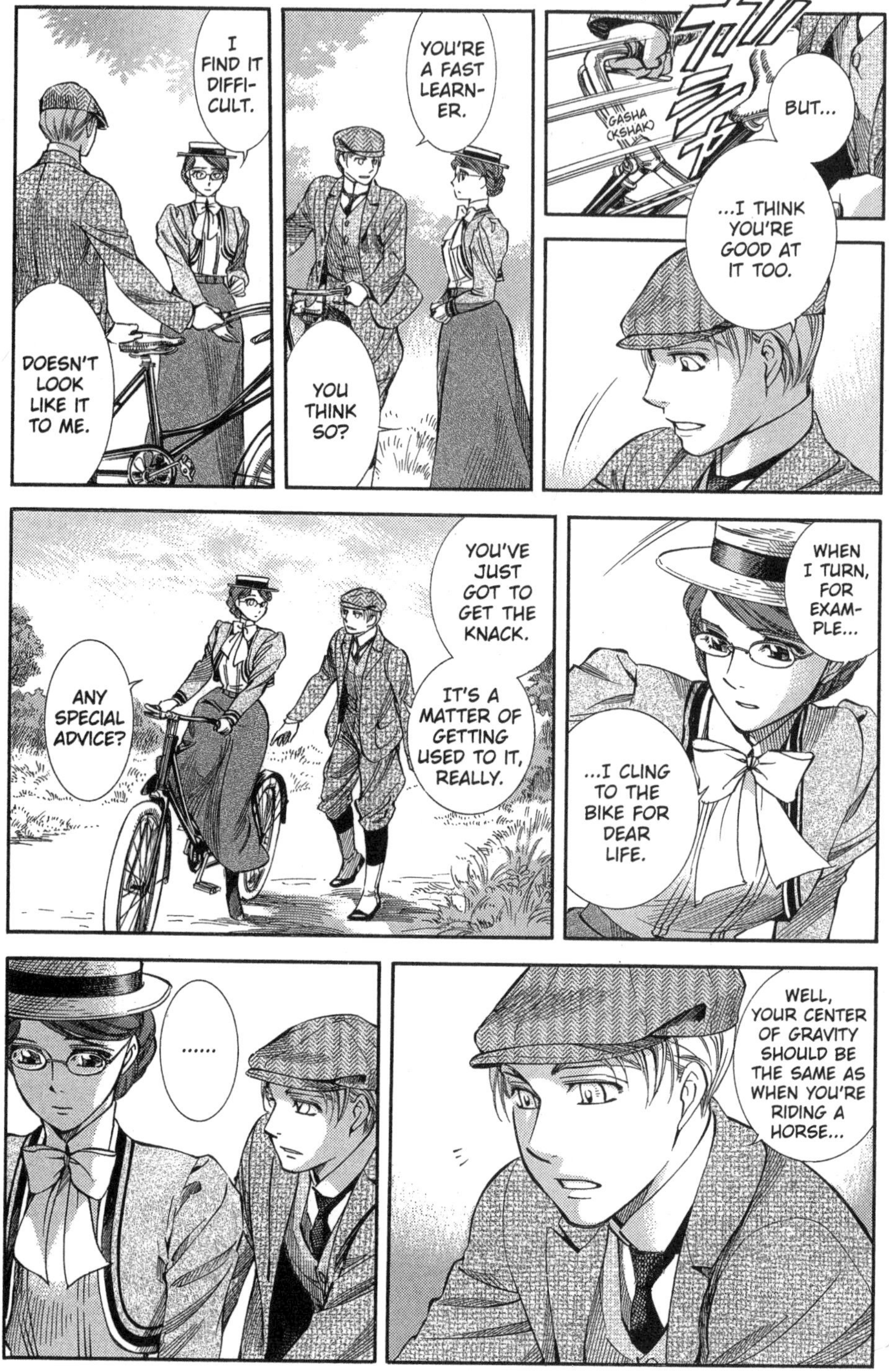
GASHA (KSHAK)
BUT...
...I THINK YOU'RE GOOD AT IT TOO.
YOU'RE A FAST LEARNER.
YOU THINK SO?
I FIND IT DIFFICULT.
DOESN'T LOOK LIKE IT TO ME.
WHEN I TURN, FOR EXAMPLE...
...I CLING TO THE BIKE FOR DEAR LIFE.
YOU'VE JUST GOT TO GET THE KNACK.
IT'S A MATTER OF GETTING USED TO IT, REALLY.
ANY SPECIAL ADVICE?
WELL, YOUR CENTER OF GRAVITY SHOULD BE THE SAME AS WHEN YOU'RE RIDING A HORSE...
......

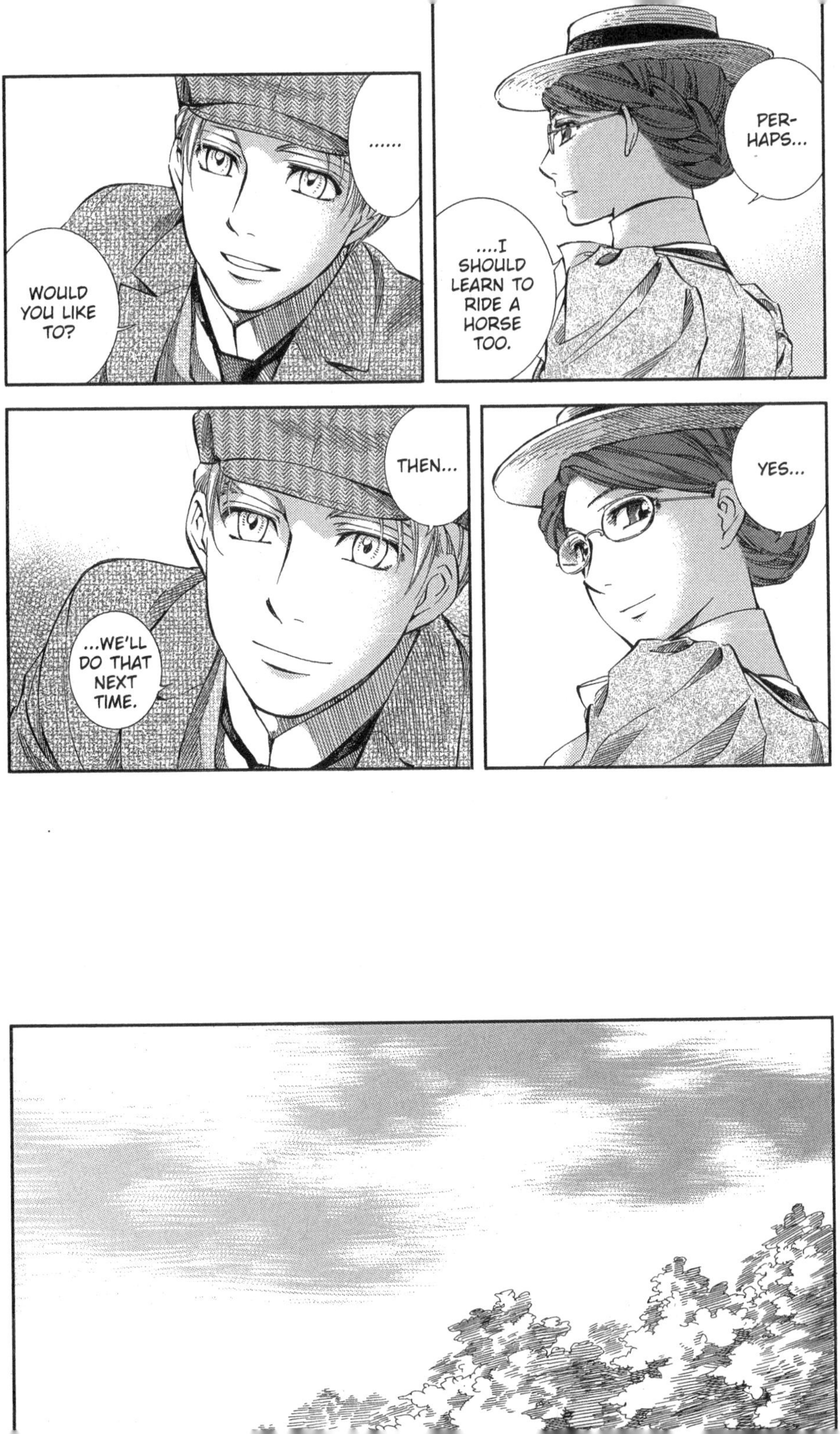
PER-HAPS...
....I SHOULD LEARN TO RIDE A HORSE TOO.
......
WOULD YOU LIKE TO?
YES...
THEN...
...WE'LL DO THAT NEXT TIME.

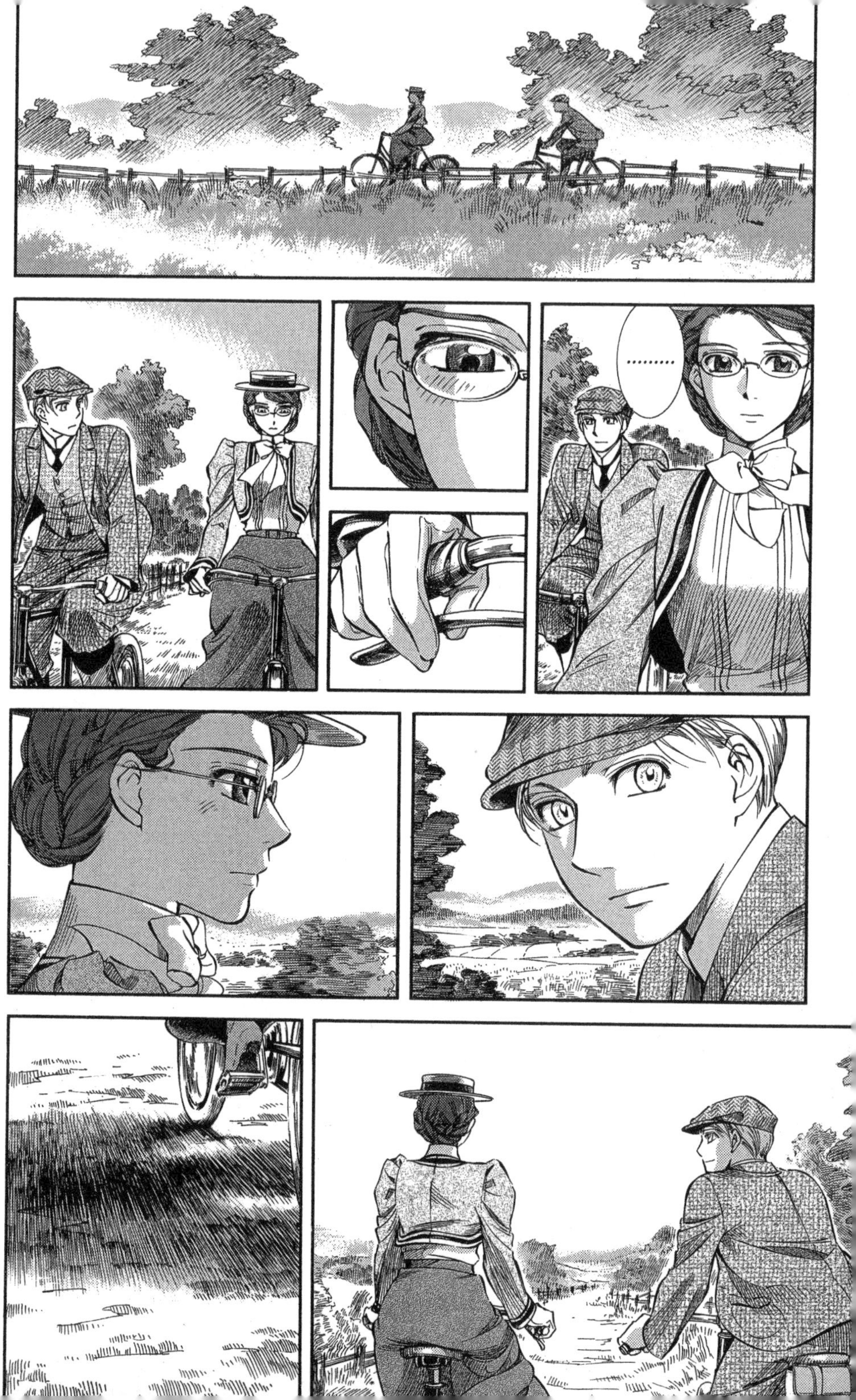
....

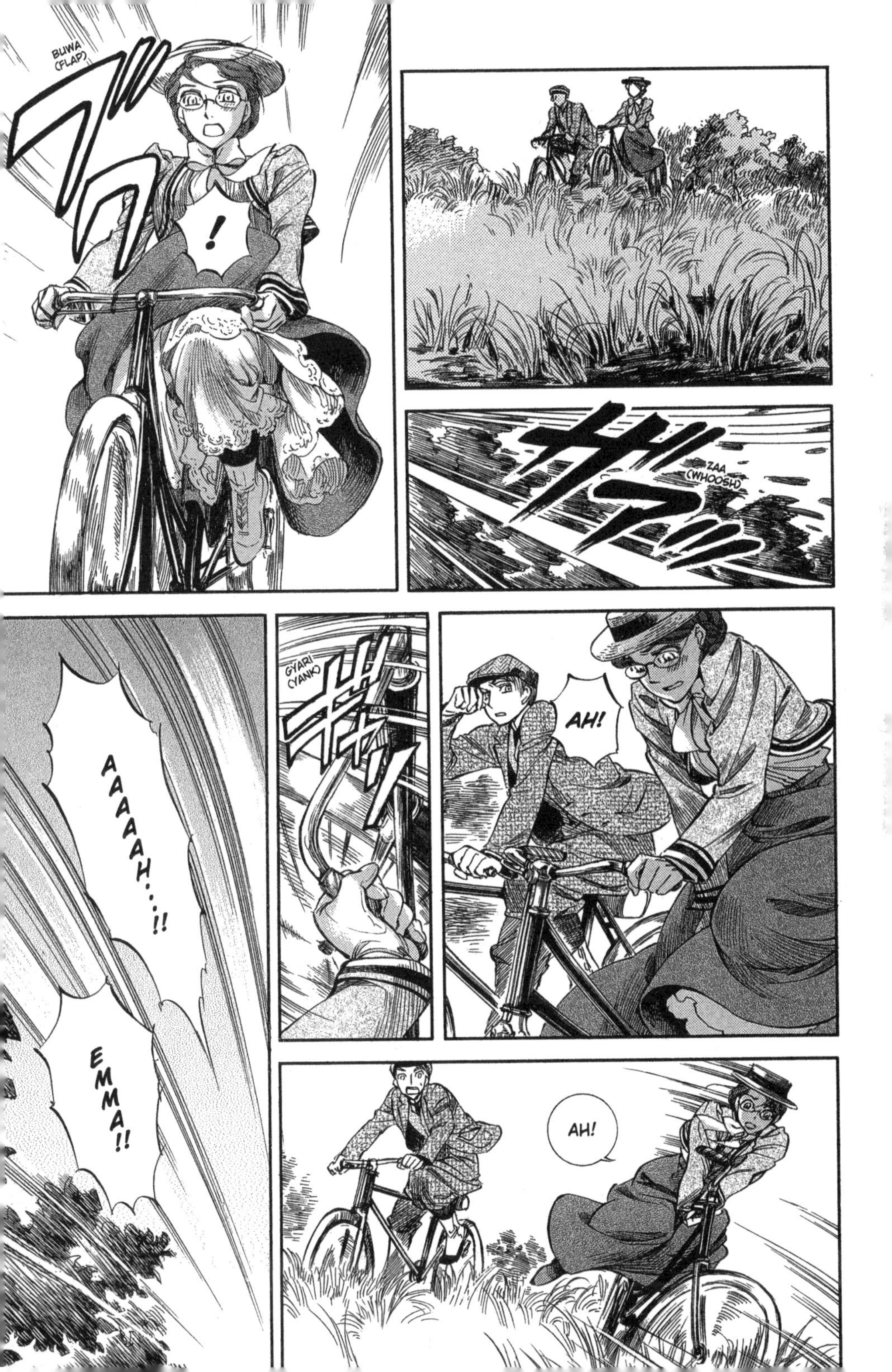
ZAA (WHOOSH)
BUWA (FLAP)
!
AH!
GYARI (YANK)
AH!
AAAAAH...!!
EMMA!!

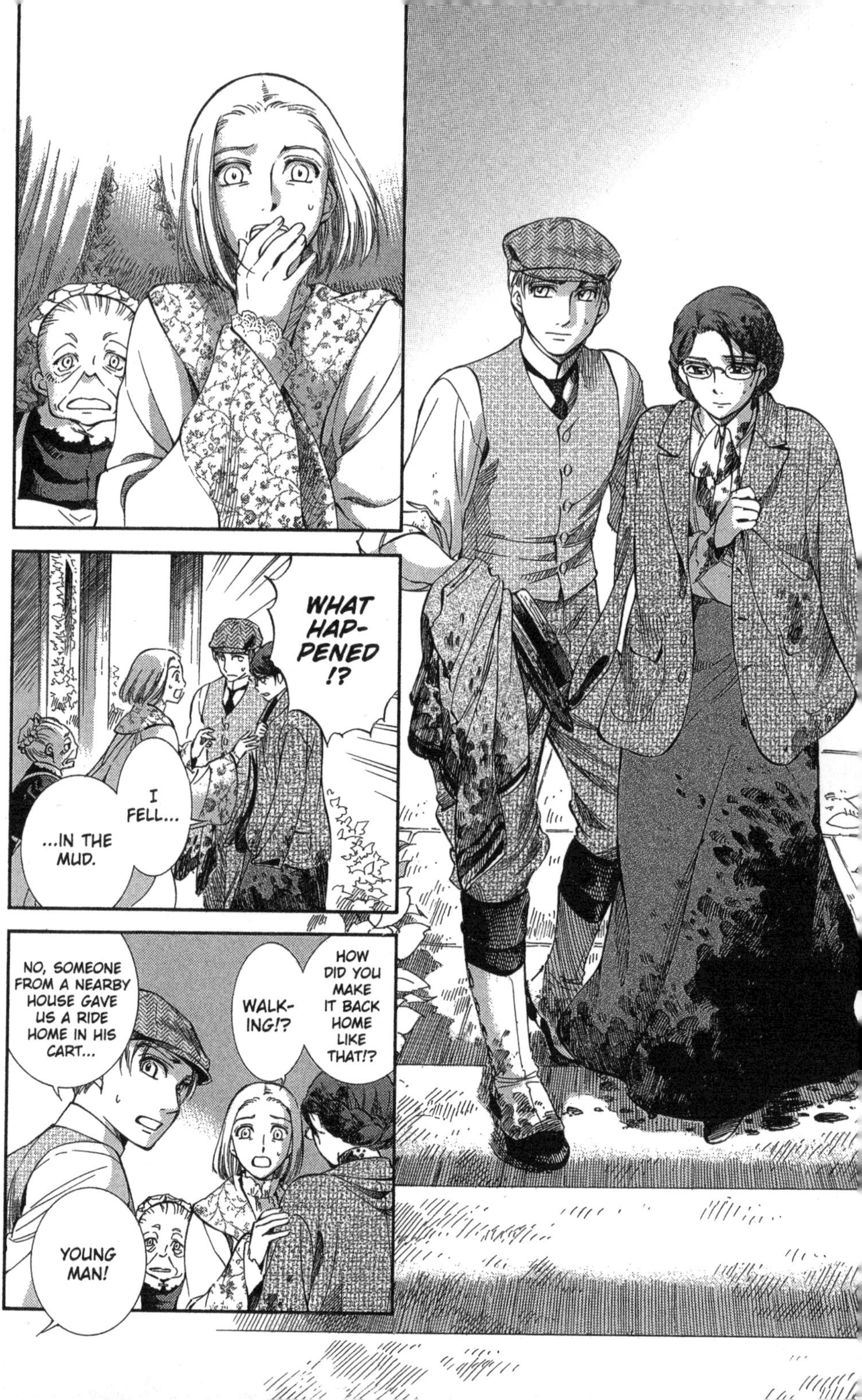
WHAT HAP-PENED!?
I FELL...
...IN THE MUD.
HOW DID YOU MAKE IT BACK HOME LIKE THAT!?
WALK-ING!?
NO, SOMEONE FROM A NEARBY HOUSE GAVE US A RIDE HOME IN HIS CART...
YOUNG MAN!

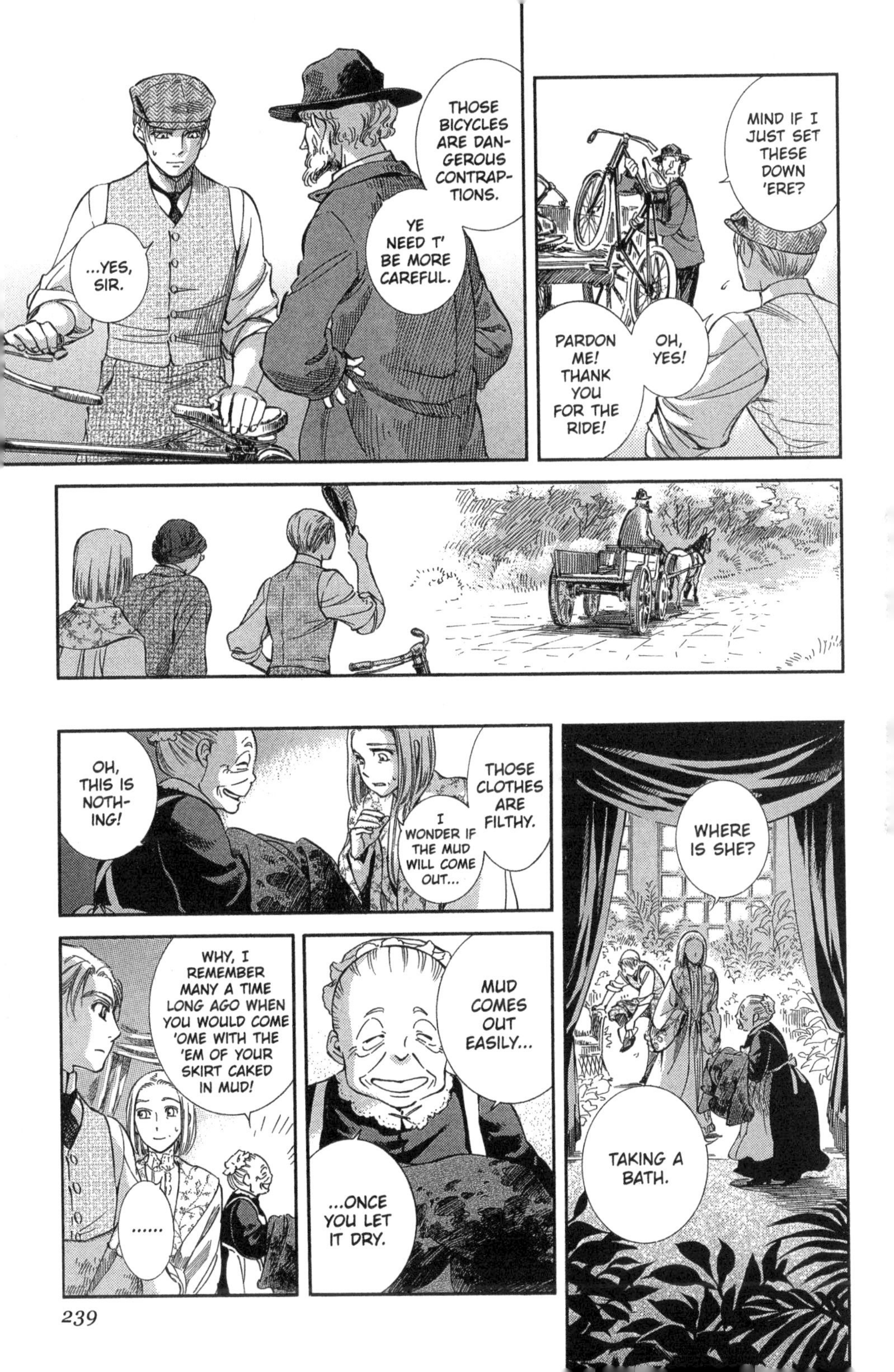
MIND IF I JUST SET THESE DOWN 'ERE?
OH, YES!
PARDON ME! THANK YOU FOR THE RIDE!
THOSE BICYCLES ARE DANGEROUS CONTRAPTIONS.
YE NEED T' BE MORE CAREFUL.
...YES, SIR.
WHERE IS SHE?
TAKING A BATH.
THOSE CLOTHES ARE FILTHY.
I WONDER IF THE MUD WILL COME OUT...
OH, THIS IS NOTHING!
MUD COMES OUT EASILY...
...ONCE YOU LET IT DRY.
WHY, I REMEMBER MANY A TIME LONG AGO WHEN YOU WOULD COME 'OME WITH THE 'EM OF YOUR SKIRT CAKED IN MUD!
......

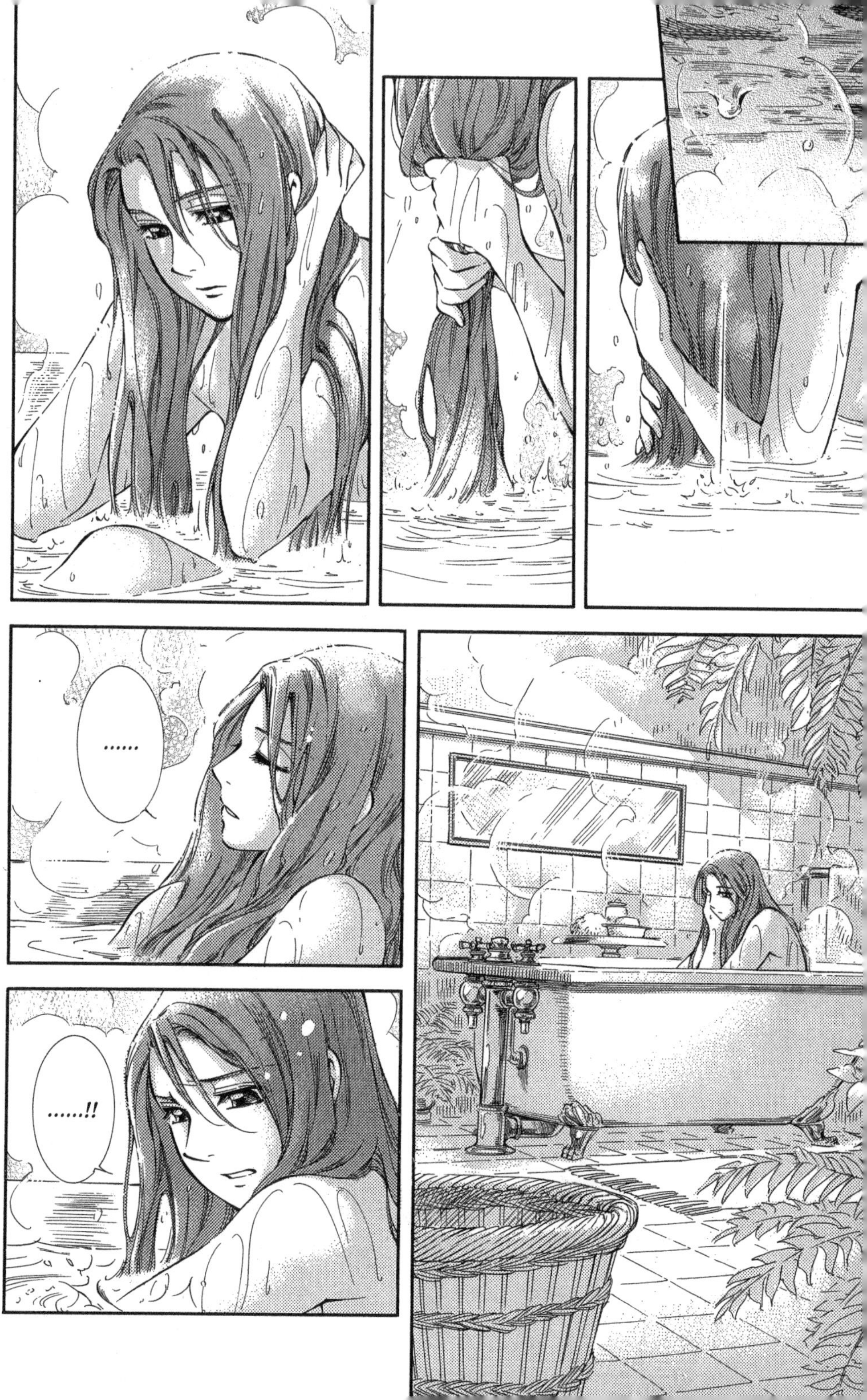
......
......!!

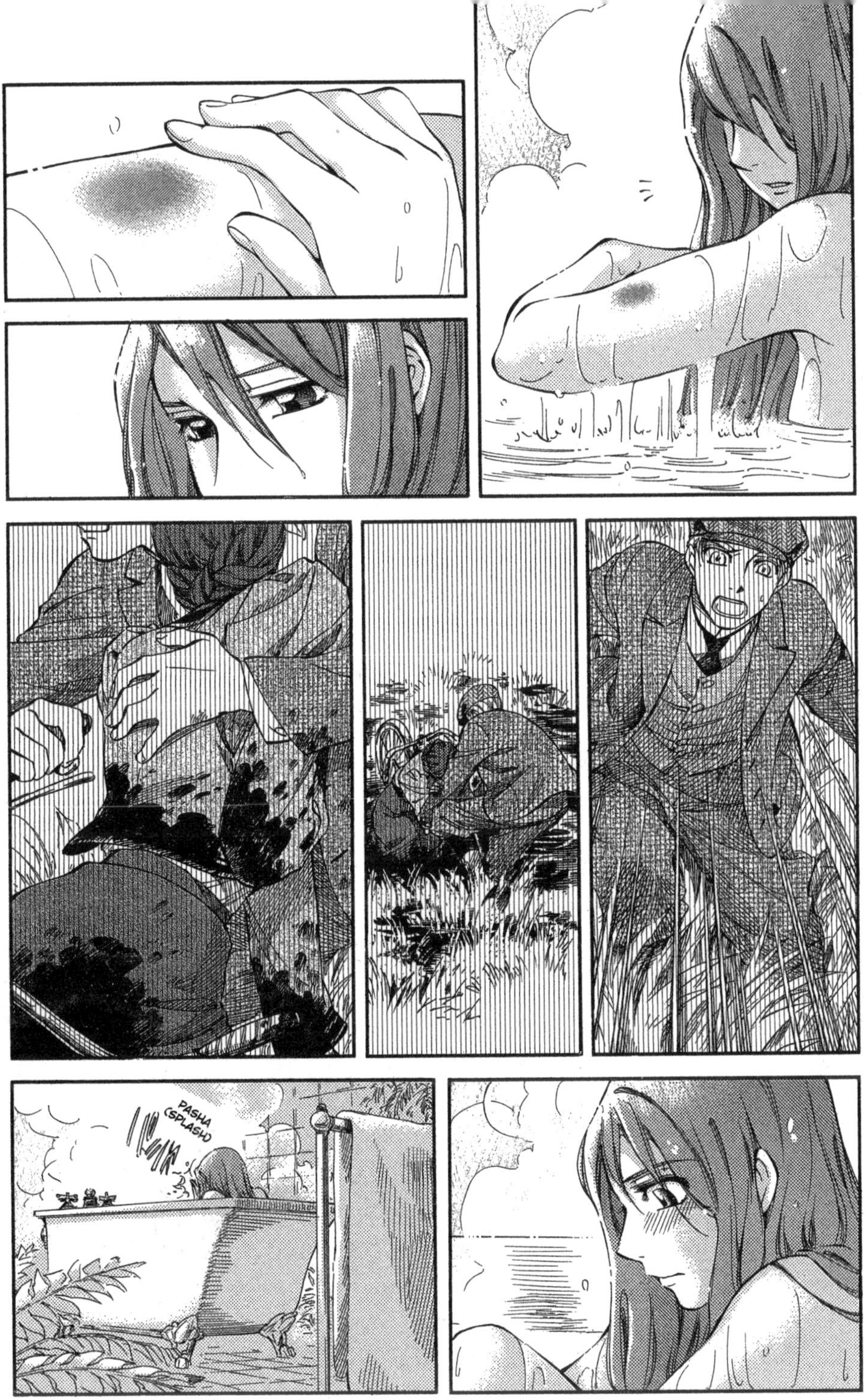
PASHA (SPLASH)

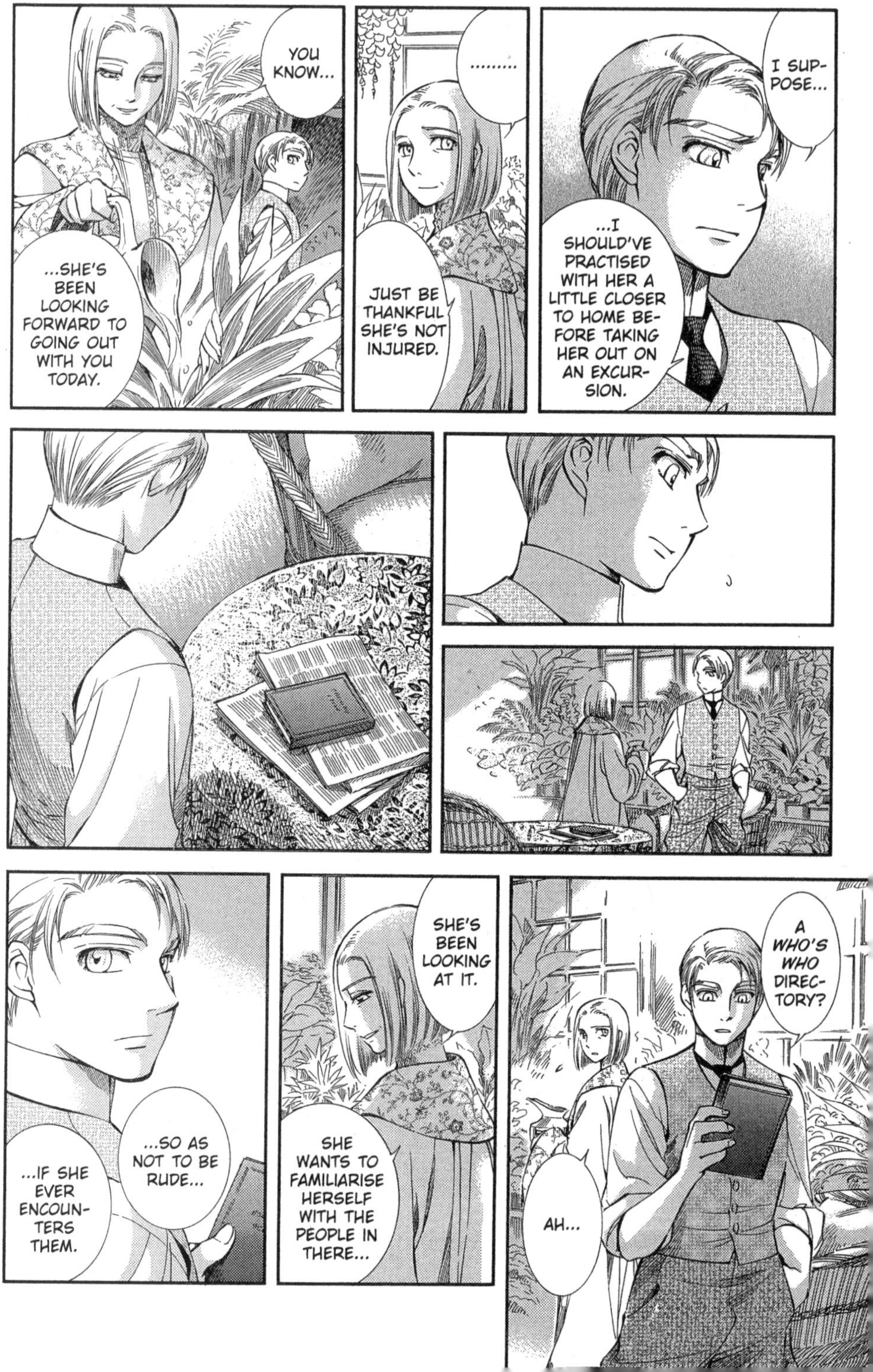
I SUPPOSE...
...I SHOULD'VE PRACTISED WITH HER A LITTLE CLOSER TO HOME BEFORE TAKING HER OUT ON AN EXCURSION.
....
JUST BE THANKFUL SHE'S NOT INJURED.
YOU KNOW...
...SHE'S BEEN LOOKING FORWARD TO GOING OUT WITH YOU TODAY.
A WHO'S WHO DIRECTORY?
AH...
SHE'S BEEN LOOKING AT IT.
SHE WANTS TO FAMILIARISE HERSELF WITH THE PEOPLE IN THERE...
...SO AS NOT TO BE RUDE...
...IF SHE EVER ENCOUNTERS THEM.

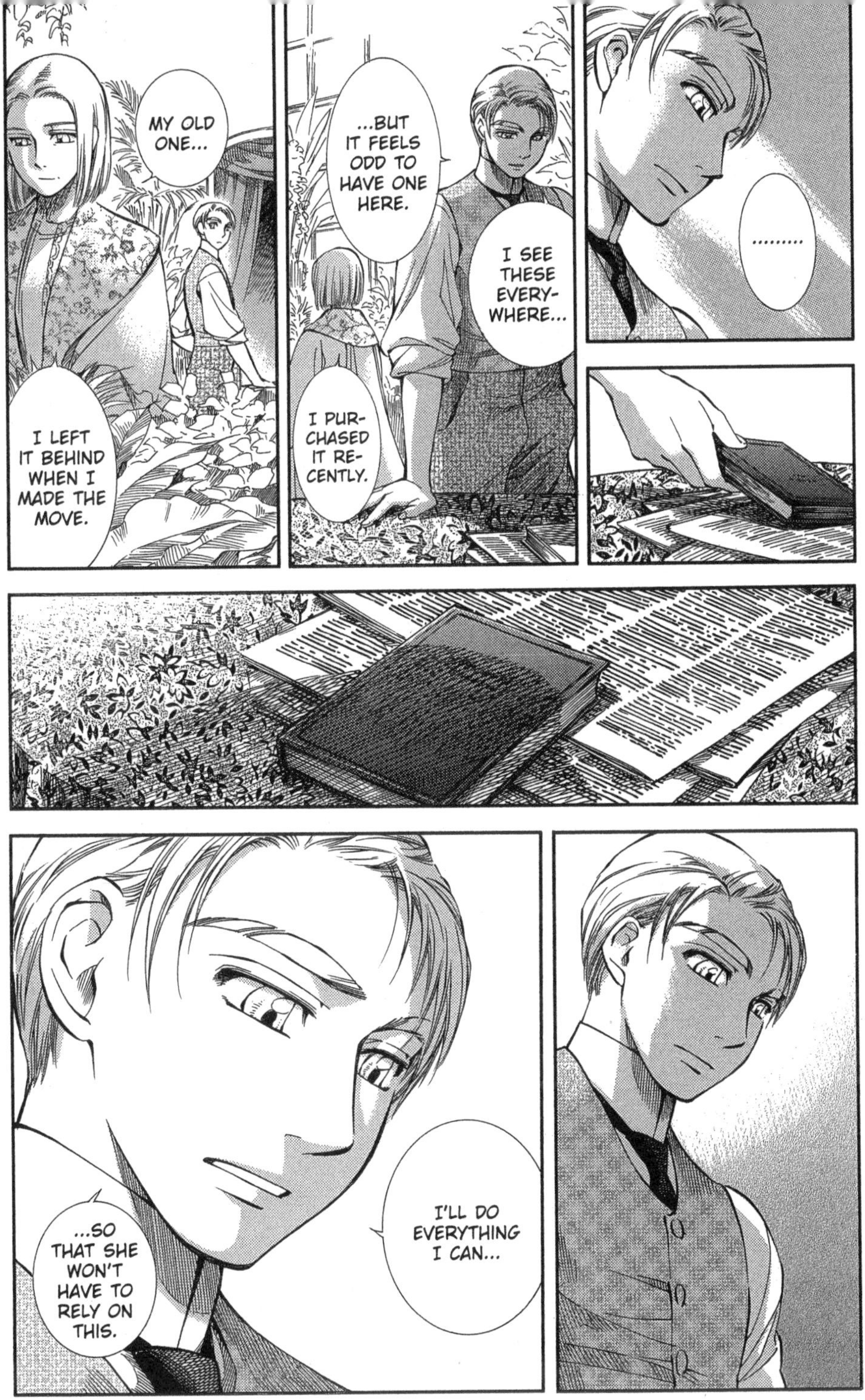
....
I SEE THESE EVERY-WHERE...
...BUT IT FEELS ODD TO HAVE ONE HERE.
I PURCHASED IT RECENTLY.
MY OLD ONE...
I LEFT IT BEHIND WHEN I MADE THE MOVE.
I'LL DO EVERYTHING I CAN...
...SO THAT SHE WON'T HAVE TO RELY ON THIS.

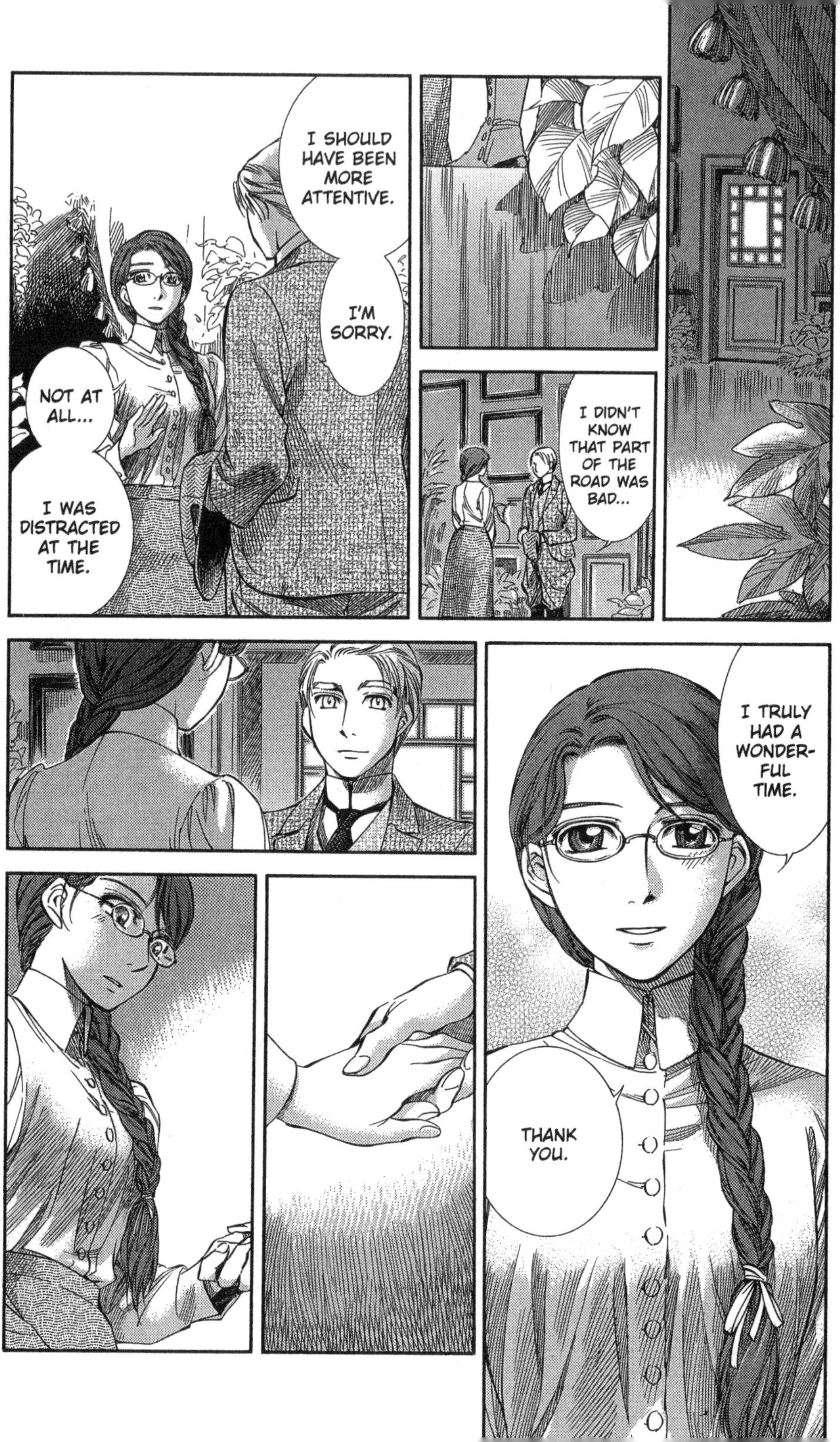
I DIDN'T KNOW THAT PART OF THE ROAD WAS BAD...
I SHOULD HAVE BEEN MORE ATTENTIVE.
I'M SORRY.
NOT AT ALL...
I WAS DISTRACTED AT THE TIME.
I TRULY HAD A WONDERFUL TIME.
THANK YOU.

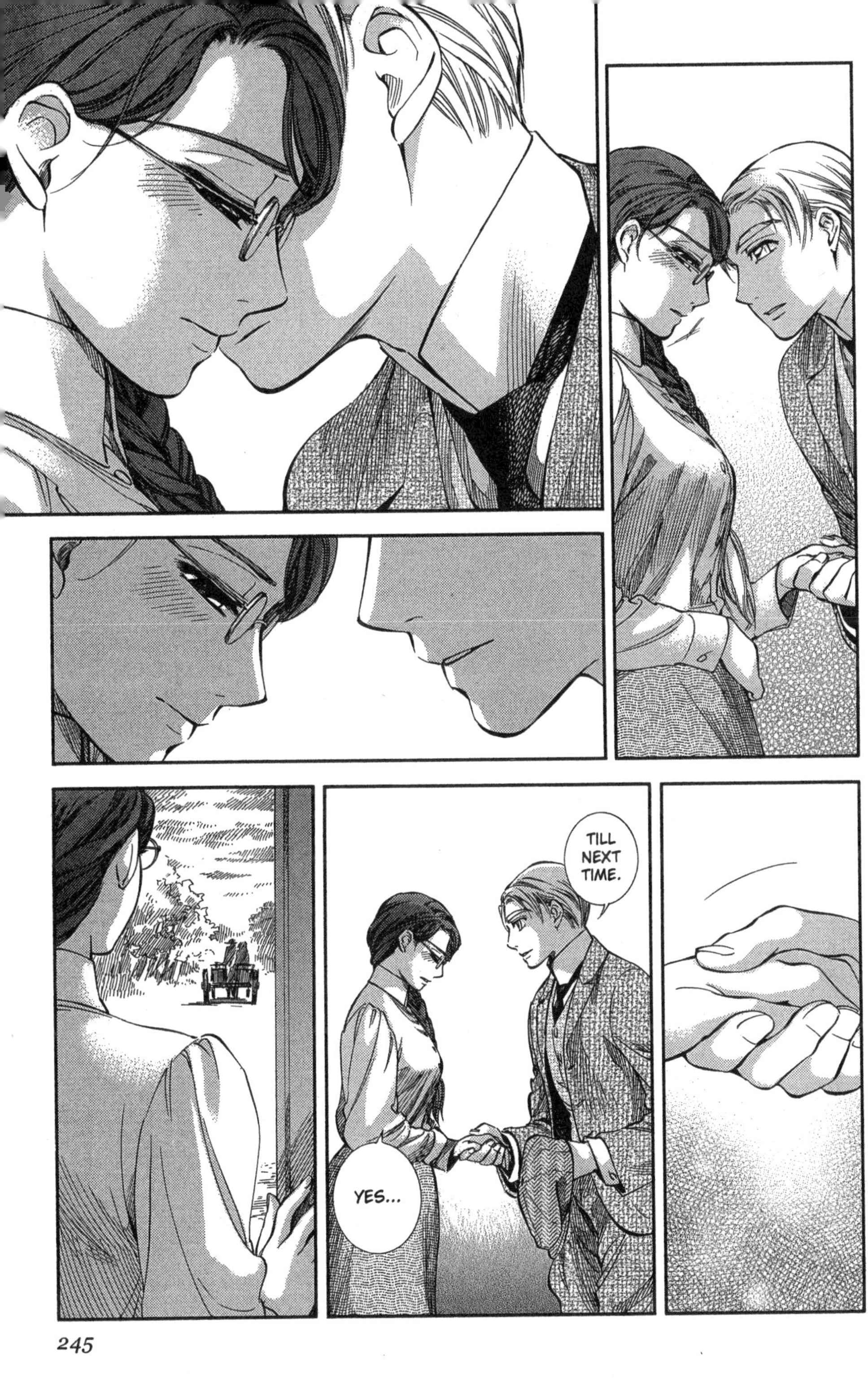
TILL NEXT TIME.
YES...

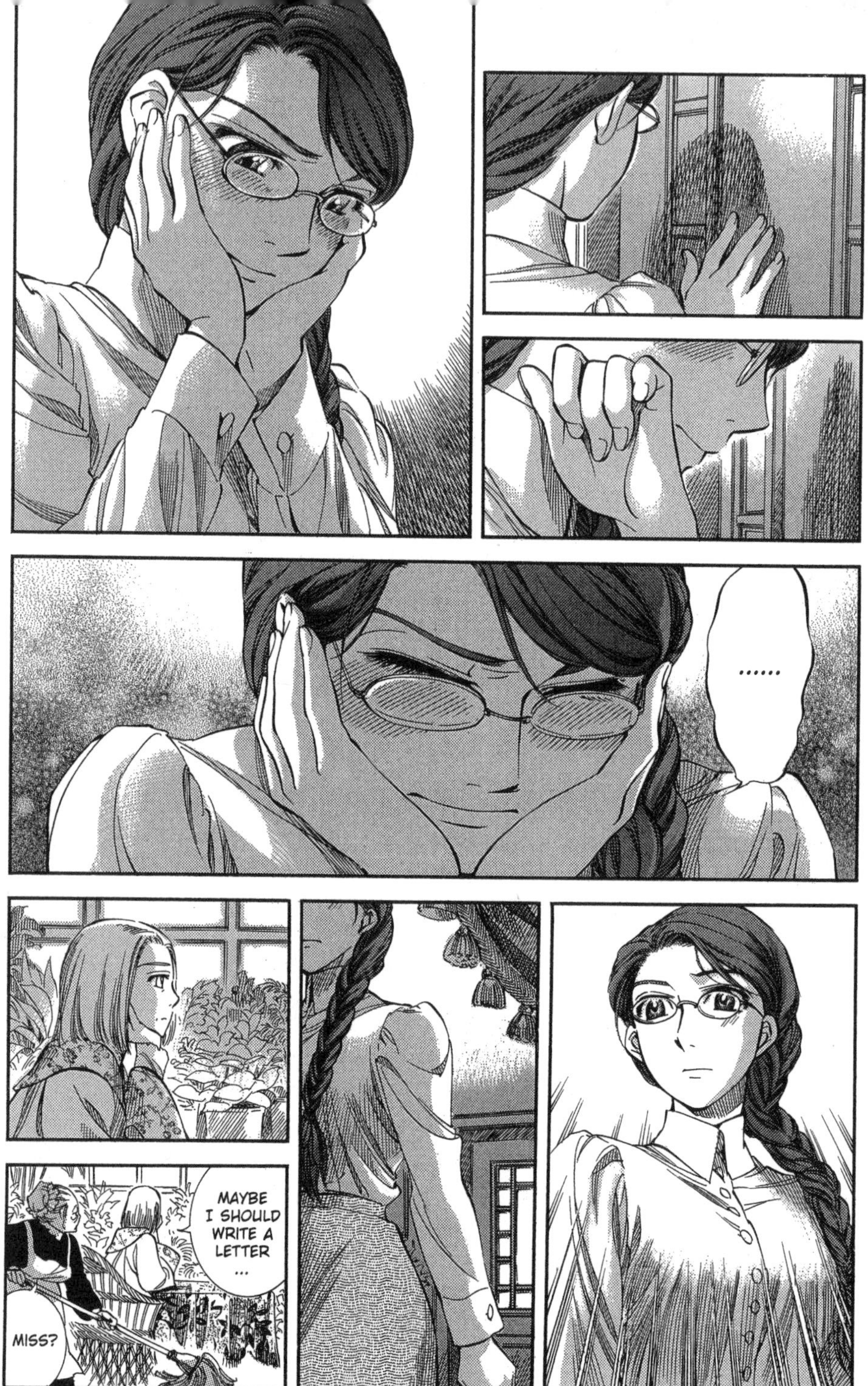
......
MAYBE I SHOULD WRITE A LETTER ...
MISS?

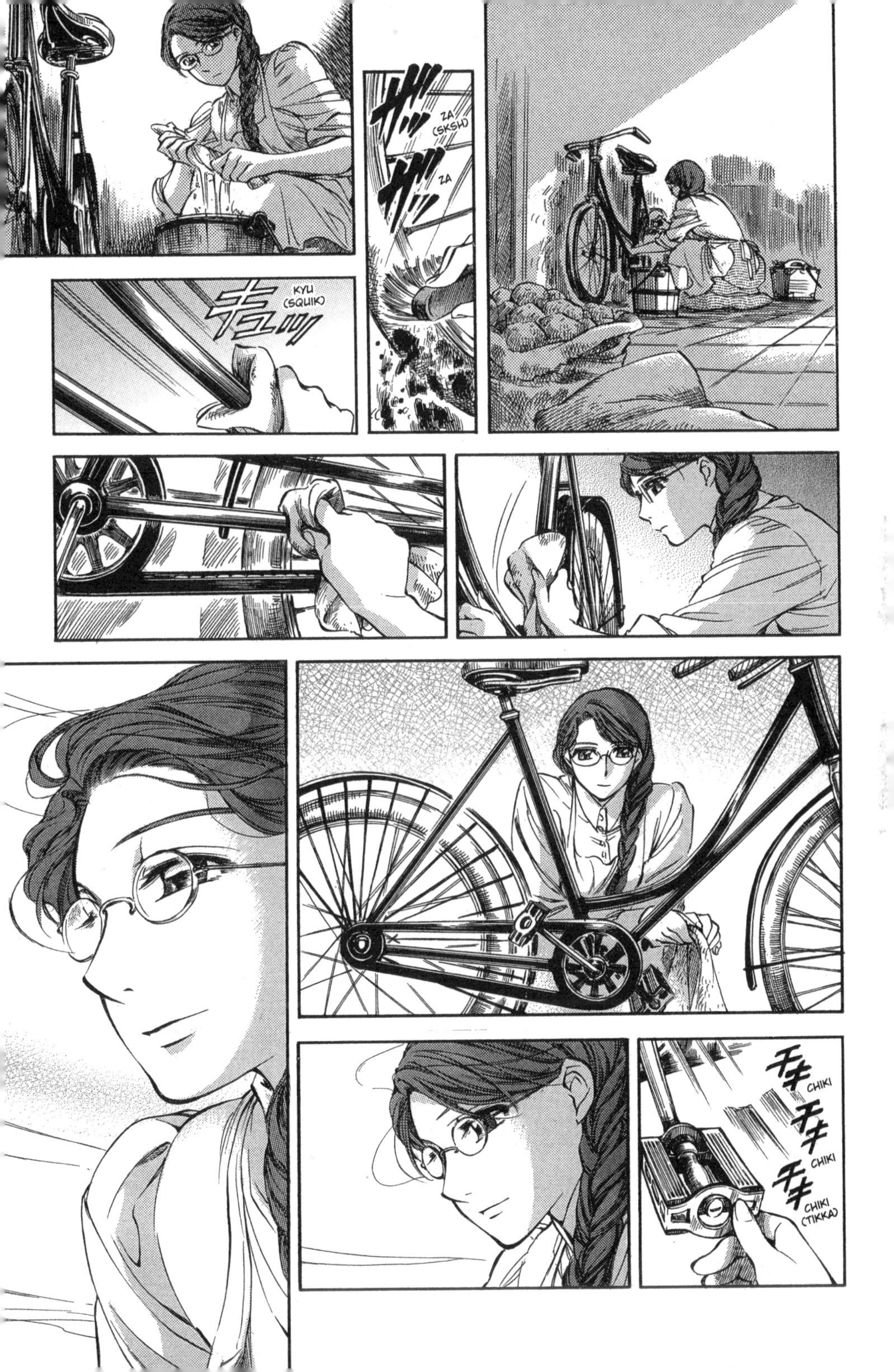

ZA (SKSH)
ZA
KYU (SQUIK)
CHIKI
CHIKI
CHIKI (TIKKA)

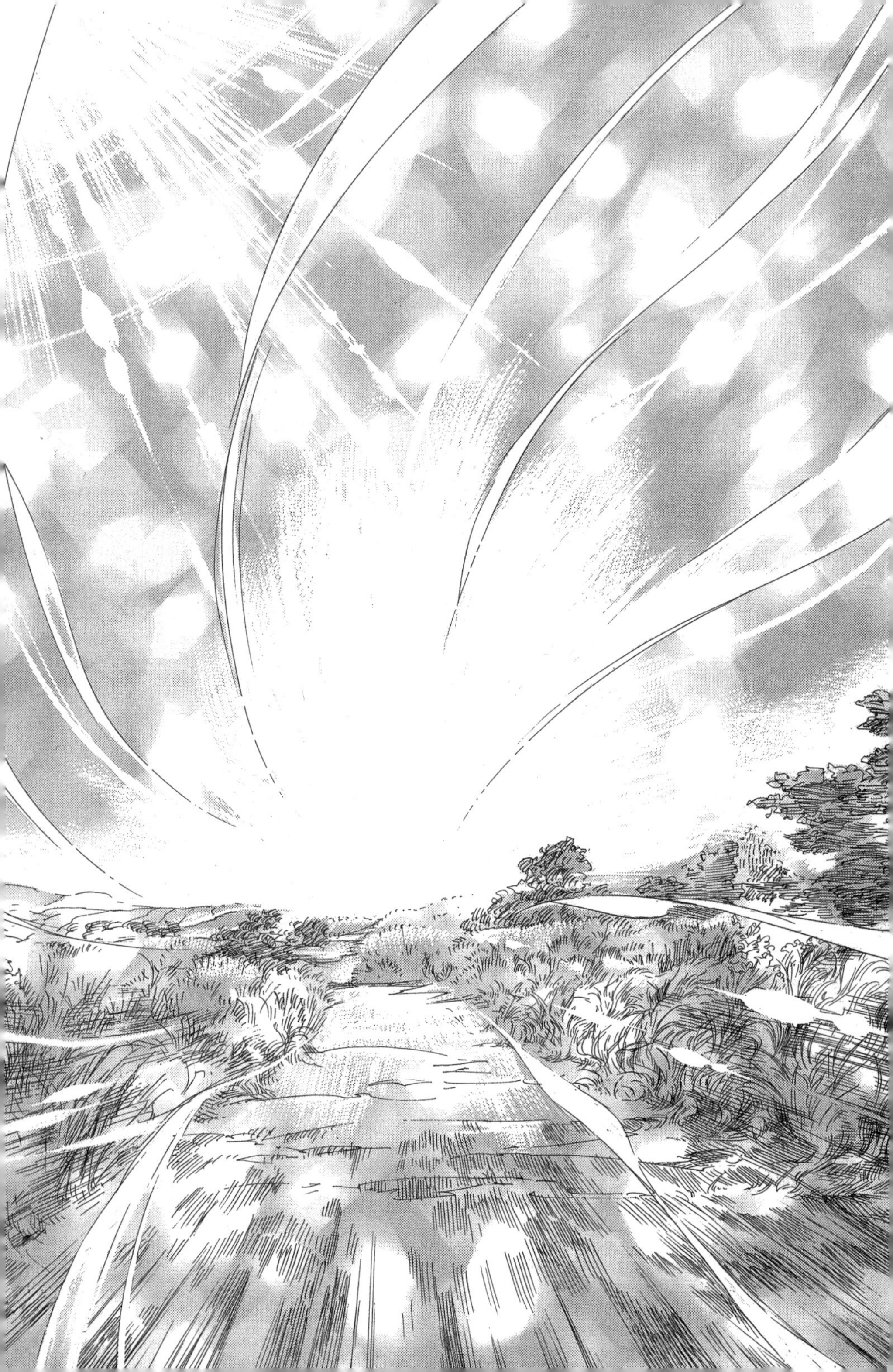

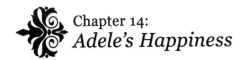

Chapter 14:
Adele's Happiness

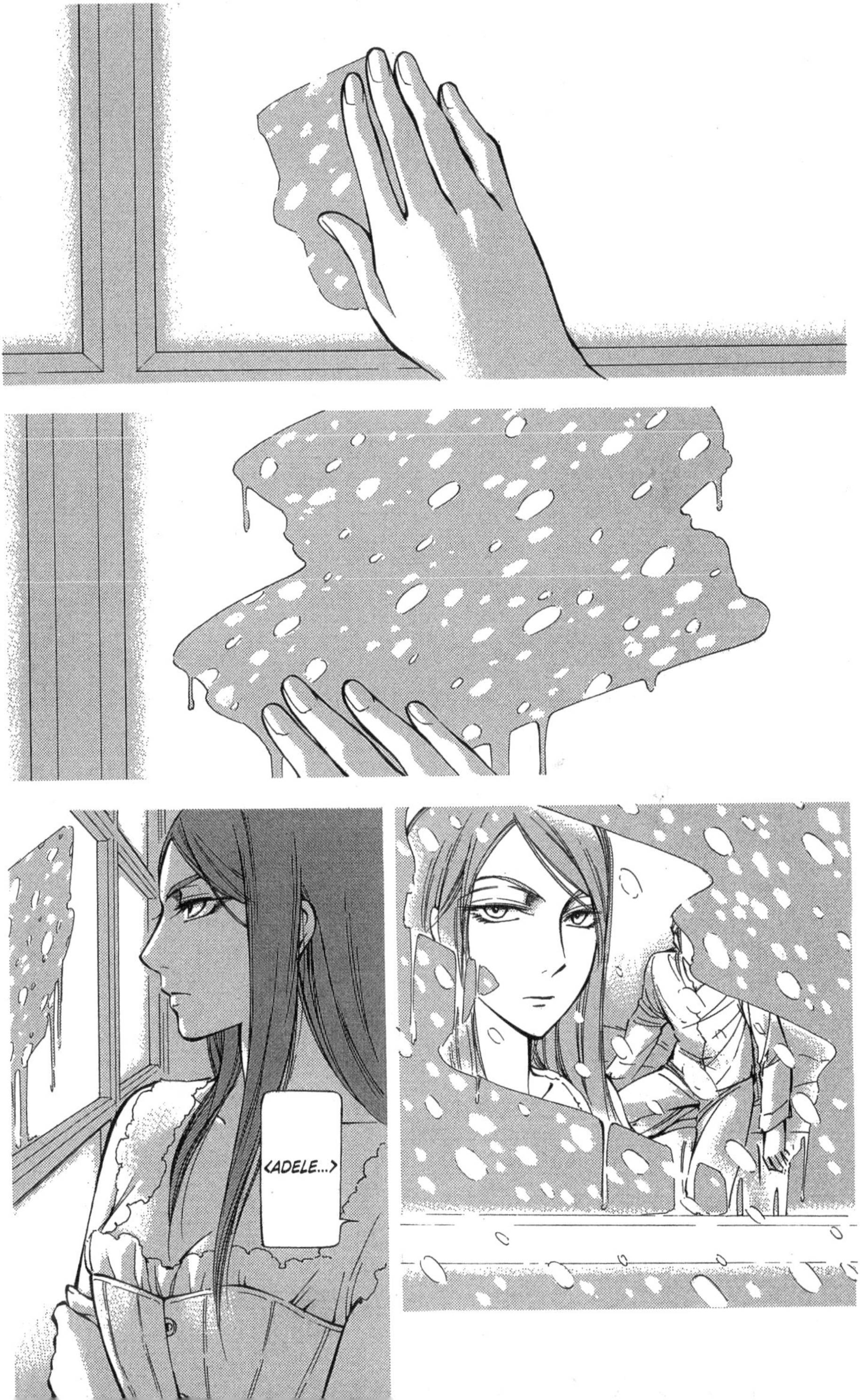
<ADELE...>

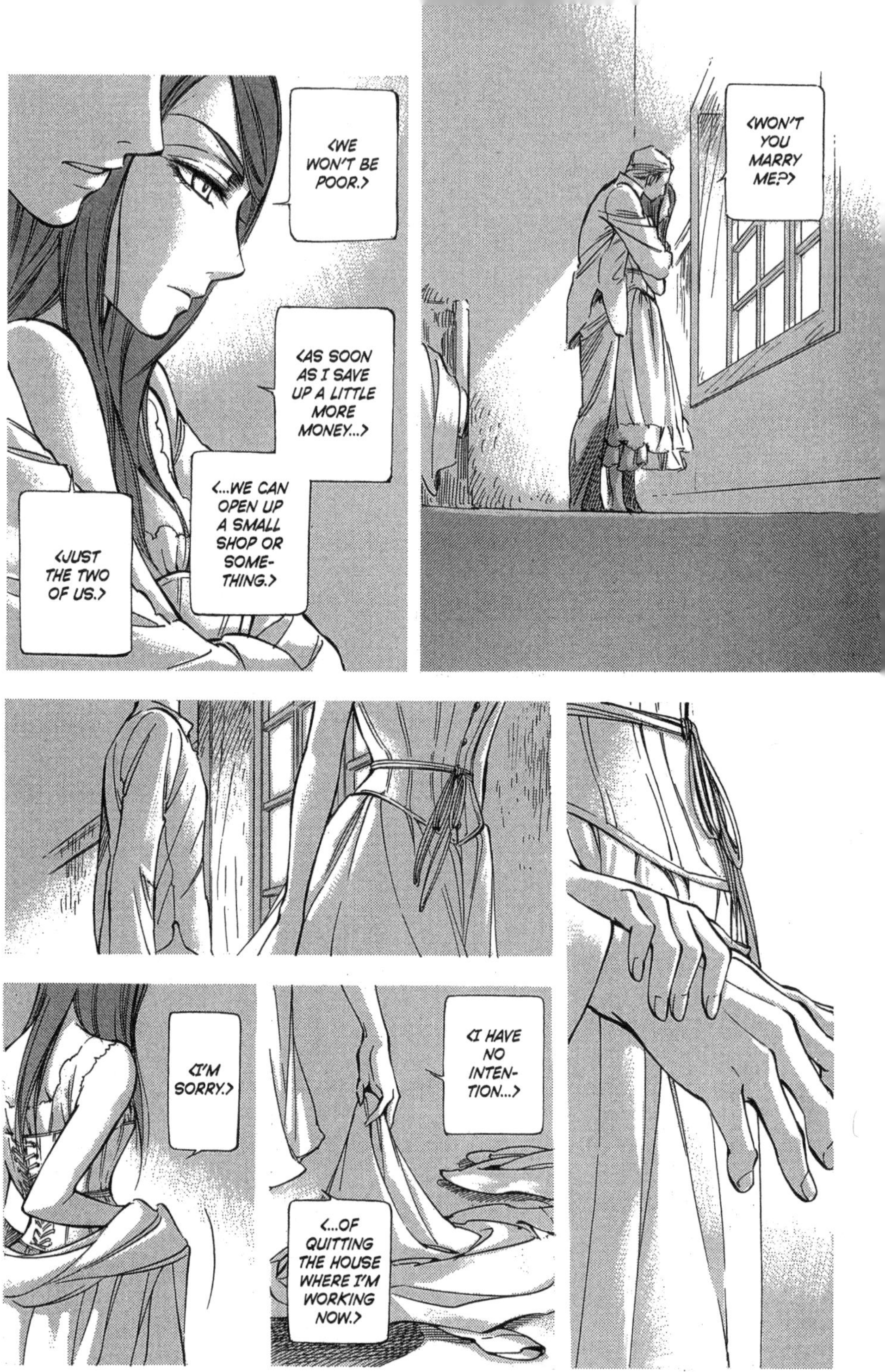
<WON'T YOU MARRY ME?>
<WE WON'T BE POOR.>
<AS SOON AS I SAVE UP A LITTLE MORE MONEY...>
<...WE CAN OPEN UP A SMALL SHOP OR SOME-THING.>
<JUST THE TWO OF US.>
<I HAVE NO INTEN-TION...>
<...OF QUITTING THE HOUSE WHERE I'M WORKING NOW.>
<I'M SORRY.>

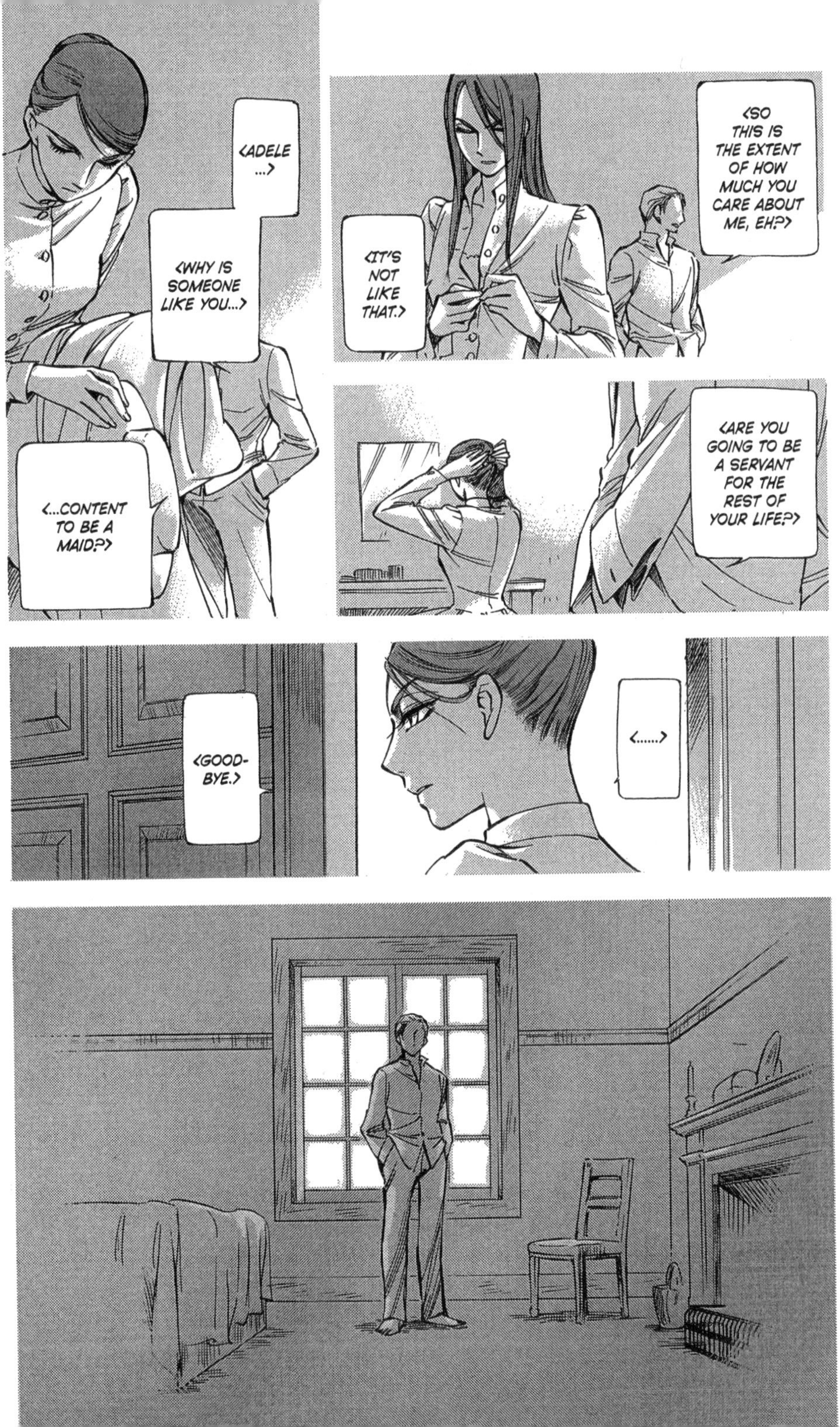

<SO THIS IS THE EXTENT OF HOW MUCH YOU CARE ABOUT ME, EH?>
<IT'S NOT LIKE THAT.>
<ARE YOU GOING TO BE A SERVANT FOR THE REST OF YOUR LIFE?>
<ADELE ...>
<WHY IS SOMEONE LIKE YOU...>
<...CONTENT TO BE A MAID?>
<......>
<GOOD-BYE.>

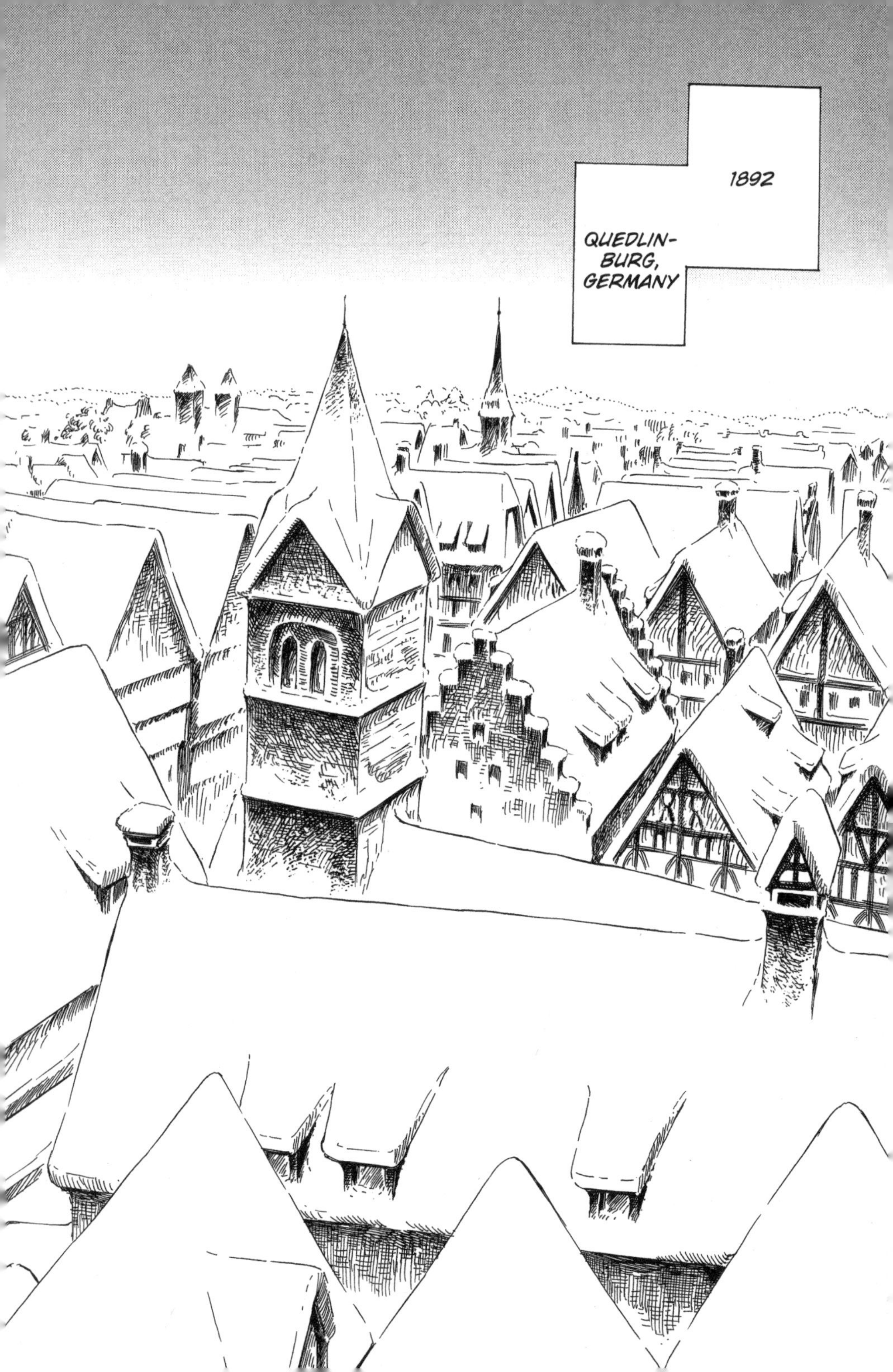
1892
QUEDLIN-BURG, GERMANY

Chapter 14:
Adele's Happiness

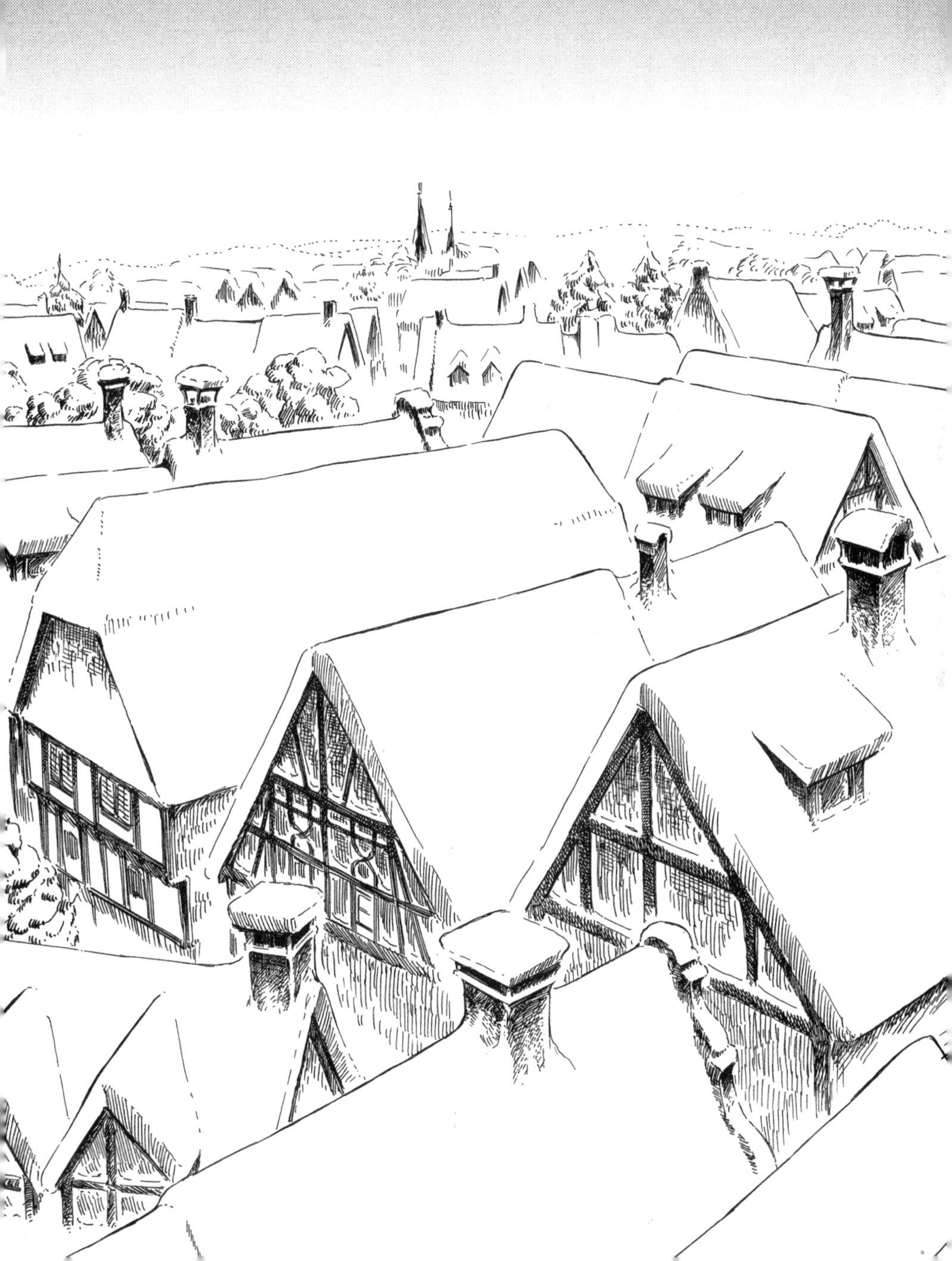

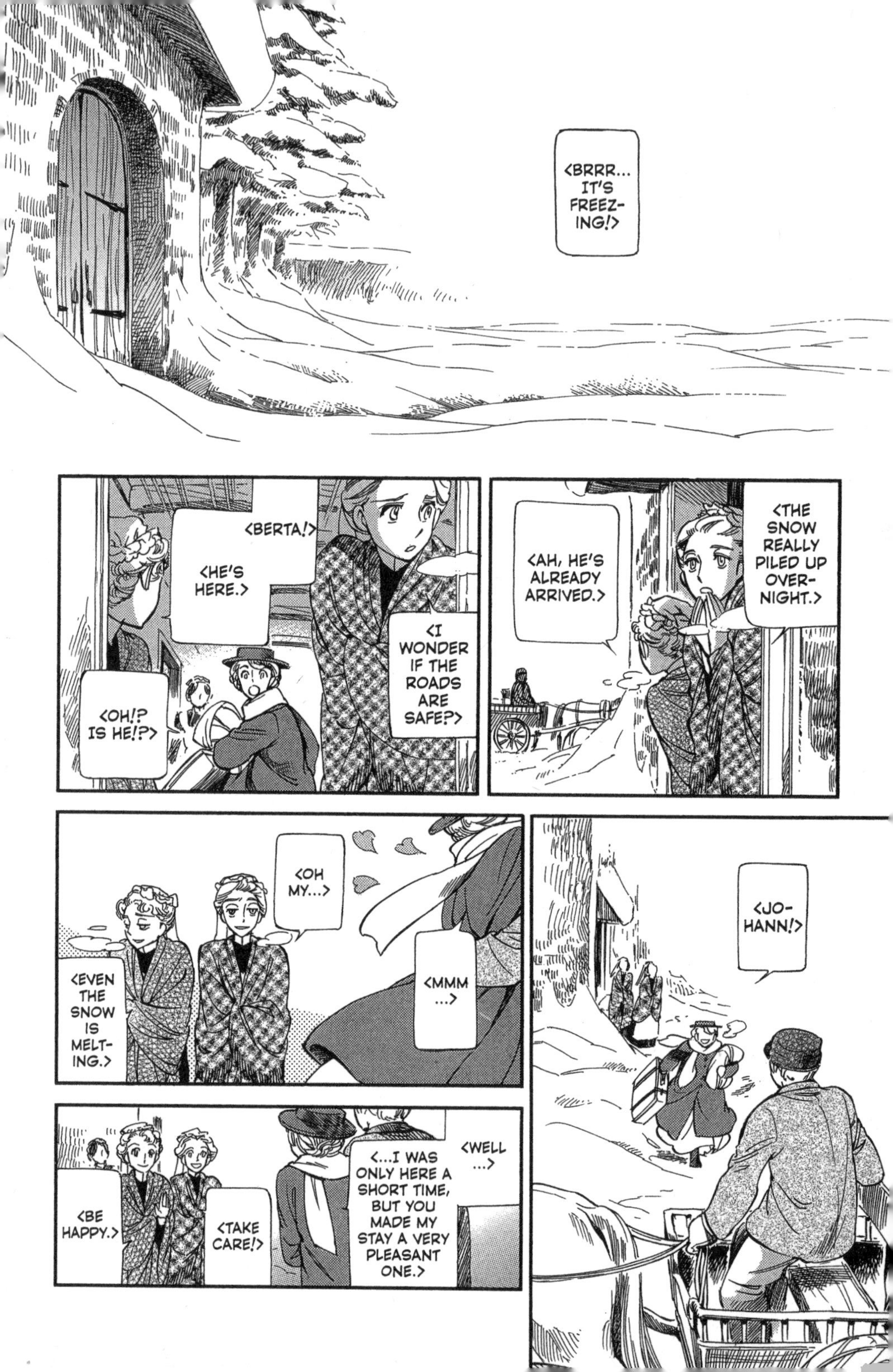
<BRRR... IT'S FREEZ-ING!>
<THE SNOW REALLY PILED UP OVER-NIGHT.>
<AH, HE'S ALREADY ARRIVED.>
<I WONDER IF THE ROADS ARE SAFE?>
<BERTA!>
<HE'S HERE.>
<OH!? IS HE!?>
<JO-HANN!>
<MMM ...>
<OH MY...>
<EVEN THE SNOW IS MELT-ING.>
<WELL ...>
<...I WAS ONLY HERE A SHORT TIME, BUT YOU MADE MY STAY A VERY PLEASANT ONE.>
<TAKE CARE!>
<BE HAPPY.>

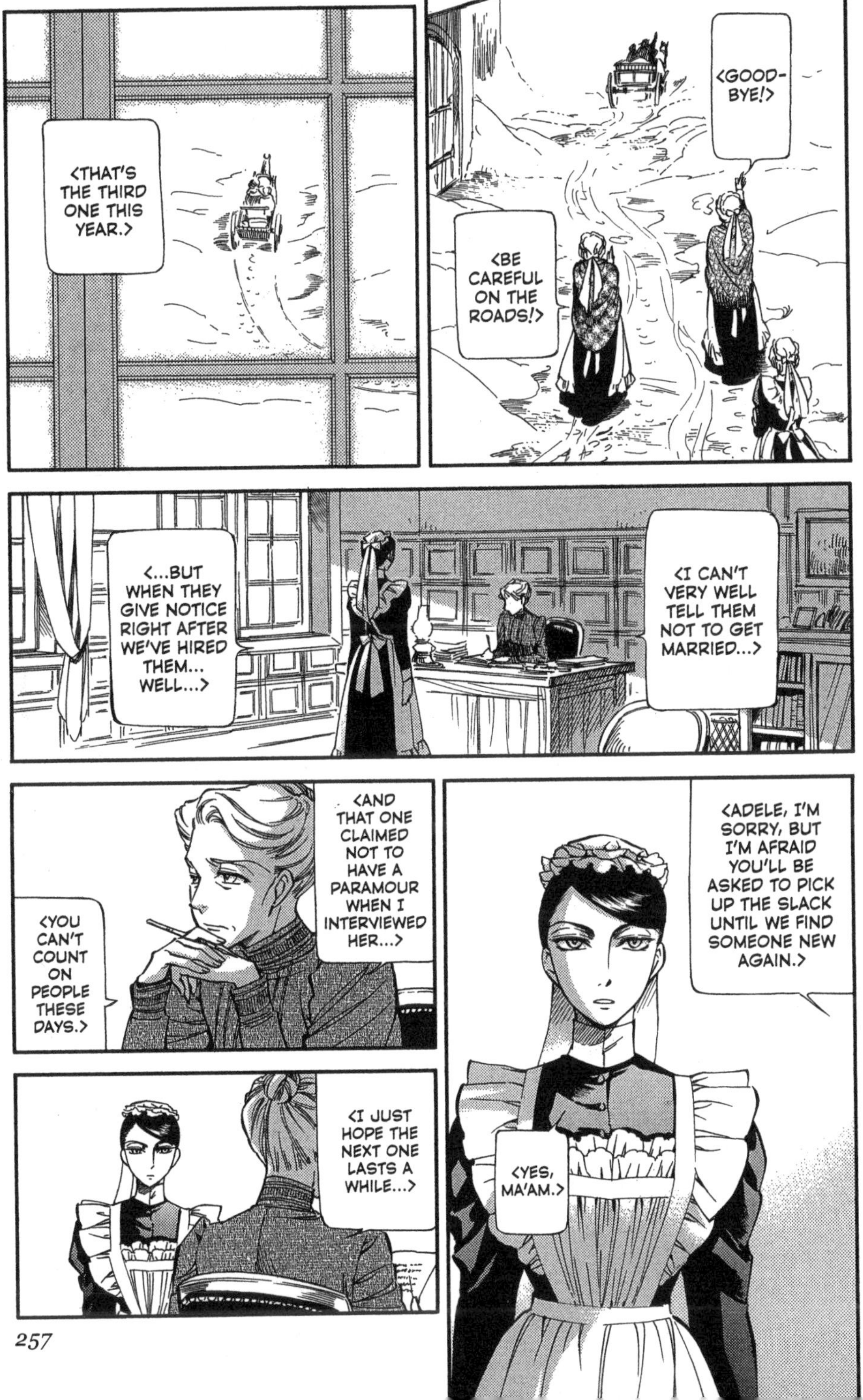
<GOOD-BYE!>
<BE CAREFUL ON THE ROADS!>
<THAT'S THE THIRD ONE THIS YEAR.>
<I CAN'T VERY WELL TELL THEM NOT TO GET MARRIED...>
<...BUT WHEN THEY GIVE NOTICE RIGHT AFTER WE'VE HIRED THEM... WELL...>
<ADELE, I'M SORRY, BUT I'M AFRAID YOU'LL BE ASKED TO PICK UP THE SLACK UNTIL WE FIND SOMEONE NEW AGAIN.>
<YES, MA'AM.>
<AND THAT ONE CLAIMED NOT TO HAVE A PARAMOUR WHEN I INTERVIEWED HER...>
<YOU CAN'T COUNT ON PEOPLE THESE DAYS.>
<I JUST HOPE THE NEXT ONE LASTS A WHILE...>

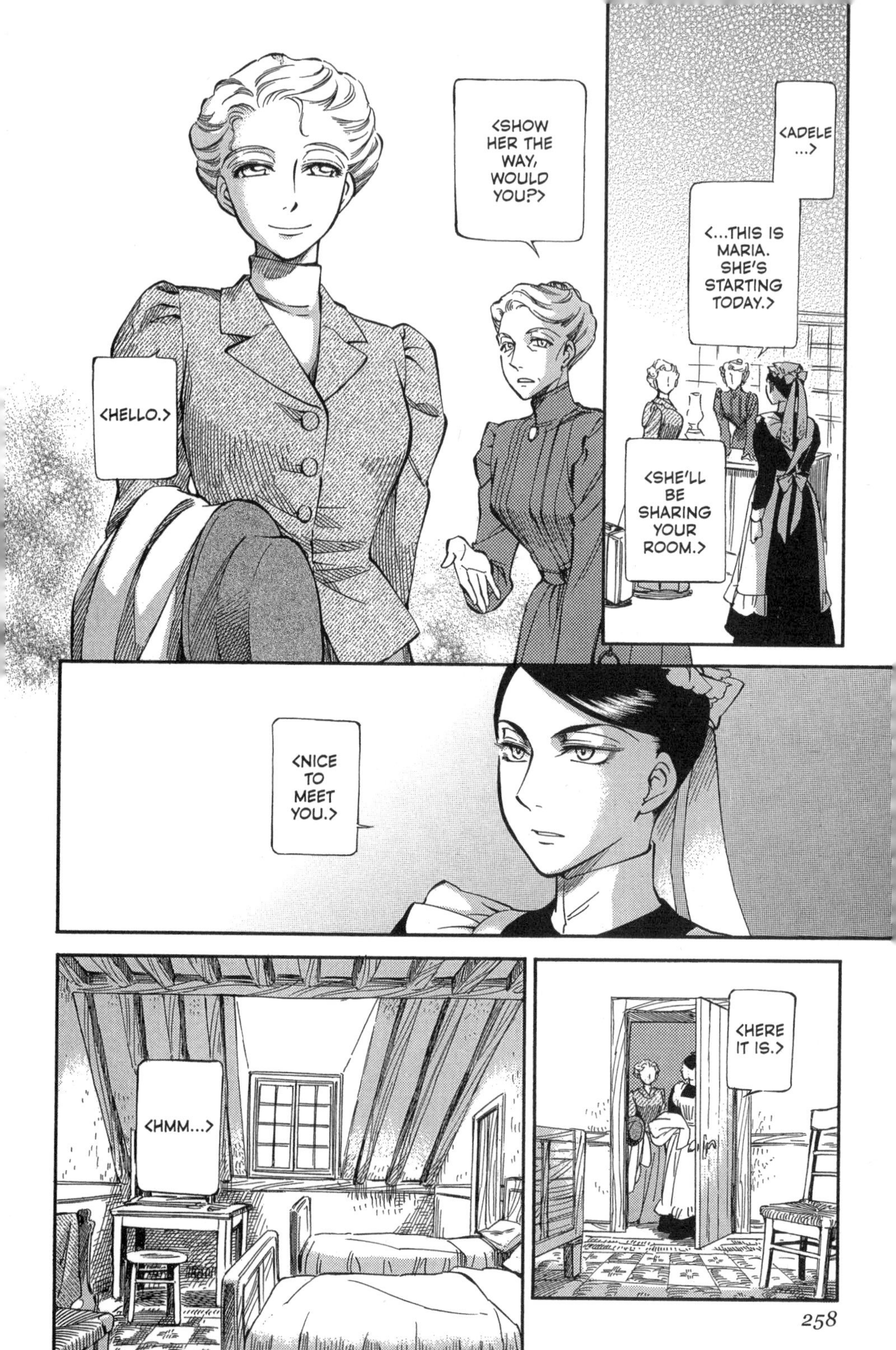
<ADELE ...>
<...THIS IS MARIA. SHE'S STARTING TODAY.>
<SHE'LL BE SHARING YOUR ROOM.>
<SHOW HER THE WAY, WOULD YOU?>
<HELLO.>
<NICE TO MEET YOU.>
<HERE IT IS.>
<HMM...>

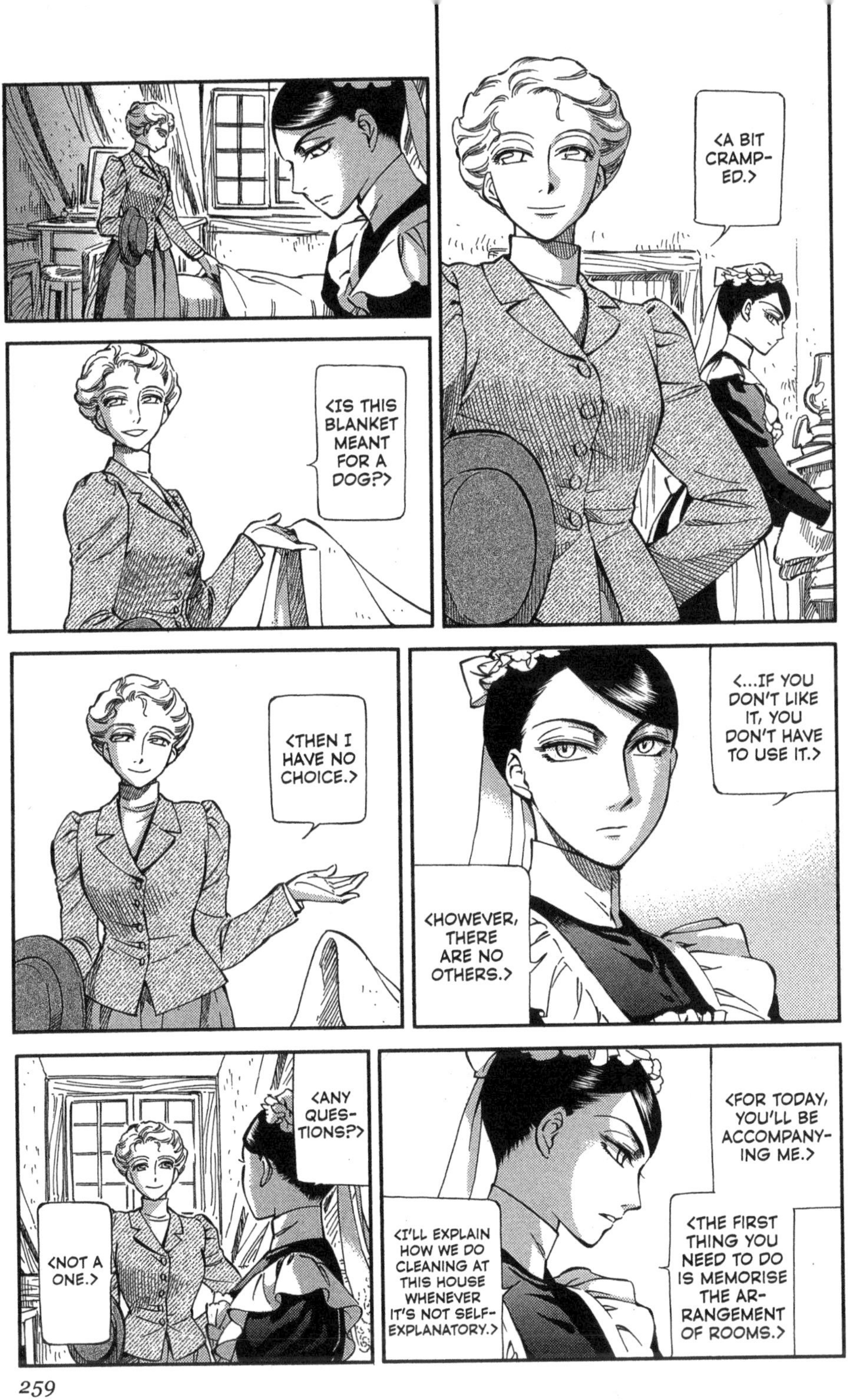
<A BIT CRAMPED.>
<IS THIS BLANKET MEANT FOR A DOG?>
<...IF YOU DON'T LIKE IT, YOU DON'T HAVE TO USE IT.>
<HOWEVER, THERE ARE NO OTHERS.>
<THEN I HAVE NO CHOICE.>
<FOR TODAY, YOU'LL BE ACCOMPANYING ME.>
<THE FIRST THING YOU NEED TO DO IS MEMORISE THE ARRANGEMENT OF ROOMS.>
<I'LL EXPLAIN HOW WE DO CLEANING AT THIS HOUSE WHENEVER IT'S NOT SELF-EXPLANATORY.>
<ANY QUESTIONS?>
<NOT A ONE.>

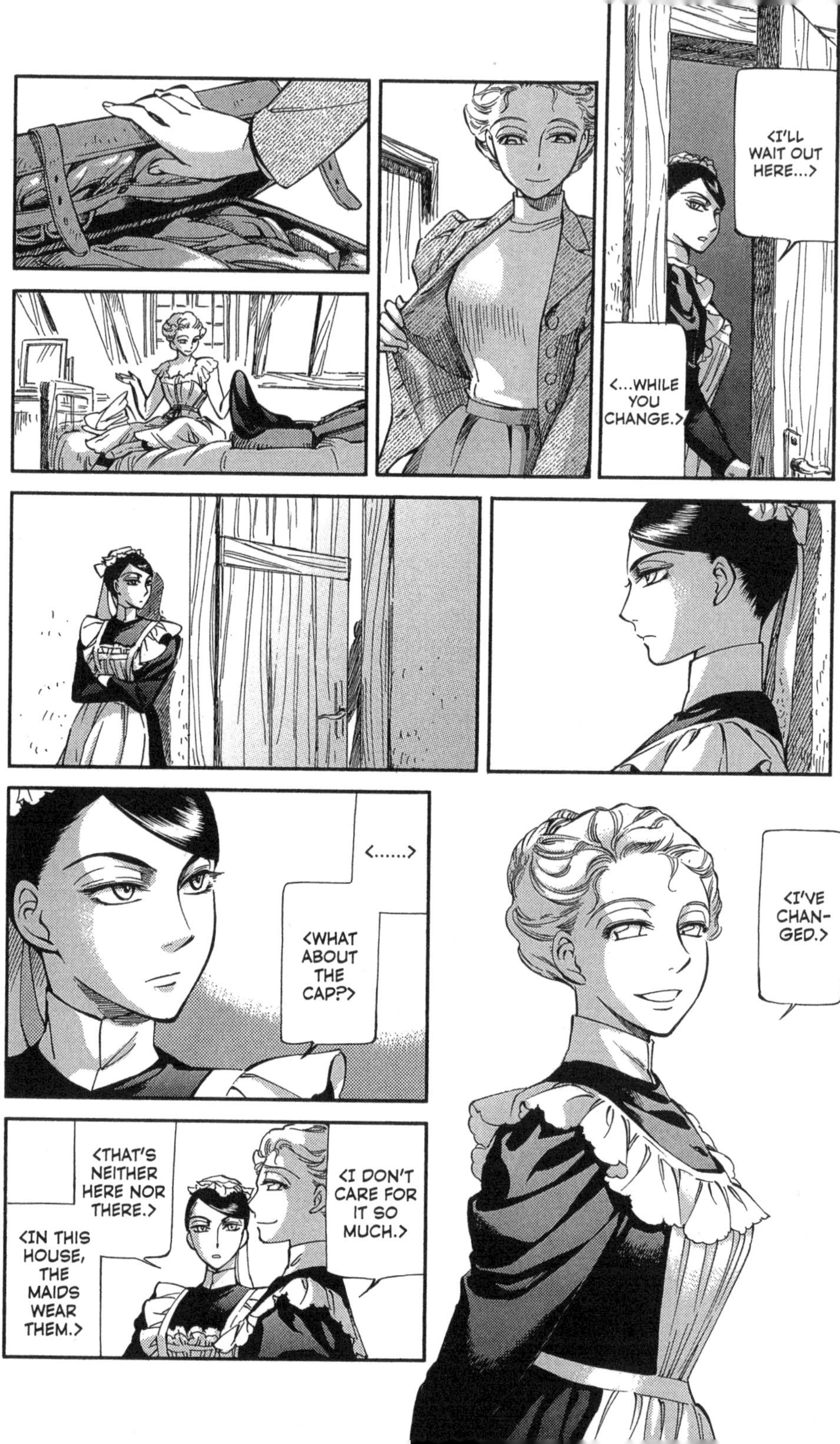
<I'LL WAIT OUT HERE...>
<...WHILE YOU CHANGE.>
<I'VE CHANGED.>
<......>
<WHAT ABOUT THE CAP?>
<I DON'T CARE FOR IT SO MUCH.>
<THAT'S NEITHER HERE NOR THERE.>
<IN THIS HOUSE, THE MAIDS WEAR THEM.>

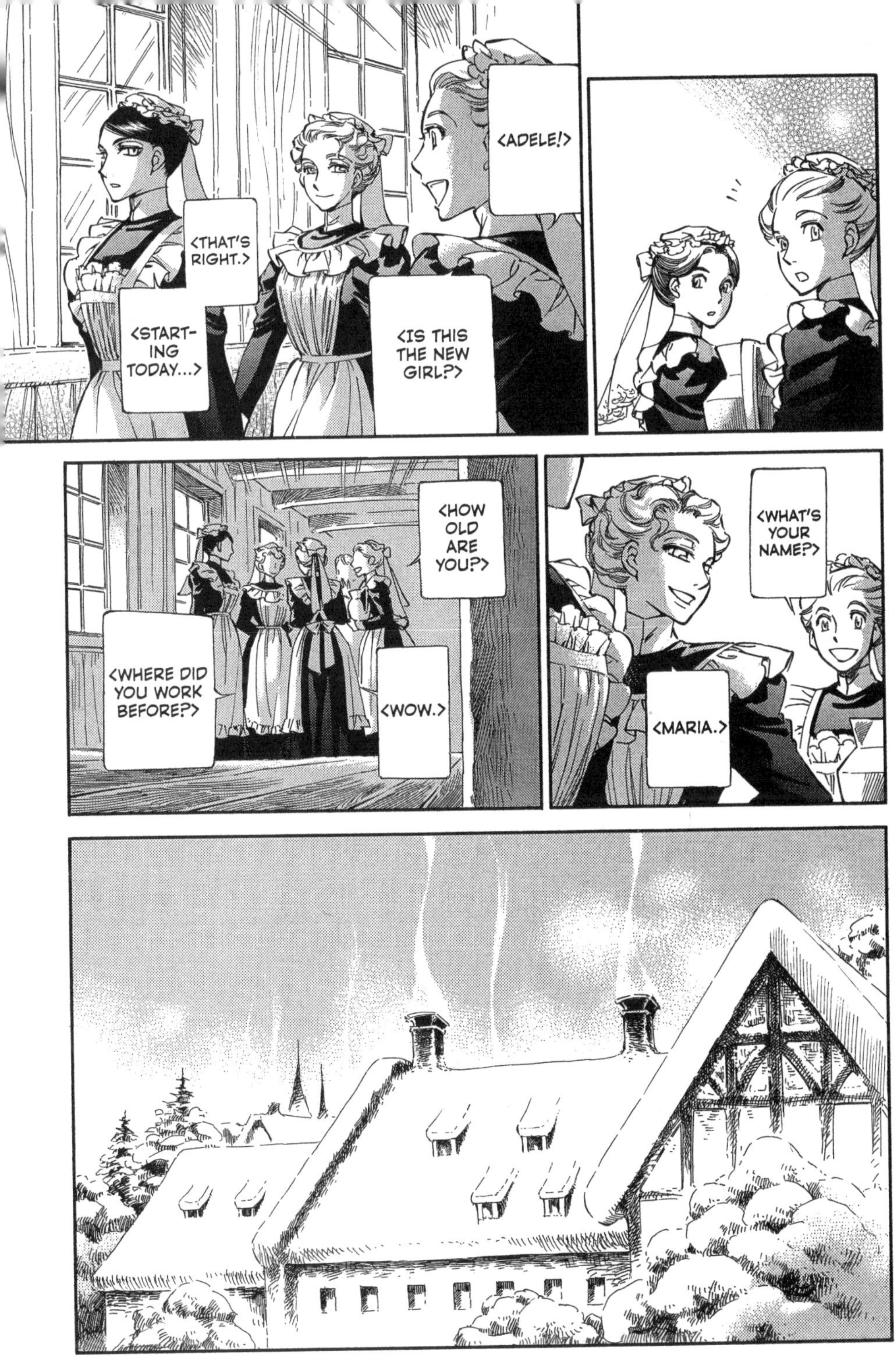
<ADELE!>
<IS THIS THE NEW GIRL?>
<THAT'S RIGHT.>
<STARTING TODAY...>
<WHAT'S YOUR NAME?>
<MARIA.>
<HOW OLD ARE YOU?>
<WOW.>
<WHERE DID YOU WORK BEFORE?>

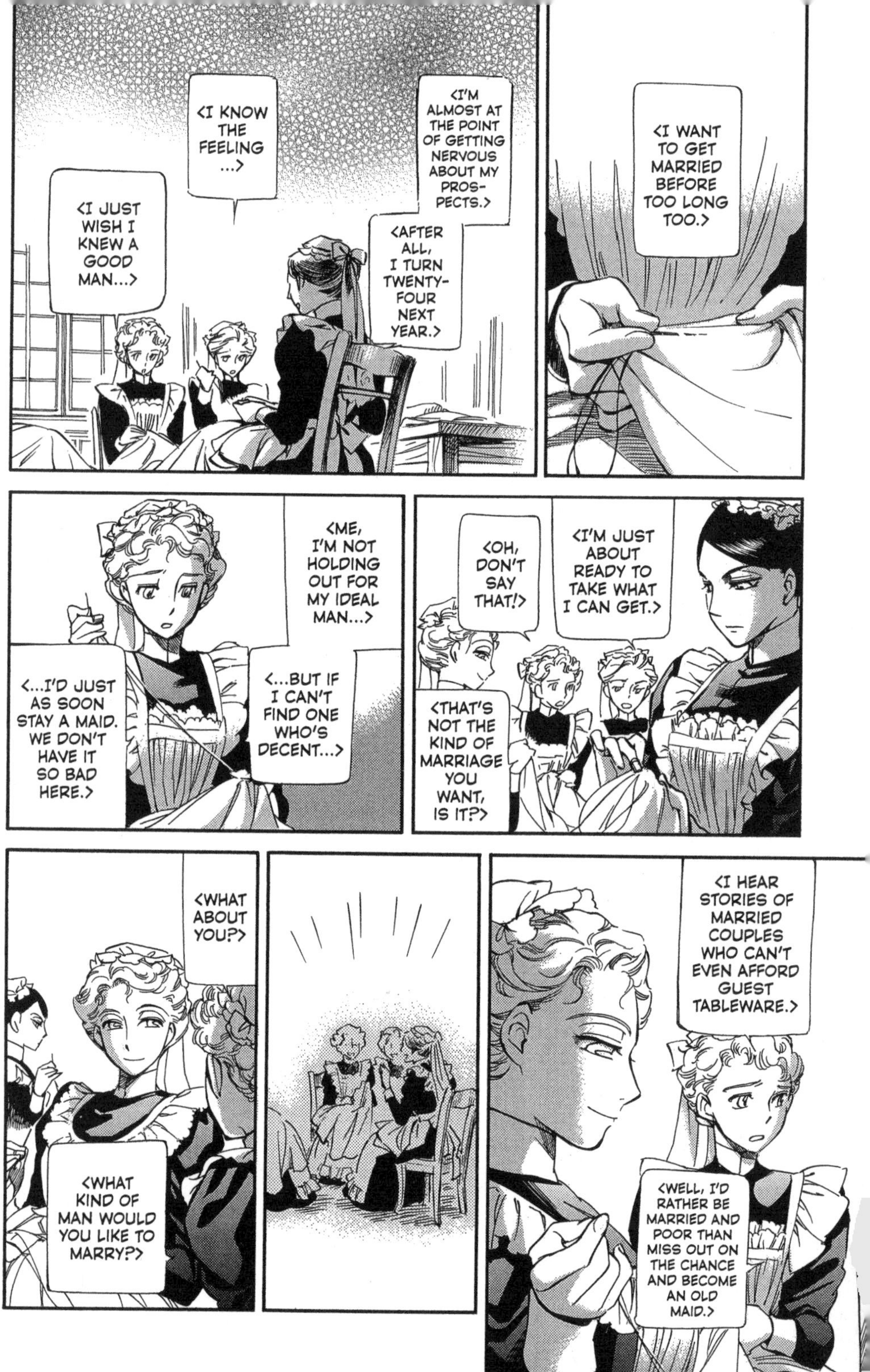
<I WANT TO GET MARRIED BEFORE TOO LONG TOO.>
<I'M ALMOST AT THE POINT OF GETTING NERVOUS ABOUT MY PROS-PECTS.>
<AFTER ALL, I TURN TWENTY-FOUR NEXT YEAR.>
<I KNOW THE FEELING ...>
<I JUST WISH I KNEW A GOOD MAN...>
<I'M JUST ABOUT READY TO TAKE WHAT I CAN GET.>
<OH, DON'T SAY THAT!>
<THAT'S NOT THE KIND OF MARRIAGE YOU WANT, IS IT?>
<ME, I'M NOT HOLDING OUT FOR MY IDEAL MAN...>
<...BUT IF I CAN'T FIND ONE WHO'S DECENT...>
<...I'D JUST AS SOON STAY A MAID. WE DON'T HAVE IT SO BAD HERE.>
<I HEAR STORIES OF MARRIED COUPLES WHO CAN'T EVEN AFFORD GUEST TABLEWARE.>
<WELL, I'D RATHER BE MARRIED AND POOR THAN MISS OUT ON THE CHANCE AND BECOME AN OLD MAID.>
<WHAT ABOUT YOU?>
<WHAT KIND OF MAN WOULD YOU LIKE TO MARRY?>

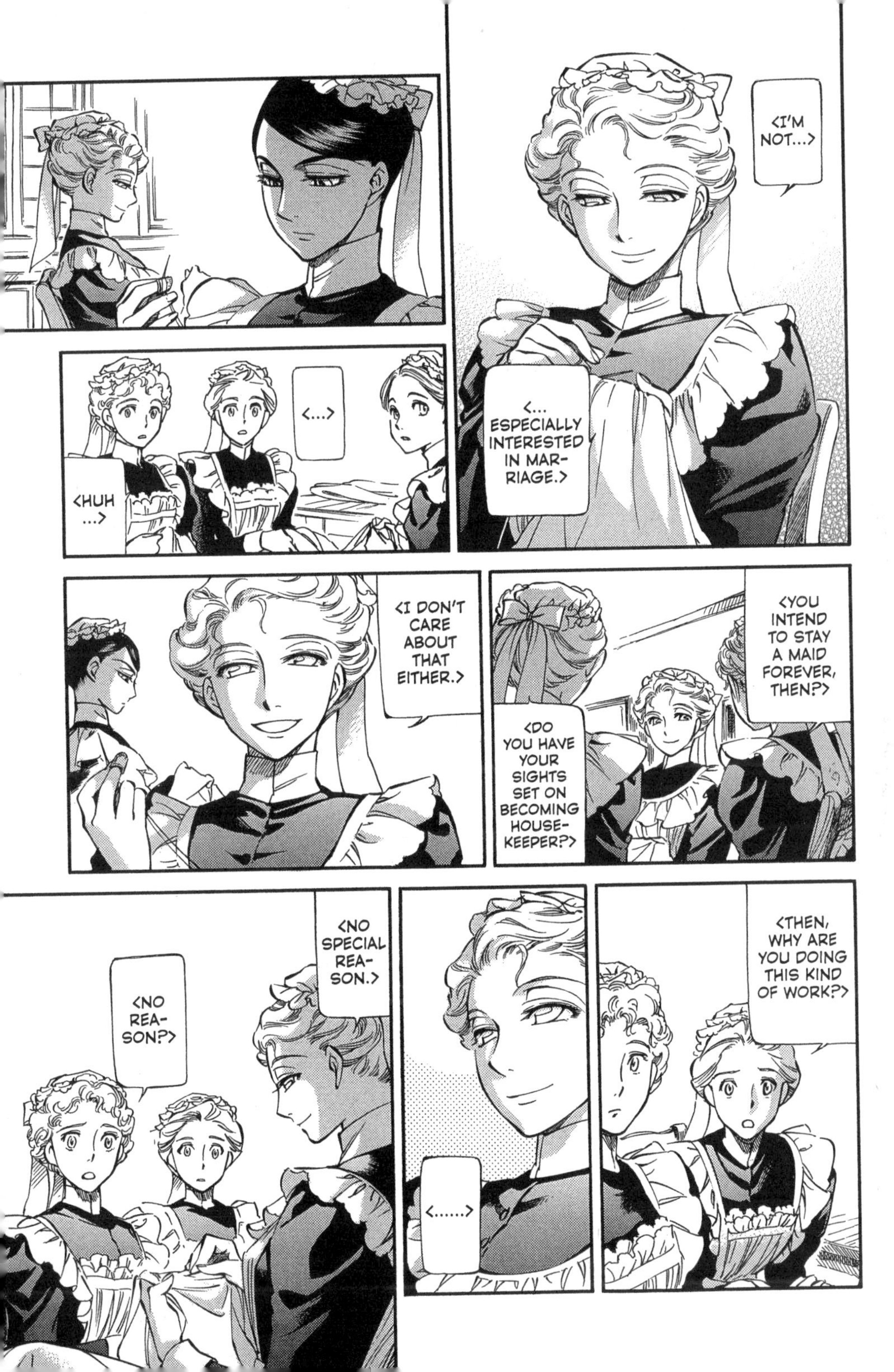
<I'M NOT...>
<... ESPECIALLY INTERESTED IN MARRIAGE.>
<...>
<HUH ...>
<YOU INTEND TO STAY A MAID FOREVER, THEN?>
<DO YOU HAVE YOUR SIGHTS SET ON BECOMING HOUSEKEEPER?>
<I DON'T CARE ABOUT THAT EITHER.>
<THEN, WHY ARE YOU DOING THIS KIND OF WORK?>
<......>
<NO SPECIAL REASON.>
<NO REASON?>

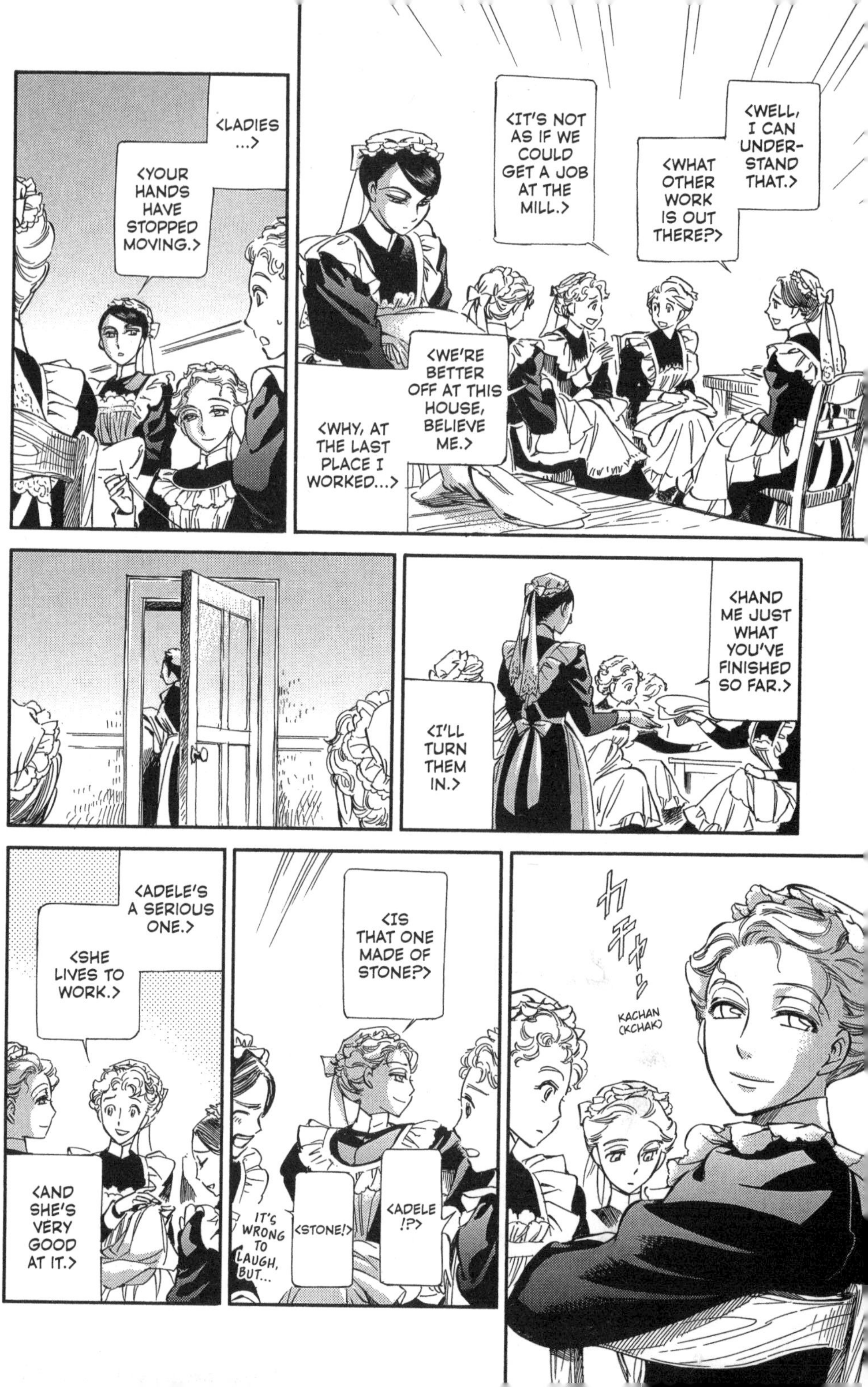

<WELL, I CAN UNDERSTAND THAT.>
<WHAT OTHER WORK IS OUT THERE?>
<IT'S NOT AS IF WE COULD GET A JOB AT THE MILL.>
<WE'RE BETTER OFF AT THIS HOUSE, BELIEVE ME.>
<WHY, AT THE LAST PLACE I WORKED...>
<LADIES ...>
<YOUR HANDS HAVE STOPPED MOVING.>
<HAND ME JUST WHAT YOU'VE FINISHED SO FAR.>
<I'LL TURN THEM IN.>
KACHAN (KCHAK)
<IS THAT ONE MADE OF STONE?>
<ADELE !?>
<STONE!>
IT'S WRONG TO LAUGH, BUT...
<ADELE'S A SERIOUS ONE.>
<SHE LIVES TO WORK.>
<AND SHE'S VERY GOOD AT IT.>

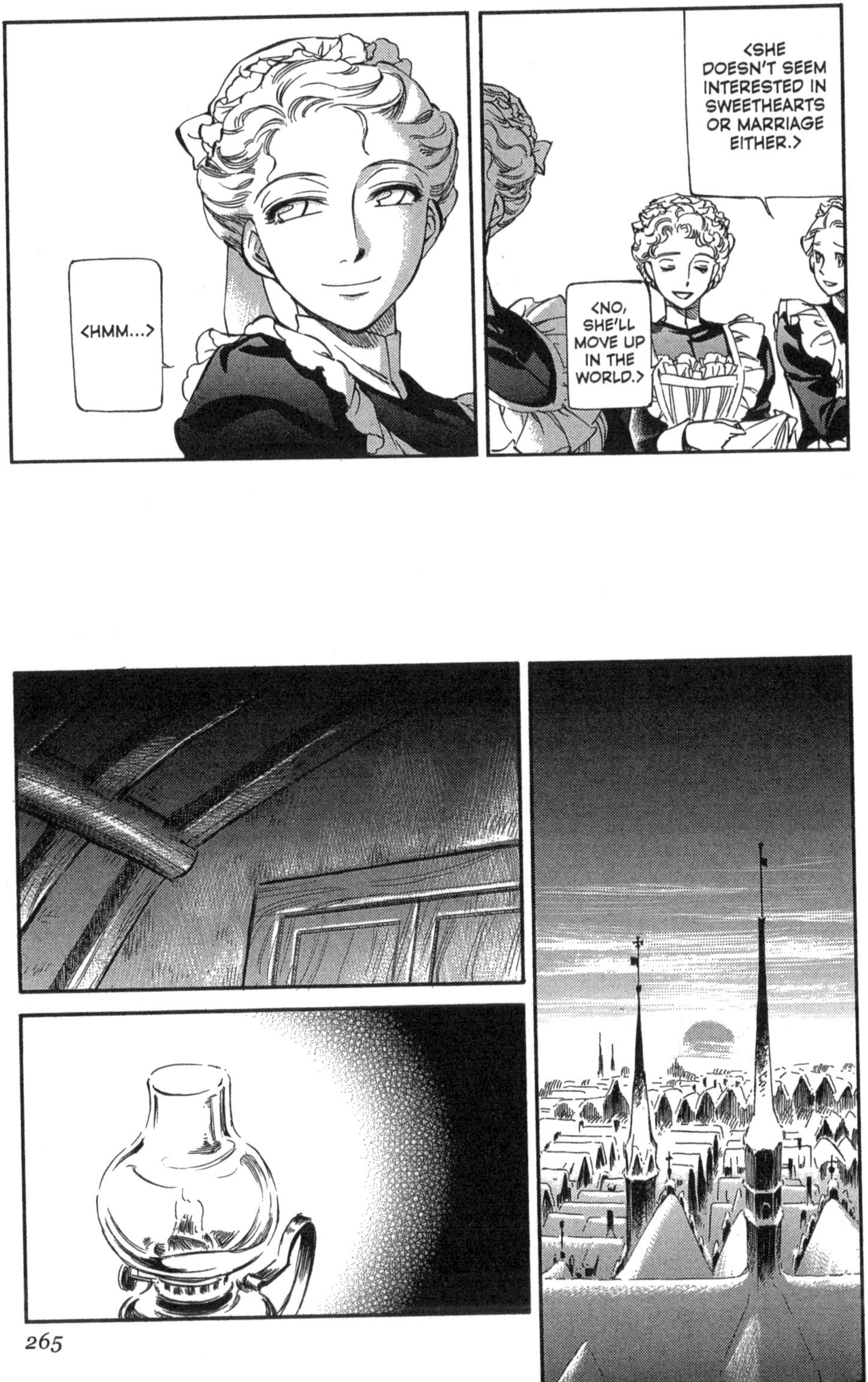
<SHE DOESN'T SEEM INTERESTED IN SWEETHEARTS OR MARRIAGE EITHER.>
<NO, SHE'LL MOVE UP IN THE WORLD.>
<HMM...>

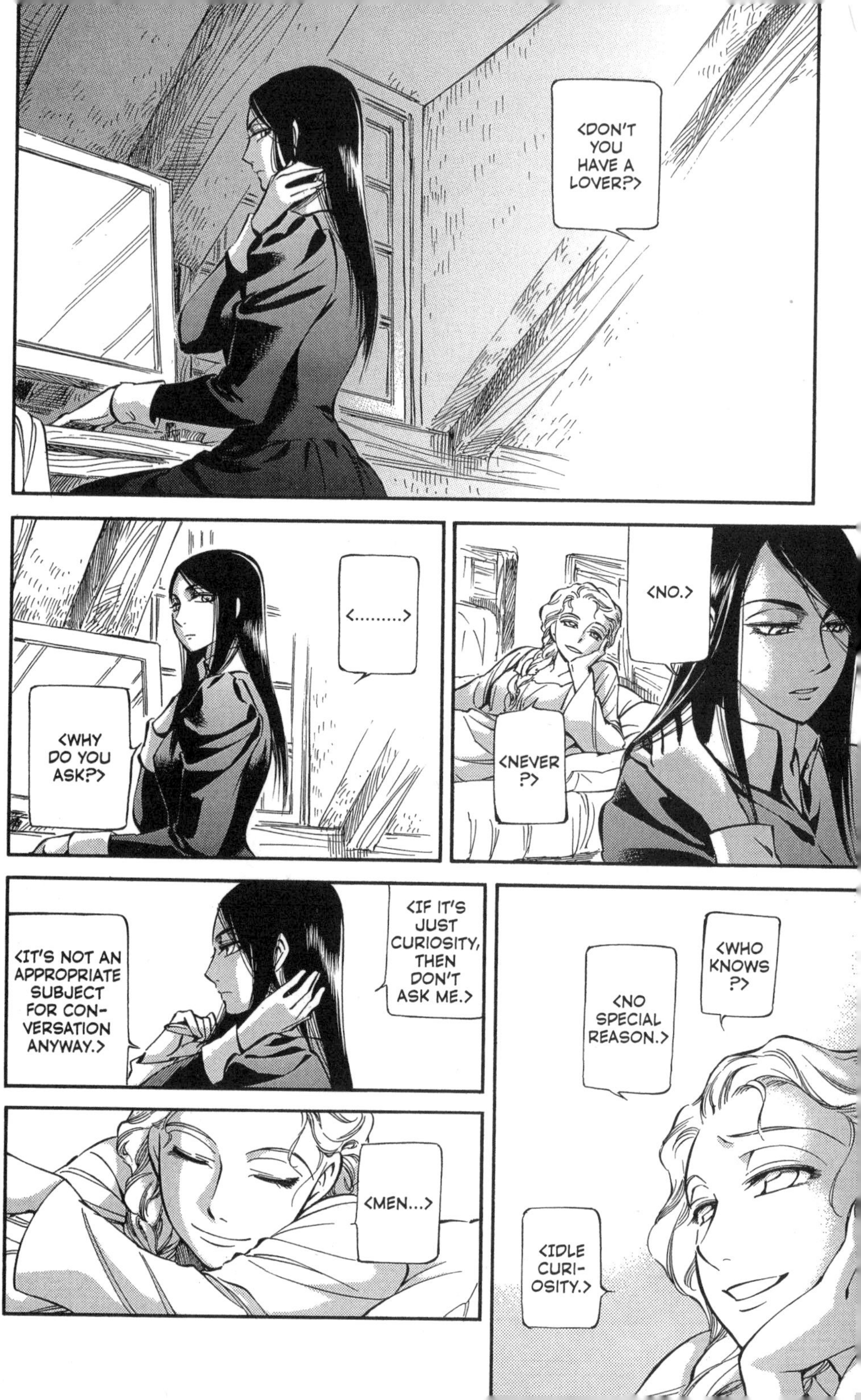
<DON'T YOU HAVE A LOVER?>
<NO.>
<NEVER?>
<.........>
<WHY DO YOU ASK?>
<WHO KNOWS?>
<NO SPECIAL REASON.>
<IDLE CURIOSITY.>
<IF IT'S JUST CURIOSITY, THEN DON'T ASK ME.>
<IT'S NOT AN APPROPRIATE SUBJECT FOR CONVERSATION ANYWAY.>
<MEN...>

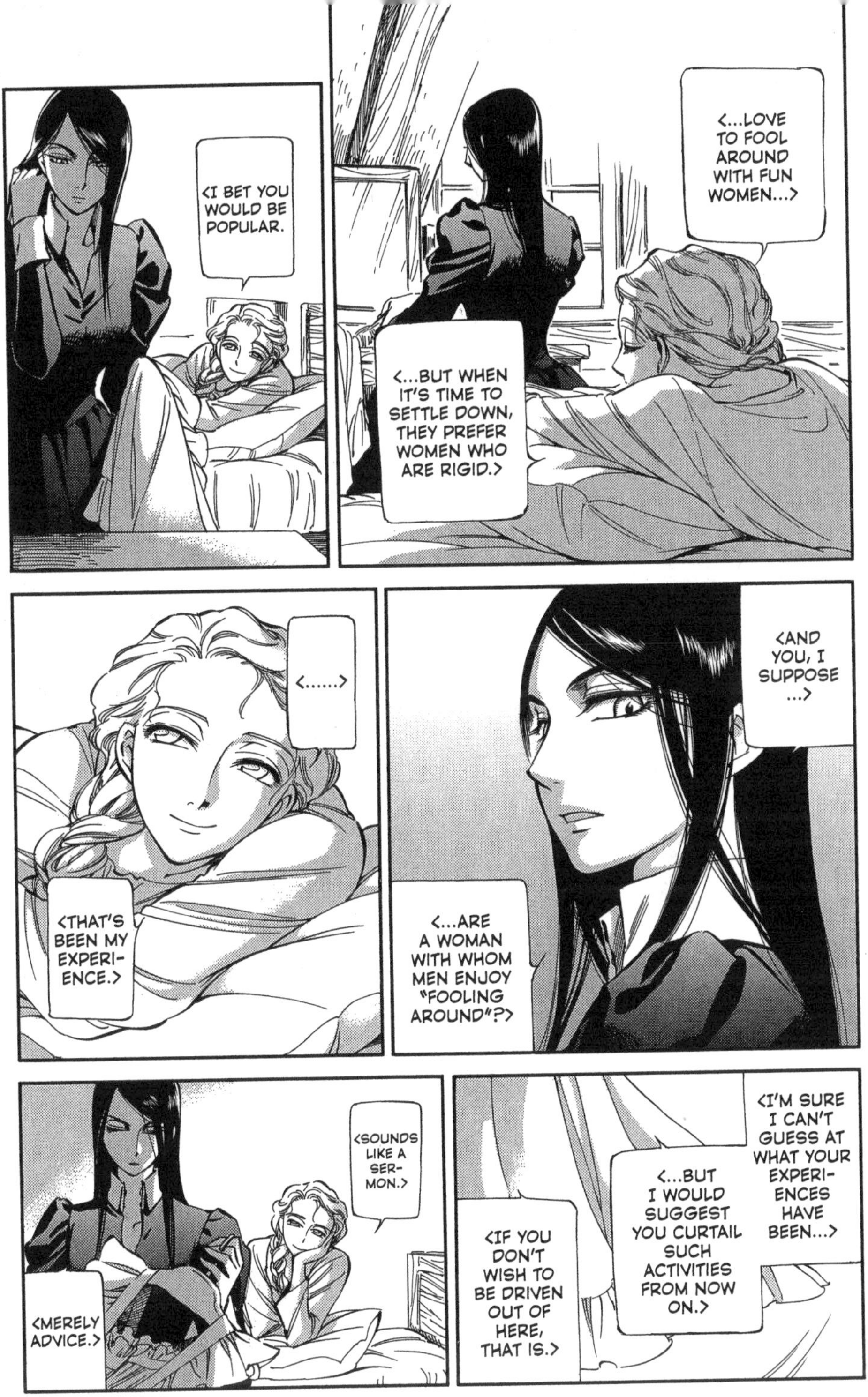
<...LOVE TO FOOL AROUND WITH FUN WOMEN...>
<...BUT WHEN IT'S TIME TO SETTLE DOWN, THEY PREFER WOMEN WHO ARE RIGID.>
<I BET YOU WOULD BE POPULAR.>
<AND YOU, I SUPPOSE ...>
<...ARE A WOMAN WITH WHOM MEN ENJOY "FOOLING AROUND"?>
<......>
<THAT'S BEEN MY EXPERI-ENCE.>
<I'M SURE I CAN'T GUESS AT WHAT YOUR EXPERI-ENCES HAVE BEEN...>
<...BUT I WOULD SUGGEST YOU CURTAIL SUCH ACTIVITIES FROM NOW ON.>
<IF YOU DON'T WISH TO BE DRIVEN OUT OF HERE, THAT IS.>
<SOUNDS LIKE A SER-MON.>
<MERELY ADVICE.>

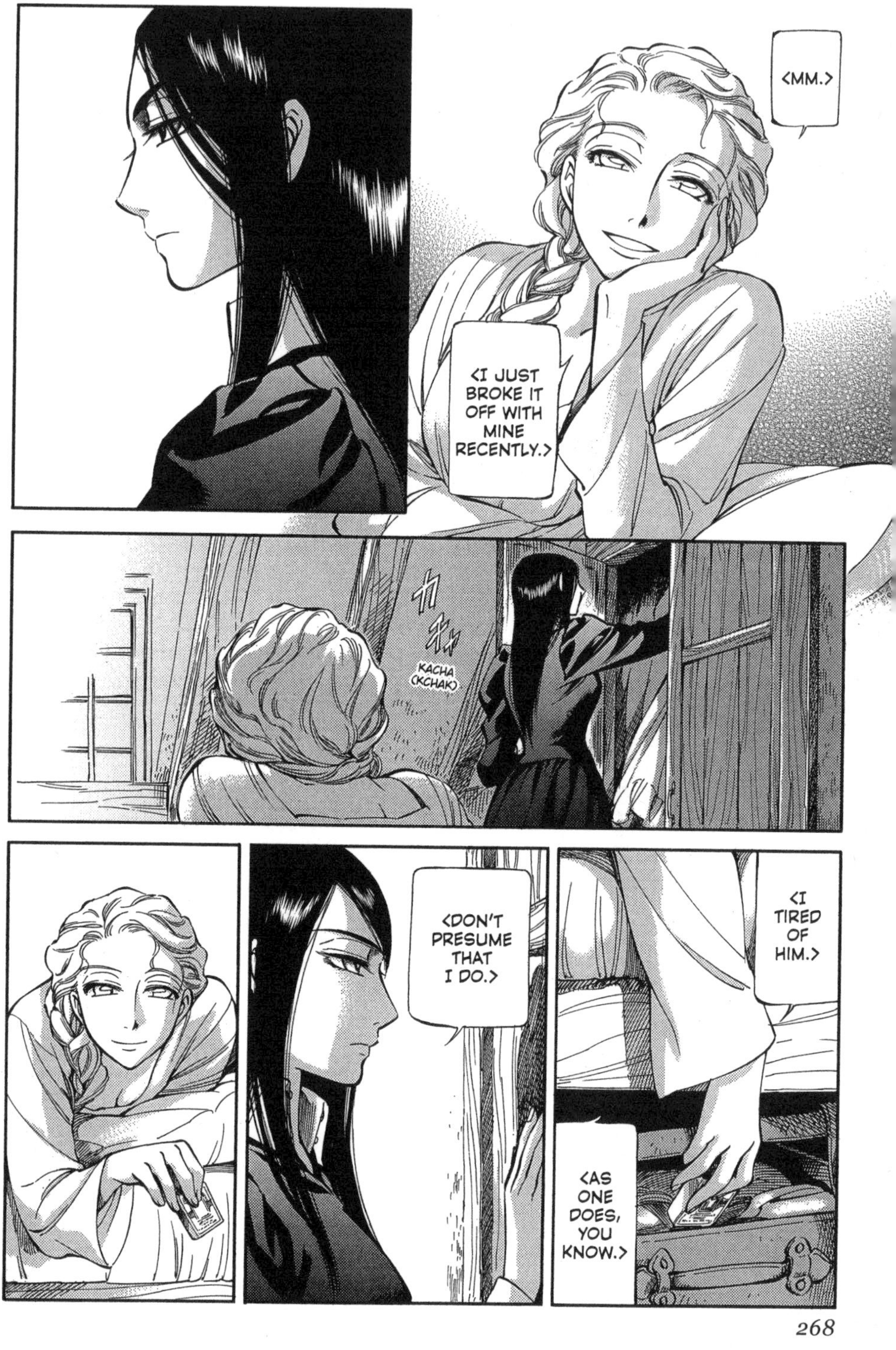

<MM.>
<I JUST BROKE IT OFF WITH MINE RECENTLY.>
KACHA (KCHAK)
<I TIRED OF HIM.>
<AS ONE DOES, YOU KNOW.>
<DON'T PRESUME THAT I DO.>

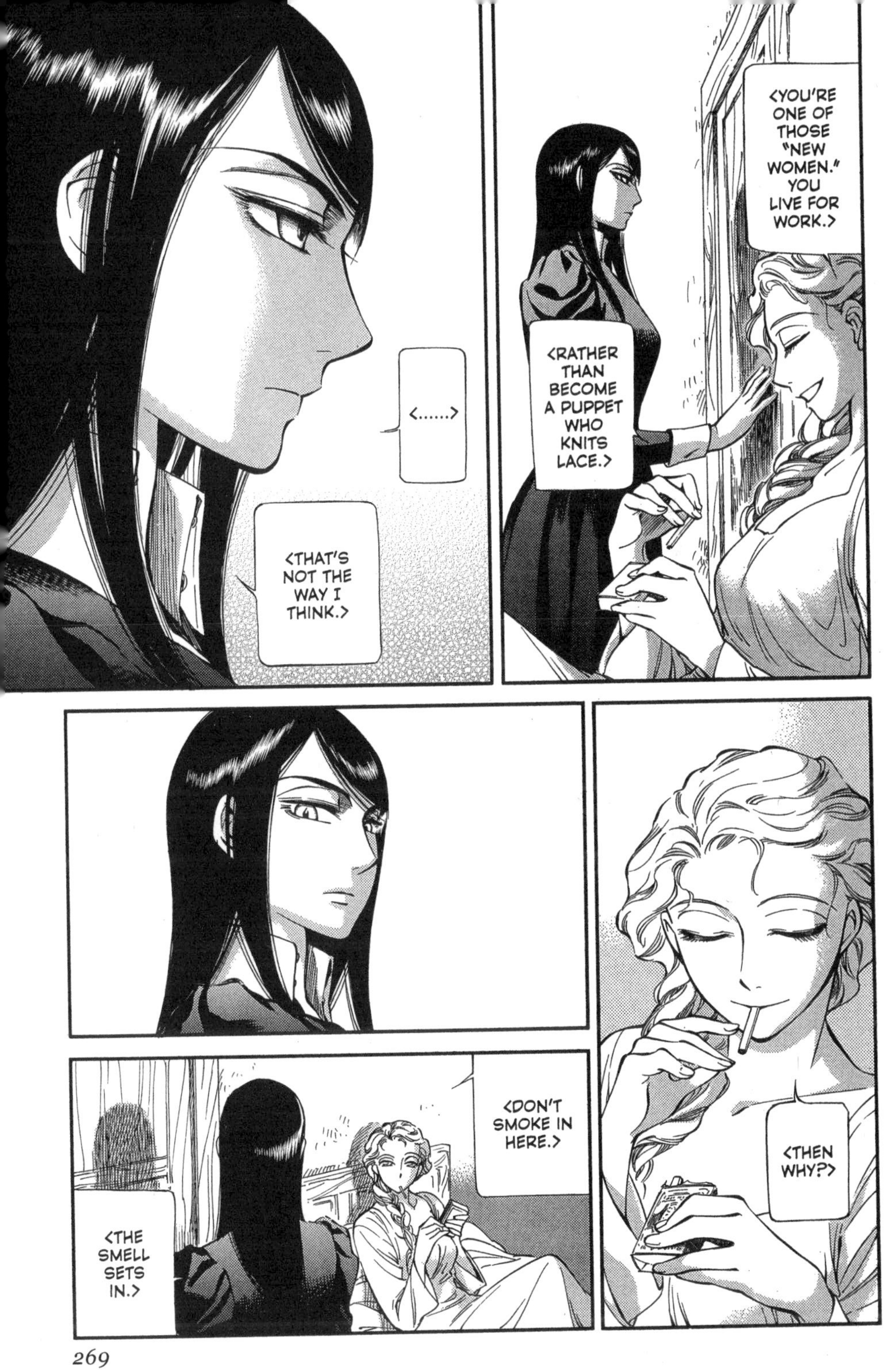
<YOU'RE ONE OF THOSE "NEW WOMEN." YOU LIVE FOR WORK.>
<RATHER THAN BECOME A PUPPET WHO KNITS LACE.>
<......>
<THAT'S NOT THE WAY I THINK.>
<THEN WHY?>
<DON'T SMOKE IN HERE.>
<THE SMELL SETS IN.>

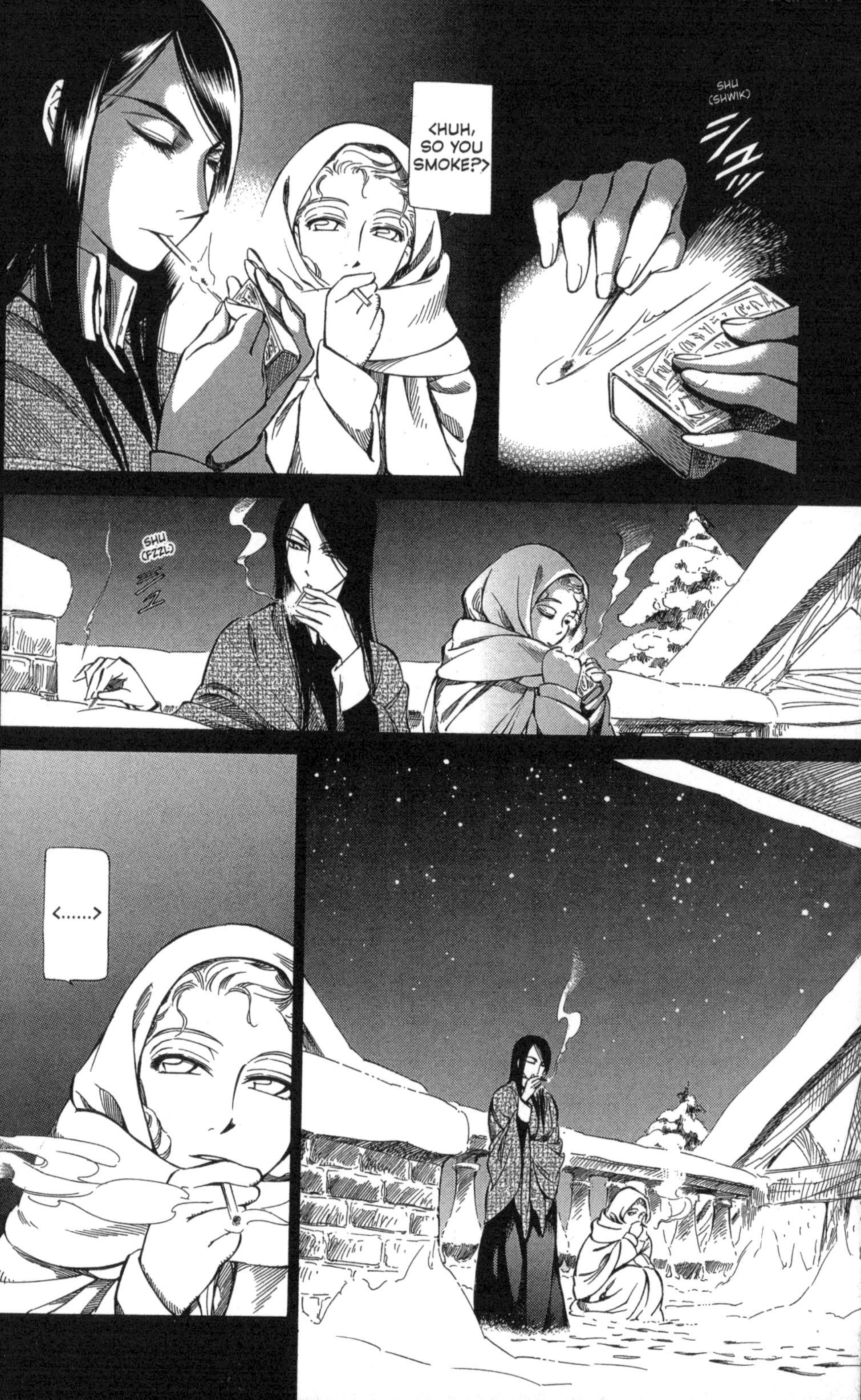
SHU (SHWIK)
<HUH, SO YOU SMOKE?>
SHU (FZZL)
<......>

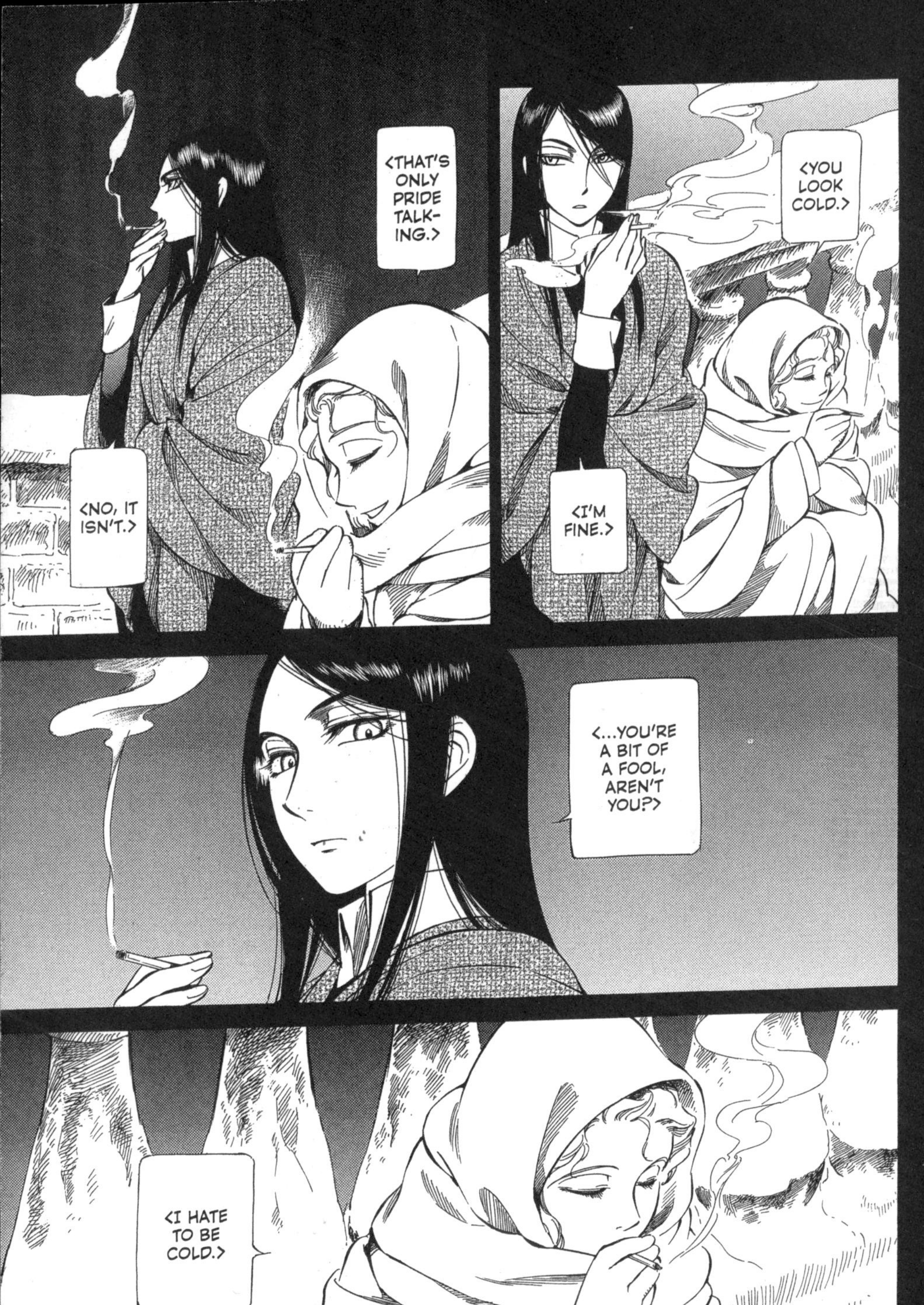
<YOU LOOK COLD.>
<I'M FINE.>
<THAT'S ONLY PRIDE TALKING.>
<NO, IT ISN'T.>
<...YOU'RE A BIT OF A FOOL, AREN'T YOU?>
<I HATE TO BE COLD.>

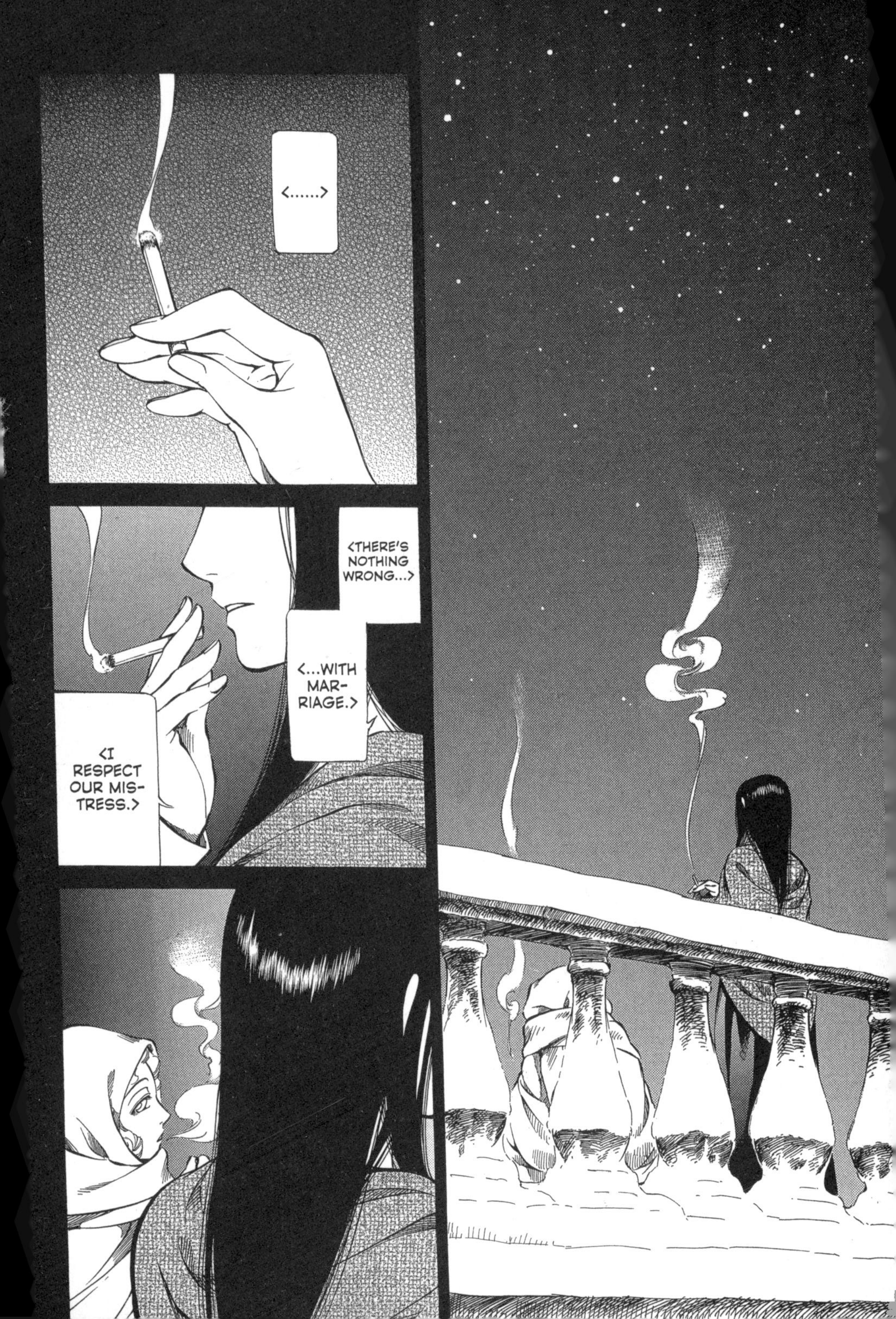
<......>
<THERE'S NOTHING WRONG...>
<...WITH MARRIAGE.>
<I RESPECT OUR MISTRESS.>

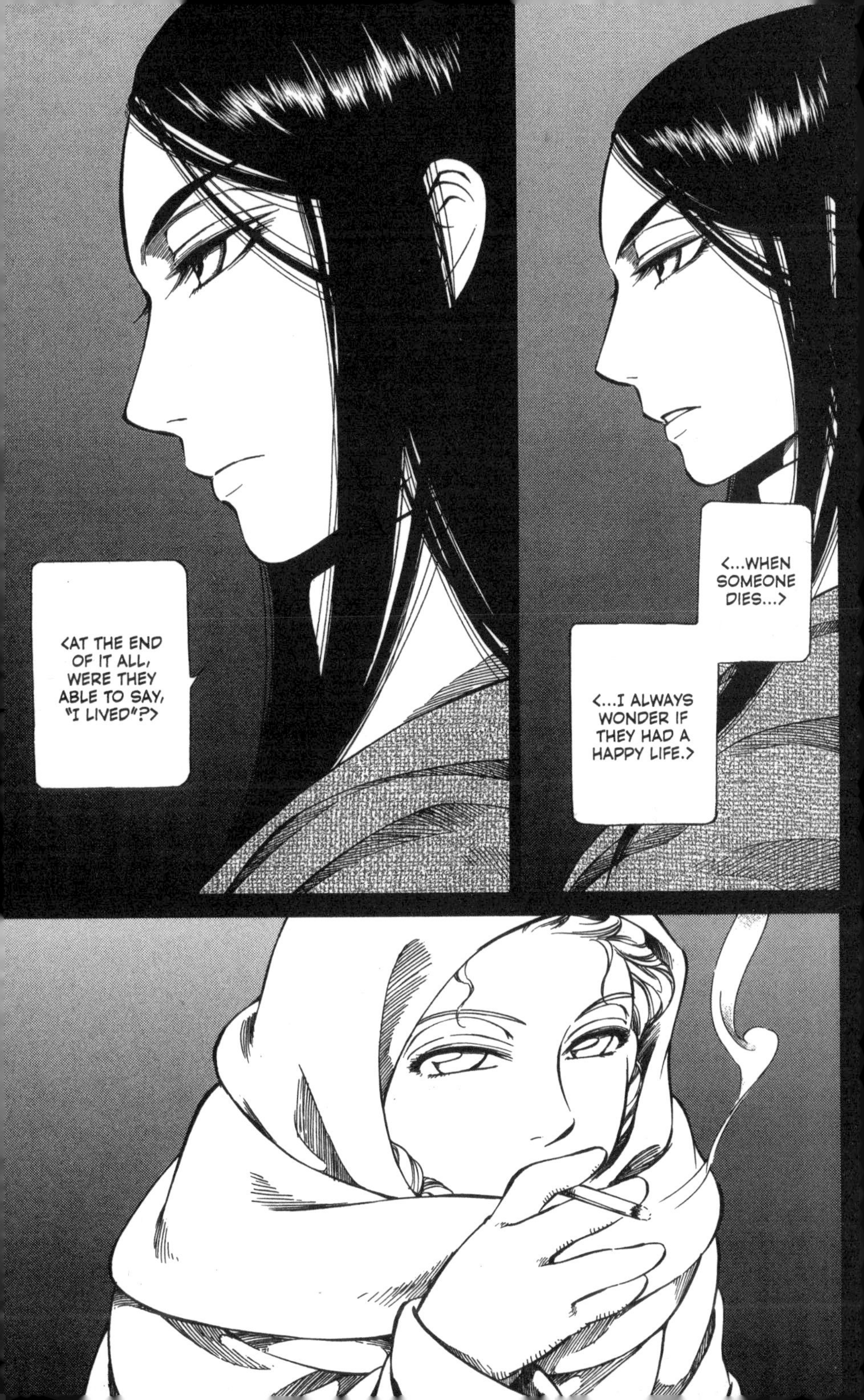
<...WHEN SOMEONE DIES...>
<...I ALWAYS WONDER IF THEY HAD A HAPPY LIFE.>
<AT THE END OF IT ALL, WERE THEY ABLE TO SAY, "I LIVED"?>

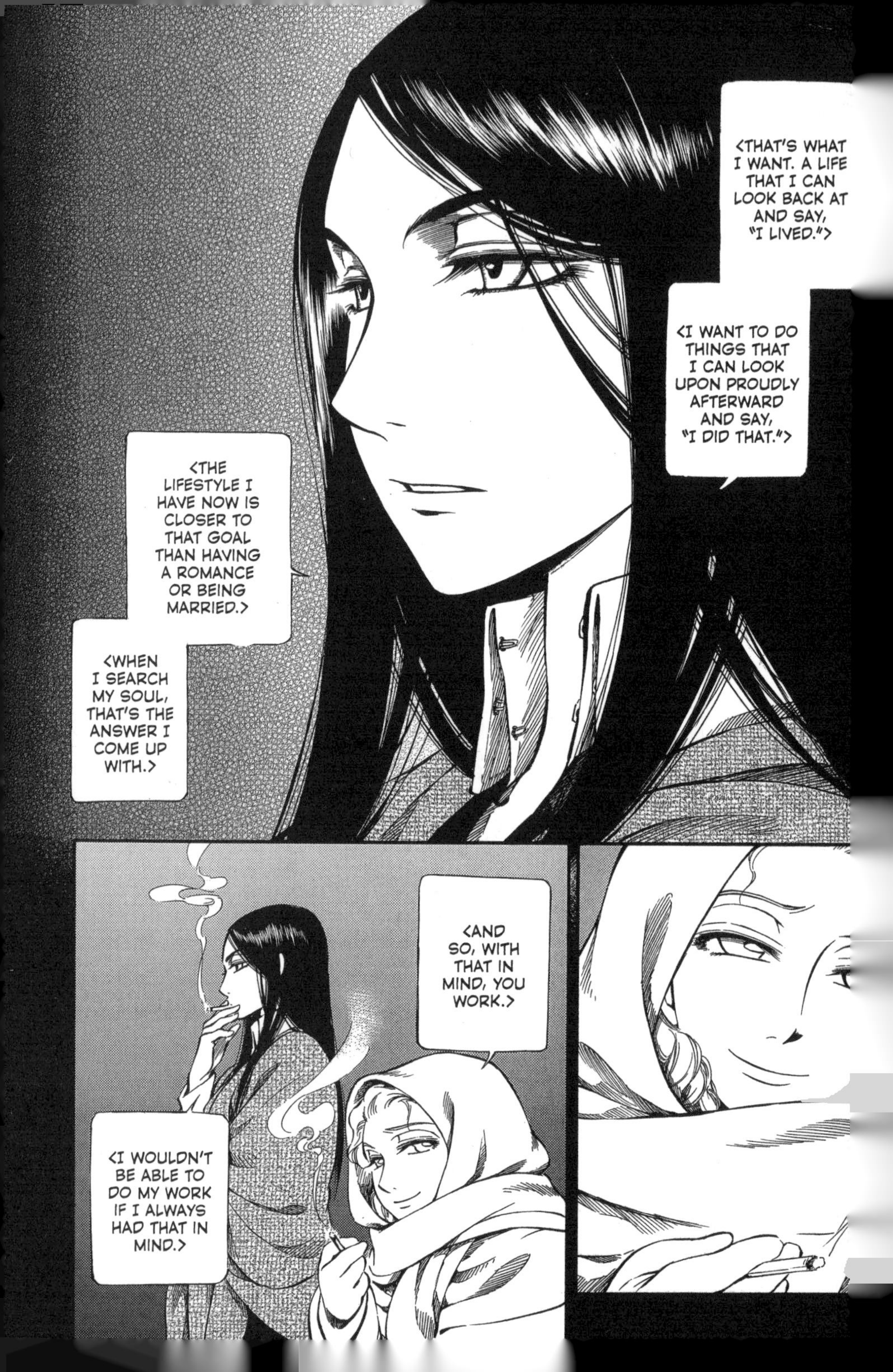
<THAT'S WHAT I WANT. A LIFE THAT I CAN LOOK BACK AT AND SAY, "I LIVED.">
<I WANT TO DO THINGS THAT I CAN LOOK UPON PROUDLY AFTERWARD AND SAY, "I DID THAT.">
<THE LIFESTYLE I HAVE NOW IS CLOSER TO THAT GOAL THAN HAVING A ROMANCE OR BEING MARRIED.>
<WHEN I SEARCH MY SOUL, THAT'S THE ANSWER I COME UP WITH.>
<AND SO, WITH THAT IN MIND, YOU WORK.>
<I WOULDN'T BE ABLE TO DO MY WORK IF I ALWAYS HAD THAT IN MIND.>

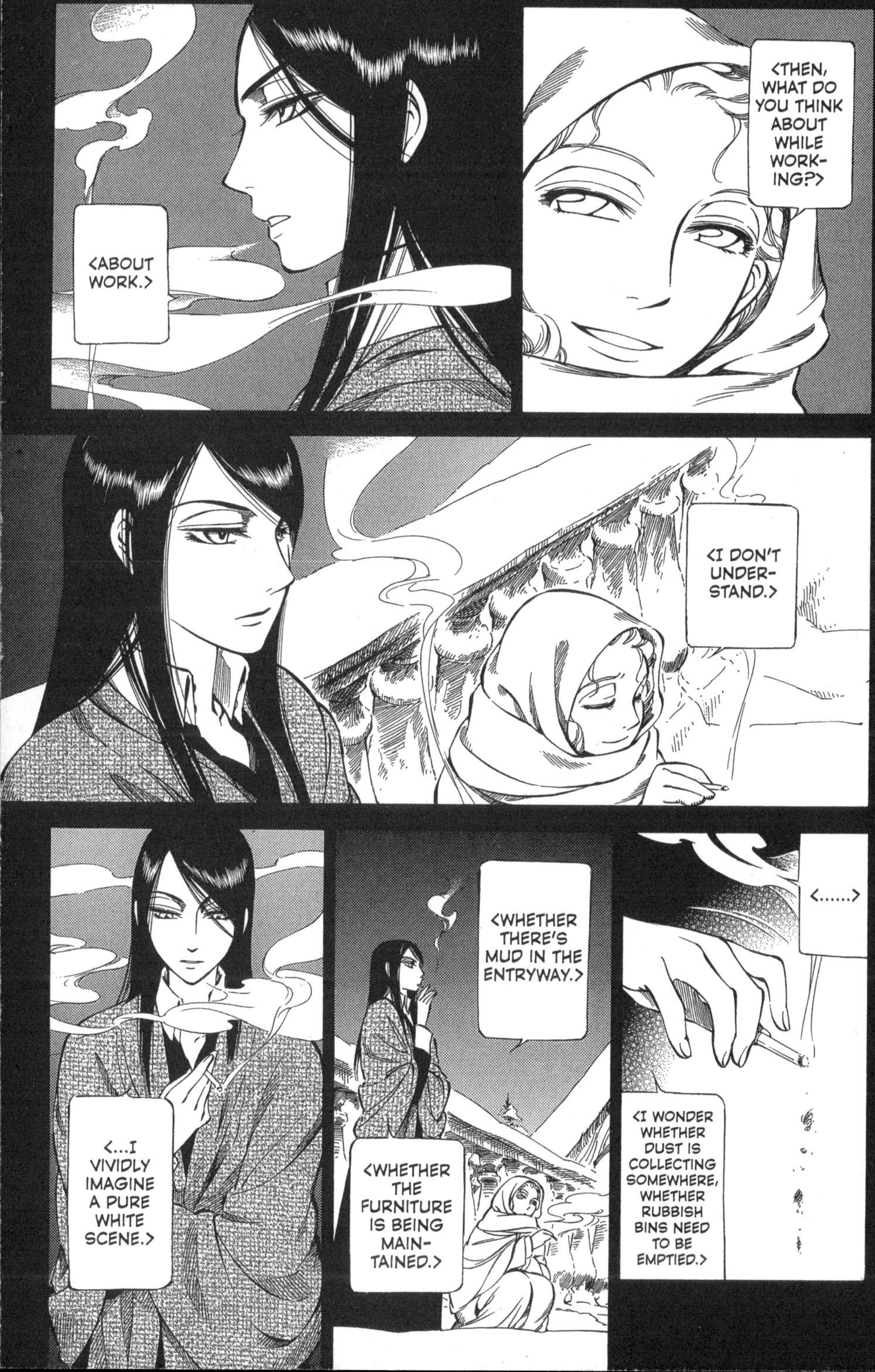
<THEN, WHAT DO YOU THINK ABOUT WHILE WORK-ING?>
<ABOUT WORK.>
<I DON'T UNDER-STAND.>
<......>
<I WONDER WHETHER DUST IS COLLECTING SOMEWHERE, WHETHER RUBBISH BINS NEED TO BE EMPTIED.>
<WHETHER THERE'S MUD IN THE ENTRYWAY.>
<WHETHER THE FURNITURE IS BEING MAIN-TAINED.>
<...I VIVIDLY IMAGINE A PURE WHITE SCENE.>

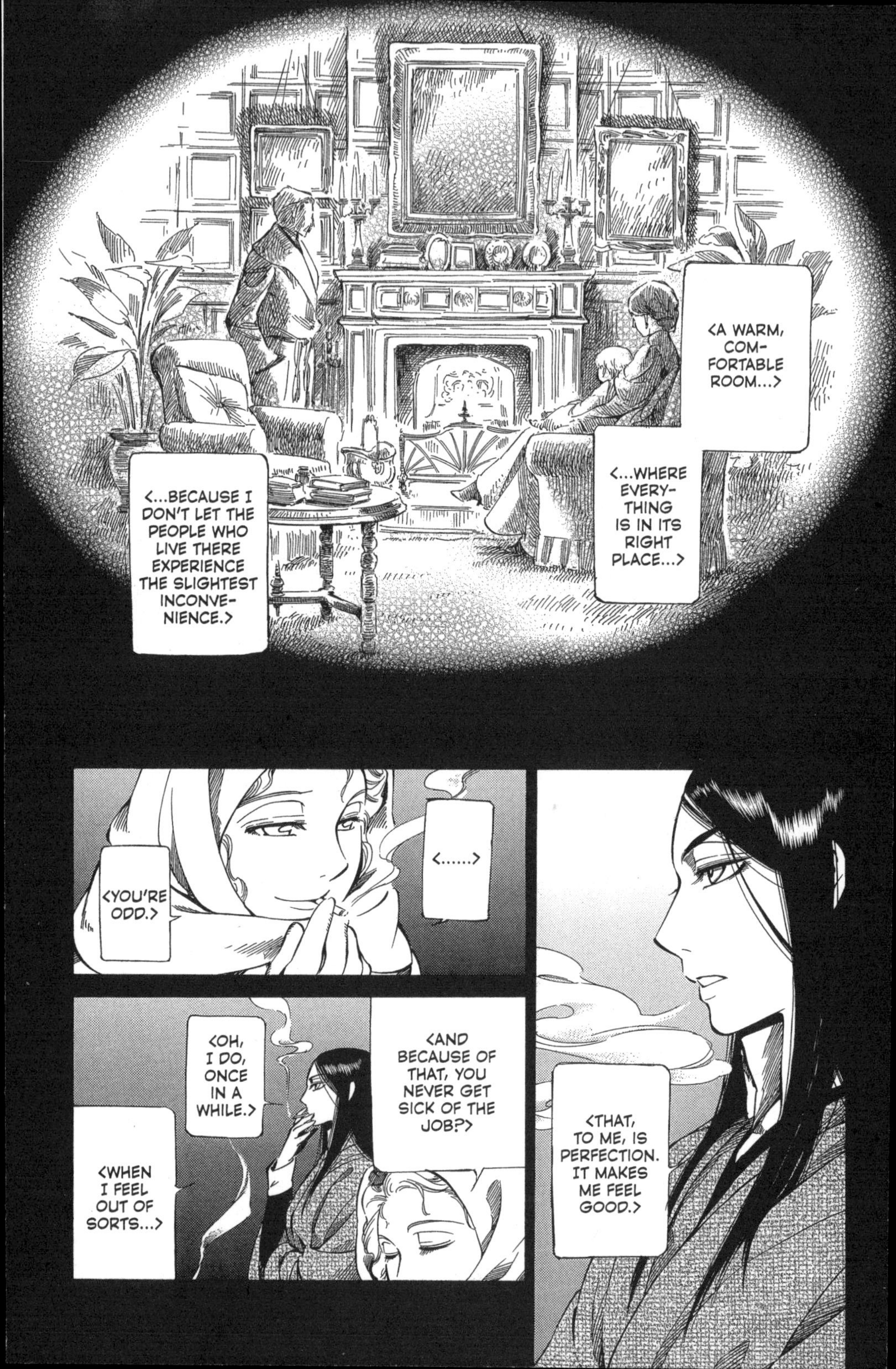
<A WARM, COMFORTABLE ROOM...>
<...WHERE EVERYTHING IS IN ITS RIGHT PLACE...>
<...BECAUSE I DON'T LET THE PEOPLE WHO LIVE THERE EXPERIENCE THE SLIGHTEST INCONVENIENCE.>
<THAT, TO ME, IS PERFECTION. IT MAKES ME FEEL GOOD.>
<......>
<YOU'RE ODD.>
<AND BECAUSE OF THAT, YOU NEVER GET SICK OF THE JOB?>
<OH, I DO, ONCE IN A WHILE.>
<WHEN I FEEL OUT OF SORTS...>

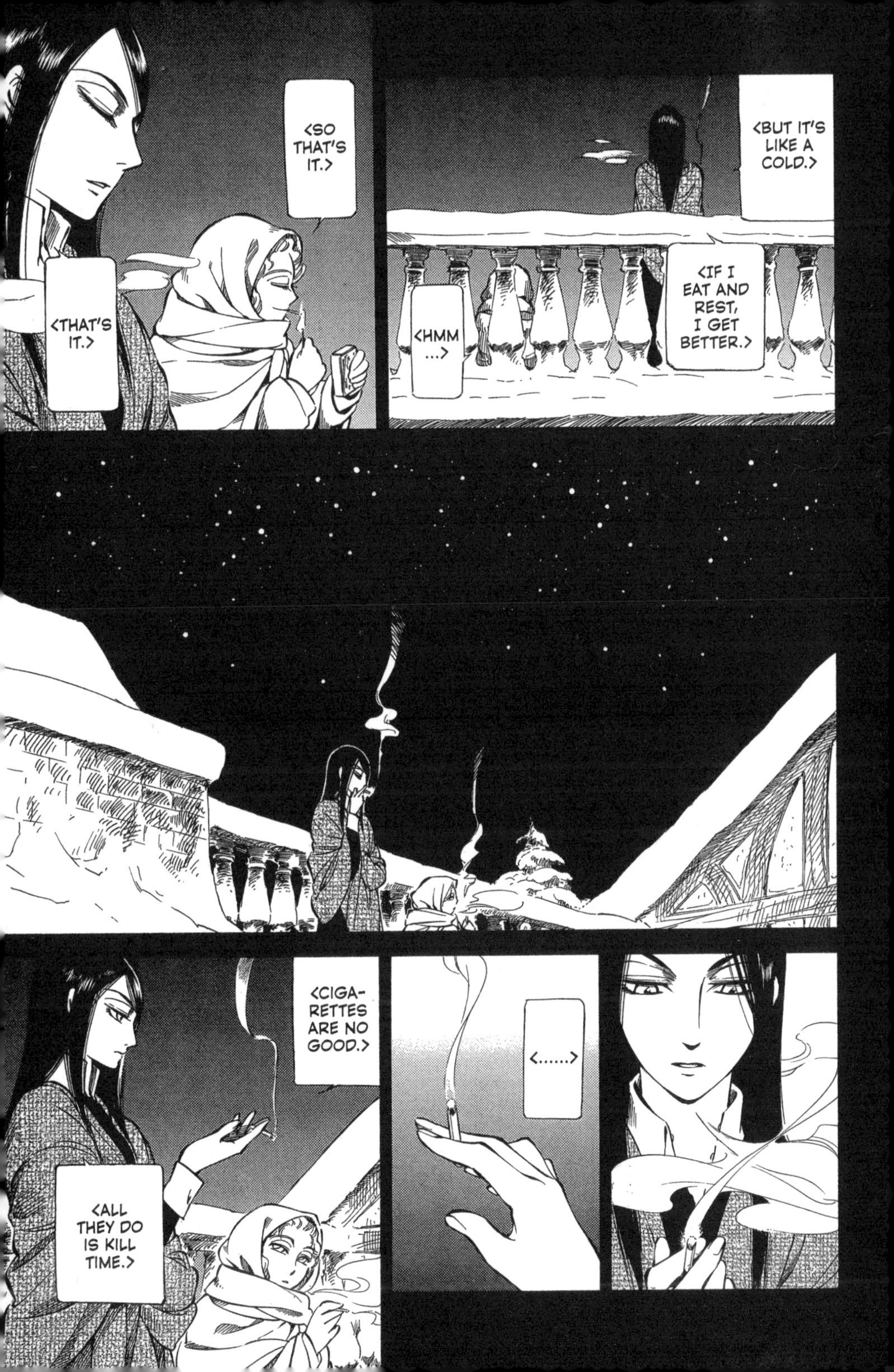
<BUT IT'S LIKE A COLD.>
<IF I EAT AND REST, I GET BETTER.>
<HMM ...>
<SO THAT'S IT.>
<THAT'S IT.>
<......>
<CIGA-RETTES ARE NO GOOD.>
<ALL THEY DO IS KILL TIME.>

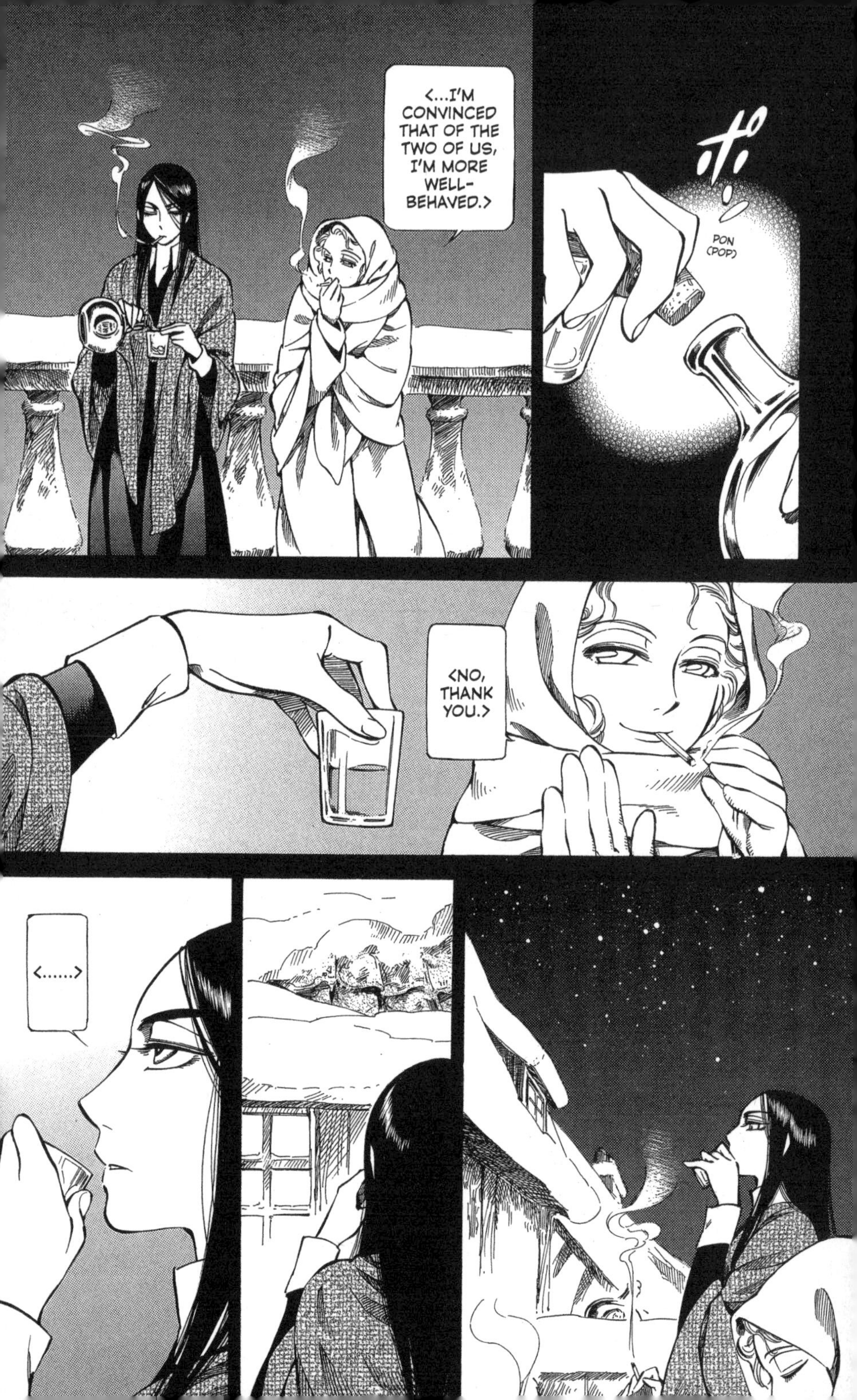
PON (POP)
<...I'M CONVINCED THAT OF THE TWO OF US, I'M MORE WELL-BEHAVED.>
<NO, THANK YOU.>
<......>

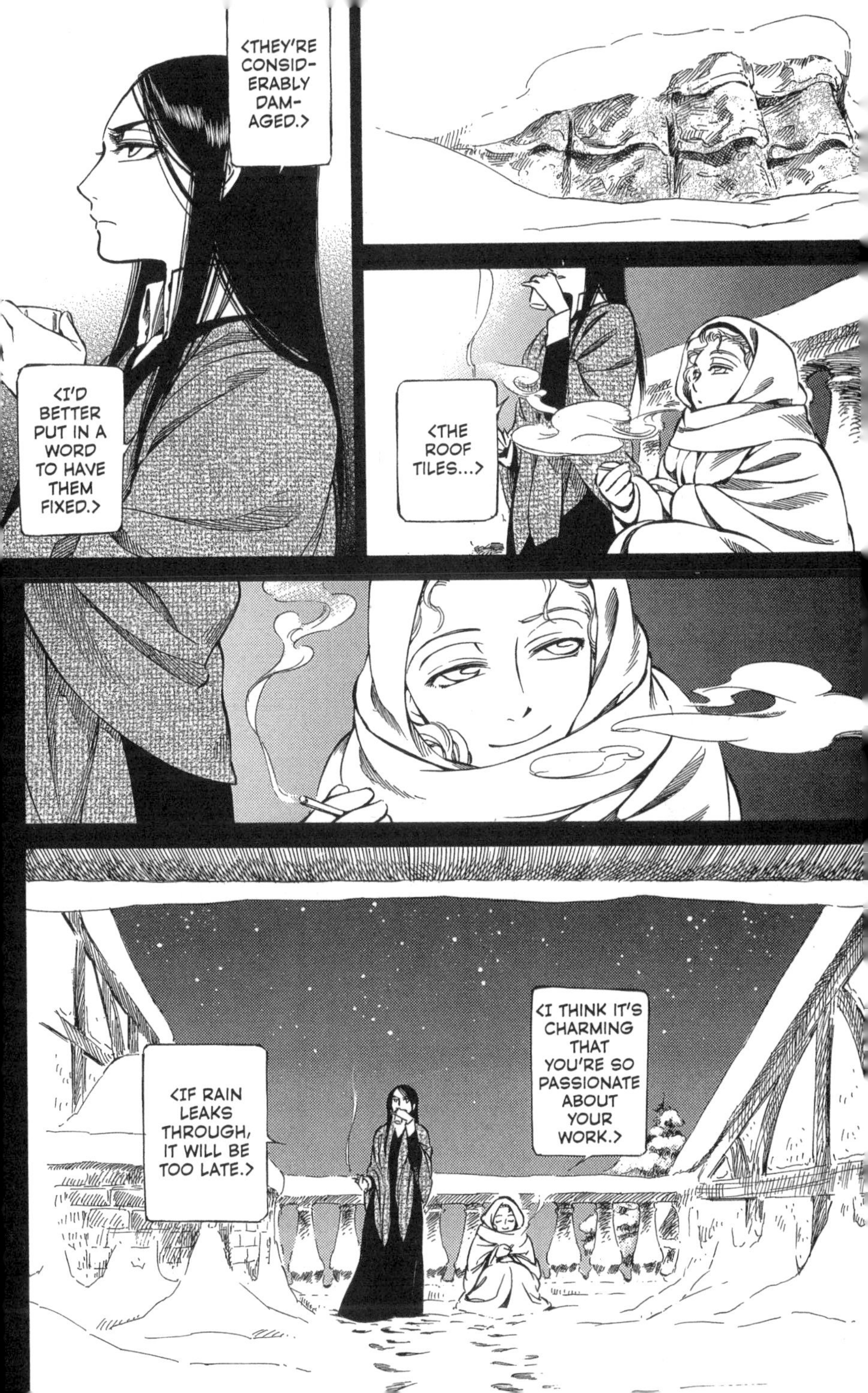
<THE ROOF TILES...>
<THEY'RE CONSIDERABLY DAMAGED.>
<I'D BETTER PUT IN A WORD TO HAVE THEM FIXED.>
<I THINK IT'S CHARMING THAT YOU'RE SO PASSIONATE ABOUT YOUR WORK.>
<IF RAIN LEAKS THROUGH, IT WILL BE TOO LATE.>

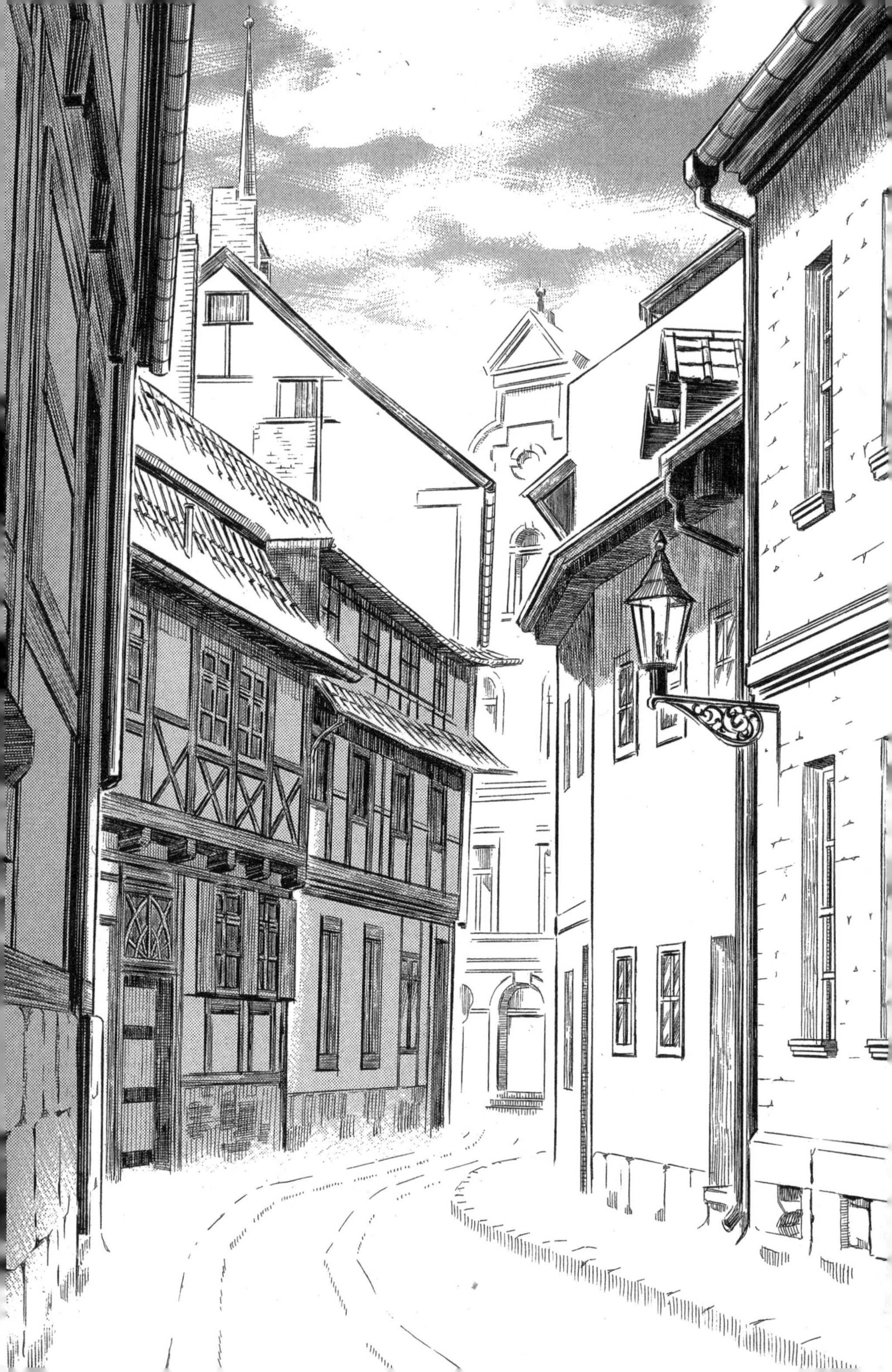

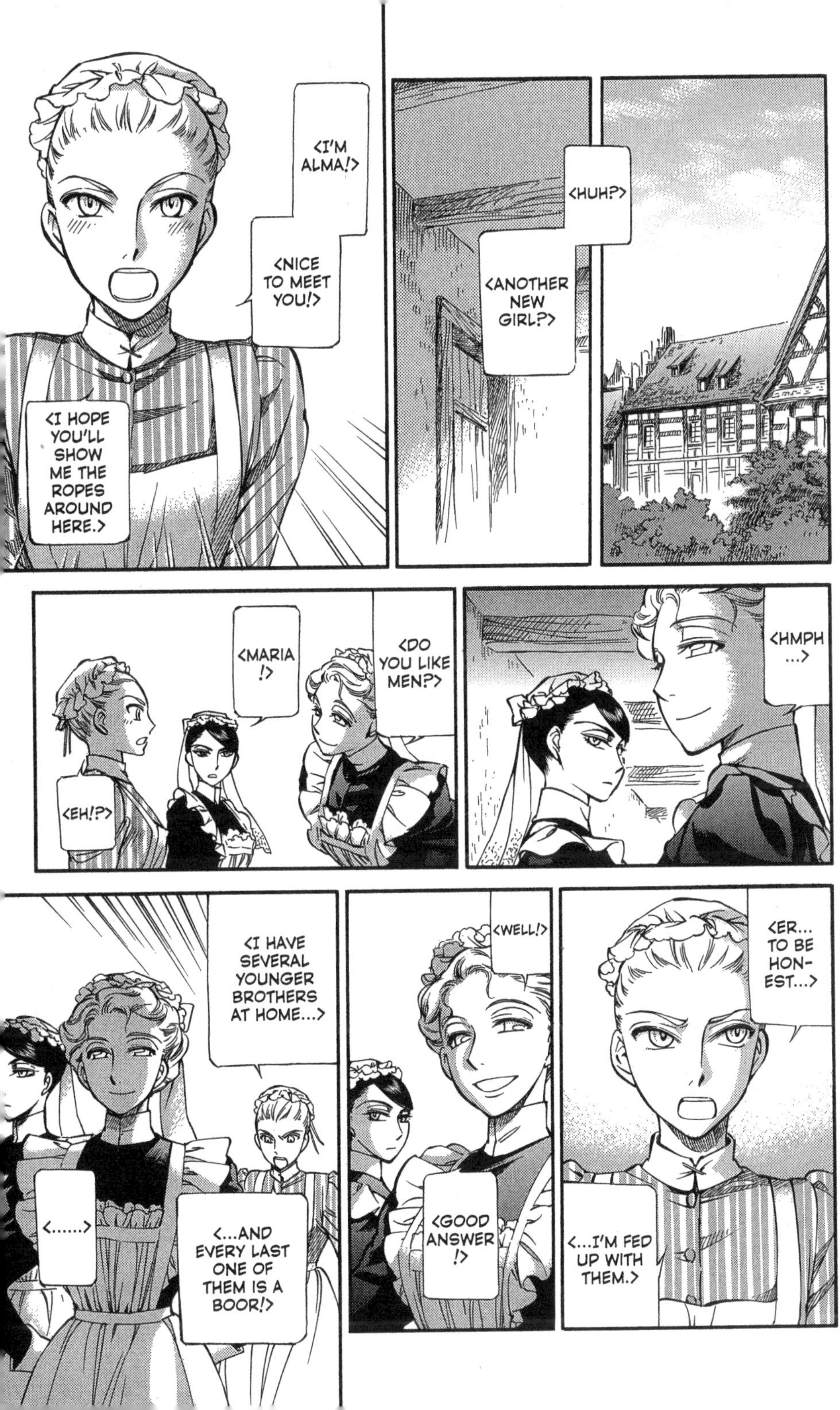
<HUH?>
<ANOTHER NEW GIRL?>
<I'M ALMA!>
<NICE TO MEET YOU!>
<I HOPE YOU'LL SHOW ME THE ROPES AROUND HERE.>
<HMPH ...>
<DO YOU LIKE MEN?>
<MARIA!>
<EH!?>
<ER... TO BE HON-EST...>
<...I'M FED UP WITH THEM.>
<WELL!>
<GOOD ANSWER!>
<I HAVE SEVERAL YOUNGER BROTHERS AT HOME...>
<......>
<...AND EVERY LAST ONE OF THEM IS A BOOR!>

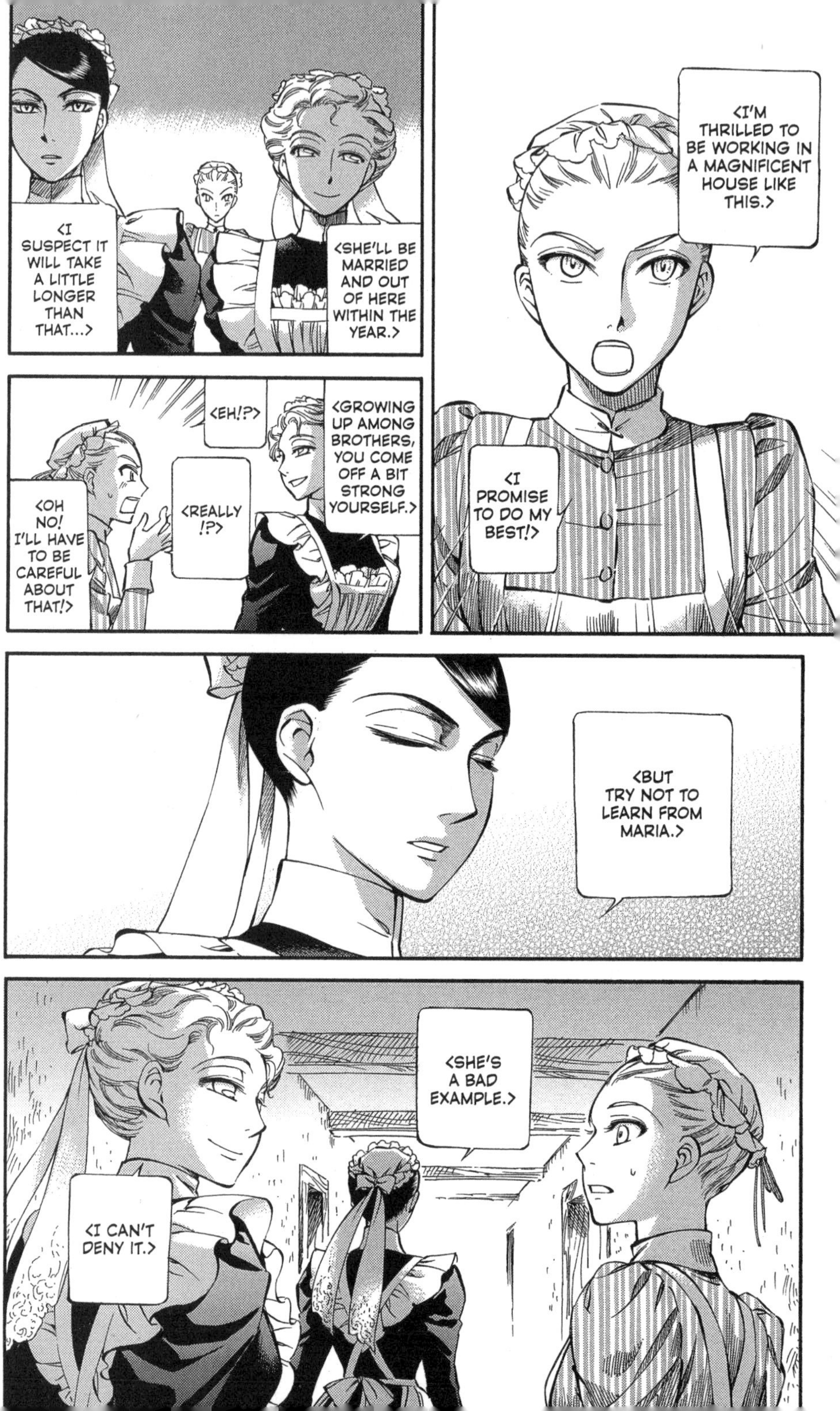

<I'M THRILLED TO BE WORKING IN A MAGNIFICENT HOUSE LIKE THIS.>
<I PROMISE TO DO MY BEST!>
<SHE'LL BE MARRIED AND OUT OF HERE WITHIN THE YEAR.>
<I SUSPECT IT WILL TAKE A LITTLE LONGER THAN THAT...>
<GROWING UP AMONG BROTHERS, YOU COME OFF A BIT STRONG YOURSELF.>
<EH!?>
<REALLY!?>
<OH NO! I'LL HAVE TO BE CAREFUL ABOUT THAT!>
<BUT TRY NOT TO LEARN FROM MARIA.>
<SHE'S A BAD EXAMPLE.>
<I CAN'T DENY IT.>

 Chapter 15:
Order

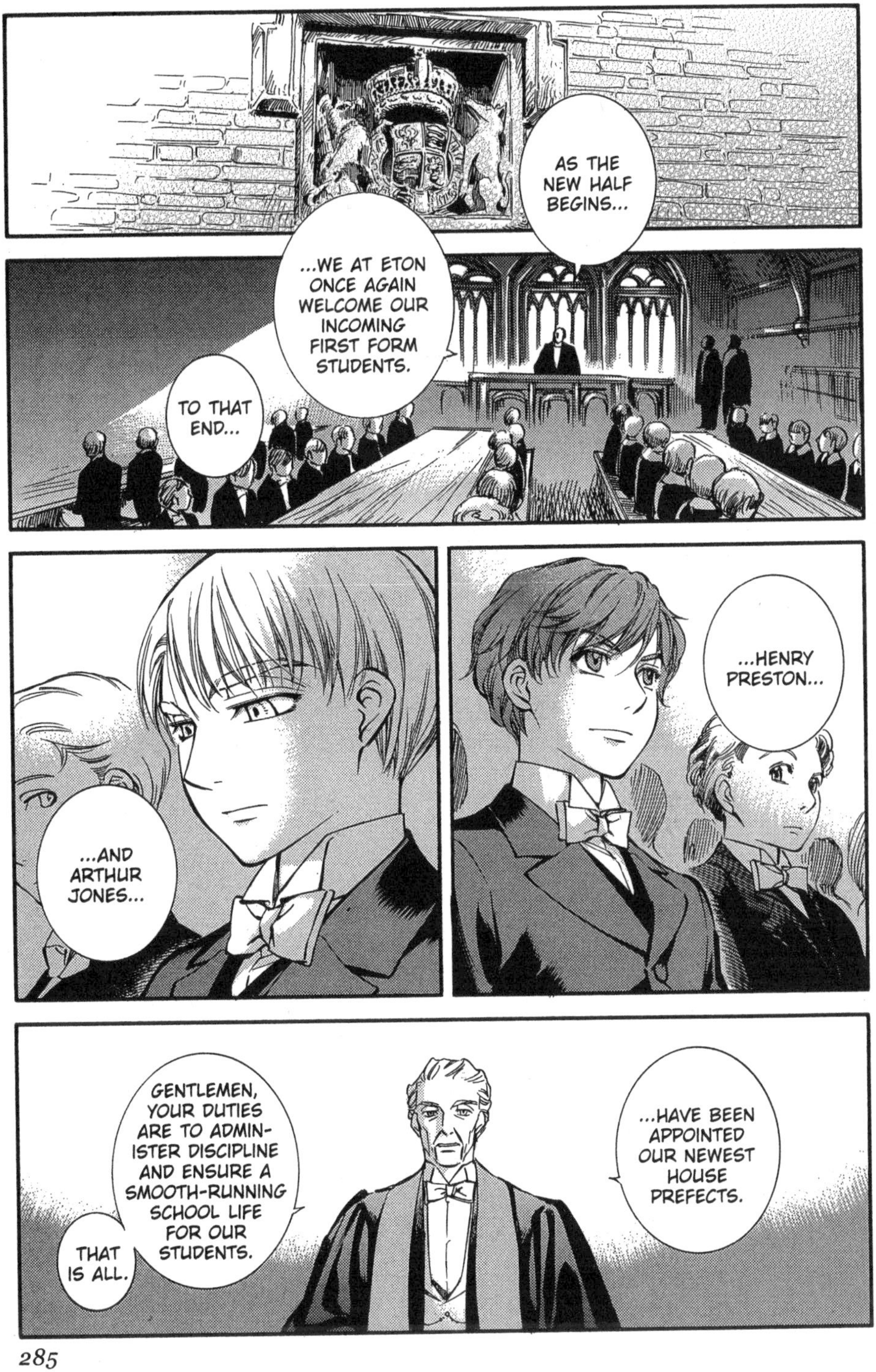
AS THE NEW HALF BEGINS...
...WE AT ETON ONCE AGAIN WELCOME OUR INCOMING FIRST FORM STUDENTS.
TO THAT END...
...HENRY PRESTON...
...AND ARTHUR JONES...
...HAVE BEEN APPOINTED OUR NEWEST HOUSE PREFECTS.
GENTLEMEN, YOUR DUTIES ARE TO ADMINISTER DISCIPLINE AND ENSURE A SMOOTH-RUNNING SCHOOL LIFE FOR OUR STUDENTS.
THAT IS ALL.

Chapter 15: *Order*

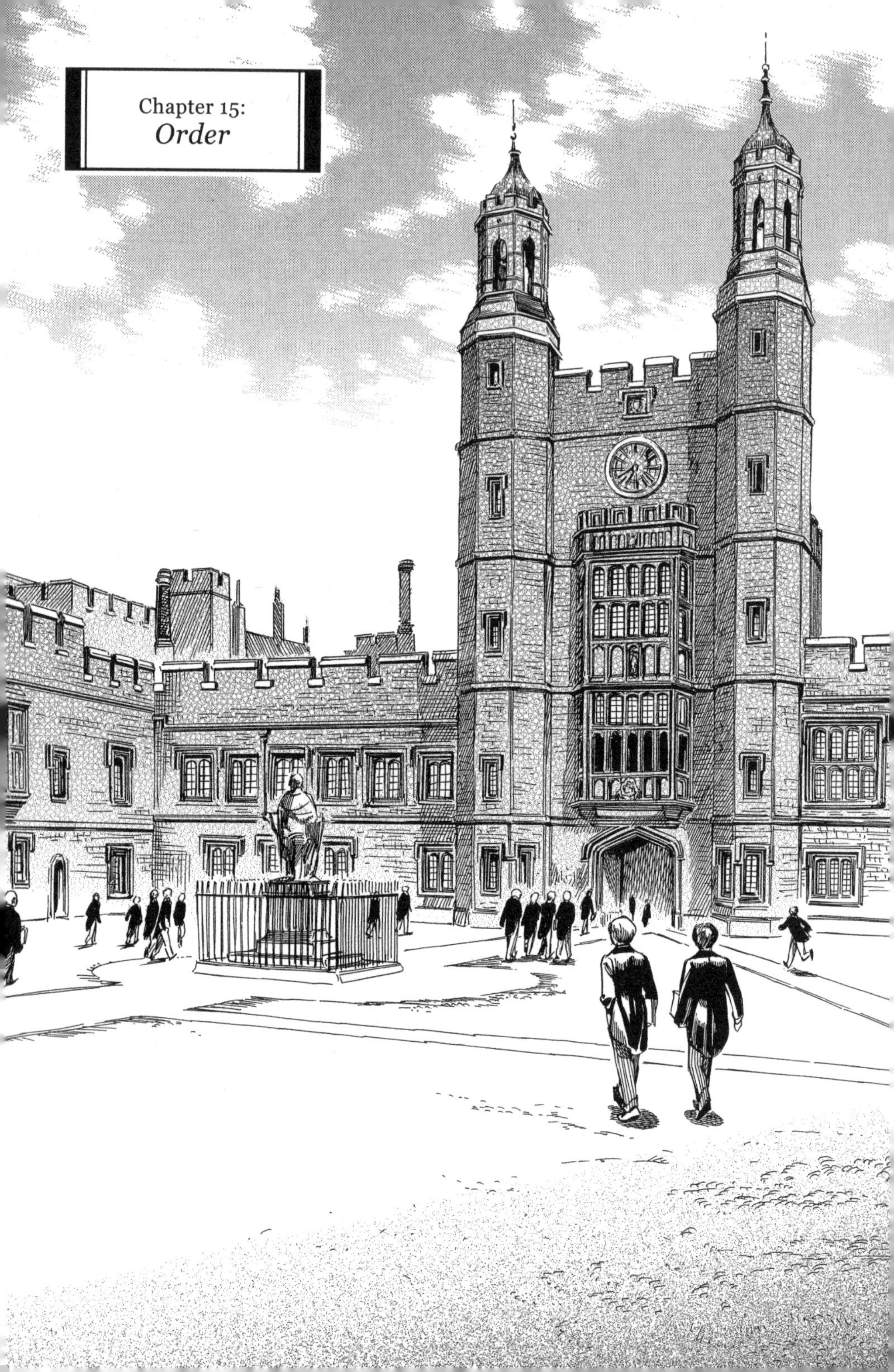

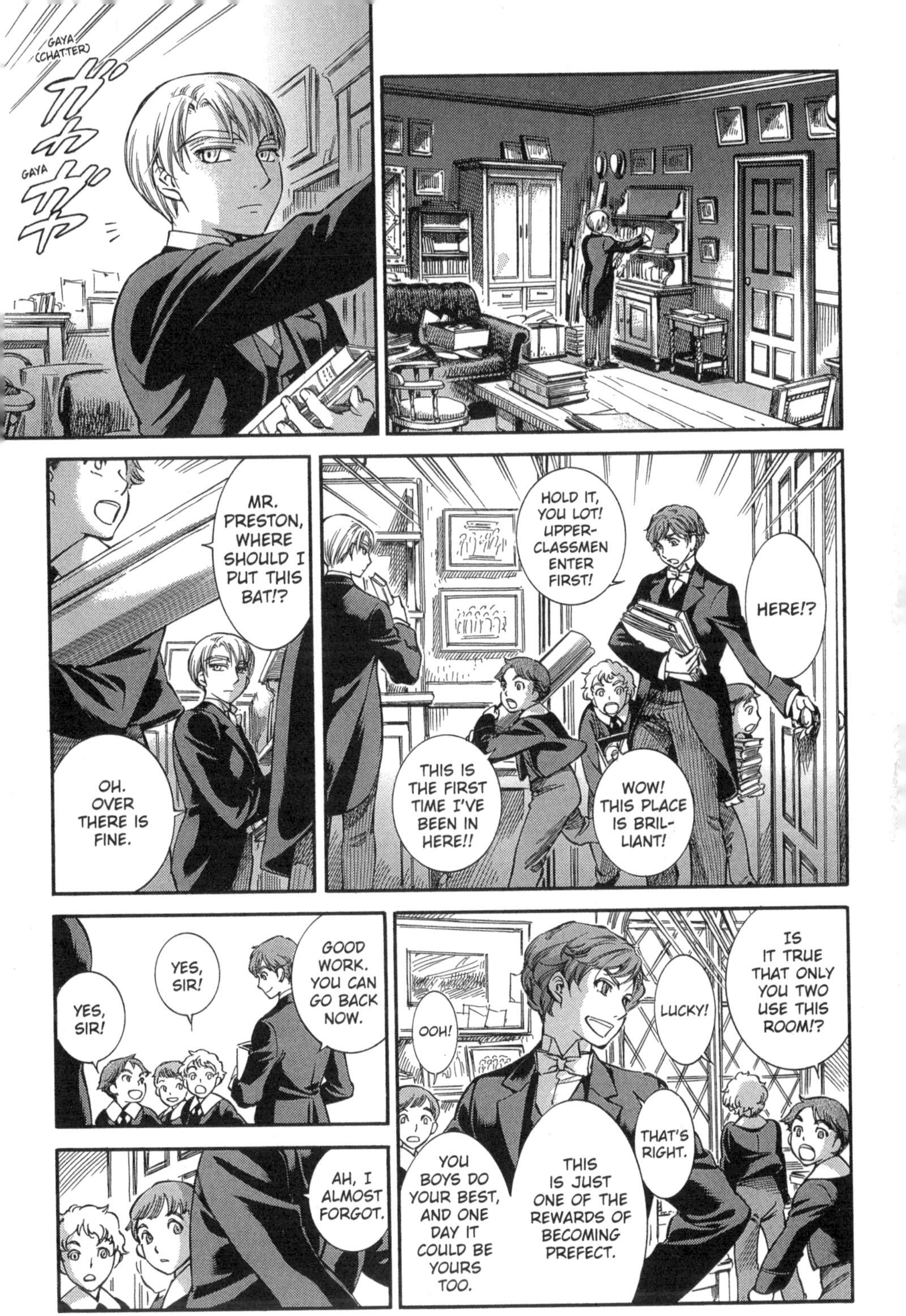
GAYA (CHATTER)
GAYA
HERE!?
HOLD IT, YOU LOT! UPPER-CLASSMEN ENTER FIRST!
WOW! THIS PLACE IS BRIL-LIANT!
THIS IS THE FIRST TIME I'VE BEEN IN HERE!!
MR. PRESTON, WHERE SHOULD I PUT THIS BAT!?
OH. OVER THERE IS FINE.
IS IT TRUE THAT ONLY YOU TWO USE THIS ROOM!?
LUCKY!
OOH!
THAT'S RIGHT.
THIS IS JUST ONE OF THE REWARDS OF BECOMING PREFECT.
YOU BOYS DO YOUR BEST, AND ONE DAY IT COULD BE YOURS TOO.
GOOD WORK. YOU CAN GO BACK NOW.
YES, SIR!
YES, SIR!
AH, I ALMOST FORGOT.

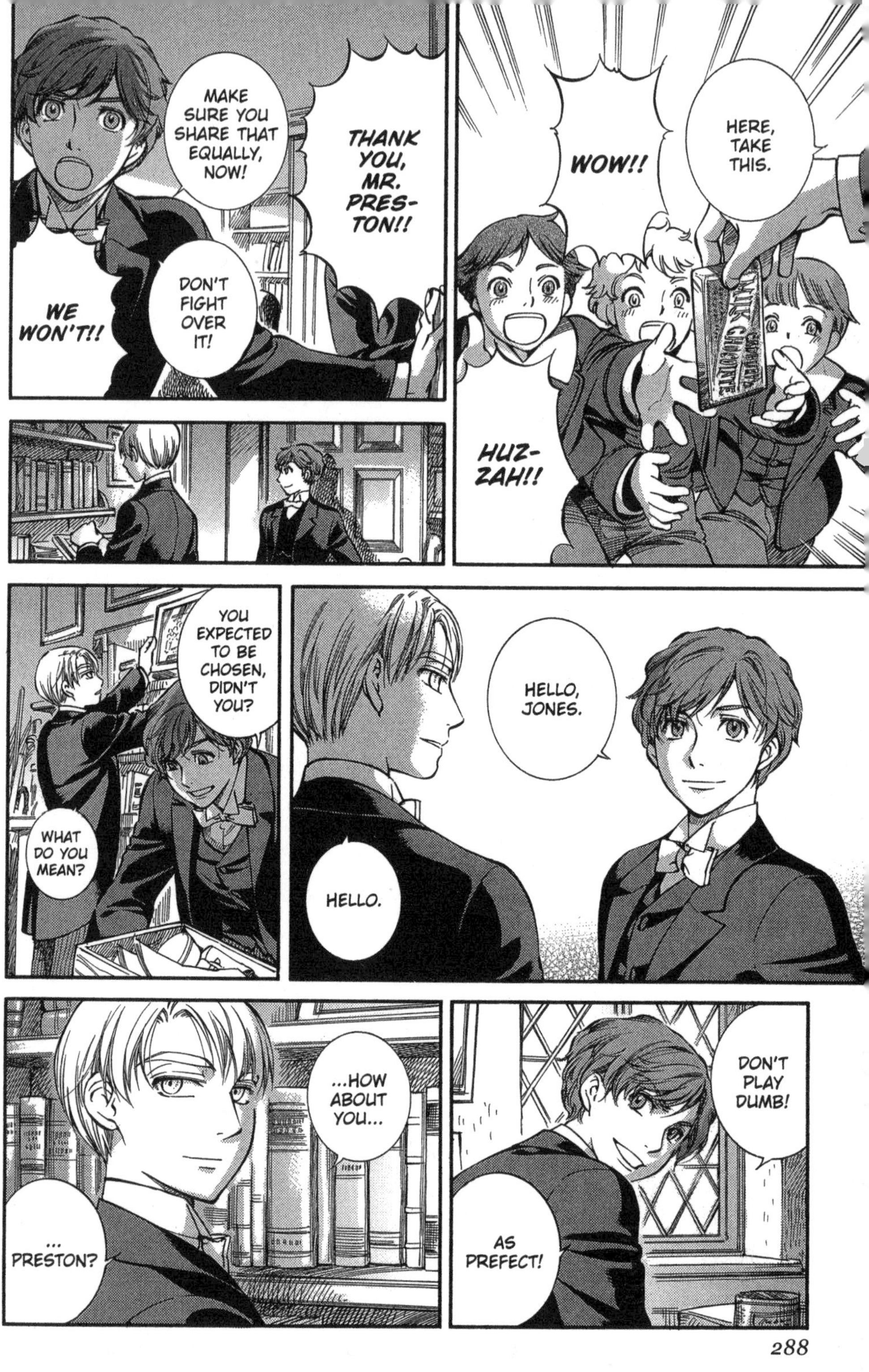
HERE, TAKE THIS.
WOW!!
HUZ-ZAH!!
THANK YOU, MR. PRES-TON!!
MAKE SURE YOU SHARE THAT EQUALLY, NOW!
DON'T FIGHT OVER IT!
WE WON'T!!
HELLO, JONES.
HELLO.
YOU EXPECTED TO BE CHOSEN, DIDN'T YOU?
WHAT DO YOU MEAN?
DON'T PLAY DUMB!
AS PREFECT!
...HOW ABOUT YOU...
...PRESTON?

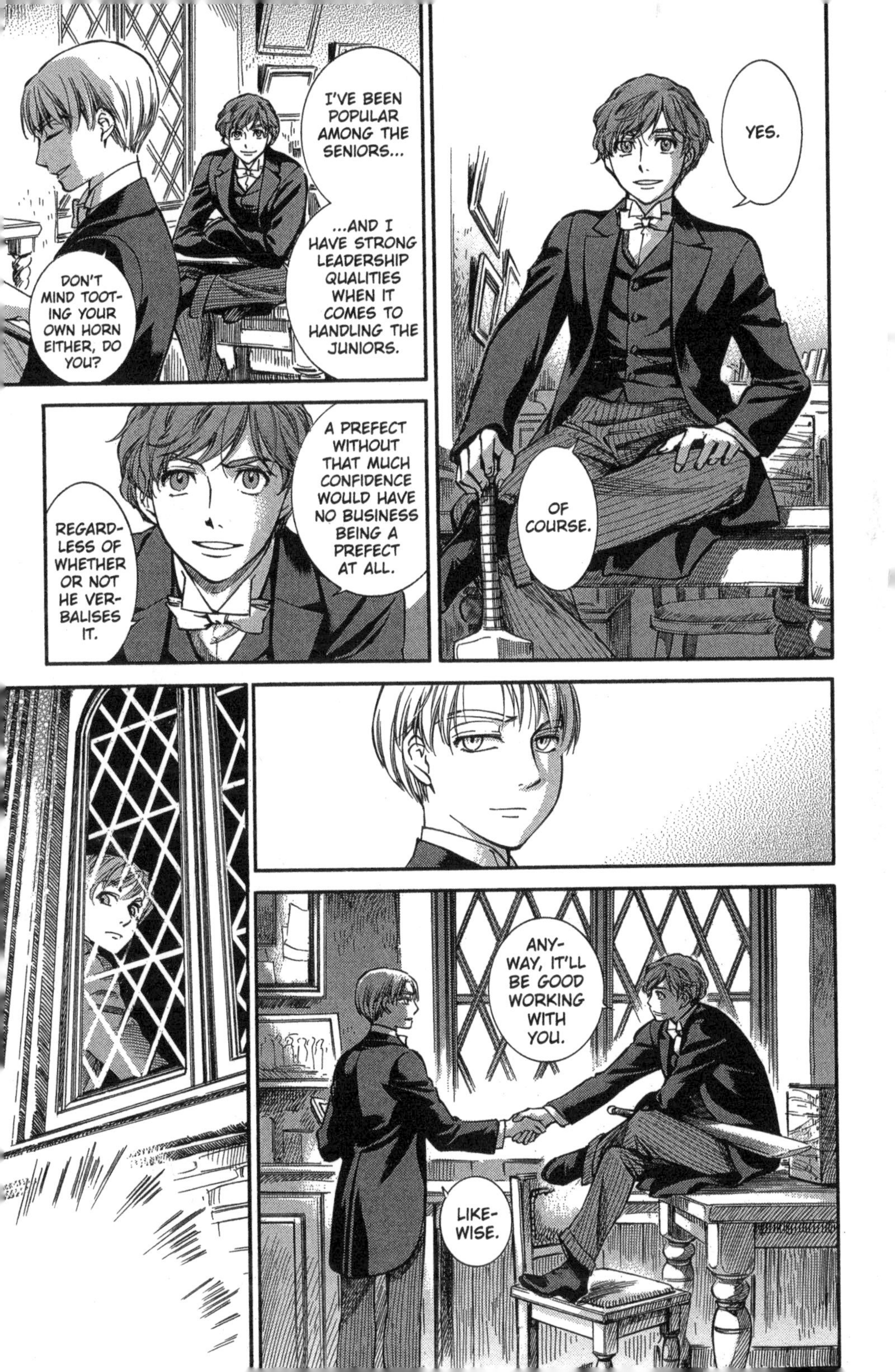
YES.
OF COURSE.
I'VE BEEN POPULAR AMONG THE SENIORS...
...AND I HAVE STRONG LEADERSHIP QUALITIES WHEN IT COMES TO HANDLING THE JUNIORS.
DON'T MIND TOOTING YOUR OWN HORN EITHER, DO YOU?
A PREFECT WITHOUT THAT MUCH CONFIDENCE WOULD HAVE NO BUSINESS BEING A PREFECT AT ALL.
REGARDLESS OF WHETHER OR NOT HE VERBALISES IT.
ANYWAY, IT'LL BE GOOD WORKING WITH YOU.
LIKEWISE.

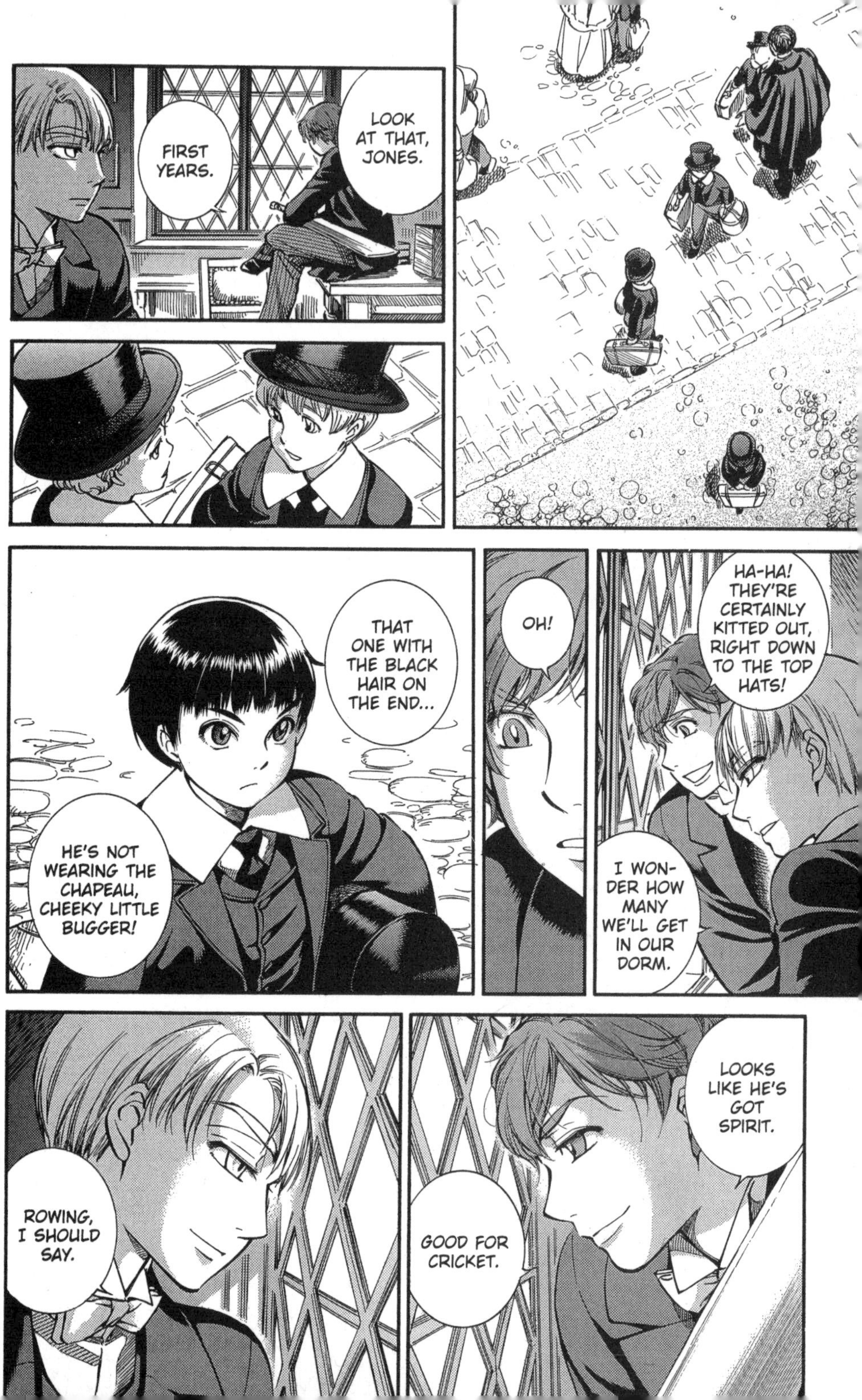
LOOK AT THAT, JONES.
FIRST YEARS.
HA-HA! THEY'RE CERTAINLY KITTED OUT, RIGHT DOWN TO THE TOP HATS!
I WONDER HOW MANY WE'LL GET IN OUR DORM.
OH!
THAT ONE WITH THE BLACK HAIR ON THE END...
HE'S NOT WEARING THE CHAPEAU, CHEEKY LITTLE BUGGER!
LOOKS LIKE HE'S GOT SPIRIT.
GOOD FOR CRICKET.
ROWING, I SHOULD SAY.

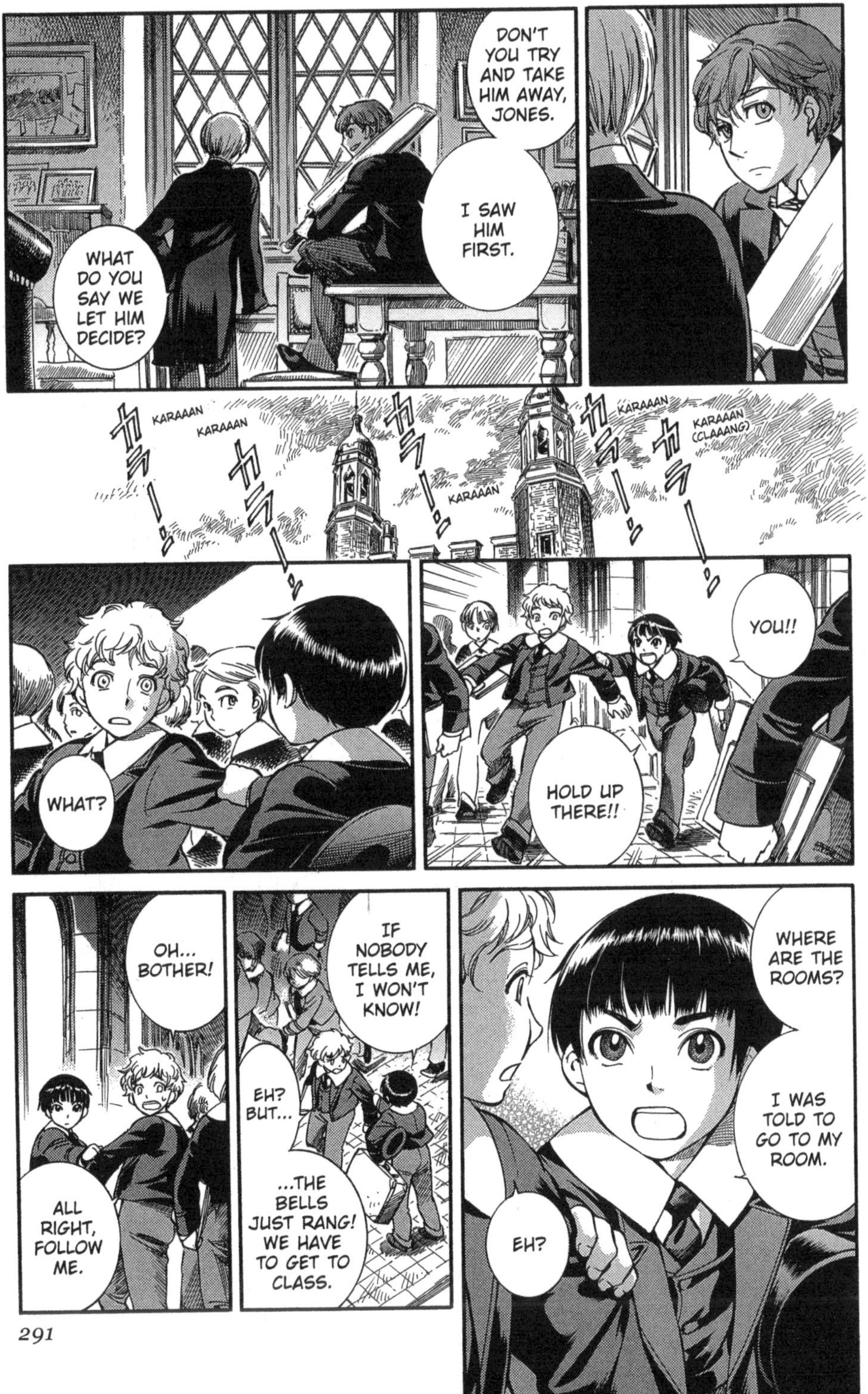
DON'T YOU TRY AND TAKE HIM AWAY, JONES.
I SAW HIM FIRST.
WHAT DO YOU SAY WE LET HIM DECIDE?
KARAAAN (CLAAANG)
KARAAAN
KARAAAN
KARAAAN
KARAAAN
YOU!!
HOLD UP THERE!!
WHAT?
WHERE ARE THE ROOMS?
I WAS TOLD TO GO TO MY ROOM.
EH?
IF NOBODY TELLS ME, I WON'T KNOW!
EH? BUT...
...THE BELLS JUST RANG! WE HAVE TO GET TO CLASS.
OH... BOTHER!
ALL RIGHT, FOLLOW ME.

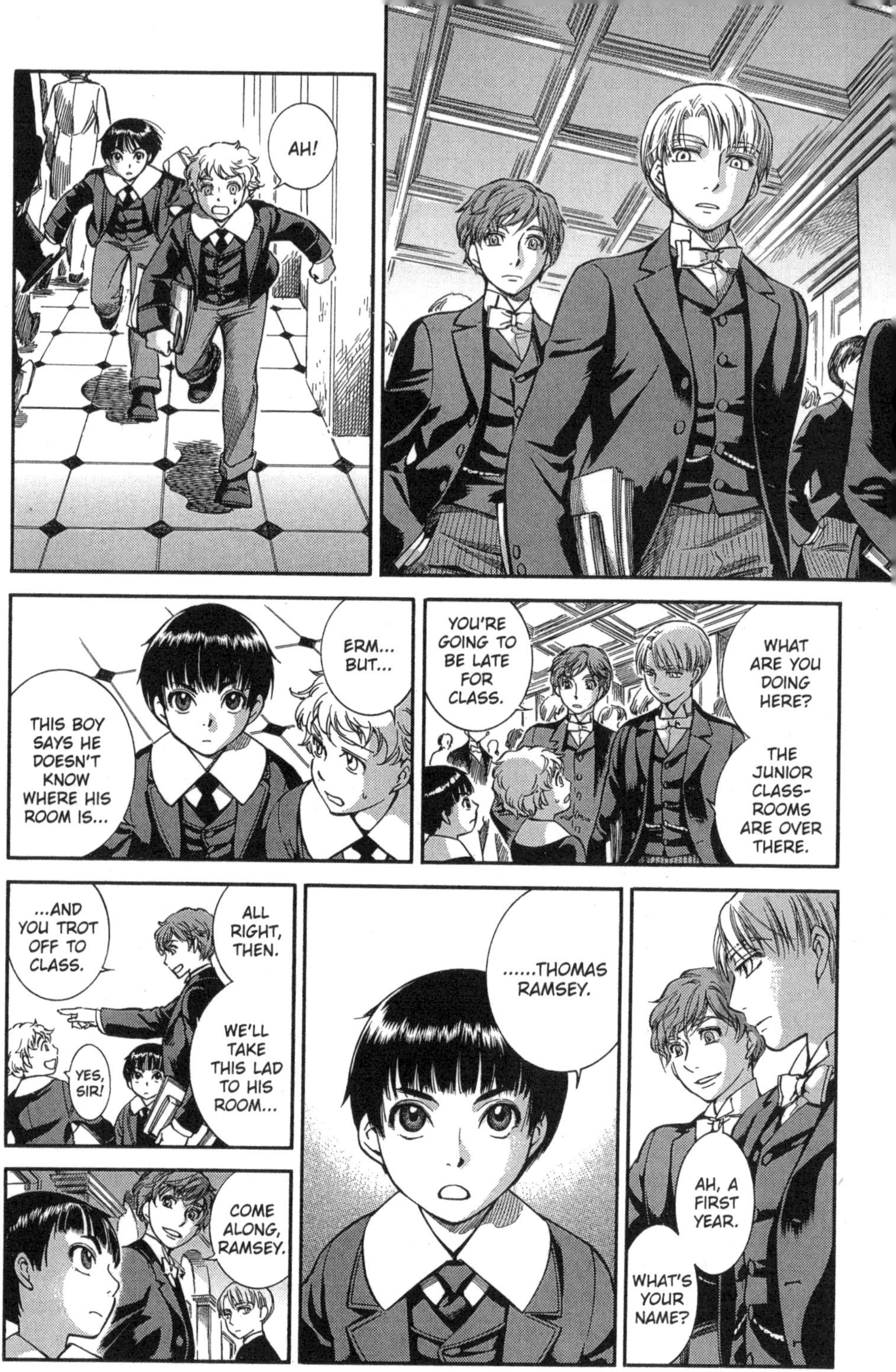
AH!
WHAT ARE YOU DOING HERE?
THE JUNIOR CLASS-ROOMS ARE OVER THERE.
YOU'RE GOING TO BE LATE FOR CLASS.
ERM... BUT...
THIS BOY SAYS HE DOESN'T KNOW WHERE HIS ROOM IS...
AH, A FIRST YEAR.
WHAT'S YOUR NAME?
......THOMAS RAMSEY.
ALL RIGHT, THEN.
...AND YOU TROT OFF TO CLASS.
WE'LL TAKE THIS LAD TO HIS ROOM...
YES, SIR!
COME ALONG, RAMSEY.

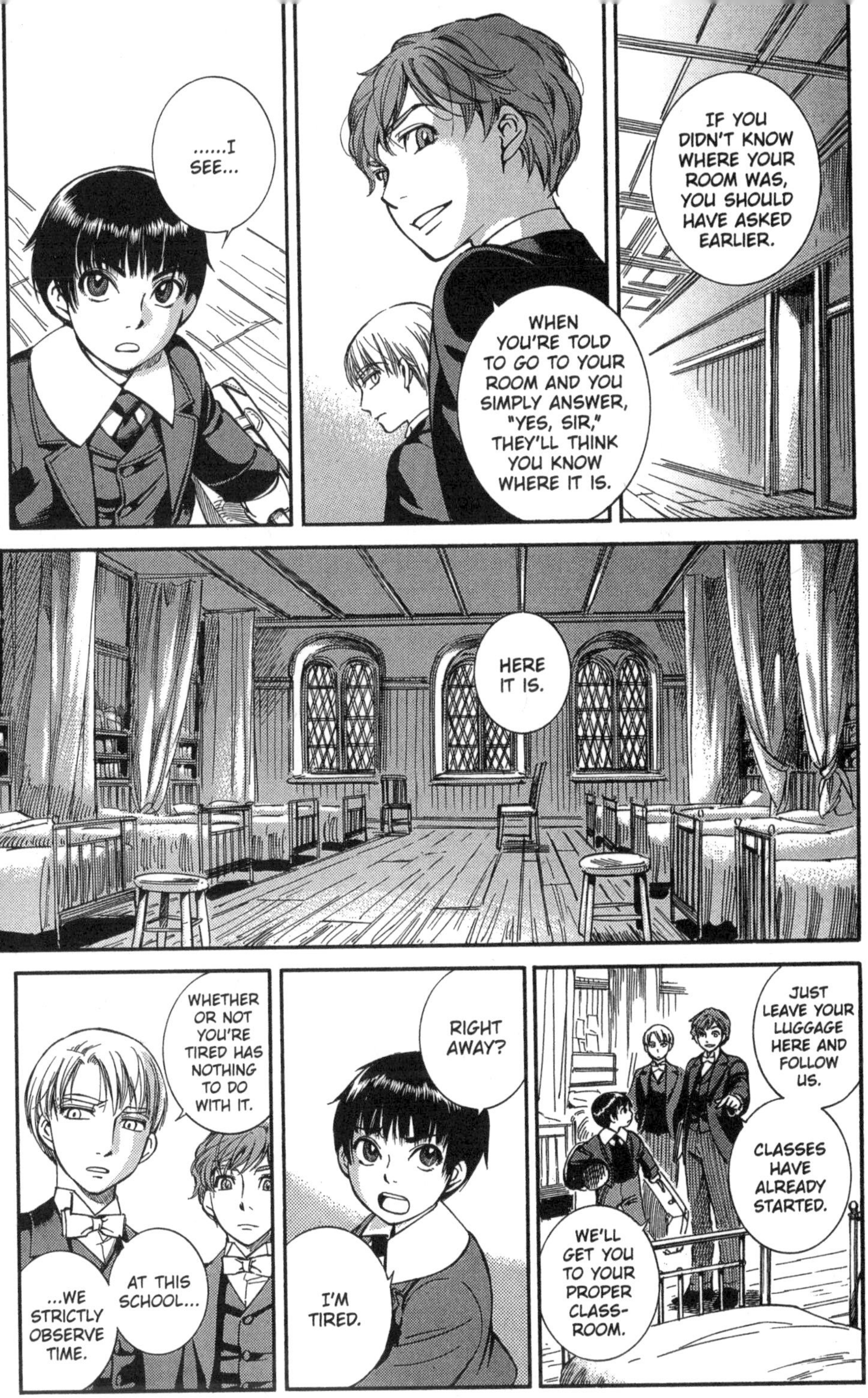
IF YOU DIDN'T KNOW WHERE YOUR ROOM WAS, YOU SHOULD HAVE ASKED EARLIER.
WHEN YOU'RE TOLD TO GO TO YOUR ROOM AND YOU SIMPLY ANSWER, "YES, SIR," THEY'LL THINK YOU KNOW WHERE IT IS.
......I SEE...
HERE IT IS.
JUST LEAVE YOUR LUGGAGE HERE AND FOLLOW US.
CLASSES HAVE ALREADY STARTED.
WE'LL GET YOU TO YOUR PROPER CLASS-ROOM.
RIGHT AWAY?
I'M TIRED.
WHETHER OR NOT YOU'RE TIRED HAS NOTHING TO DO WITH IT.
AT THIS SCHOOL...
...WE STRICTLY OBSERVE TIME.

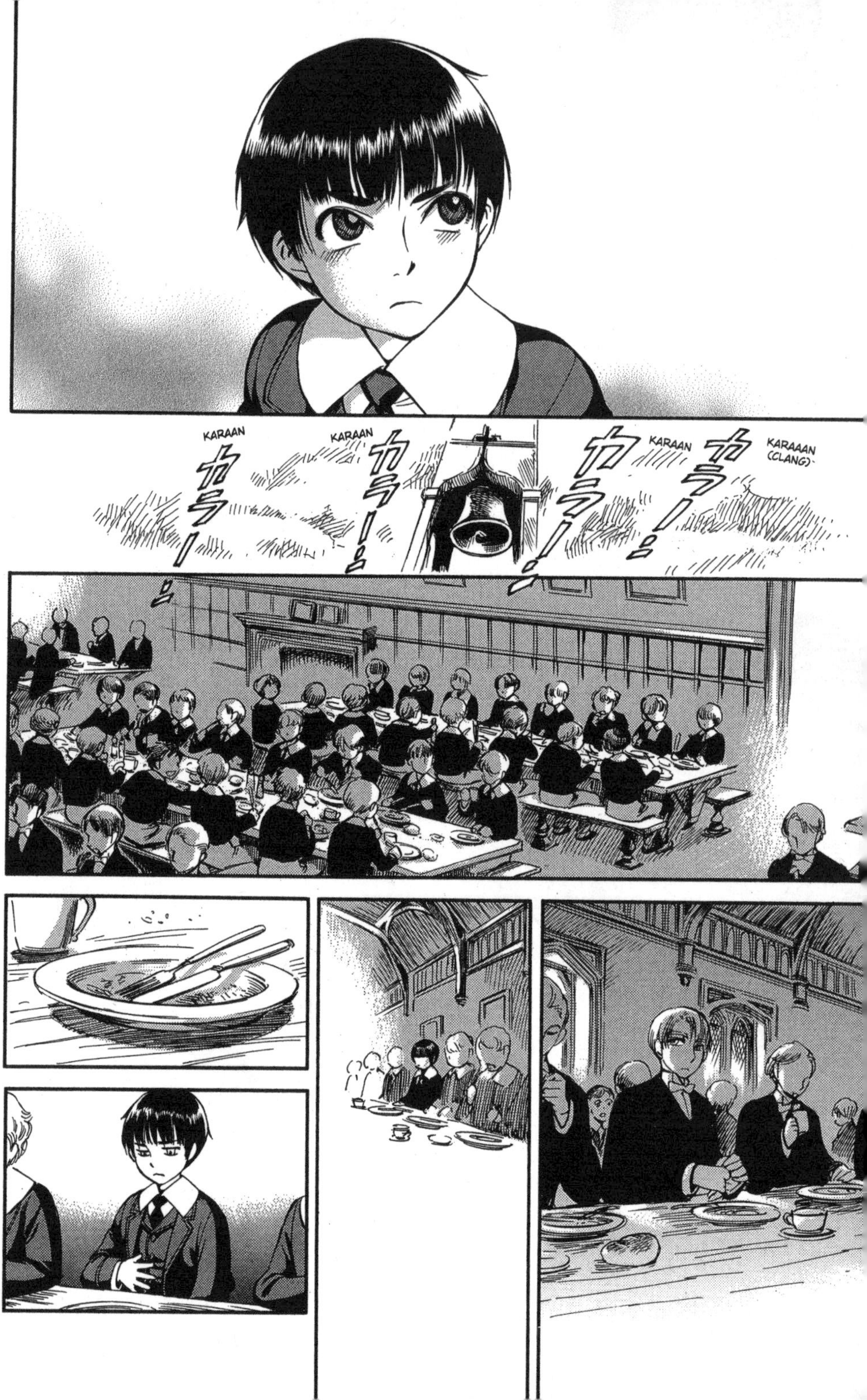
KARAAAN (CLANG)
カラーン!!
KARAAN
カラーン!!
KARAAN
カラーン!!
KARAAN
カラーン!!

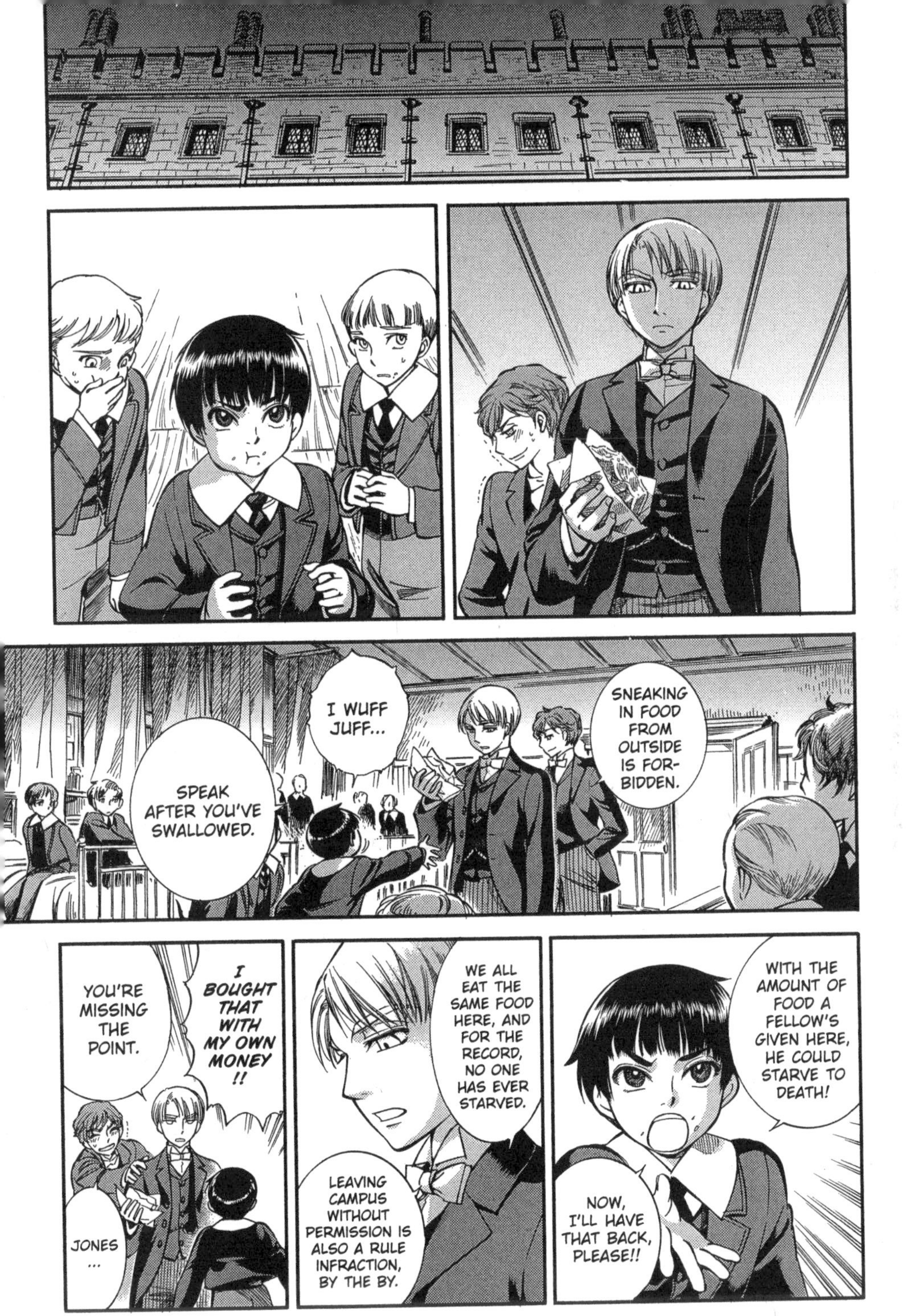
SNEAKING IN FOOD FROM OUTSIDE IS FOR-BIDDEN.
I WUFF JUFF...
SPEAK AFTER YOU'VE SWALLOWED.
WITH THE AMOUNT OF FOOD A FELLOW'S GIVEN HERE, HE COULD STARVE TO DEATH!
NOW, I'LL HAVE THAT BACK, PLEASE!!
WE ALL EAT THE SAME FOOD HERE, AND FOR THE RECORD, NO ONE HAS EVER STARVED.
LEAVING CAMPUS WITHOUT PERMISSION IS ALSO A RULE INFRACTION, BY THE BY.
I BOUGHT THAT WITH MY OWN MONEY!!
YOU'RE MISSING THE POINT.
JONES ...

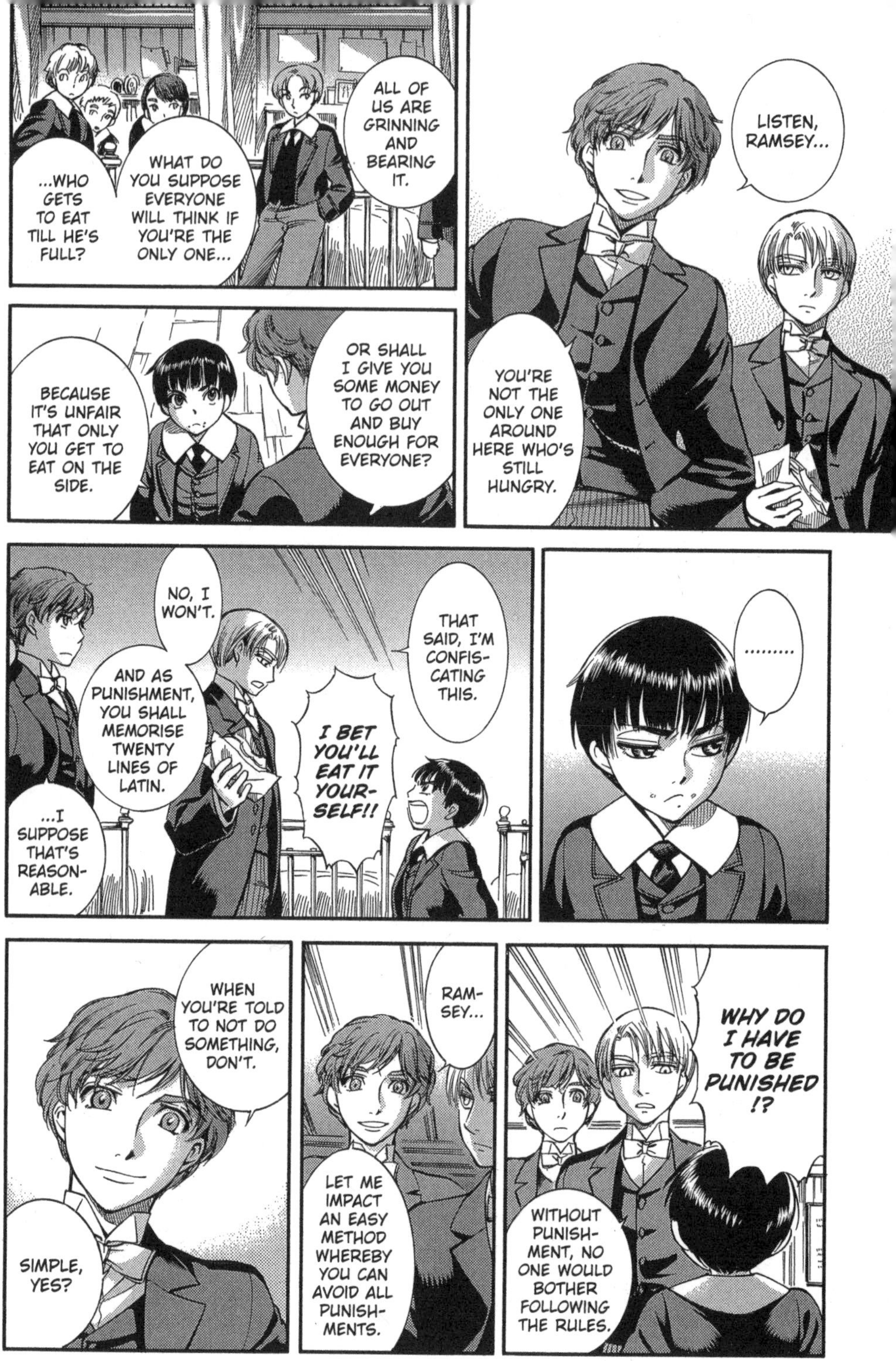
LISTEN, RAMSEY...
YOU'RE NOT THE ONLY ONE AROUND HERE WHO'S STILL HUNGRY.
ALL OF US ARE GRINNING AND BEARING IT.
WHAT DO YOU SUPPOSE EVERYONE WILL THINK IF YOU'RE THE ONLY ONE...
...WHO GETS TO EAT TILL HE'S FULL?
OR SHALL I GIVE YOU SOME MONEY TO GO OUT AND BUY ENOUGH FOR EVERYONE?
BECAUSE IT'S UNFAIR THAT ONLY YOU GET TO EAT ON THE SIDE.
....
NO, I WON'T.
THAT SAID, I'M CONFISCATING THIS.
I BET YOU'LL EAT IT YOURSELF!!
AND AS PUNISHMENT, YOU SHALL MEMORISE TWENTY LINES OF LATIN.
...I SUPPOSE THAT'S REASONABLE.
WHY DO I HAVE TO BE PUNISHED!?
WITHOUT PUNISHMENT, NO ONE WOULD BOTHER FOLLOWING THE RULES.
RAMSEY...
LET ME IMPACT AN EASY METHOD WHEREBY YOU CAN AVOID ALL PUNISHMENTS.
WHEN YOU'RE TOLD TO NOT DO SOMETHING, DON'T.
SIMPLE, YES?

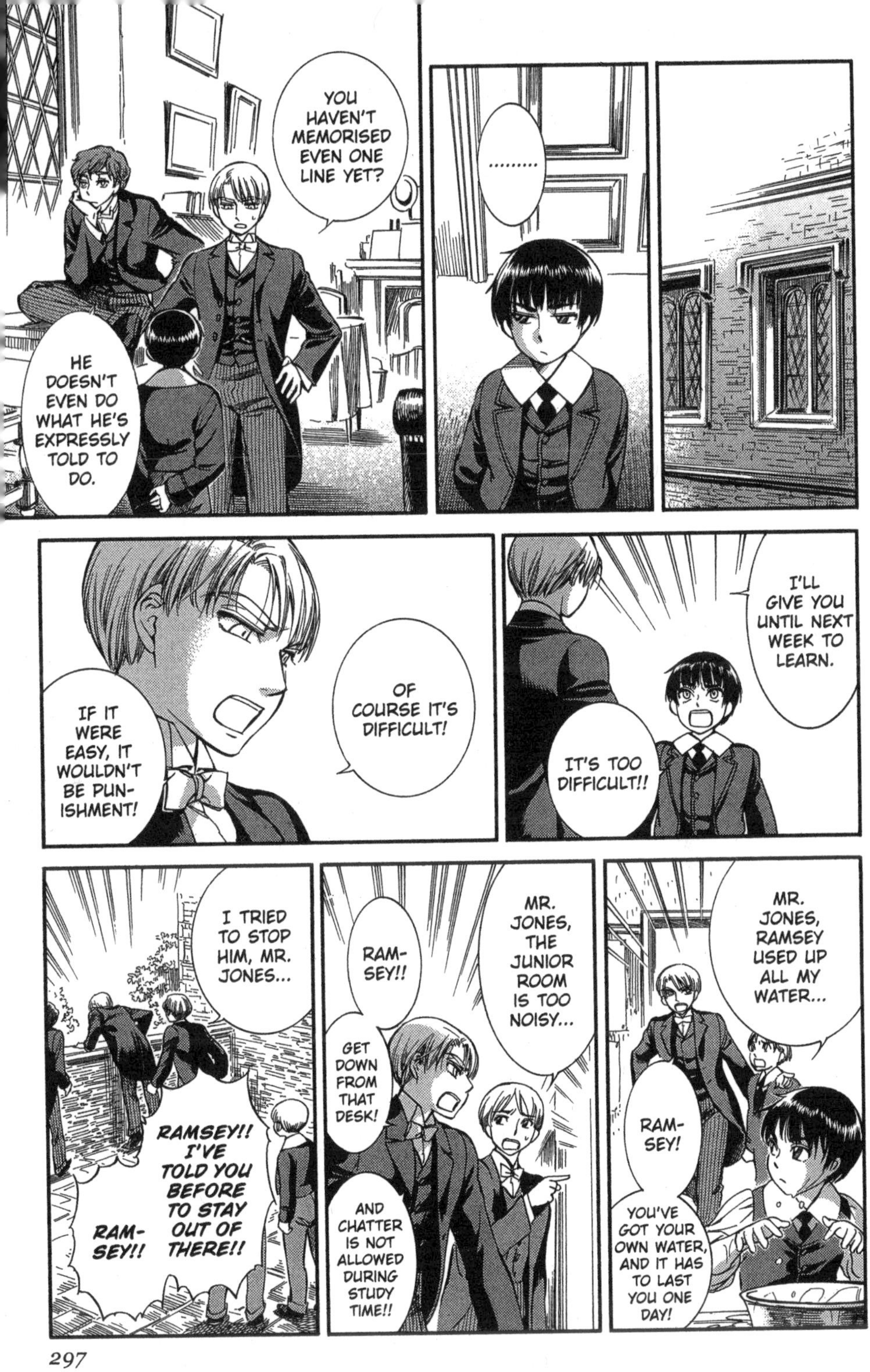
....
YOU HAVEN'T MEMORISED EVEN ONE LINE YET?
HE DOESN'T EVEN DO WHAT HE'S EXPRESSLY TOLD TO DO.
I'LL GIVE YOU UNTIL NEXT WEEK TO LEARN.
IT'S TOO DIFFICULT!!
OF COURSE IT'S DIFFICULT!
IF IT WERE EASY, IT WOULDN'T BE PUNISHMENT!
MR. JONES, RAMSEY USED UP ALL MY WATER...
RAMSEY!
YOU'VE GOT YOUR OWN WATER, AND IT HAS TO LAST YOU ONE DAY!
MR. JONES, THE JUNIOR ROOM IS TOO NOISY...
RAMSEY!!
GET DOWN FROM THAT DESK!
AND CHATTER IS NOT ALLOWED DURING STUDY TIME!!
I TRIED TO STOP HIM, MR. JONES...
RAMSEY!! I'VE TOLD YOU BEFORE TO STAY OUT OF THERE!!
RAMSEY!!

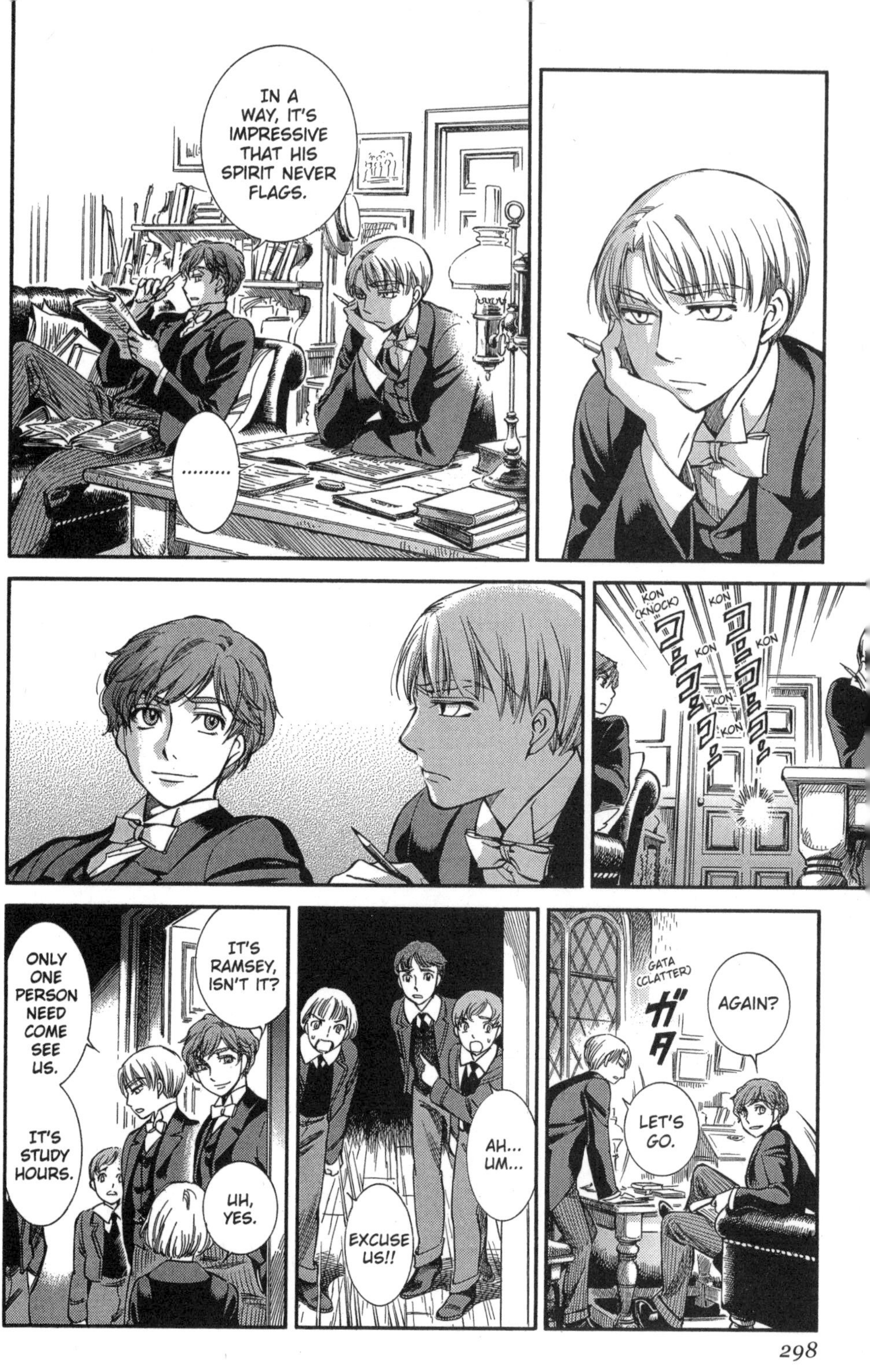

IN A WAY, IT'S IMPRESSIVE THAT HIS SPIRIT NEVER FLAGS.
....
KON (KNOCK)
KON
KON
KON
KON
KON
GATA (CLATTER)
ガタ
AGAIN?
LET'S GO.
AH... UM...
EXCUSE US!!
IT'S RAMSEY, ISN'T IT?
ONLY ONE PERSON NEED COME SEE US.
IT'S STUDY HOURS.
UH, YES.

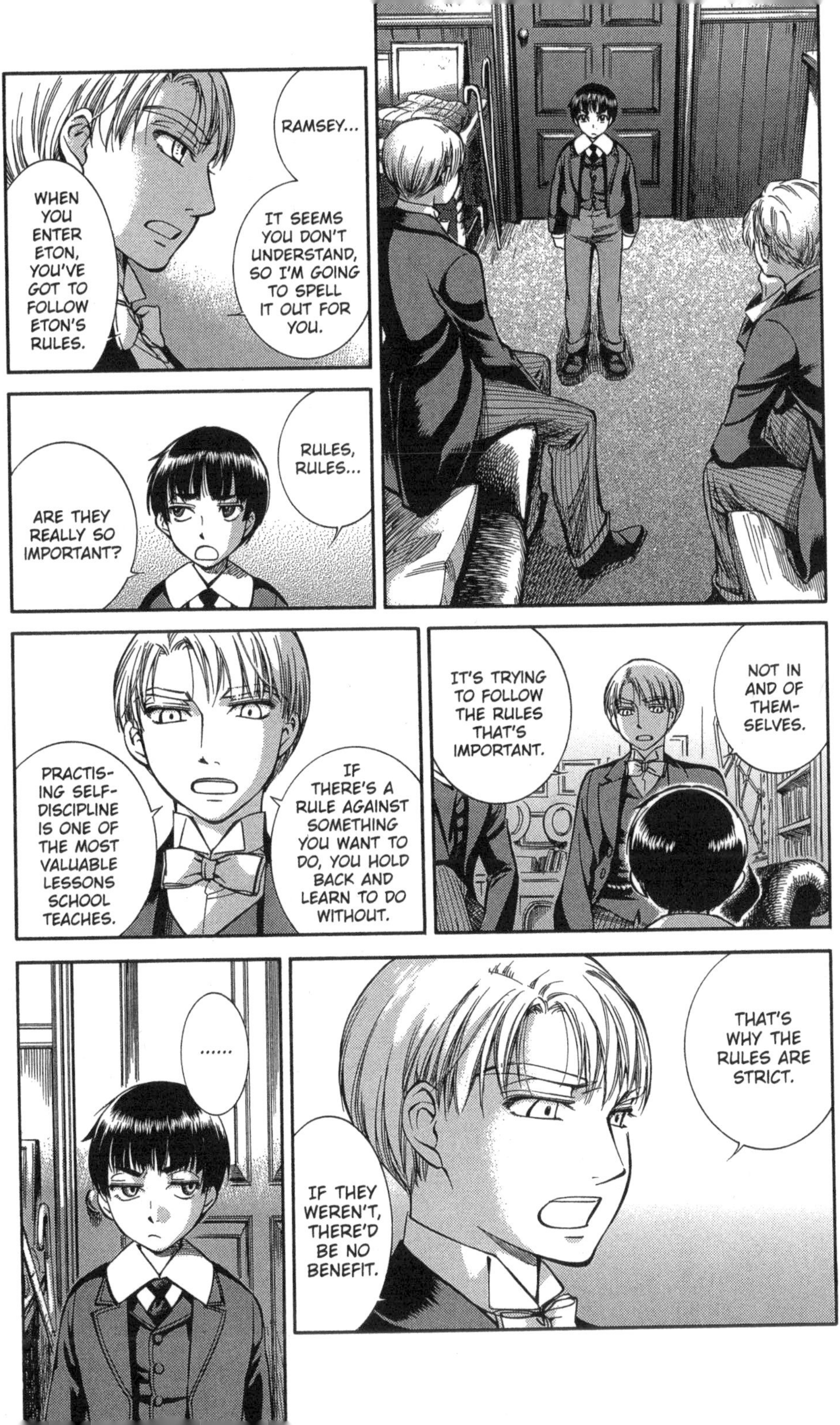
RAMSEY...
IT SEEMS YOU DON'T UNDERSTAND, SO I'M GOING TO SPELL IT OUT FOR YOU.
WHEN YOU ENTER ETON, YOU'VE GOT TO FOLLOW ETON'S RULES.
RULES, RULES...
ARE THEY REALLY SO IMPORTANT?
NOT IN AND OF THEM-SELVES.
IT'S TRYING TO FOLLOW THE RULES THAT'S IMPORTANT.
IF THERE'S A RULE AGAINST SOMETHING YOU WANT TO DO, YOU HOLD BACK AND LEARN TO DO WITHOUT.
PRACTIS-ING SELF-DISCIPLINE IS ONE OF THE MOST VALUABLE LESSONS SCHOOL TEACHES.
THAT'S WHY THE RULES ARE STRICT.
IF THEY WEREN'T, THERE'D BE NO BENEFIT.
......

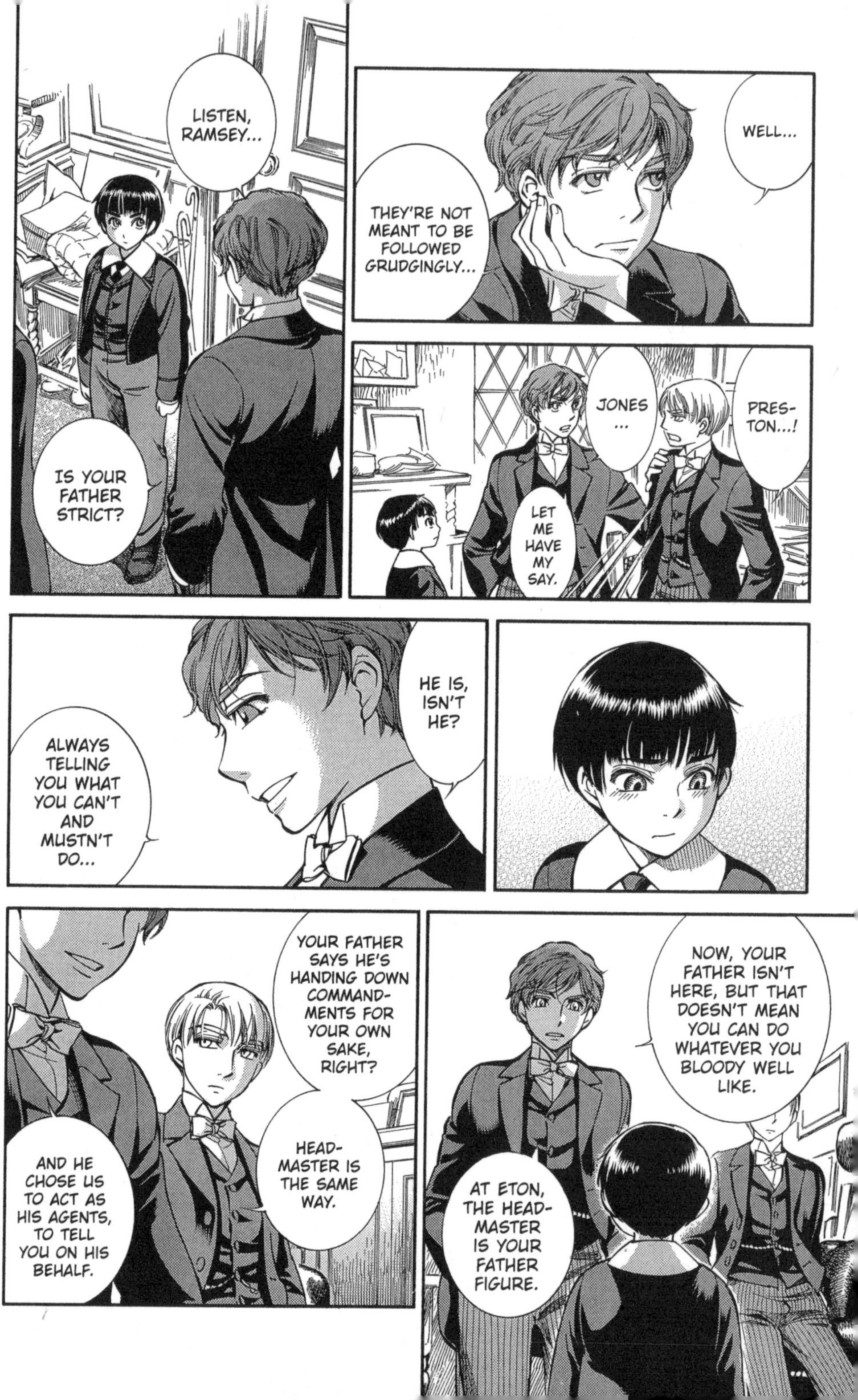
WELL...
THEY'RE NOT MEANT TO BE FOLLOWED GRUDGINGLY...
PRES-TON...!
JONES...
LET ME HAVE MY SAY.
LISTEN, RAMSEY...
IS YOUR FATHER STRICT?
HE IS, ISN'T HE?
ALWAYS TELLING YOU WHAT YOU CAN'T AND MUSTN'T DO...
NOW, YOUR FATHER ISN'T HERE, BUT THAT DOESN'T MEAN YOU CAN DO WHATEVER YOU BLOODY WELL LIKE.
AT ETON, THE HEAD-MASTER IS YOUR FATHER FIGURE.
YOUR FATHER SAYS HE'S HANDING DOWN COMMAND-MENTS FOR YOUR OWN SAKE, RIGHT?
HEAD-MASTER IS THE SAME WAY.
AND HE CHOSE US TO ACT AS HIS AGENTS, TO TELL YOU ON HIS BEHALF.

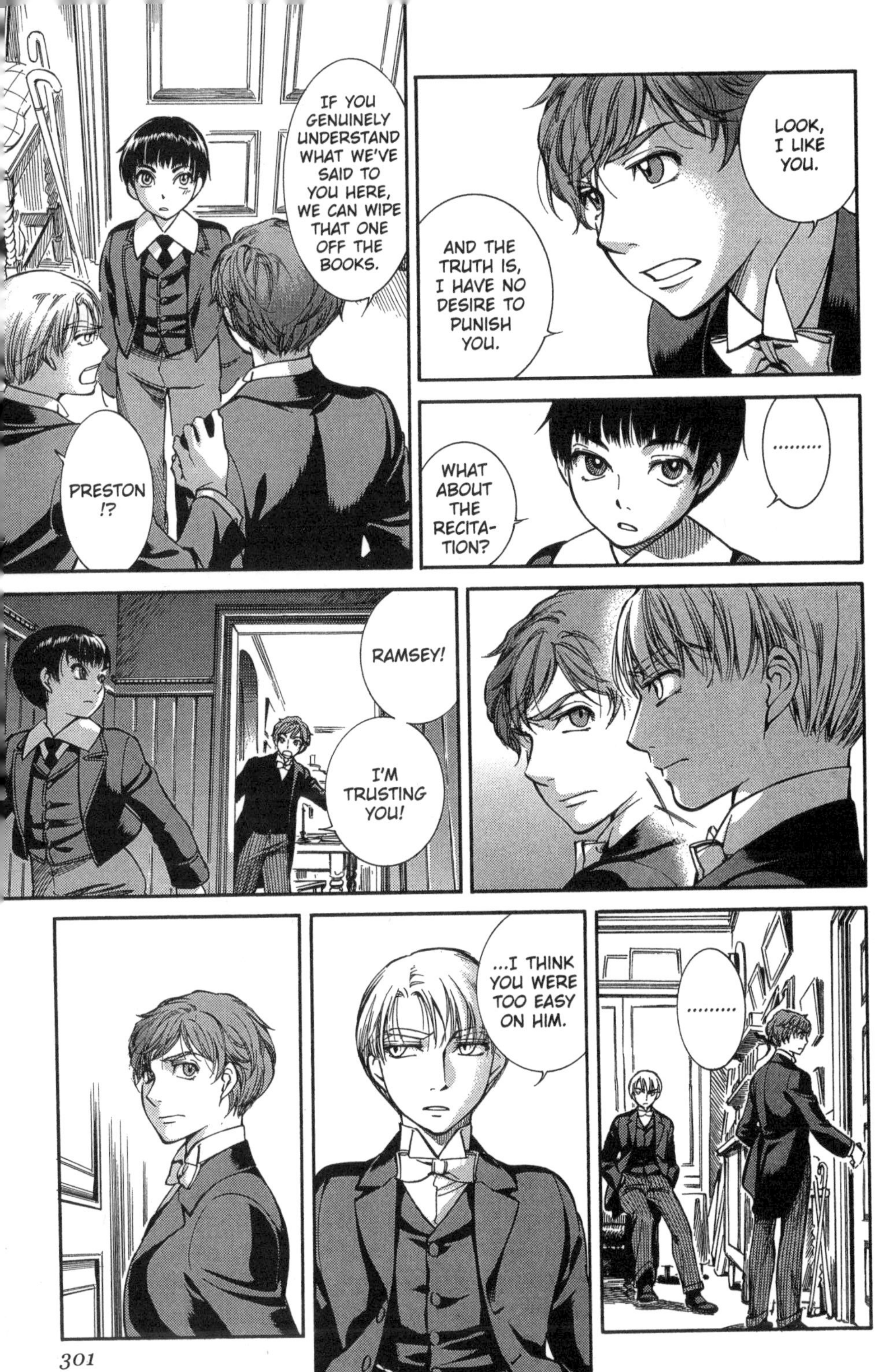
LOOK, I LIKE YOU.
AND THE TRUTH IS, I HAVE NO DESIRE TO PUNISH YOU.
....
WHAT ABOUT THE RECITATION?
IF YOU GENUINELY UNDERSTAND WHAT WE'VE SAID TO YOU HERE, WE CAN WIPE THAT ONE OFF THE BOOKS.
PRESTON!?
RAMSEY!
I'M TRUSTING YOU!
....
...I THINK YOU WERE TOO EASY ON HIM.

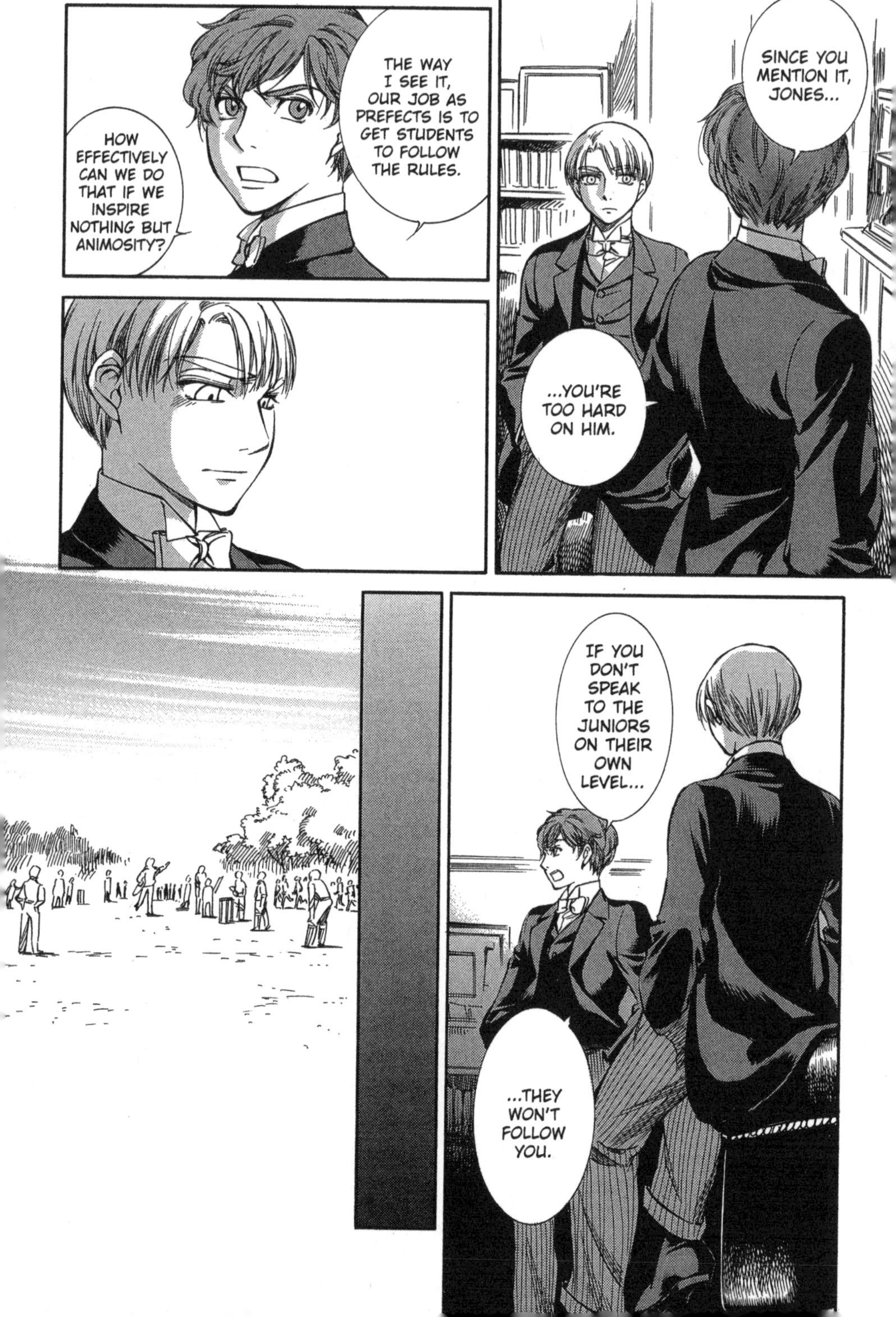
SINCE YOU MENTION IT, JONES...
...YOU'RE TOO HARD ON HIM.
THE WAY I SEE IT, OUR JOB AS PREFECTS IS TO GET STUDENTS TO FOLLOW THE RULES.
HOW EFFECTIVELY CAN WE DO THAT IF WE INSPIRE NOTHING BUT ANIMOSITY?
IF YOU DON'T SPEAK TO THE JUNIORS ON THEIR OWN LEVEL...
...THEY WON'T FOLLOW YOU.

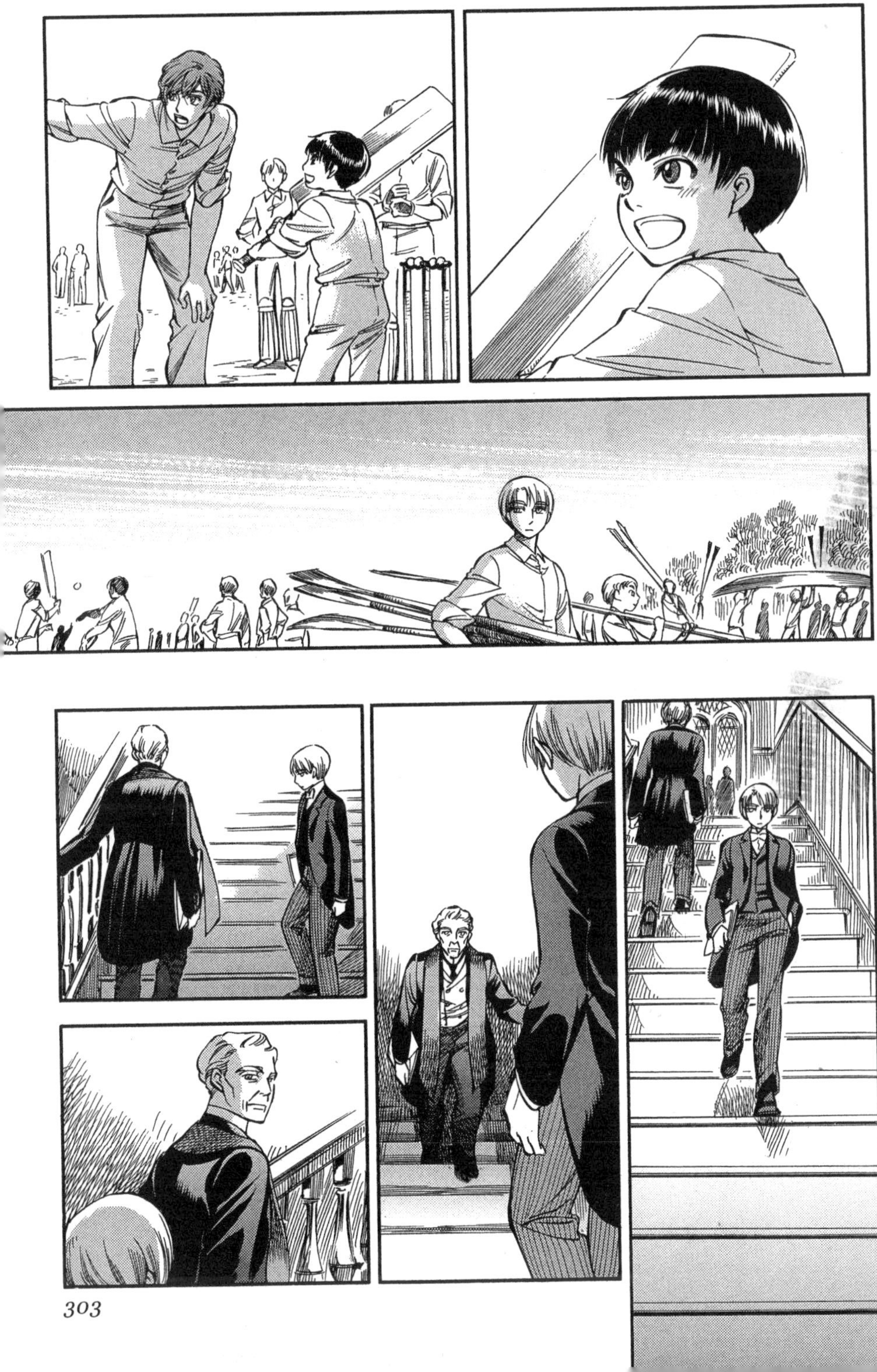

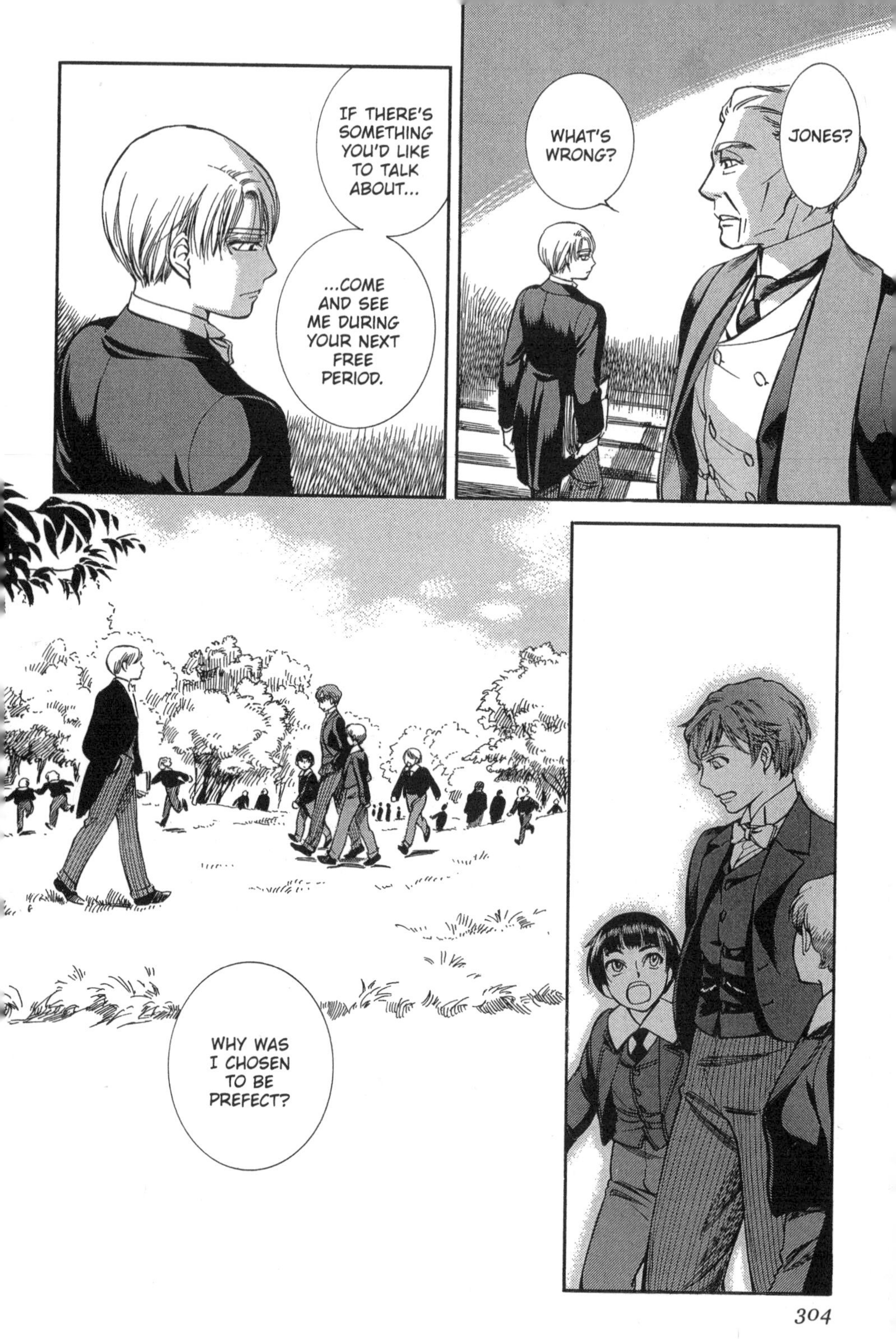
JONES?
WHAT'S WRONG?
IF THERE'S SOMETHING YOU'D LIKE TO TALK ABOUT...
...COME AND SEE ME DURING YOUR NEXT FREE PERIOD.
WHY WAS I CHOSEN TO BE PREFECT?

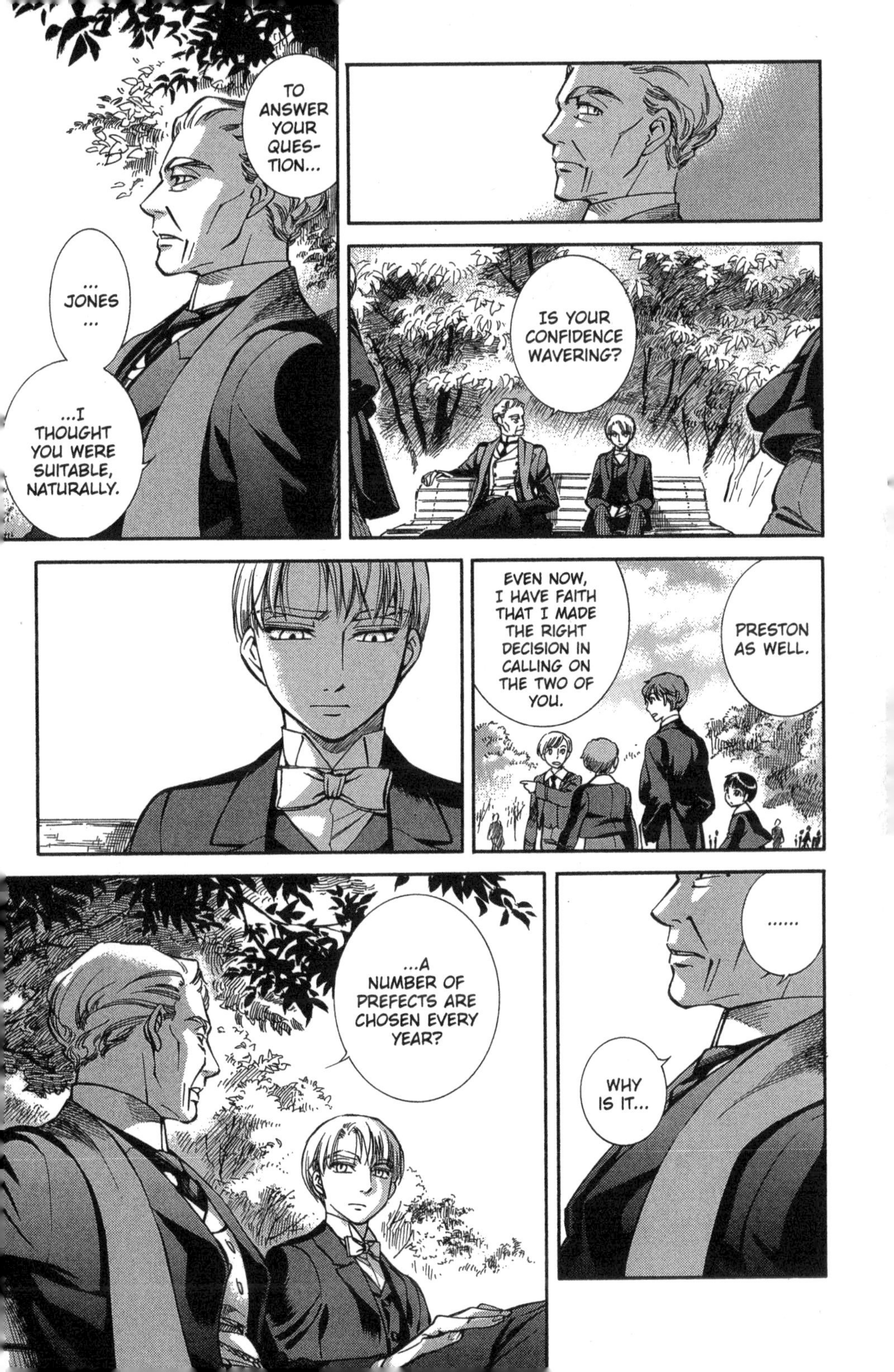
IS YOUR CONFIDENCE WAVERING?
TO ANSWER YOUR QUESTION...
...JONES...
...I THOUGHT YOU WERE SUITABLE, NATURALLY.
PRESTON AS WELL.
EVEN NOW, I HAVE FAITH THAT I MADE THE RIGHT DECISION IN CALLING ON THE TWO OF YOU.
......
WHY IS IT...
...A NUMBER OF PREFECTS ARE CHOSEN EVERY YEAR?

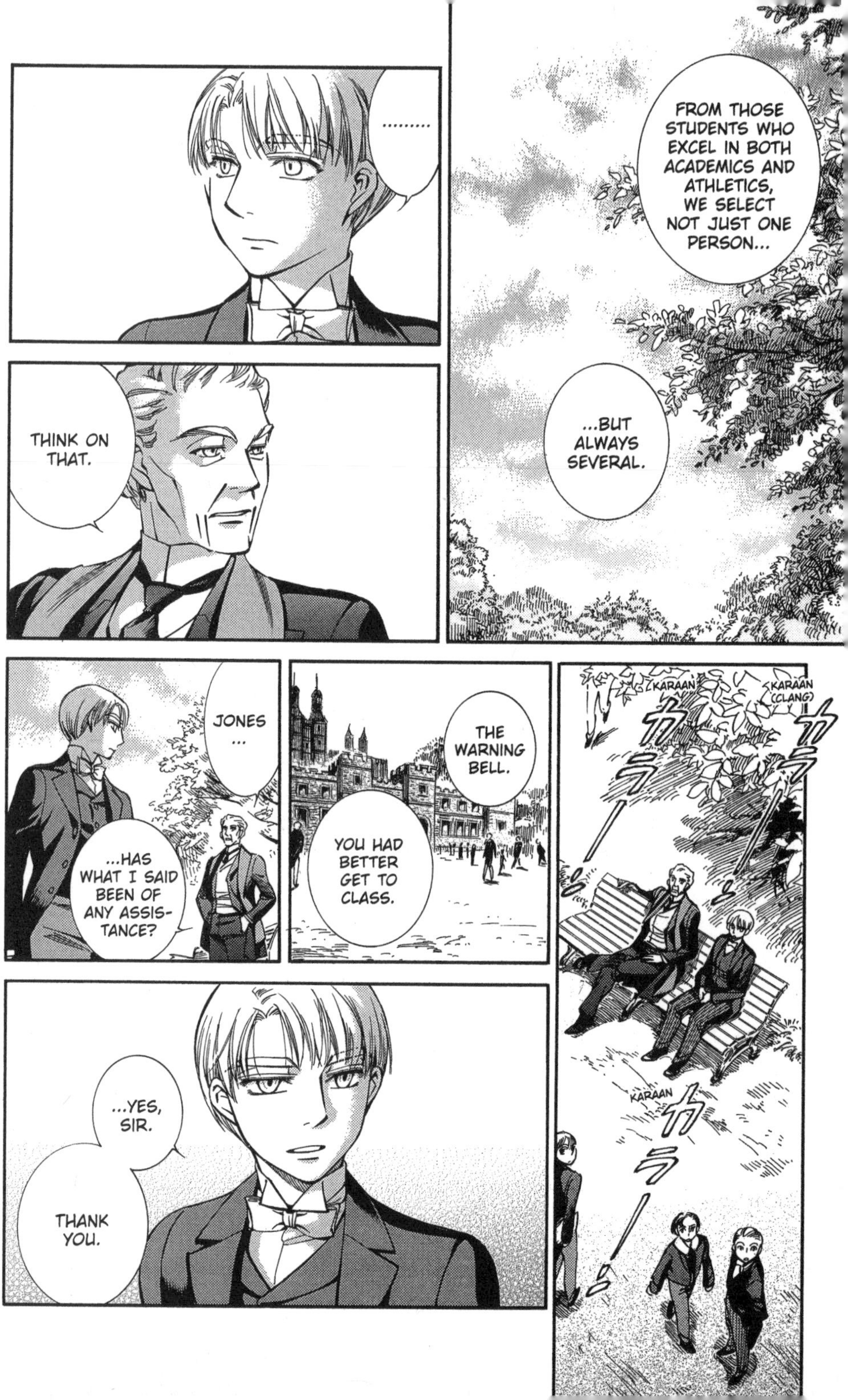
FROM THOSE STUDENTS WHO EXCEL IN BOTH ACADEMICS AND ATHLETICS, WE SELECT NOT JUST ONE PERSON...
...BUT ALWAYS SEVERAL.
....
THINK ON THAT.
KARAAN (CLANG)
KARAAN
KARAAN
THE WARNING BELL.
YOU HAD BETTER GET TO CLASS.
JONES ...
...HAS WHAT I SAID BEEN OF ANY ASSISTANCE?
...YES, SIR.
THANK YOU.

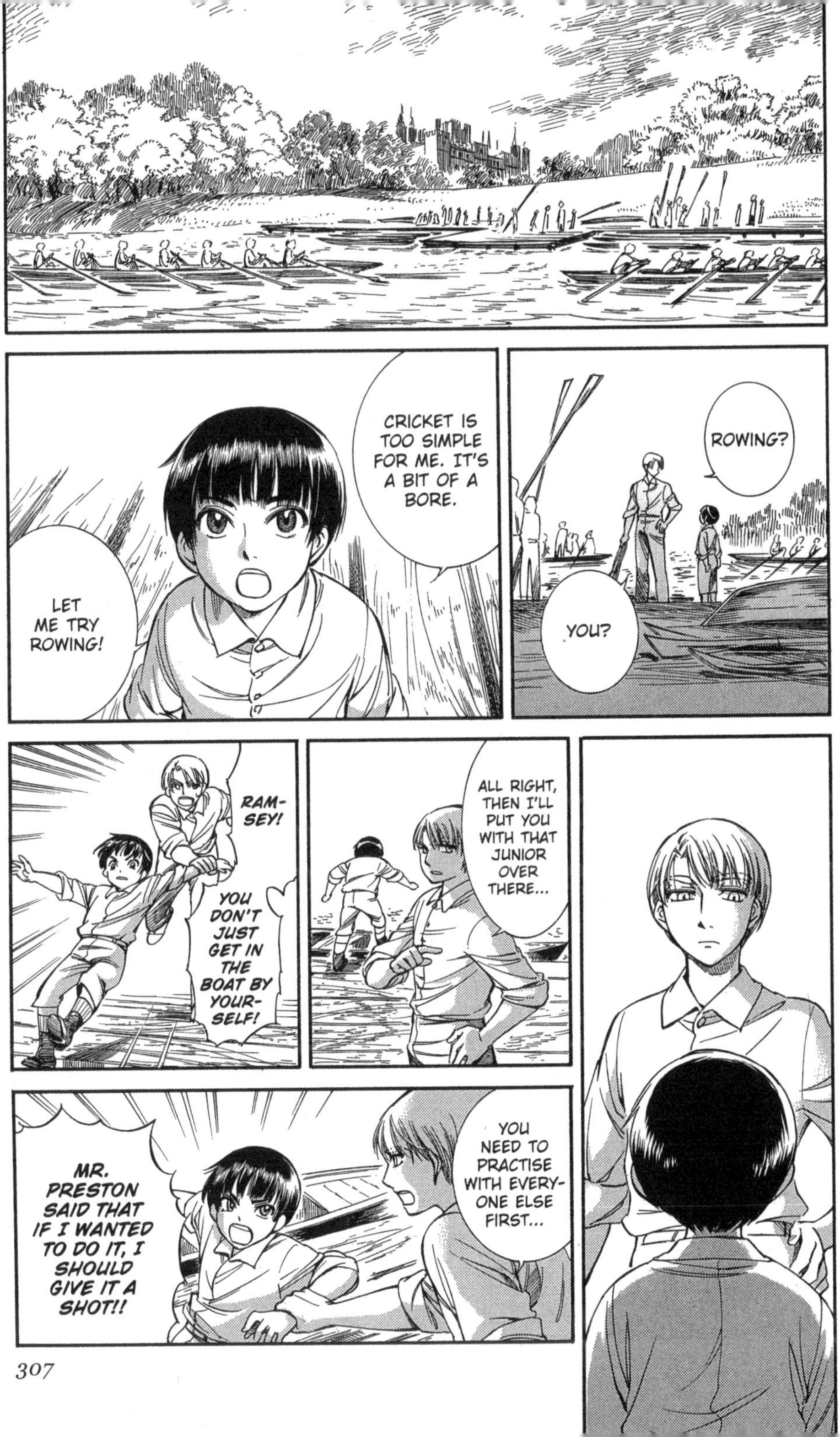
ROWING?
YOU?
CRICKET IS TOO SIMPLE FOR ME. IT'S A BIT OF A BORE.
LET ME TRY ROWING!
ALL RIGHT, THEN I'LL PUT YOU WITH THAT JUNIOR OVER THERE...
RAM-SEY!
YOU DON'T JUST GET IN THE BOAT BY YOUR-SELF!
YOU NEED TO PRACTISE WITH EVERY-ONE ELSE FIRST...
MR. PRESTON SAID THAT IF I WANTED TO DO IT, I SHOULD GIVE IT A SHOT!!

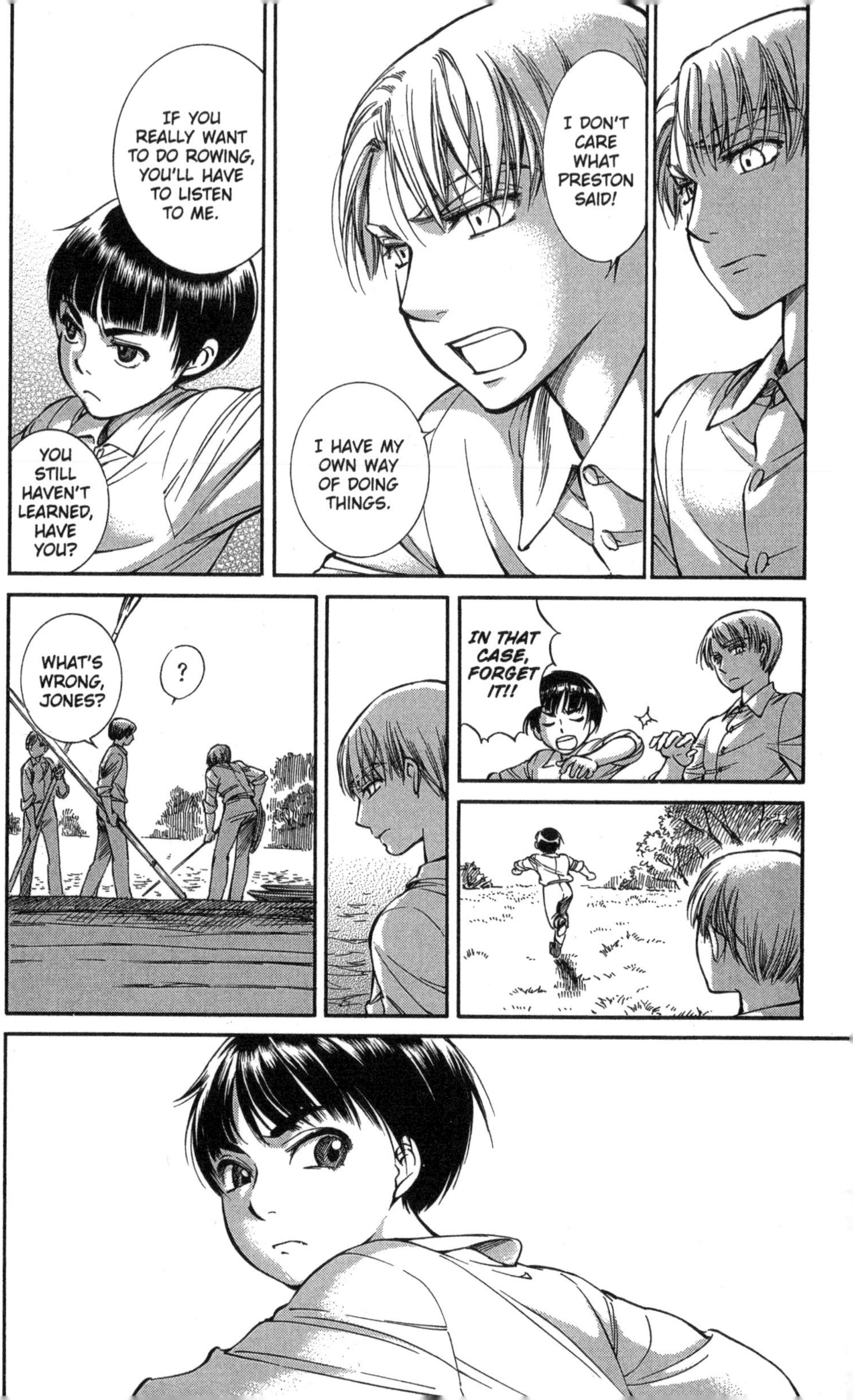
I DON'T CARE WHAT PRESTON SAID!
I HAVE MY OWN WAY OF DOING THINGS.
IF YOU REALLY WANT TO DO ROWING, YOU'LL HAVE TO LISTEN TO ME.
YOU STILL HAVEN'T LEARNED, HAVE YOU?
IN THAT CASE, FORGET IT!!
?
WHAT'S WRONG, JONES?

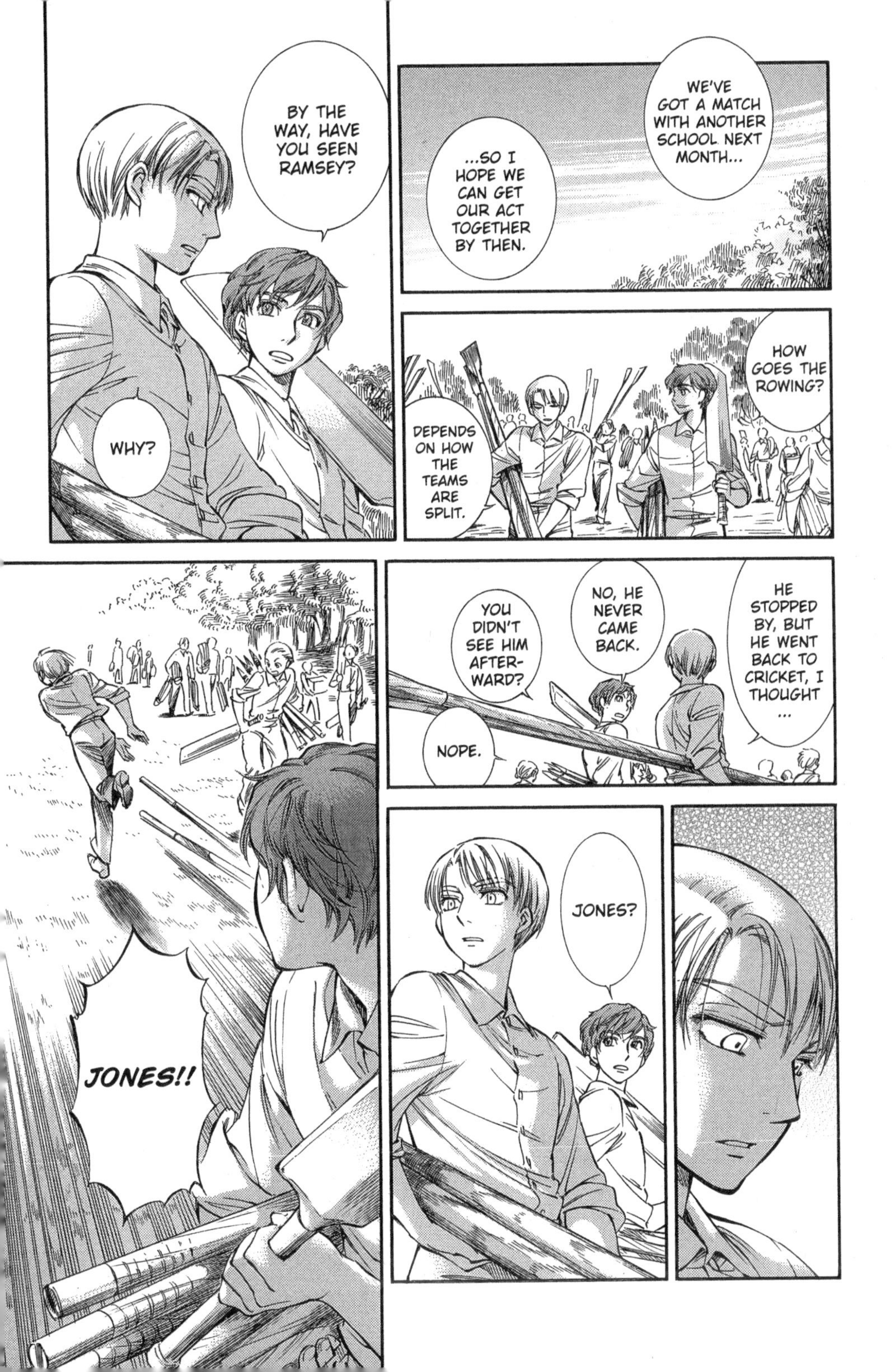
WE'VE GOT A MATCH WITH ANOTHER SCHOOL NEXT MONTH...
...SO I HOPE WE CAN GET OUR ACT TOGETHER BY THEN.
HOW GOES THE ROWING?
DEPENDS ON HOW THE TEAMS ARE SPLIT.
BY THE WAY, HAVE YOU SEEN RAMSEY?
WHY?
HE STOPPED BY, BUT HE WENT BACK TO CRICKET, I THOUGHT...
NO, HE NEVER CAME BACK.
YOU DIDN'T SEE HIM AFTER-WARD?
NOPE.
JONES?
JONES!!

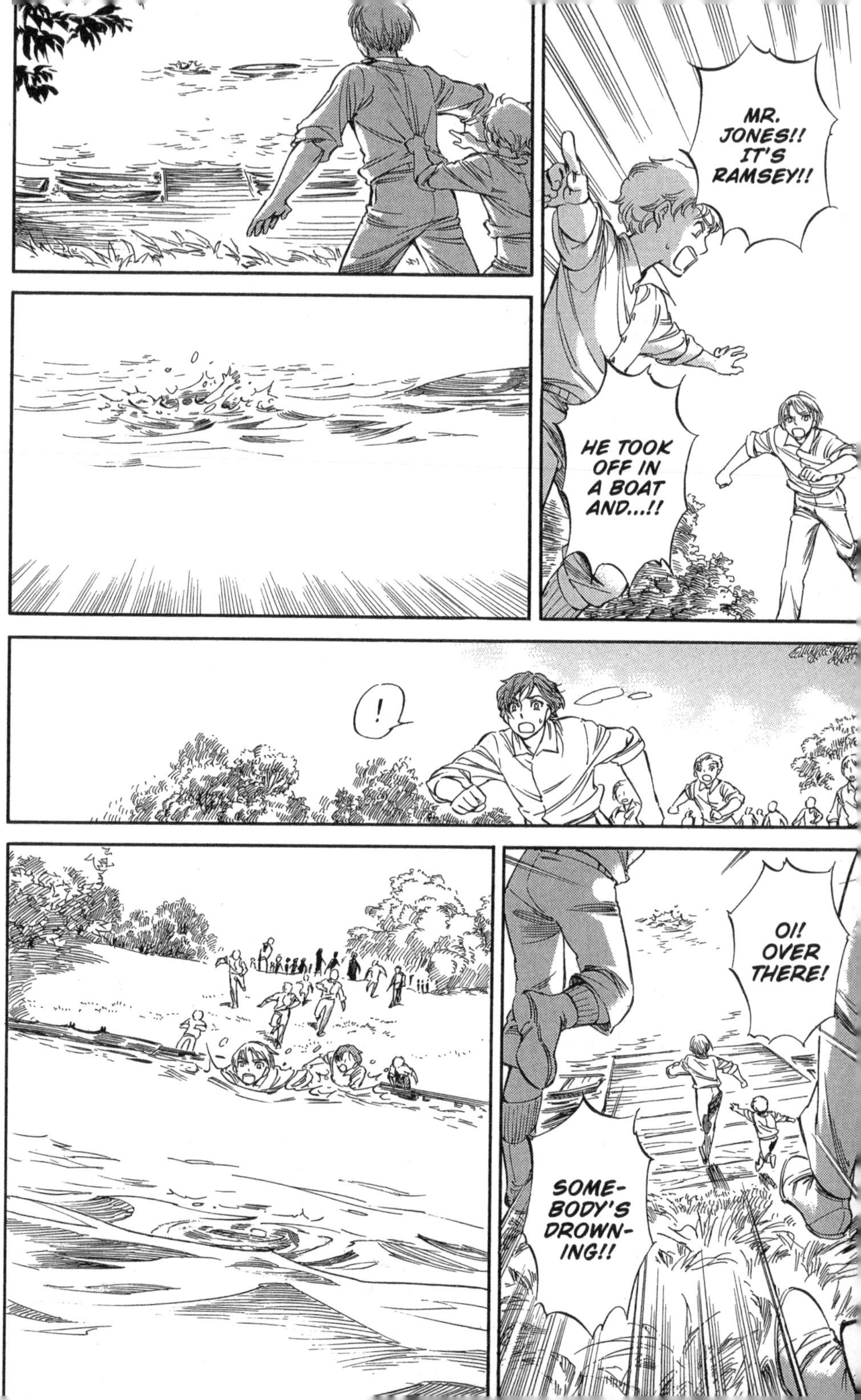
MR. JONES!! IT'S RAMSEY!!
HE TOOK OFF IN A BOAT AND...!!
!
OI! OVER THERE!
SOME-BODY'S DROWN-ING!!

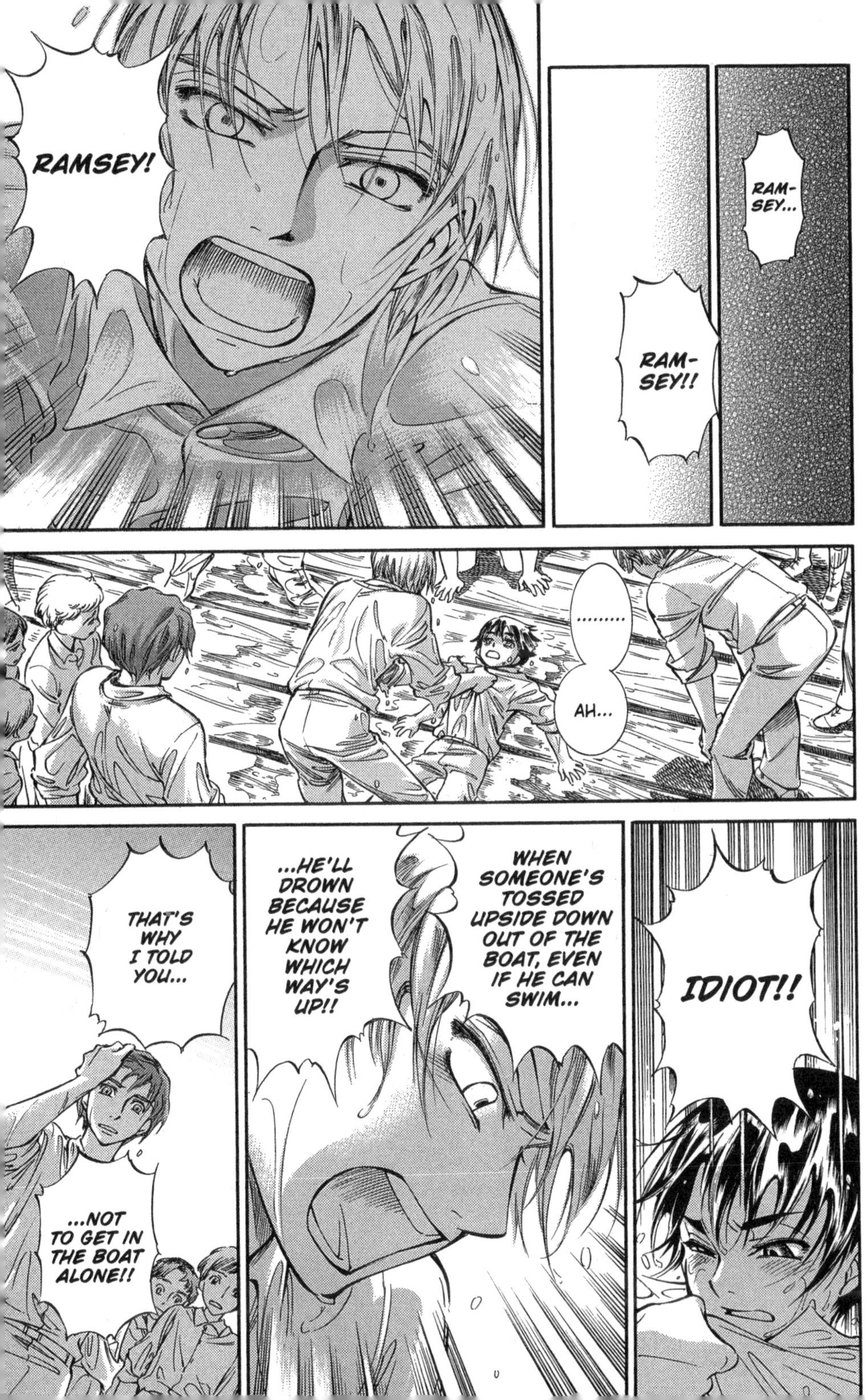
RAM-SEY...
RAM-SEY!!
RAMSEY!
....
AH...
IDIOT!!
WHEN SOMEONE'S TOSSED UPSIDE DOWN OUT OF THE BOAT, EVEN IF HE CAN SWIM...
...HE'LL DROWN BECAUSE HE WON'T KNOW WHICH WAY'S UP!!
THAT'S WHY I TOLD YOU...
...NOT TO GET IN THE BOAT ALONE!!

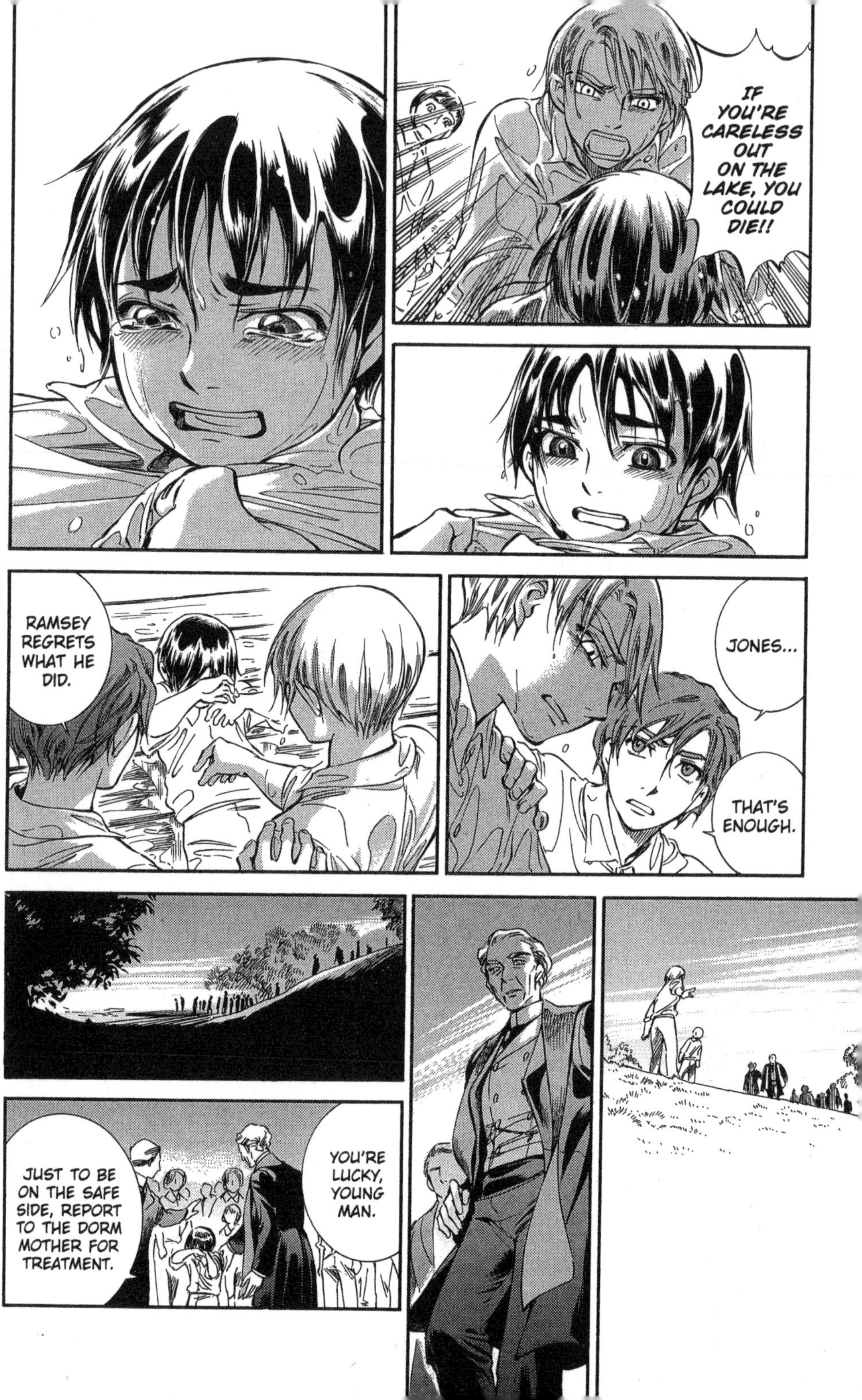
IF YOU'RE CARELESS OUT ON THE LAKE, YOU COULD DIE!!
JONES...
THAT'S ENOUGH.
RAMSEY REGRETS WHAT HE DID.
YOU'RE LUCKY, YOUNG MAN.
JUST TO BE ON THE SAFE SIDE, REPORT TO THE DORM MOTHER FOR TREATMENT.

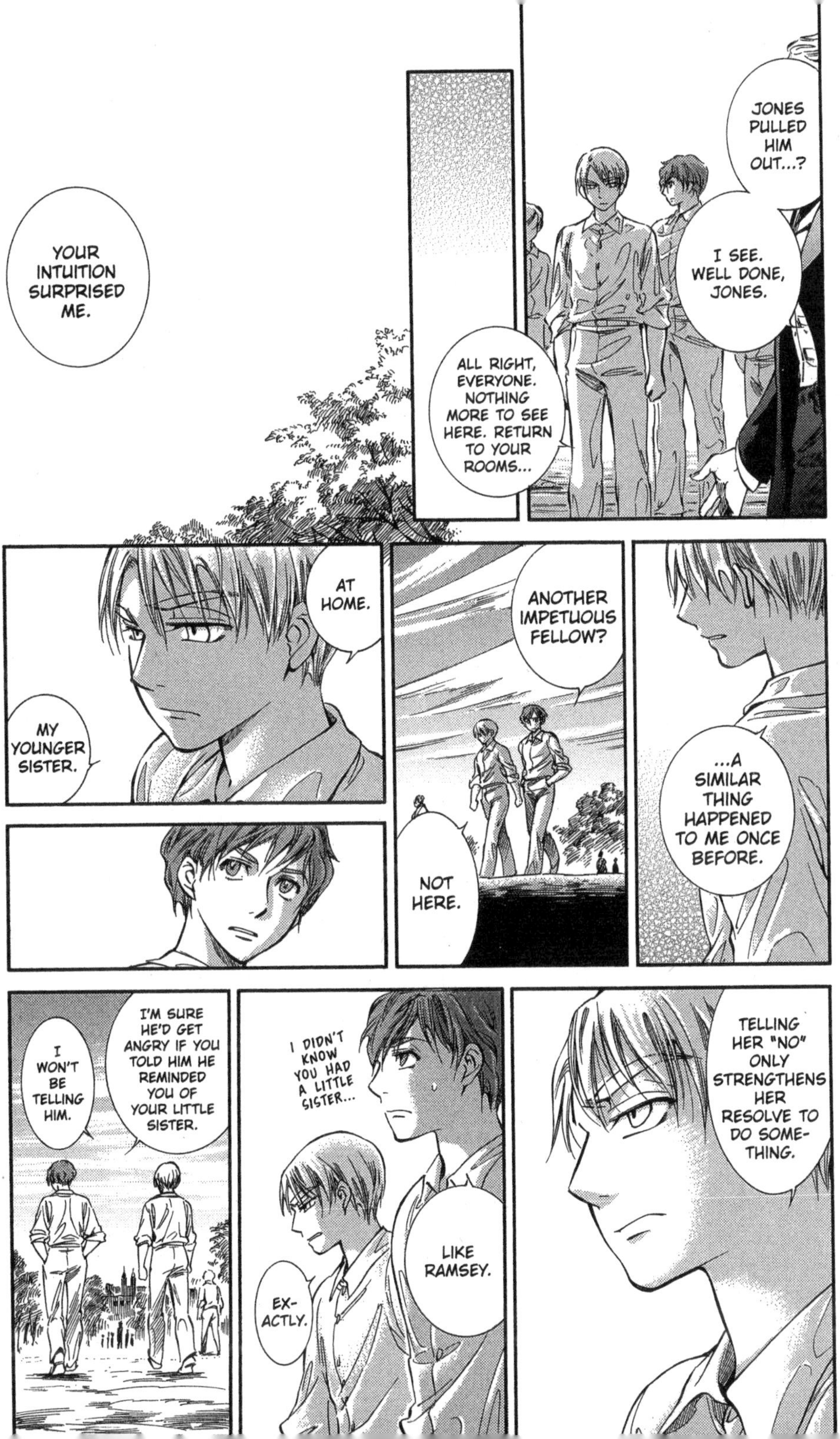
JONES PULLED HIM OUT...?
I SEE. WELL DONE, JONES.
ALL RIGHT, EVERYONE. NOTHING MORE TO SEE HERE. RETURN TO YOUR ROOMS...
YOUR INTUITION SURPRISED ME.
...A SIMILAR THING HAPPENED TO ME ONCE BEFORE.
ANOTHER IMPETUOUS FELLOW?
NOT HERE.
AT HOME.
MY YOUNGER SISTER.
TELLING HER "NO" ONLY STRENGTHENS HER RESOLVE TO DO SOMETHING.
I DIDN'T KNOW YOU HAD A LITTLE SISTER...
LIKE RAMSEY.
EX-ACTLY.
I'M SURE HE'D GET ANGRY IF YOU TOLD HIM HE REMINDED YOU OF YOUR LITTLE SISTER.
I WON'T BE TELLING HIM.

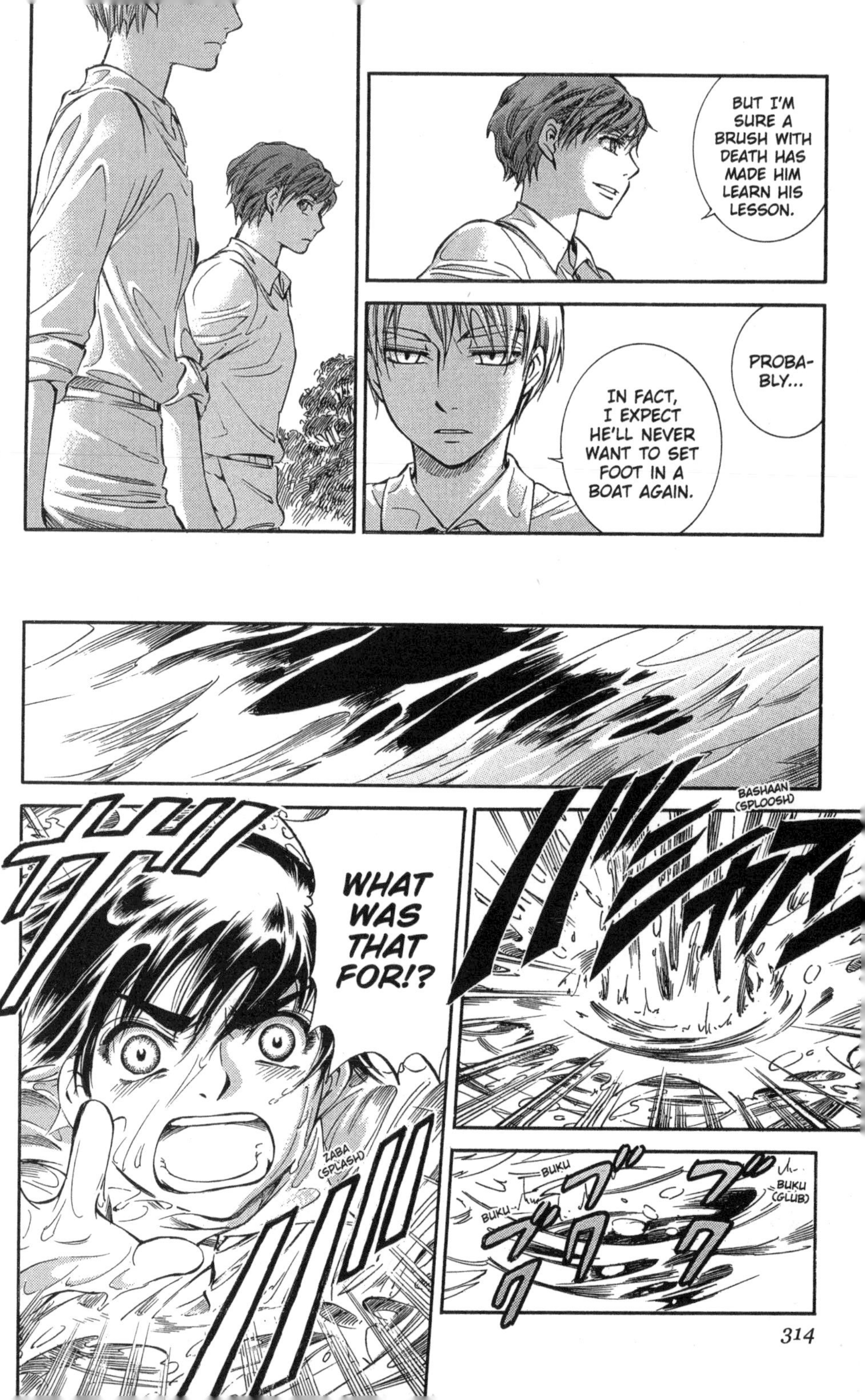
BUT I'M SURE A BRUSH WITH DEATH HAS MADE HIM LEARN HIS LESSON.
PROBA-BLY...
IN FACT, I EXPECT HE'LL NEVER WANT TO SET FOOT IN A BOAT AGAIN.
BASHAAN (SPLOOSH)
BUKU
BUKU (GLUB)
BUKU
WHAT WAS THAT FOR!?
ZABA (SPLASH)

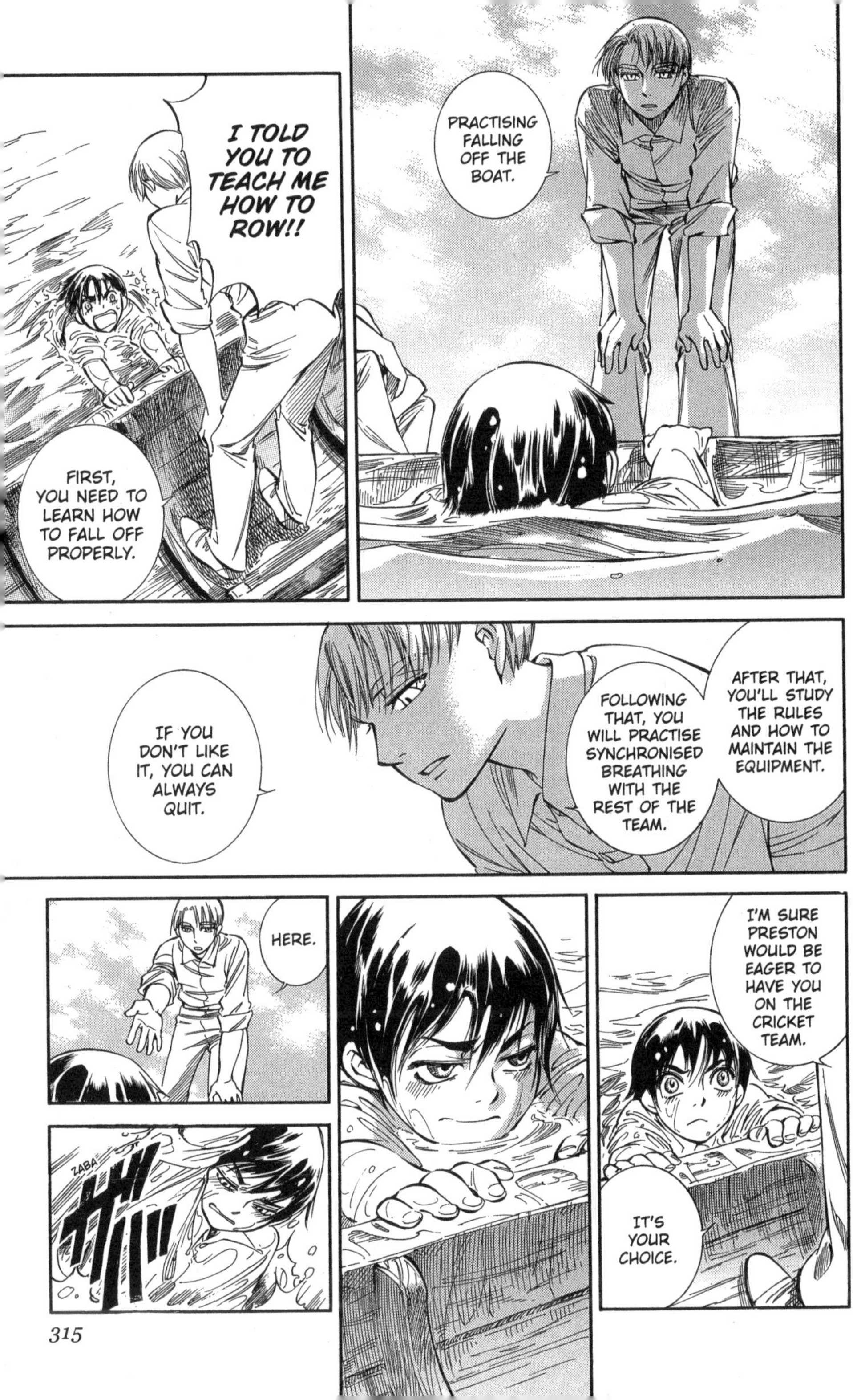
PRACTISING FALLING OFF THE BOAT.
I TOLD YOU TO TEACH ME HOW TO ROW!!
FIRST, YOU NEED TO LEARN HOW TO FALL OFF PROPERLY.
AFTER THAT, YOU'LL STUDY THE RULES AND HOW TO MAINTAIN THE EQUIPMENT.
FOLLOWING THAT, YOU WILL PRACTISE SYNCHRONISED BREATHING WITH THE REST OF THE TEAM.
IF YOU DON'T LIKE IT, YOU CAN ALWAYS QUIT.
I'M SURE PRESTON WOULD BE EAGER TO HAVE YOU ON THE CRICKET TEAM.
IT'S YOUR CHOICE.
HERE.
ZABA

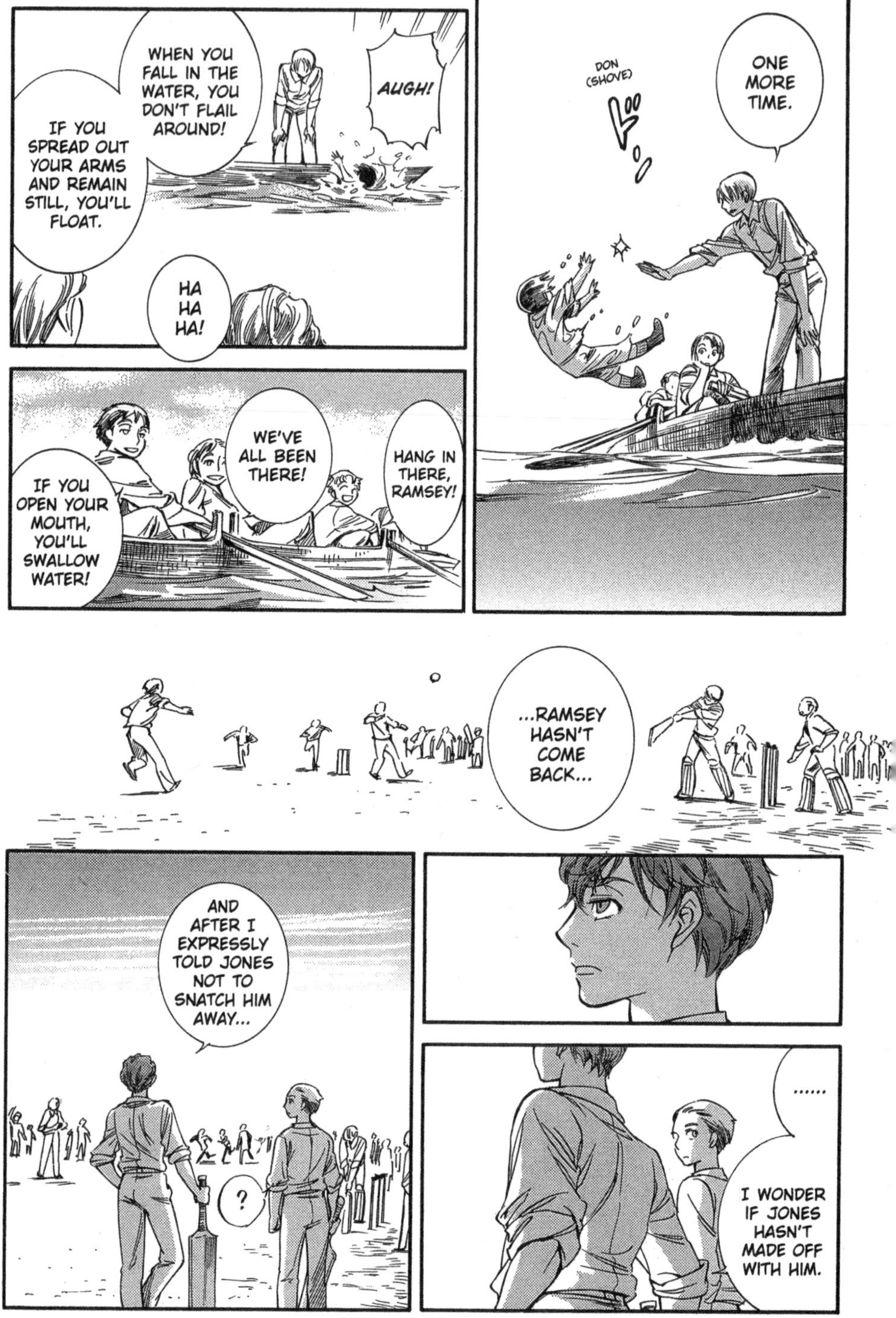
ONE MORE TIME.
DON (SHOVE)
AUGH!
WHEN YOU FALL IN THE WATER, YOU DON'T FLAIL AROUND!
IF YOU SPREAD OUT YOUR ARMS AND REMAIN STILL, YOU'LL FLOAT.
HA HA HA!
HANG IN THERE, RAMSEY!
WE'VE ALL BEEN THERE!
IF YOU OPEN YOUR MOUTH, YOU'LL SWALLOW WATER!
...RAMSEY HASN'T COME BACK...
......
I WONDER IF JONES HASN'T MADE OFF WITH HIM.
AND AFTER I EXPRESSLY TOLD JONES NOT TO SNATCH HIM AWAY...
?

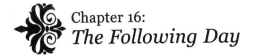

Chapter 16:
The Following Day

Chapter 16: *The Following Day*

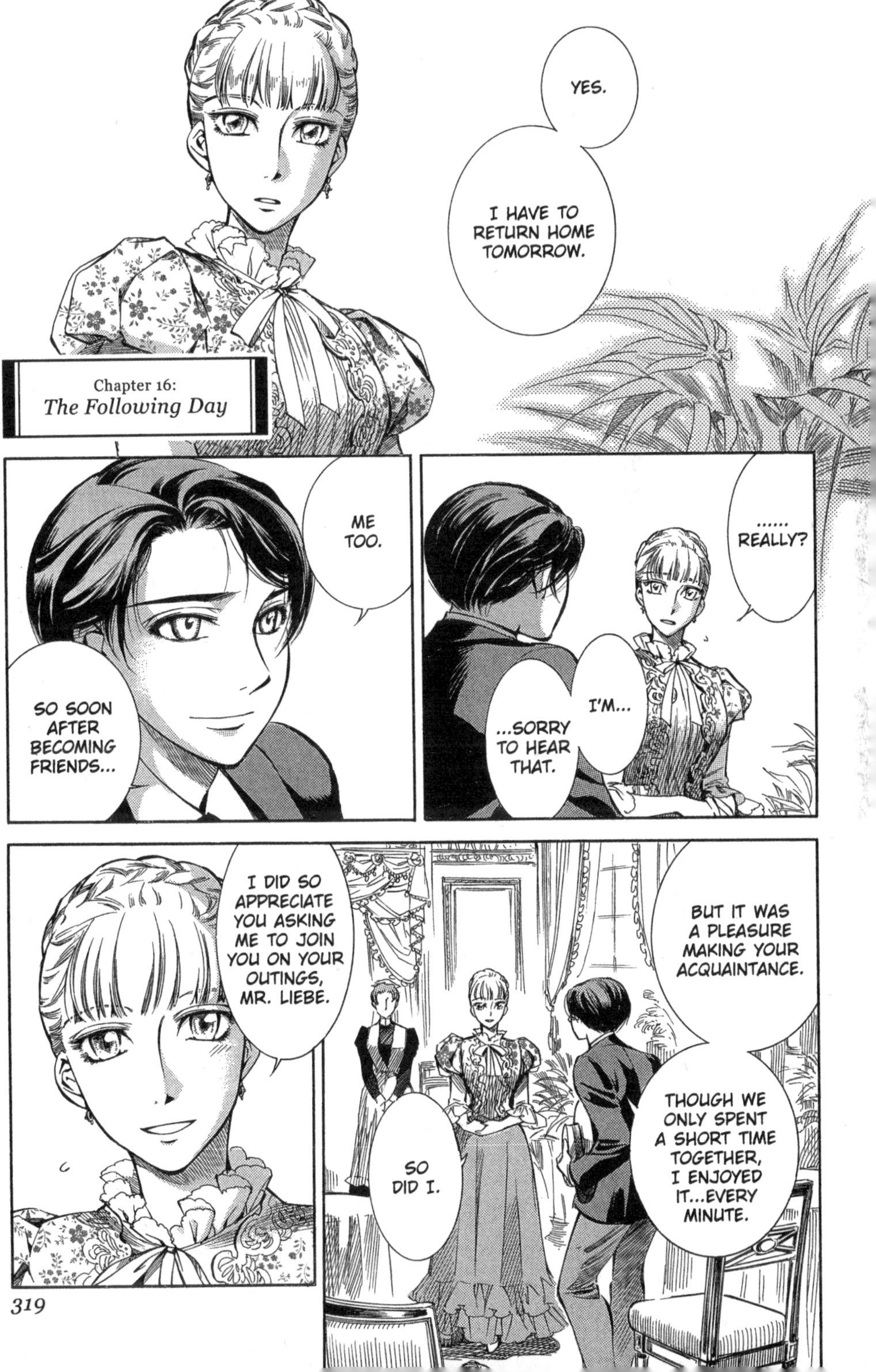
YES.
I HAVE TO RETURN HOME TOMORROW.
...... REALLY?
I'M...
...SORRY TO HEAR THAT.
ME TOO.
SO SOON AFTER BECOMING FRIENDS...
BUT IT WAS A PLEASURE MAKING YOUR ACQUAINTANCE.
THOUGH WE ONLY SPENT A SHORT TIME TOGETHER, I ENJOYED IT...EVERY MINUTE.
SO DID I.
I DID SO APPRECIATE YOU ASKING ME TO JOIN YOU ON YOUR OUTINGS, MR. LIEBE.

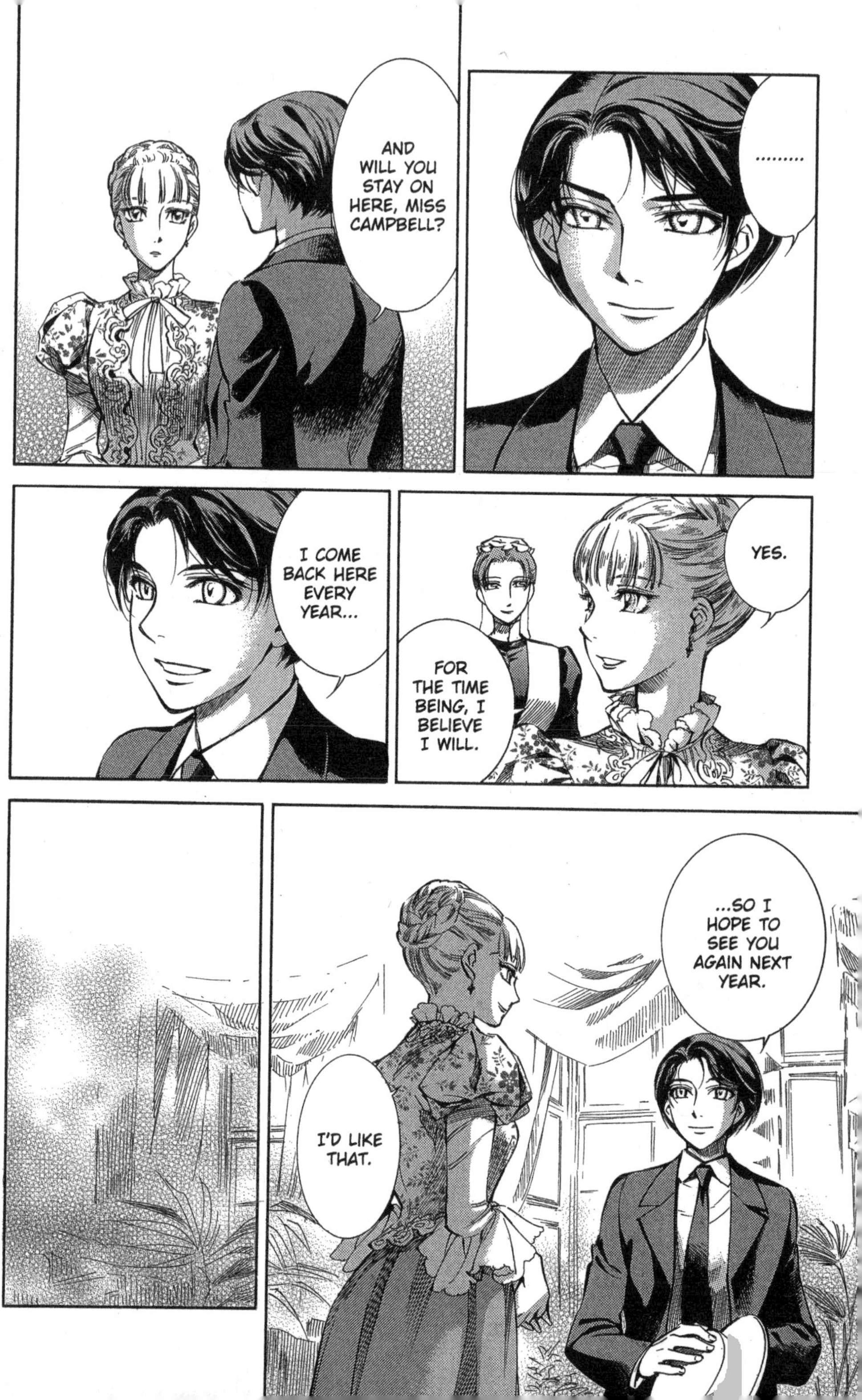

....
AND WILL YOU STAY ON HERE, MISS CAMPBELL?
YES.
FOR THE TIME BEING, I BELIEVE I WILL.
I COME BACK HERE EVERY YEAR...
...SO I HOPE TO SEE YOU AGAIN NEXT YEAR.
I'D LIKE THAT.

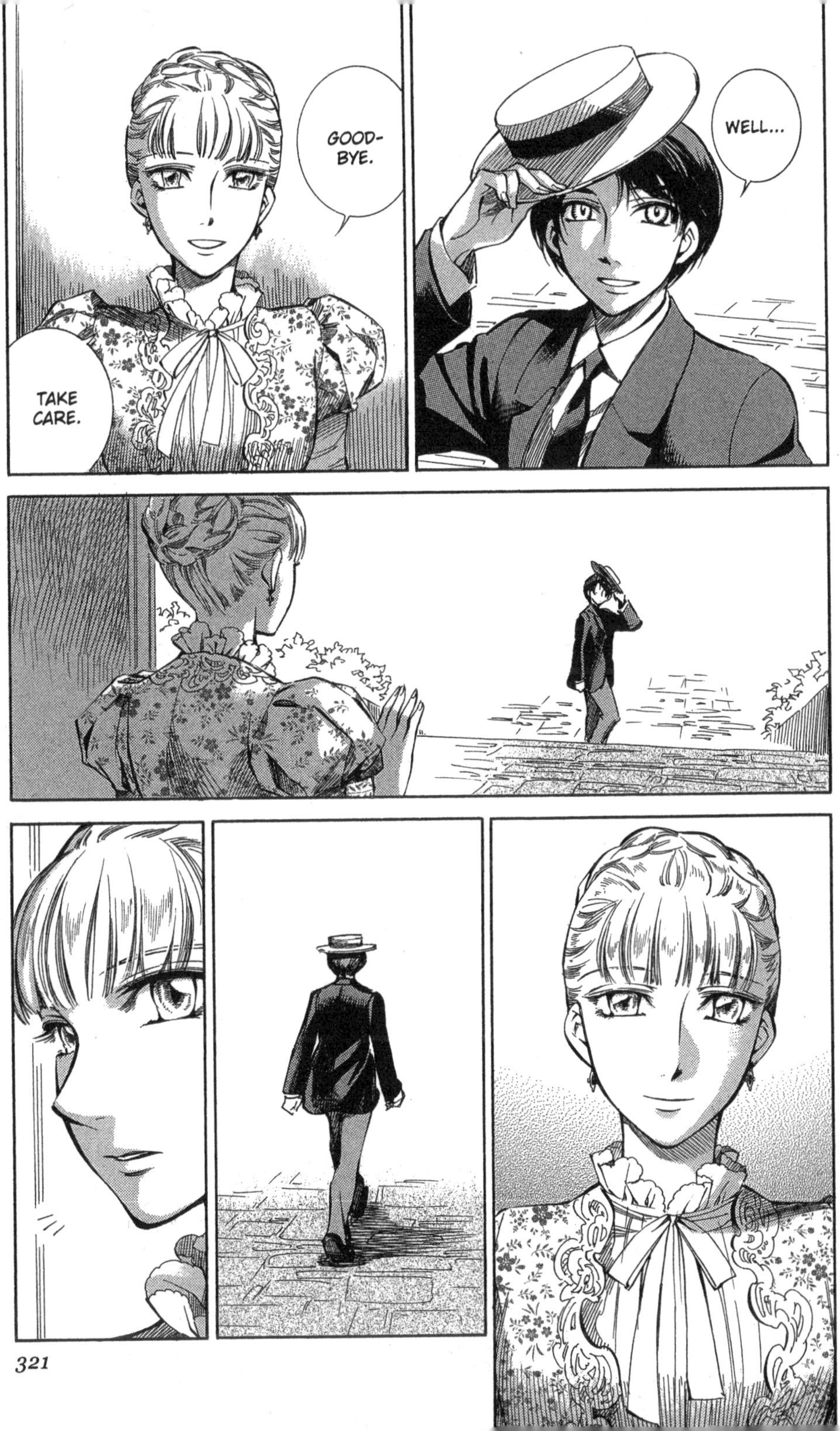
WELL...
GOOD-BYE.
TAKE CARE.

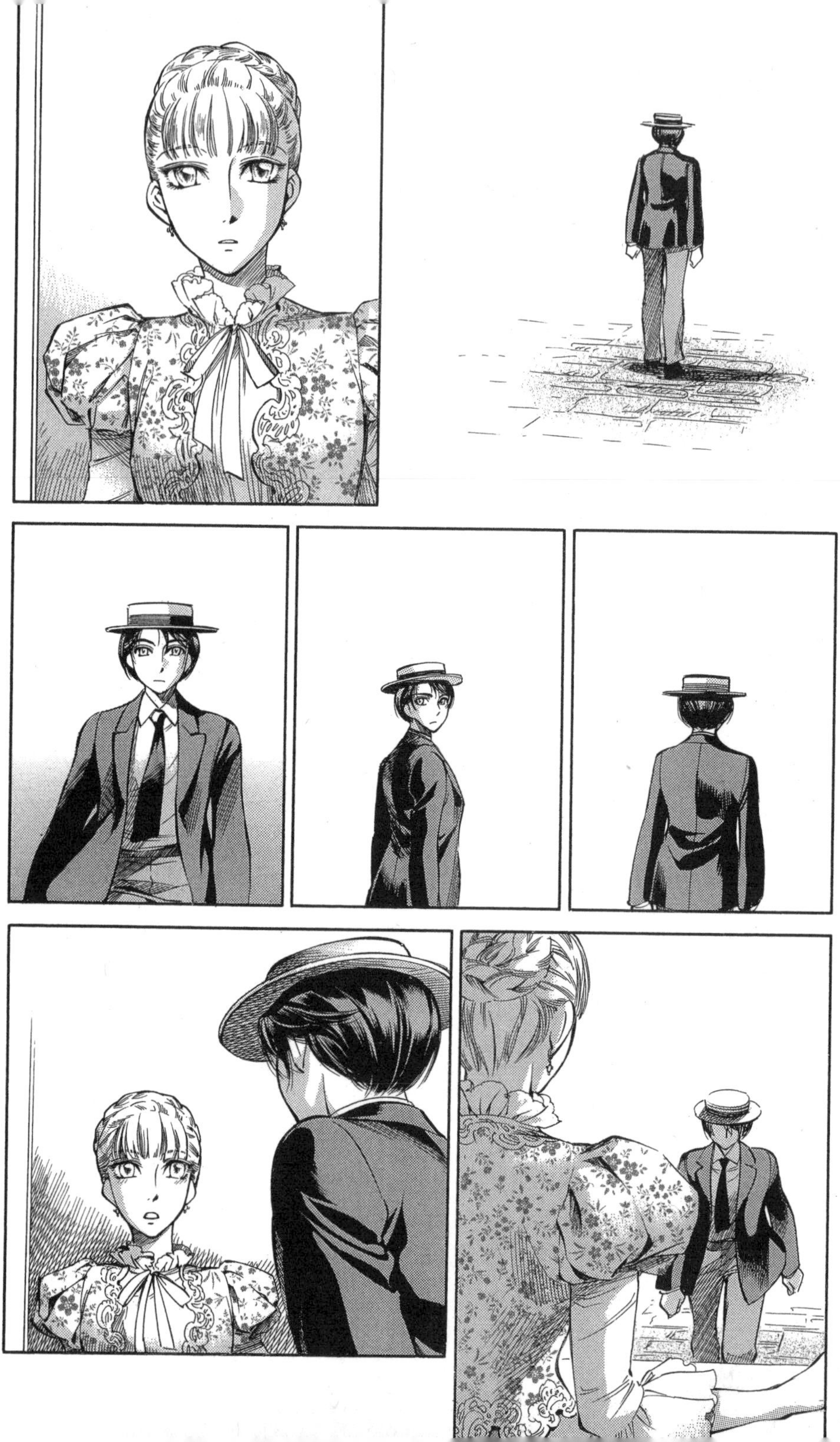

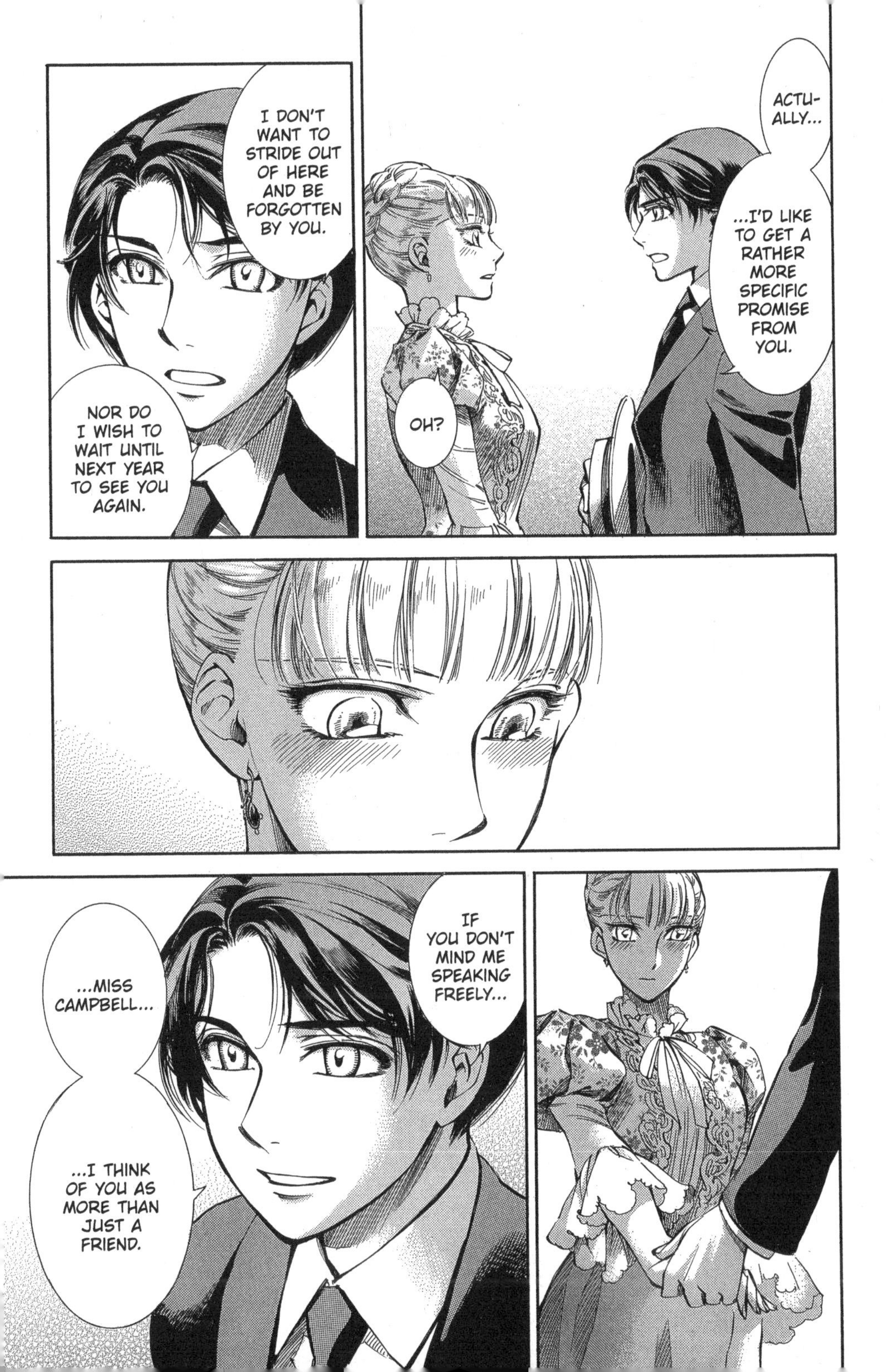
ACTU-ALLY...
...I'D LIKE TO GET A RATHER MORE SPECIFIC PROMISE FROM YOU.
OH?
I DON'T WANT TO STRIDE OUT OF HERE AND BE FORGOTTEN BY YOU.
NOR DO I WISH TO WAIT UNTIL NEXT YEAR TO SEE YOU AGAIN.
IF YOU DON'T MIND ME SPEAKING FREELY...
...MISS CAMPBELL...
...I THINK OF YOU AS MORE THAN JUST A FRIEND.

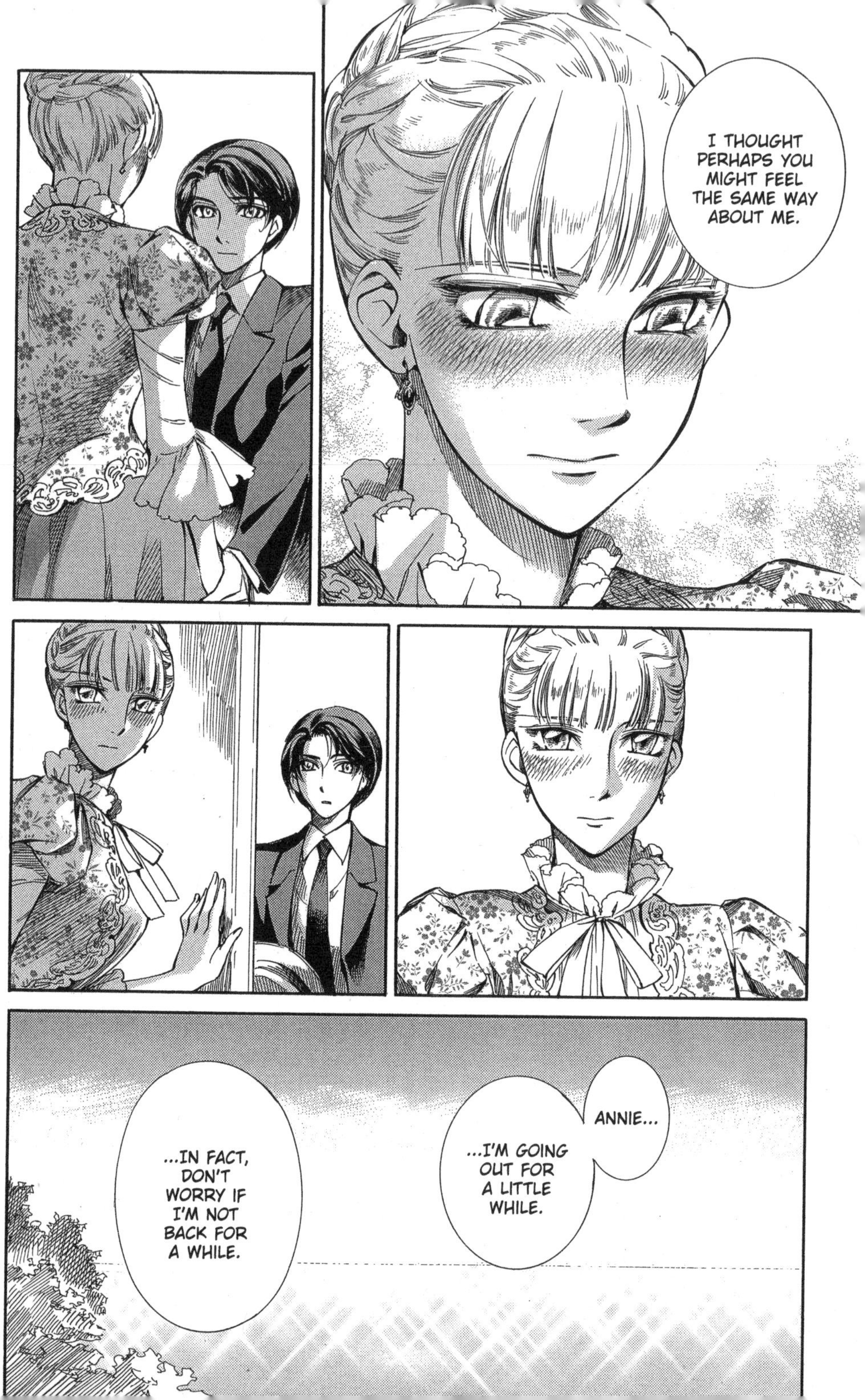
I THOUGHT PERHAPS YOU MIGHT FEEL THE SAME WAY ABOUT ME.
ANNIE...
...I'M GOING OUT FOR A LITTLE WHILE.
...IN FACT, DON'T WORRY IF I'M NOT BACK FOR A WHILE.

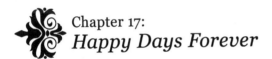

Chapter 17:
Happy Days Forever

Chapter 17: *Happy Days Forever*

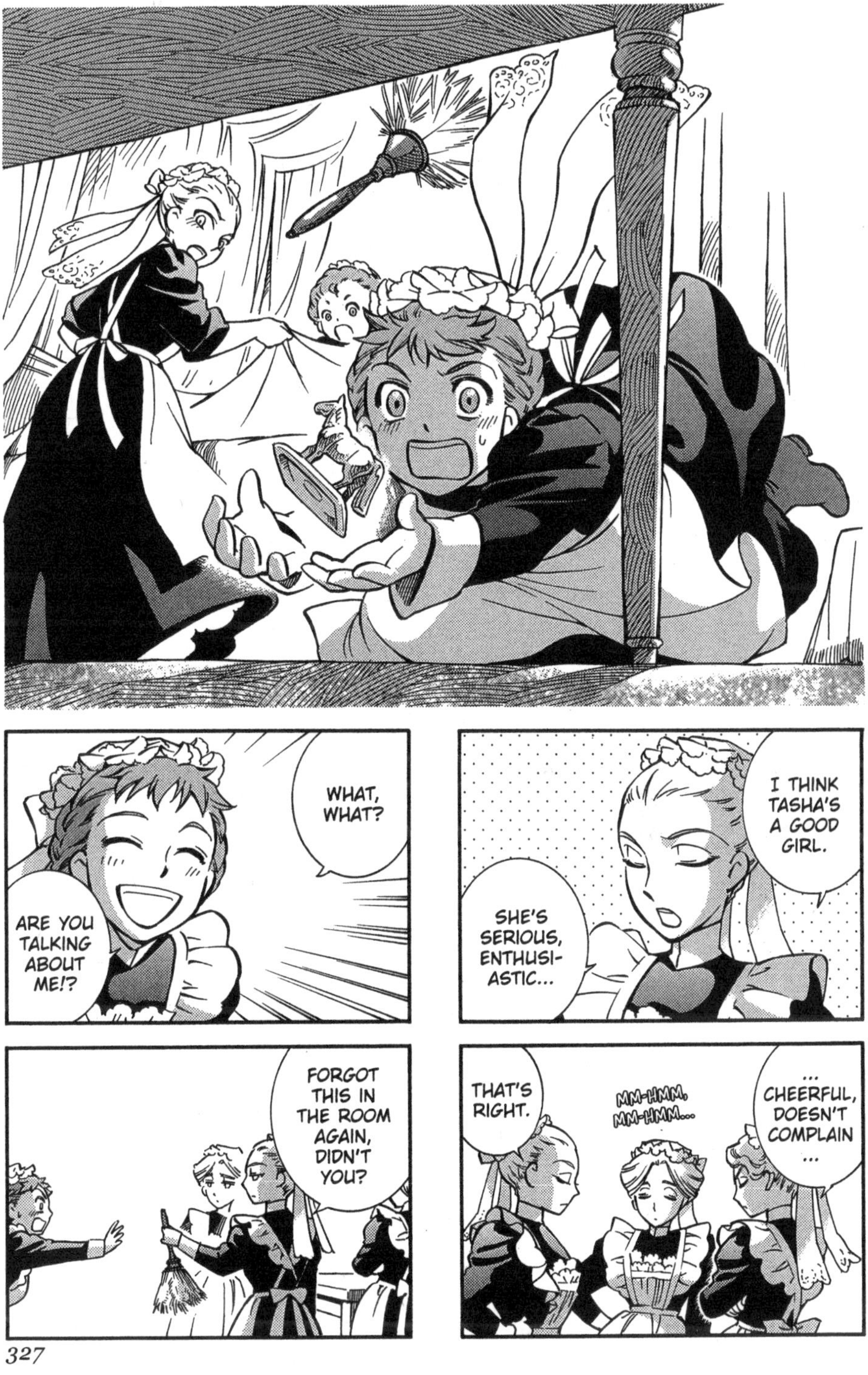

I THINK TASHA'S A GOOD GIRL.
SHE'S SERIOUS, ENTHUSI-ASTIC...
WHAT, WHAT?
ARE YOU TALKING ABOUT ME!?
... CHEERFUL, DOESN'T COMPLAIN ...
MM-HMM, MM-HMM...
THAT'S RIGHT.
FORGOT THIS IN THE ROOM AGAIN, DIDN'T YOU?

....

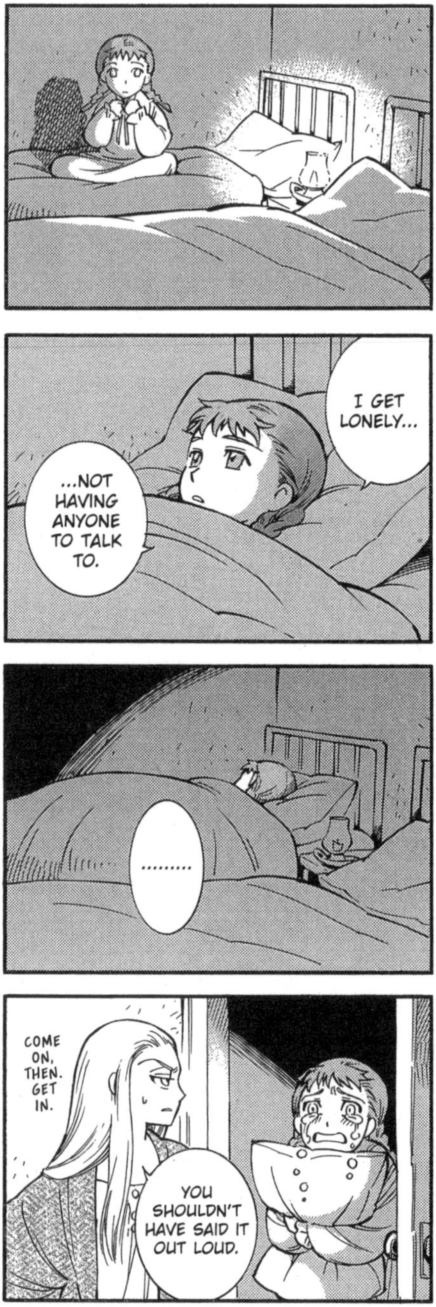
I GET LONELY...
...NOT HAVING ANYONE TO TALK TO.
....
COME ON, THEN. GET IN.
YOU SHOULDN'T HAVE SAID IT OUT LOUD.

I'm Sorry

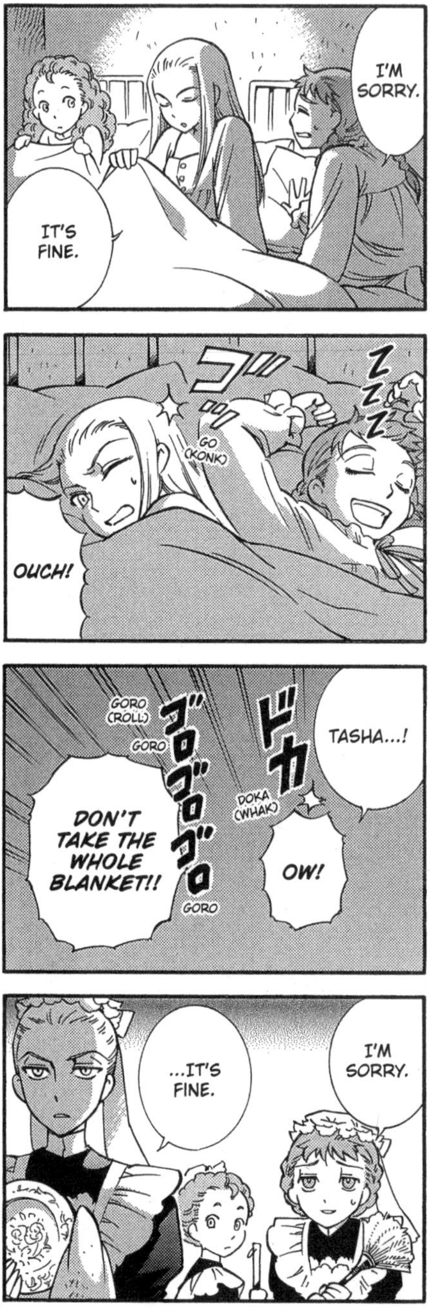
I'M SORRY.
IT'S FINE.
ZZZ
ゴッ
GO (KONK)
OUCH!
TASHA...!
ドカ
DOKA (WHAK)
OW!
ゴロゴロゴロ
GORO (ROLL)
GORO
GORO
DON'T TAKE THE WHOLE BLANKET!!
I'M SORRY.
...IT'S FINE.

Again

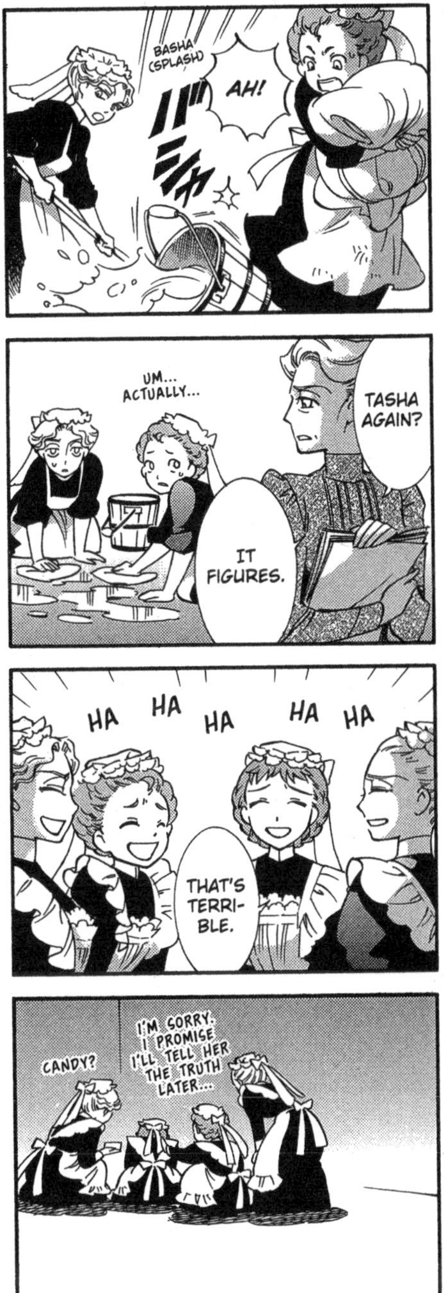
AH!
BASHA (SPLASH)
TASHA AGAIN?
UM... ACTUALLY...
IT FIGURES.
HA HA HA HA HA
THAT'S TERRIBLE.
I'M SORRY. I PROMISE I'LL TELL HER THE TRUTH LATER...
CANDY?

Resolve

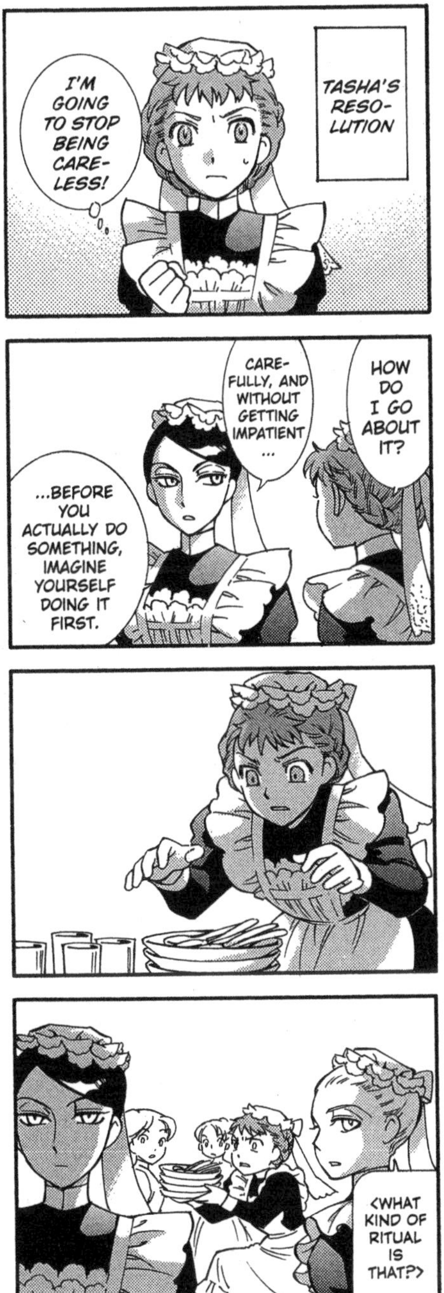
TASHA'S RESOLUTION
I'M GOING TO STOP BEING CARELESS!
HOW DO I GO ABOUT IT?
CAREFULLY, AND WITHOUT GETTING IMPATIENT...
...BEFORE YOU ACTUALLY DO SOMETHING, IMAGINE YOURSELF DOING IT FIRST.
<WHAT KIND OF RITUAL IS THAT?>

Who Did It?

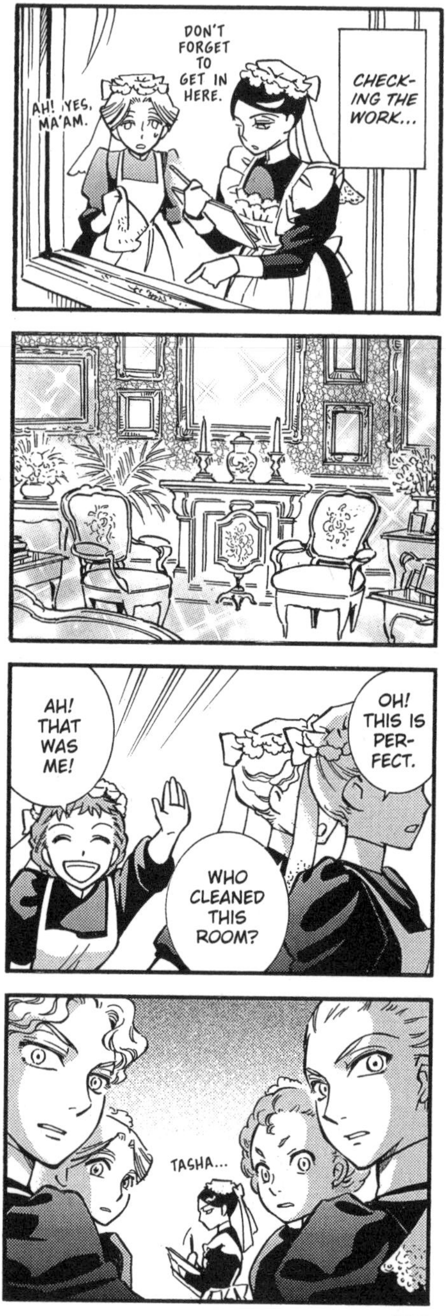

CHECKING THE WORK...
DON'T FORGET TO GET IN HERE.
AH! YES, MA'AM.
OH! THIS IS PERFECT.
WHO CLEANED THIS ROOM?
AH! THAT WAS ME!
TASHA...

If You Put Your Mind to It...

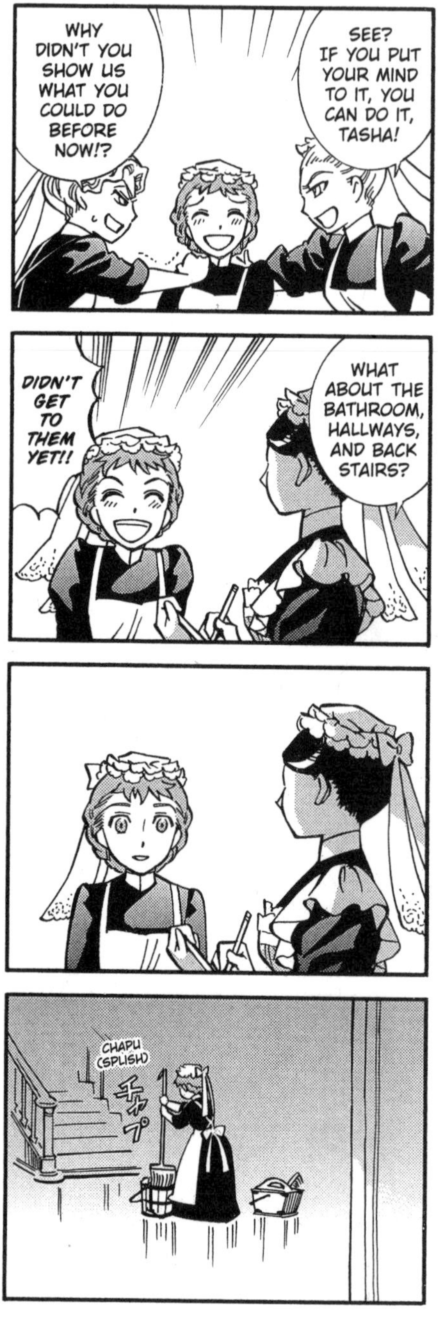

SEE? IF YOU PUT YOUR MIND TO IT, YOU CAN DO IT, TASHA!
WHY DIDN'T YOU SHOW US WHAT YOU COULD DO BEFORE NOW!?
WHAT ABOUT THE BATHROOM, HALLWAYS, AND BACK STAIRS?
DIDN'T GET TO THEM YET!!
CHAPU (SPLISH)
チャプ

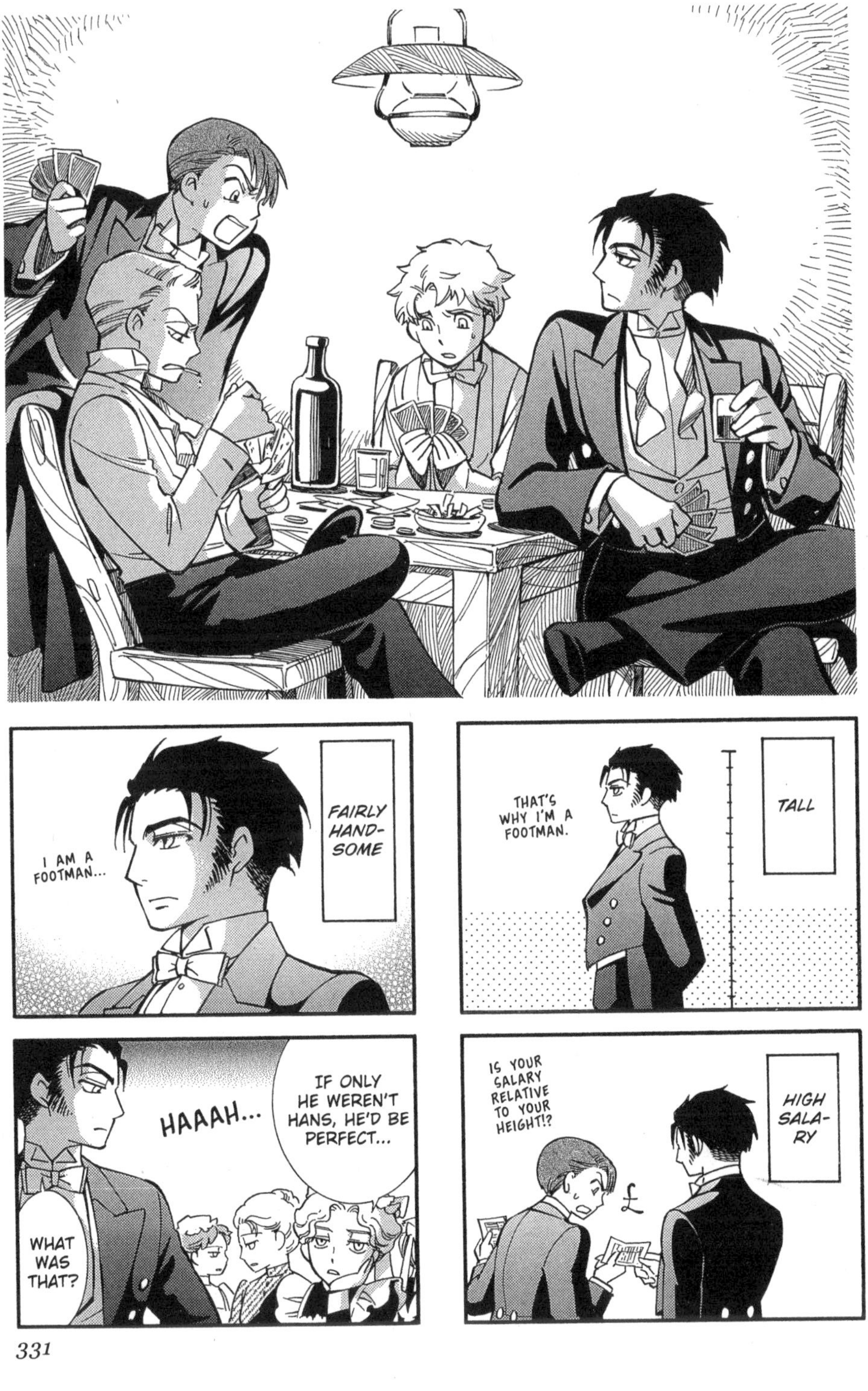
TALL
THAT'S WHY I'M A FOOTMAN.
FAIRLY HAND-SOME
I AM A FOOTMAN...
HIGH SALA-RY
IS YOUR SALARY RELATIVE TO YOUR HEIGHT!?
£
IF ONLY HE WEREN'T HANS, HE'D BE PERFECT...
HAAAH...
WHAT WAS THAT?

Book

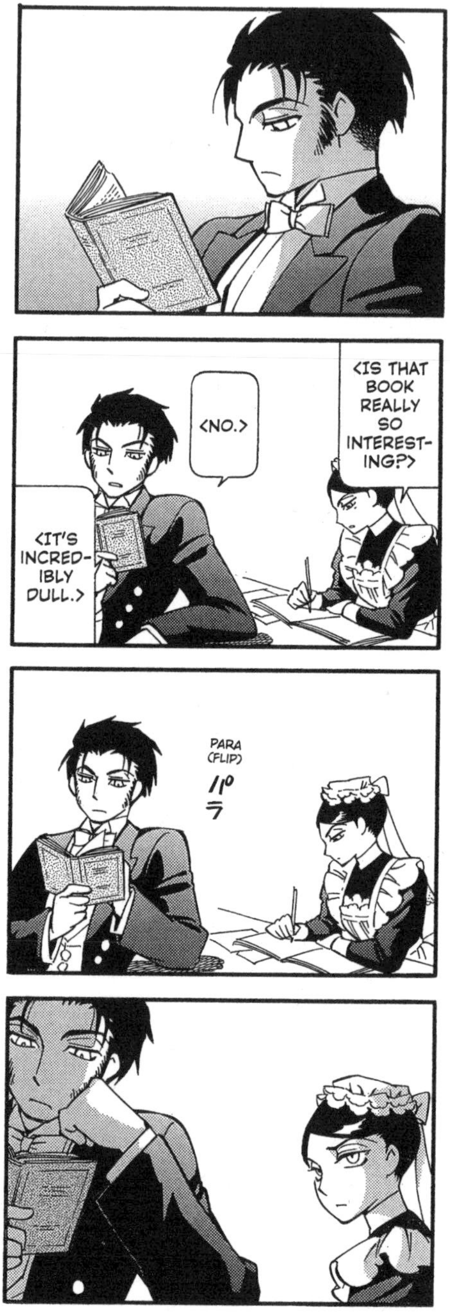
<IS THAT BOOK REALLY SO INTERESTING?>
<NO.>
<IT'S INCREDIBLY DULL.>
PARA (FLIP)
パラ

Child

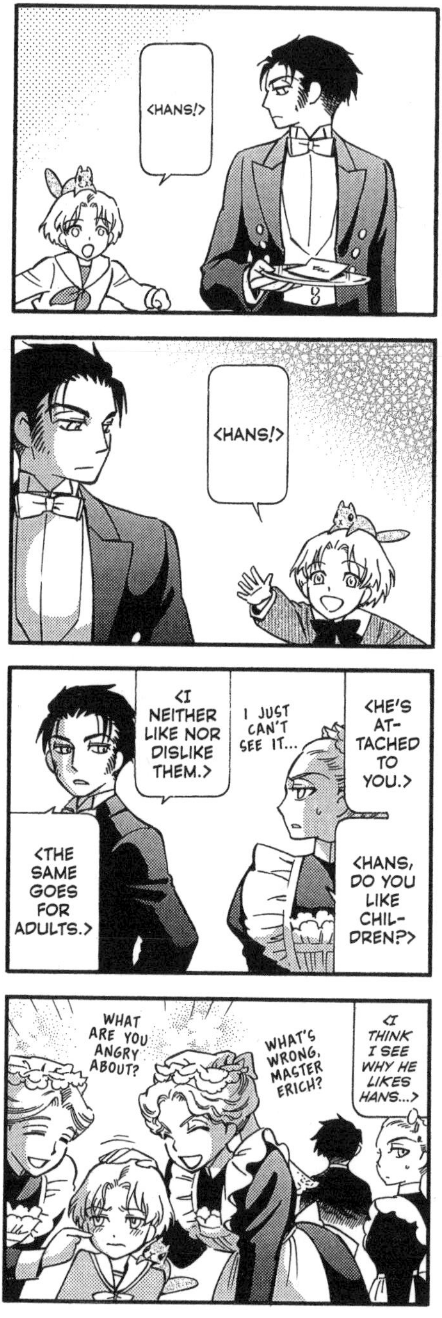
<HANS!>
<HANS!>
<HE'S ATTACHED TO YOU.>
I JUST CAN'T SEE IT...
<I NEITHER LIKE NOR DISLIKE THEM.>
<HANS, DO YOU LIKE CHILDREN?>
<THE SAME GOES FOR ADULTS.>
<I THINK I SEE WHY HE LIKES HANS...>
WHAT'S WRONG, MASTER ERICH?
WHAT ARE YOU ANGRY ABOUT?

Insurance

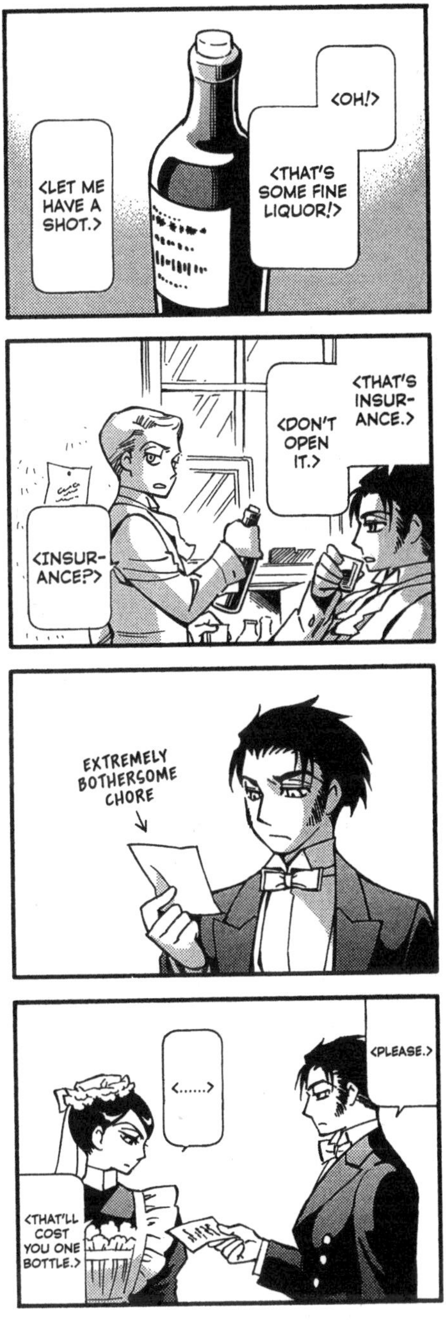

<OH!>
<THAT'S SOME FINE LIQUOR!>
<LET ME HAVE A SHOT.>
<THAT'S INSURANCE.>
<DON'T OPEN IT.>
<INSURANCE?>
EXTREMELY BOTHERSOME CHORE
<PLEASE.>
<......>
<THAT'LL COST YOU ONE BOTTLE.>

Nothing

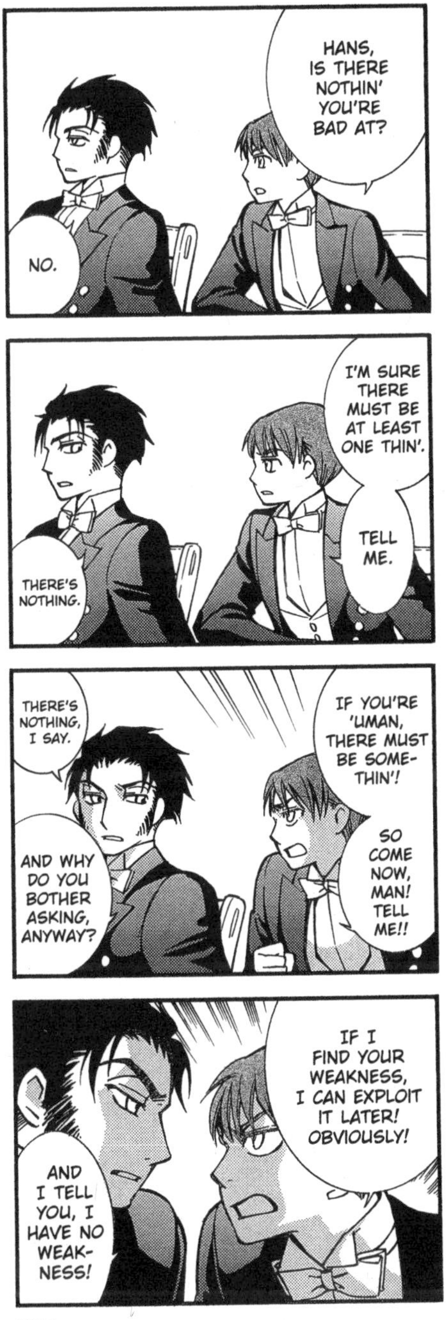

HANS, IS THERE NOTHIN' YOU'RE BAD AT?
NO.
I'M SURE THERE MUST BE AT LEAST ONE THIN'.
TELL ME.
THERE'S NOTHING.
IF YOU'RE 'UMAN, THERE MUST BE SOMETHIN'!
THERE'S NOTHING, I SAY.
SO COME NOW, MAN! TELL ME!!
AND WHY DO YOU BOTHER ASKING, ANYWAY?
IF I FIND YOUR WEAKNESS, I CAN EXPLOIT IT LATER! OBVIOUSLY!
AND I TELL YOU, I HAVE NO WEAKNESS!

Tell Me

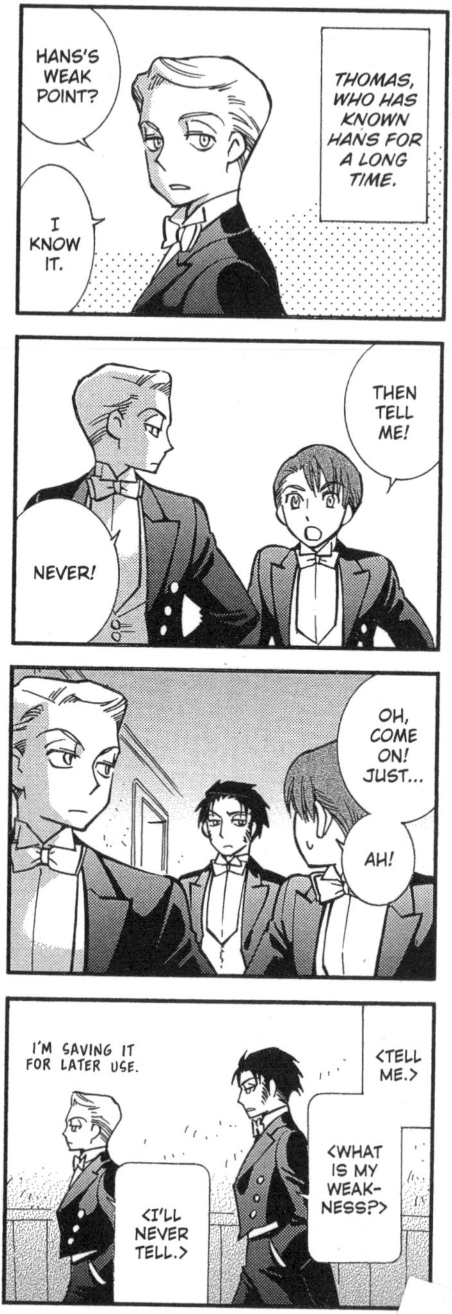
THOMAS, WHO HAS KNOWN HANS FOR A LONG TIME.
HANS'S WEAK POINT?
I KNOW IT.
THEN TELL ME!
NEVER!
OH, COME ON! JUST...
AH!
<TELL ME.>
<WHAT IS MY WEAKNESS?>
<I'LL NEVER TELL.>
I'M SAVING IT FOR LATER USE.

Weakness

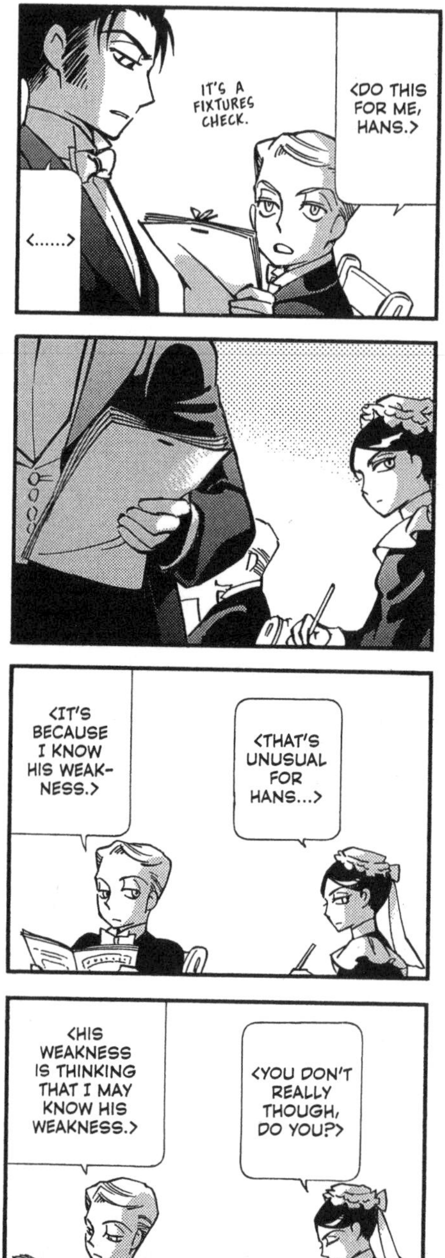
<DO THIS FOR ME, HANS.>
IT'S A FIXTURES CHECK.
<......>
<THAT'S UNUSUAL FOR HANS...>
<IT'S BECAUSE I KNOW HIS WEAKNESS.>
<YOU DON'T REALLY THOUGH, DO YOU?>
<HIS WEAKNESS IS THINKING THAT I MAY KNOW HIS WEAKNESS.>

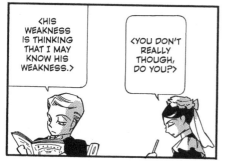

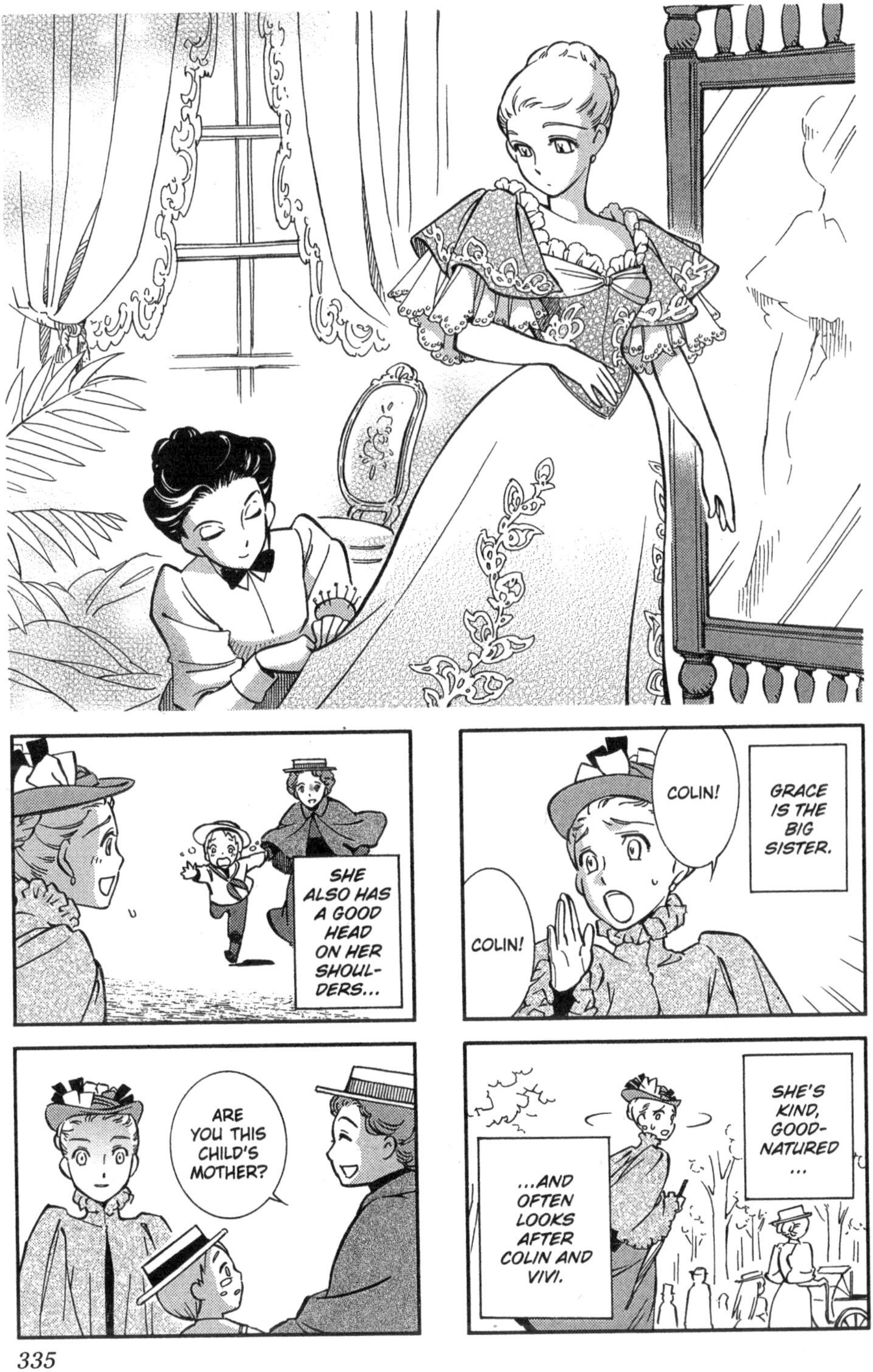
GRACE IS THE BIG SISTER.
COLIN!
COLIN!
SHE ALSO HAS A GOOD HEAD ON HER SHOUL-DERS...
SHE'S KIND, GOOD-NATURED ...
...AND OFTEN LOOKS AFTER COLIN AND VIVI.
ARE YOU THIS CHILD'S MOTHER?

Hairstyle

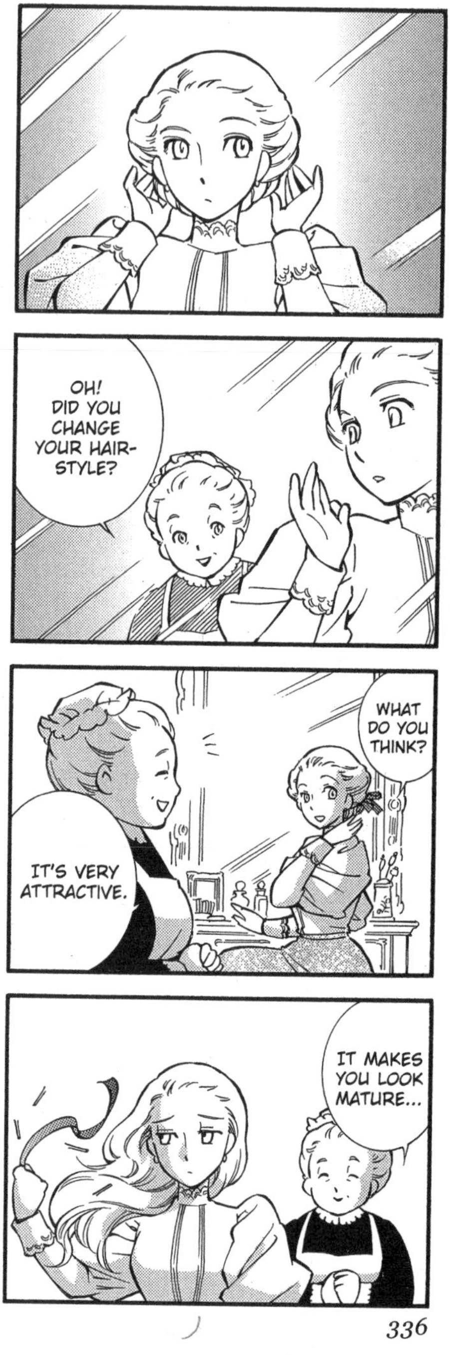

OH! DID YOU CHANGE YOUR HAIR-STYLE?
WHAT DO YOU THINK?
IT'S VERY ATTRACTIVE.
IT MAKES YOU LOOK MATURE...

Not the Way You Look

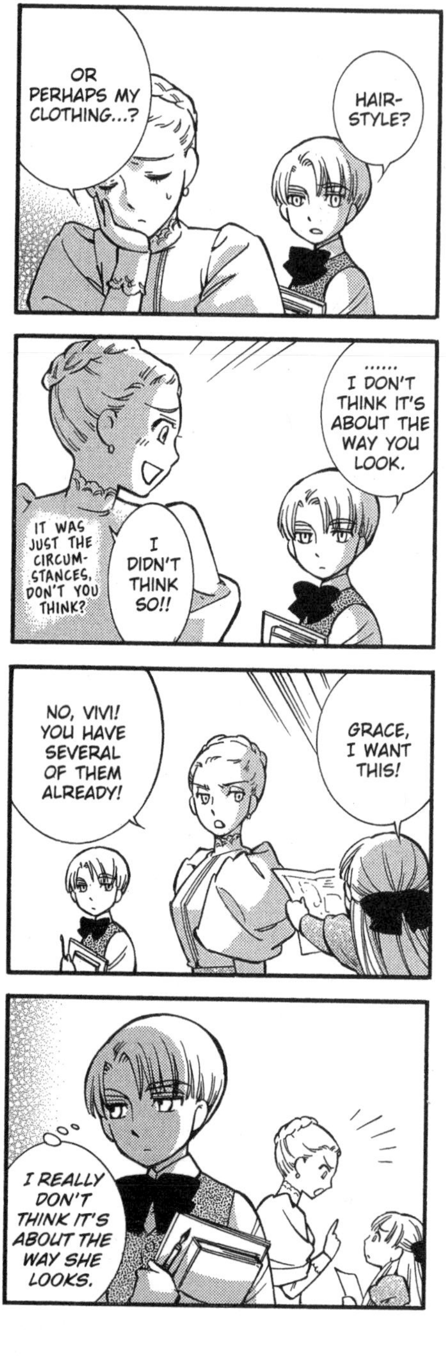

HAIR-STYLE?
OR PERHAPS MY CLOTHING...?
...... I DON'T THINK IT'S ABOUT THE WAY YOU LOOK.
I DIDN'T THINK SO!!
IT WAS JUST THE CIRCUM-STANCES, DON'T YOU THINK?
GRACE, I WANT THIS!
NO, VIVI! YOU HAVE SEVERAL OF THEM ALREADY!
I REALLY DON'T THINK IT'S ABOUT THE WAY SHE LOOKS.

Draw

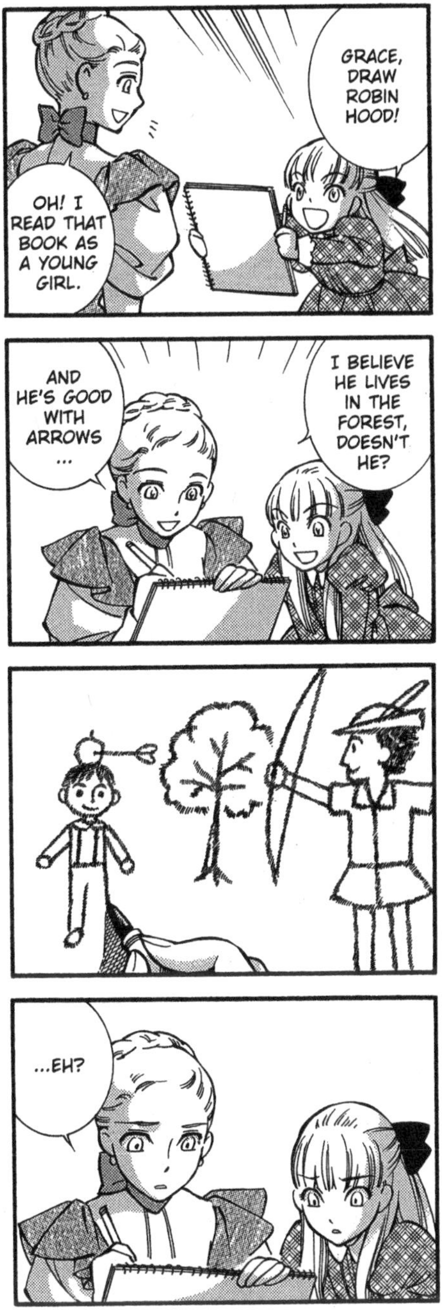
GRACE, DRAW ROBIN HOOD!
OH! I READ THAT BOOK AS A YOUNG GIRL.
I BELIEVE HE LIVES IN THE FOREST, DOESN'T HE?
AND HE'S GOOD WITH ARROWS ...
...EH?

Birdcage

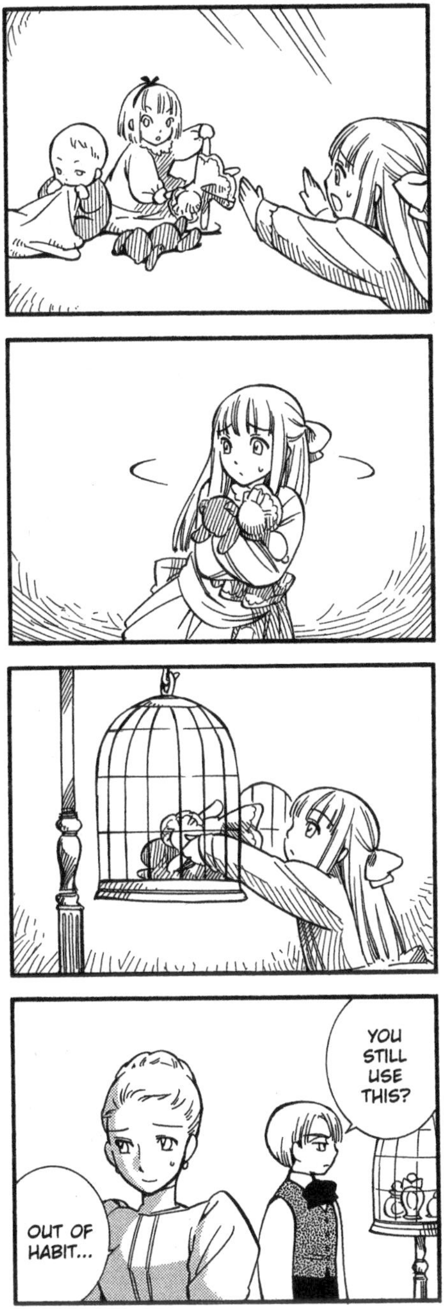
YOU STILL USE THIS?
OUT OF HABIT...

Eh?

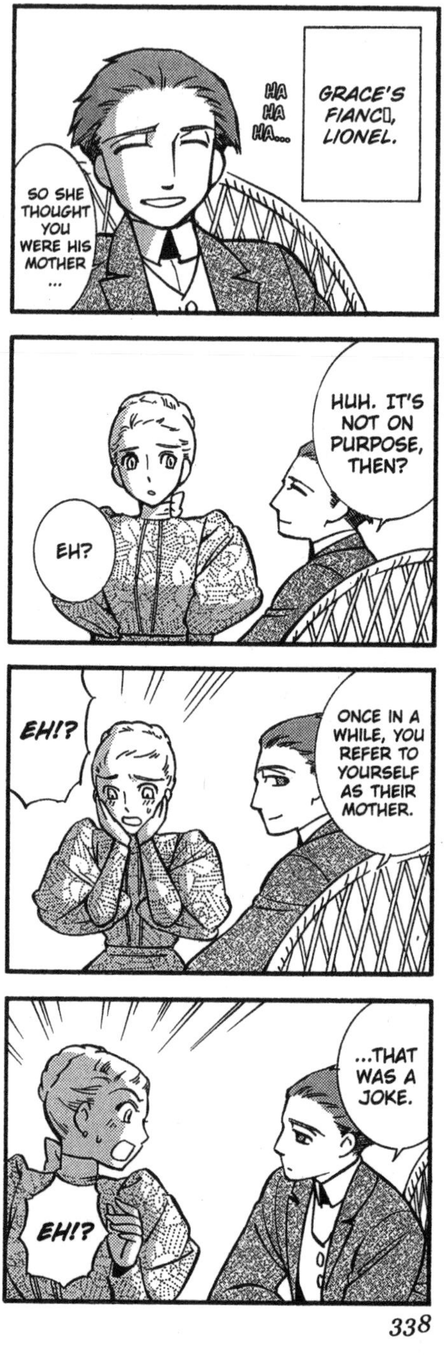
GRACE'S FIANC□, LIONEL.
HA HA HA...
SO SHE THOUGHT YOU WERE HIS MOTHER...
HUH. IT'S NOT ON PURPOSE, THEN?
EH?
ONCE IN A WHILE, YOU REFER TO YOURSELF AS THEIR MOTHER.
EH!?
...THAT WAS A JOKE.
EH!?

Why?

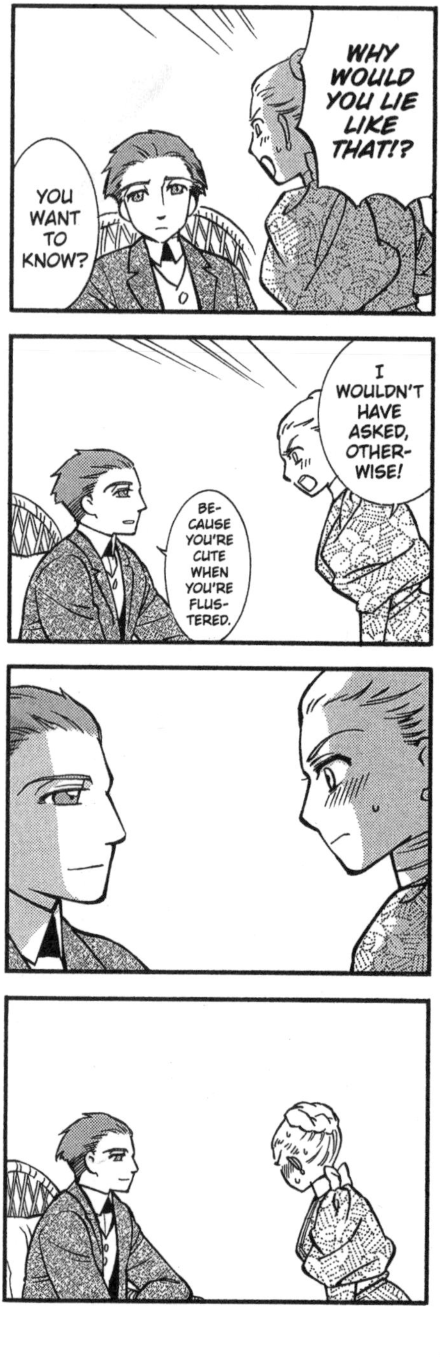
WHY WOULD YOU LIE LIKE THAT!?
YOU WANT TO KNOW?
I WOULDN'T HAVE ASKED, OTHER-WISE!
BE-CAUSE YOU'RE CUTE WHEN YOU'RE FLUS-TERED.

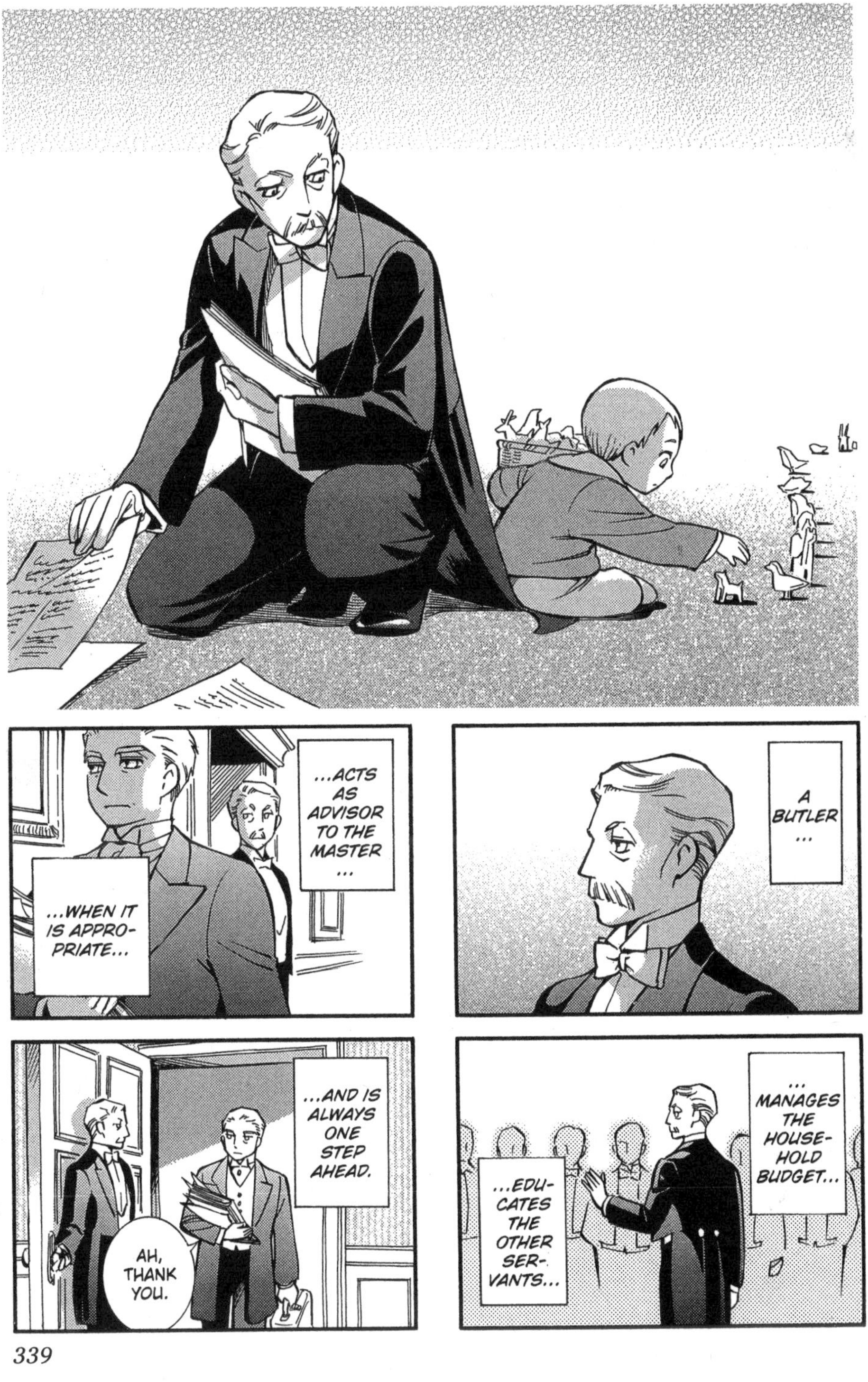
A BUTLER...
...ACTS AS ADVISOR TO THE MASTER...
...WHEN IT IS APPROPRIATE...
...MANAGES THE HOUSEHOLD BUDGET...
...EDUCATES THE OTHER SERVANTS...
...AND IS ALWAYS ONE STEP AHEAD.
AH, THANK YOU.

Chair

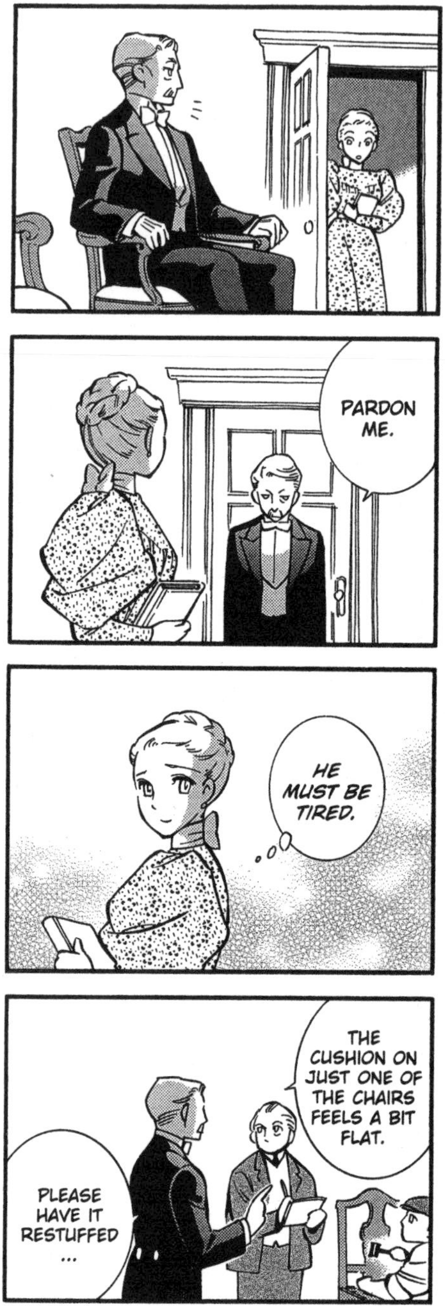
PARDON ME.
HE MUST BE TIRED.
THE CUSHION ON JUST ONE OF THE CHAIRS FEELS A BIT FLAT.
PLEASE HAVE IT RESTUFFED ...

Stevens

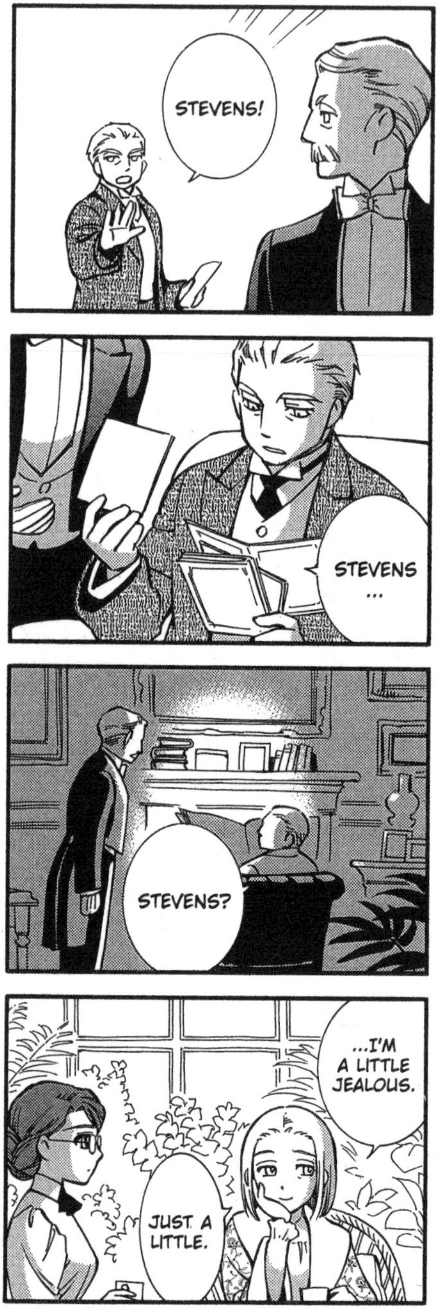
STEVENS!
STEVENS ...
STEVENS?
...I'M A LITTLE JEALOUS.
JUST A LITTLE.

Baby

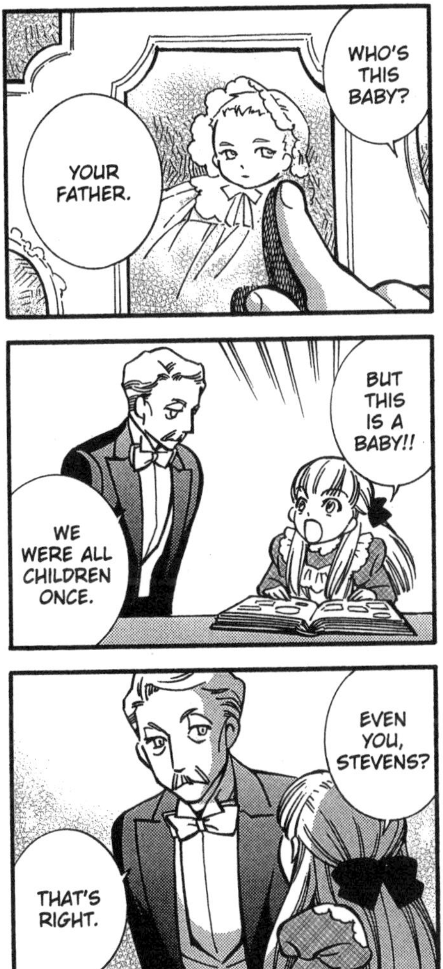
WHO'S THIS BABY?
YOUR FATHER.
BUT THIS IS A BABY!!
WE WERE ALL CHILDREN ONCE.
EVEN YOU, STEVENS?
THAT'S RIGHT.
WHERE!?
I DON'T SEE ANY CHILDREN WITH MOUS-TACHES IN HERE!!
BARA (FLIPP)
バラ
BARA
バラ
バラ
BARA
BOYS CAN GROW MOUS-TACHES WHEN THEY BECOME ADULTS.

Drawing

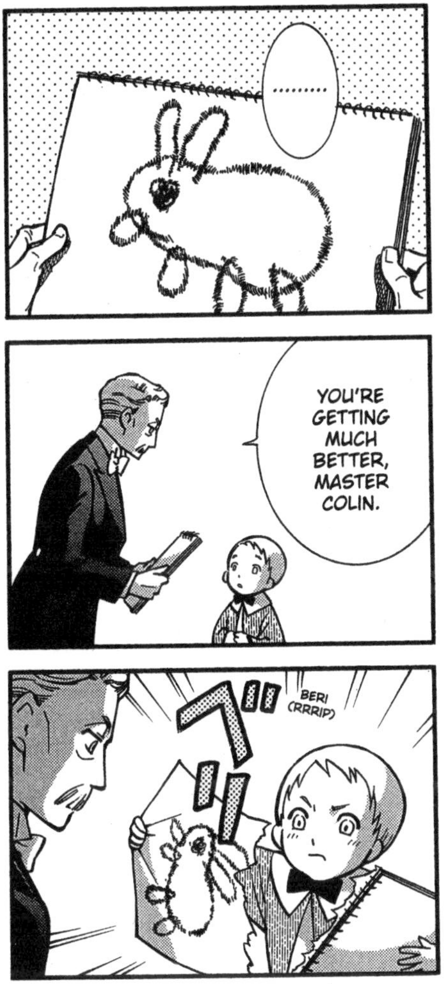
......
YOU'RE GETTING MUCH BETTER, MASTER COLIN.
ベリ
BERI (RRRIP)
...YOU'RE GIVING IT TO ME?

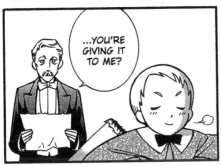

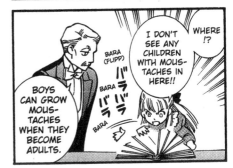

Drawing, Later

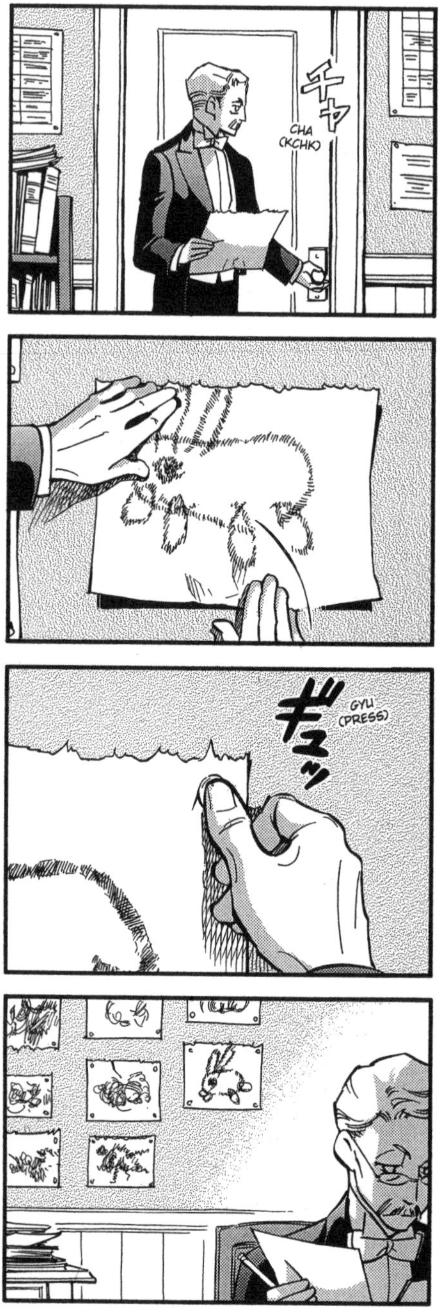
チャ
CHA (KCHK)
ギュッ
GYU (PRESS)

And Then...

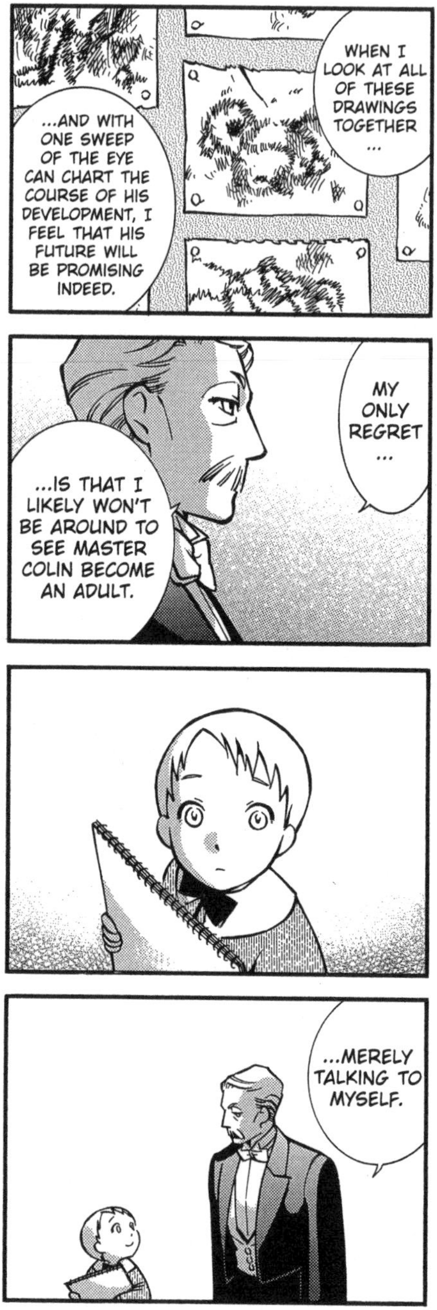
WHEN I LOOK AT ALL OF THESE DRAWINGS TOGETHER ...
...AND WITH ONE SWEEP OF THE EYE CAN CHART THE COURSE OF HIS DEVELOPMENT, I FEEL THAT HIS FUTURE WILL BE PROMISING INDEED.
MY ONLY REGRET ...
...IS THAT I LIKELY WON'T BE AROUND TO SEE MASTER COLIN BECOME AN ADULT.
...MERELY TALKING TO MYSELF.

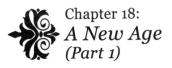

Chapter 18:
A New Age
(Part 1)

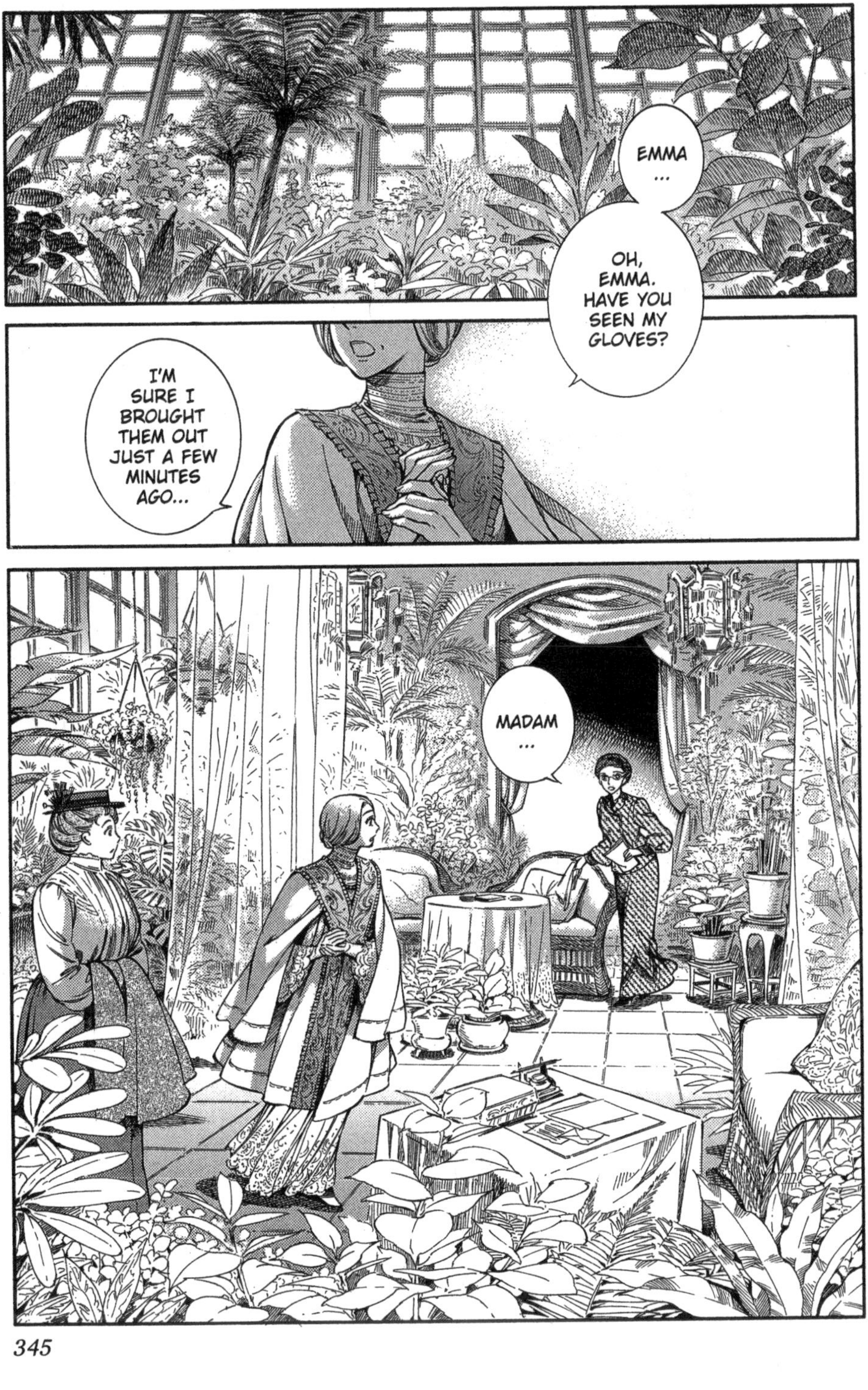
EMMA...
OH, EMMA. HAVE YOU SEEN MY GLOVES?
I'M SURE I BROUGHT THEM OUT JUST A FEW MINUTES AGO...
MADAM...

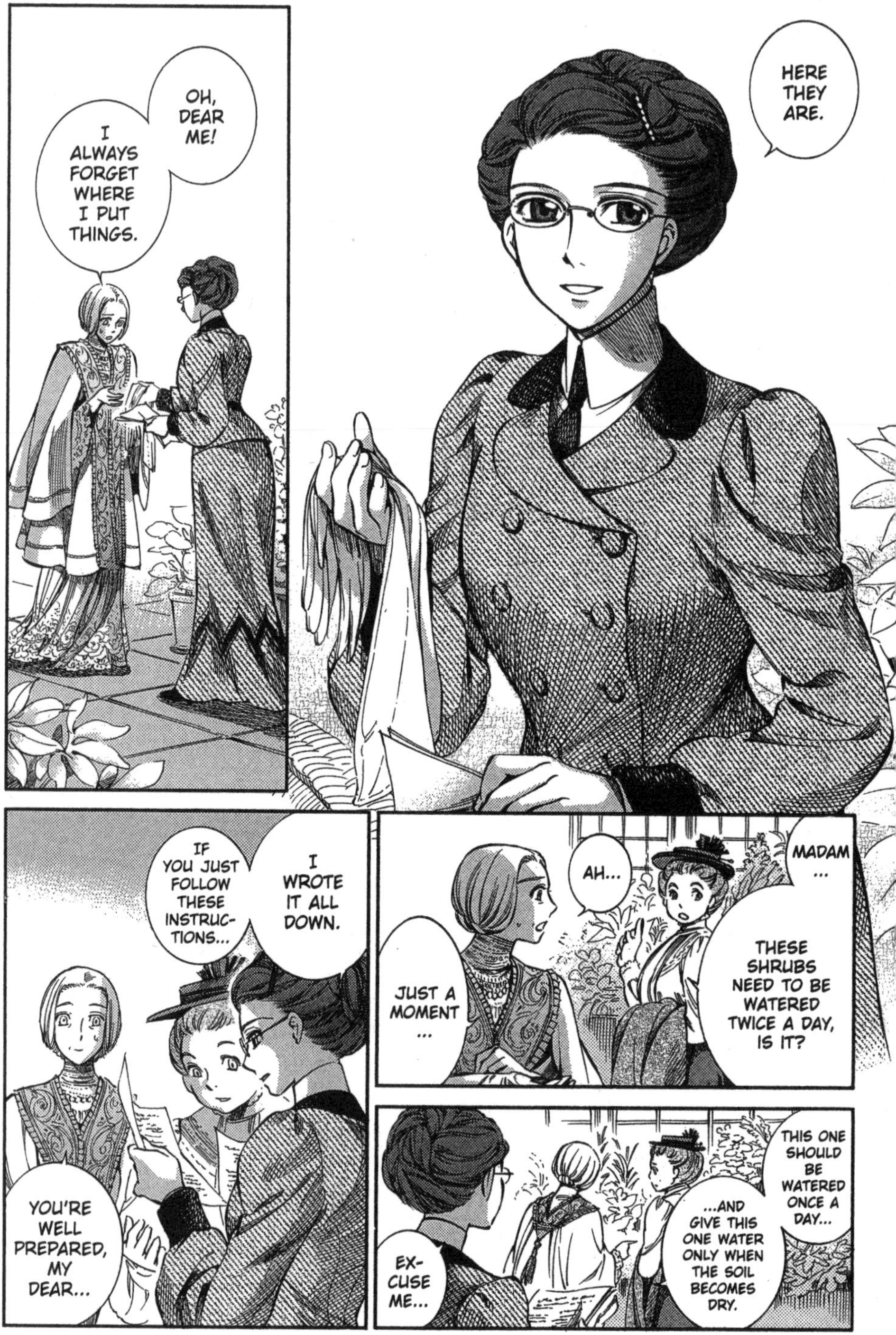
HERE THEY ARE.
OH, DEAR ME!
I ALWAYS FORGET WHERE I PUT THINGS.
MADAM ...
THESE SHRUBS NEED TO BE WATERED TWICE A DAY, IS IT?
AH...
JUST A MOMENT ...
THIS ONE SHOULD BE WATERED ONCE A DAY...
...AND GIVE THIS ONE WATER ONLY WHEN THE SOIL BECOMES DRY.
EX-CUSE ME...
I WROTE IT ALL DOWN.
IF YOU JUST FOLLOW THESE INSTRUC-TIONS...
YOU'RE WELL PREPARED, MY DEAR...

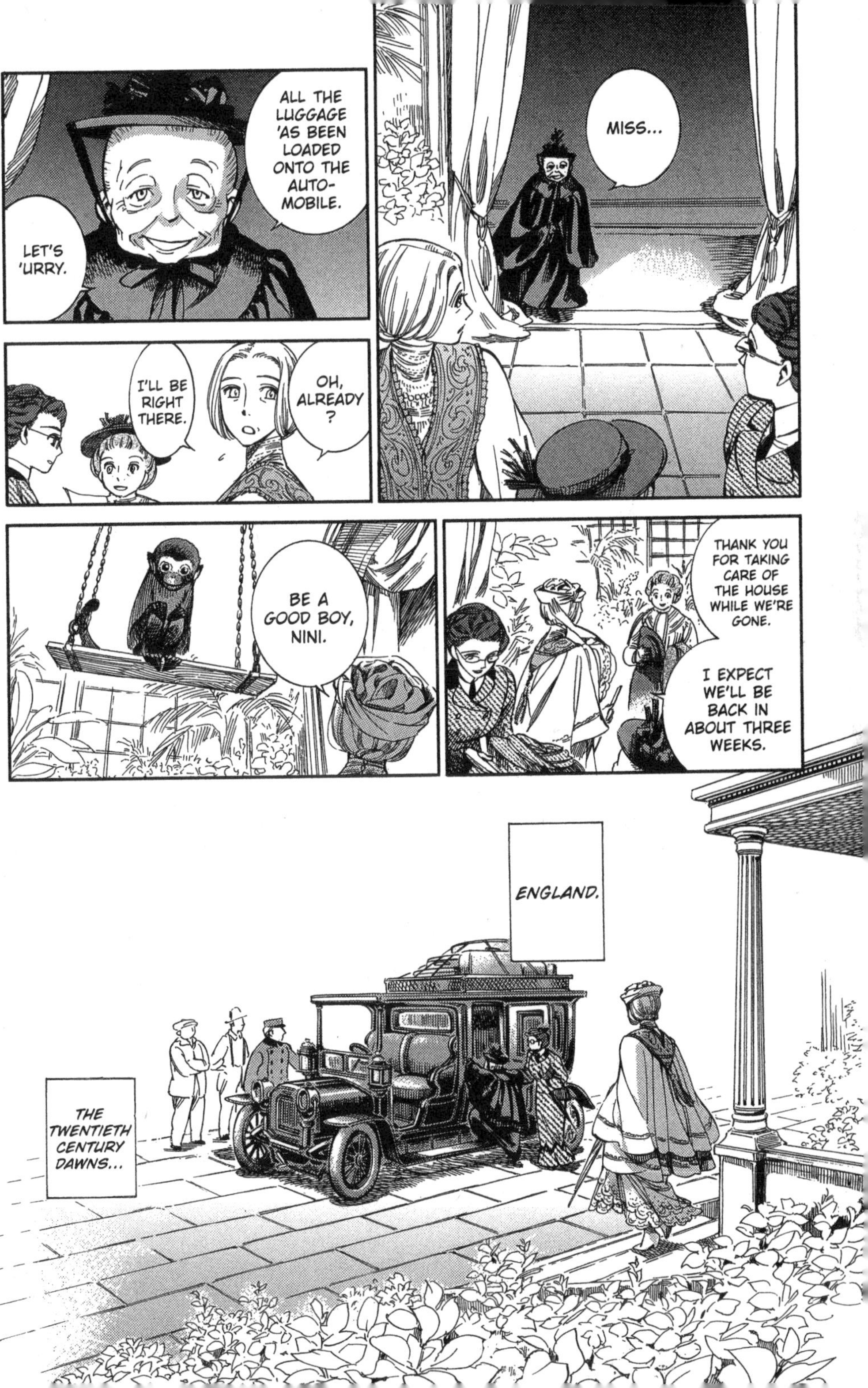
MISS...
ALL THE LUGGAGE 'AS BEEN LOADED ONTO THE AUTO-MOBILE.
LET'S 'URRY.
OH, ALREADY?
I'LL BE RIGHT THERE.
THANK YOU FOR TAKING CARE OF THE HOUSE WHILE WE'RE GONE.
I EXPECT WE'LL BE BACK IN ABOUT THREE WEEKS.
BE A GOOD BOY, NINI.
ENGLAND.
THE TWENTIETH CENTURY DAWNS...

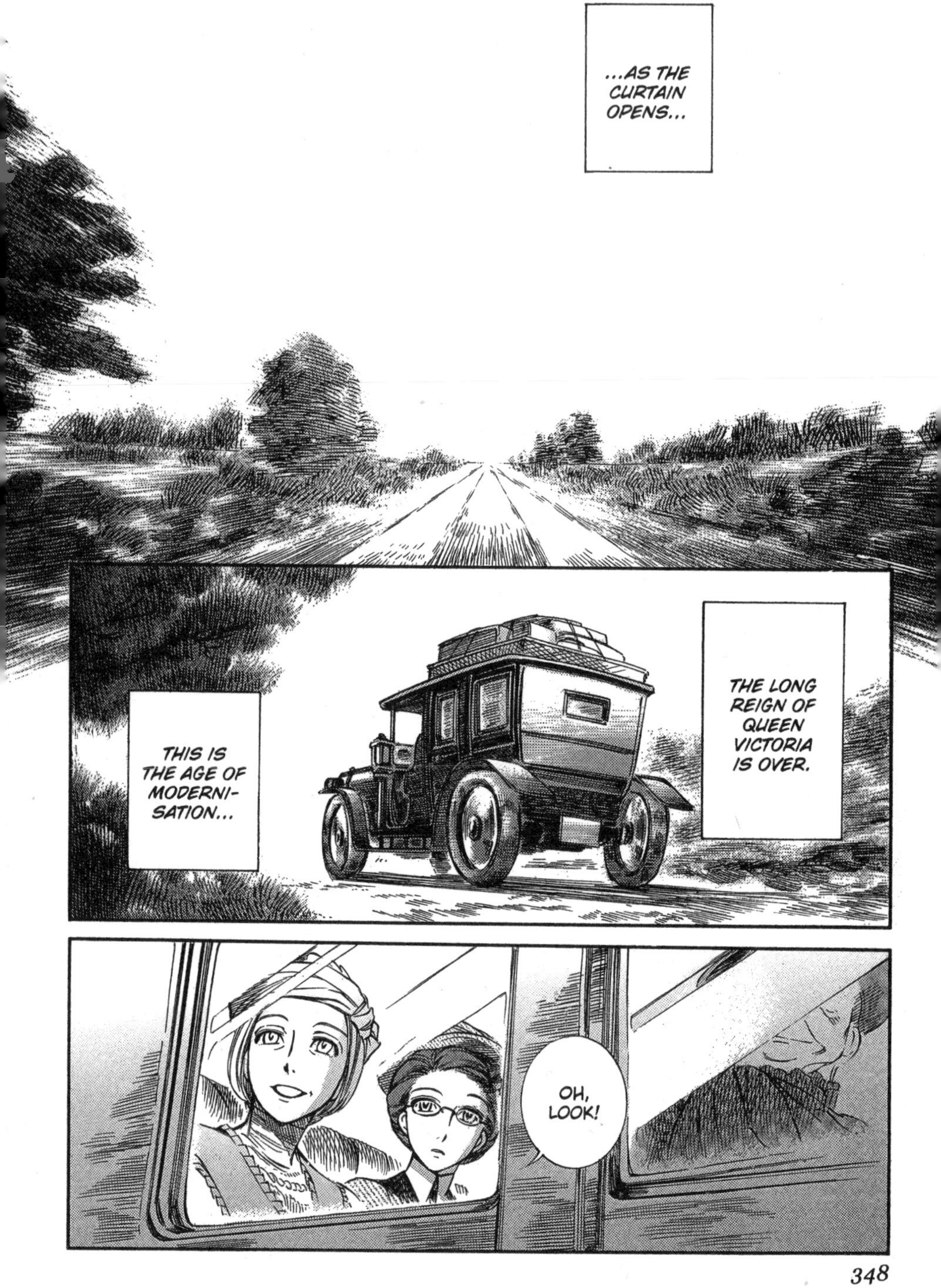
...AS THE CURTAIN OPENS...
THE LONG REIGN OF QUEEN VICTORIA IS OVER.
THIS IS THE AGE OF MODERNI-SATION...
OH, LOOK!

Chapter 18: *A New Age* (Part 1)

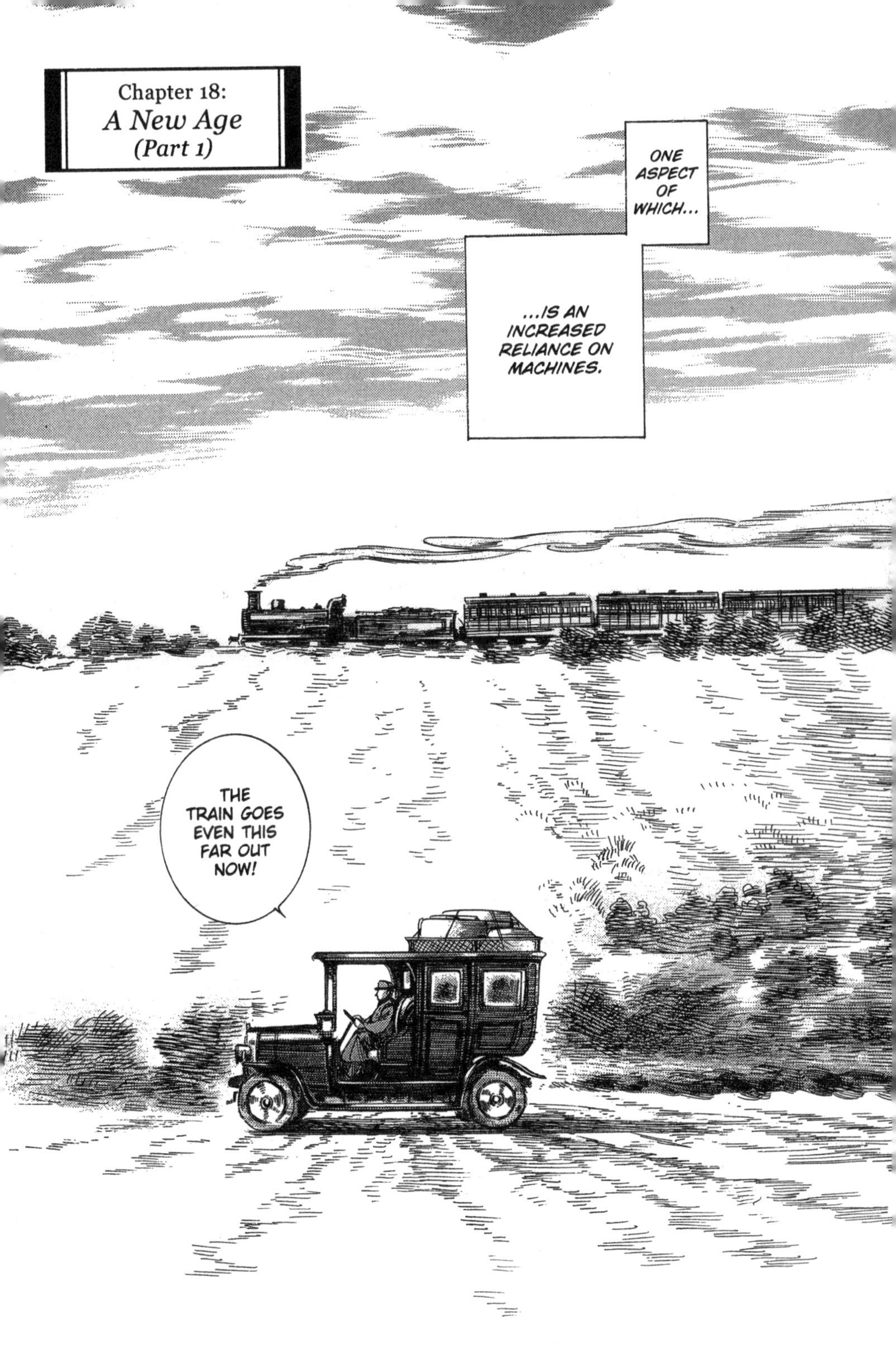
ONE ASPECT OF WHICH...
...IS AN INCREASED RELIANCE ON MACHINES.
THE TRAIN GOES EVEN THIS FAR OUT NOW!

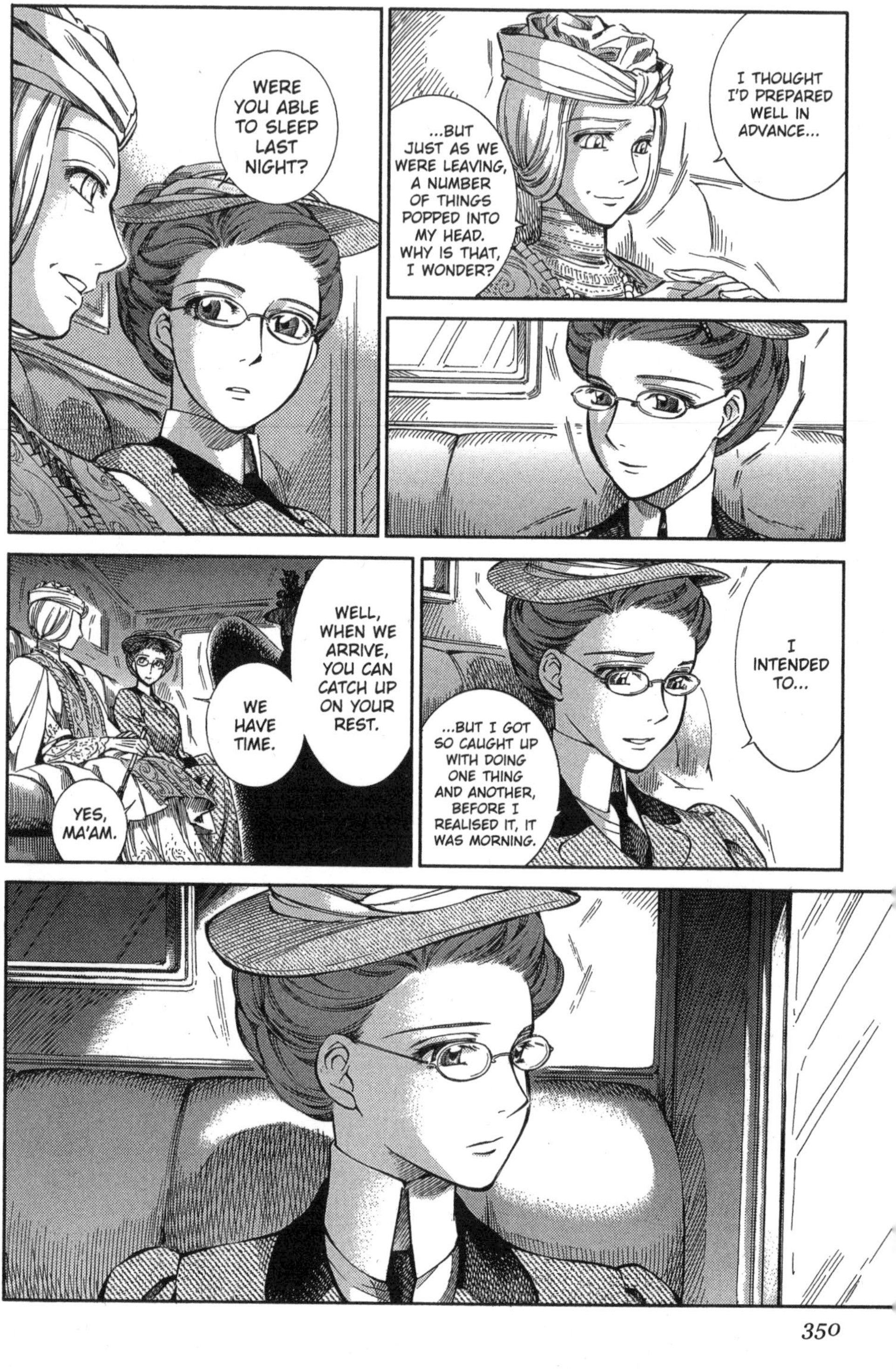
I THOUGHT I'D PREPARED WELL IN ADVANCE...
...BUT JUST AS WE WERE LEAVING, A NUMBER OF THINGS POPPED INTO MY HEAD. WHY IS THAT, I WONDER?
WERE YOU ABLE TO SLEEP LAST NIGHT?
I INTENDED TO...
...BUT I GOT SO CAUGHT UP WITH DOING ONE THING AND ANOTHER, BEFORE I REALISED IT, IT WAS MORNING.
WELL, WHEN WE ARRIVE, YOU CAN CATCH UP ON YOUR REST.
WE HAVE TIME.
YES, MA'AM.

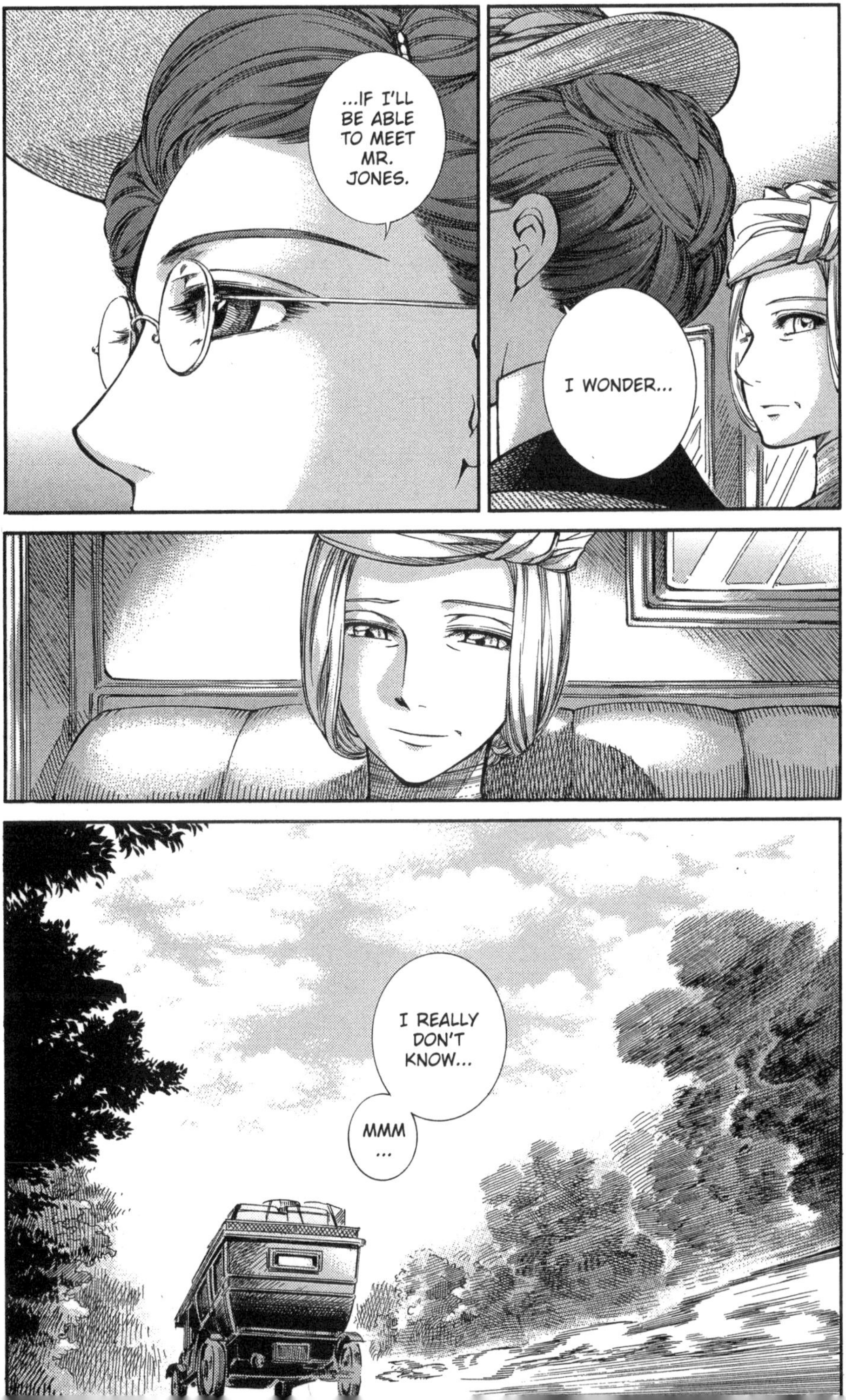
I WONDER...
...IF I'LL BE ABLE TO MEET MR. JONES.
I REALLY DON'T KNOW...
MMM ...

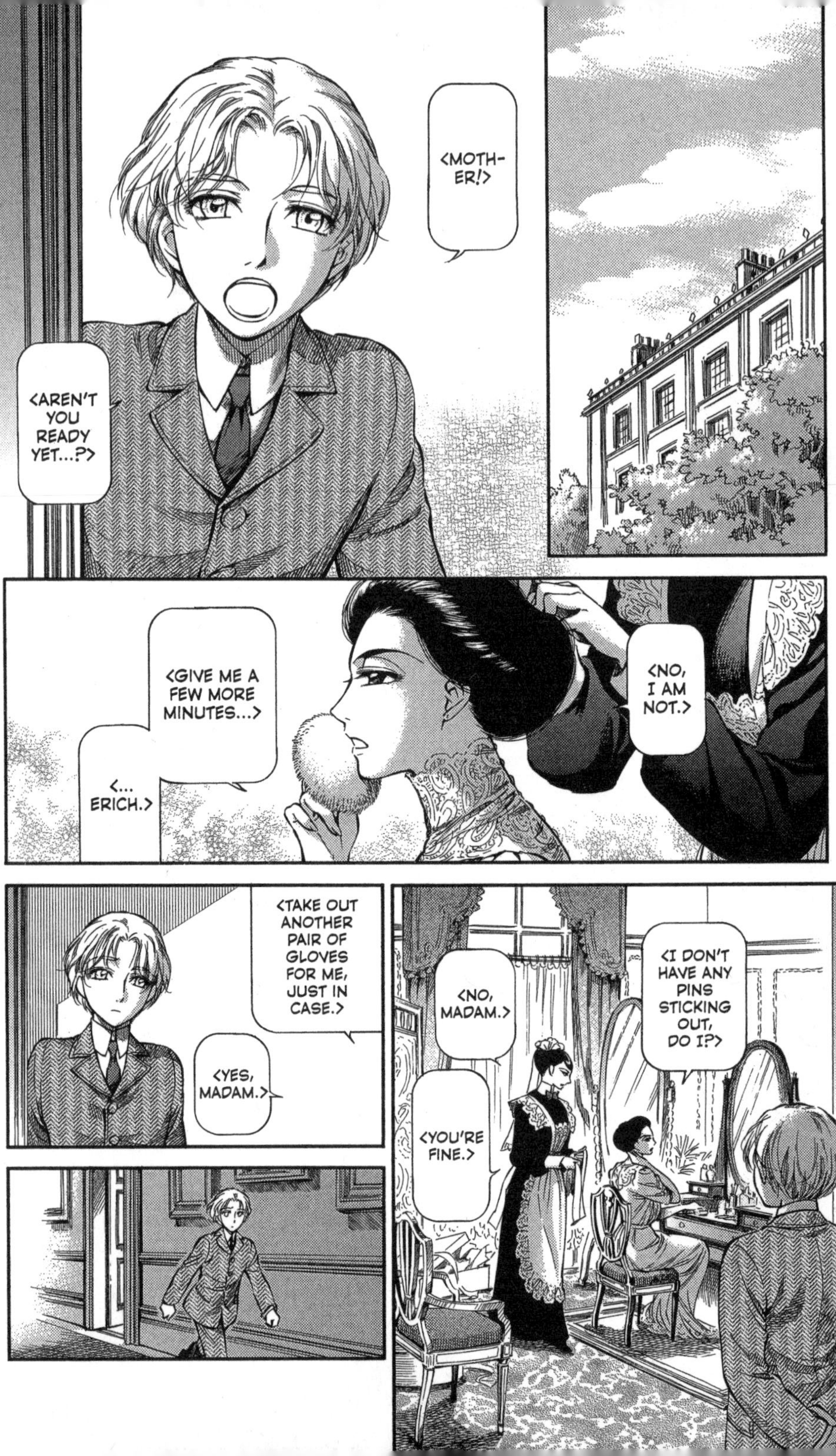
<MOTH-ER!>
<AREN'T YOU READY YET...?>
<NO, I AM NOT.>
<GIVE ME A FEW MORE MINUTES...>
<... ERICH.>
<I DON'T HAVE ANY PINS STICKING OUT, DO I?>
<NO, MADAM.>
<YOU'RE FINE.>
<TAKE OUT ANOTHER PAIR OF GLOVES FOR ME, JUST IN CASE.>
<YES, MADAM.>

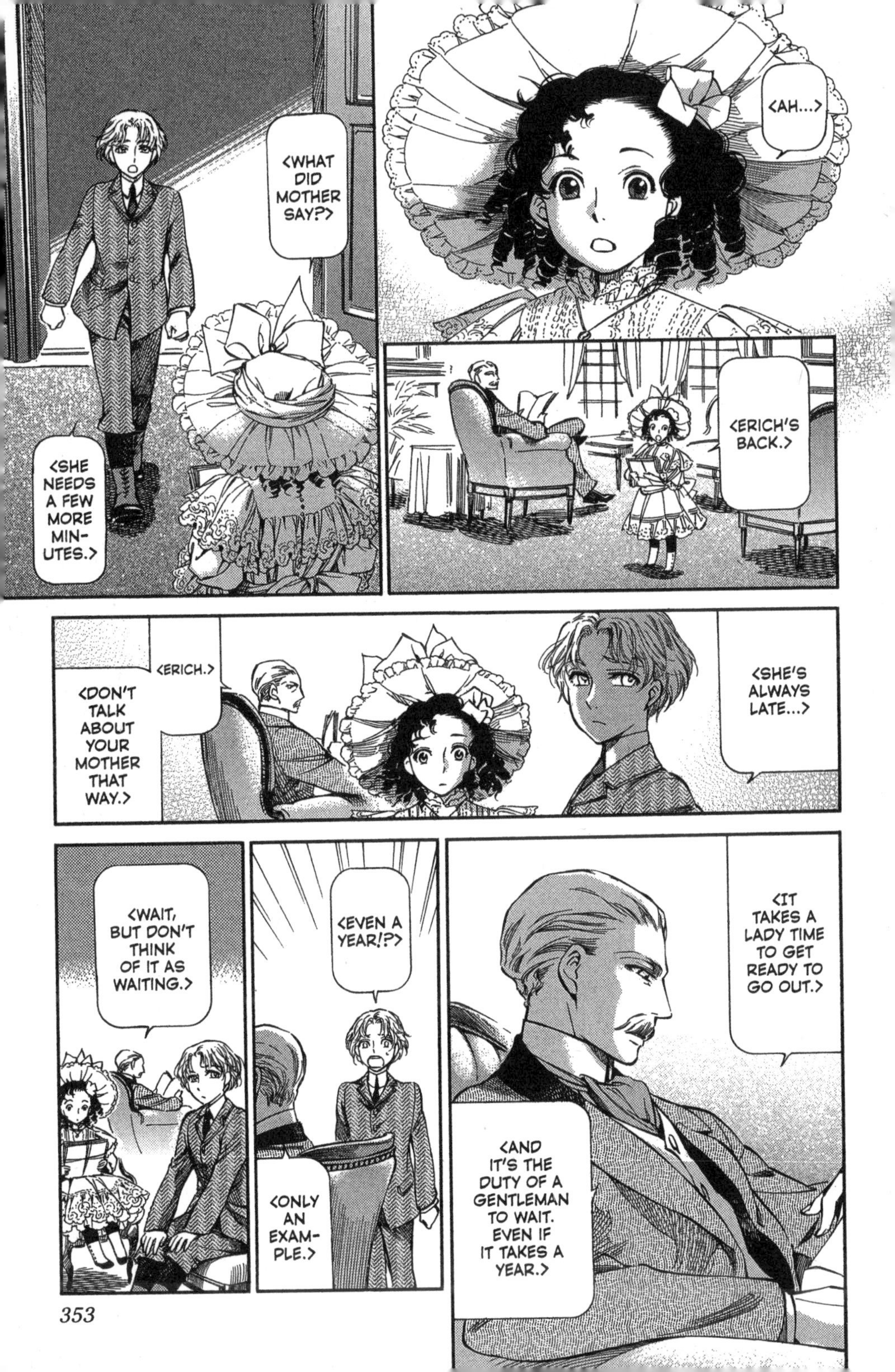
<AH...>
<ERICH'S BACK.>
<WHAT DID MOTHER SAY?>
<SHE NEEDS A FEW MORE MIN-UTES.>
<SHE'S ALWAYS LATE...>
<ERICH.>
<DON'T TALK ABOUT YOUR MOTHER THAT WAY.>
<IT TAKES A LADY TIME TO GET READY TO GO OUT.>
<AND IT'S THE DUTY OF A GENTLEMAN TO WAIT. EVEN IF IT TAKES A YEAR.>
<EVEN A YEAR!?>
<ONLY AN EXAMPLE.>
<WAIT, BUT DON'T THINK OF IT AS WAITING.>

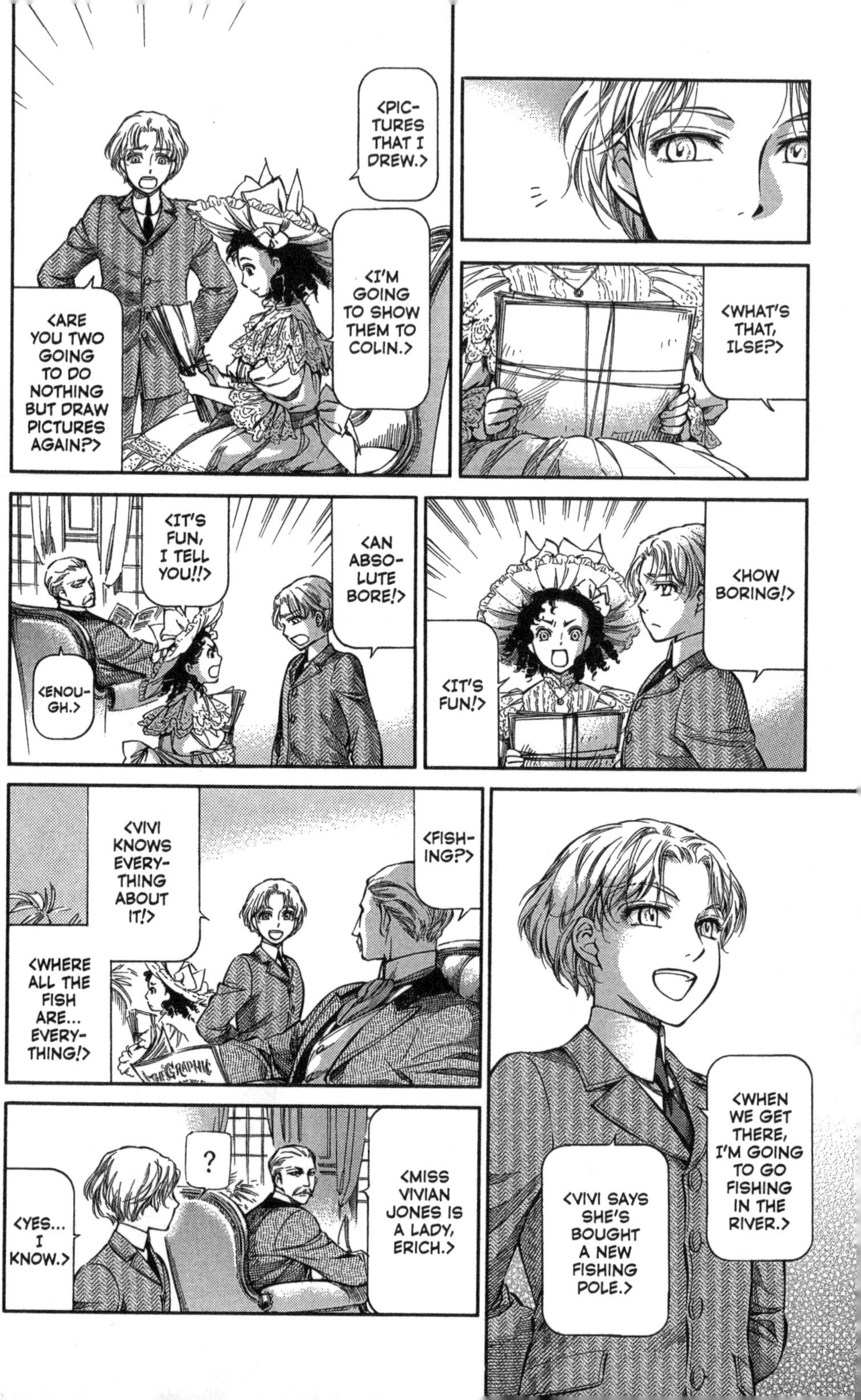
<WHAT'S THAT, ILSE?>
<PICTURES THAT I DREW.>
<I'M GOING TO SHOW THEM TO COLIN.>
<ARE YOU TWO GOING TO DO NOTHING BUT DRAW PICTURES AGAIN?>
<HOW BORING!>
<IT'S FUN!>
<AN ABSOLUTE BORE!>
<IT'S FUN, I TELL YOU!!>
<ENOUGH.>
<WHEN WE GET THERE, I'M GOING TO GO FISHING IN THE RIVER.>
<VIVI SAYS SHE'S BOUGHT A NEW FISHING POLE.>
<FISHING?>
<VIVI KNOWS EVERYTHING ABOUT IT!>
<WHERE ALL THE FISH ARE... EVERYTHING!>
THE GRAPHIC
<MISS VIVIAN JONES IS A LADY, ERICH.>
?
<YES... I KNOW.>

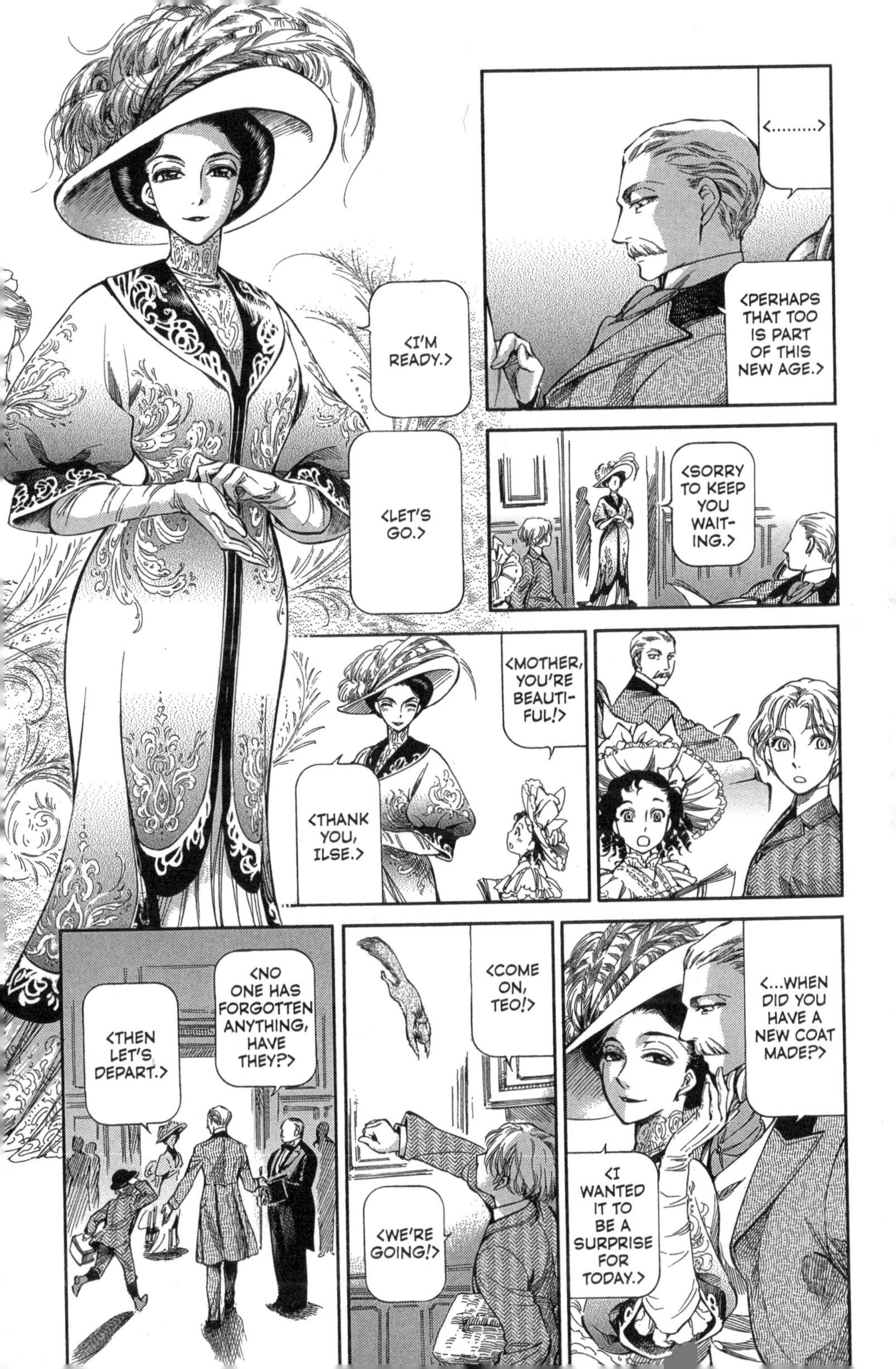
<.........>
<PERHAPS THAT TOO IS PART OF THIS NEW AGE.>
<SORRY TO KEEP YOU WAITING.>
<MOTHER, YOU'RE BEAUTIFUL!>
<THANK YOU, ILSE.>
<I'M READY.>
<LET'S GO.>
<...WHEN DID YOU HAVE A NEW COAT MADE?>
<I WANTED IT TO BE A SURPRISE FOR TODAY.>
<COME ON, TEO!>
<WE'RE GOING!>
<NO ONE HAS FORGOTTEN ANYTHING, HAVE THEY?>
<THEN LET'S DEPART.>

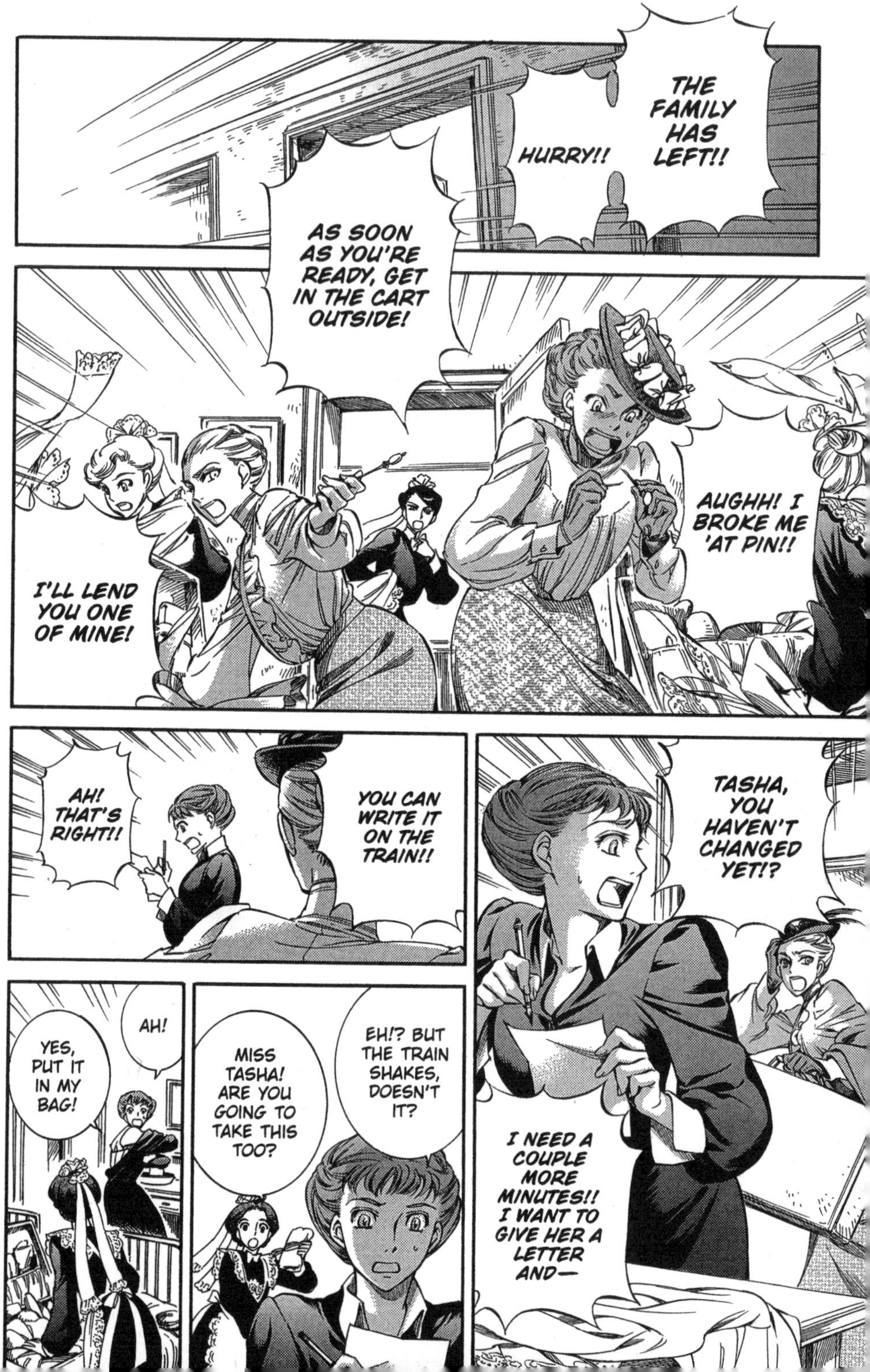
THE FAMILY HAS LEFT!!
HURRY!!
AS SOON AS YOU'RE READY, GET IN THE CART OUTSIDE!
AUGHH! I BROKE ME 'AT PIN!!
I'LL LEND YOU ONE OF MINE!
TASHA, YOU HAVEN'T CHANGED YET!?
I NEED A COUPLE MORE MINUTES!! I WANT TO GIVE HER A LETTER AND—
YOU CAN WRITE IT ON THE TRAIN!!
AH! THAT'S RIGHT!!
EH!? BUT THE TRAIN SHAKES, DOESN'T IT?
MISS TASHA! ARE YOU GOING TO TAKE THIS TOO?
AH!
YES, PUT IT IN MY BAG!

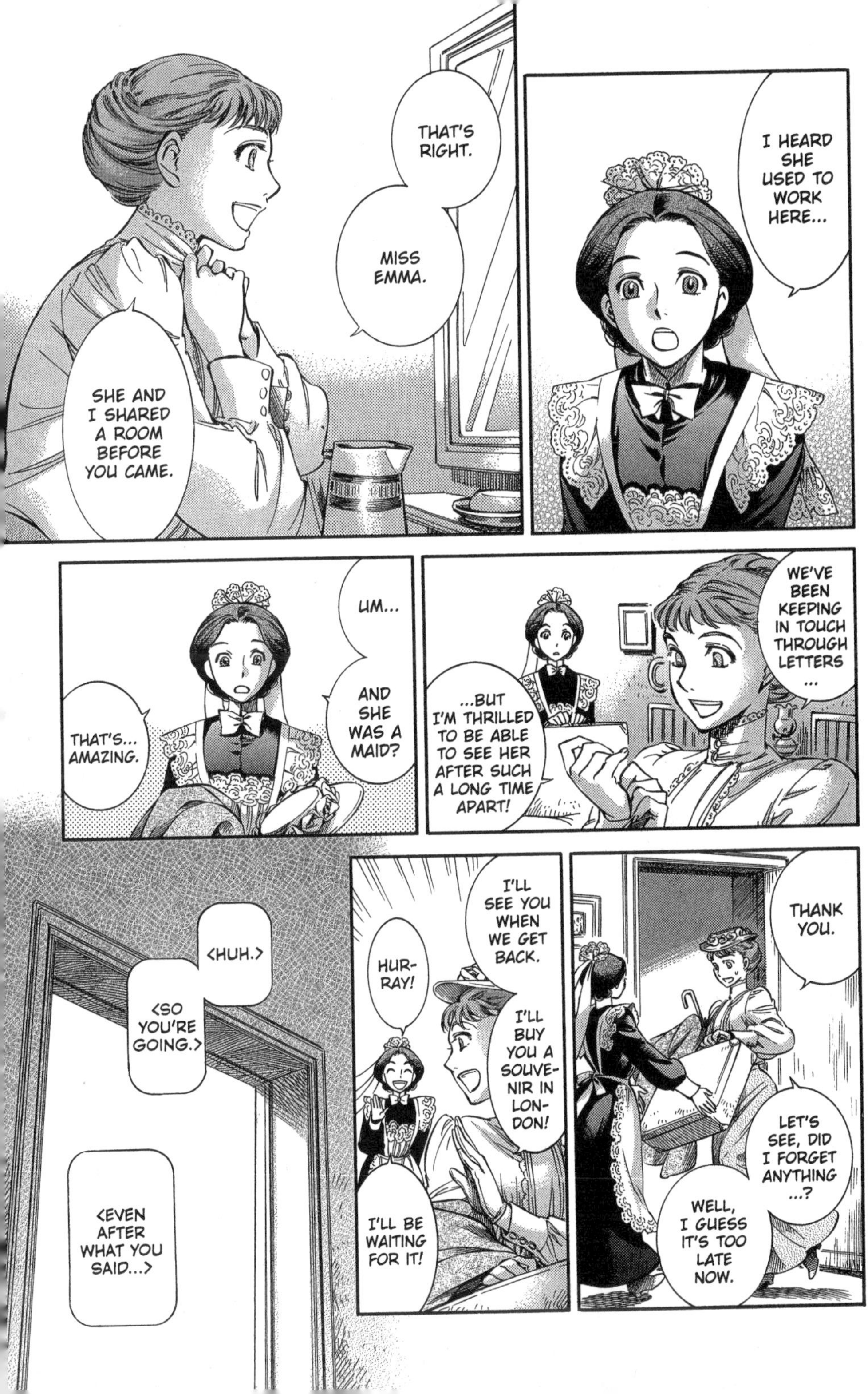
I HEARD SHE USED TO WORK HERE...
THAT'S RIGHT.
MISS EMMA.
SHE AND I SHARED A ROOM BEFORE YOU CAME.
WE'VE BEEN KEEPING IN TOUCH THROUGH LETTERS...
...BUT I'M THRILLED TO BE ABLE TO SEE HER AFTER SUCH A LONG TIME APART!
UM...
AND SHE WAS A MAID?
THAT'S... AMAZING.
THANK YOU.
LET'S SEE, DID I FORGET ANYTHING...?
WELL, I GUESS IT'S TOO LATE NOW.
I'LL SEE YOU WHEN WE GET BACK.
I'LL BUY YOU A SOUVENIR IN LONDON!
HUR-RAY!
I'LL BE WAITING FOR IT!
<HUH.>
<SO YOU'RE GOING.>
<EVEN AFTER WHAT YOU SAID...>

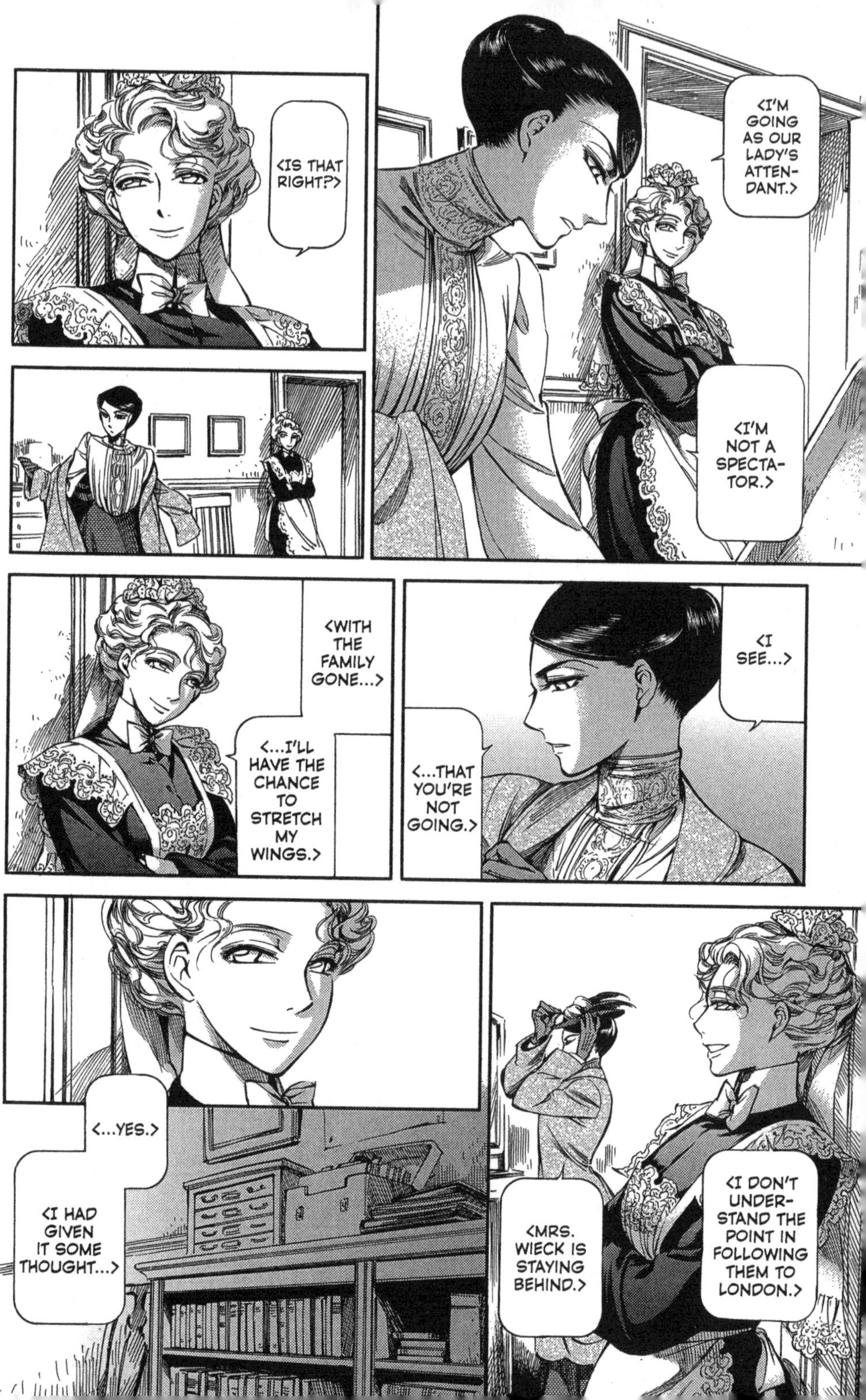
<I'M GOING AS OUR LADY'S ATTEN-DANT.>
<I'M NOT A SPECTA-TOR.>
<IS THAT RIGHT?>
<I SEE...>
<...THAT YOU'RE NOT GOING.>
<WITH THE FAMILY GONE...>
<...I'LL HAVE THE CHANCE TO STRETCH MY WINGS.>
<I DON'T UNDER-STAND THE POINT IN FOLLOWING THEM TO LONDON.>
<MRS. WIECK IS STAYING BEHIND.>
<...YES.>
<I HAD GIVEN IT SOME THOUGHT...>

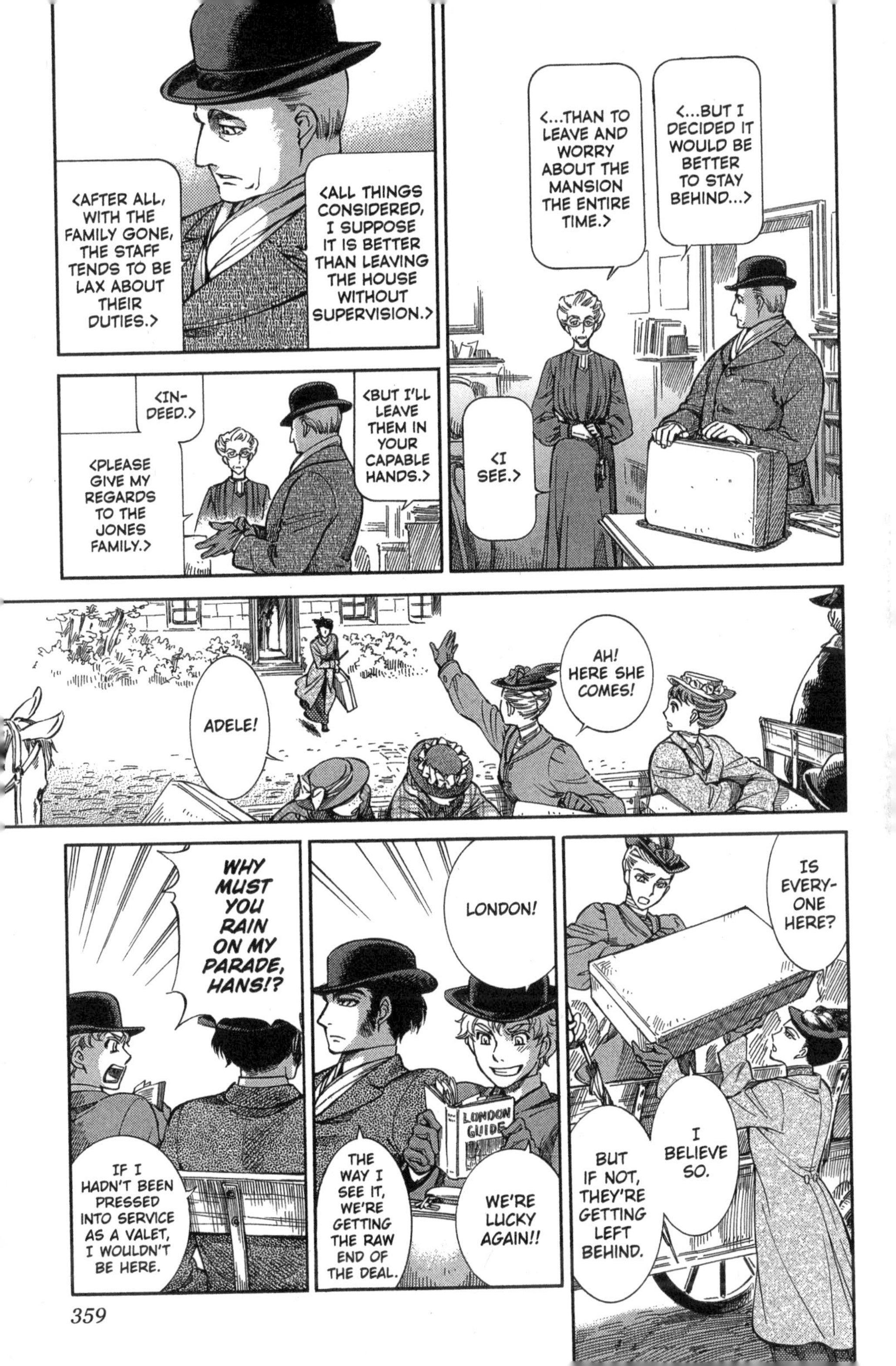

<...BUT I DECIDED IT WOULD BE BETTER TO STAY BEHIND...>
<...THAN TO LEAVE AND WORRY ABOUT THE MANSION THE ENTIRE TIME.>
<I SEE.>
<ALL THINGS CONSIDERED, I SUPPOSE IT IS BETTER THAN LEAVING THE HOUSE WITHOUT SUPERVISION.>
<AFTER ALL, WITH THE FAMILY GONE, THE STAFF TENDS TO BE LAX ABOUT THEIR DUTIES.>
<BUT I'LL LEAVE THEM IN YOUR CAPABLE HANDS.>
<IN-DEED.>
<PLEASE GIVE MY REGARDS TO THE JONES FAMILY.>
AH! HERE SHE COMES!
ADELE!
IS EVERY-ONE HERE?
I BELIEVE SO.
BUT IF NOT, THEY'RE GETTING LEFT BEHIND.
LONDON!
LONDON GUIDE
WE'RE LUCKY AGAIN!!
THE WAY I SEE IT, WE'RE GETTING THE RAW END OF THE DEAL.
WHY MUST YOU RAIN ON MY PARADE, HANS!?
IF I HADN'T BEEN PRESSED INTO SERVICE AS A VALET, I WOULDN'T BE HERE.

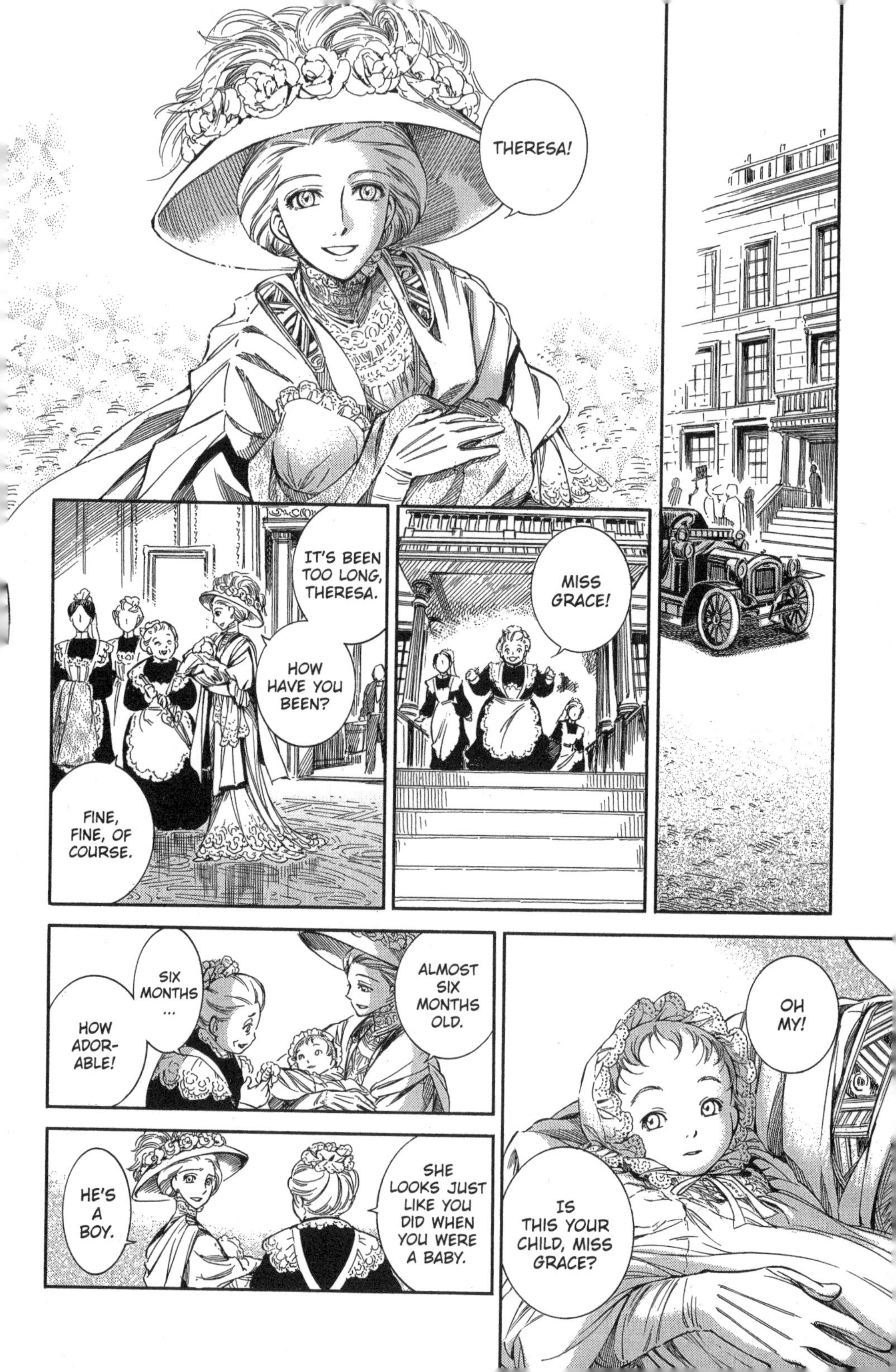
THERESA!
MISS GRACE!
IT'S BEEN TOO LONG, THERESA.
HOW HAVE YOU BEEN?
FINE, FINE, OF COURSE.
OH MY!
IS THIS YOUR CHILD, MISS GRACE?
ALMOST SIX MONTHS OLD.
SIX MONTHS ...
HOW ADORABLE!
SHE LOOKS JUST LIKE YOU DID WHEN YOU WERE A BABY.
HE'S A BOY.

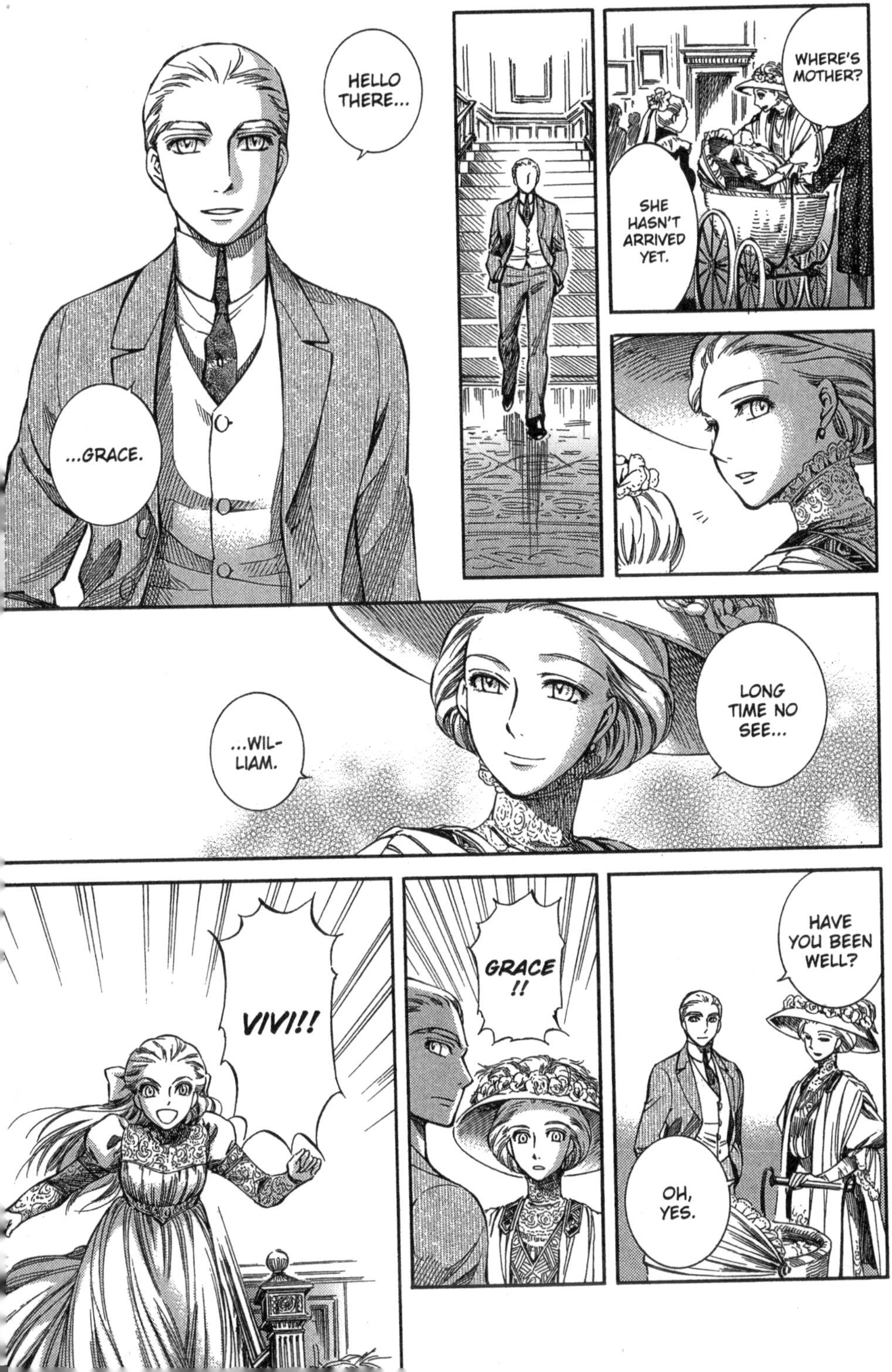
WHERE'S MOTHER?
SHE HASN'T ARRIVED YET.
HELLO THERE...
...GRACE.
LONG TIME NO SEE...
...WIL-LIAM.
HAVE YOU BEEN WELL?
OH, YES.
GRACE !!
VIVI!!

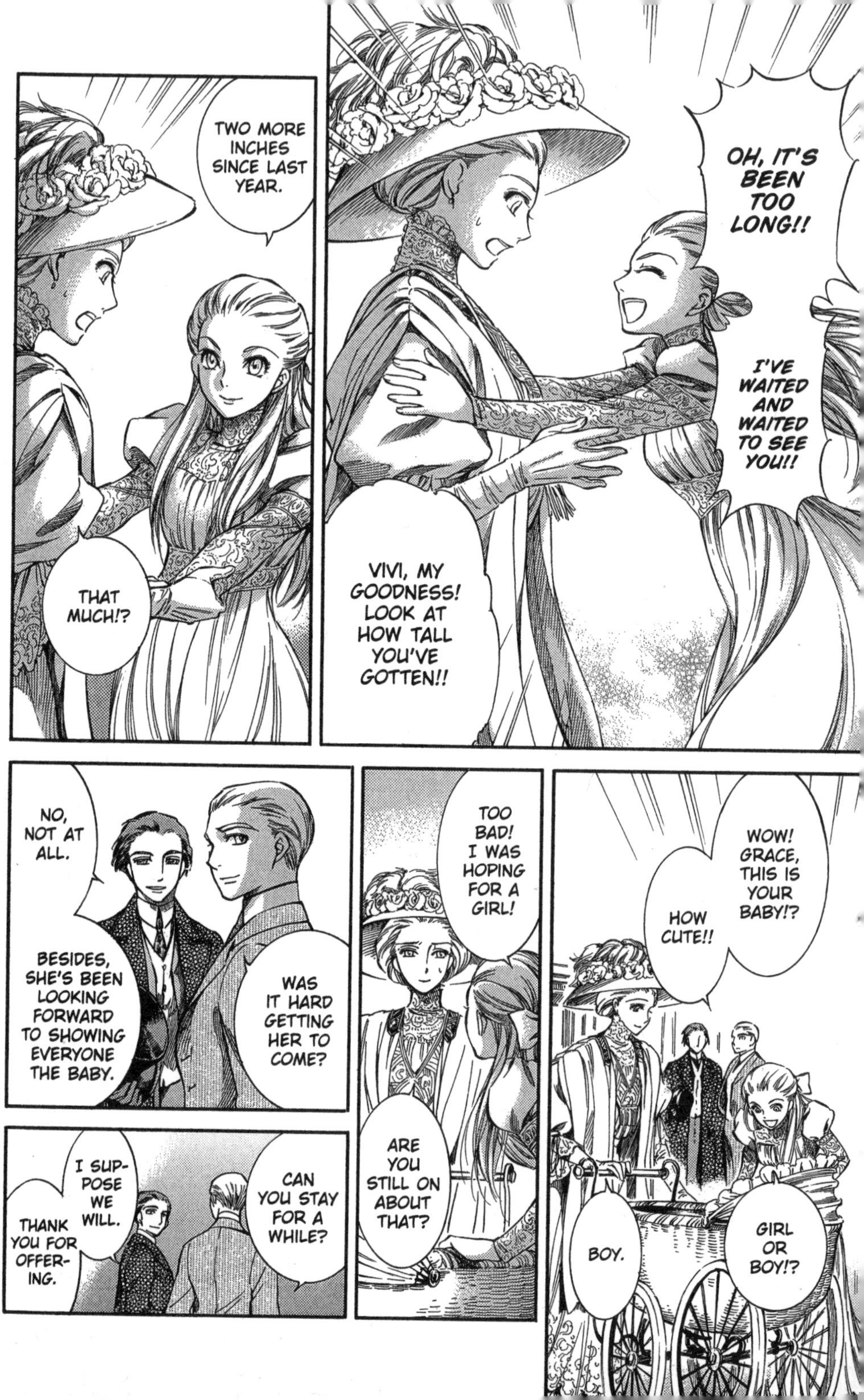
OH, IT'S BEEN TOO LONG!!
I'VE WAITED AND WAITED TO SEE YOU!!
VIVI, MY GOODNESS! LOOK AT HOW TALL YOU'VE GOTTEN!!
TWO MORE INCHES SINCE LAST YEAR.
THAT MUCH!?
WOW! GRACE, THIS IS YOUR BABY!?
HOW CUTE!!
GIRL OR BOY!?
BOY.
TOO BAD! I WAS HOPING FOR A GIRL!
ARE YOU STILL ON ABOUT THAT?
WAS IT HARD GETTING HER TO COME?
NO, NOT AT ALL.
BESIDES, SHE'S BEEN LOOKING FORWARD TO SHOWING EVERYONE THE BABY.
CAN YOU STAY FOR A WHILE?
I SUPPOSE WE WILL.
THANK YOU FOR OFFERING.

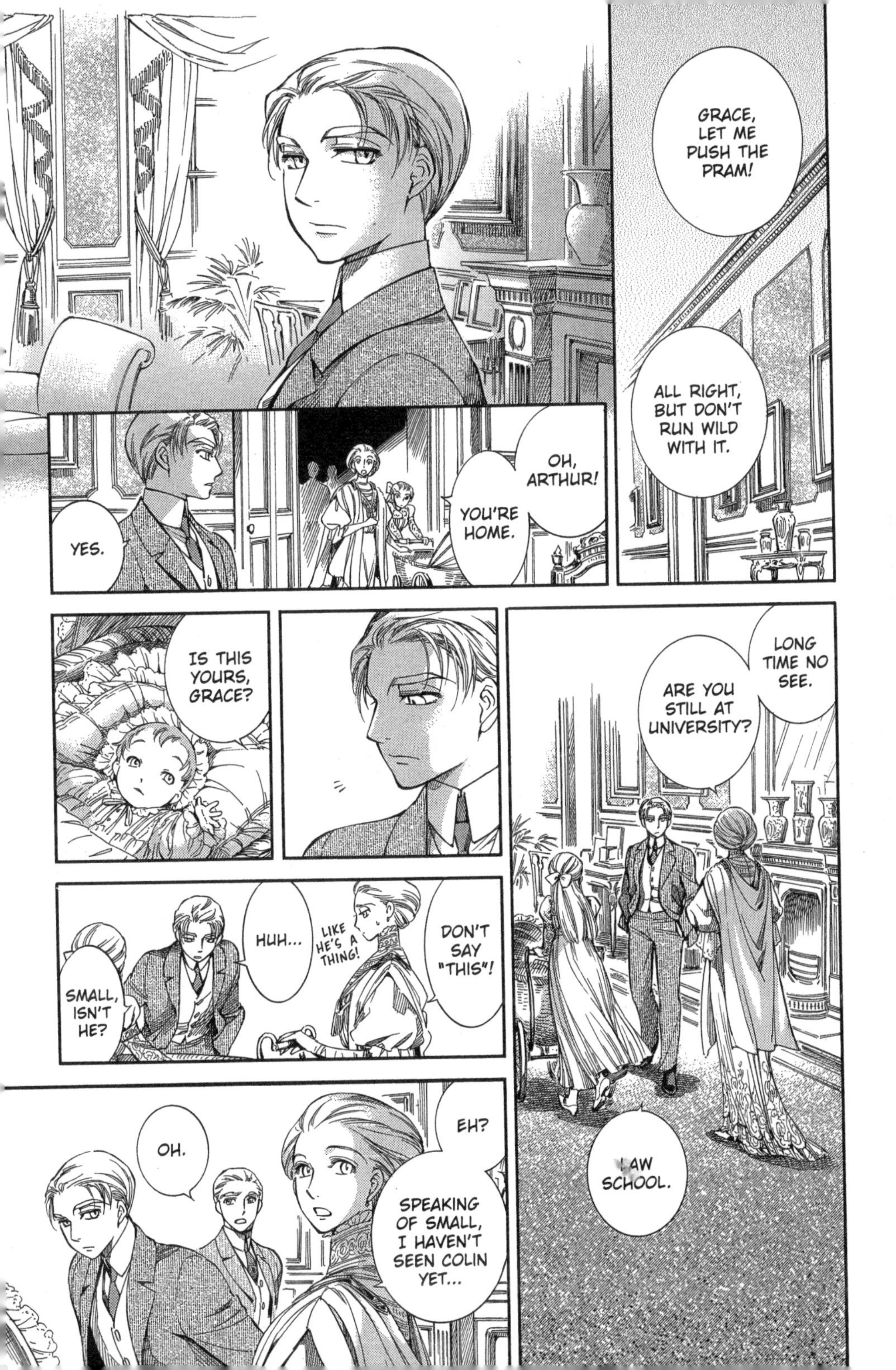
GRACE, LET ME PUSH THE PRAM!
ALL RIGHT, BUT DON'T RUN WILD WITH IT.
OH, ARTHUR!
YOU'RE HOME.
YES.
LONG TIME NO SEE.
ARE YOU STILL AT UNIVERSITY?
LAW SCHOOL.
IS THIS YOURS, GRACE?
DON'T SAY "THIS"!
LIKE HE'S A THING!
HUH...
SMALL, ISN'T HE?
EH?
SPEAKING OF SMALL, I HAVEN'T SEEN COLIN YET...
OH.

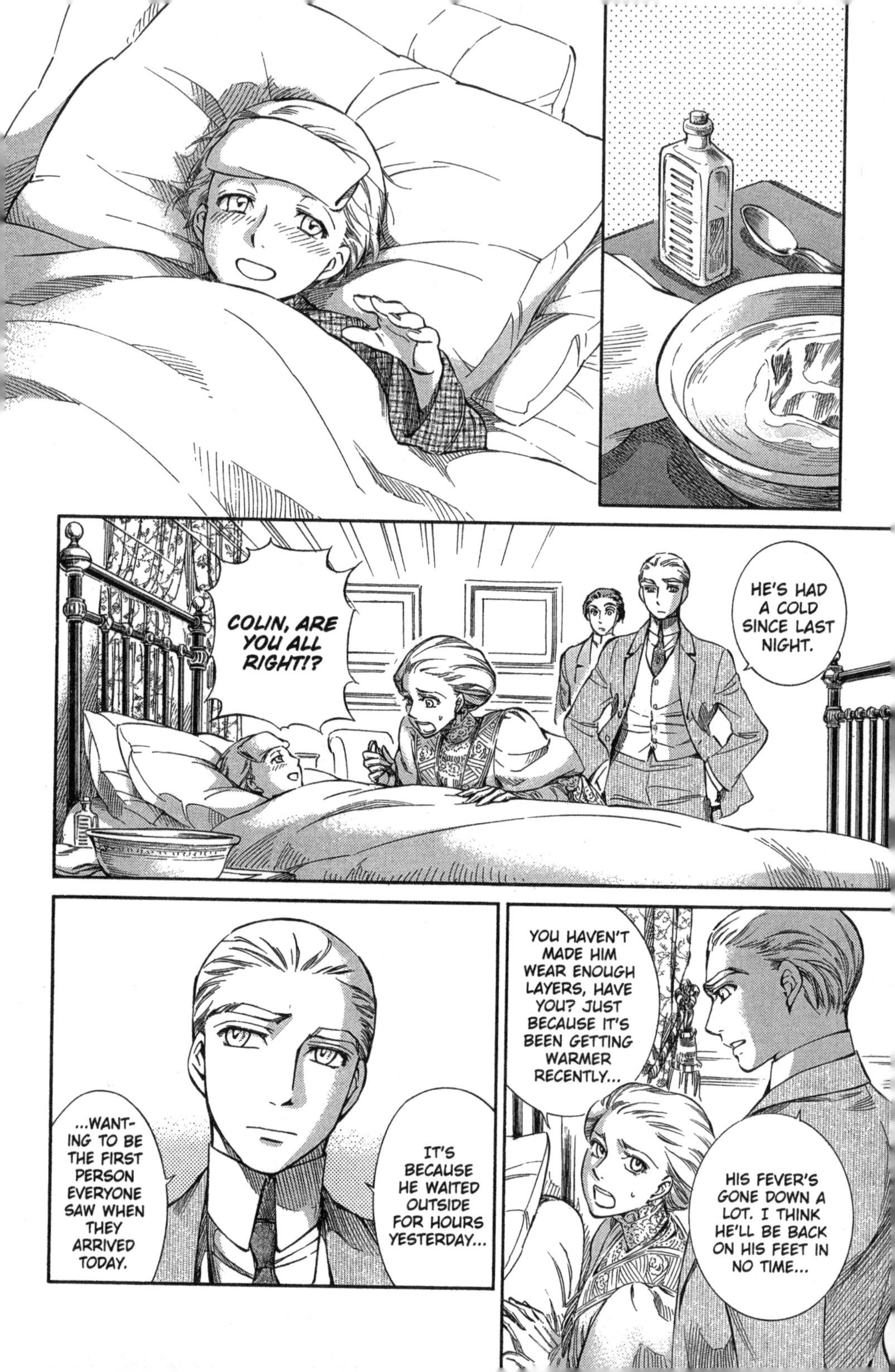
HE'S HAD A COLD SINCE LAST NIGHT.
COLIN, ARE YOU ALL RIGHT!?
YOU HAVEN'T MADE HIM WEAR ENOUGH LAYERS, HAVE YOU? JUST BECAUSE IT'S BEEN GETTING WARMER RECENTLY...
HIS FEVER'S GONE DOWN A LOT. I THINK HE'LL BE BACK ON HIS FEET IN NO TIME...
IT'S BECAUSE HE WAITED OUTSIDE FOR HOURS YESTERDAY...
...WANT-ING TO BE THE FIRST PERSON EVERYONE SAW WHEN THEY ARRIVED TODAY.

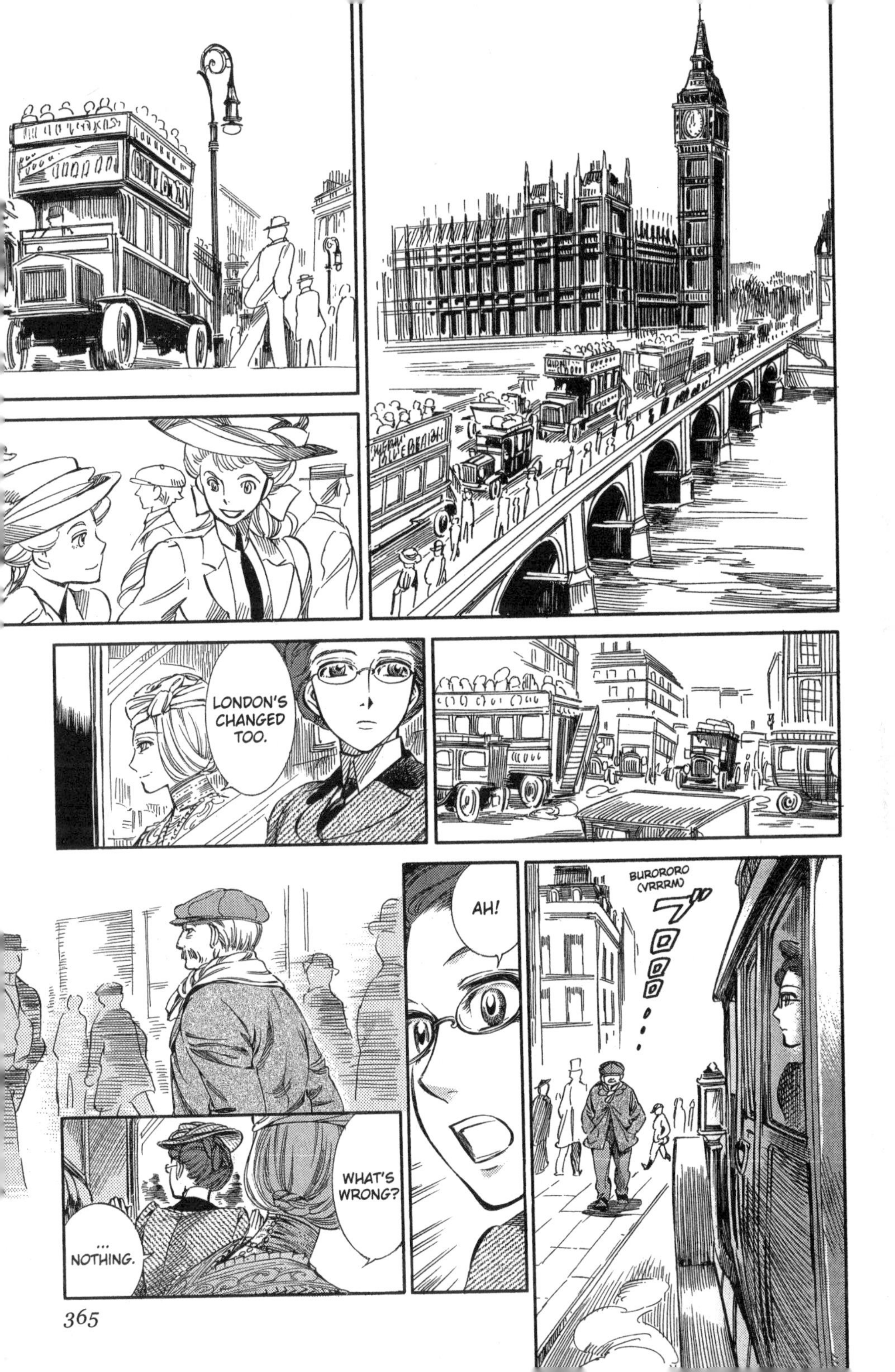
LONDON'S CHANGED TOO.
BURORORO (VRRRM)
AH!
WHAT'S WRONG?
... NOTHING.

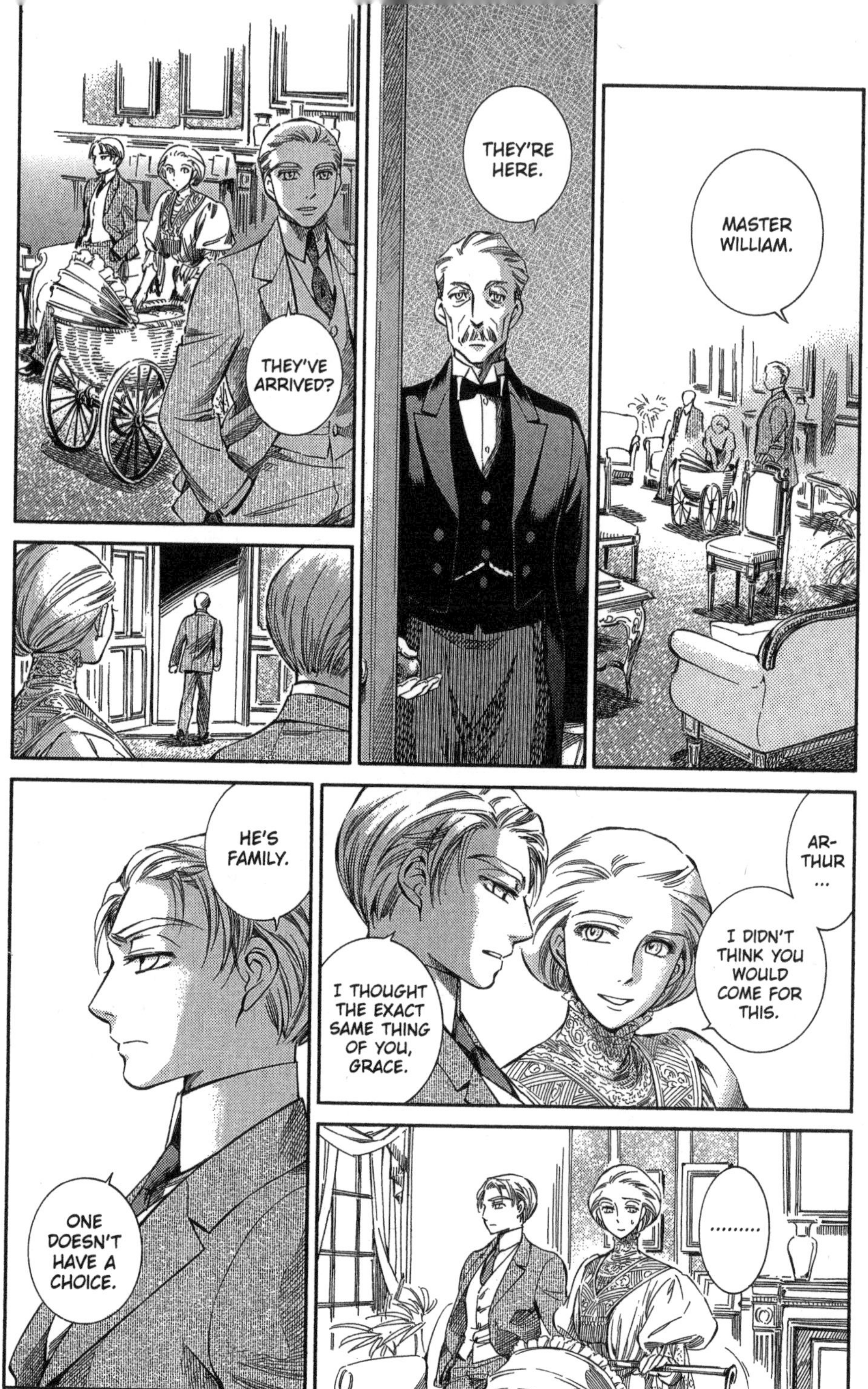
MASTER WILLIAM.
THEY'RE HERE.
THEY'VE ARRIVED?
ARTHUR ...
I DIDN'T THINK YOU WOULD COME FOR THIS.
I THOUGHT THE EXACT SAME THING OF YOU, GRACE.
....
HE'S FAMILY.
ONE DOESN'T HAVE A CHOICE.

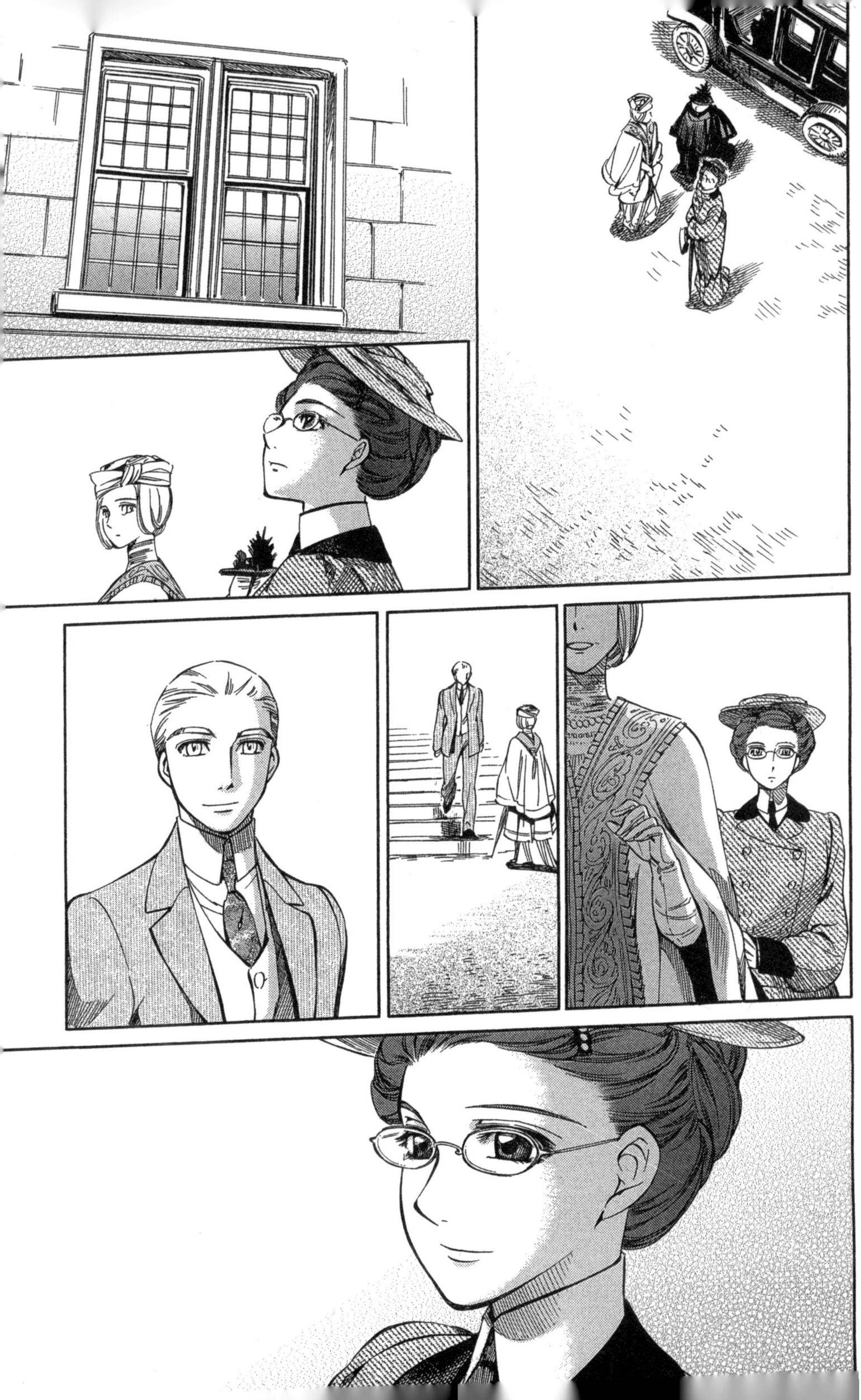

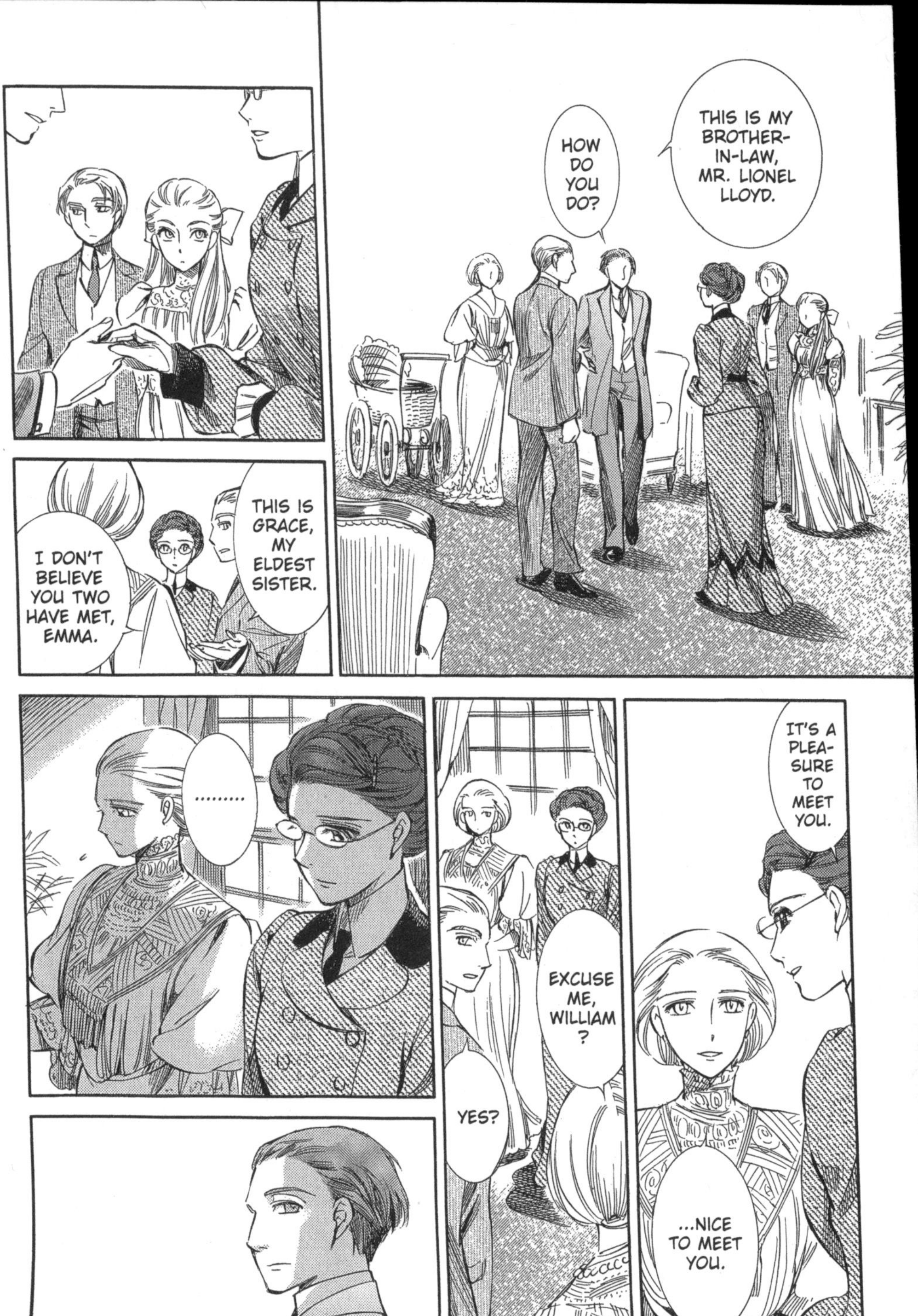
THIS IS MY BROTHER-IN-LAW, MR. LIONEL LLOYD.
HOW DO YOU DO?
THIS IS GRACE, MY ELDEST SISTER.
I DON'T BELIEVE YOU TWO HAVE MET, EMMA.
IT'S A PLEASURE TO MEET YOU.
...NICE TO MEET YOU.
EXCUSE ME, WILLIAM?
YES?
....

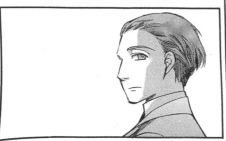

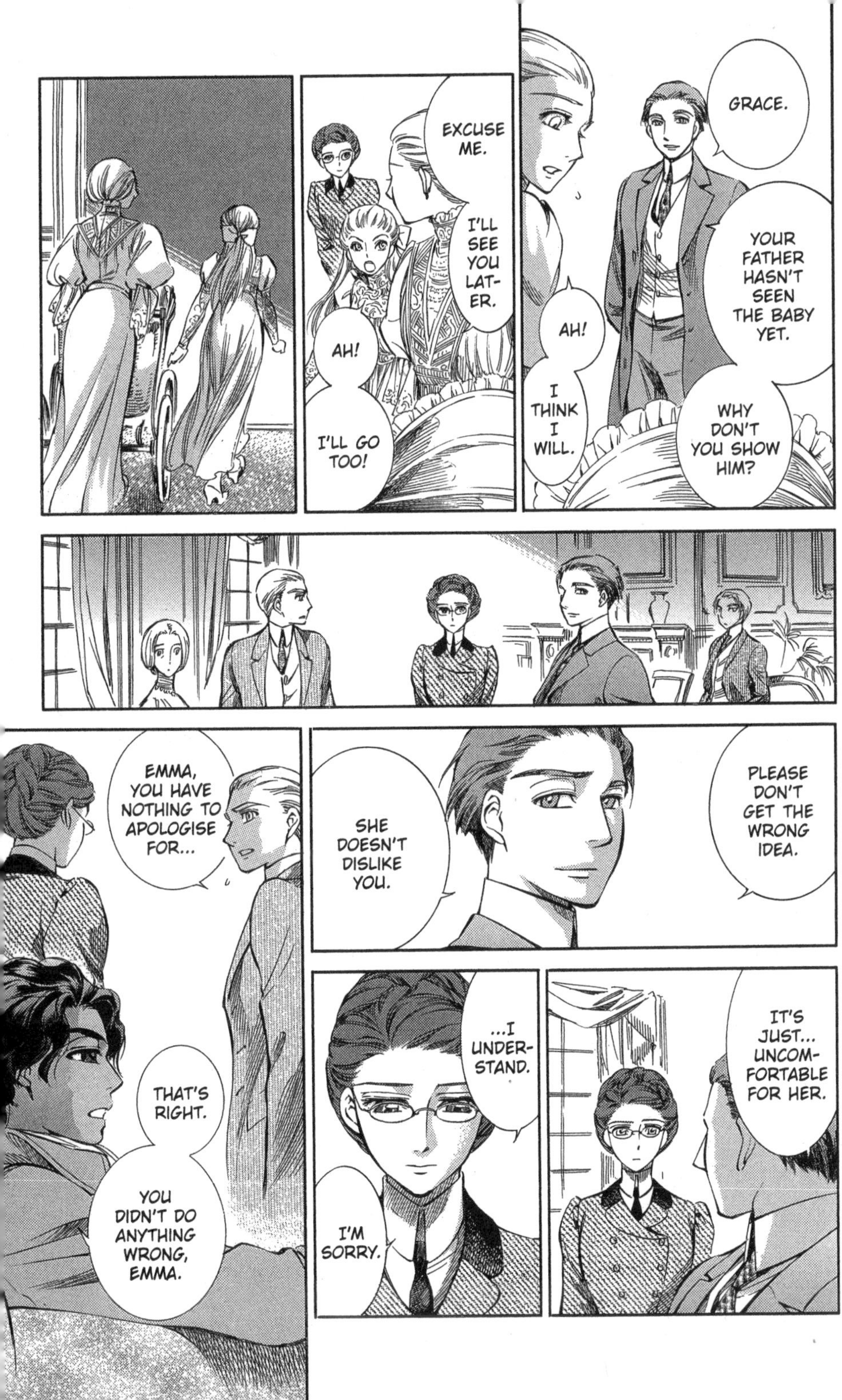
GRACE.
YOUR FATHER HASN'T SEEN THE BABY YET.
WHY DON'T YOU SHOW HIM?
AH!
I THINK I WILL.
EXCUSE ME.
I'LL SEE YOU LAT-ER.
AH!
I'LL GO TOO!
PLEASE DON'T GET THE WRONG IDEA.
SHE DOESN'T DISLIKE YOU.
IT'S JUST... UNCOM-FORTABLE FOR HER.
...I UNDER-STAND.
I'M SORRY.
EMMA, YOU HAVE NOTHING TO APOLOGISE FOR...
THAT'S RIGHT.
YOU DIDN'T DO ANYTHING WRONG, EMMA.

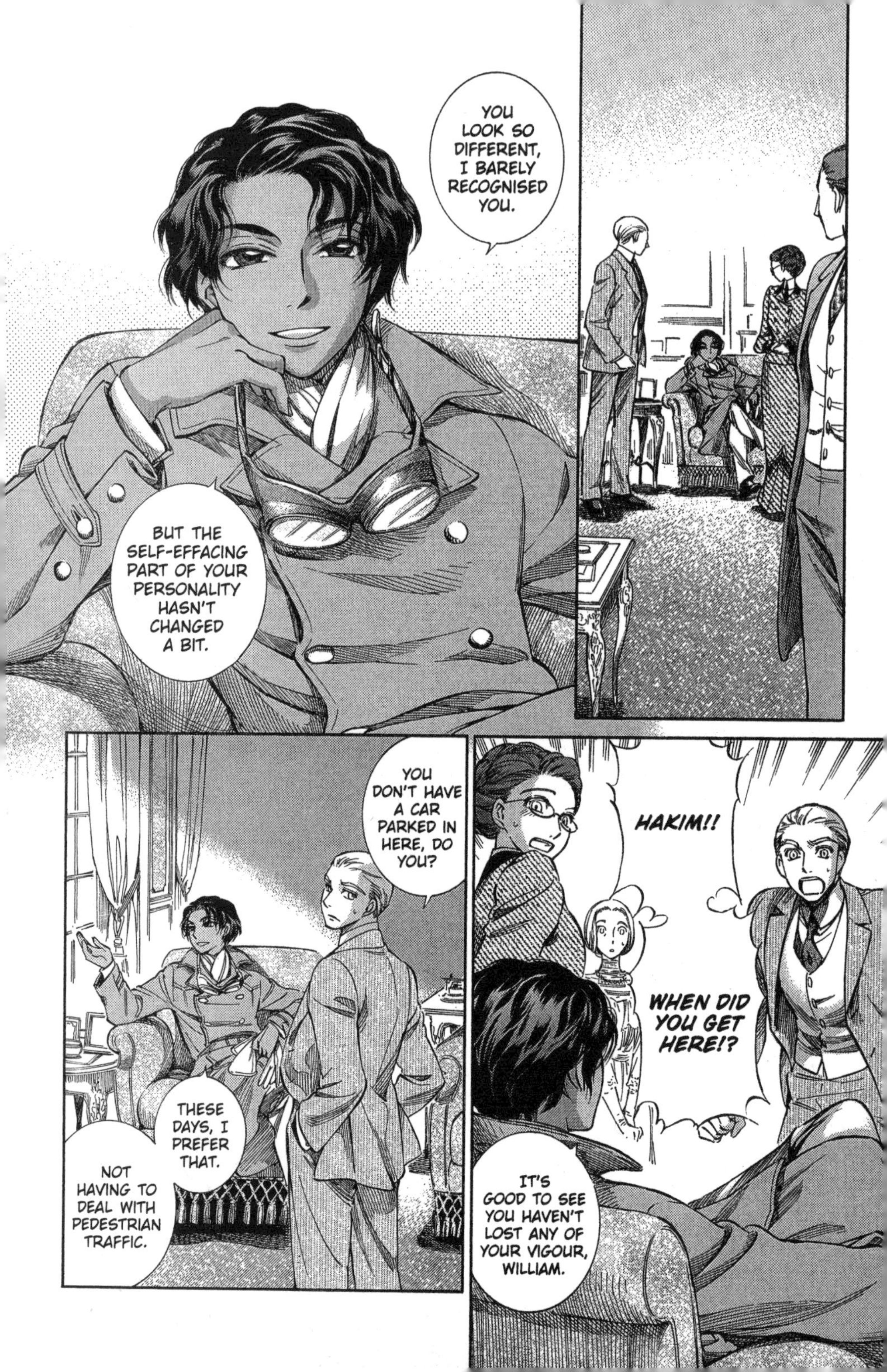
YOU LOOK SO DIFFERENT, I BARELY RECOGNISED YOU.
BUT THE SELF-EFFACING PART OF YOUR PERSONALITY HASN'T CHANGED A BIT.
HAKIM!!
WHEN DID YOU GET HERE!?
IT'S GOOD TO SEE YOU HAVEN'T LOST ANY OF YOUR VIGOUR, WILLIAM.
YOU DON'T HAVE A CAR PARKED IN HERE, DO YOU?
THESE DAYS, I PREFER THAT.
NOT HAVING TO DEAL WITH PEDESTRIAN TRAFFIC.

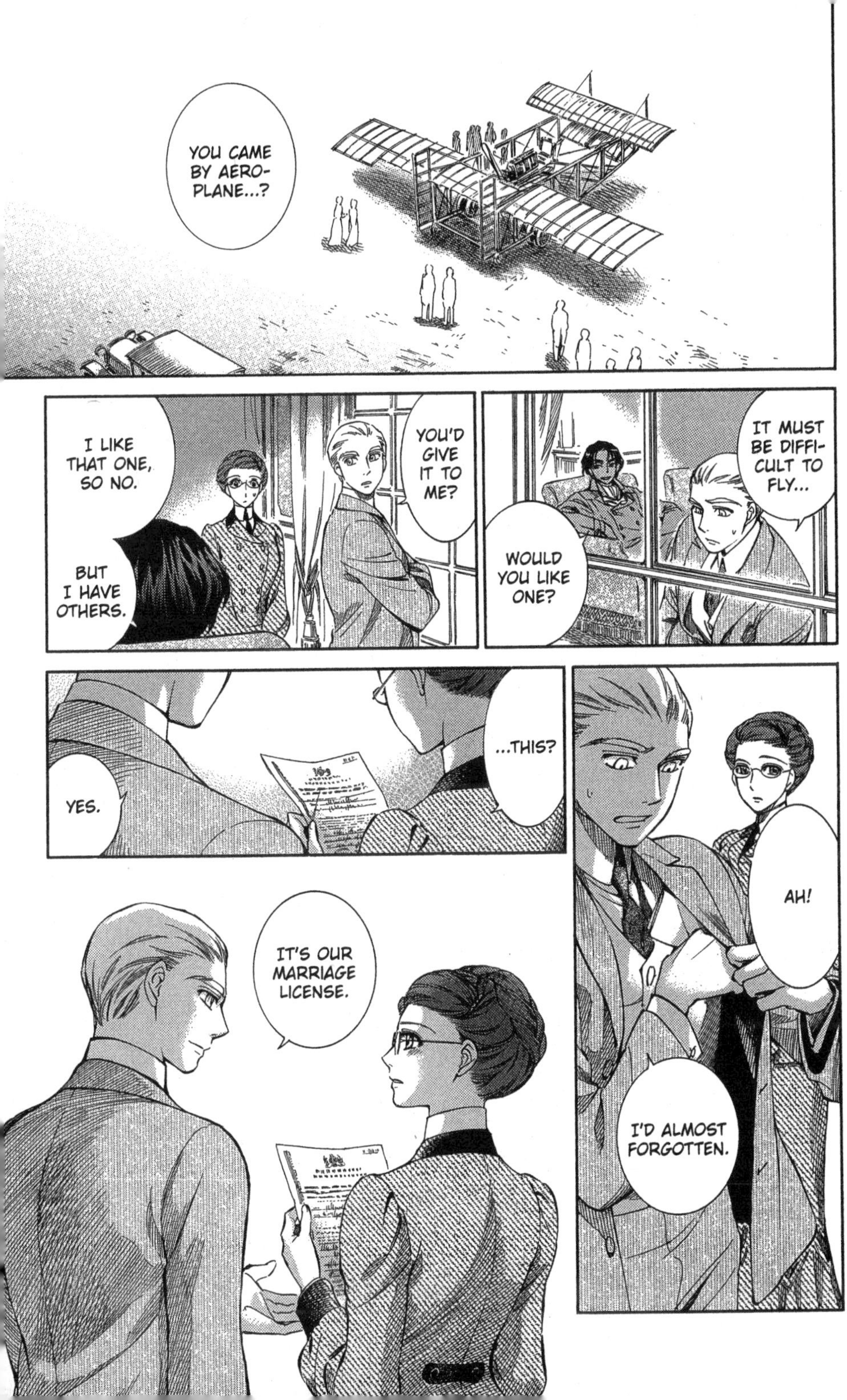
YOU CAME BY AERO-PLANE...?
IT MUST BE DIFFI-CULT TO FLY...
WOULD YOU LIKE ONE?
YOU'D GIVE IT TO ME?
I LIKE THAT ONE, SO NO.
BUT I HAVE OTHERS.
AH!
I'D ALMOST FORGOTTEN.
...THIS?
YES.
IT'S OUR MARRIAGE LICENSE.

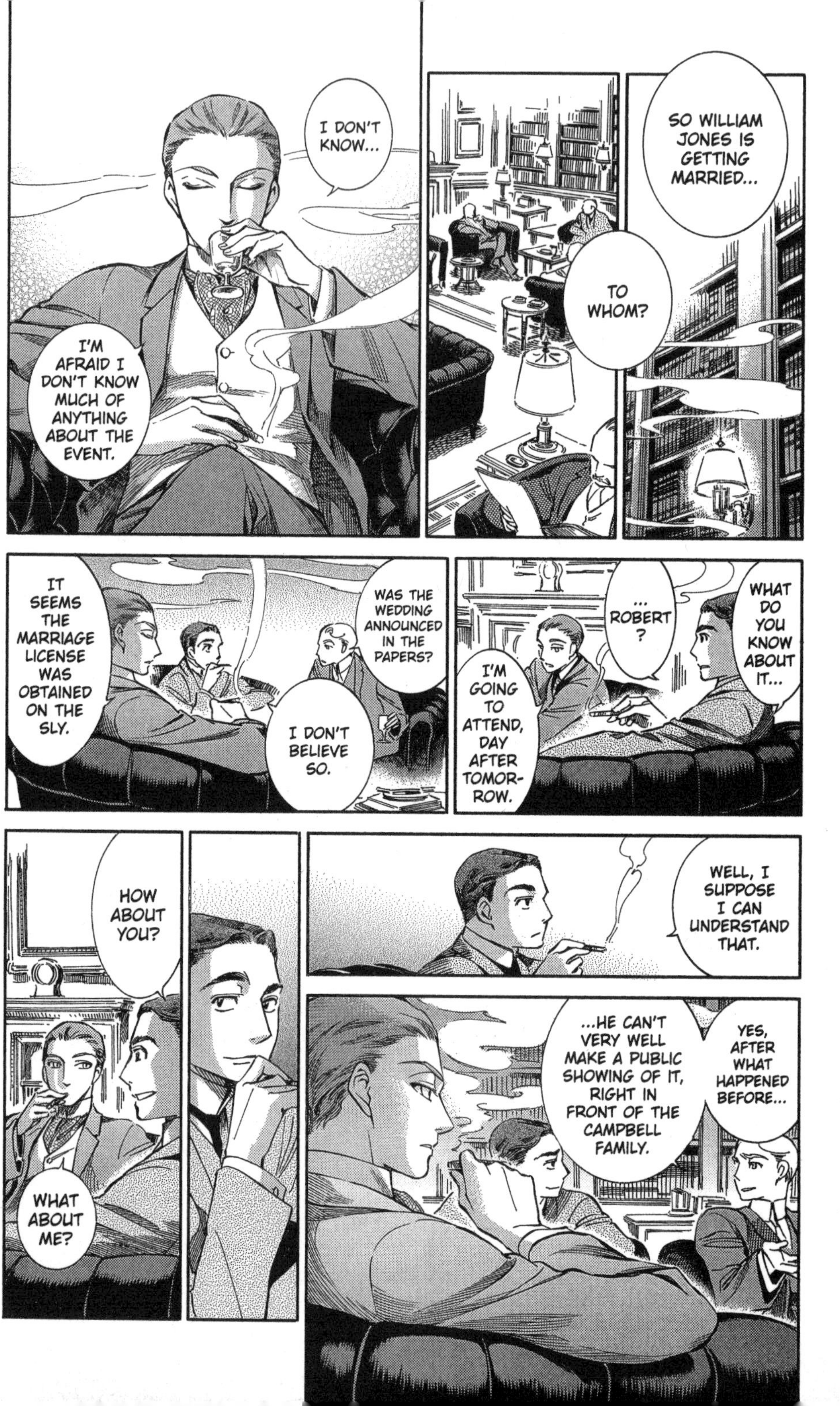
SO WILLIAM JONES IS GETTING MARRIED...
TO WHOM?
I DON'T KNOW...
I'M AFRAID I DON'T KNOW MUCH OF ANYTHING ABOUT THE EVENT.
WHAT DO YOU KNOW ABOUT IT...
... ROBERT?
I'M GOING TO ATTEND, DAY AFTER TOMOR-ROW.
WAS THE WEDDING ANNOUNCED IN THE PAPERS?
I DON'T BELIEVE SO.
IT SEEMS THE MARRIAGE LICENSE WAS OBTAINED ON THE SLY.
WELL, I SUPPOSE I CAN UNDERSTAND THAT.
YES, AFTER WHAT HAPPENED BEFORE...
...HE CAN'T VERY WELL MAKE A PUBLIC SHOWING OF IT, RIGHT IN FRONT OF THE CAMPBELL FAMILY.
HOW ABOUT YOU?
WHAT ABOUT ME?

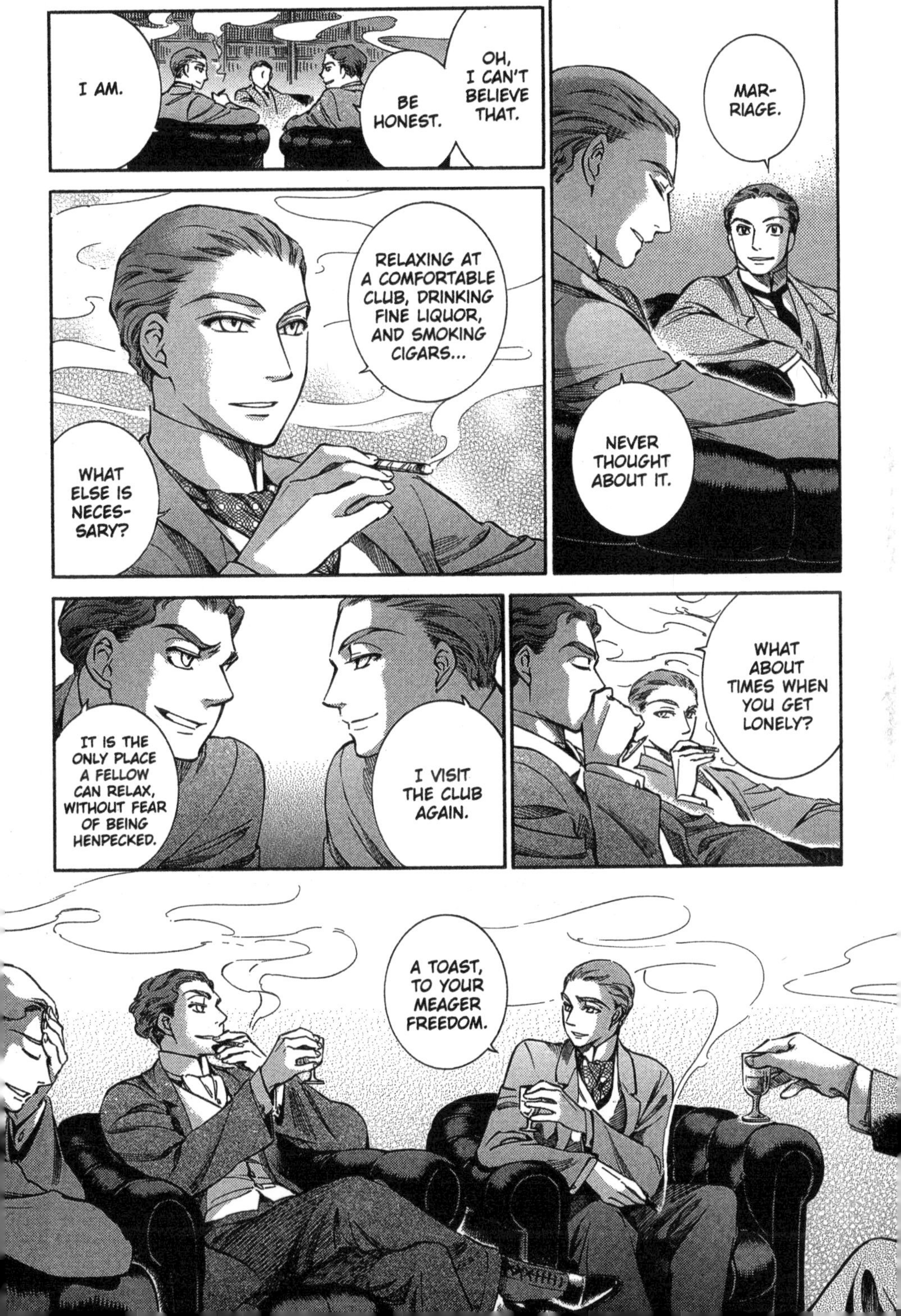
MAR-RIAGE.
NEVER THOUGHT ABOUT IT.
OH, I CAN'T BELIEVE THAT.
BE HONEST.
I AM.
RELAXING AT A COMFORTABLE CLUB, DRINKING FINE LIQUOR, AND SMOKING CIGARS...
WHAT ELSE IS NECES-SARY?
WHAT ABOUT TIMES WHEN YOU GET LONELY?
I VISIT THE CLUB AGAIN.
IT IS THE ONLY PLACE A FELLOW CAN RELAX, WITHOUT FEAR OF BEING HENPECKED.
A TOAST, TO YOUR MEAGER FREEDOM.

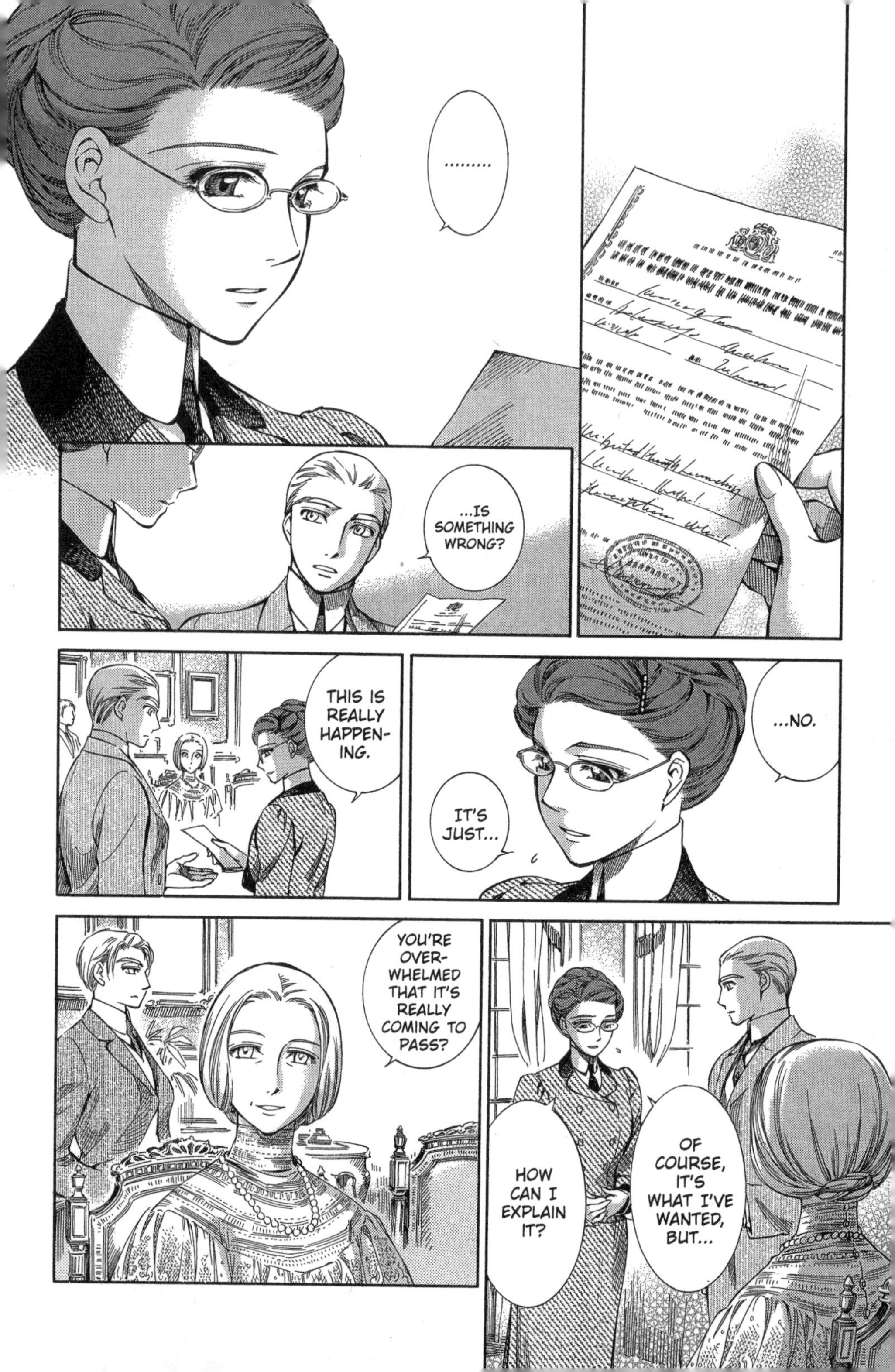
....
...IS SOMETHING WRONG?
...NO.
IT'S JUST...
THIS IS REALLY HAPPENING.
OF COURSE, IT'S WHAT I'VE WANTED, BUT...
HOW CAN I EXPLAIN IT?
YOU'RE OVERWHELMED THAT IT'S REALLY COMING TO PASS?

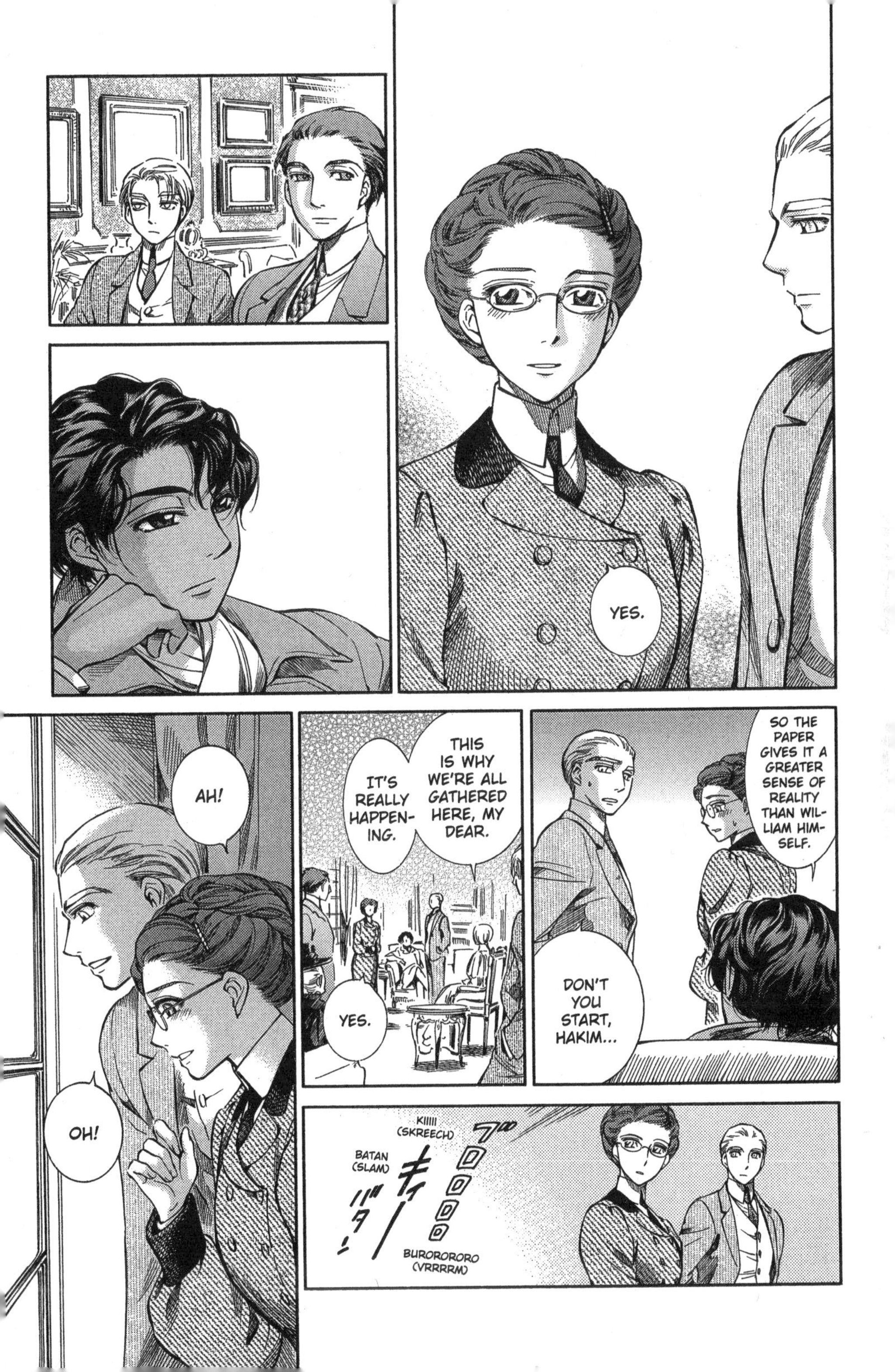
YES.
SO THE PAPER GIVES IT A GREATER SENSE OF REALITY THAN WIL-LIAM HIM-SELF.
DON'T YOU START, HAKIM...
THIS IS WHY WE'RE ALL GATHERED HERE, MY DEAR.
IT'S REALLY HAPPEN-ING.
YES.
BURORORORO (VRRRRM)
KIIII (SKREECH)
BATAN (SLAM)
AH!
OH!

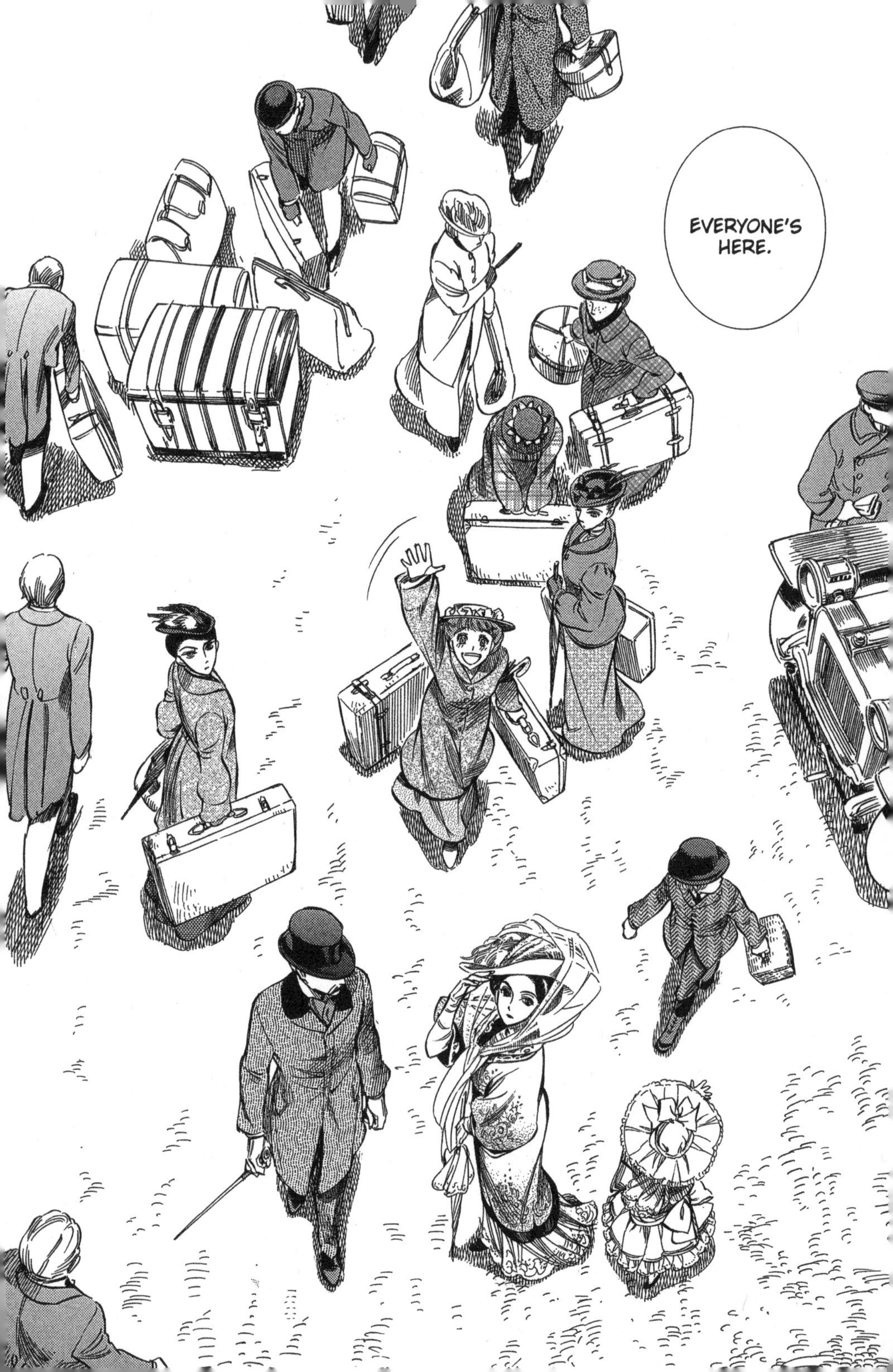
EVERYONE'S HERE.

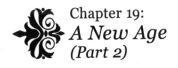

Chapter 19:
A New Age
(Part 2)

Chapter 19: *A New Age (Part 2)*

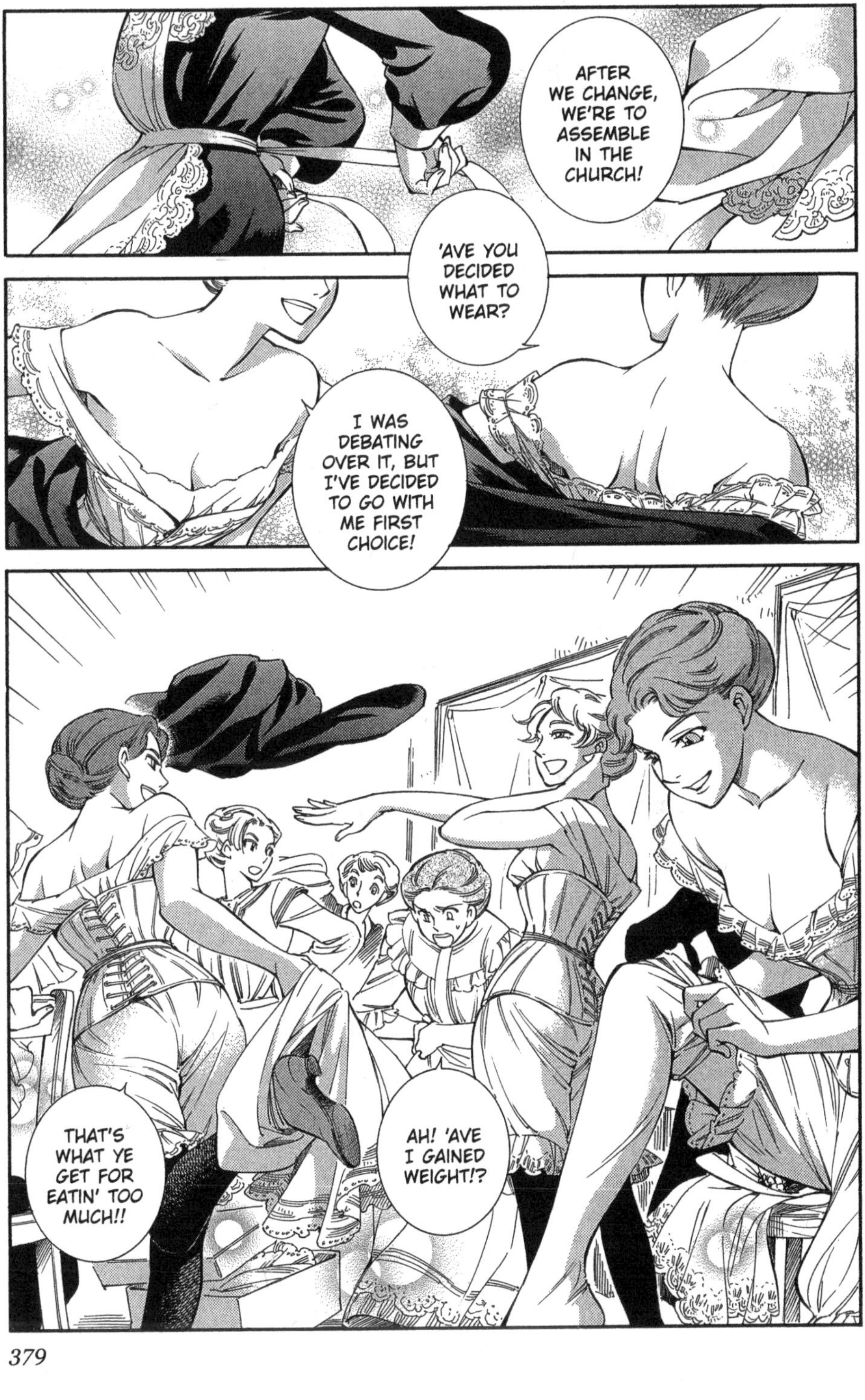
AFTER WE CHANGE, WE'RE TO ASSEMBLE IN THE CHURCH!
'AVE YOU DECIDED WHAT TO WEAR?
I WAS DEBATING OVER IT, BUT I'VE DECIDED TO GO WITH ME FIRST CHOICE!
AH! 'AVE I GAINED WEIGHT!?
THAT'S WHAT YE GET FOR EATIN' TOO MUCH!!

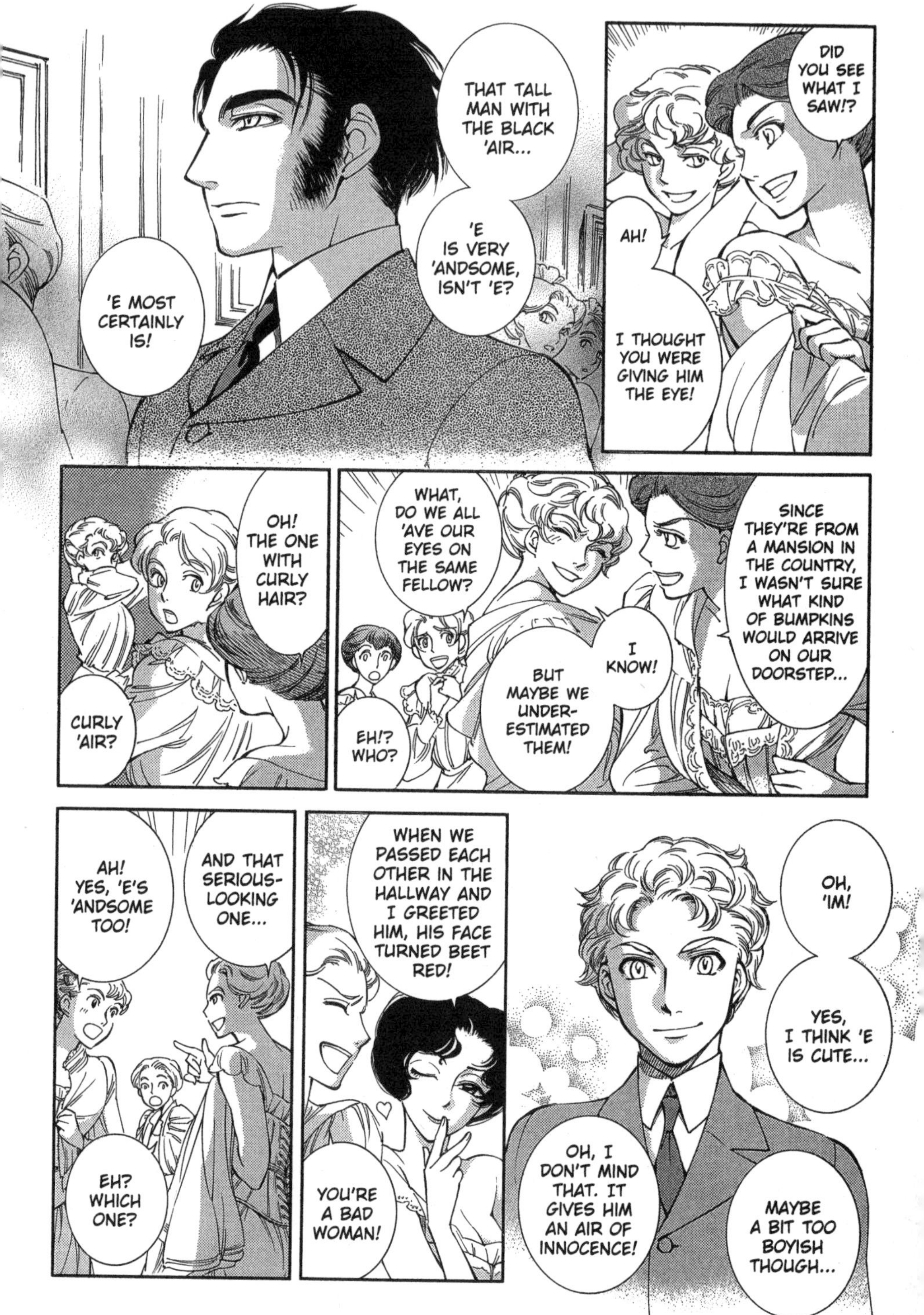
DID YOU SEE WHAT I SAW!?
AH!
I THOUGHT YOU WERE GIVING HIM THE EYE!
THAT TALL MAN WITH THE BLACK 'AIR...
'E IS VERY 'ANDSOME, ISN'T 'E?
'E MOST CERTAINLY IS!
SINCE THEY'RE FROM A MANSION IN THE COUNTRY, I WASN'T SURE WHAT KIND OF BUMPKINS WOULD ARRIVE ON OUR DOORSTEP...
WHAT, DO WE ALL 'AVE OUR EYES ON THE SAME FELLOW?
I KNOW!
BUT MAYBE WE UNDERESTIMATED THEM!
EH!? WHO?
OH! THE ONE WITH CURLY HAIR?
CURLY 'AIR?
OH, 'IM!
YES, I THINK 'E IS CUTE...
MAYBE A BIT TOO BOYISH THOUGH...
OH, I DON'T MIND THAT. IT GIVES HIM AN AIR OF INNOCENCE!
WHEN WE PASSED EACH OTHER IN THE HALLWAY AND I GREETED HIM, HIS FACE TURNED BEET RED!
YOU'RE A BAD WOMAN!
AND THAT SERIOUS-LOOKING ONE...
AH! YES, 'E'S 'ANDSOME TOO!
EH? WHICH ONE?

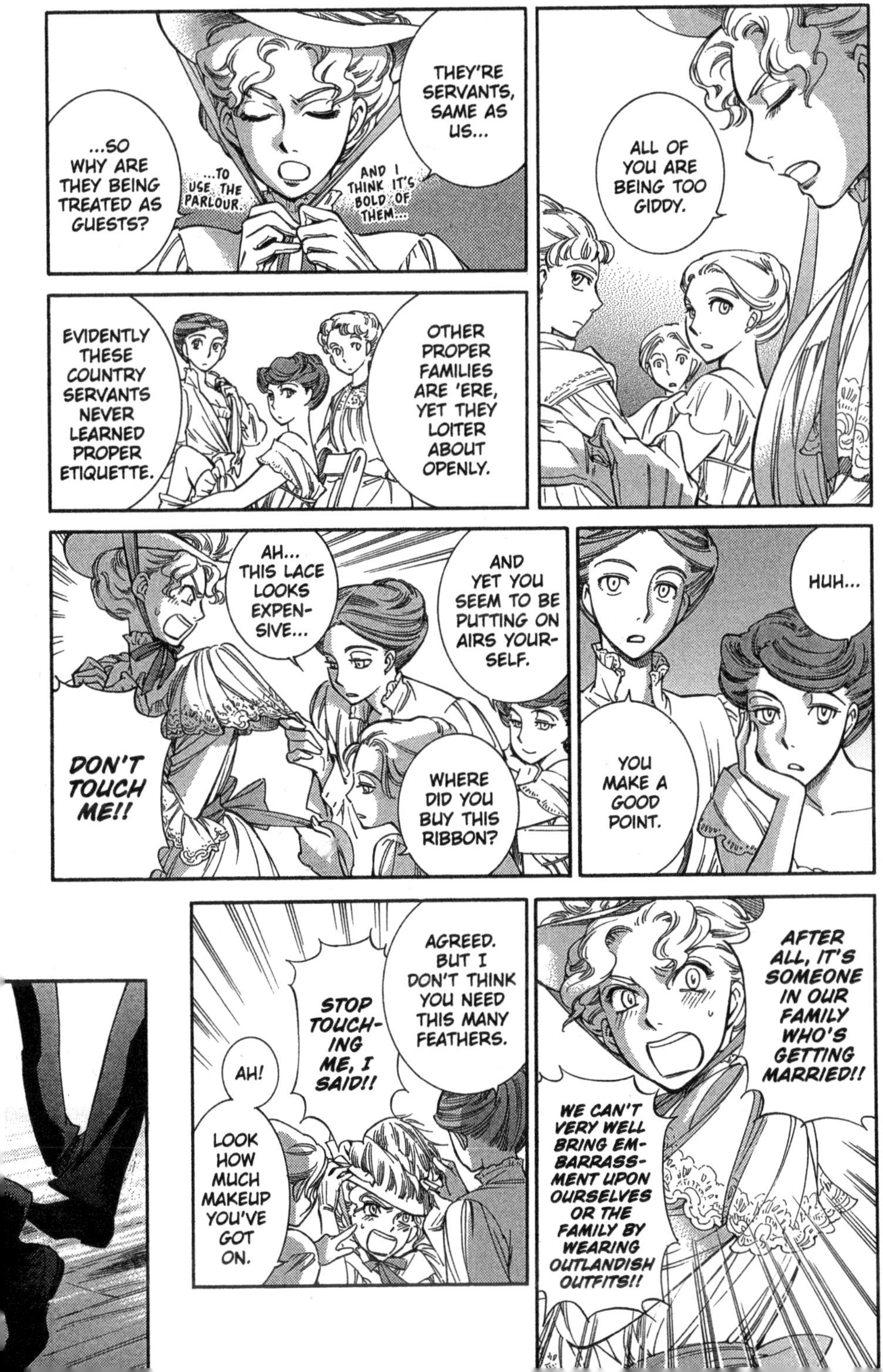

ALL OF YOU ARE BEING TOO GIDDY.
THEY'RE SERVANTS, SAME AS US...
AND I THINK IT'S BOLD OF THEM...
...TO USE THE PARLOUR.
...SO WHY ARE THEY BEING TREATED AS GUESTS?
OTHER PROPER FAMILIES ARE 'ERE, YET THEY LOITER ABOUT OPENLY.
EVIDENTLY THESE COUNTRY SERVANTS NEVER LEARNED PROPER ETIQUETTE.
HUH...
YOU MAKE A GOOD POINT.
AND YET YOU SEEM TO BE PUTTING ON AIRS YOUR-SELF.
AH... THIS LACE LOOKS EXPEN-SIVE...
WHERE DID YOU BUY THIS RIBBON?
DON'T TOUCH ME!!
AFTER ALL, IT'S SOMEONE IN OUR FAMILY WHO'S GETTING MARRIED!!
WE CAN'T VERY WELL BRING EM-BARRASS-MENT UPON OURSELVES OR THE FAMILY BY WEARING OUTLANDISH OUTFITS!!
AGREED. BUT I DON'T THINK YOU NEED THIS MANY FEATHERS.
STOP TOUCH-ING ME, I SAID!!
AH!
LOOK HOW MUCH MAKEUP YOU'VE GOT ON.

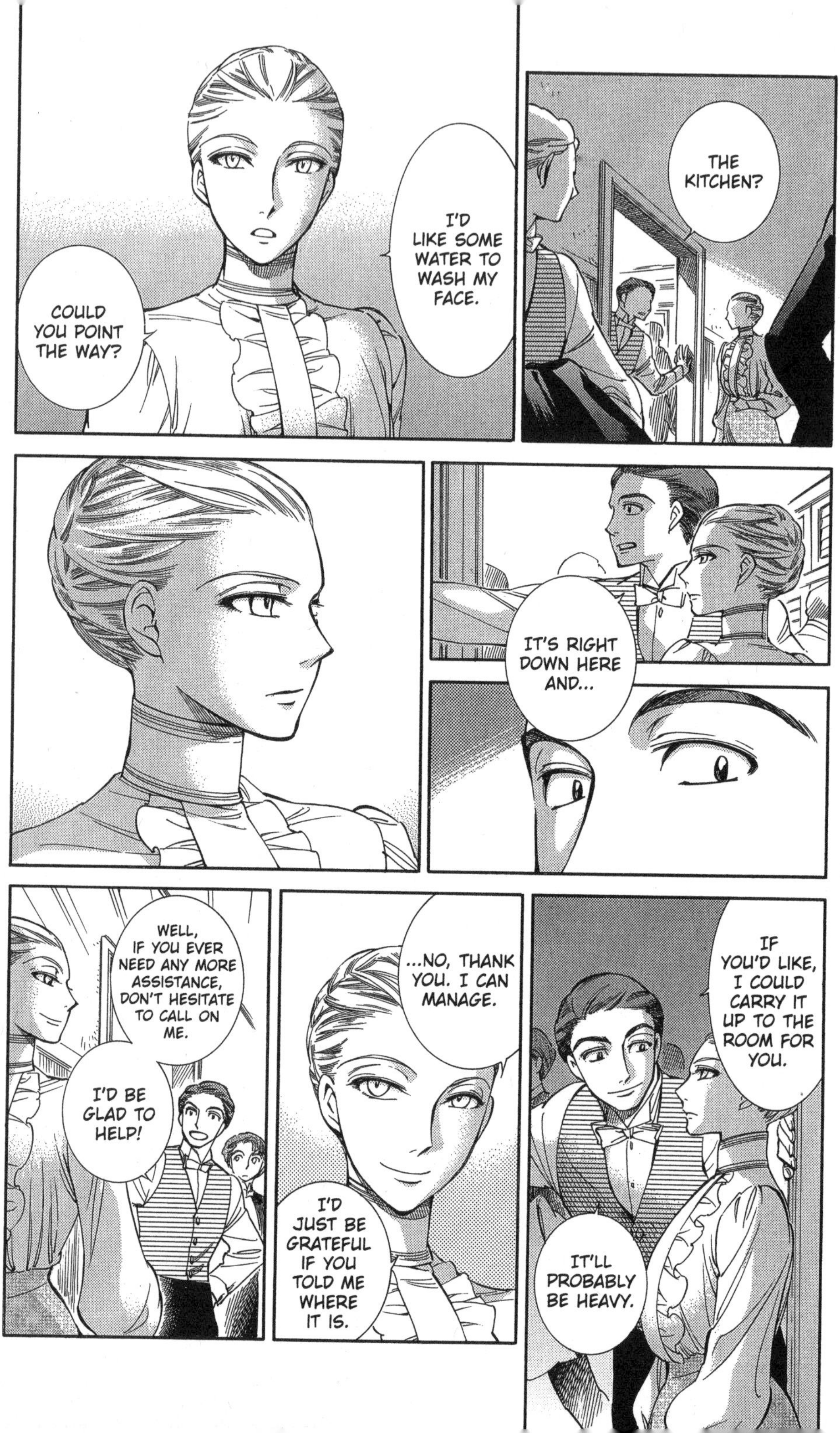
THE KITCHEN?
I'D LIKE SOME WATER TO WASH MY FACE.
COULD YOU POINT THE WAY?
IT'S RIGHT DOWN HERE AND...
IF YOU'D LIKE, I COULD CARRY IT UP TO THE ROOM FOR YOU.
IT'LL PROBABLY BE HEAVY.
...NO, THANK YOU. I CAN MANAGE.
I'D JUST BE GRATEFUL IF YOU TOLD ME WHERE IT IS.
WELL, IF YOU EVER NEED ANY MORE ASSISTANCE, DON'T HESITATE TO CALL ON ME.
I'D BE GLAD TO HELP!

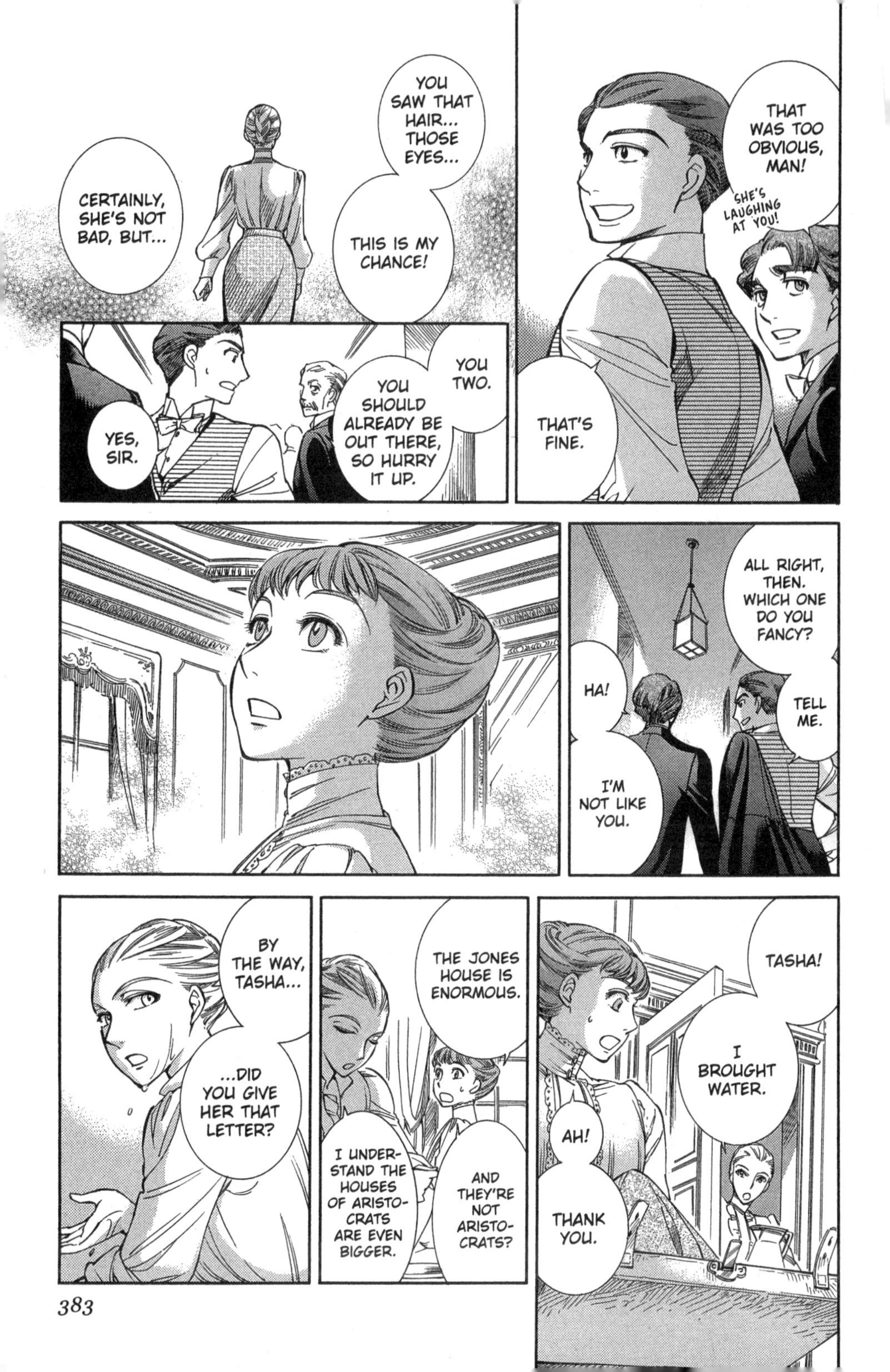
THAT WAS TOO OBVIOUS, MAN!
SHE'S LAUGHING AT YOU!
THAT'S FINE.
YOU SAW THAT HAIR... THOSE EYES...
THIS IS MY CHANCE!
CERTAINLY, SHE'S NOT BAD, BUT...
YOU TWO.
YOU SHOULD ALREADY BE OUT THERE, SO HURRY IT UP.
YES, SIR.
ALL RIGHT, THEN. WHICH ONE DO YOU FANCY?
TELL ME.
HA!
I'M NOT LIKE YOU.
TASHA!
I BROUGHT WATER.
AH!
THANK YOU.
THE JONES HOUSE IS ENORMOUS.
AND THEY'RE NOT ARISTOCRATS?
I UNDERSTAND THE HOUSES OF ARISTOCRATS ARE EVEN BIGGER.
BY THE WAY, TASHA...
...DID YOU GIVE HER THAT LETTER?

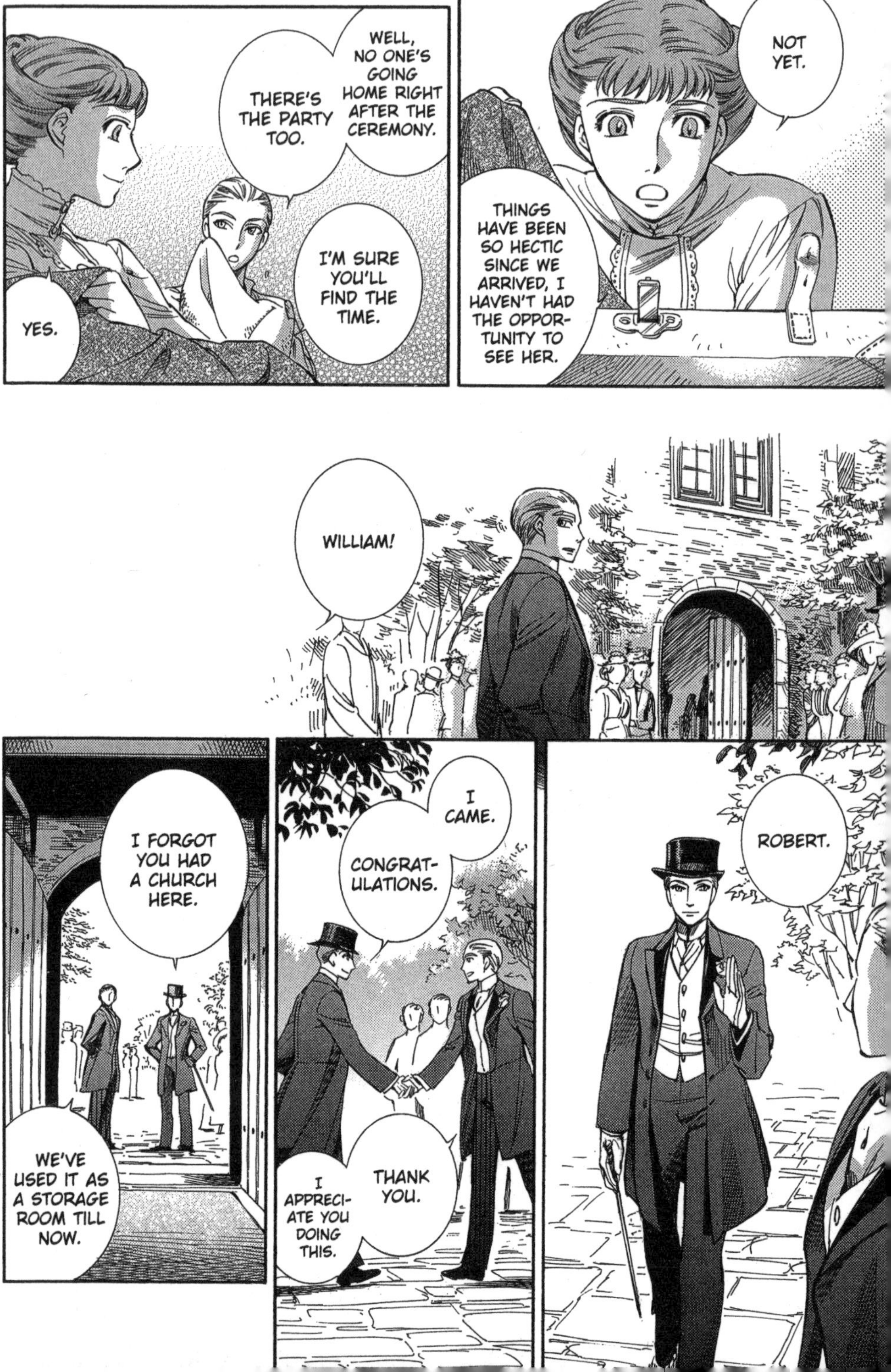
NOT YET.
THINGS HAVE BEEN SO HECTIC SINCE WE ARRIVED, I HAVEN'T HAD THE OPPORTUNITY TO SEE HER.
WELL, NO ONE'S GOING HOME RIGHT AFTER THE CEREMONY.
THERE'S THE PARTY TOO.
I'M SURE YOU'LL FIND THE TIME.
YES.
WILLIAM!
ROBERT.
I CAME.
CONGRAT-ULATIONS.
THANK YOU.
I APPRECI-ATE YOU DOING THIS.
I FORGOT YOU HAD A CHURCH HERE.
WE'VE USED IT AS A STORAGE ROOM TILL NOW.

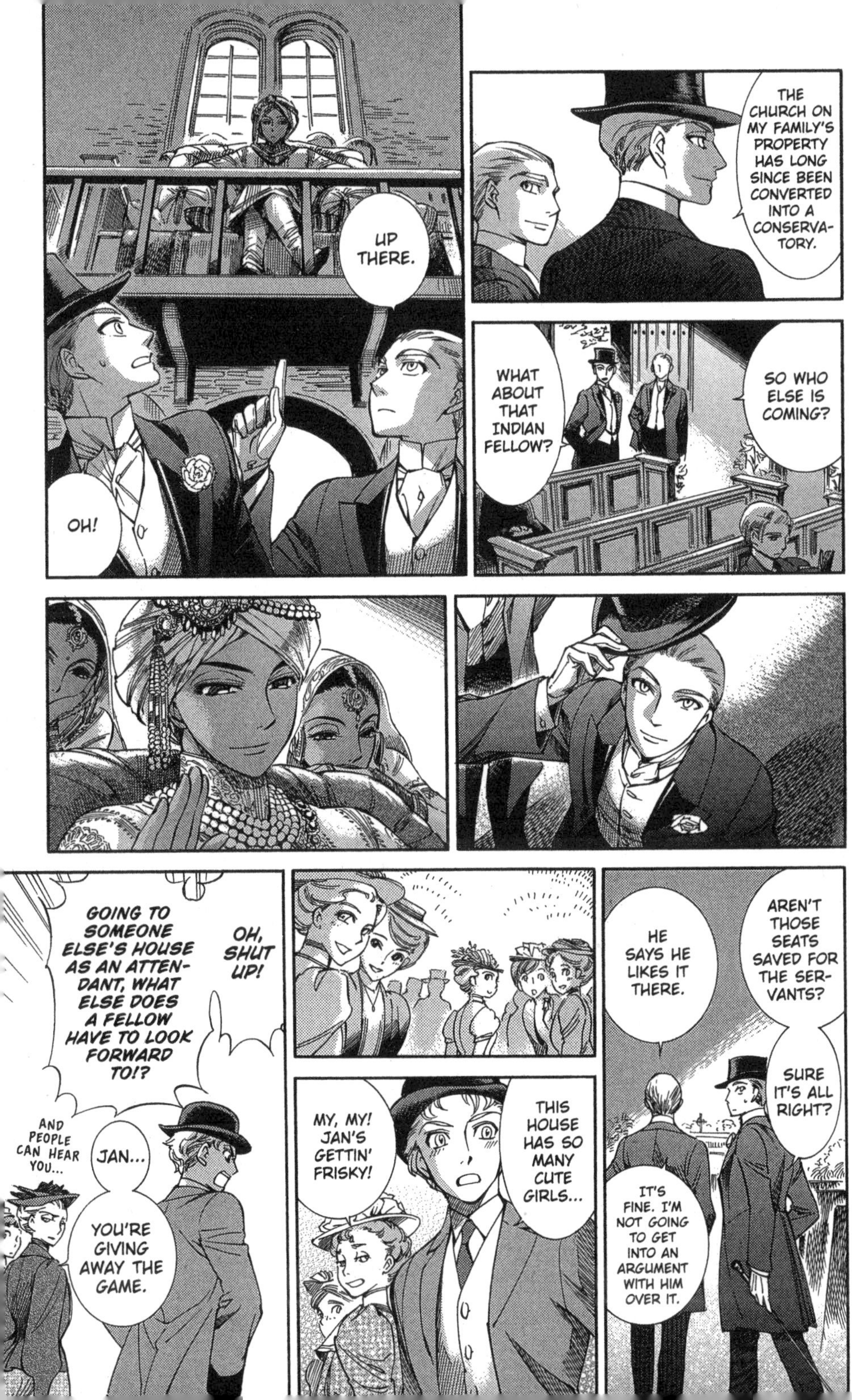
THE CHURCH ON MY FAMILY'S PROPERTY HAS LONG SINCE BEEN CONVERTED INTO A CONSERVATORY.
SO WHO ELSE IS COMING?
WHAT ABOUT THAT INDIAN FELLOW?
UP THERE.
OH!
AREN'T THOSE SEATS SAVED FOR THE SERVANTS?
HE SAYS HE LIKES IT THERE.
SURE IT'S ALL RIGHT?
IT'S FINE. I'M NOT GOING TO GET INTO AN ARGUMENT WITH HIM OVER IT.
THIS HOUSE HAS SO MANY CUTE GIRLS...
MY, MY! JAN'S GETTIN' FRISKY!
OH, SHUT UP!
GOING TO SOMEONE ELSE'S HOUSE AS AN ATTENDANT, WHAT ELSE DOES A FELLOW HAVE TO LOOK FORWARD TO!?
JAN...
YOU'RE GIVING AWAY THE GAME.
AND PEOPLE CAN HEAR YOU...

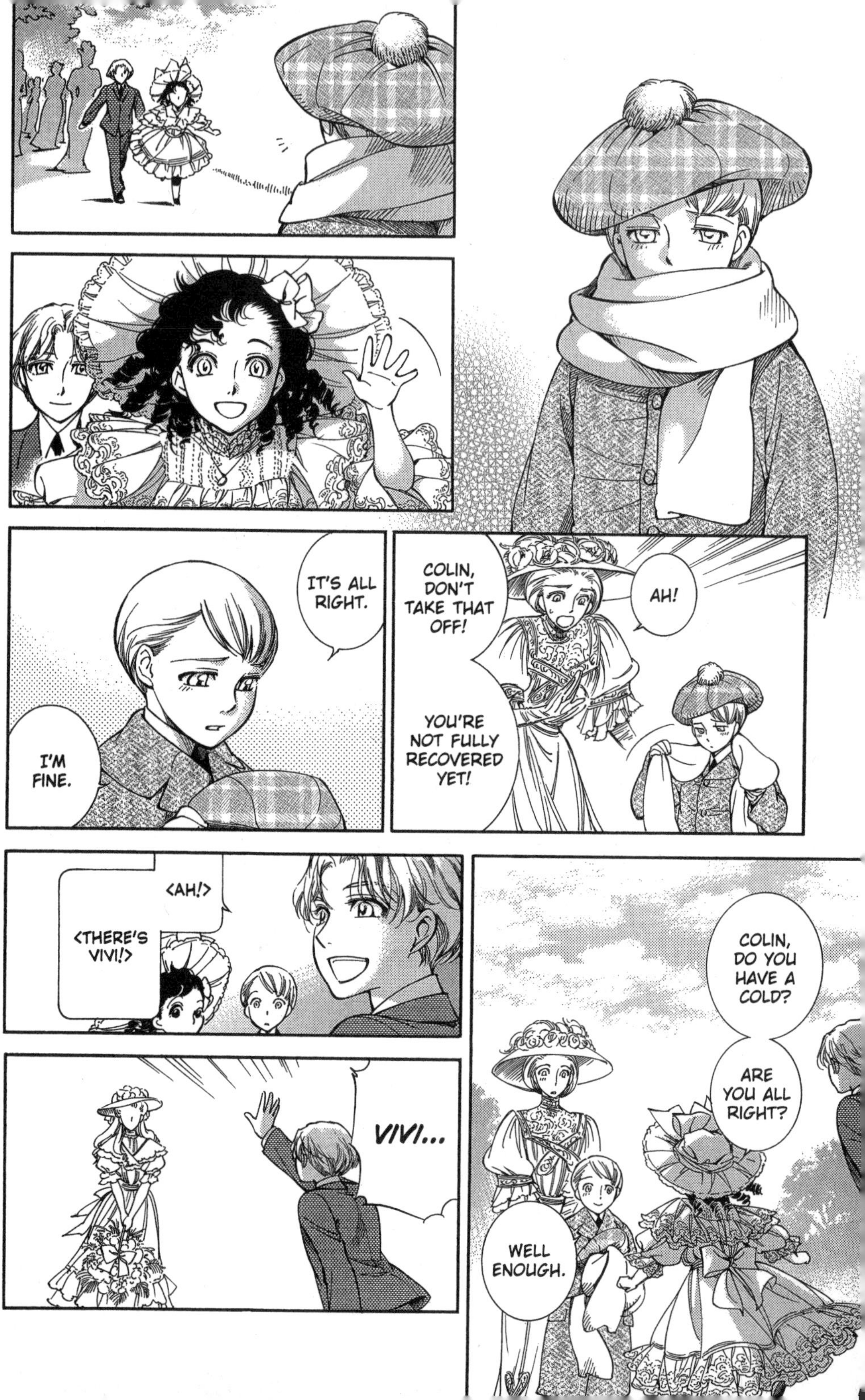
AH!
COLIN, DON'T TAKE THAT OFF!
YOU'RE NOT FULLY RECOVERED YET!
IT'S ALL RIGHT.
I'M FINE.
COLIN, DO YOU HAVE A COLD?
ARE YOU ALL RIGHT?
WELL ENOUGH.
<AH!>
<THERE'S VIVI!>
VIVI...

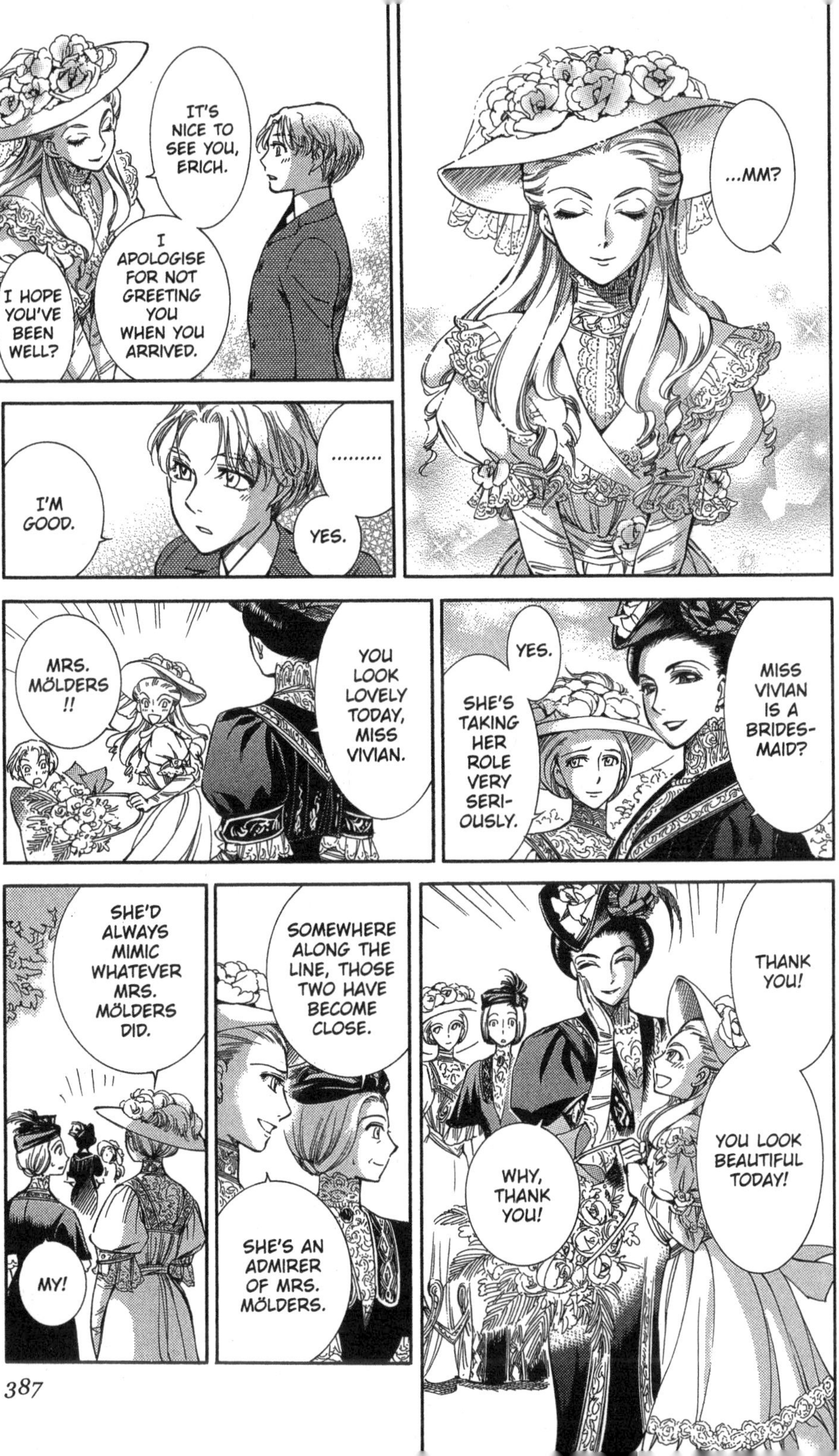
...MM?
IT'S NICE TO SEE YOU, ERICH.
I APOLOGISE FOR NOT GREETING YOU WHEN YOU ARRIVED.
I HOPE YOU'VE BEEN WELL?
....
YES.
I'M GOOD.
MISS VIVIAN IS A BRIDES-MAID?
YES.
SHE'S TAKING HER ROLE VERY SERI-OUSLY.
YOU LOOK LOVELY TODAY, MISS VIVIAN.
MRS. MÖLDERS !!
THANK YOU!
YOU LOOK BEAUTIFUL TODAY!
WHY, THANK YOU!
SOMEWHERE ALONG THE LINE, THOSE TWO HAVE BECOME CLOSE.
SHE'S AN ADMIRER OF MRS. MÖLDERS.
SHE'D ALWAYS MIMIC WHATEVER MRS. MÖLDERS DID.
MY!

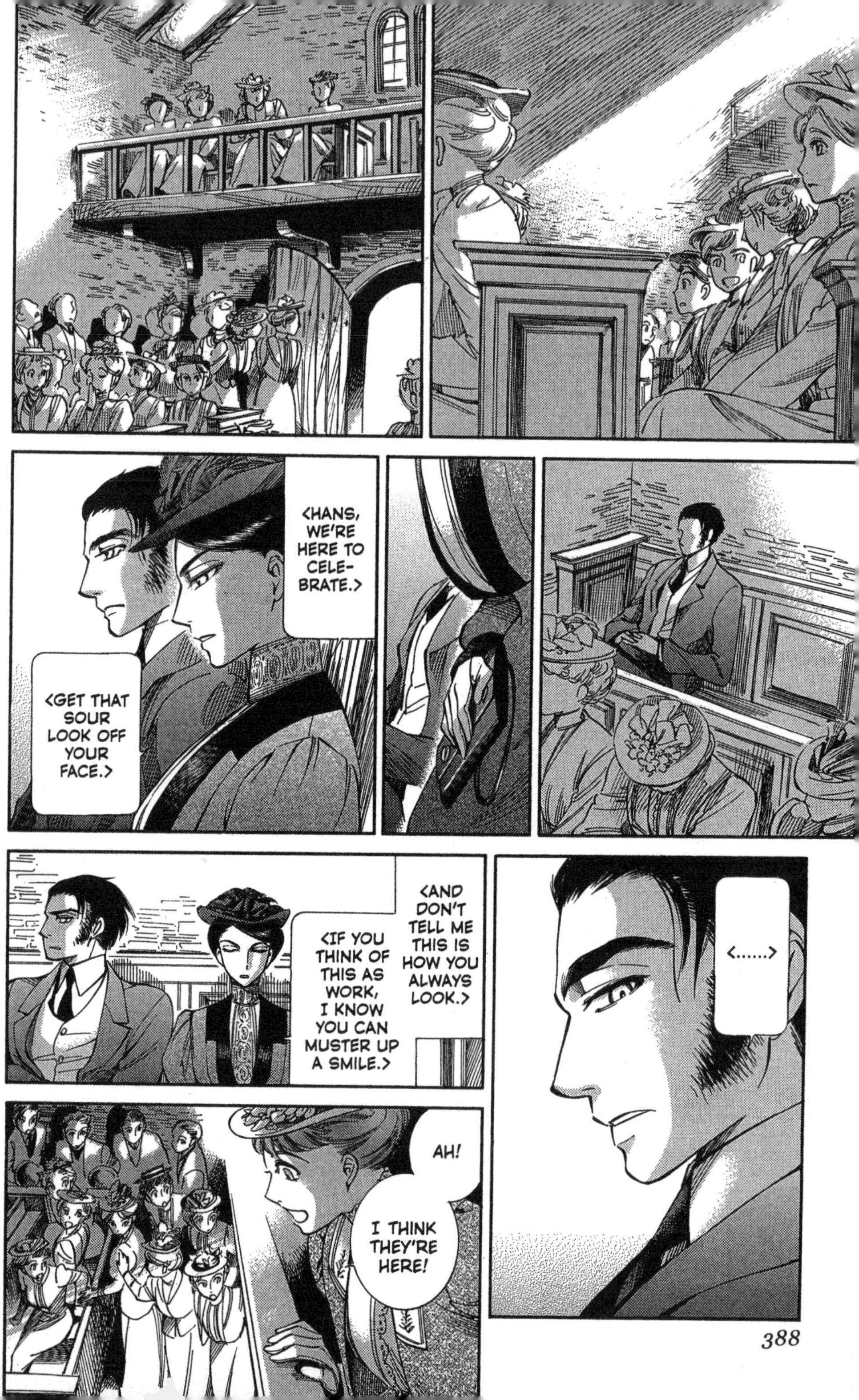

<HANS, WE'RE HERE TO CELEBRATE.>
<GET THAT SOUR LOOK OFF YOUR FACE.>
<......>
<AND DON'T TELL ME THIS IS HOW YOU ALWAYS LOOK.>
<IF YOU THINK OF THIS AS WORK, I KNOW YOU CAN MUSTER UP A SMILE.>
AH!
I THINK THEY'RE HERE!

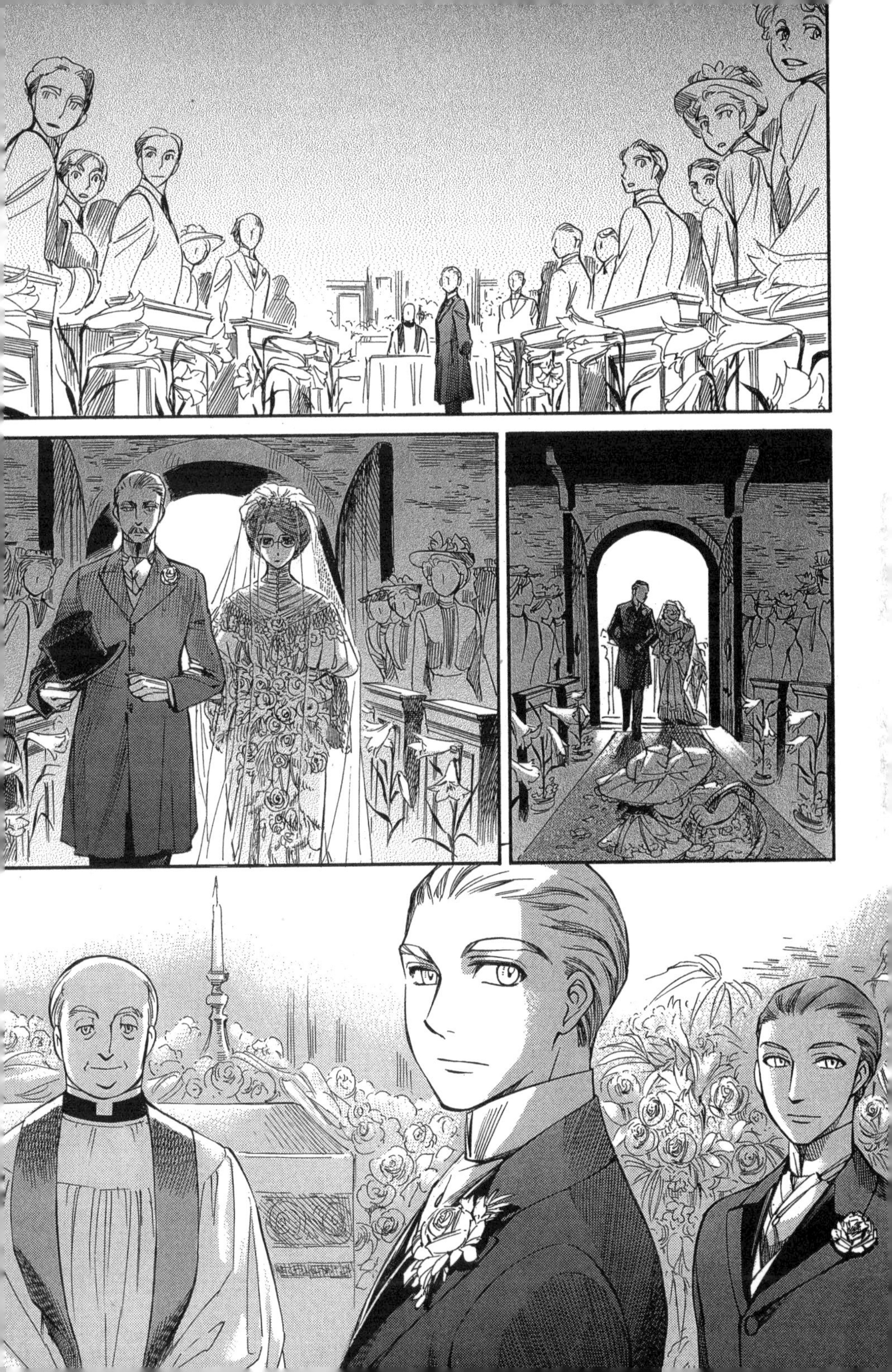

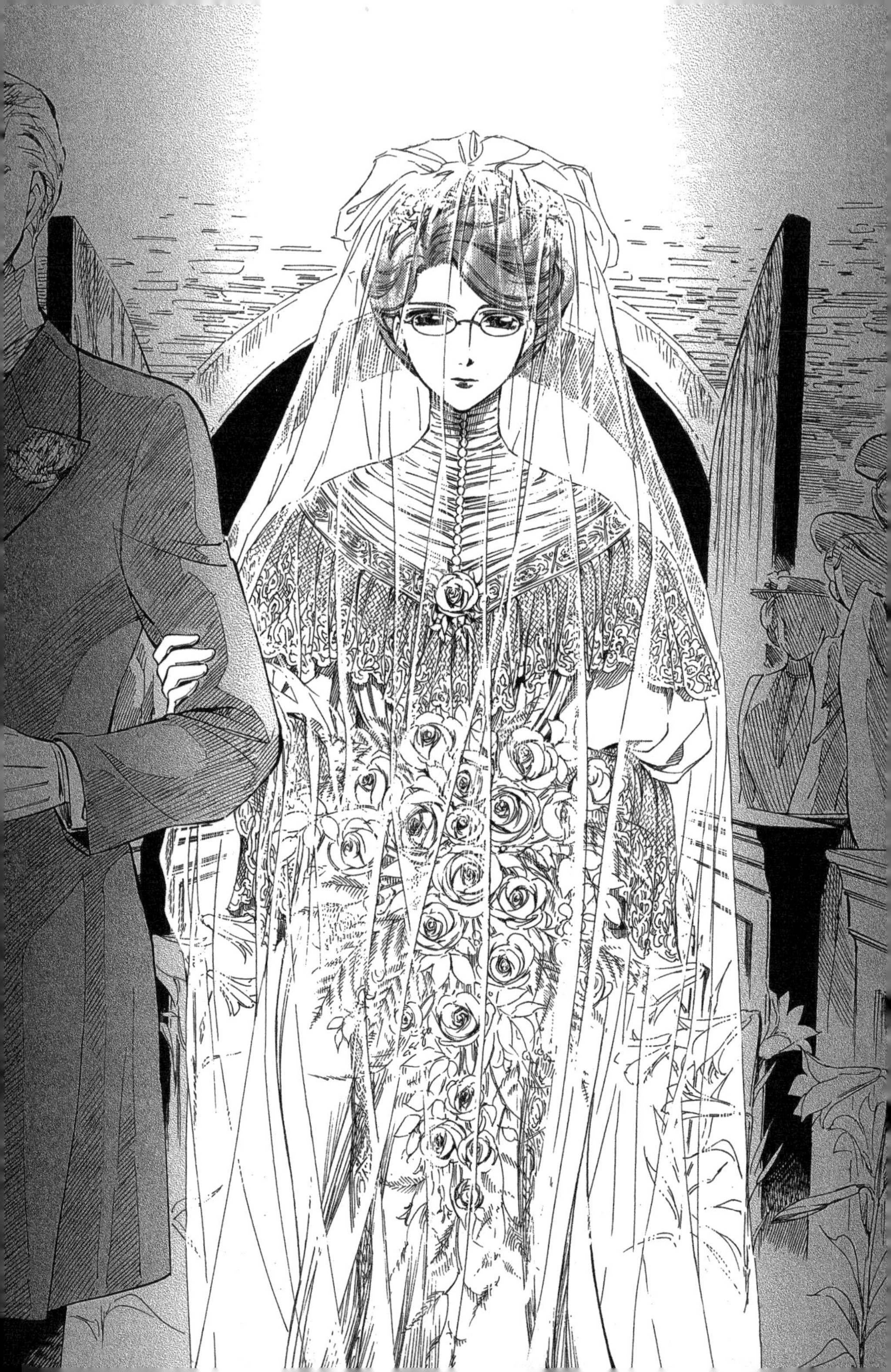

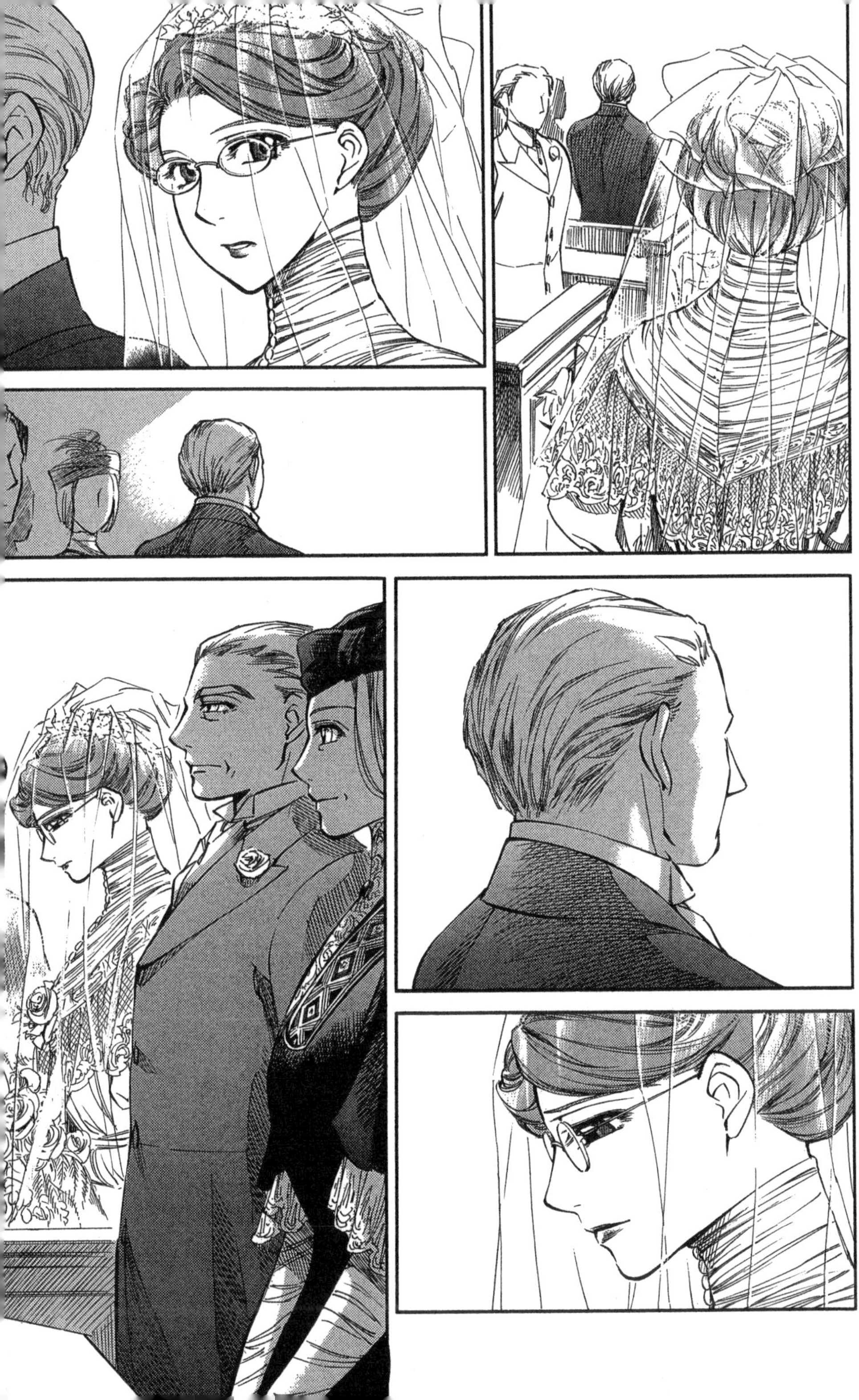

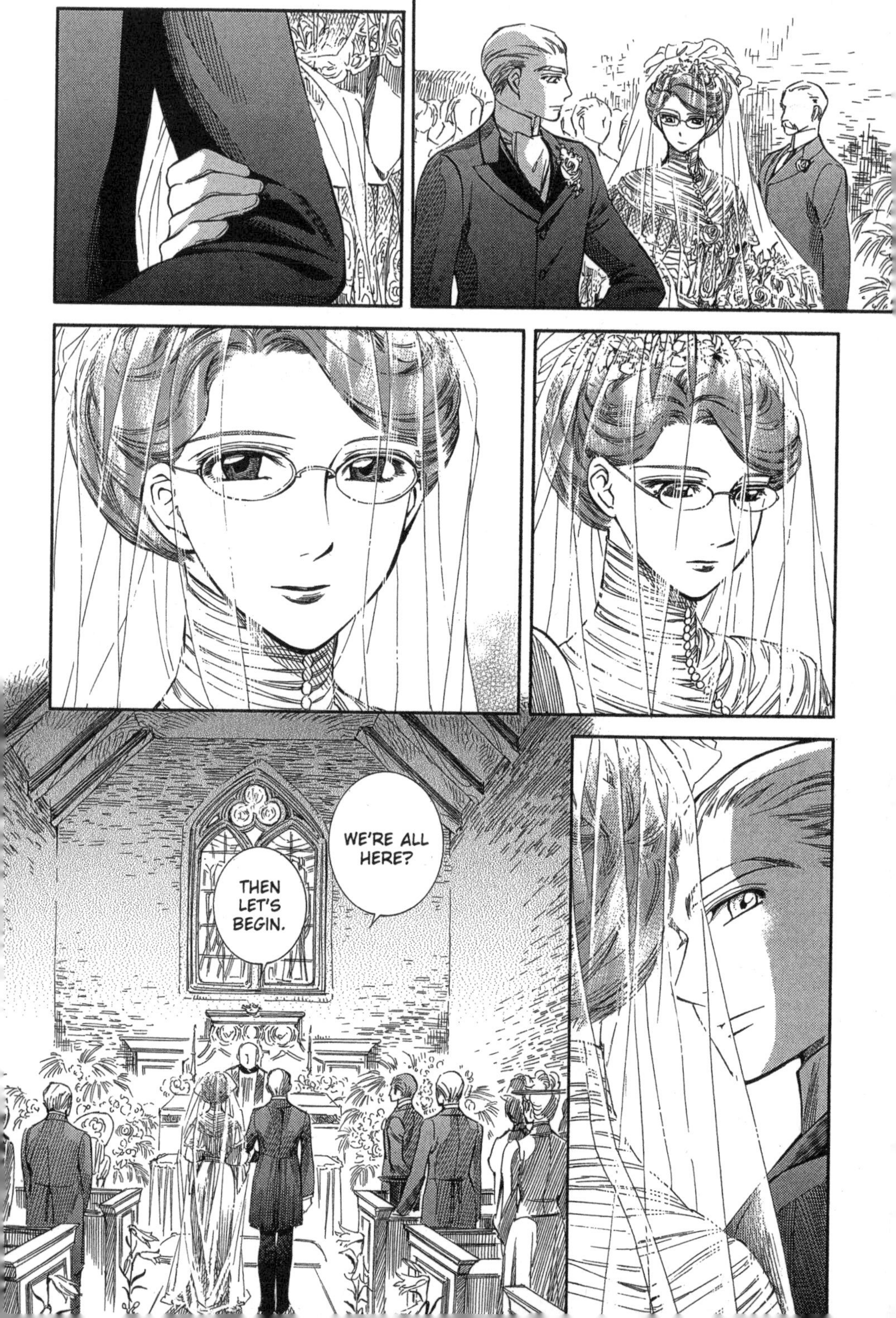
WE'RE ALL HERE?
THEN LET'S BEGIN.

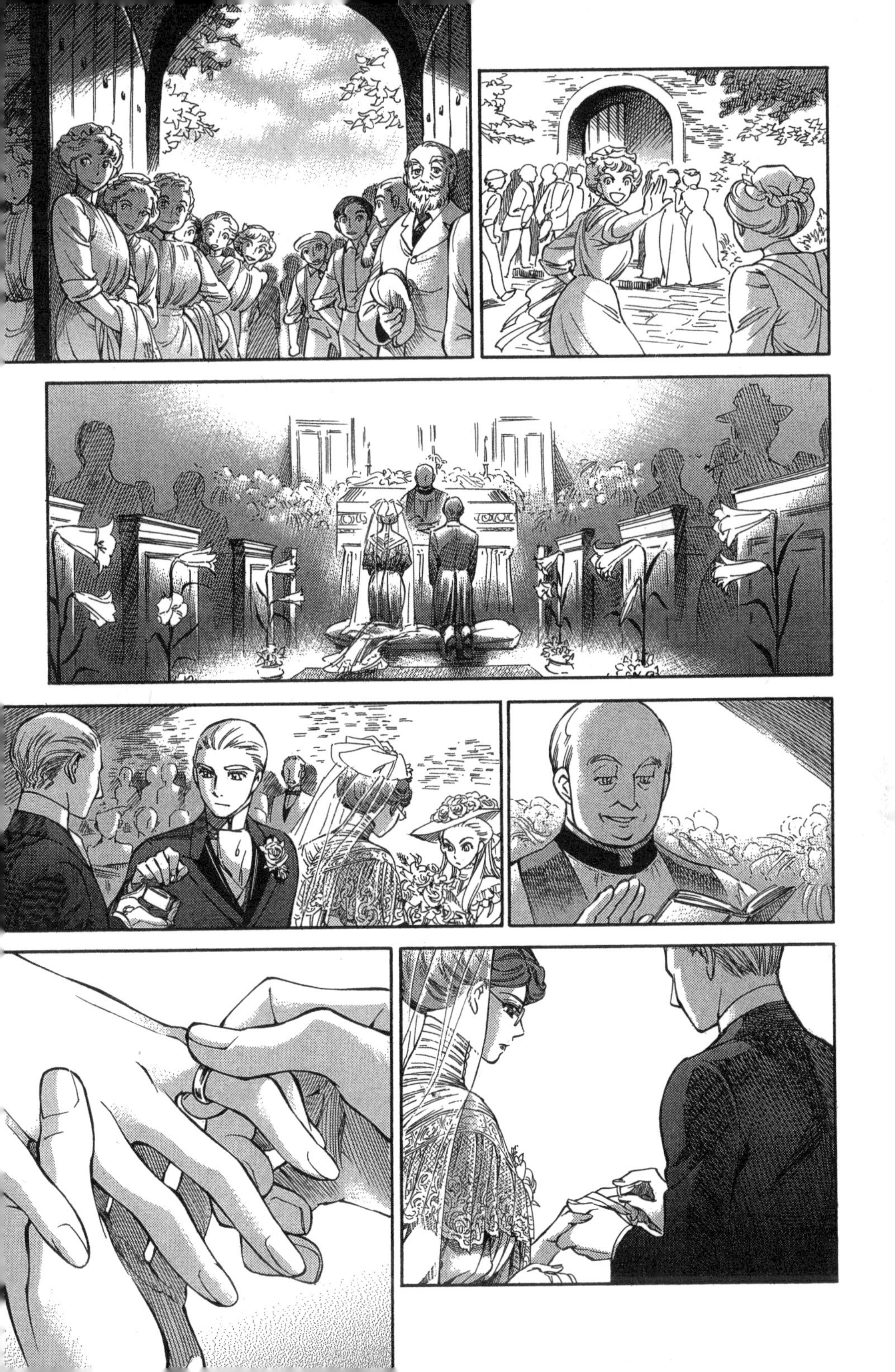

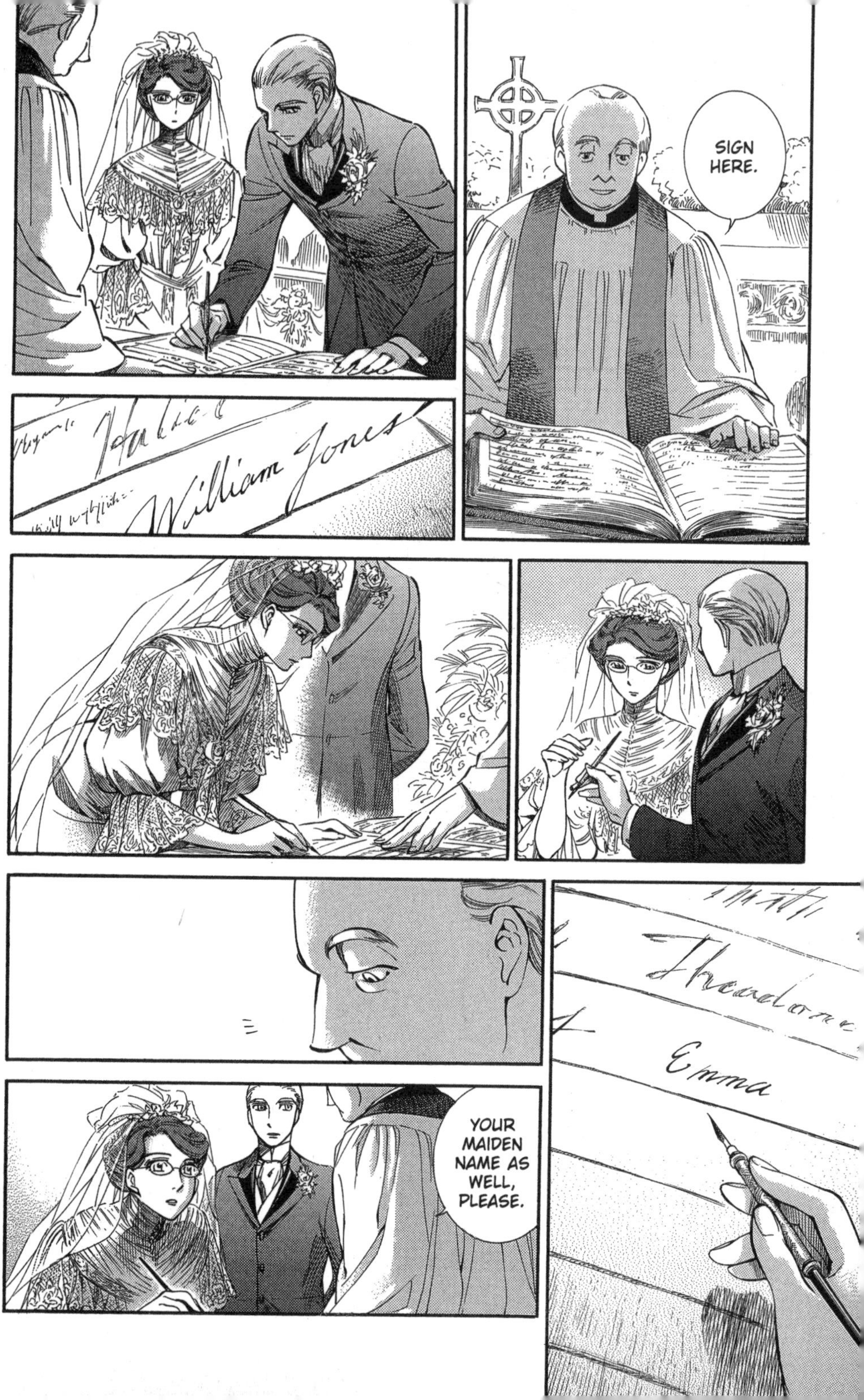
SIGN HERE.
William Jones
Emma
YOUR MAIDEN NAME AS WELL, PLEASE.

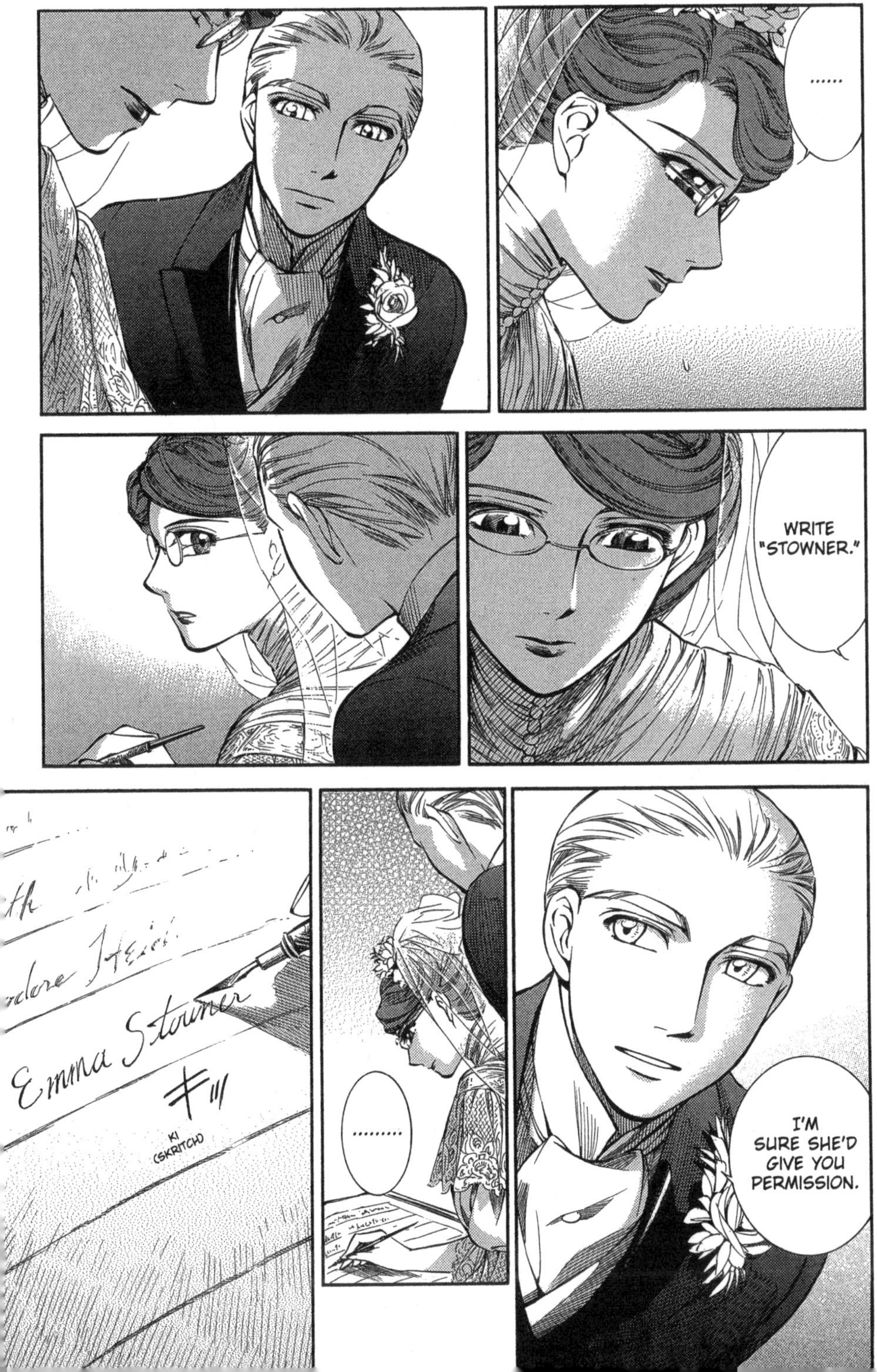
......
WRITE "STOWNER."
I'M SURE SHE'D GIVE YOU PERMISSION.
....
Emma Stowner
KI (SKRITCH)

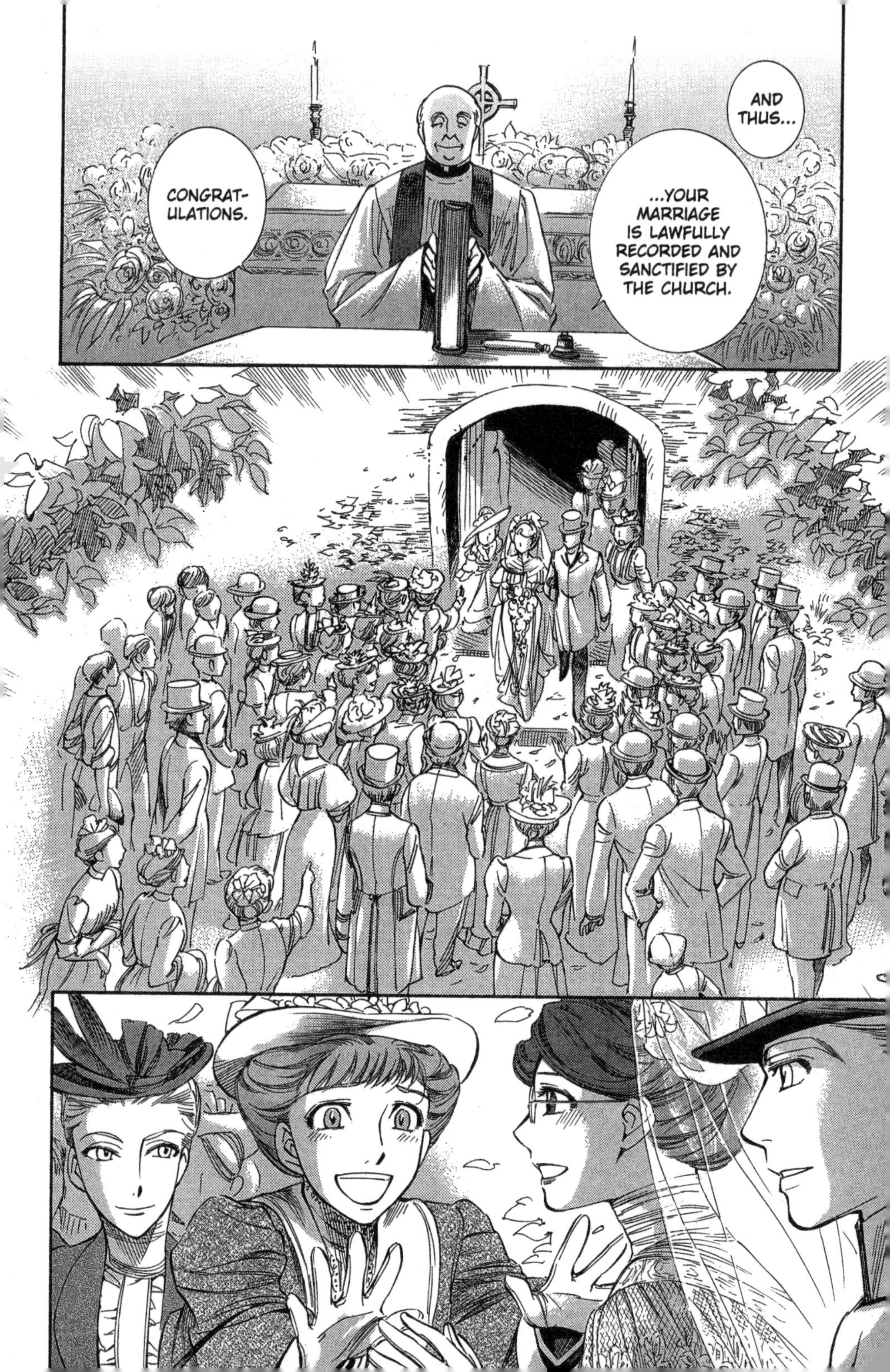
AND THUS...
...YOUR MARRIAGE IS LAWFULLY RECORDED AND SANCTIFIED BY THE CHURCH.
CONGRAT-ULATIONS.

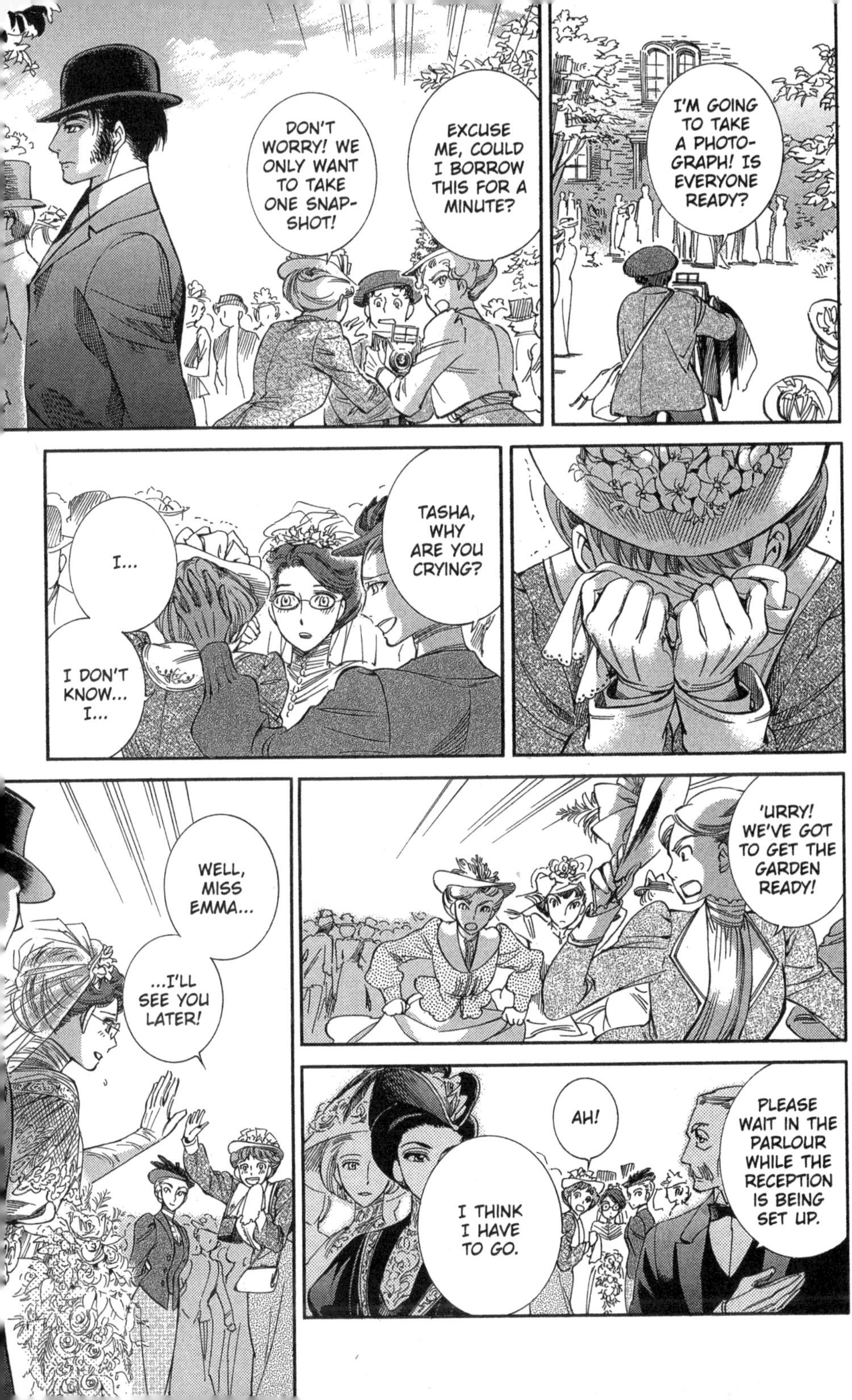
I'M GOING TO TAKE A PHOTOGRAPH! IS EVERYONE READY?
EXCUSE ME, COULD I BORROW THIS FOR A MINUTE?
DON'T WORRY! WE ONLY WANT TO TAKE ONE SNAPSHOT!
TASHA, WHY ARE YOU CRYING?
I...
I DON'T KNOW... I...
'URRY! WE'VE GOT TO GET THE GARDEN READY!
PLEASE WAIT IN THE PARLOUR WHILE THE RECEPTION IS BEING SET UP.
AH!
I THINK I HAVE TO GO.
WELL, MISS EMMA...
...I'LL SEE YOU LATER!

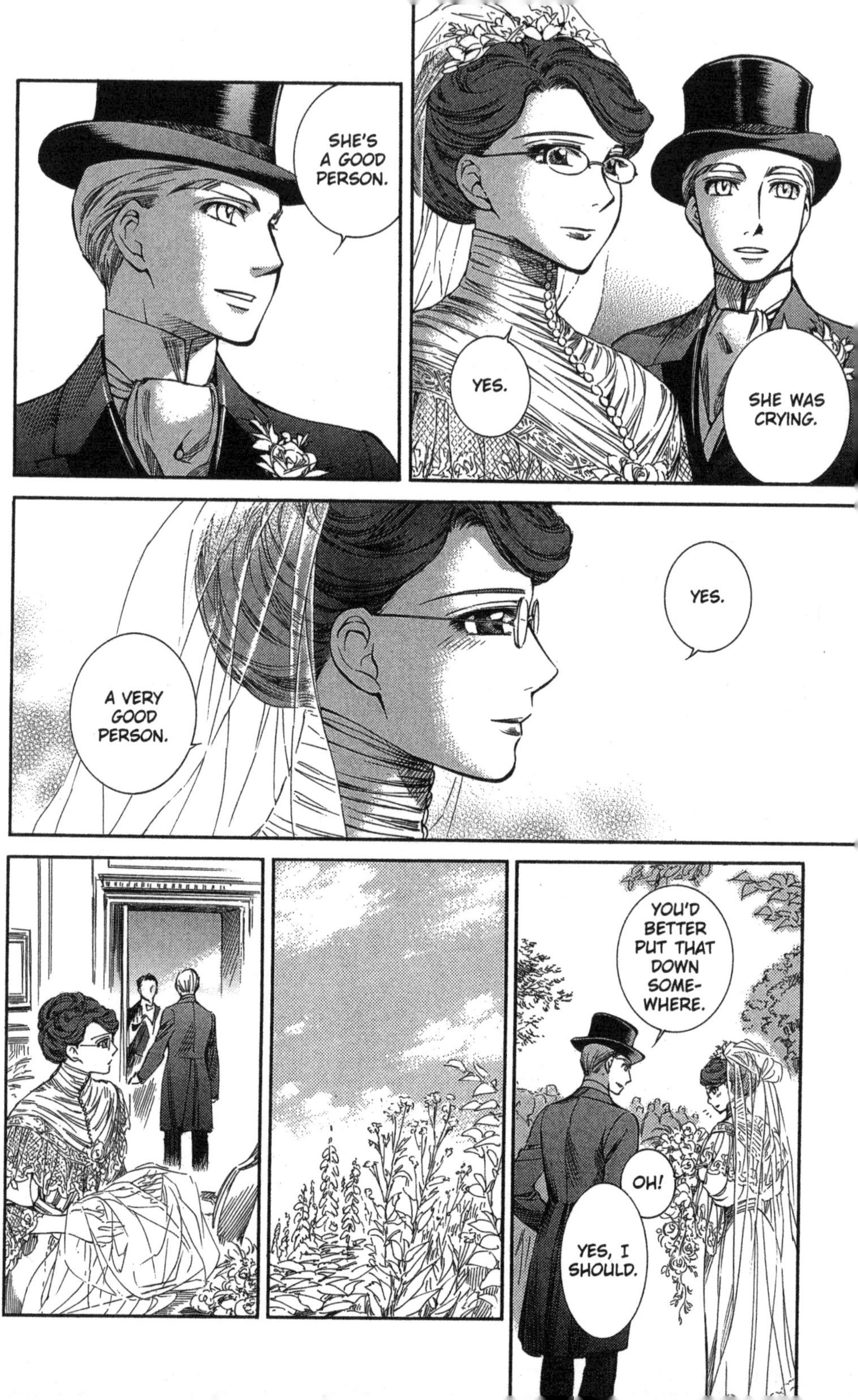
SHE WAS CRYING.
YES.
SHE'S A GOOD PERSON.
YES.
A VERY GOOD PERSON.
YOU'D BETTER PUT THAT DOWN SOME-WHERE.
OH!
YES, I SHOULD.

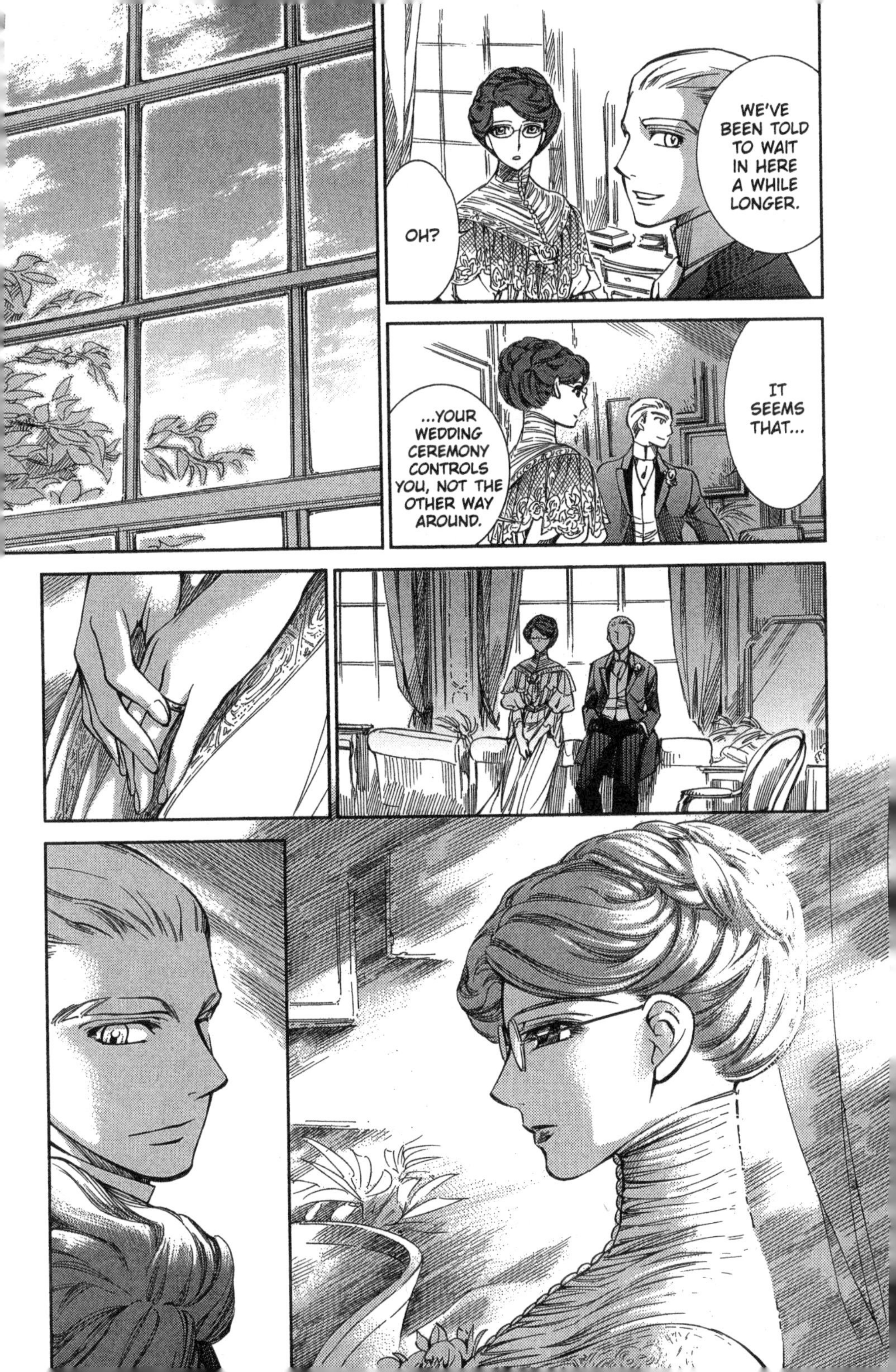
WE'VE BEEN TOLD TO WAIT IN HERE A WHILE LONGER.
OH?
IT SEEMS THAT...
...YOUR WEDDING CEREMONY CONTROLS YOU, NOT THE OTHER WAY AROUND.

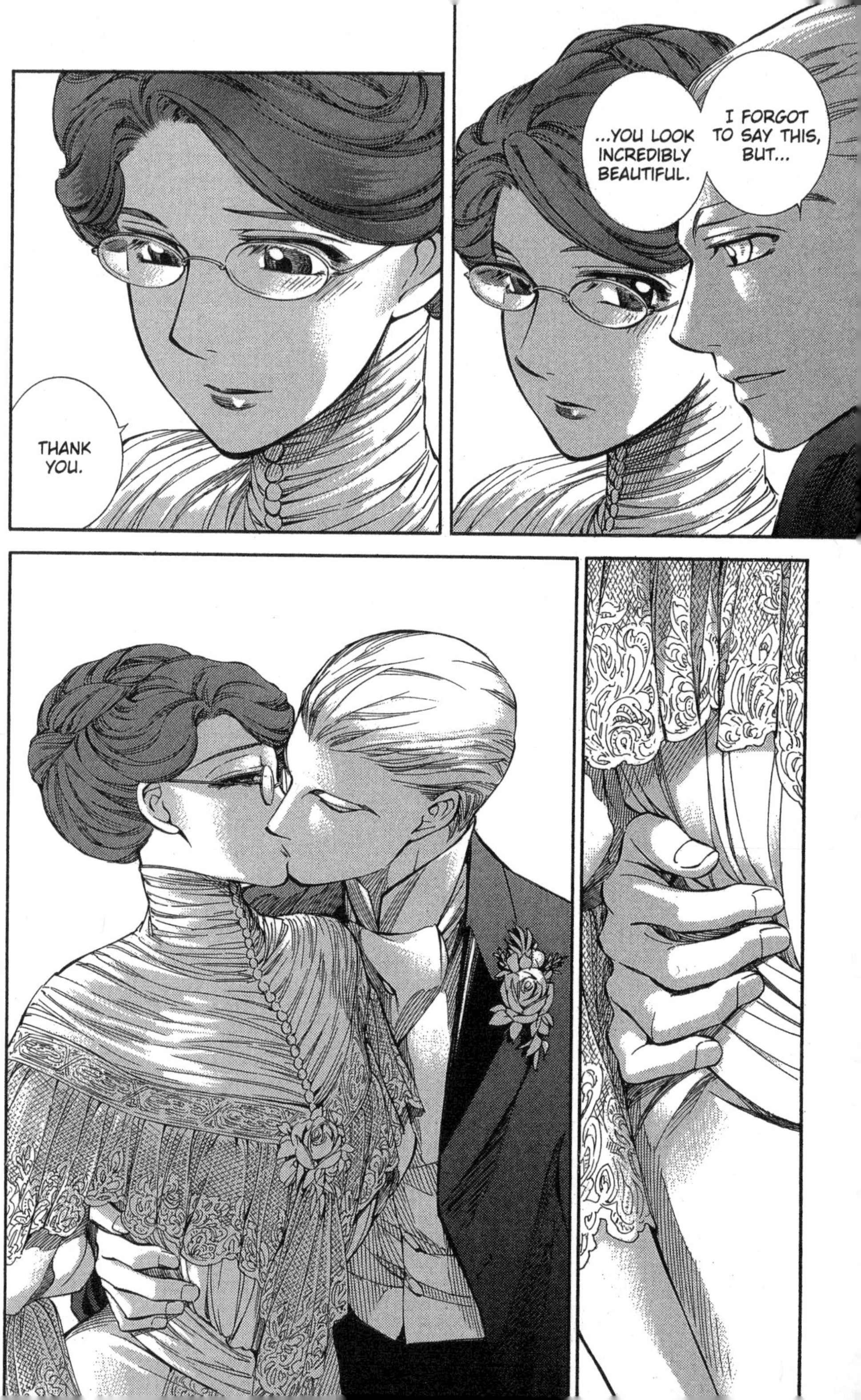
I FORGOT TO SAY THIS, BUT...
...YOU LOOK INCREDIBLY BEAUTIFUL.
THANK YOU.

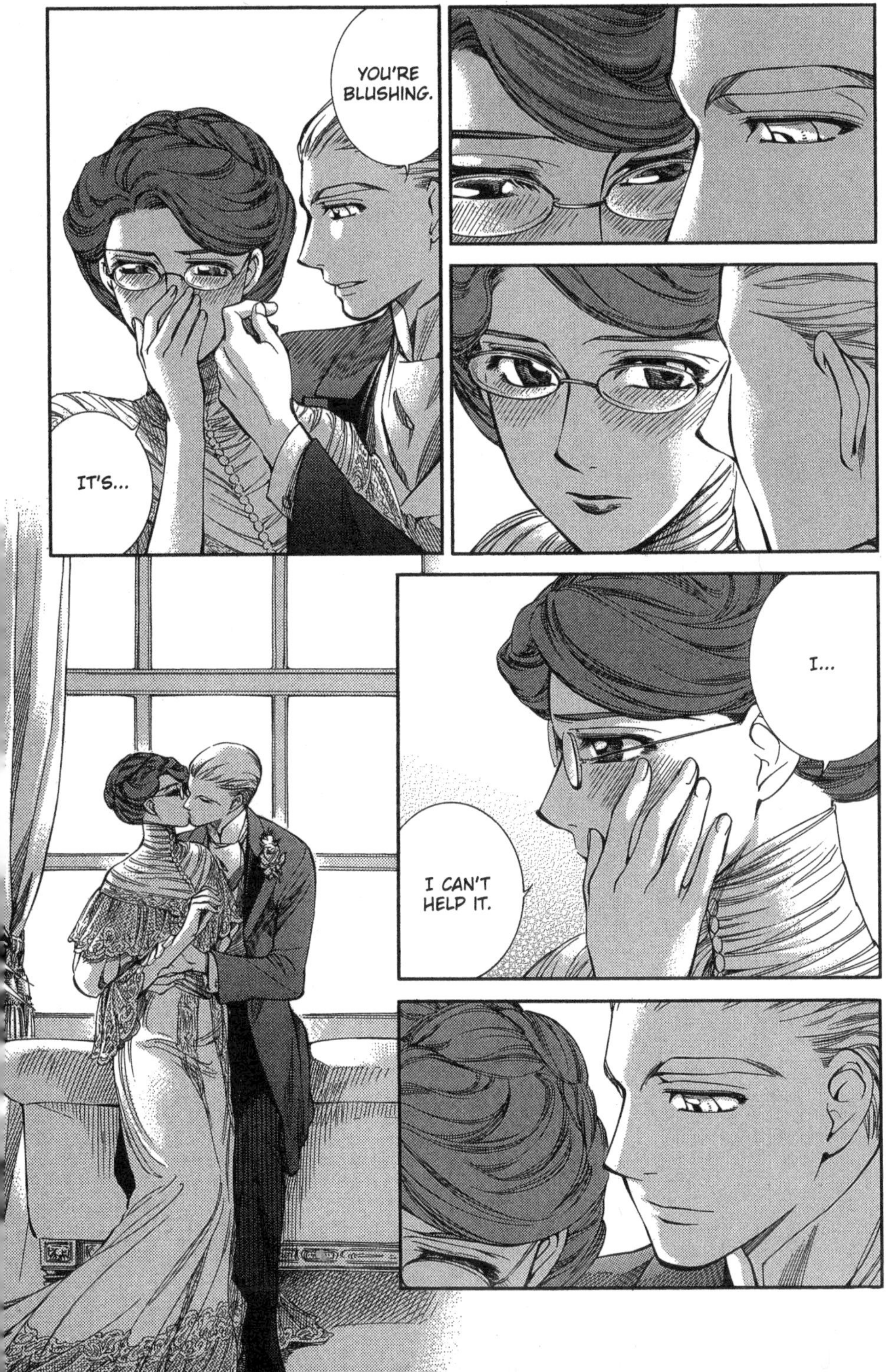
YOU'RE BLUSHING.
IT'S...
I...
I CAN'T HELP IT.

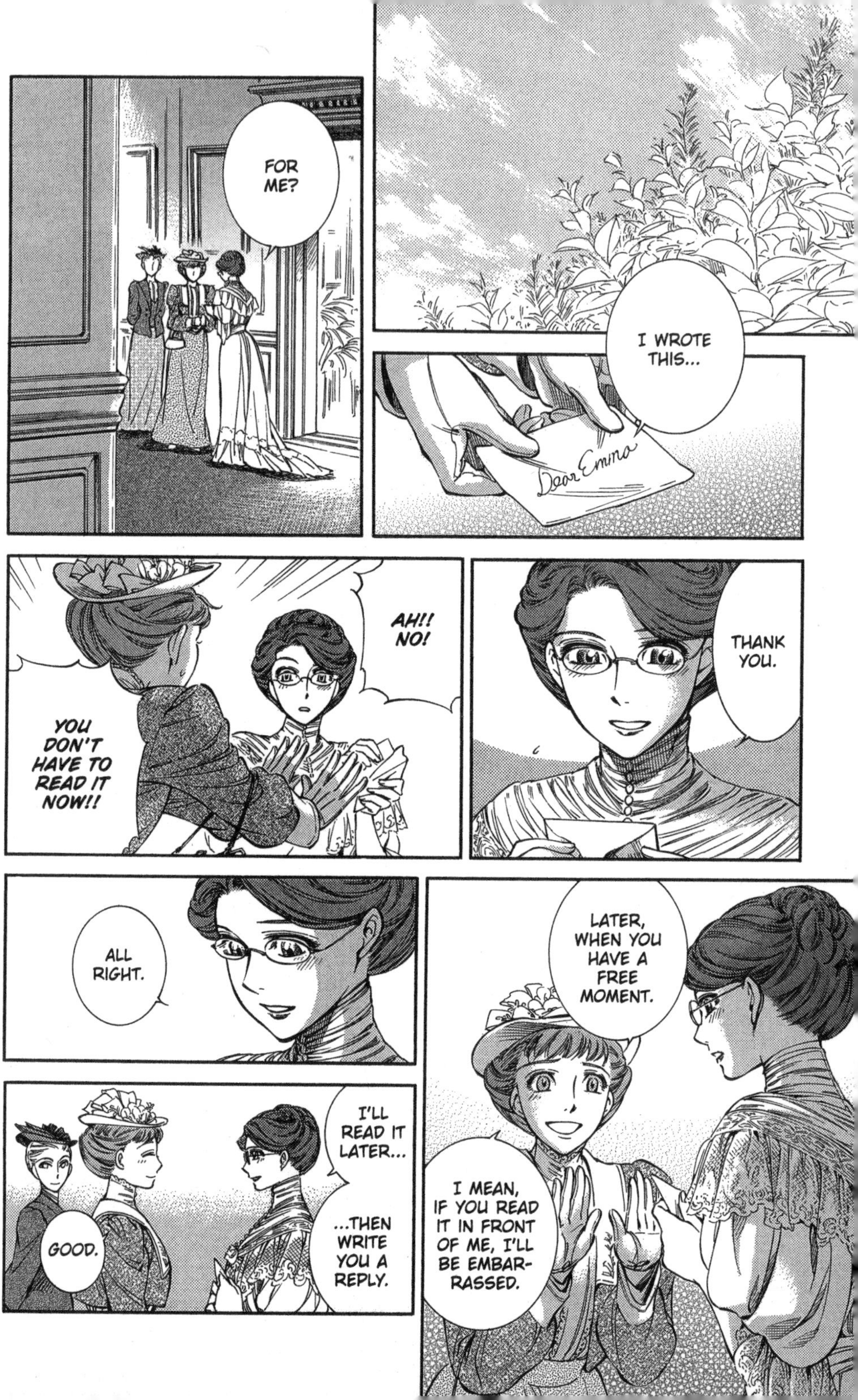
I WROTE THIS...
Dear Emma
FOR ME?
THANK YOU.
AH!! NO!
YOU DON'T HAVE TO READ IT NOW!!
LATER, WHEN YOU HAVE A FREE MOMENT.
I MEAN, IF YOU READ IT IN FRONT OF ME, I'LL BE EMBARRASSED.
ALL RIGHT.
I'LL READ IT LATER...
...THEN WRITE YOU A REPLY.
GOOD.

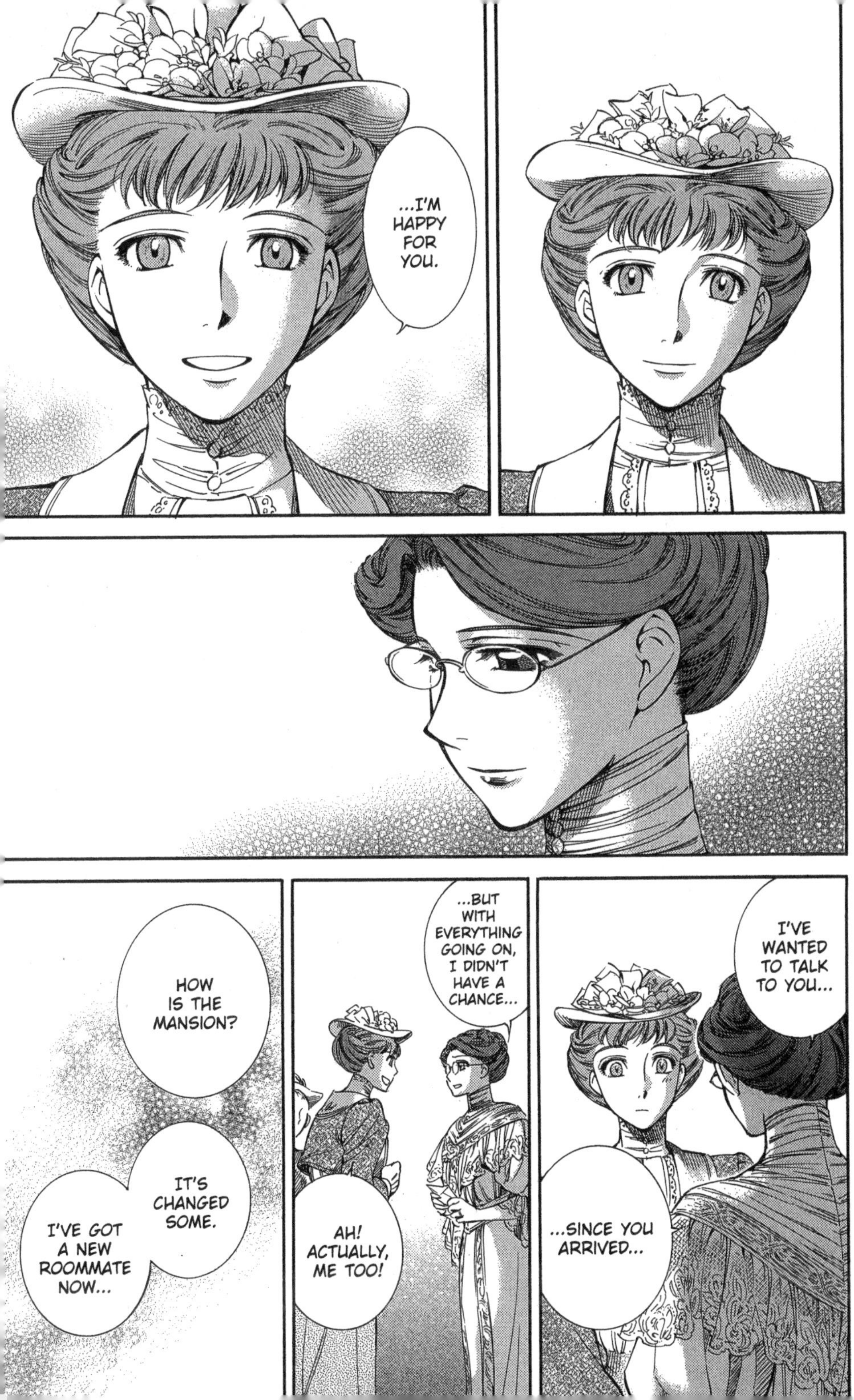
...I'M HAPPY FOR YOU.
I'VE WANTED TO TALK TO YOU...
...SINCE YOU ARRIVED...
...BUT WITH EVERYTHING GOING ON, I DIDN'T HAVE A CHANCE...
AH! ACTUALLY, ME TOO!
HOW IS THE MANSION?
IT'S CHANGED SOME.
I'VE GOT A NEW ROOMMATE NOW...

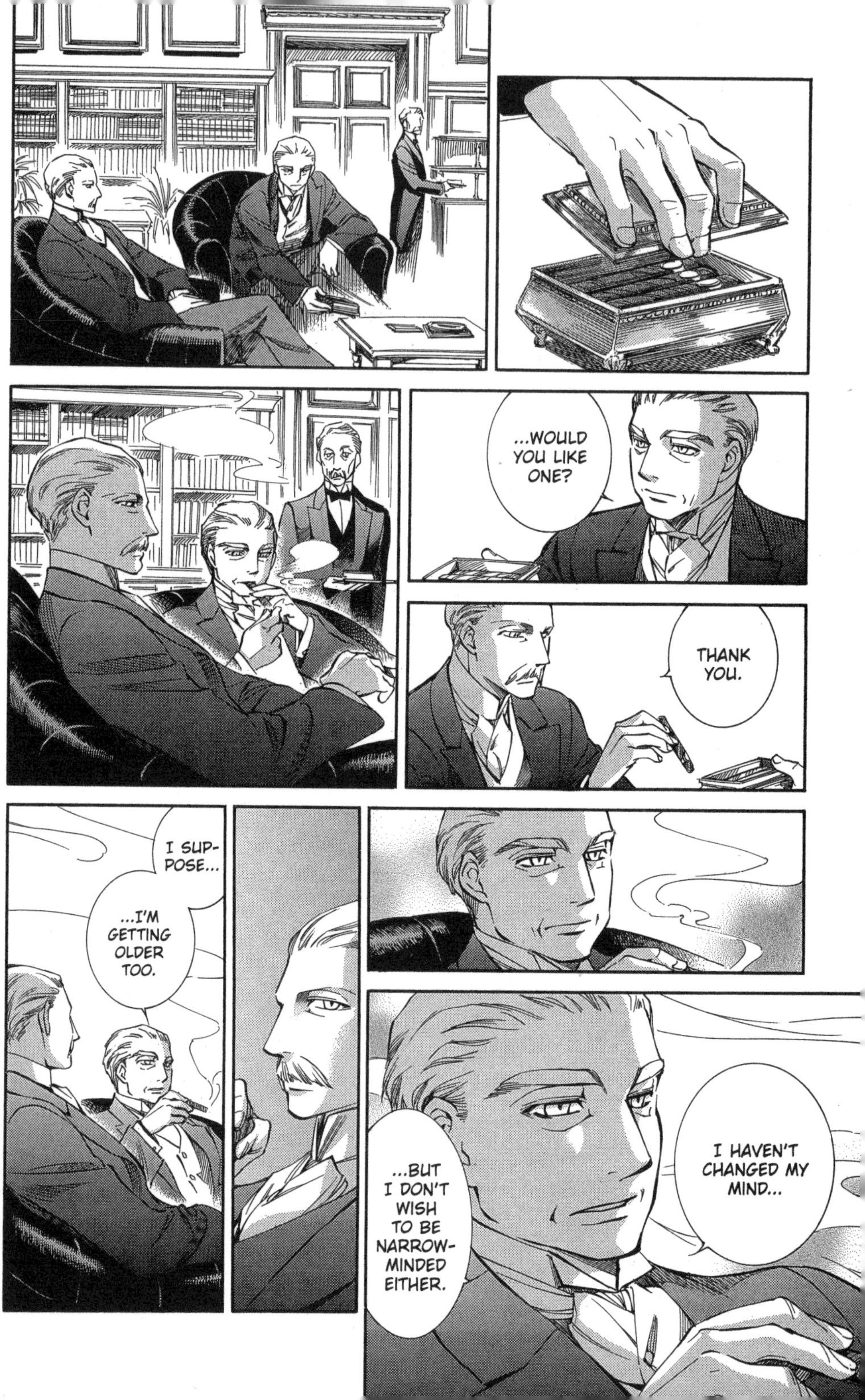
...WOULD YOU LIKE ONE?
THANK YOU.
I HAVEN'T CHANGED MY MIND...
...BUT I DON'T WISH TO BE NARROW-MINDED EITHER.
I SUP-POSE...
...I'M GETTING OLDER TOO.

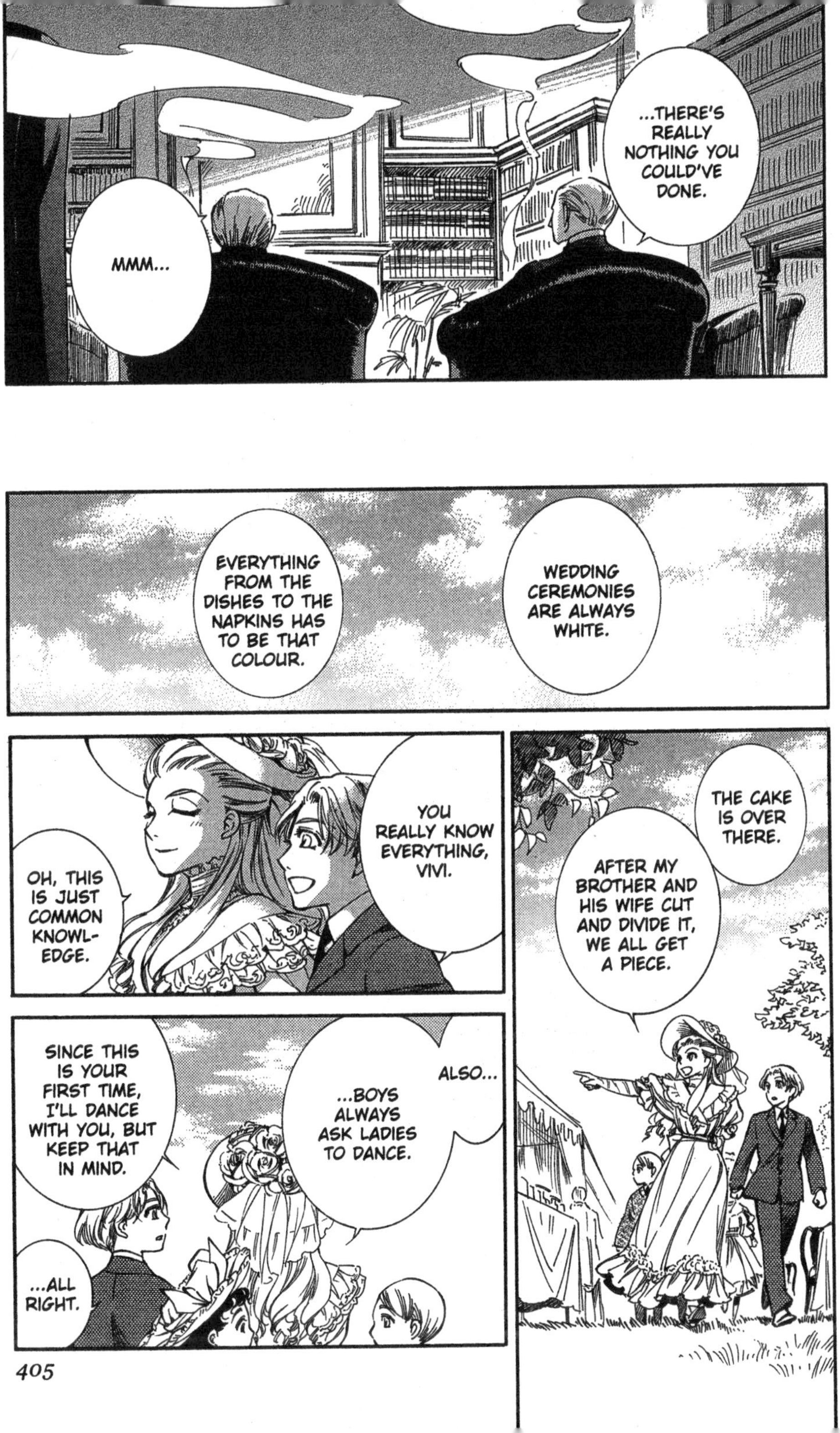
...THERE'S REALLY NOTHING YOU COULD'VE DONE.
MMM...
WEDDING CEREMONIES ARE ALWAYS WHITE.
EVERYTHING FROM THE DISHES TO THE NAPKINS HAS TO BE THAT COLOUR.
THE CAKE IS OVER THERE.
AFTER MY BROTHER AND HIS WIFE CUT AND DIVIDE IT, WE ALL GET A PIECE.
YOU REALLY KNOW EVERYTHING, VIVI.
OH, THIS IS JUST COMMON KNOWL-EDGE.
ALSO...
...BOYS ALWAYS ASK LADIES TO DANCE.
SINCE THIS IS YOUR FIRST TIME, I'LL DANCE WITH YOU, BUT KEEP THAT IN MIND.
...ALL RIGHT.

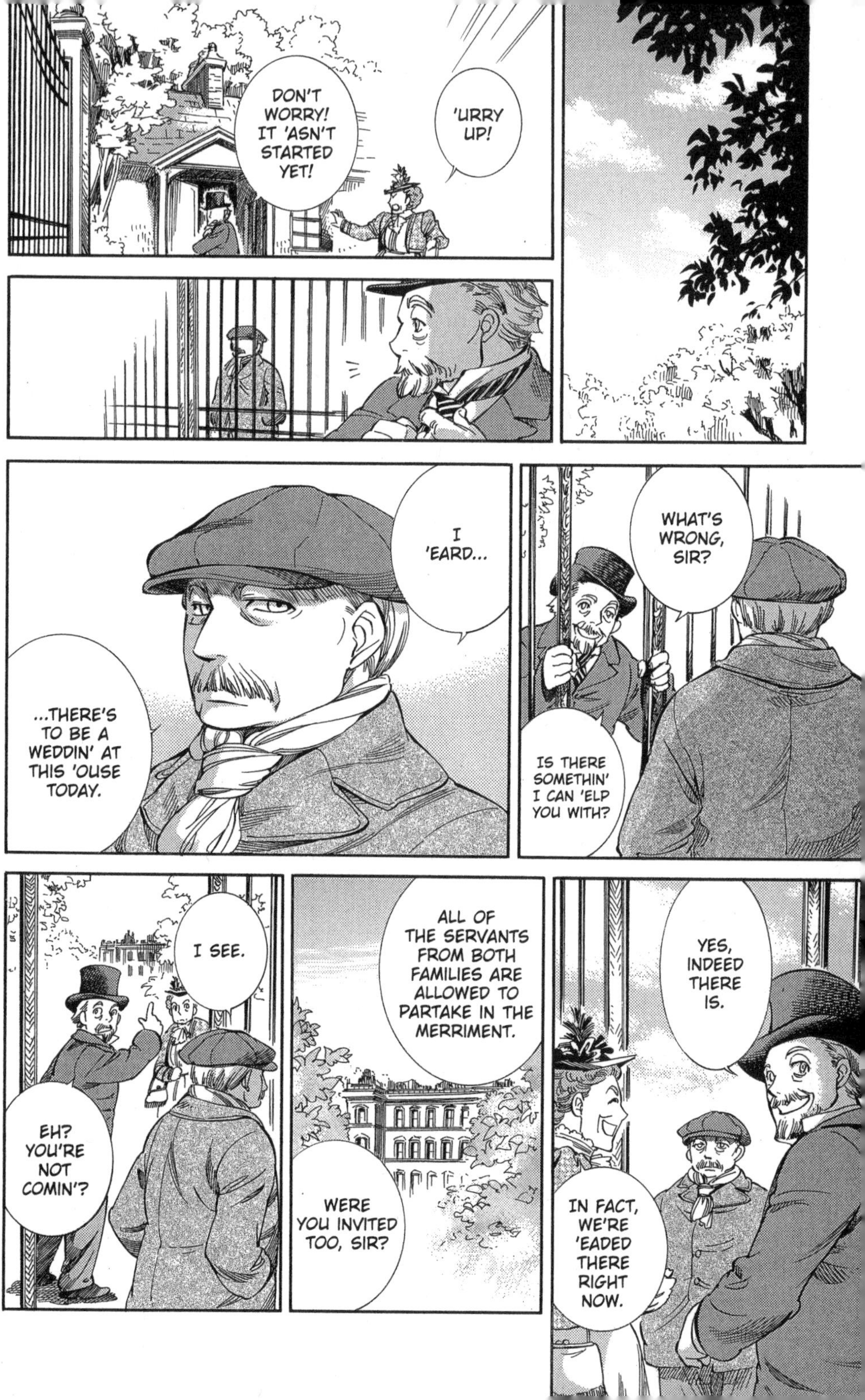
'URRY UP!
DON'T WORRY! IT 'ASN'T STARTED YET!
WHAT'S WRONG, SIR?
IS THERE SOMETHIN' I CAN 'ELP YOU WITH?
I 'EARD...
...THERE'S TO BE A WEDDIN' AT THIS 'OUSE TODAY.
YES, INDEED THERE IS.
IN FACT, WE'RE 'EADED THERE RIGHT NOW.
ALL OF THE SERVANTS FROM BOTH FAMILIES ARE ALLOWED TO PARTAKE IN THE MERRIMENT.
WERE YOU INVITED TOO, SIR?
I SEE.
EH? YOU'RE NOT COMIN'?

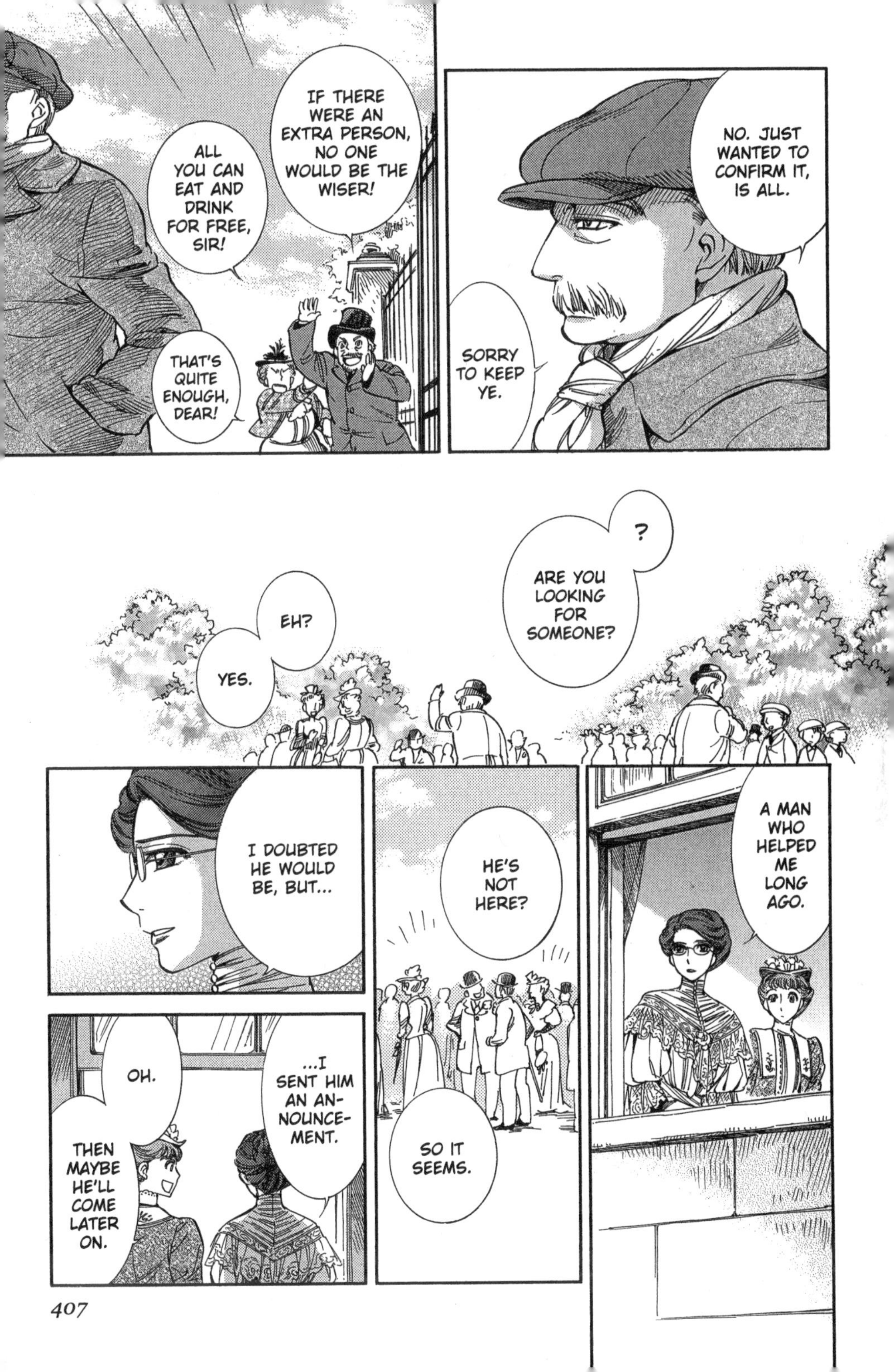
NO. JUST WANTED TO CONFIRM IT, IS ALL.
SORRY TO KEEP YE.
IF THERE WERE AN EXTRA PERSON, NO ONE WOULD BE THE WISER!
ALL YOU CAN EAT AND DRINK FOR FREE, SIR!
THAT'S QUITE ENOUGH, DEAR!
?
ARE YOU LOOKING FOR SOMEONE?
EH?
YES.
A MAN WHO HELPED ME LONG AGO.
HE'S NOT HERE?
SO IT SEEMS.
I DOUBTED HE WOULD BE, BUT...
...I SENT HIM AN AN-NOUNCE-MENT.
OH.
THEN MAYBE HE'LL COME LATER ON.

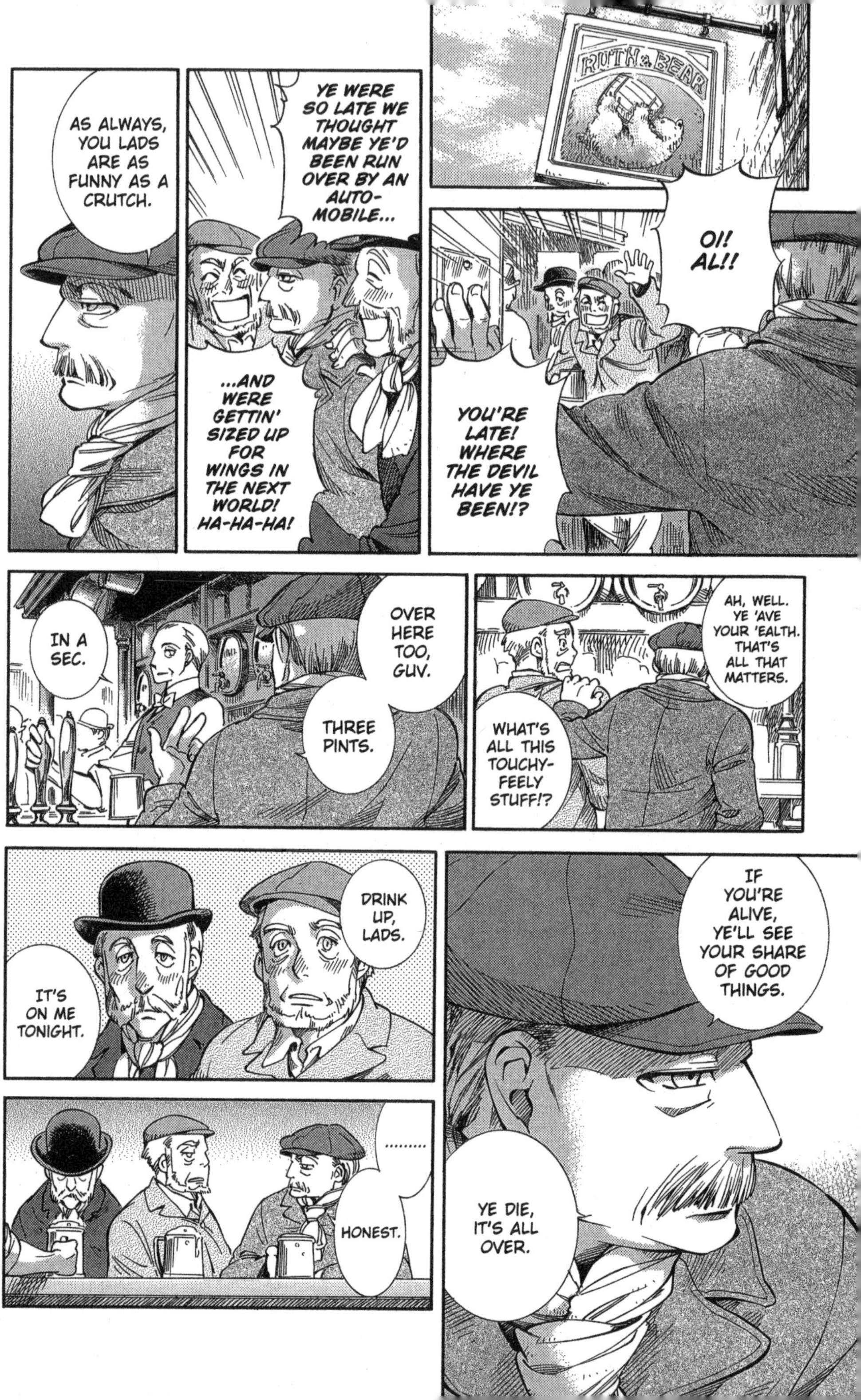
RUTH & BEAR
OI! AL!!
YOU'RE LATE! WHERE THE DEVIL HAVE YE BEEN!?
YE WERE SO LATE WE THOUGHT MAYBE YE'D BEEN RUN OVER BY AN AUTO-MOBILE...
...AND WERE GETTIN' SIZED UP FOR WINGS IN THE NEXT WORLD! HA-HA-HA!
AS ALWAYS, YOU LADS ARE AS FUNNY AS A CRUTCH.
AH, WELL. YE 'AVE YOUR 'EALTH. THAT'S ALL THAT MATTERS.
WHAT'S ALL THIS TOUCHY-FEELY STUFF!?
OVER HERE TOO, GUV.
THREE PINTS.
IN A SEC.
IF YOU'RE ALIVE, YE'LL SEE YOUR SHARE OF GOOD THINGS.
YE DIE, IT'S ALL OVER.
DRINK UP, LADS.
IT'S ON ME TONIGHT.
....
HONEST.

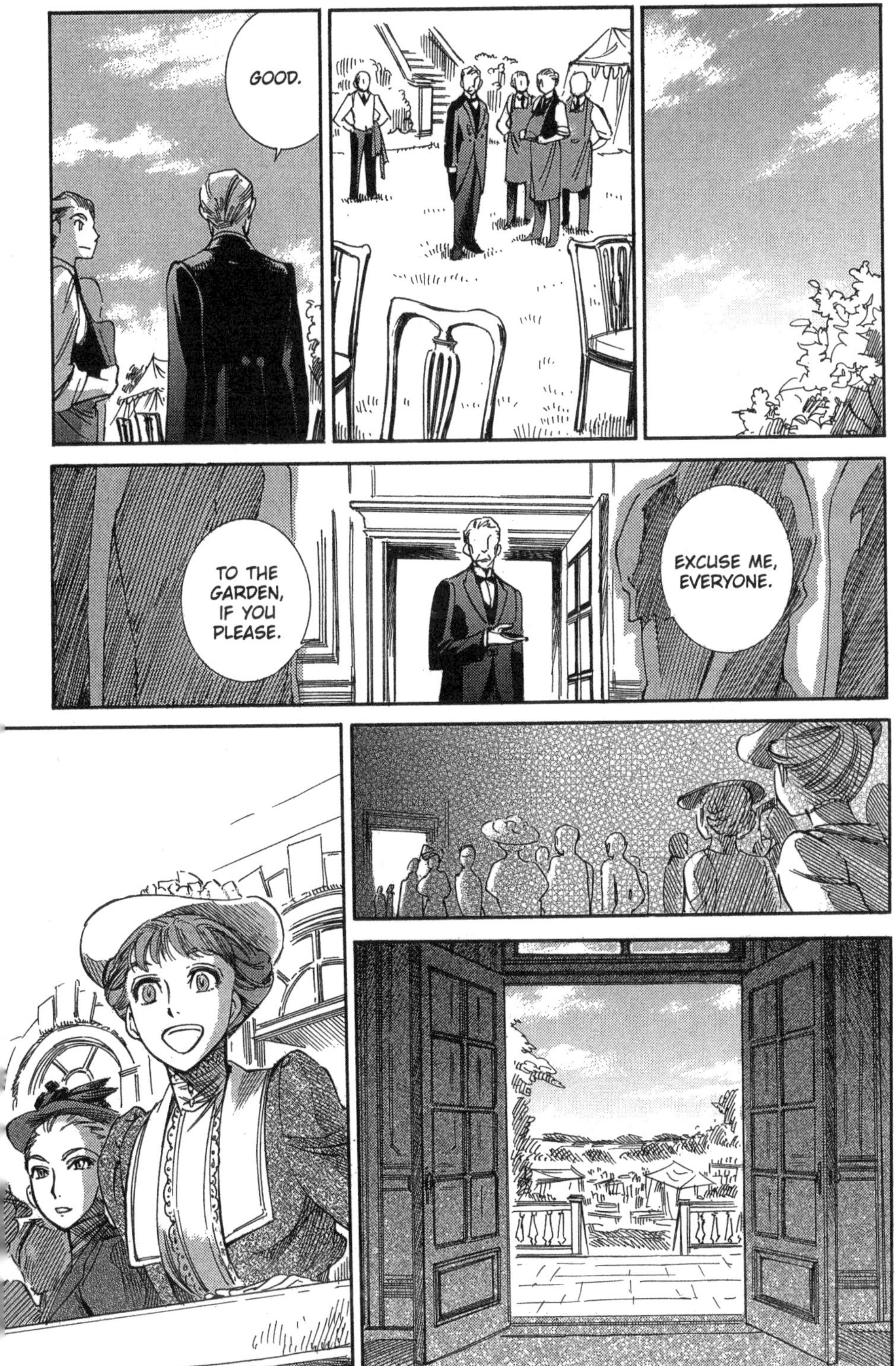
GOOD.
EXCUSE ME, EVERYONE.
TO THE GARDEN, IF YOU PLEASE.

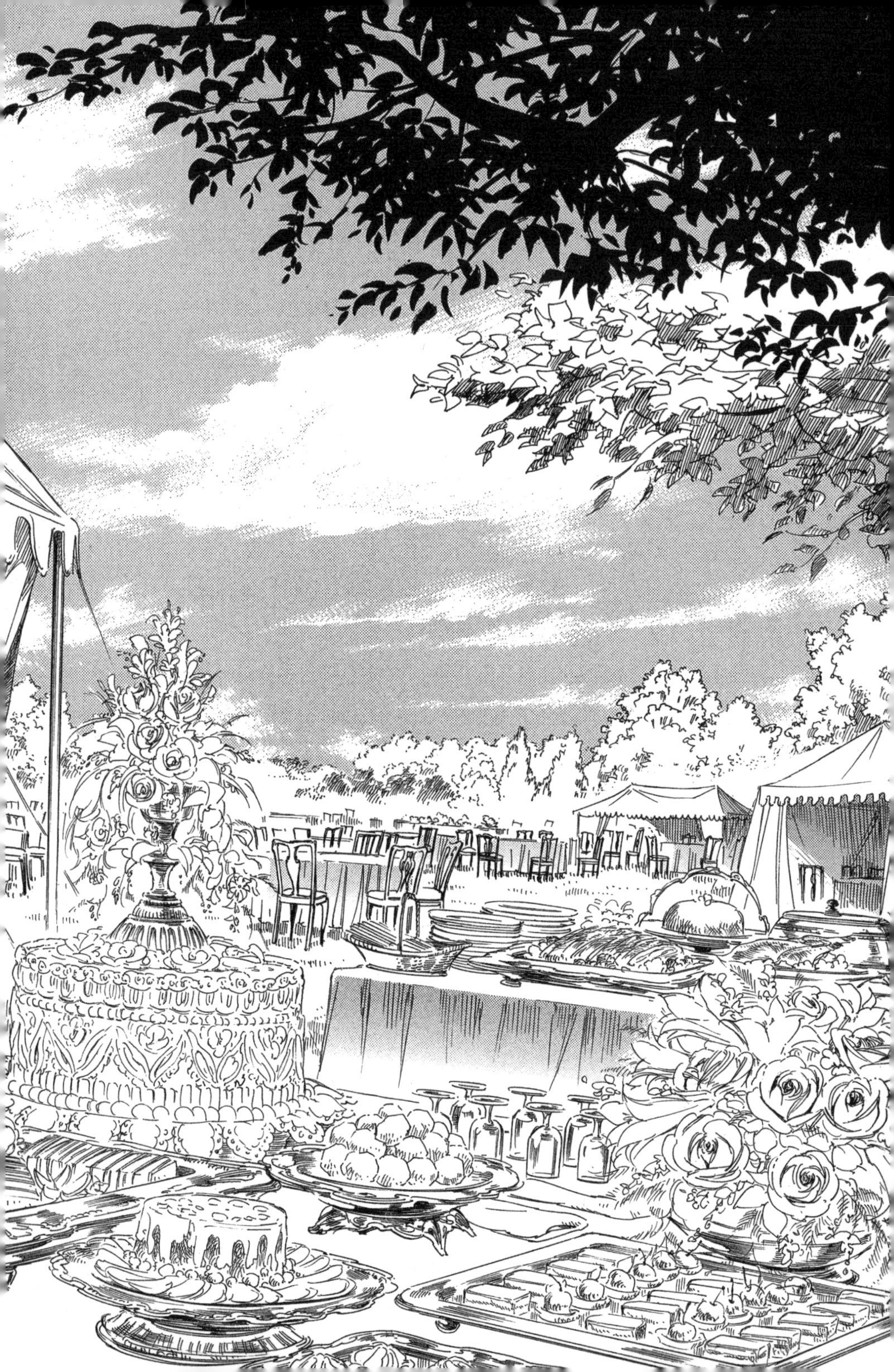

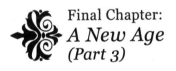

Final Chapter:
A New Age
(Part 3)

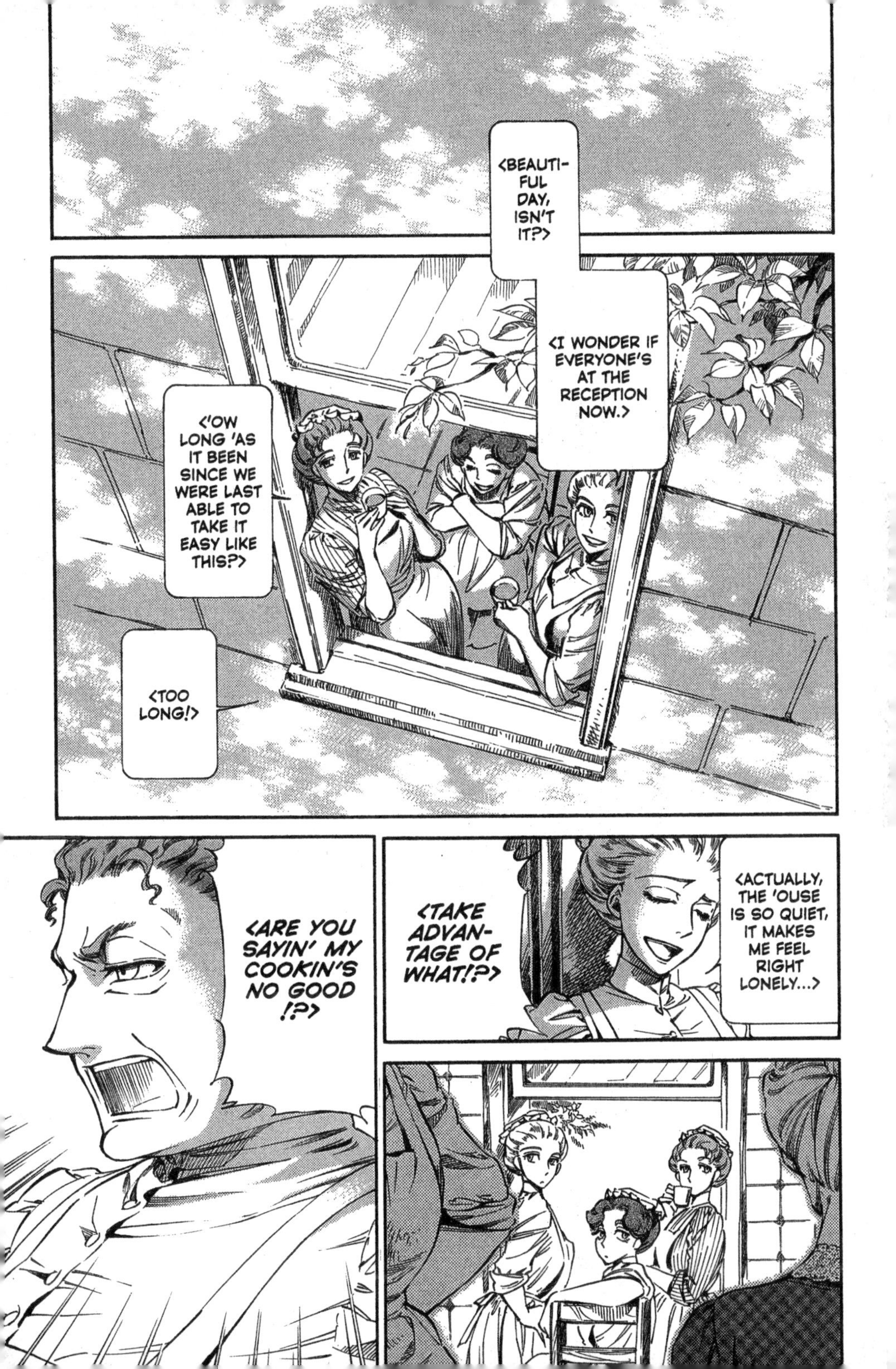
<BEAUTIFUL DAY, ISN'T IT?>
<I WONDER IF EVERYONE'S AT THE RECEPTION NOW.>
<'OW LONG 'AS IT BEEN SINCE WE WERE LAST ABLE TO TAKE IT EASY LIKE THIS?>
<TOO LONG!>
<ACTUALLY, THE 'OUSE IS SO QUIET, IT MAKES ME FEEL RIGHT LONELY...>
<TAKE ADVANTAGE OF WHAT!?>
<ARE YOU SAYIN' MY COOKIN'S NO GOOD!?>

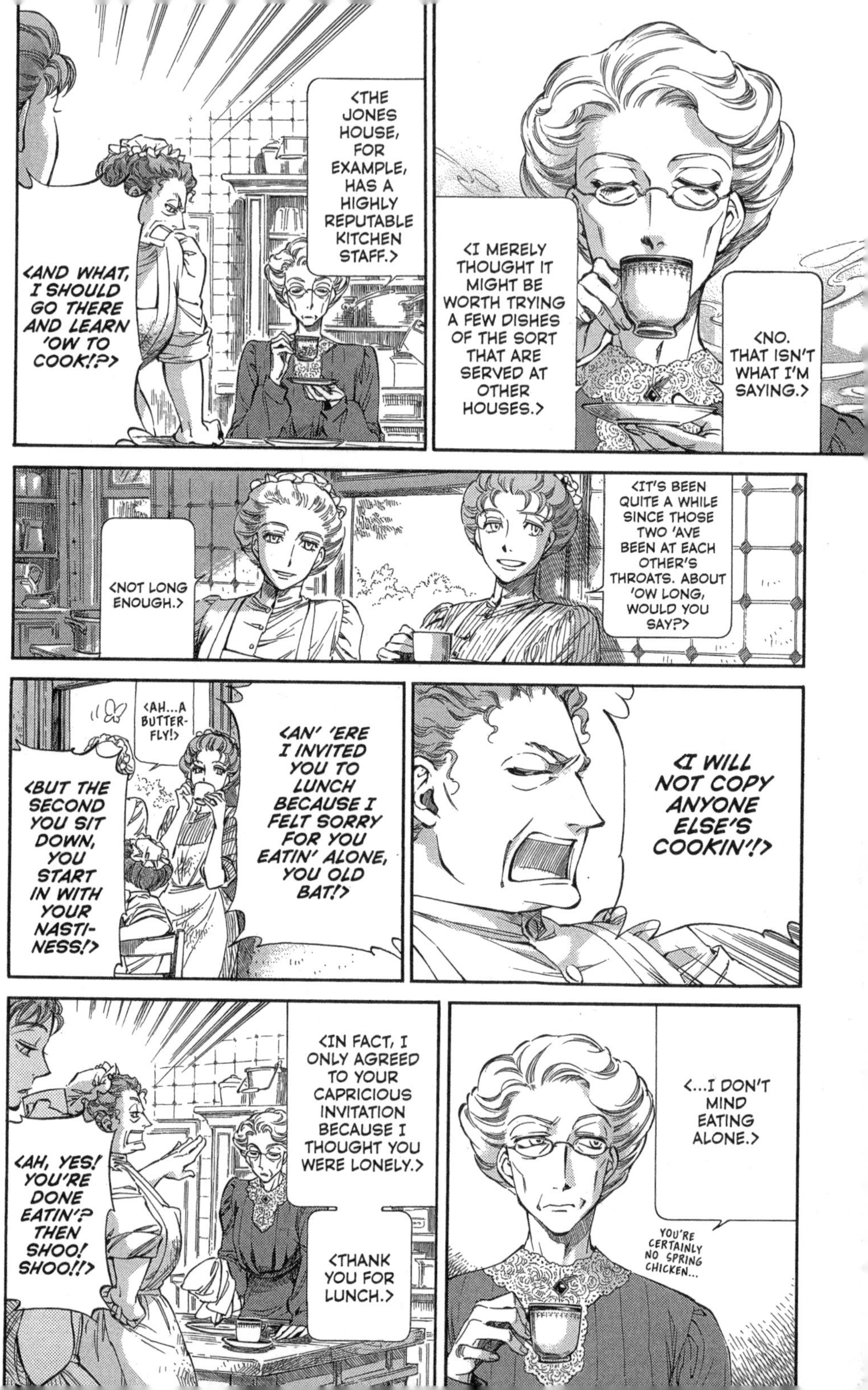

<NO. THAT ISN'T WHAT I'M SAYING.>
<I MERELY THOUGHT IT MIGHT BE WORTH TRYING A FEW DISHES OF THE SORT THAT ARE SERVED AT OTHER HOUSES.>
<THE JONES HOUSE, FOR EXAMPLE, HAS A HIGHLY REPUTABLE KITCHEN STAFF.>
<AND WHAT, I SHOULD GO THERE AND LEARN 'OW TO COOK!?>
<IT'S BEEN QUITE A WHILE SINCE THOSE TWO 'AVE BEEN AT EACH OTHER'S THROATS. ABOUT 'OW LONG, WOULD YOU SAY?>
<NOT LONG ENOUGH.>
<I WILL NOT COPY ANYONE ELSE'S COOKIN'!>
<AH...A BUTTERFLY!>
<AN' 'ERE I INVITED YOU TO LUNCH BECAUSE I FELT SORRY FOR YOU EATIN' ALONE, YOU OLD BAT!>
<BUT THE SECOND YOU SIT DOWN, YOU START IN WITH YOUR NASTINESS!>
<...I DON'T MIND EATING ALONE.>
YOU'RE CERTAINLY NO SPRING CHICKEN...
<IN FACT, I ONLY AGREED TO YOUR CAPRICIOUS INVITATION BECAUSE I THOUGHT YOU WERE LONELY.>
<THANK YOU FOR LUNCH.>
<AH, YES! YOU'RE DONE EATIN'? THEN SHOO! SHOO!!>

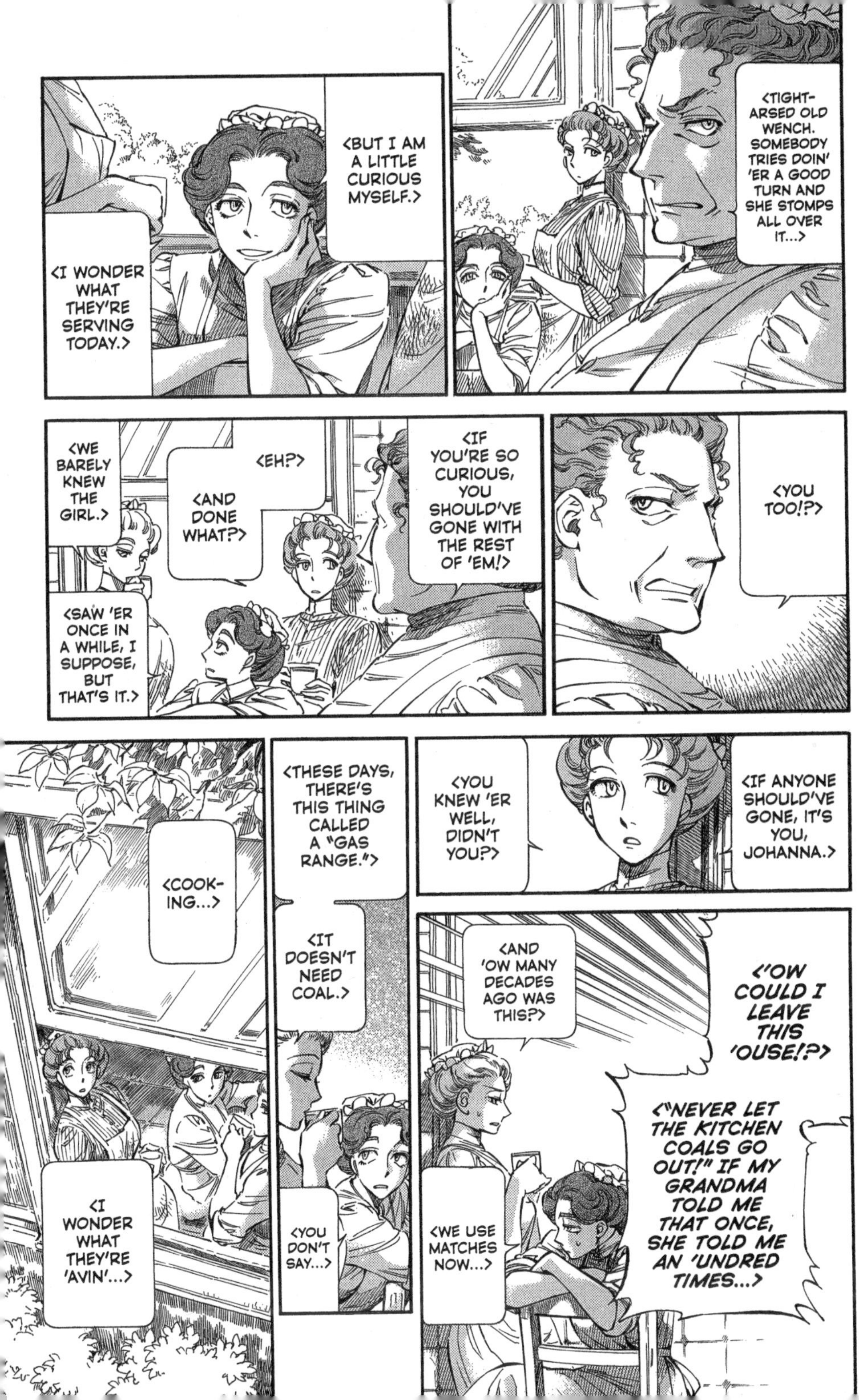
<TIGHT-ARSED OLD WENCH. SOMEBODY TRIES DOIN' 'ER A GOOD TURN AND SHE STOMPS ALL OVER IT...>
<BUT I AM A LITTLE CURIOUS MYSELF.>
<I WONDER WHAT THEY'RE SERVING TODAY.>
<YOU TOO!?>
<IF YOU'RE SO CURIOUS, YOU SHOULD'VE GONE WITH THE REST OF 'EM!>
<EH?>
<AND DONE WHAT?>
<WE BARELY KNEW THE GIRL.>
<SAW 'ER ONCE IN A WHILE, I SUPPOSE, BUT THAT'S IT.>
<IF ANYONE SHOULD'VE GONE, IT'S YOU, JOHANNA.>
<YOU KNEW 'ER WELL, DIDN'T YOU?>
<'OW COULD I LEAVE THIS 'OUSE!?>
<AND 'OW MANY DECADES AGO WAS THIS?>
<"NEVER LET THE KITCHEN COALS GO OUT!" IF MY GRANDMA TOLD ME THAT ONCE, SHE TOLD ME AN 'UNDRED TIMES...>
<WE USE MATCHES NOW...>
<THESE DAYS, THERE'S THIS THING CALLED A "GAS RANGE.">
<IT DOESN'T NEED COAL.>
<YOU DON'T SAY...>
<COOK-ING...>
<I WONDER WHAT THEY'RE 'AVIN'...>

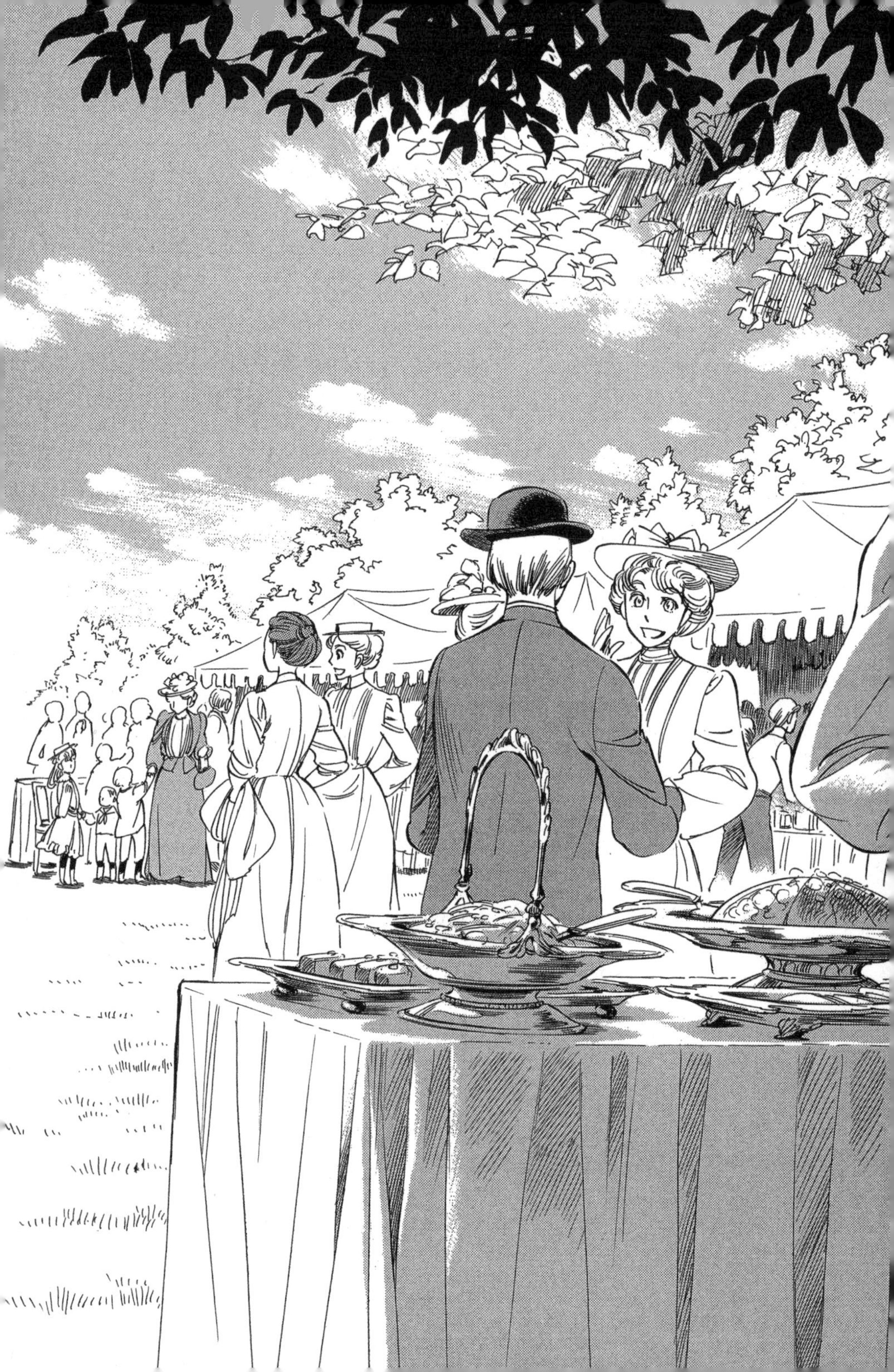

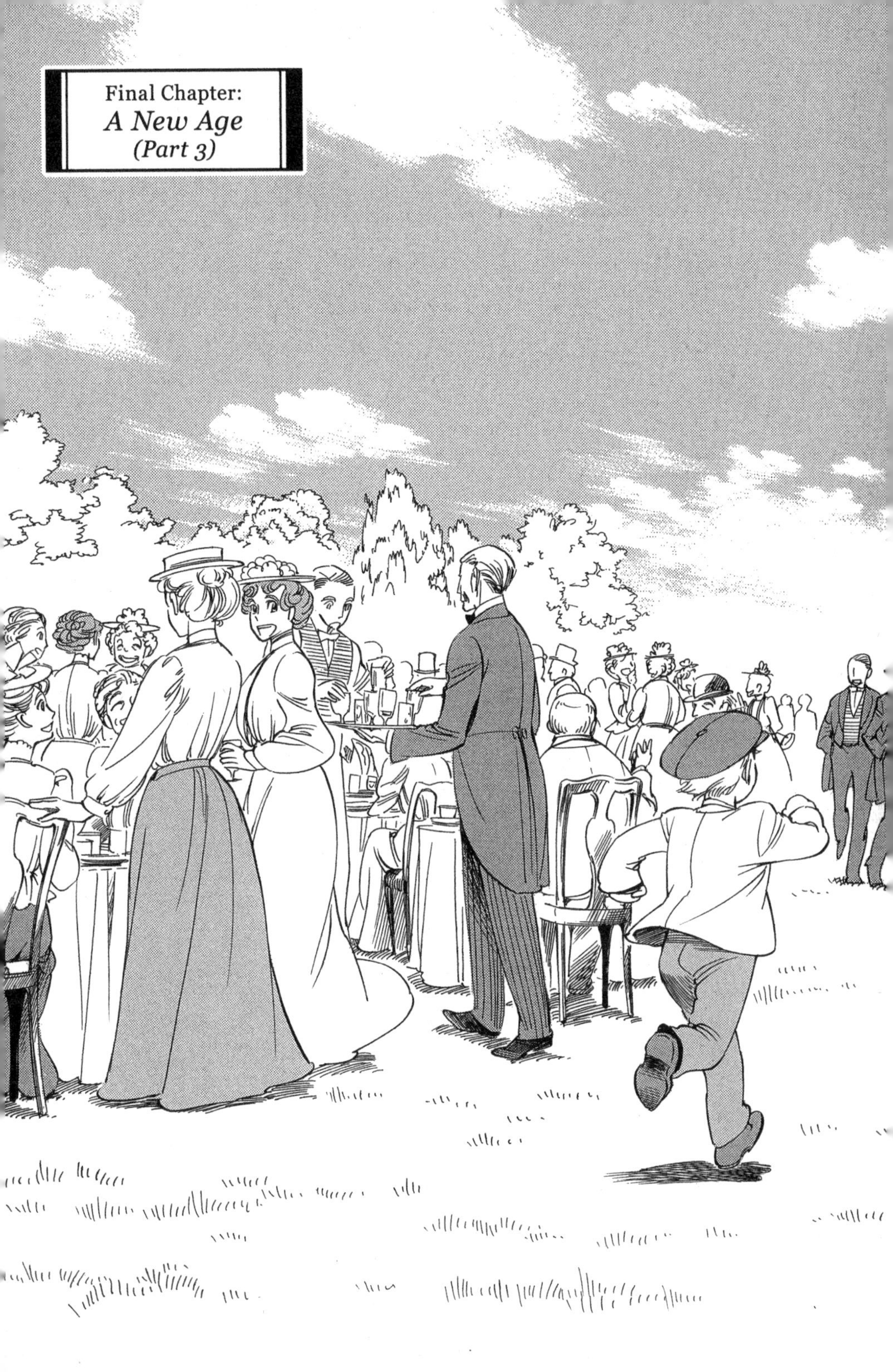
Final Chapter:
A New Age
(Part 3)

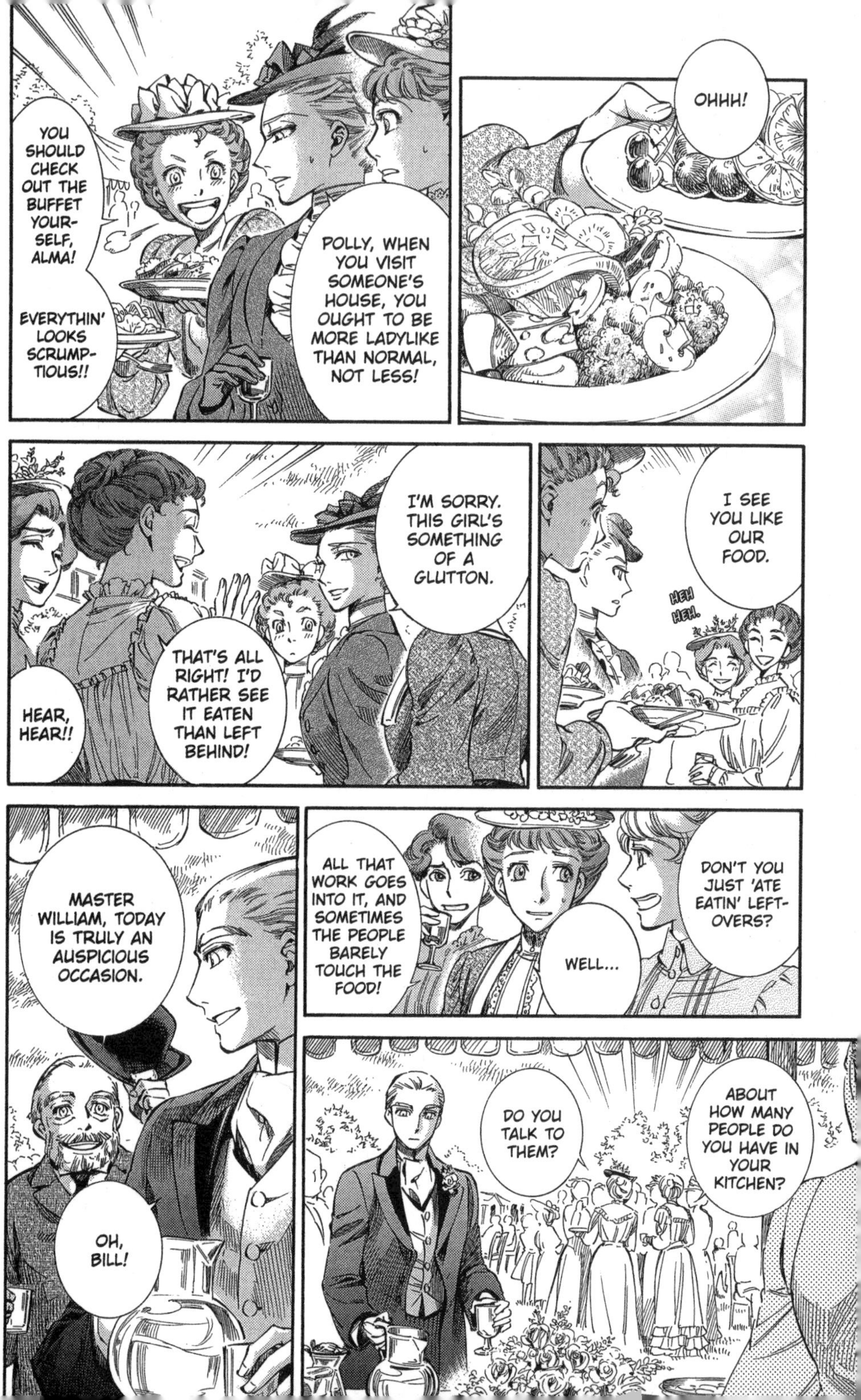

OHHH!
YOU SHOULD CHECK OUT THE BUFFET YOUR-SELF, ALMA!
EVERYTHIN' LOOKS SCRUMP-TIOUS!!
POLLY, WHEN YOU VISIT SOMEONE'S HOUSE, YOU OUGHT TO BE MORE LADYLIKE THAN NORMAL, NOT LESS!
I SEE YOU LIKE OUR FOOD.
HEH HEH.
I'M SORRY. THIS GIRL'S SOMETHING OF A GLUTTON.
THAT'S ALL RIGHT! I'D RATHER SEE IT EATEN THAN LEFT BEHIND!
HEAR, HEAR!!
DON'T YOU JUST 'ATE EATIN' LEFT-OVERS?
WELL...
ALL THAT WORK GOES INTO IT, AND SOMETIMES THE PEOPLE BARELY TOUCH THE FOOD!
ABOUT HOW MANY PEOPLE DO YOU HAVE IN YOUR KITCHEN?
DO YOU TALK TO THEM?
MASTER WILLIAM, TODAY IS TRULY AN AUSPICIOUS OCCASION.
OH, BILL!

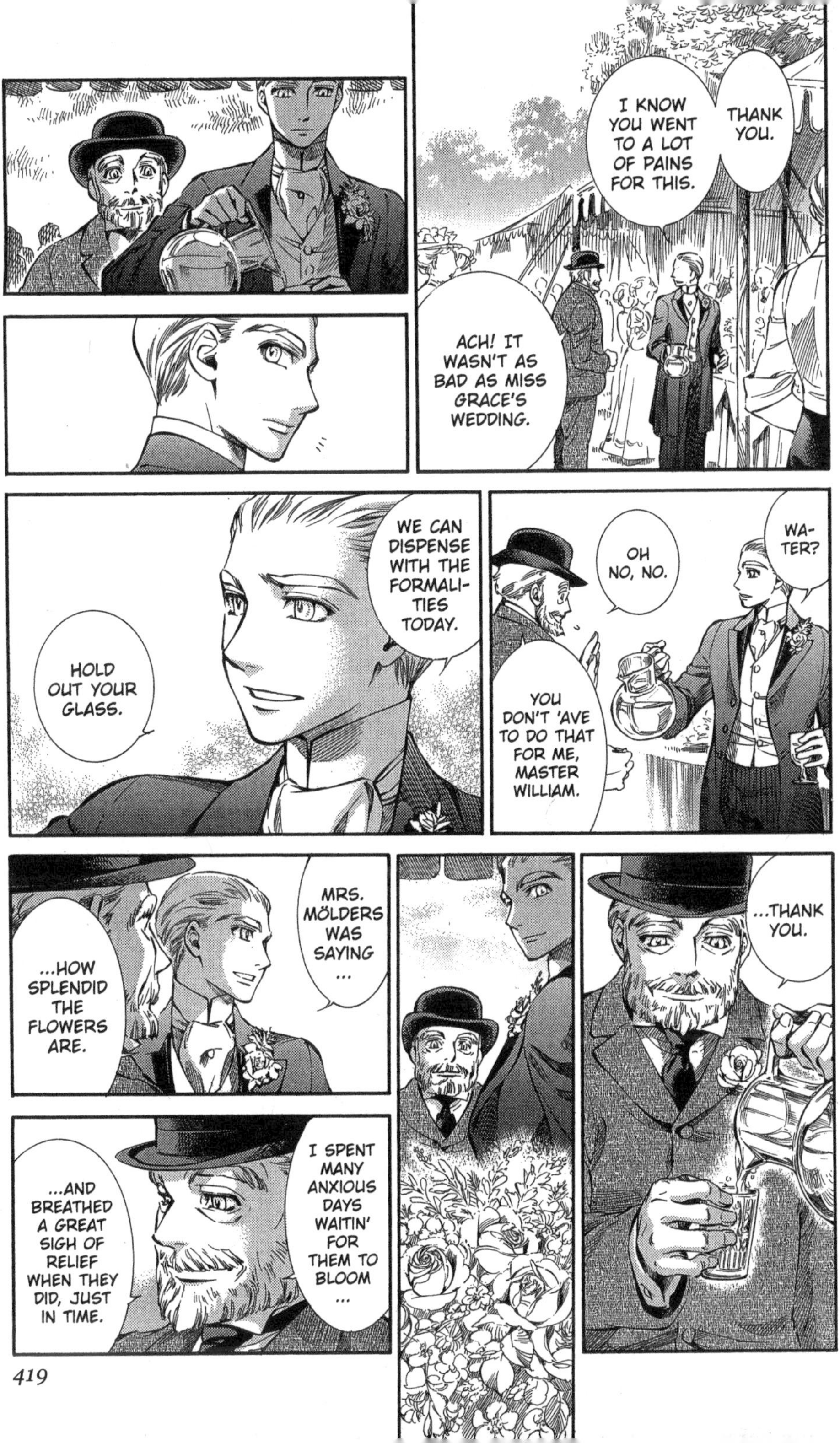
THANK YOU.
I KNOW YOU WENT TO A LOT OF PAINS FOR THIS.
ACH! IT WASN'T AS BAD AS MISS GRACE'S WEDDING.
WA-TER?
OH NO, NO.
YOU DON'T 'AVE TO DO THAT FOR ME, MASTER WILLIAM.
WE CAN DISPENSE WITH THE FORMALI-TIES TODAY.
HOLD OUT YOUR GLASS.
...THANK YOU.
MRS. MÖLDERS WAS SAYING ...
...HOW SPLENDID THE FLOWERS ARE.
I SPENT MANY ANXIOUS DAYS WAITIN' FOR THEM TO BLOOM ...
...AND BREATHED A GREAT SIGH OF RELIEF WHEN THEY DID, JUST IN TIME.

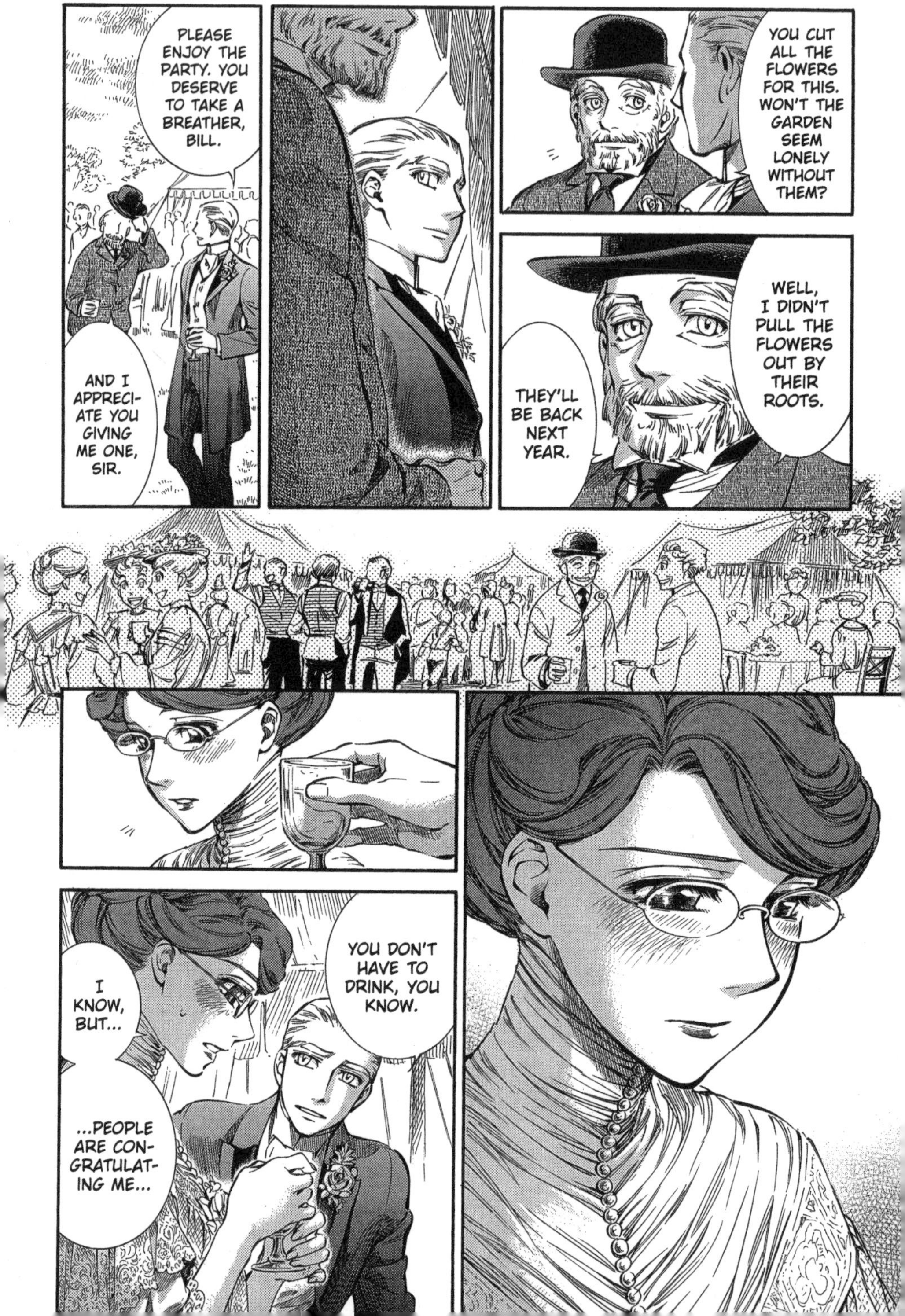
YOU CUT ALL THE FLOWERS FOR THIS. WON'T THE GARDEN SEEM LONELY WITHOUT THEM?
WELL, I DIDN'T PULL THE FLOWERS OUT BY THEIR ROOTS.
THEY'LL BE BACK NEXT YEAR.
PLEASE ENJOY THE PARTY. YOU DESERVE TO TAKE A BREATHER, BILL.
AND I APPRECIATE YOU GIVING ME ONE, SIR.
YOU DON'T HAVE TO DRINK, YOU KNOW.
I KNOW, BUT...
...PEOPLE ARE CONGRATULATING ME...

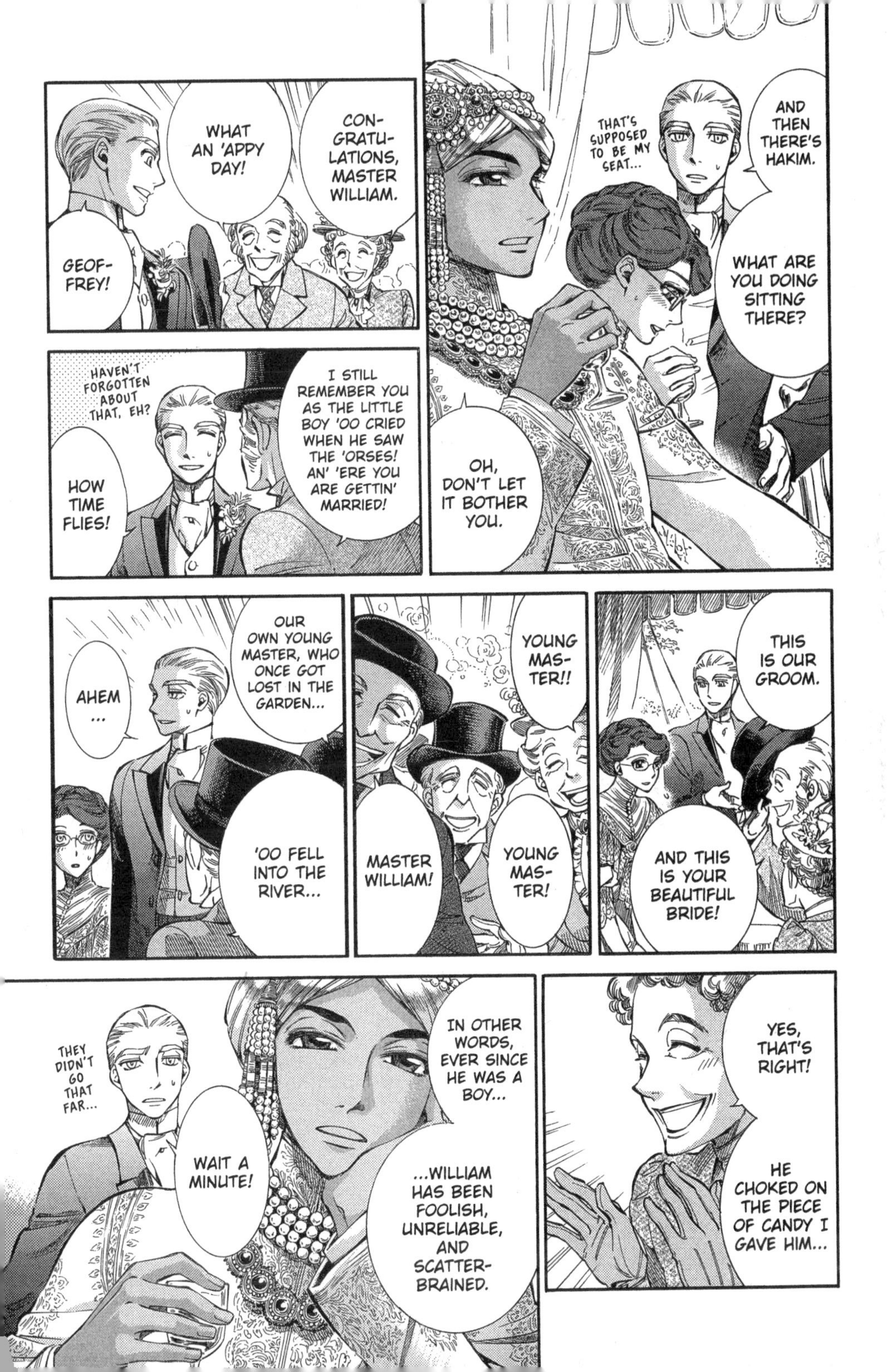
AND THEN THERE'S HAKIM.
THAT'S SUPPOSED TO BE MY SEAT...
WHAT ARE YOU DOING SITTING THERE?
OH, DON'T LET IT BOTHER YOU.
CON-GRATU-LATIONS, MASTER WILLIAM.
WHAT AN 'APPY DAY!
GEOF-FREY!
I STILL REMEMBER YOU AS THE LITTLE BOY 'OO CRIED WHEN HE SAW THE 'ORSES! AN' 'ERE YOU ARE GETTIN' MARRIED!
HAVEN'T FORGOTTEN ABOUT THAT, EH?
HOW TIME FLIES!
THIS IS OUR GROOM.
AND THIS IS YOUR BEAUTIFUL BRIDE!
YOUNG MAS-TER!!
YOUNG MAS-TER!
MASTER WILLIAM!
OUR OWN YOUNG MASTER, WHO ONCE GOT LOST IN THE GARDEN...
'OO FELL INTO THE RIVER...
AHEM ...
YES, THAT'S RIGHT!
HE CHOKED ON THE PIECE OF CANDY I GAVE HIM...
IN OTHER WORDS, EVER SINCE HE WAS A BOY...
...WILLIAM HAS BEEN FOOLISH, UNRELIABLE, AND SCATTER-BRAINED.
WAIT A MINUTE!
THEY DIDN'T GO THAT FAR...

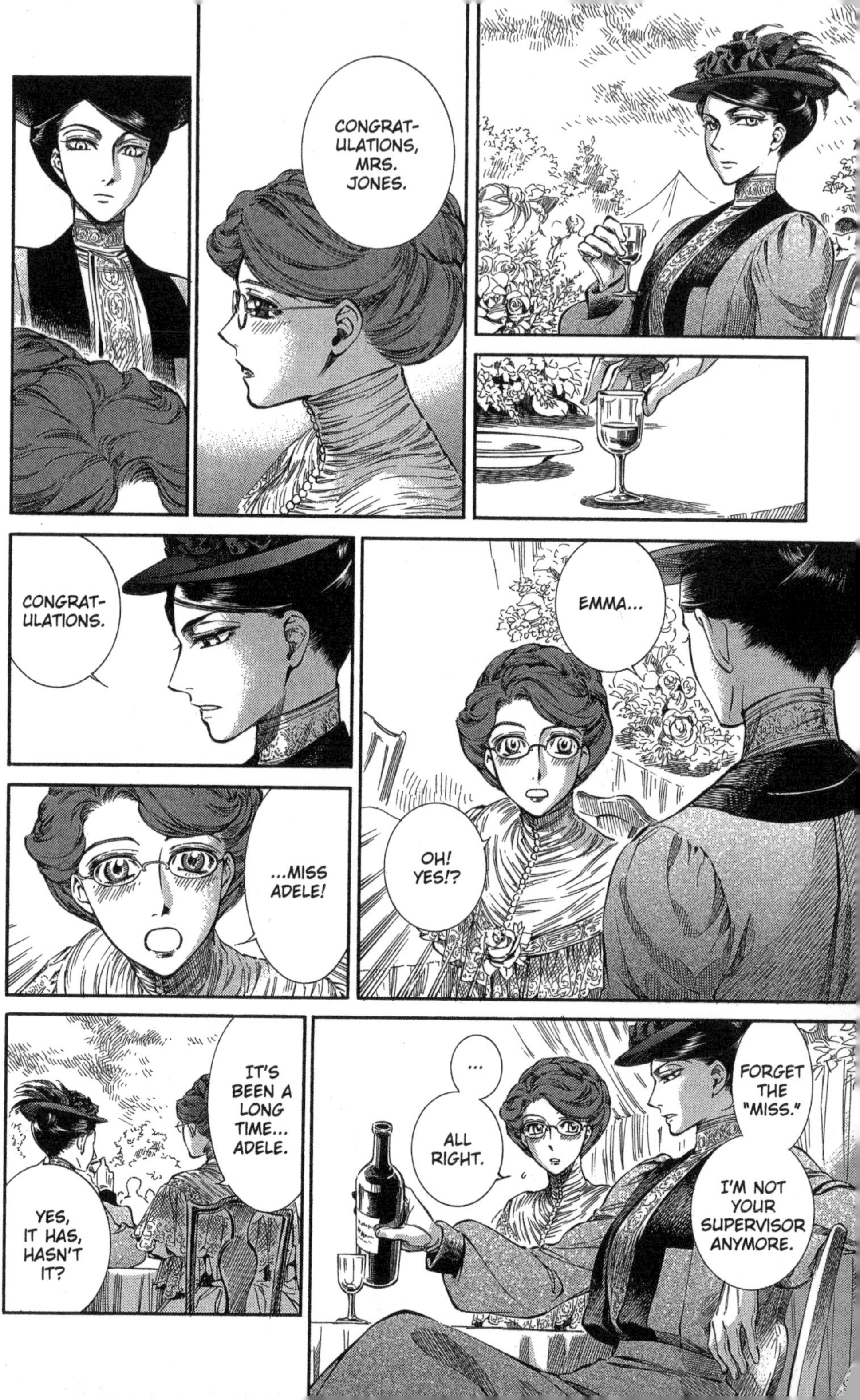
CONGRAT-ULATIONS, MRS. JONES.
EMMA...
OH! YES!?
CONGRAT-ULATIONS.
...MISS ADELE!
FORGET THE "MISS."
I'M NOT YOUR SUPERVISOR ANYMORE.
...
ALL RIGHT.
IT'S BEEN A LONG TIME... ADELE.
YES, IT HAS, HASN'T IT?

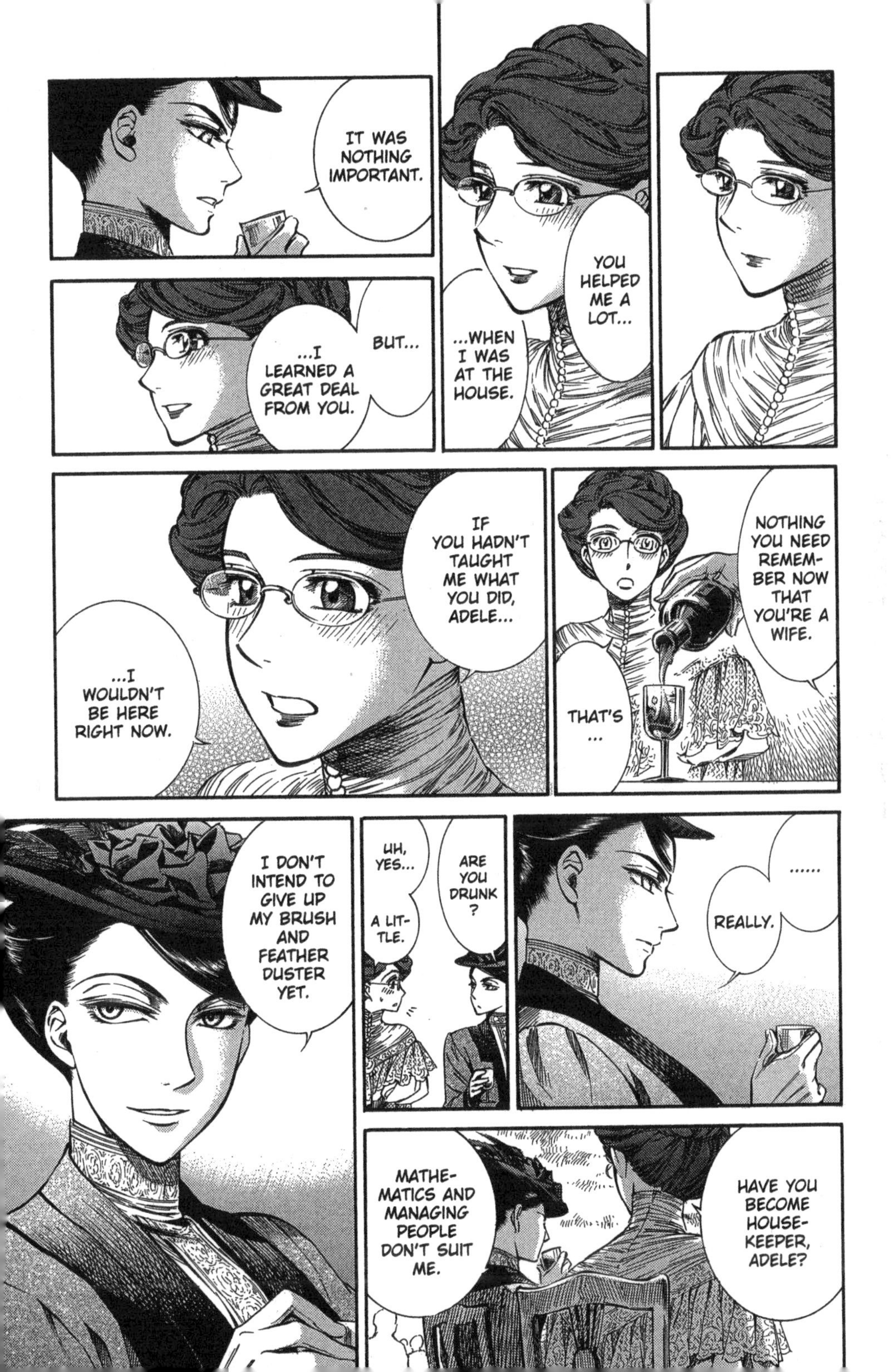
YOU HELPED ME A LOT...
...WHEN I WAS AT THE HOUSE.
IT WAS NOTHING IMPORTANT.
BUT...
...I LEARNED A GREAT DEAL FROM YOU.
NOTHING YOU NEED REMEMBER NOW THAT YOU'RE A WIFE.
THAT'S ...
IF YOU HADN'T TAUGHT ME WHAT YOU DID, ADELE...
...I WOULDN'T BE HERE RIGHT NOW.
......
REALLY.
ARE YOU DRUNK?
UH, YES...
A LITTLE.
HAVE YOU BECOME HOUSEKEEPER, ADELE?
MATHEMATICS AND MANAGING PEOPLE DON'T SUIT ME.
I DON'T INTEND TO GIVE UP MY BRUSH AND FEATHER DUSTER YET.

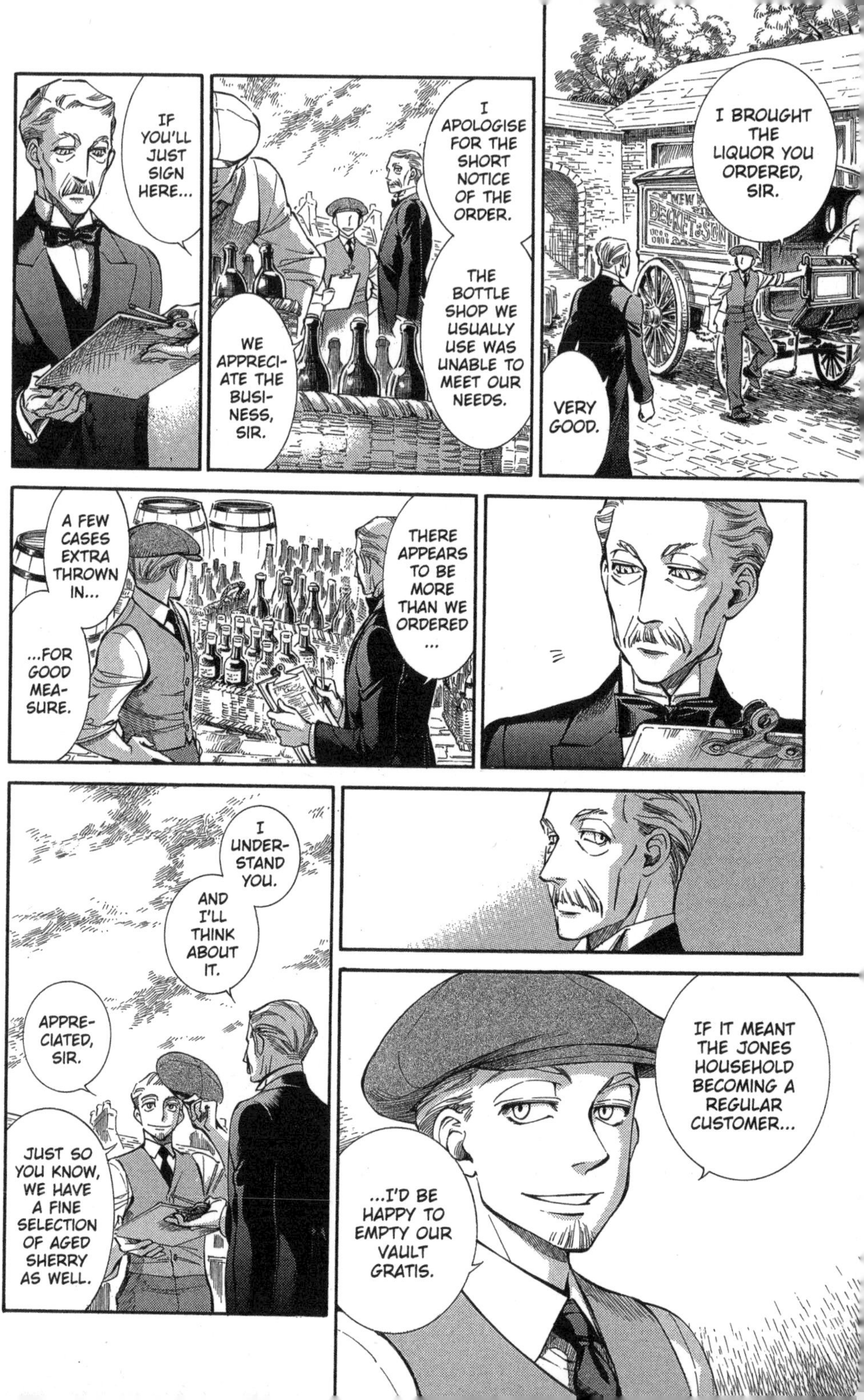
I BROUGHT THE LIQUOR YOU ORDERED, SIR.
BECKET & SON
VERY GOOD.
I APOLOGISE FOR THE SHORT NOTICE OF THE ORDER.
THE BOTTLE SHOP WE USUALLY USE WAS UNABLE TO MEET OUR NEEDS.
WE APPRECIATE THE BUSINESS, SIR.
IF YOU'LL JUST SIGN HERE...
THERE APPEARS TO BE MORE THAN WE ORDERED...
A FEW CASES EXTRA THROWN IN...
...FOR GOOD MEASURE.
IF IT MEANT THE JONES HOUSEHOLD BECOMING A REGULAR CUSTOMER...
...I'D BE HAPPY TO EMPTY OUR VAULT GRATIS.
I UNDERSTAND YOU.
AND I'LL THINK ABOUT IT.
APPRECIATED, SIR.
JUST SO YOU KNOW, WE HAVE A FINE SELECTION OF AGED SHERRY AS WELL.

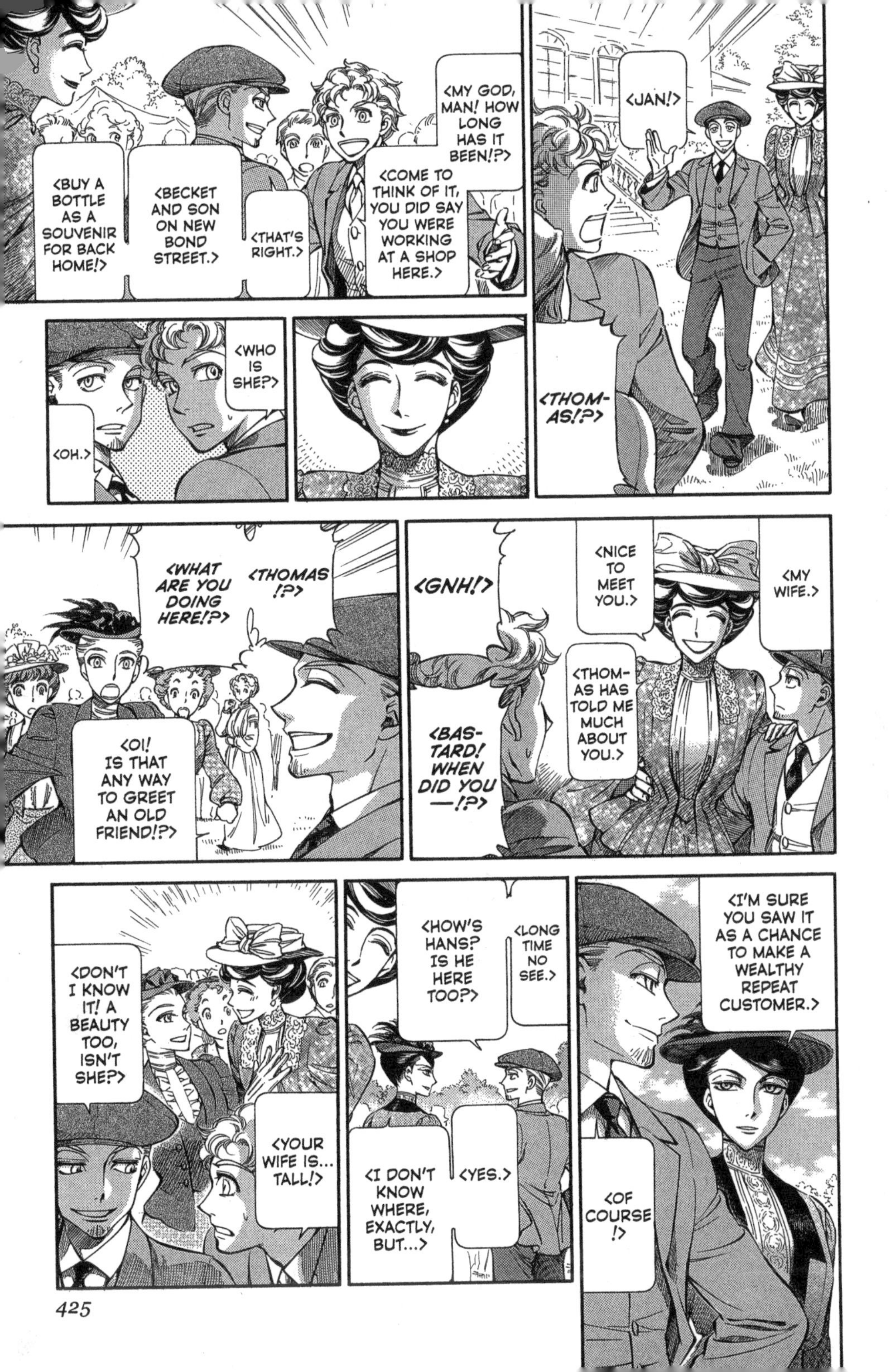

<JAN!>
<THOMAS!?>
<MY GOD, MAN! HOW LONG HAS IT BEEN!?>
<COME TO THINK OF IT, YOU DID SAY YOU WERE WORKING AT A SHOP HERE.>
<THAT'S RIGHT.>
<BECKET AND SON ON NEW BOND STREET.>
<BUY A BOTTLE AS A SOUVENIR FOR BACK HOME!>
<WHO IS SHE?>
<OH.>
<MY WIFE.>
<NICE TO MEET YOU.>
<THOMAS HAS TOLD ME MUCH ABOUT YOU.>
<GNH!>
<BASTARD! WHEN DID YOU—!?>
<THOMAS!?>
<WHAT ARE YOU DOING HERE!?>
<OI! IS THAT ANY WAY TO GREET AN OLD FRIEND!?>
<I'M SURE YOU SAW IT AS A CHANCE TO MAKE A WEALTHY REPEAT CUSTOMER.>
<OF COURSE!>
<LONG TIME NO SEE.>
<HOW'S HANS? IS HE HERE TOO?>
<YES.>
<I DON'T KNOW WHERE, EXACTLY, BUT...>
<YOUR WIFE IS... TALL!>
<DON'T I KNOW IT! A BEAUTY TOO, ISN'T SHE?>

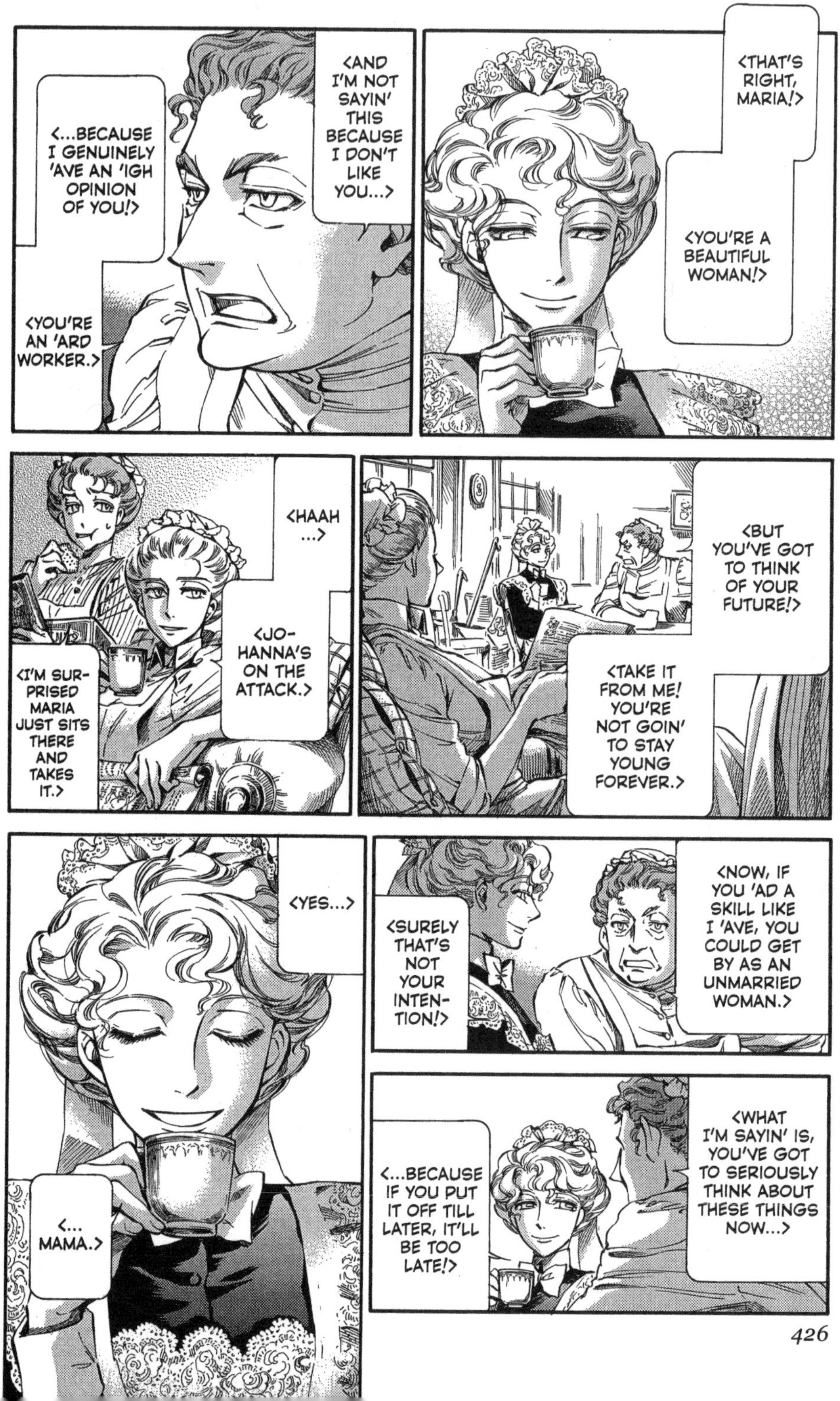
<THAT'S RIGHT, MARIA!>
<YOU'RE A BEAUTIFUL WOMAN!>
<AND I'M NOT SAYIN' THIS BECAUSE I DON'T LIKE YOU...>
<...BECAUSE I GENUINELY 'AVE AN 'IGH OPINION OF YOU!>
<YOU'RE AN 'ARD WORKER.>
<BUT YOU'VE GOT TO THINK OF YOUR FUTURE!>
<TAKE IT FROM ME! YOU'RE NOT GOIN' TO STAY YOUNG FOREVER.>
<HAAH ...>
<JO-HANNA'S ON THE ATTACK.>
<I'M SUR-PRISED MARIA JUST SITS THERE AND TAKES IT.>
<NOW, IF YOU 'AD A SKILL LIKE I 'AVE, YOU COULD GET BY AS AN UNMARRIED WOMAN.>
<SURELY THAT'S NOT YOUR INTEN-TION!>
<WHAT I'M SAYIN' IS, YOU'VE GOT TO SERIOUSLY THINK ABOUT THESE THINGS NOW...>
<...BECAUSE IF YOU PUT IT OFF TILL LATER, IT'LL BE TOO LATE!>
<YES...>
<... MAMA.>

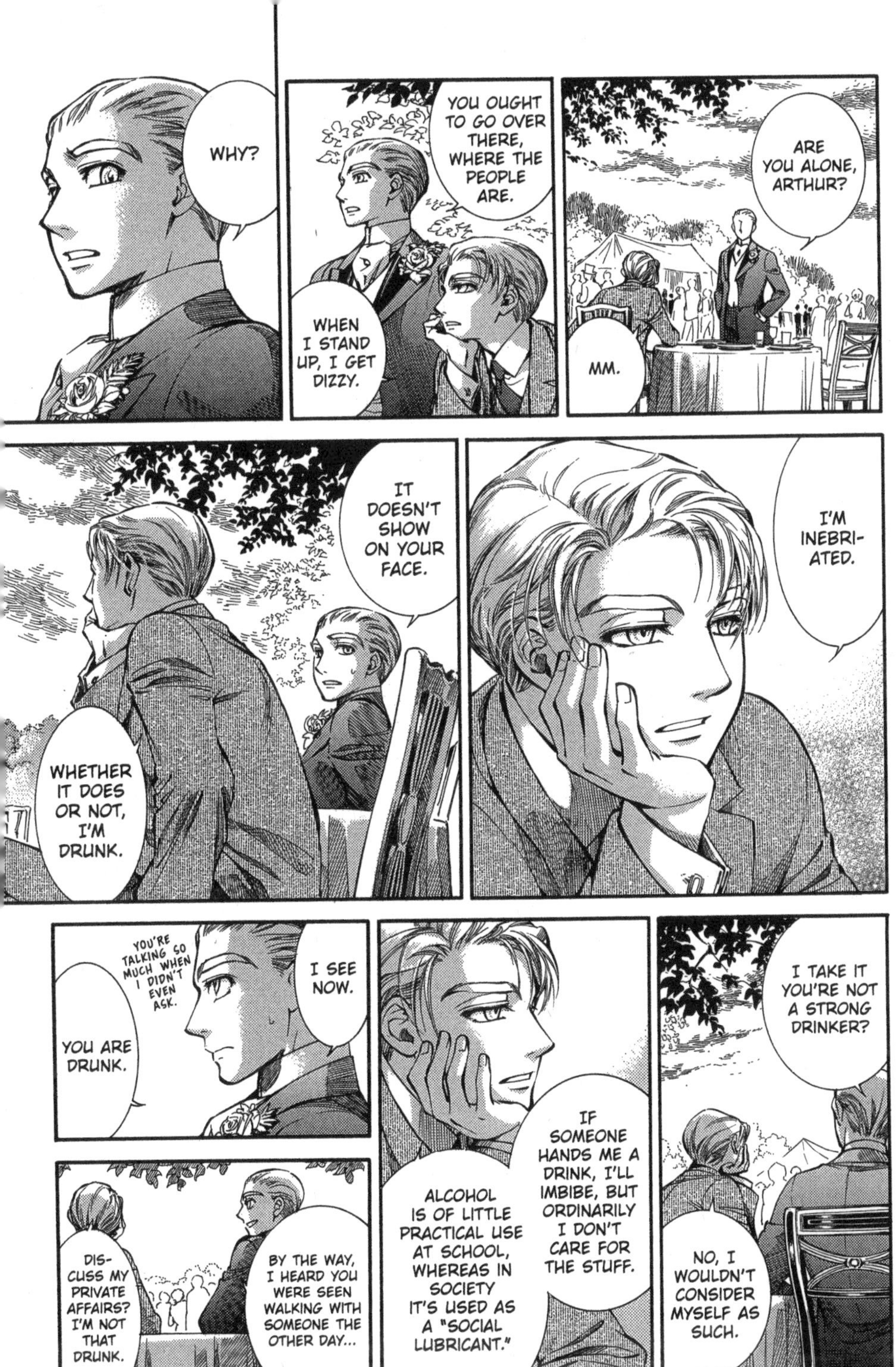
ARE YOU ALONE, ARTHUR?
MM.
YOU OUGHT TO GO OVER THERE, WHERE THE PEOPLE ARE.
WHEN I STAND UP, I GET DIZZY.
WHY?
I'M INEBRIATED.
IT DOESN'T SHOW ON YOUR FACE.
WHETHER IT DOES OR NOT, I'M DRUNK.
I TAKE IT YOU'RE NOT A STRONG DRINKER?
NO, I WOULDN'T CONSIDER MYSELF AS SUCH.
IF SOMEONE HANDS ME A DRINK, I'LL IMBIBE, BUT ORDINARILY I DON'T CARE FOR THE STUFF.
ALCOHOL IS OF LITTLE PRACTICAL USE AT SCHOOL, WHEREAS IN SOCIETY IT'S USED AS A "SOCIAL LUBRICANT."
I SEE NOW.
YOU'RE TALKING SO MUCH WHEN I DIDN'T EVEN ASK.
YOU ARE DRUNK.
BY THE WAY, I HEARD YOU WERE SEEN WALKING WITH SOMEONE THE OTHER DAY...
DIS-CUSS MY PRIVATE AFFAIRS? I'M NOT THAT DRUNK.

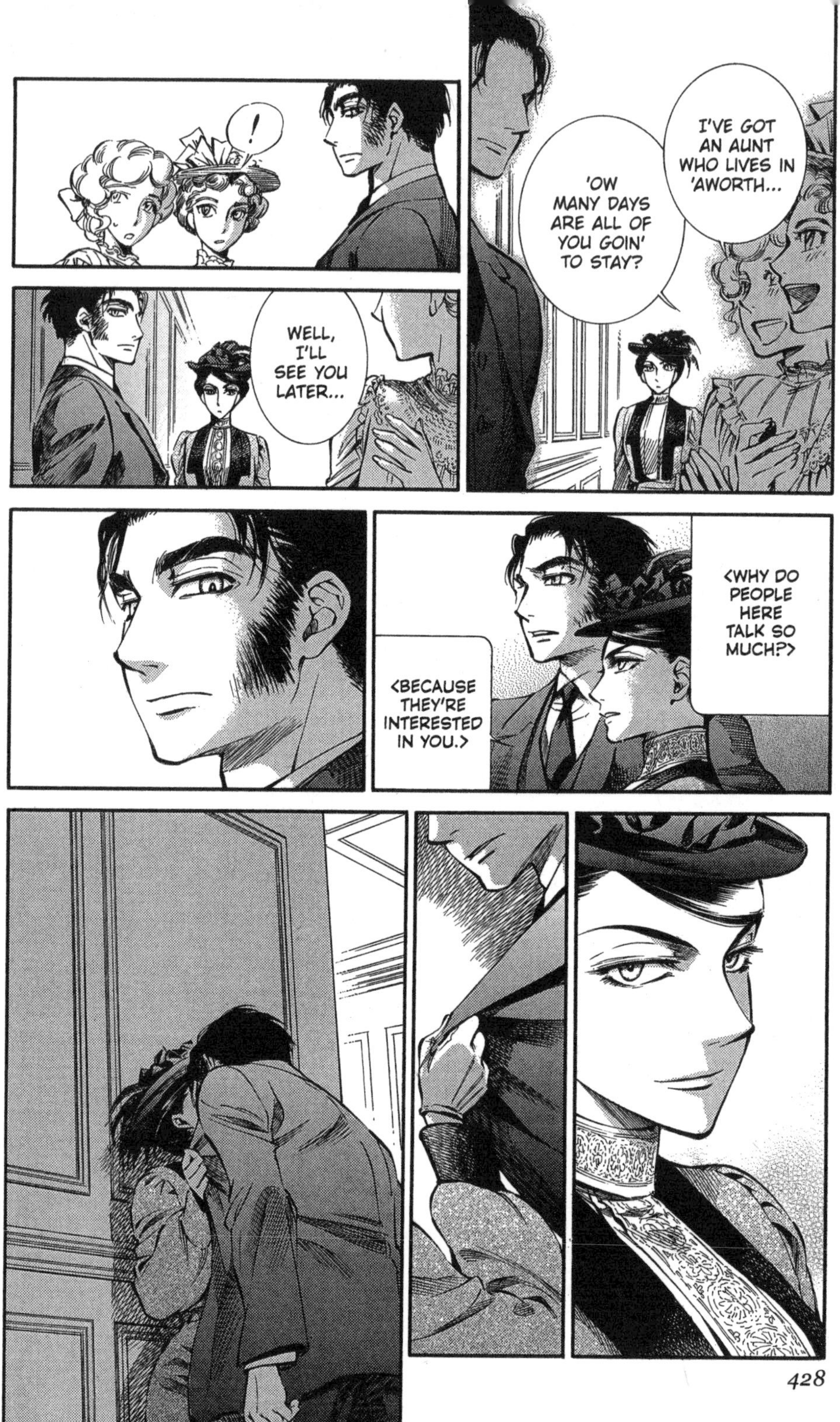
I'VE GOT AN AUNT WHO LIVES IN 'AWORTH...
'OW MANY DAYS ARE ALL OF YOU GOIN' TO STAY?
!
WELL, I'LL SEE YOU LATER...
<WHY DO PEOPLE HERE TALK SO MUCH?>
<BECAUSE THEY'RE INTERESTED IN YOU.>

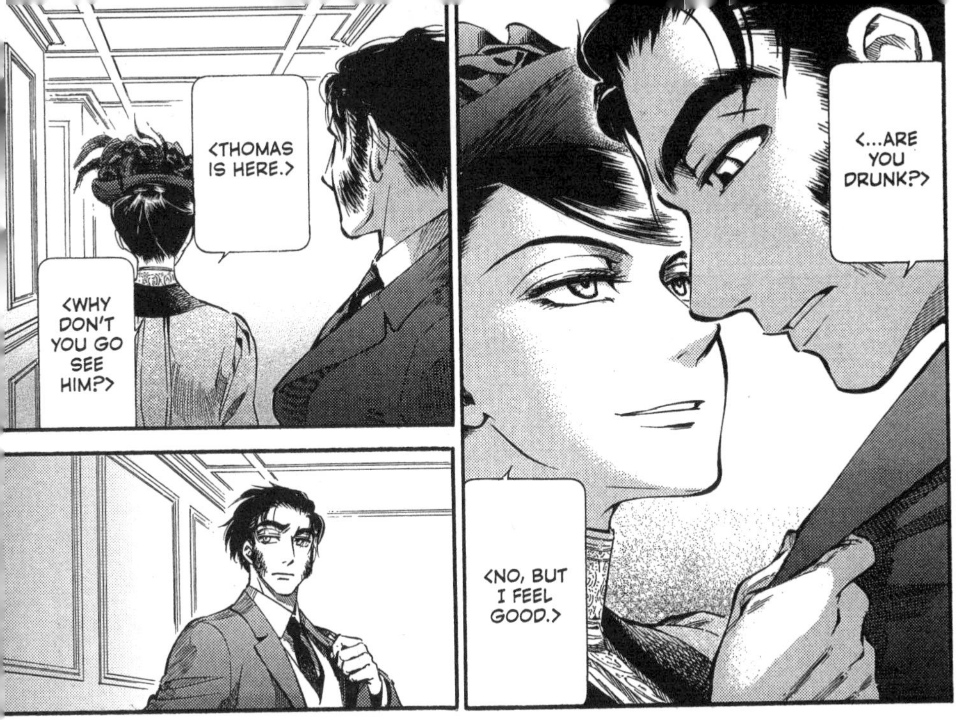
<...ARE YOU DRUNK?>
<NO, BUT I FEEL GOOD.>
<THOMAS IS HERE.>
<WHY DON'T YOU GO SEE HIM?>

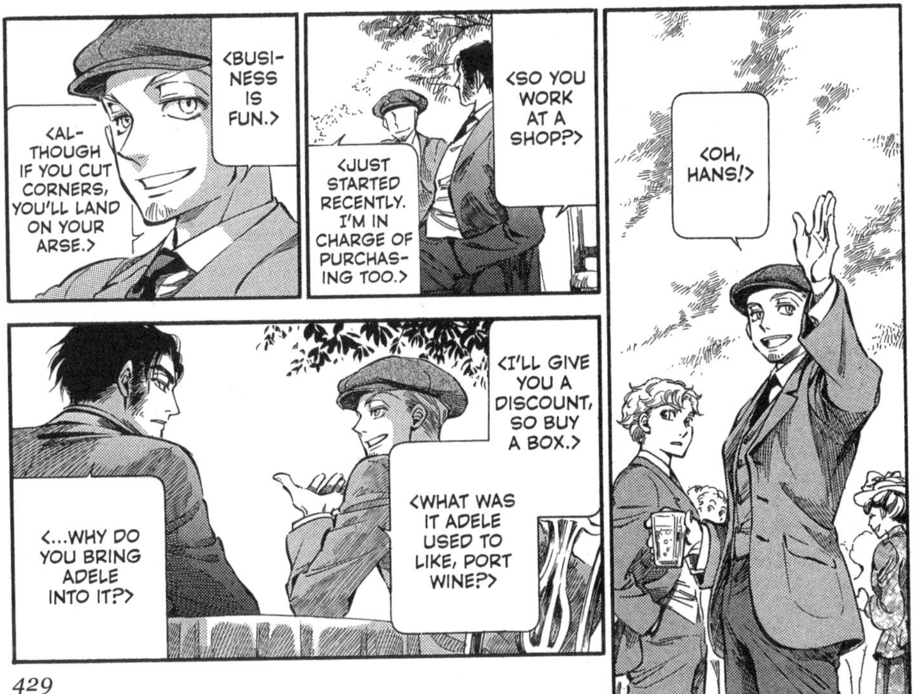
<OH, HANS!>
<SO YOU WORK AT A SHOP?>
<JUST STARTED RECENTLY. I'M IN CHARGE OF PURCHASING TOO.>
<BUSINESS IS FUN.>
<ALTHOUGH IF YOU CUT CORNERS, YOU'LL LAND ON YOUR ARSE.>
<I'LL GIVE YOU A DISCOUNT, SO BUY A BOX.>
<WHAT WAS IT ADELE USED TO LIKE, PORT WINE?>
<...WHY DO YOU BRING ADELE INTO IT?>

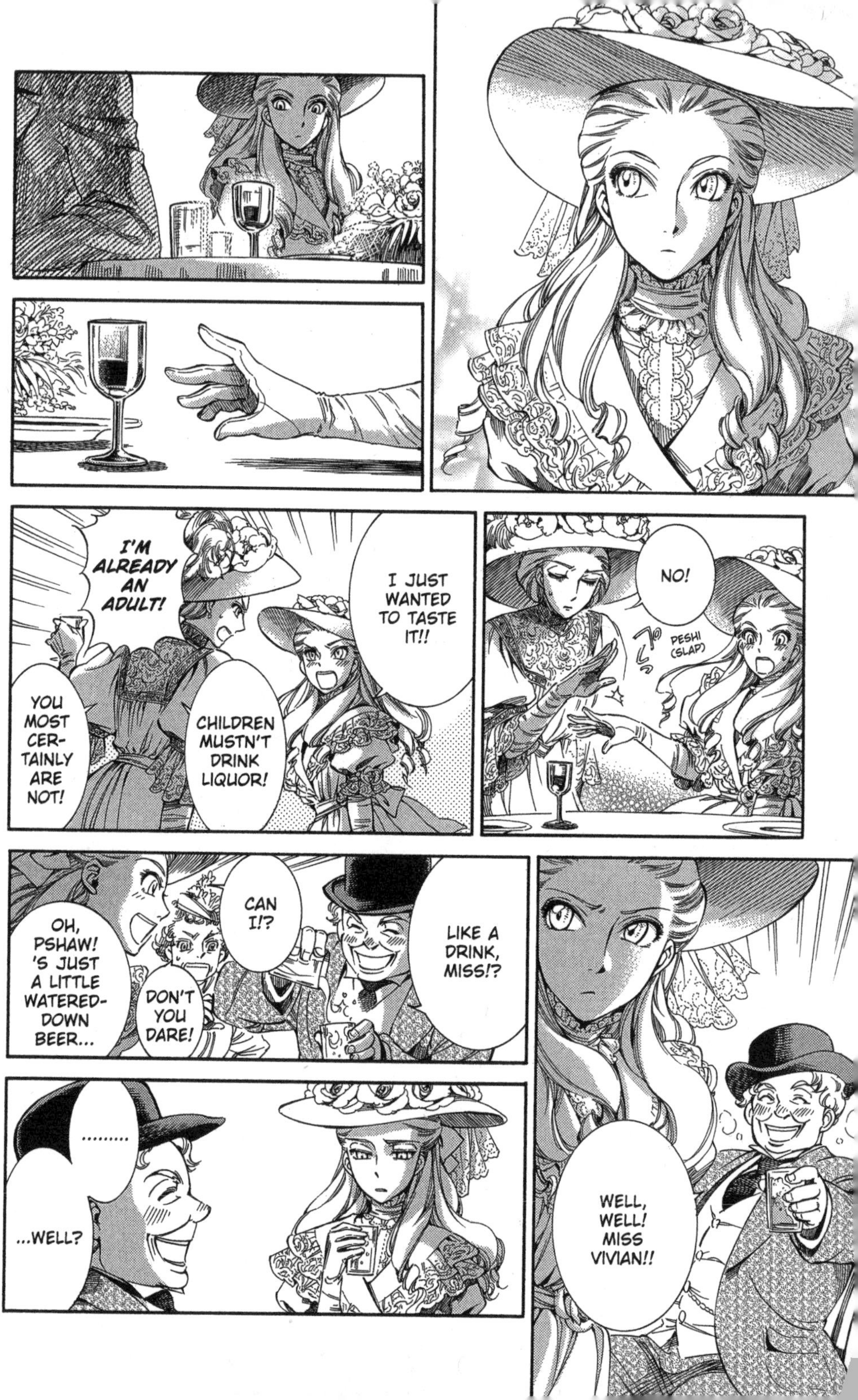
NO!
PESHI (SLAP)
I JUST WANTED TO TASTE IT!!
I'M ALREADY AN ADULT!
CHILDREN MUSTN'T DRINK LIQUOR!
YOU MOST CER-TAINLY ARE NOT!
WELL, WELL! MISS VIVIAN!!
LIKE A DRINK, MISS!?
CAN I!?
DON'T YOU DARE!
OH, PSHAW! 'S JUST A LITTLE WATERED-DOWN BEER...
....
...WELL?

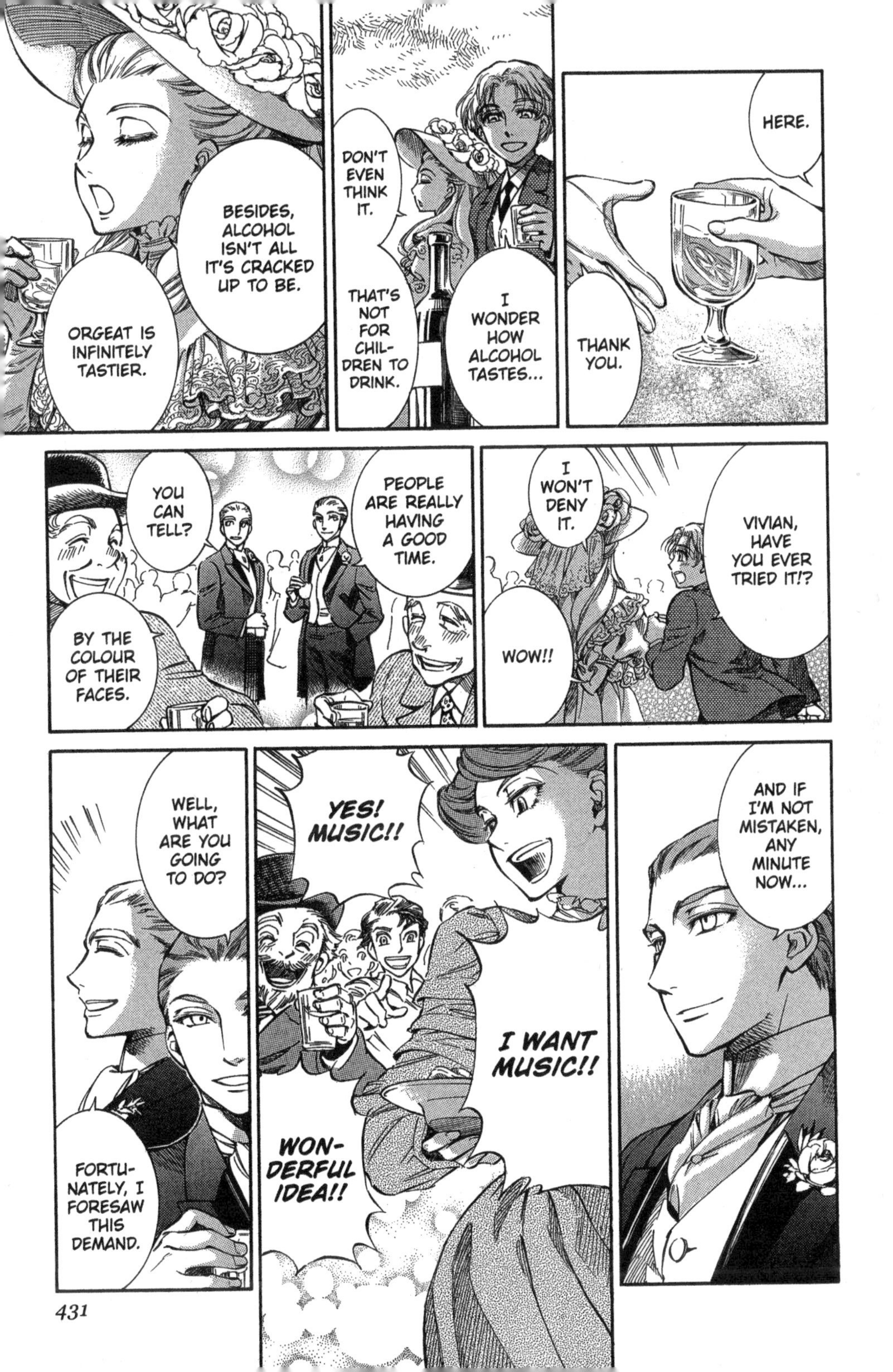
HERE.
THANK YOU.
I WONDER HOW ALCOHOL TASTES...
THAT'S NOT FOR CHIL-DREN TO DRINK.
DON'T EVEN THINK IT.
BESIDES, ALCOHOL ISN'T ALL IT'S CRACKED UP TO BE.
ORGEAT IS INFINITELY TASTIER.
VIVIAN, HAVE YOU EVER TRIED IT!?
I WON'T DENY IT.
WOW!!
PEOPLE ARE REALLY HAVING A GOOD TIME.
YOU CAN TELL?
BY THE COLOUR OF THEIR FACES.
AND IF I'M NOT MISTAKEN, ANY MINUTE NOW...
I WANT MUSIC!!
YES! MUSIC!!
WON-DERFUL IDEA!!
WELL, WHAT ARE YOU GOING TO DO?
FORTU-NATELY, I FORESAW THIS DEMAND.

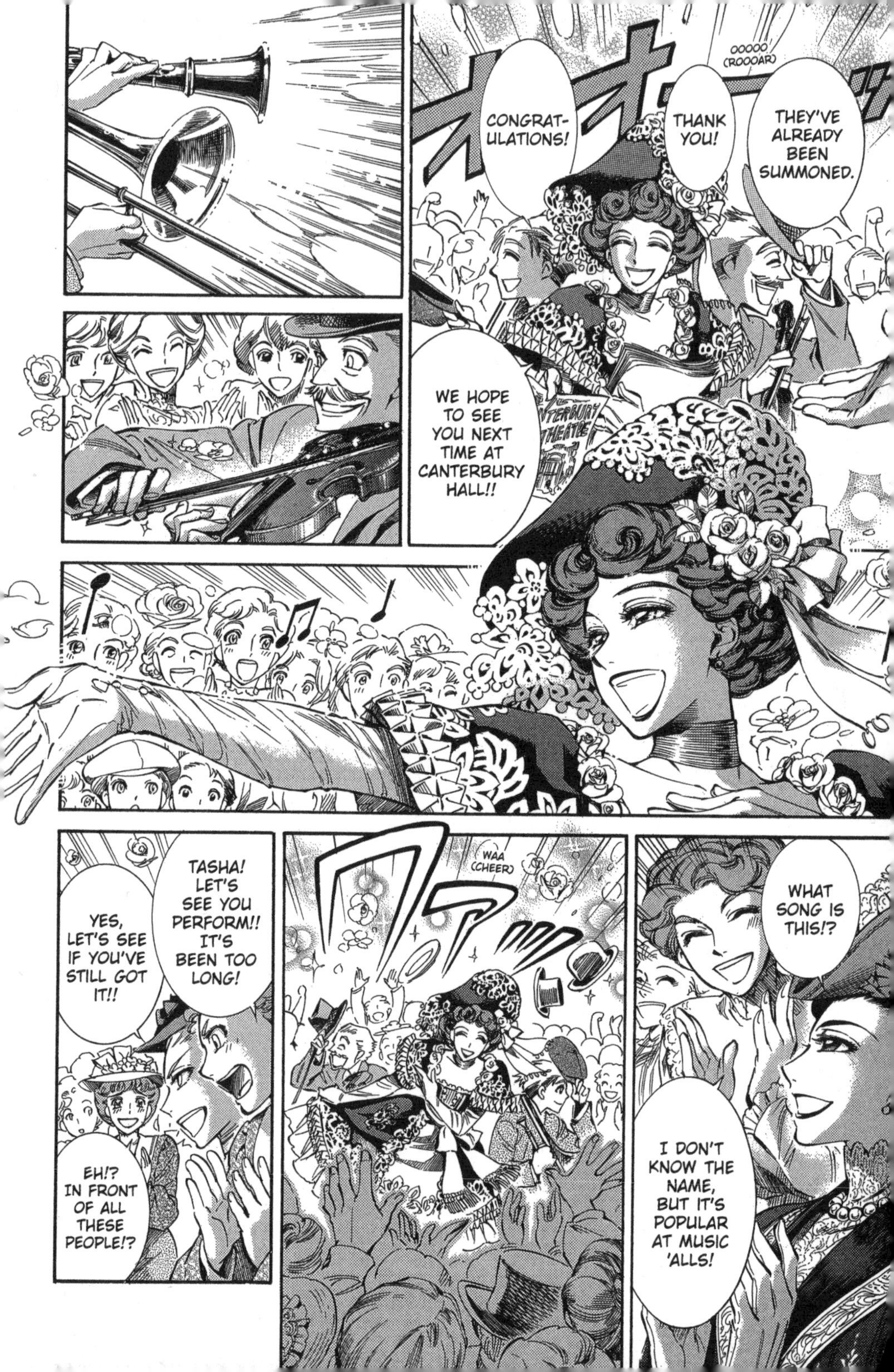
OOOOO (ROOOAR)
THEY'VE ALREADY BEEN SUMMONED.
THANK YOU!
CONGRAT-ULATIONS!
WE HOPE TO SEE YOU NEXT TIME AT CANTERBURY HALL!!
WHAT SONG IS THIS!?
I DON'T KNOW THE NAME, BUT IT'S POPULAR AT MUSIC 'ALLS!
WAA (CHEER)
TASHA! LET'S SEE YOU PERFORM!! IT'S BEEN TOO LONG!
YES, LET'S SEE IF YOU'VE STILL GOT IT!!
EH!? IN FRONT OF ALL THESE PEOPLE!?

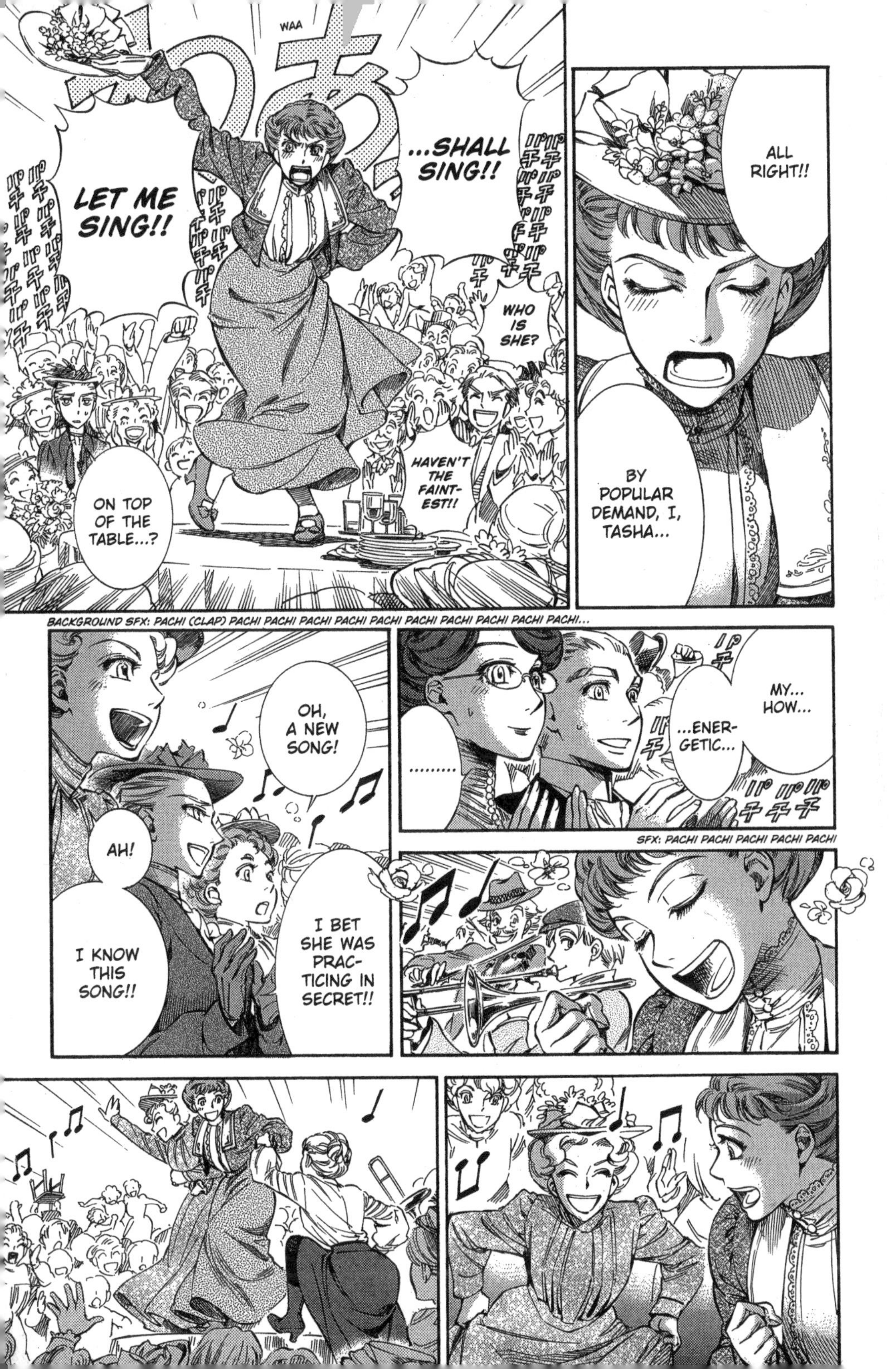
ALL RIGHT!!
BY POPULAR DEMAND, I, TASHA...
WAA
...SHALL SING!!
LET ME SING!!
WHO IS SHE?
HAVEN'T THE FAINTEST!!
ON TOP OF THE TABLE...?
BACKGROUND SFX: PACHI (CLAP) PACHI PACHI PACHI PACHI PACHI PACHI PACHI PACHI PACHI PACHI...
MY... HOW...
...ENER-GETIC...
....
SFX: PACHI PACHI PACHI PACHI PACHI
OH, A NEW SONG!
AH!
I BET SHE WAS PRAC-TICING IN SECRET!!
I KNOW THIS SONG!!

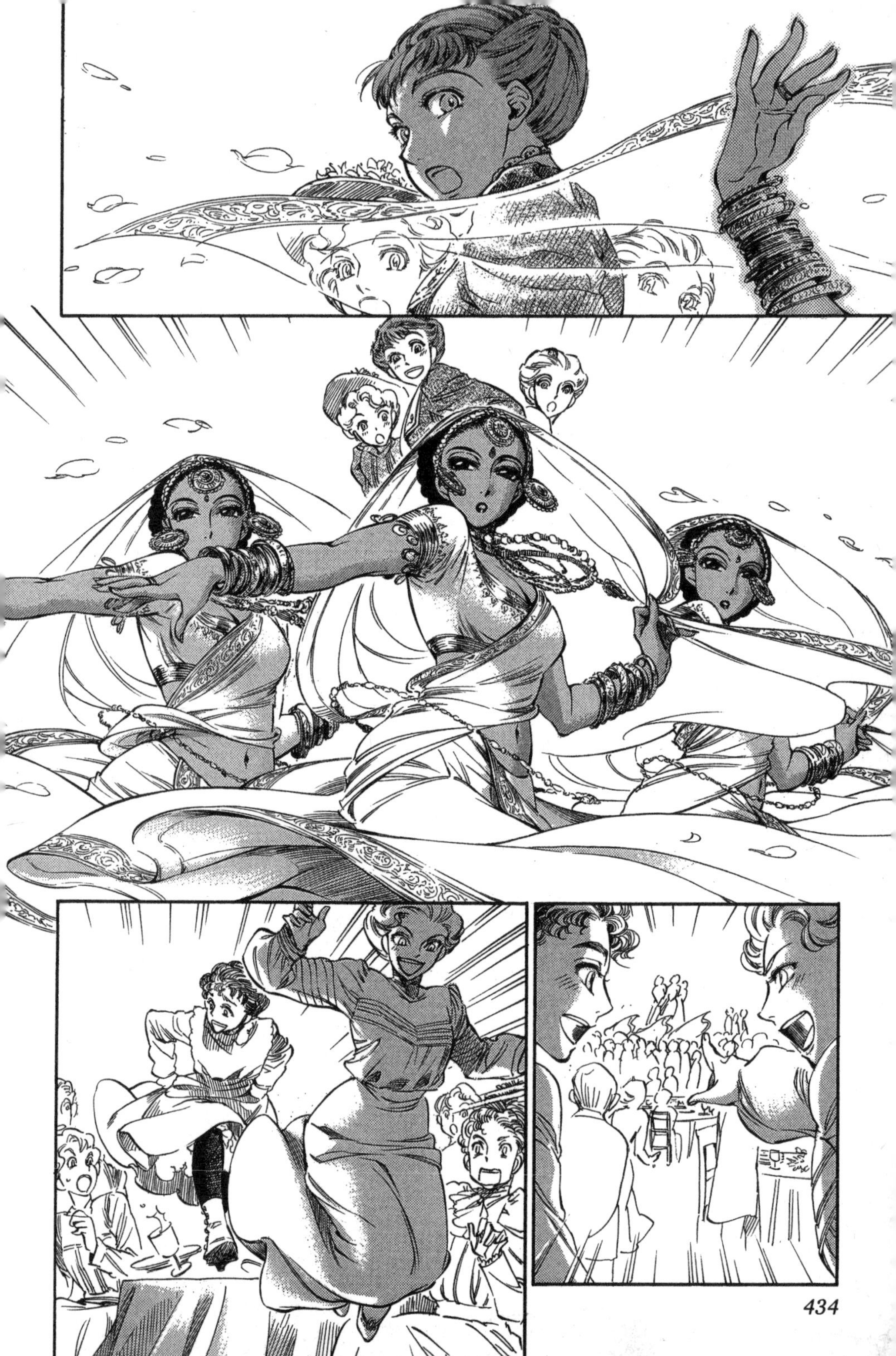

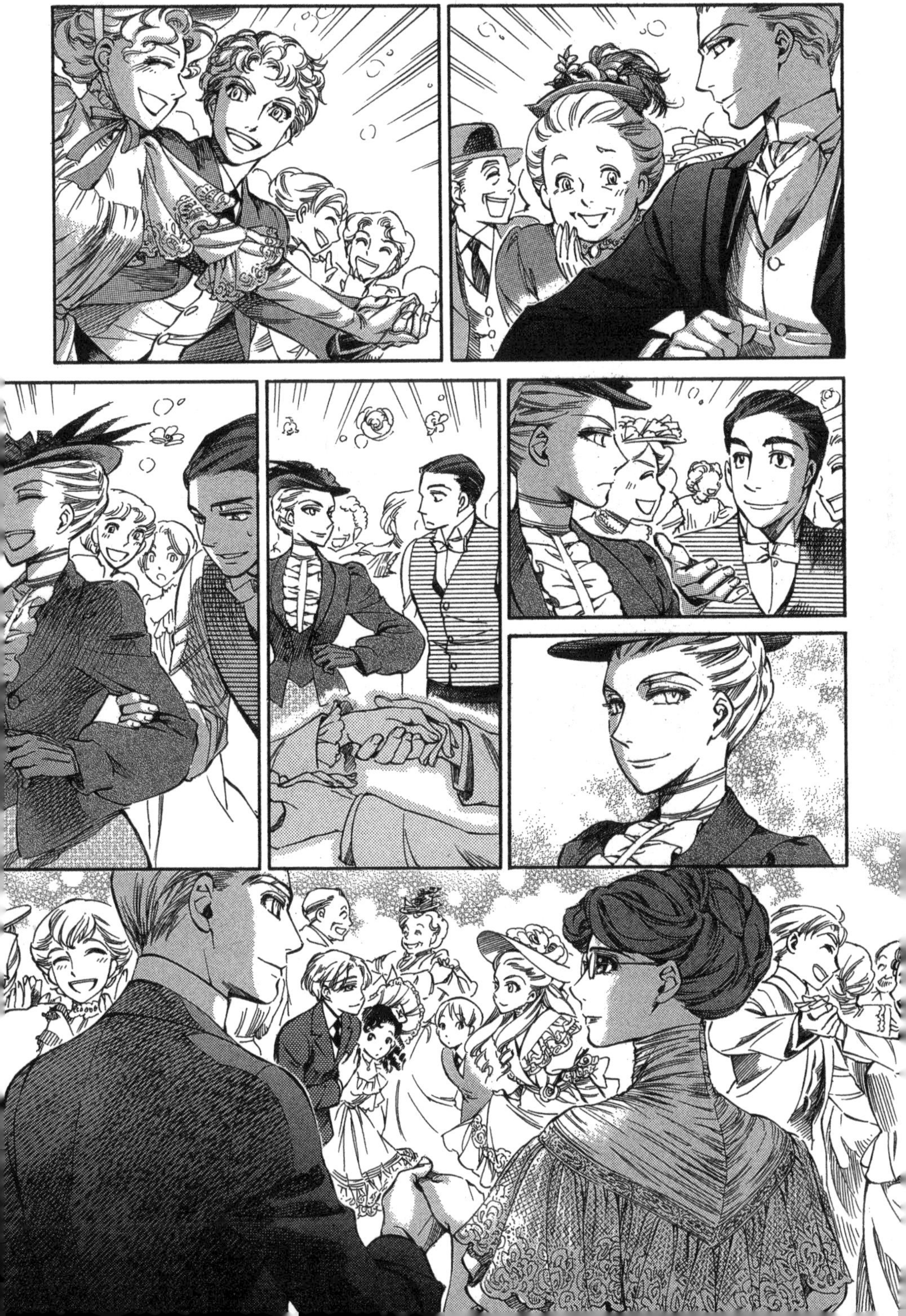

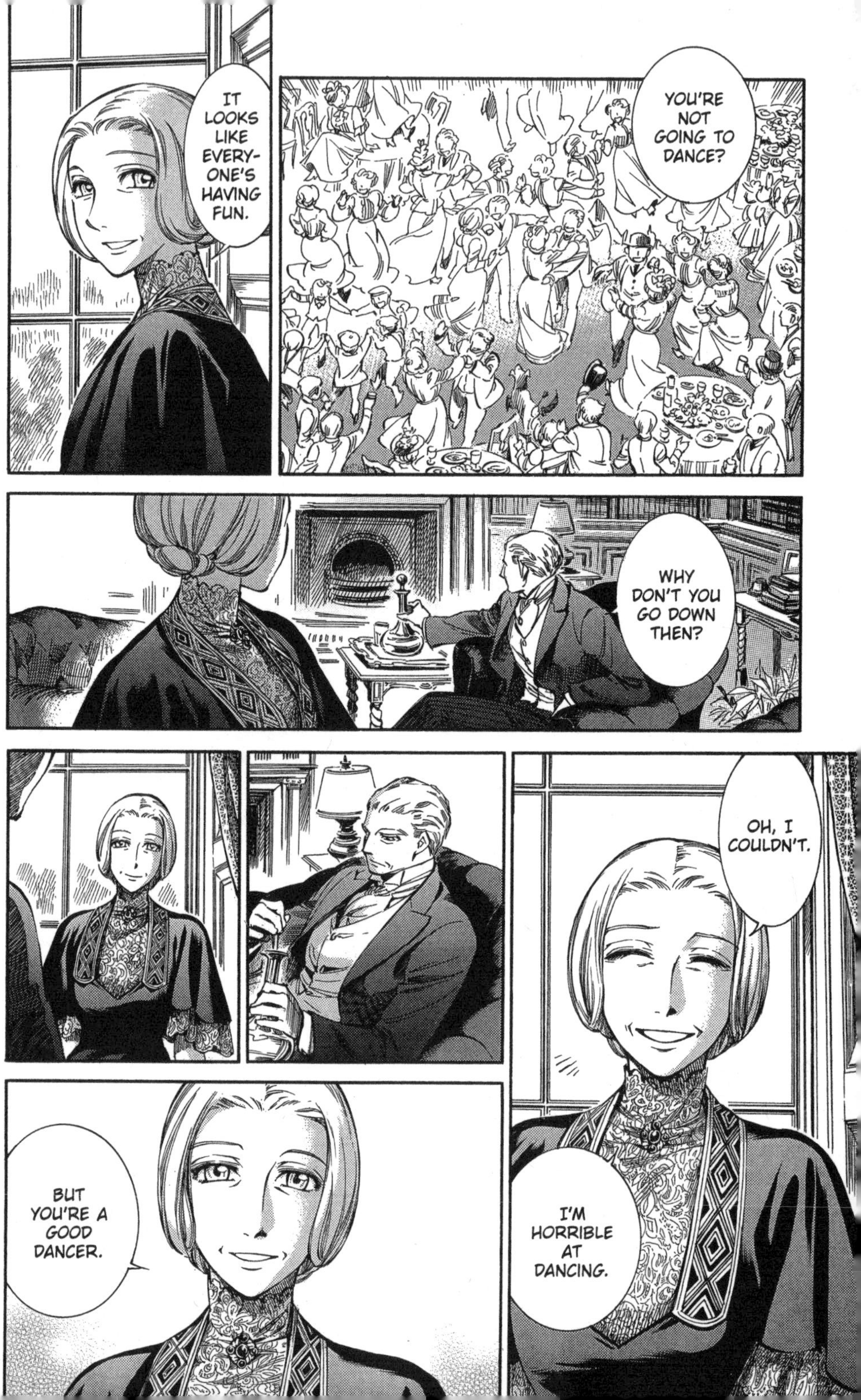

YOU'RE NOT GOING TO DANCE?
IT LOOKS LIKE EVERY-ONE'S HAVING FUN.
WHY DON'T YOU GO DOWN THEN?
OH, I COULDN'T.
I'M HORRIBLE AT DANCING.
BUT YOU'RE A GOOD DANCER.

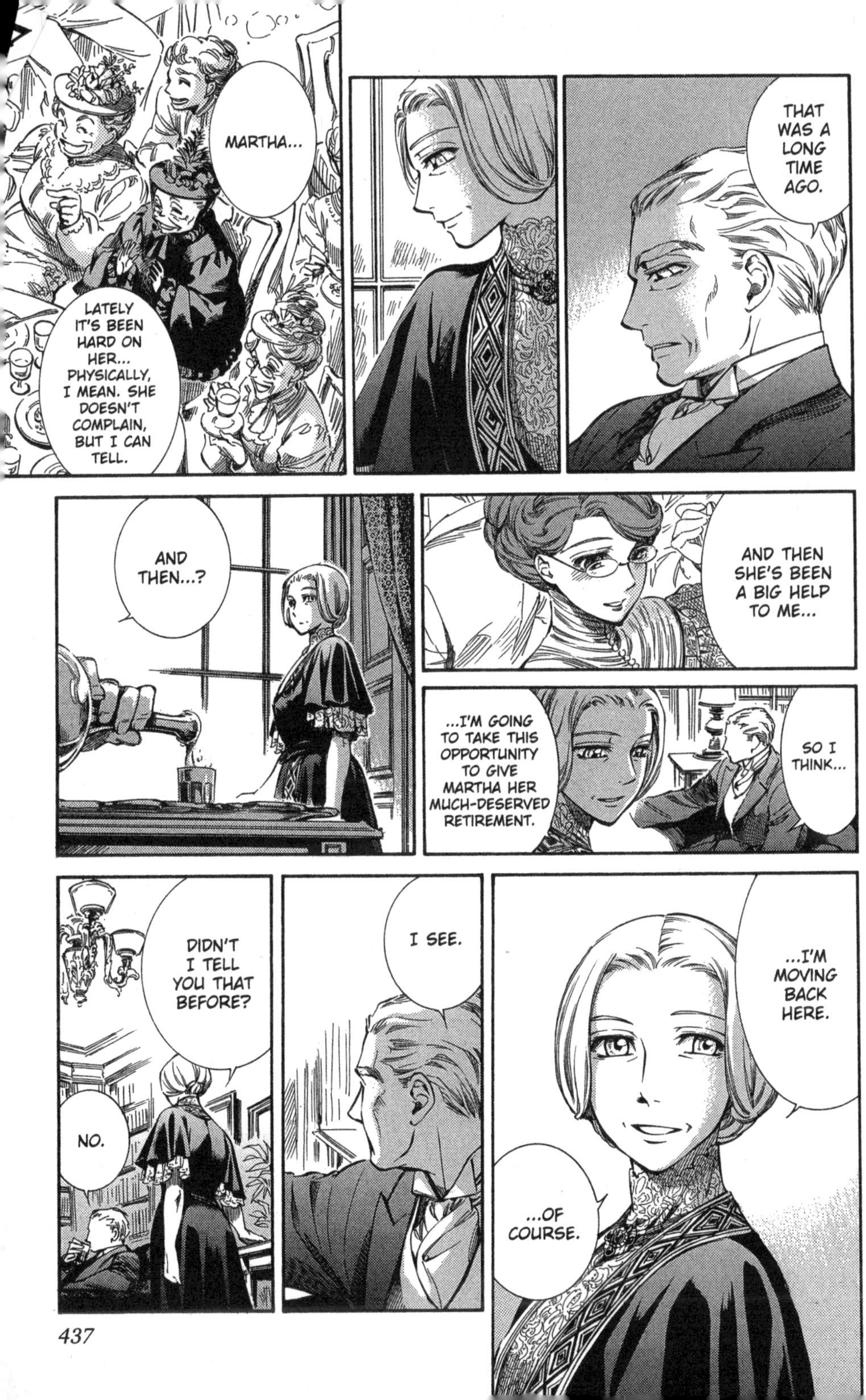
THAT WAS A LONG TIME AGO.
MARTHA...
LATELY IT'S BEEN HARD ON HER... PHYSICALLY, I MEAN. SHE DOESN'T COMPLAIN, BUT I CAN TELL.
AND THEN SHE'S BEEN A BIG HELP TO ME...
SO I THINK...
...I'M GOING TO TAKE THIS OPPORTUNITY TO GIVE MARTHA HER MUCH-DESERVED RETIREMENT.
AND THEN...?
...I'M MOVING BACK HERE.
...OF COURSE.
I SEE.
DIDN'T I TELL YOU THAT BEFORE?
NO.

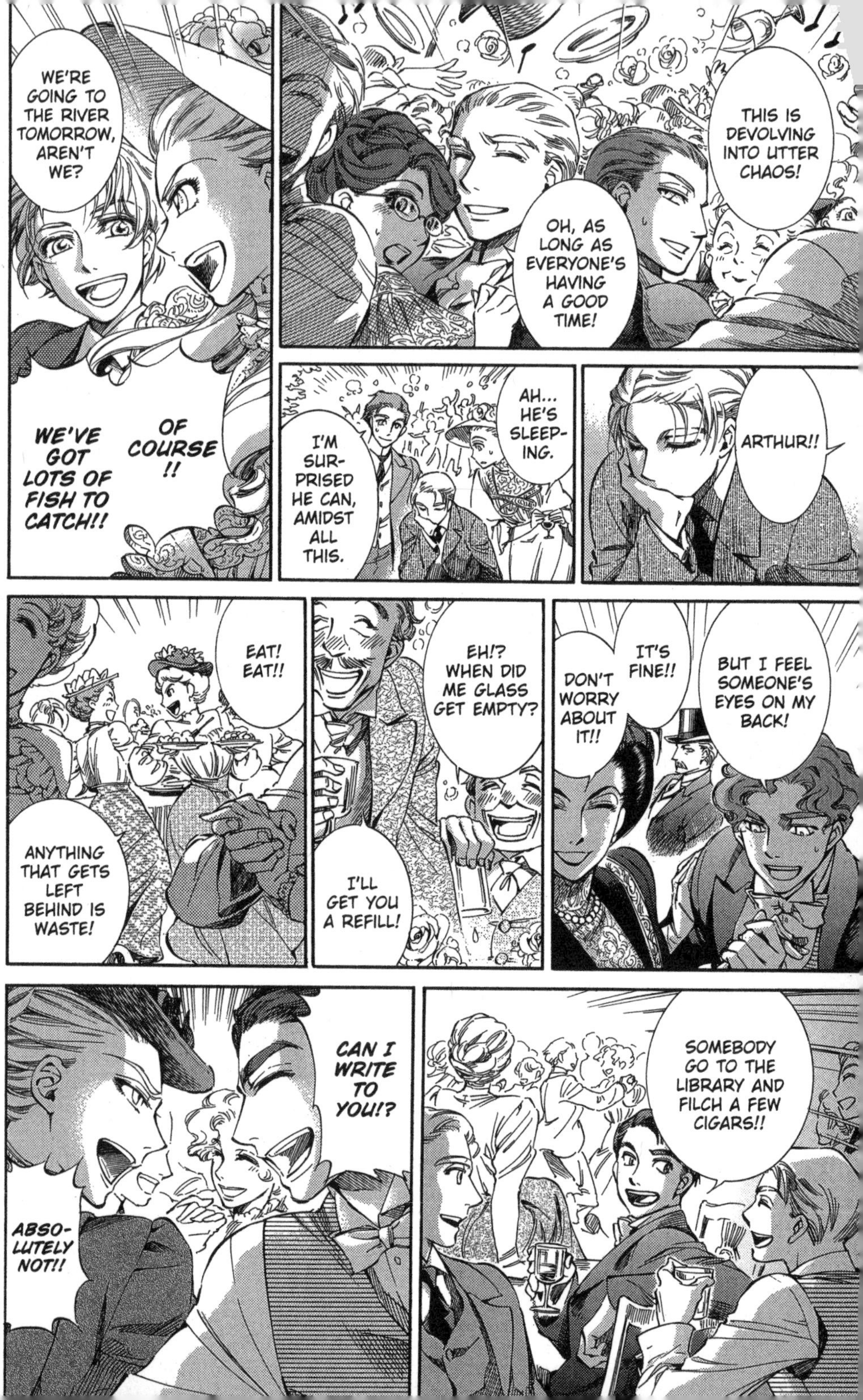
THIS IS DEVOLVING INTO UTTER CHAOS!
OH, AS LONG AS EVERYONE'S HAVING A GOOD TIME!
ARTHUR!!
AH... HE'S SLEEP-ING.
I'M SUR-PRISED HE CAN, AMIDST ALL THIS.
WE'RE GOING TO THE RIVER TOMORROW, AREN'T WE?
OF COURSE!!
WE'VE GOT LOTS OF FISH TO CATCH!!
BUT I FEEL SOMEONE'S EYES ON MY BACK!
IT'S FINE!!
DON'T WORRY ABOUT IT!!
EH!? WHEN DID ME GLASS GET EMPTY?
I'LL GET YOU A REFILL!
EAT! EAT!!
ANYTHING THAT GETS LEFT BEHIND IS WASTE!
SOMEBODY GO TO THE LIBRARY AND FILCH A FEW CIGARS!!
CAN I WRITE TO YOU!?
ABSO-LUTELY NOT!!

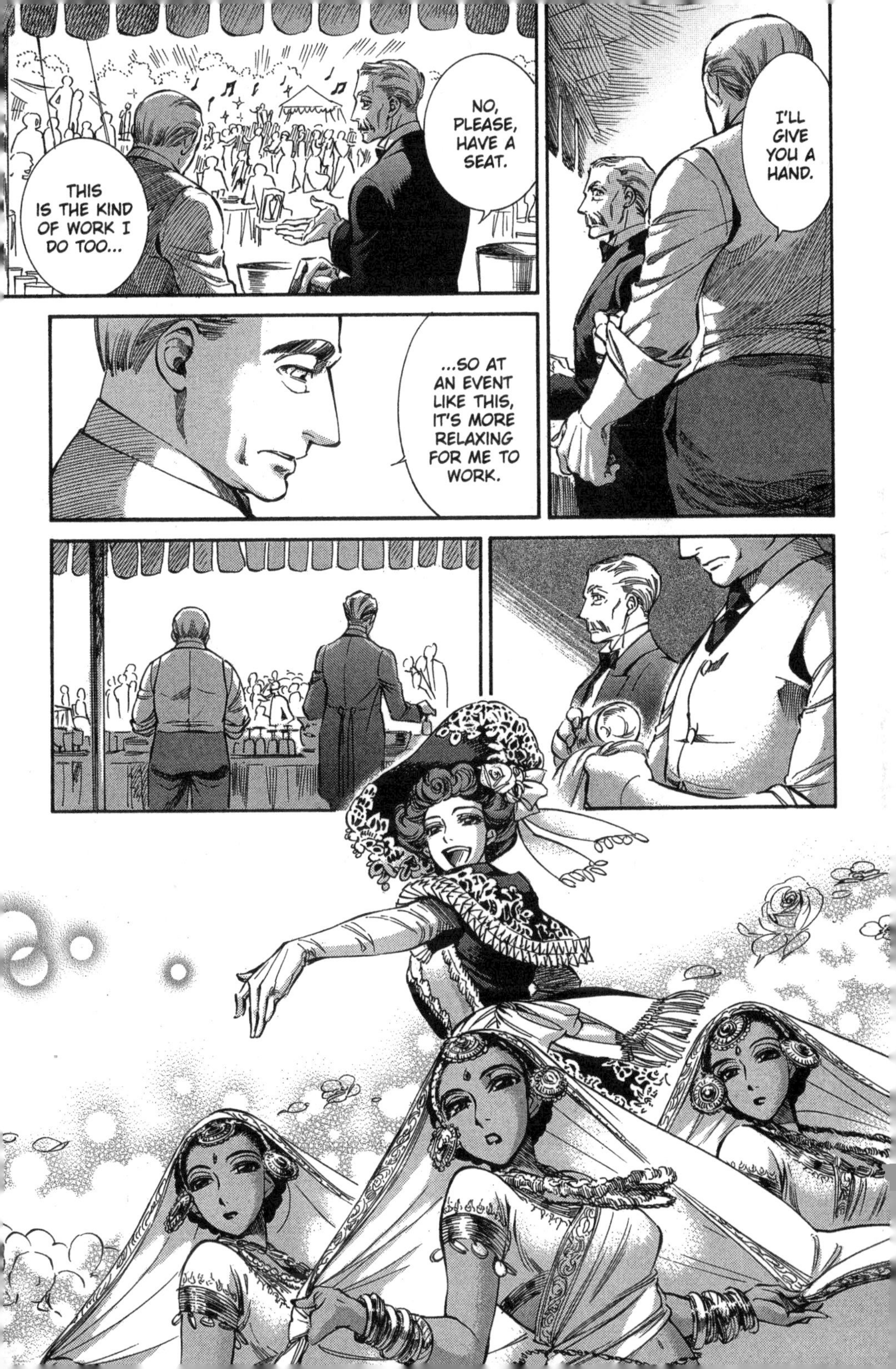
I'LL GIVE YOU A HAND.
NO, PLEASE, HAVE A SEAT.
THIS IS THE KIND OF WORK I DO TOO...
...SO AT AN EVENT LIKE THIS, IT'S MORE RELAXING FOR ME TO WORK.

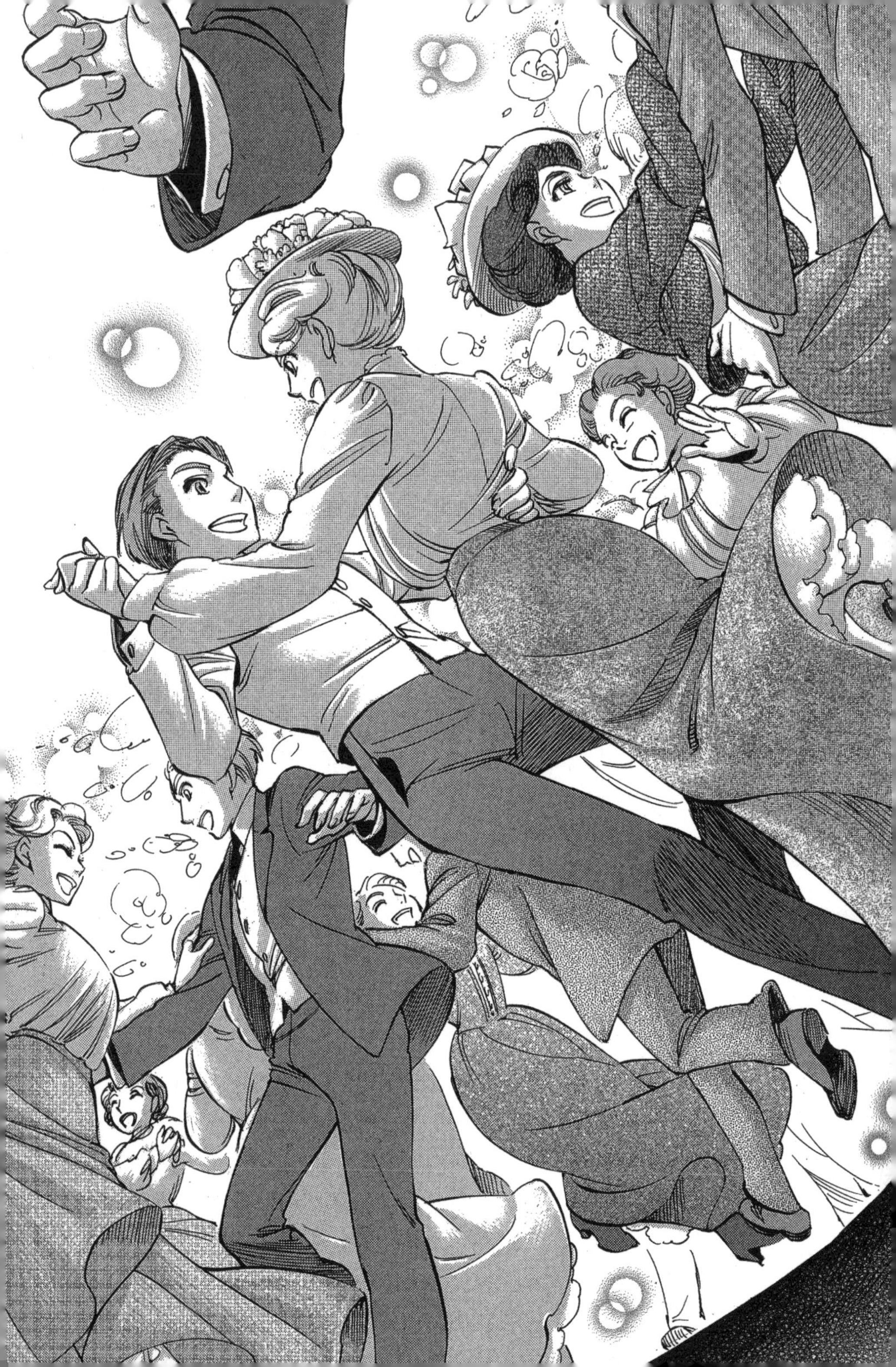

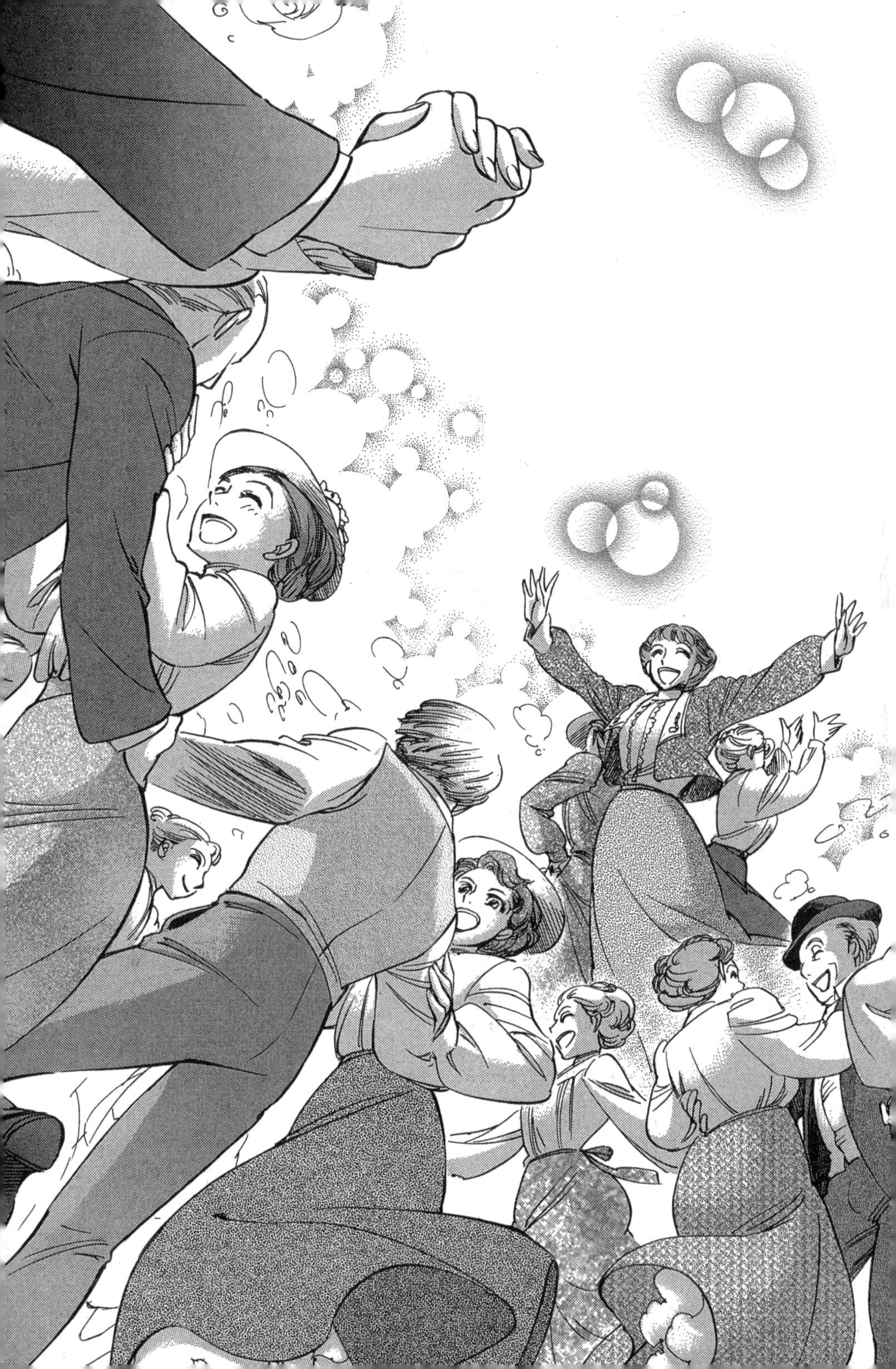

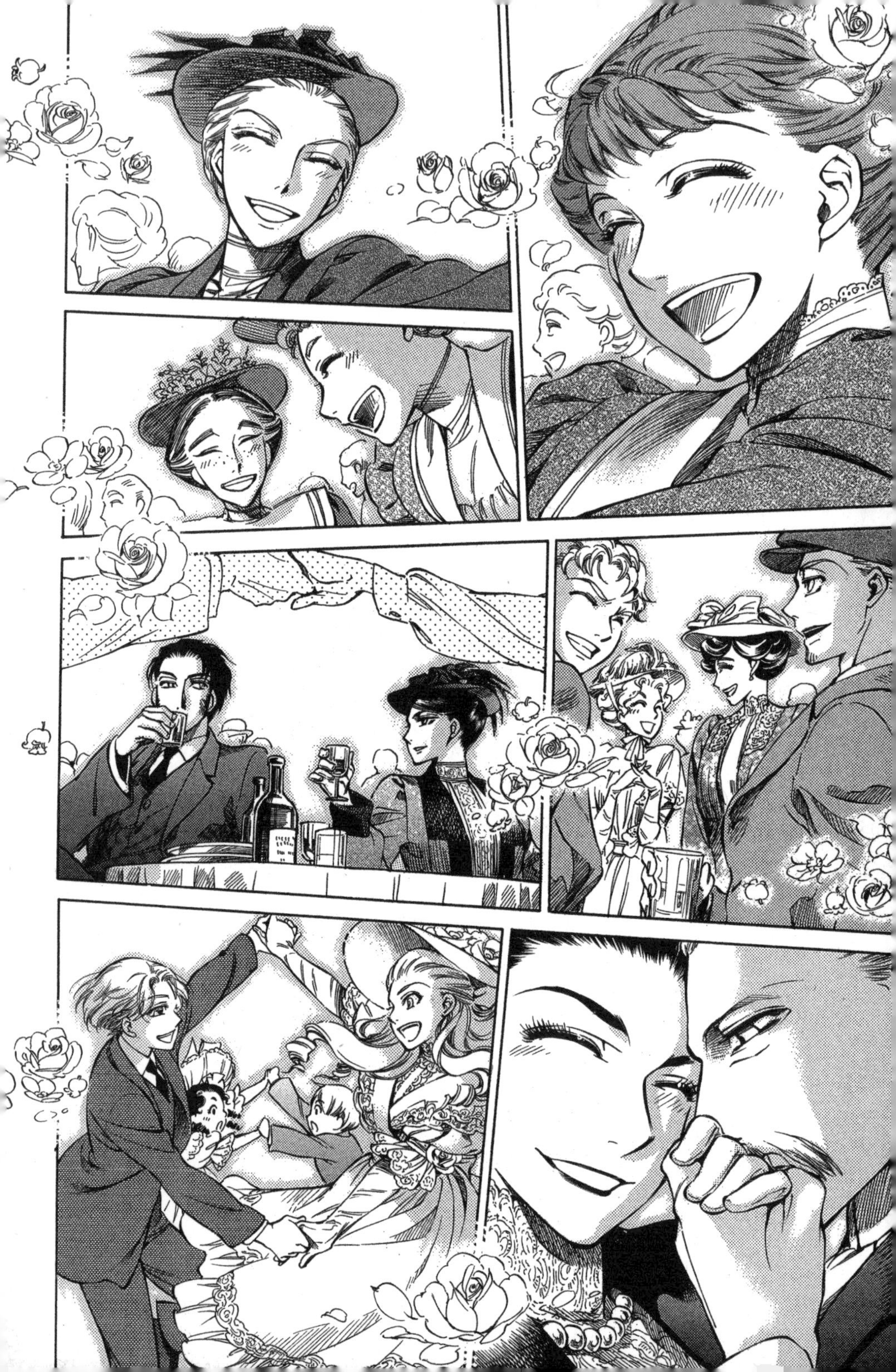

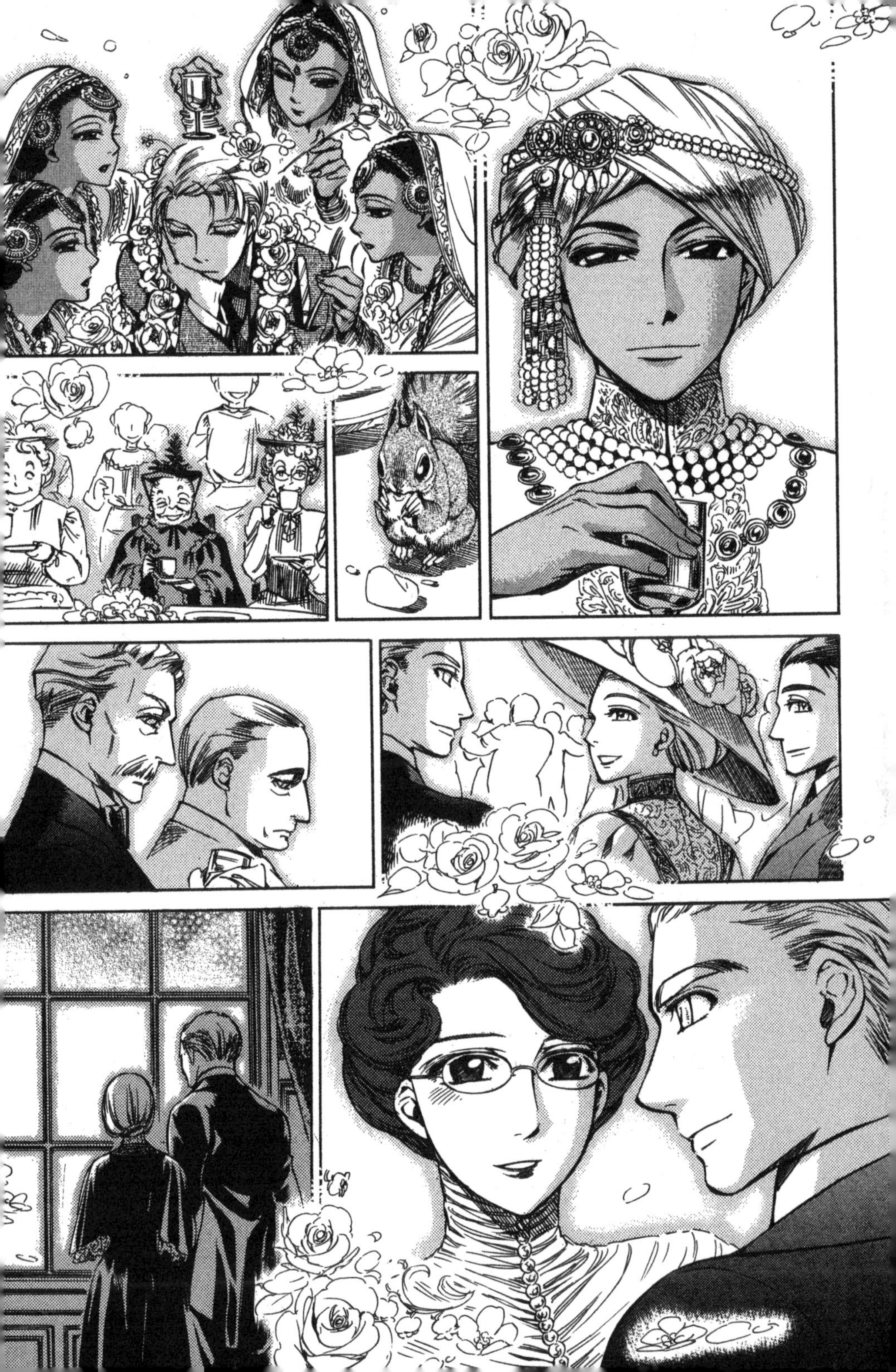

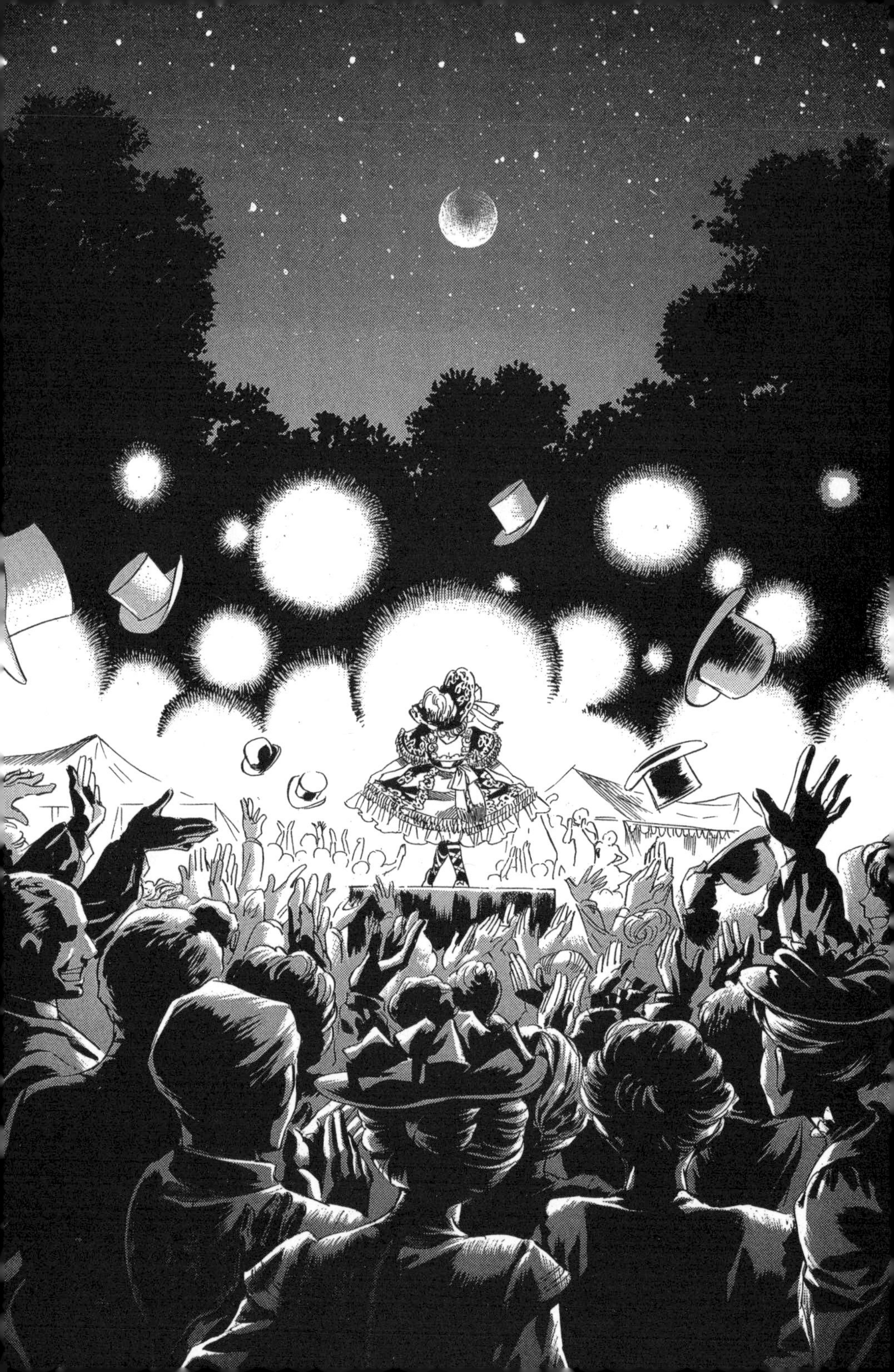

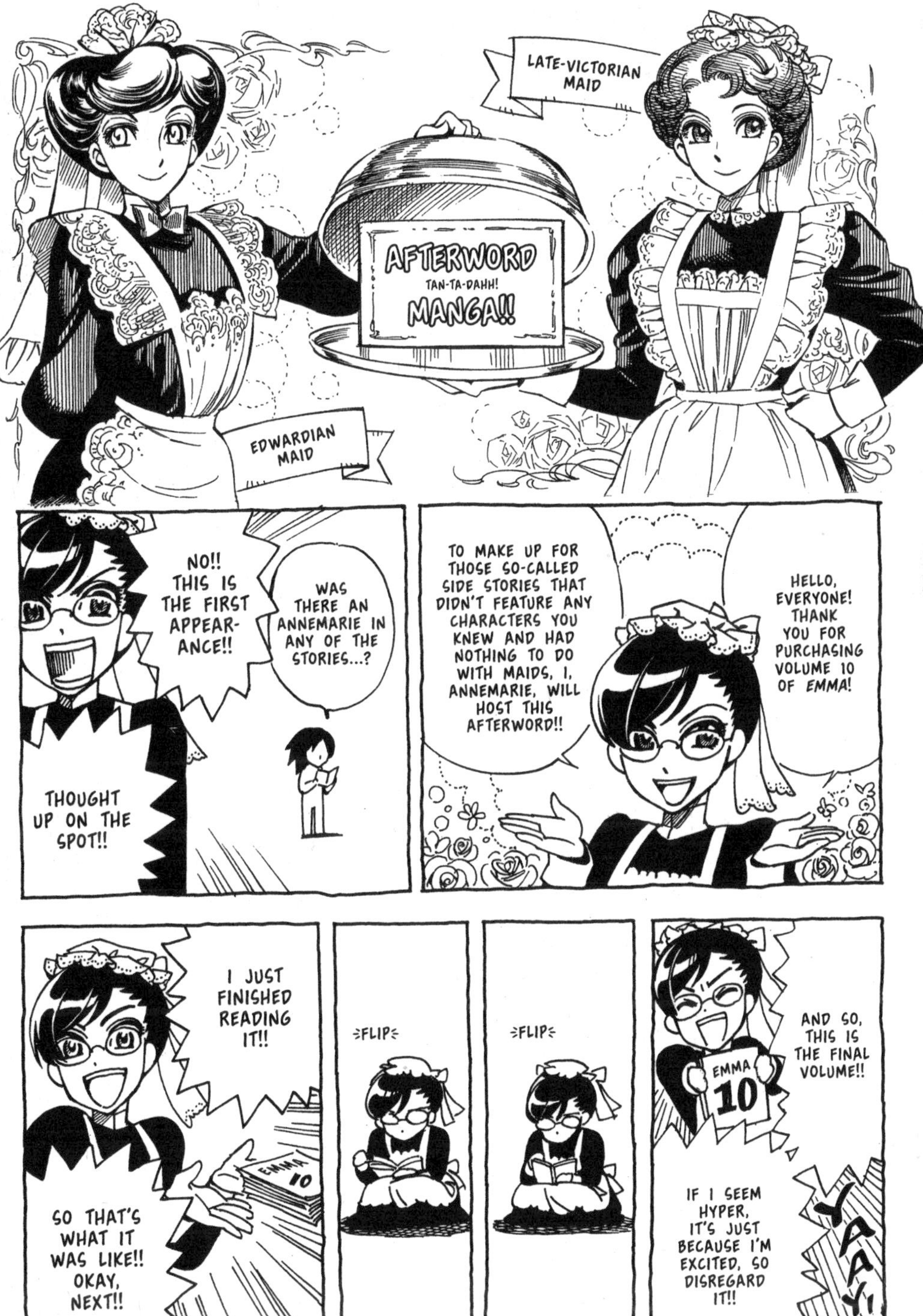

LATE-VICTORIAN MAID
AFTERWORD
TAN-TA-DAHH!
MANGA!!
EDWARDIAN MAID
HELLO, EVERYONE! THANK YOU FOR PURCHASING VOLUME 10 OF *EMMA*!
TO MAKE UP FOR THOSE SO-CALLED SIDE STORIES THAT DIDN'T FEATURE ANY CHARACTERS YOU KNEW AND HAD NOTHING TO DO WITH MAIDS, I, ANNEMARIE, WILL HOST THIS AFTERWORD!!
WAS THERE AN ANNEMARIE IN ANY OF THE STORIES...?
NO!! THIS IS THE FIRST APPEAR-ANCE!!
THOUGHT UP ON THE SPOT!!
AND SO, THIS IS THE FINAL VOLUME!!
EMMA 10
YAY!
IF I SEEM HYPER, IT'S JUST BECAUSE I'M EXCITED, SO DISREGARD IT!!
FLIP
FLIP
I JUST FINISHED READING IT!!
EMMA 10
SO THAT'S WHAT IT WAS LIKE!! OKAY, NEXT!!

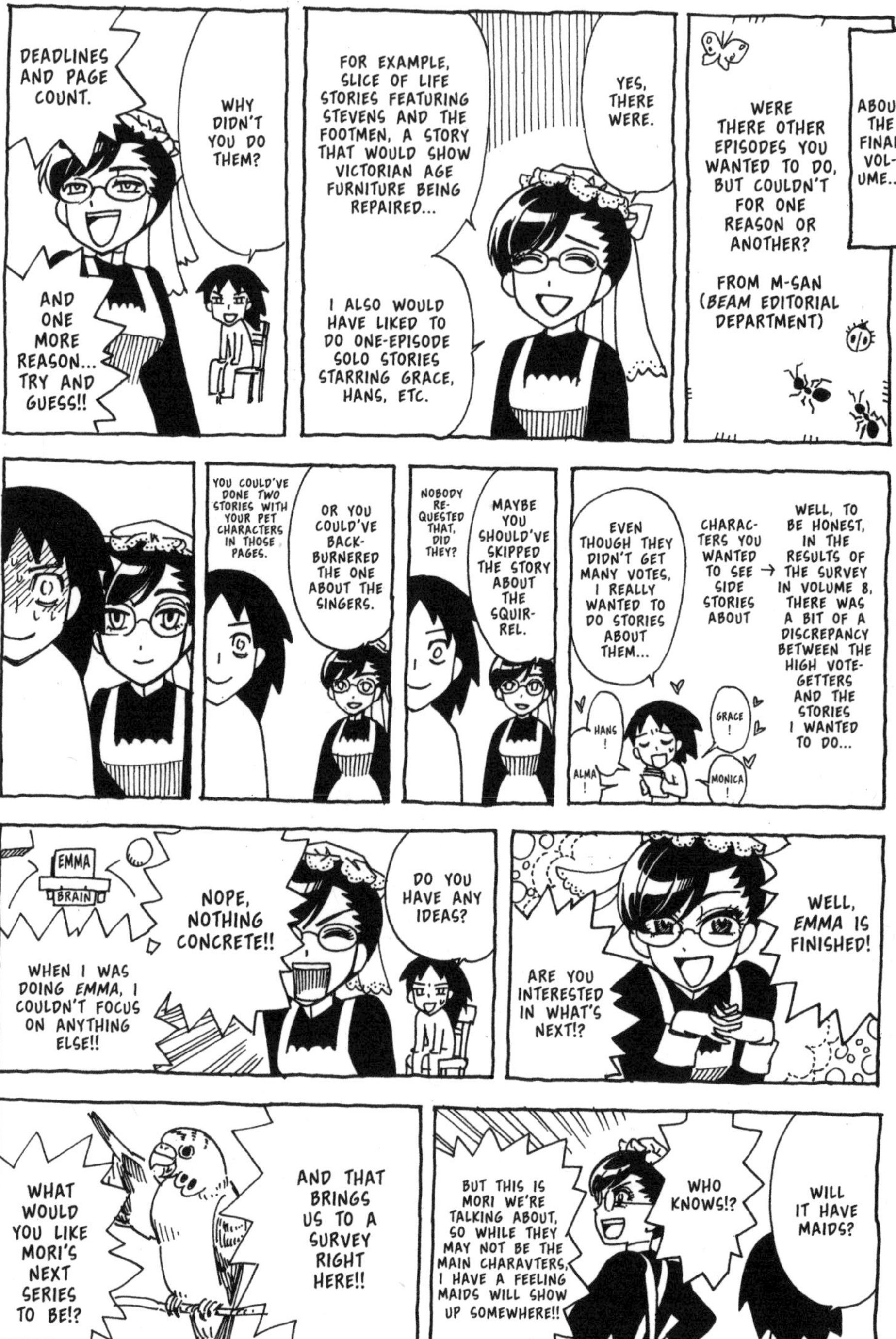
ABOUT THE FINAL VOLUME...
WERE THERE OTHER EPISODES YOU WANTED TO DO, BUT COULDN'T FOR ONE REASON OR ANOTHER?
FROM M-SAN (*BEAM* EDITORIAL DEPARTMENT)
YES, THERE WERE.
FOR EXAMPLE, SLICE OF LIFE STORIES FEATURING STEVENS AND THE FOOTMEN, A STORY THAT WOULD SHOW VICTORIAN AGE FURNITURE BEING REPAIRED...
I ALSO WOULD HAVE LIKED TO DO ONE-EPISODE SOLO STORIES STARRING GRACE, HANS, ETC.
WHY DIDN'T YOU DO THEM?
DEADLINES AND PAGE COUNT.
AND ONE MORE REASON... TRY AND GUESS!!
WELL, TO BE HONEST, IN THE RESULTS OF THE SURVEY IN VOLUME 8, THERE WAS A BIT OF A DISCREPANCY BETWEEN THE HIGH VOTE-GETTERS AND THE STORIES I WANTED TO DO...
CHARACTERS YOU WANTED TO SEE SIDE STORIES ABOUT →
EVEN THOUGH THEY DIDN'T GET MANY VOTES, I REALLY WANTED TO DO STORIES ABOUT THEM...
GRACE!
MONICA!
HANS!
ALMA!
MAYBE YOU SHOULD'VE SKIPPED THE STORY ABOUT THE SQUIRREL.
NOBODY REQUESTED THAT, DID THEY?
OR YOU COULD'VE BACKBURNERED THE ONE ABOUT THE SINGERS.
YOU COULD'VE DONE *TWO* STORIES WITH YOUR PET CHARACTERS IN THOSE PAGES.
WELL, *EMMA* IS FINISHED!
ARE YOU INTERESTED IN WHAT'S NEXT!?
DO YOU HAVE ANY IDEAS?
NOPE, NOTHING CONCRETE!!
EMMA
BRAIN
WHEN I WAS DOING *EMMA*, I COULDN'T FOCUS ON ANYTHING ELSE!!
WILL IT HAVE MAIDS?
WHO KNOWS!?
BUT THIS IS MORI WE'RE TALKING ABOUT, SO WHILE THEY MAY NOT BE THE MAIN CHARAVTERS, I HAVE A FEELING MAIDS WILL SHOW UP SOMEWHERE!!
AND THAT BRINGS US TO A SURVEY RIGHT HERE!!
WHAT WOULD YOU LIKE MORI'S NEXT SERIES TO BE!?

LATE-VICTORIAN MAID

AFTERWORD
TAN-TA-DAHH!
MANGA!!

EDWARDIAN MAID

NO!! THIS IS THE FIRST APPEARANCE!!

WAS THERE AN ANNEMARIE IN ANY OF THE STORIES...?

THOUGHT UP ON THE SPOT!!

TO MAKE UP FOR THOSE SO-CALLED SIDE STORIES THAT DIDN'T FEATURE ANY CHARACTERS YOU KNEW AND HAD NOTHING TO DO WITH MAIDS, I, ANNEMARIE, WILL HOST THIS AFTERWORD!!

HELLO, EVERYONE! THANK YOU FOR PURCHASING VOLUME 10 OF EMMA!

I JUST FINISHED READING IT!!

SO THAT'S WHAT IT WAS LIKE!! OKAY, NEXT!!

≈FLIP≈

≈FLIP≈

AND SO, THIS IS THE FINAL VOLUME!!

IF I SEEM HYPER, IT'S JUST BECAUSE I'M EXCITED, SO DISREGARD IT!!

EMMA 10

YAY!

445

Panel 1:

DEADLINES AND PAGE COUNT.

WHY DIDN'T YOU DO THEM?

AND ONE MORE REASON... TRY AND GUESS!!

Panel 2:

FOR EXAMPLE, SLICE OF LIFE STORIES FEATURING STEVENS AND THE FOOTMEN, A STORY THAT WOULD SHOW VICTORIAN AGE FURNITURE BEING REPAIRED...

I ALSO WOULD HAVE LIKED TO DO ONE-EPISODE SOLO STORIES STARRING GRACE, HANS, ETC.

YES, THERE WERE.

Panel 3:

WERE THERE OTHER EPISODES YOU WANTED TO DO, BUT COULDN'T FOR ONE REASON OR ANOTHER?

FROM M-SAN (BEAM EDITORIAL DEPARTMENT)

ABOUT THE FINAL VOLUME...

Panel 4:

YOU COULD'VE DONE *TWO* STORIES WITH YOUR PET CHARACTERS IN THOSE PAGES.

OR YOU COULD'VE BACK-BURNERED THE ONE ABOUT THE SINGERS.

NOBODY RE-QUESTED THAT, DID THEY?

MAYBE YOU SHOULD'VE SKIPPED THE STORY ABOUT THE SQUIRREL.

EVEN THOUGH THEY DIDN'T GET MANY VOTES, I REALLY WANTED TO DO STORIES ABOUT THEM...

CHARACTERS YOU WANTED TO SEE → SIDE STORIES ABOUT

WELL, TO BE HONEST, IN THE RESULTS OF THE SURVEY IN VOLUME 8, THERE WAS A BIT OF A DISCREPANCY BETWEEN THE HIGH VOTE-GETTERS AND THE STORIES I WANTED TO DO...

HANS!
ALMA!
GRACE!
MONICA!

Panel 5:

EMMA
BRAIN

WHEN I WAS DOING EMMA, I COULDN'T FOCUS ON ANYTHING ELSE!!

NOPE, NOTHING CONCRETE!!

DO YOU HAVE ANY IDEAS?

Panel 6:

ARE YOU INTERESTED IN WHAT'S NEXT!?

WELL, EMMA IS FINISHED!

Panel 7:

WHAT WOULD YOU LIKE MORI'S NEXT SERIES TO BE!?

AND THAT BRINGS US TO A SURVEY RIGHT HERE!!

Panel 8:

BUT THIS IS MORI WE'RE TALKING ABOUT, SO WHILE THEY MAY NOT BE THE MAIN CHARAVTERS, I HAVE A FEELING MAIDS WILL SHOW UP SOMEWHERE!!

WHO KNOWS!?

WILL IT HAVE MAIDS?

446

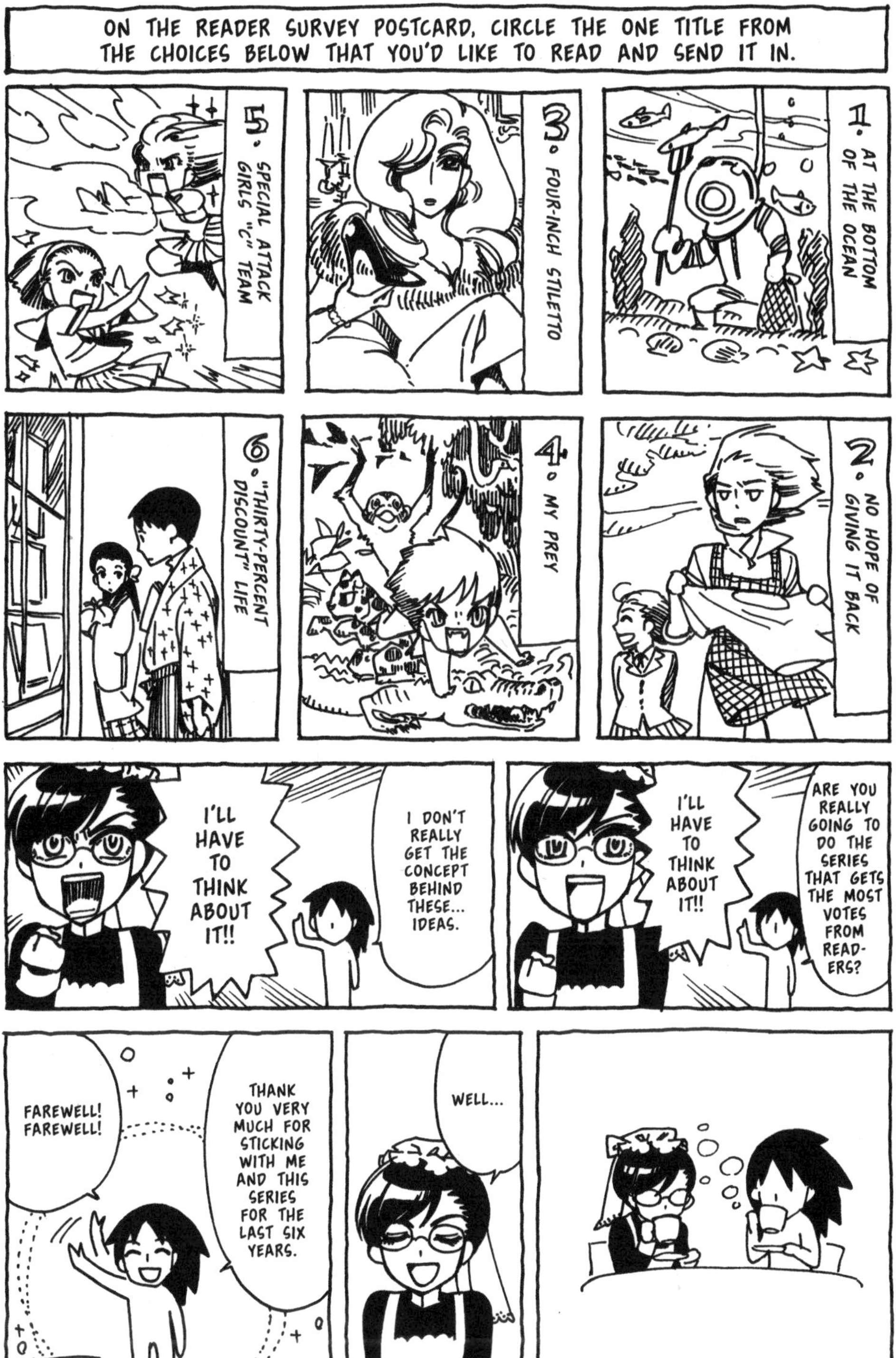
ON THE READER SURVEY POSTCARD, CIRCLE THE ONE TITLE FROM THE CHOICES BELOW THAT YOU'D LIKE TO READ AND SEND IT IN.
1. AT THE BOTTOM OF THE OCEAN
3. FOUR-INCH STILETTO
5. SPECIAL ATTACK GIRLS "C" TEAM
2. NO HOPE OF GIVING IT BACK
4. MY PREY
6. "THIRTY-PERCENT DISCOUNT" LIFE
ARE YOU REALLY GOING TO DO THE SERIES THAT GETS THE MOST VOTES FROM READERS?
I'LL HAVE TO THINK ABOUT IT!!
I DON'T REALLY GET THE CONCEPT BEHIND THESE... IDEAS.
I'LL HAVE TO THINK ABOUT IT!!
WELL...
THANK YOU VERY MUCH FOR STICKING WITH ME AND THIS SERIES FOR THE LAST SIX YEARS.
FAREWELL! FAREWELL!
THE END.

EMMA ⑤

KAORU MORI

TRANSLATION: SHELDON DRZKA

LETTERING: ABIGAIL BLACKMAN

EMMA Volume 9, 10
© 2007, 2008 Kaoru Mori.
First published in Japan in 2007, 2008 by KADOKAWA CORPORATION, Tokyo.
English translation rights arranged with KADOKAWA CORPORATION, Tokyo through Tuttle-Mori Agency, Inc., Tokyo.

English translation © 2016 by Yen Press, LLC

Yen Press
1290 Avenue of the Americas
New York, NY 10104

Visit us at yenpress.com
facebook.com/yenpress
twitter.com/yenpress
yenpress.tumblr.com

First Yen Press Edition: August 2016

Yen Press is an imprint of Yen Press, LLC.
The Yen Press name and logo are trademarks of Yen Press, LLC.

Library of Congress Control Number: 2016297057

ISBN: 978-0-316-30447-4

10 9 8 7 6 5 4 3 2 1

BVG

Printed in the United States of America